HUMAN DEVELOPMENT
THE SPAN OF LIFE

HUMAN DEVELOPMENT
THE SPAN OF LIFE

GEORGE KALUGER, Ph.D.
Professor and Chairman, Department of Psychology, Shippensburg State College, Shippensburg, Pennsylvania

MERIEM FAIR KALUGER, Litt.M.
Psycho/Educational Consultant, Shippensburg, Pennsylvania

with 44 illustrations

THE C. V. MOSBY COMPANY
SAINT LOUIS   1974

Cover photo courtesy Flint Laboratories, Division of Baxter/Travenol, Deerfield, Illinois.

Copyright © 1974 by The C. V. Mosby Company

All rights reserved. No part of this book may be reproduced in any manner without written permission of the publisher.

Printed in the United States of America

Distributed in Great Britain by Henry Kimpton, London

Library of Congress Cataloging in Publication Data

Kaluger, George.
    Human development; the span of life.

    1. Developmental psychology. I. Kaluger,
Meriem Fair, 1921-   joint author. II. Title.
[DNLM: 1. Growth. 2. Personality development.
3. Psychology. BF701 K14h 1974]
BF713.K34   155   74-1059
ISBN 0-8016-2611-0

VH/VH/VH   9 8 7 6 5 4 3 2 1

To our parents,
who, by precepts and examples,
taught us the joy of living, the goodness
of man, and the love of God.

Preface

We live in a world in which rapid change of ideas, values, and products seems to be the main characteristic of the times. It is commonplace to hear someone say, "Fifteen to twenty years ago this information (or whatever) did not exist." Children born since 1955 are growing up in a sensory and conceptual world that never existed before, one with which their parents are quite unfamiliar, unaware, and possibly unconcerned. A strange new society is erupting in our midst. Adults must look to the children and their environment for a glimpse of the future. Yet, some things have not and will not change. The fundamental organic patterns of growth and development continue to be universal and interminable in nature. Only the external conditions wherein these patterns develop change. This factor, however, is enough to be a matter of concern.

In part, this text has evolved from our interaction with children and adults of all ages. We have done clinical work with children as young as 4 weeks and with adults in their eighties and nineties. The bulk of our work has been with individuals between the ages of 5 and 50 years. We have taught in elementary schools, secondary schools, college, and graduate school. We have both served as teachers, counselors, and psychologists. For over a decade we have taught a course in developmental psychology to graduate students. From these experiences have come many ideas for this book. Many of the topics included in this text were derived from the questions most frequently asked by students from a wide variety of disciplines. In a sense, the subject matter is directed to what we perceived to be the interests, needs, and desires of students studying human development and behavior.

The life-span approach, based on chronological development, was chosen because it helped make the individual seem more "real" than he was under the dimensional or topical approach. However, on each age level there is a treatment of certain topics that are presented throughout the entire life-span. Our basic theme is that an individual grows in five ways: physically, mentally, socially, emotionally, and morally. These five ways of development are considered at each stage. Developmental tasks are presented for each age division as are age level characteristics of behavior and development, living patterns, and personality development. Special emphasis is given to topics particularly important to that age level.

A thorough review of current knowledge of growth and development at each stage would have been a difficult if not an impossible task in one volume. Indeed, it is not our intent to present all of the literature. Our aim is to present basic universals of development while maintaining a continuous recognition of individual differences and the factors responsible for these differences. We selected research and factual material that was in keeping with that purpose. Focus throughout is on processes and not on isolated research content. We acknowledge and accept the dynamic influences of biological foundations, psychosocial factors, and individual experience. Prominent new research dealing with learning, perception, and personality is included.

If there is any bias or position it would be that we tend to emphasize universal principles of total growth and development while recognizing the dynamic forces of individualization. Seminars with some very great men have no doubt influenced our thinking. From Arnold Gesell we learned about the orderly, sequential manner of the maturational process and how the mind manifests itself. From Carl R. Rogers we acquired insights concerning the dignity of the individual and his total being. Jean Piaget says much to us, as do Donald Hebb, Jerome Kagan, and Paul Mussen.

We read somewhere of an author who once said "I hate writing but I love having written." We love having written but we loved writing too. Part of the reason for it being a pleasant task was that we lived so many parts of the book. The text is "people centered"; it deals with live persons, not with statistics. Thus personalizing comments are included. We permitted ourselves to do interpretative writing of some of the research. We often had to curb our enthusiasm for nonessential conversation. We have allowed some commentaries and editorializing to be included. We have sought to label all personal observations and opinions as our own thinking so that readers would not be misled. We have tried to make the text meaningful as well as informative for readers who would probably take only one course in developmental psychology.

We express our appreciation to the many graduate and undergraduate students with whom we have worked over the years. Their questions and interests are reflected in many parts of the book. We thank the Unity Hi-Y Club of Butler, Pennsylvania, who accepted us as their advisors and enabled us to closely observe thirty-five boys growing from prepuberty to manhood and to families of their own. Our colleagues were most helpful and encouraging. We appreciate all of their expressions of support. Special thanks and appreciation go to Norma Strassburger for her masterful typing of the manuscript, often from very rough copy. To Mary Lou Orndorff, who read our original manuscript, and to Patricia Felix, our graduate assistant, we express our sincere appreciation for their wonderful help. To our readers, have a nice day—and a nicer tomorrow.

George Kaluger
Meriem Fair Kaluger

Contents

1 **Foundations of human development, 1**

   Individuality and universality, 1
   Developmental principles, 2
   Basic processes related to efficient living, 5
   Physiological basis of development, 10
   Psychosocial influences of development, 18

2 **Prenatal development, 24**

   Life begins, 24
   Pregnancy, 29
   Prenatal development and behavior, 32

3 **Birth of the baby, 42**

   Birth process, 43
   Influences on prenatal development, 49
   Conditions at birth affecting development, 53

4 **Infant motor and cognitive development, 61**

   The neonate, 63
   Motor development during infancy, 69
   Development of intelligence, 74
   Development of the perceptual processes, 78

5 **Psychosocial development in infancy, 82**

   Infant speech and language, 84
   Emotional and social development, 87
   Nature and origins of personality, 93

6 **Early childhood: 3 to 5 years of age, 100**

   Physical characteristics and motor skills, 102
   Perceptual-motor processes for learning, 105
   Cognitive development, 110
   Development of language, 114
   Psychosocial development, 115
   Organization of personality, 120
   Concepts of morality, 122

7 **Middle childhood: 6 to 8 years of age, 125**

   Physical development, 127
   Social growth, 129
   Intelligence, language, and thought, 134
   Personality, self-concept, and sex role, 138
   Emotional and moral development, 141

8 **Late childhood: 9 to 11 years of age, 147**

   Physical growth and motor development, 149
   Sexual awareness and sex information, 154
   Social behavior, 157
   Cognitive development and school learning, 160
   Affective and moral development, 162

9 **Puberty and early adolescence: 12 to 14 years of age, 167**

   Pubertal and physical development, 170
   Emotional characteristics, 177
   Social development, 179

ix

Teen culture and interests, 187
Personal problems and concerns, 189
Awakening of reasoning, 192

10 **Middle and later adolescence: 15 to 18 years of age, 195**

Adolescence and the coming of age, 197
Physical growth and development, 198
Achieving independence from home, 199
Establishing heterosexual relationships, 202
Love relationships, 206
Maturing intellectual operations, 208
Emotionality, 209
Need for a value judgment system, 211
Problems of middle adolescence, 212
Adolescence in disadvantaged environments, 215
The youth market, 217

11 **Emerging adulthood: the awakening years, 220**

Developmental self, 224
Identity and self, 226
Moral and religious uncertainty, 228
Youth and society, 231
A final word, 236

12 **Early adulthood: the developing years, 238**

Getting married, 243
Being married, 250
The unmarried young adult, 258
Maturity and the early adult, 259

13 **Middle adulthood: the years of stability, 264**

Life in the middle years, 269
The change of life, 278

14 **Later adulthood: age of recompense, 284**

Life in later adulthood, 289
Age level changes, 296
Dying and death, 304

Glossary, 308

HUMAN DEVELOPMENT
THE SPAN OF LIFE

1 Foundations of human development

An ancient philosopher observed that one of the most significant questions one person can ask of another is "What do you see when you see a man?" The answer to this question will reflect the person's degree of understanding and insight, as well as his faith and acceptance, concerning the dignity of nature and human worthiness.

As a seed develops, changes, and matures into a tree by following a specified pattern of growth, so does an infant change and mature into an adult by following an established pattern of principles relating to growth and development. This maturational sequence is specific enough so that it can be identified, observed, and recorded. The sequence is the same for all individuals. The developmental process is not limited to one aspect of growth, however, since each child grows in five ways—physically, mentally, emotionally, socially, and spiritually. The environment makes an impact on this growth mechanism, but the step-by-step process remains the same. Adults ascribe positive or negative values to this developing personality. The insight that an adult possesses concerning human growth and development largely determines "what he sees when he sees a man."

INDIVIDUALITY AND UNIVERSALITY

A Vermont farmer is quoted as having said "People are mostly alike, but what difference they are can be powerful important." In one statement is the general concept of individuality and universality. "People are mostly alike . . ." reflects a sameness, a "universal likeness" of world man in his development. ". . . But what difference they are can be powerful important" suggests the magnitude and depth of individual differences that can be found in people.

The facts of human individuality are astounding. Each one of us is built in a highly distinctive way in every particular—physically, mentally, emotionally, socially, and morally—and these differences form the bases of individuality. It is well known that each individual has distinctive fingerprints and a natural odor, distinctive enough for a bloodhound to follow. It has also been determined that man has distinctive voice prints, lip prints, and footprints. A person can disguise himself in all kinds of wearing apparel and cosmetics, but "you can't fool Mother Nature." More startling are the differences that are inside people.

There are variations in the size, shape, and operations of stomachs of normal people. There are also large differences in hearts and endocrine glands. Diversity of structure of the brain and nervous system is as great from man to man as is diversity between related species of animals. Each individual is "extra-ordinary." Although the illustrations given all pertain to physical growth, they could have been given equally well of any aspect of growth.

Universality refers to the commonality of man. Everyone can give examples of ways in which men and women the world over are alike. Under the facade of cultural influences man is pretty much the same physically, mentally, emotionally, socially, and spiritually. The five ways of growing up are purposely being emphasized so that the total developmental pattern of man can be realized instead of relegating it to just one or two areas of growth. The universality of man is deeply ingrained within the developmental processes. Babies are conceived and born the same way the world over. They go through the same stages in learning to walk and to talk. Children develop their self-concept, their processes of learning, and their adjustive patterns of behavior in much the same way. In other words, there are some basic, fundamental principles of laws governing growth and development to which earthly man is subjected, whether he knows about them or not, whether he agrees with them or not, and whether he is ready for them or not. The scientific laws governing growth are universal and eternal.

The implications of individuality and universality are manifold. For one thing they state that man is like others in some very basic ways. Yet he is different enough in other ways to make him a unique being. The ultimate implication is to recognize the individual worth of each human being, understanding and accepting him, and at the same time understanding and accepting ourselves, seeking to make the most of ourselves with whatever traits we may have.

DEVELOPMENTAL PRINCIPLES

The principles of growth and development that follow reflect the universality of the laws by which man grows and develops. The maturational process, the sequential stages of development, and the directions of growth are fundamental to all human life everywhere and at any point in time in history.

Growth gradients

Human growth and development relate to physiological, psychological, and environmental processes that, by nature, are continuous and orderly. They bring about changes in the physical, mental, emotional, social, and moral components of being. Growth refers to organic changes and is basically quantitative in nature. Development generally refers to functional or nonorganic changes and is usually qualitative in nature. Development, therefore, is a lifelong process that covers the entire pattern of human existence, whereas some aspects of growth do reach a point of maturity from which no further change is anticipated. The word *development*, however, has several meanings, some of which are not related to the developmental process, and the reader should be aware of these different uses.

There are three principles related to directions of growth and development. The first direction of growth is the *cephalocaudal sequence*, which is sometimes referred to as the law of developmental direction. The cephalocaudal sequence suggests that the direction of growth occurs from the head end to the foot (the tail end). The development of the major aspects of growth takes place in the head first, the trunk next, and the legs last. (See Fig. 1-1.) This direction is vividly illustrated in both prenatal and postnatal stages of development. In the embryonic state the

Foundations of human development 3

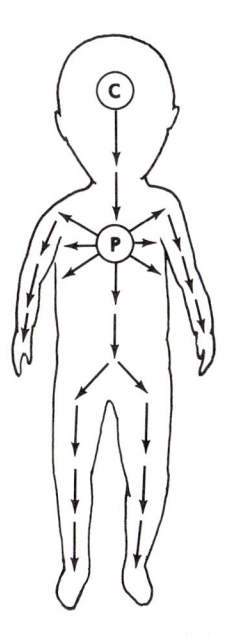

Fig. 1-1. Direction of cephalocaudal sequence, Ⓒ, of growth and development is from maturation and control of head movement to trunk, to legs, and to feet movements and development. Direction of growth of proximodistal sequence, Ⓟ, is from maturation of the center of the body to development of peripheral parts of the body.

brain and central nervous system start to develop first, followed by features of the head, then the region of the trunk with its organs. The development of the head proceeds more rapidly than that of any other part of the body because of the importance of the brain and central nervous system to the operation of the rest of the body. At birth the head constitutes 20% of the body length. After the rest of the body grows to maturity the head will be only 8% of the body length. After birth the baby first gains control of the head, eyes, mouth, and neck; then he gains control over the trunk. The baby can sit before he can stand, and he can stand before he can walk.

The second direction of growth is the *proximodistal sequence*. The proximodistal direction of development states that controlled movements proximal to the body axis (the parts of bodily members that lie closest to the center of the body) mature before those that are distal (further away). Progression is from the central parts of the body maturing earlier and functioning before those located nearer the periphery. A baby gains control of his shoulder before his hand. He can control his thigh before he can control his foot. The central nervous system develops more rapidly than the peripheral nervous system.

The third direction of growth is expressed by the principle of *differentiation*. This principle states that the trend of the direction of growth proceeds from mass to specific activities of development. Generalized development will occur before specific or specialized development can occur. In other words, development is from simple operations to more complex performances. For example, there will be a development of gross muscle usage before fine muscle control can take place. When the new baby cries, he seems to cry with his whole body (general); later, the child cries only with the upper part of his body, with his shoulders and chest heaving and his face all red. Even later in development he cries only with his face and eyes. Eventually, only the eyes cry, and, perhaps, only a tear escapes without the eyes moving at all. The baby learns to grasp with his whole hand before making use of his thumb and forefinger. He crawls before he creeps, and he creeps before he walks. Socially, he responds to many people before he decides that he really prefers his mother. Development in all areas—mentally, socially, emotionally, physically, and morally—proceeds from general to specific.

Specific principles

There are several significant facts about development that are fundamental and predictable and thus important to the understanding of growth and development. The first principle indicates that development follows a definite, orderly, sequential, predictable pattern. Growth is a continuous process following a predetermined maturational pattern. Normally, each child passes through each stage in the developmental process. Although individual differences exist within the developmental pattern, they are slight and, for the most part, do not appreciably influence the general trend of development.[1] Individual cases may be exceptions, however, because of environmental interference.

A second principle is that development comes from both maturation and learning. The maturational pattern is genetically programmed so that certain aspects of physiological growth take place innately. The learning process and opportunities for learning may hinder or aid the maturational process in developing organic elements to their maximum. The maturational process is, in turn, influential in determining when and if certain types of learning are ready to take place. For example, a child will be unable to be toilet trained, walk, read, or respond to conceptual development until the "teachable moment," as established by physiological maturation, has arrived. Parents and teachers should be happy to know that behavior patterns can be changed by maturation and learning, but the child must learn the new behavior pattern.

A third principle states that although all individuals follow a definite pattern of growth and development, each individual does so in his own style. Individual differences are partly due to differences in hereditary endowment, to the manner or rate in which the maturational process manifests itself, and to environmental influences and the nature of learning that has taken place. Factors that may be responsible for producing differences in rate of development include innate sex differences (male or female), appropriateness of glandular functions, adequacy of nutrition, genetic endowment, rate of intellectual development, nature of health, amount of fresh air and sunshine, position of the child within the family as regards siblings, incentive and motivational drive, and parental attitudes, interest, and support. The rate of growth is not the same for all children, or is it consistent for a specific child. Although there is some correlation between different types of growth, as for example, a heavy child may be a late walker, a child may differ in the rate of growth physically, mentally, socially, emotionally, and morally.

A fourth developmental principle suggests that each phase or stage of life has characteristic traits that are typical of that phase. The phases of life in chronological order are as follows: germinal, embryonic, and fetal before birth, neonatal, infancy (0 to 2 years), early childhood (3 to 5 years), middle childhood (6 to 8 years), late childhood (9 to 11 years), early adolescence (12 to 15 years), middle or late adolescence (16 to 18 years), late adolescence or emerging adulthood (19 to 22 years), early adulthood (23 to 42 years), middle adulthood (43 to 64 years), and late adulthood (65 years and older). Each stage has its own psychology, distinguishing traits and features, and developmental tasks to be achieved.

The fifth principle stresses that it is during infancy and early childhood that basic attitudes, traits, life styles, behaviors, and patterns of growth are formed. These factors will determine how the individual will develop as he grows older. Different physical and psychological traits have their roots in the earlier stages of life. Basic personality patterns may be set during the first five years of life.[2] The role that the child plays in the family and in the peer group will determine whether he develops into a leader, follower, or a nonresponder.[3] Because of the plasticity of the central nervous system of the early child, he is capable of being molded into a wide variety of developmental patterns.

Developmental tasks

As the individual proceeds from the neonatal stage of development to infancy and through the other stages of life, he is confronted with the need to master certain skills and to learn certain behavior patterns that are essential to personal and social adjustment at those ages.[4] Indeed some of the tasks that he must learn are pertinent to his very survival, especially in the earlier years. The skills, habits, attitudes, and behaviors that must be learned are known as "developmental tasks." Each phase or stage of development has a number of tasks or organizational (intellectual) patterns that must be learned or accomplished for the individual to achieve the level of maturity expected of him by his cultural group. The expectations and requirements that the culture holds over the child or adult change at each stage of development.

Havighurst,[5] who developed a widely accepted list of developmental tasks for the different age levels, states that "A developmental task is a task which arises at or about a certain period in the life of the individual, successful achievement of which leads to his happiness and to success with later tasks, while failure leads to unhappiness in the individual, disapproval by the society and difficulty with later tasks." Examples of developmental tasks in infancy and early childhood are learning to take solid food, to achieve physiological stability, and to form simple concepts of social and physical reality. In middle childhood some tasks are to learn physical skills necessary for games and to learn appropriate sex roles. In adolescence, tasks include developing new relations with age mates of both sexes and developing intellectual skills necessary for civic competence. Early adulthood tasks may include selecting a mate and getting started in an occupation. Some middle adulthood tasks are establishing and maintaining an economic standard of living and, if married, relating oneself to one's spouse as a person. In later maturity, tasks include adjusting to retirement and reduced income and establishing satisfactory physical living arrangements. In this book developmental tasks will be presented for each age level discussed.

BASIC PROCESSES RELATED TO EFFICIENT LIVING

There are many processes at work within the human body, but none of them is as fundamental as the processes of homeostasis, motivation, and learning. These processes are responsible for man's physical and psychological well-being and are instrumental in initiating behavior for a variety of purposes. They are crucial for survival. Many other processes function as a result of these three processes. For man's body and mind to operate at a high level of efficiency and effectiveness it is necessary for homeostasis, maturation, and learning to function at a peak level of performance.

Homeostasis

In general, the physical scientific laws of the universe operate in precise and specific ways. As long as these laws operate as they were intended to, according to nature, all will be well. However, whenever anything interferes with the effective, efficient operation of these laws, unpleasant, even dire consequences result. Natural forces then seek to bring about conditions that will restore the initial balance of nature so that the principles once again can operate as they were intended to. To provide an equilibrium, to restore a balance, to be in harmony with the underlying principles and laws by which the universe operates is fundamental to the very essence of life and the universe itself.

Homeostasis is a principle that proclaims that there is a tendency for the body to seek to maintain a relatively stable, constant state of equilibrium of its internal environment, even under changing external or internal circumstances. The purpose of this equilibrium is to maintain a state of constancy of the physiological processes so that all of the "laws" governing the body will "work in harmony" and permit the individual to perform at an efficient and effective level of being. For example, normal body temperature is 98.6° F. It is interesting to note that the body maintains that temperature rather well, whether the air temperature is 120° or 32° F. In general, rapid adjustments are made by the autonomic nervous system to restore or maintain the balance while slower adjustments occur through chemical and hormonal influences.

This demand for a steady, balanced internal constitution, however, does allow for necessary responses of the body to meet the needs of tissues. In some ways it may be said that "Mother Nature," in her wisdom, uses the principle of homeostasis to keep the body in good working order while, at the same time, providing the means by which the person is compelled to do those things that help to keep individual tissues and organisms in good condition. To illustrate, the tissues of the body need to have food to function. A person cannot eat enough food at one sitting to last him for a lifetime. In fact, he cannot eat enough food to last him for a whole month, or even a whole week. So on the one hand there is a need to maintain a stable, constant balance, and, on the other hand, there is a "built-in" process by which "tissue needs" go out of equilibrium. Means are provided by which behavior that can restore the balance is initiated.

Fig. 1-2 seeks to interpret how the homeostatic principle operates. At the outset it must be said that we are taking some liberties with the technical definition of homeostasis by including psychological processes in its coverage. Actually, there is a seeking of balance in promoting mental well-being, just as there is in achieving physical well-being. Therefore there is a similarity involved when one considers "that which is responsible for initiating behavior." The term *adjustive behavior* is used to indicate

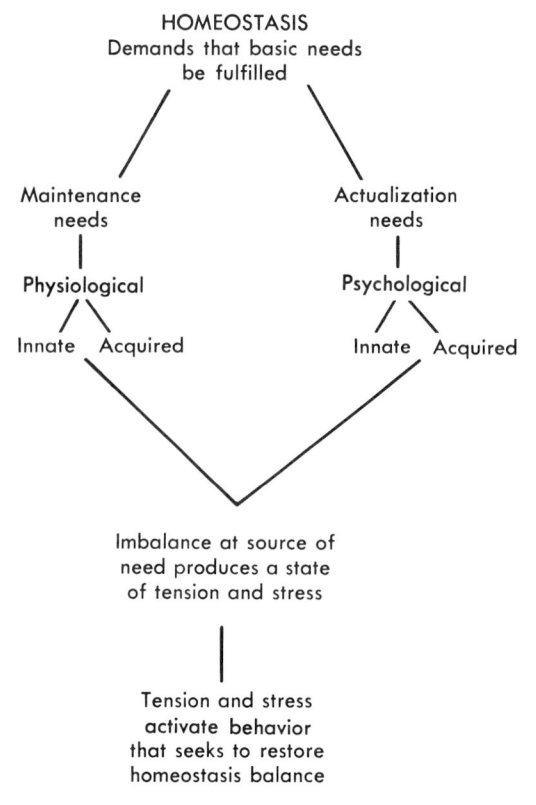

Fig. 1-2. The principle of homeostasis and how it operates to provide a relatively stable, constant state of physiological and psychological balance.

the process that sets in motion activities that tend to restore mental, or emotional, equilibrium. The difference between homeostatic activity and adjustive behavior is the means by which the action is pursued. Homeostasis uses the autonomic nervous system and some glandular activity; adjustive behavior may use these same elements, but it also uses cognitive (intellectual) and ego functions. Consider Fig. 1-2 as presenting the principle that seeks to explain what it is that initiates the need for some form of behavior to take place.

There are two major aims or goals of the human organism. One is to maintain a physiological well-being for the purpose of survival, and the other is to strive for self-actualization and enhancement of one's psychological well-being. The conditions that must be satisfied may be innate, ones with which a person is born, or they may be acquired by learning or experiencing within the environment. Most physiological demands are innate, but the body may learn to crave some things, such as certain drugs, that develop physiological cravings. Innate needs, or genetically programmed behavior, are within themselves a necessary and sufficient condition for the survival of man.[6] Some psychological needs, such as a need for love, security, and recognition, are considered by many psychologists to be innate. However, many emotional needs are acquired by interacting with people and conditions in the environment as one works his way through the growing-up process. In either area, physical or emotional, when conditions are not as they should be (according to the laws that indicate what is needed to maintain a state of well-being), an imbalance occurs, indicating that there is a deficiency or insufficiency of something needed for an equilibrium to exist. Whenever a disequilibrium occurs, stress or anxieties are created. These, in turn, bring about energy mobilization, which activates the organism to action or behavior. Behavior is actually initiated by the process of motivation.

Motivation

There is a reason or cause responsible for everything that a person does. Behind each action is an explanation, and included in that explanation will be an element of the motivational process. The term *motivation* is used to refer to the process by which behavior is initiated in response to a need, a deficiency, or a lack in the organism or person. Need-instigated behavior is goal-oriented in the sense that the behavior initiated is directed toward a goal or objective that, when attained, will satisfy the need by overcoming the deficiency and restoring the balance (Fig. 1-3). The type of behavior initiated depends on the type of need encountered, physiological or psychological. If the need is physiological, the behavior becomes task oriented in the sense of "I have a task to fulfill, I must get some food" (or water, sleep, release of bowel or bladder tension, or whatever the biological need may be). If the need is psychological, a defense mechanism is used. Such behavior may be an aggressive action to get what one needs or may be a withdrawal reaction to get away from the problem. Defense mechanisms are identifiable forms of normal behavior, utilized to consciously or unconsciously meet psychological needs.

In any case if the goal is reached and it is a proper goal (in the sense of providing what it was thought it would provide), the deficiency is overcome, balance is restored, and the individual no longer has any stress or anxiety on that account. If the goal is not appropriate or if the individual is prevented from attaining the goal for some reason, such as use of the wrong behavior, obstacles that have not been overcome, or personal limitations that restrict the use of appropriate behavior, then the inability to gain the needed goal produces a frustration. The frustration, in turn, produces more stress and anxiety, since the need has not been relieved, and more behavior is produced.

Learning

How does a person know what behavior is appropriate for reaching a desired aim? What would be behavior that would be instrumental in restoring the physiological or psychological balance? Nature provides some simple behaviors for this purpose, such as the sucking reflex, but most behavior is determined by the reasoning, cognitive process. "I know I have a need for some water, I am thirsty. My mouth is dry, my lips are parched, and I recognize those symptoms from the past as indicating that I am thirsty. Let's see, now, where is there a faucet or a fountain." This individual has

MOTIVATION

I. Successful goal-seeking behavior

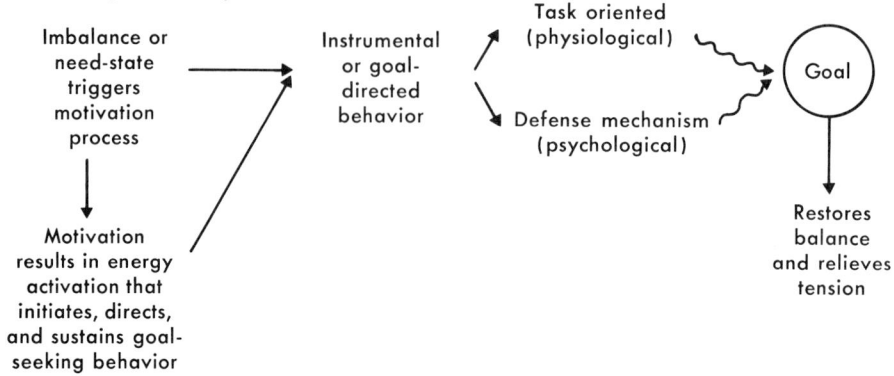

Imbalance or need-state triggers motivation process → Motivation results in energy activation that initiates, directs, and sustains goal-seeking behavior → Instrumental or goal-directed behavior → Task oriented (physiological) / Defense mechanism (psychological) → Goal → Restores balance and relieves tension

II. Unsuccessful goal-seeking behavior

Need-state → Goal-directed behavior → Barrier to reaching goal → Frustration → Produces more tension and stress → Results in more goal-seeking behavior → Aggressive behavior / Withdrawal behavior / Compromise behavior

Energy activation initiates behavior

Fig. 1-3. Motivation process and behavior produced.

learned what the symptoms of thirst were and what could produce water. An aborigine who has never been out of the wilds of his native homeland could perish from a lack of water if he were trapped in a room in a modern building, even if a drinking fountain were in that room. He may never have learned what a drinking fountain is or how to operate it to get water.

Learning provides man with cognitive and apperceptive materials that enable him to determine appropriate behavior for reaching a desired goal.

Learning is fundamental to the good life. There is a need to learn those things that will help one to survive and to actualize in his culture and environment. The more complex the society or culture within which

```
                            LEARNING
                    Helps determine appropriate
                        goal-seeking behavior

Learning            Learning            Learning            Learning
processes           methods             outcomes            modes
• perceptual        • trial and         • facts             • adaptive
• cognition           error             • skills              perception
• language          • conditioning      • attitudes           communication
• socialization       classical         • behavior            social
• creative            operant             patterns          • adjustive
                    • associative                             coping
                      insight                                 mechanisms

                    Contribute to fund of knowledge and
                    development of reasoning and decision-
                    making ability
```

Fig. 1-4. Component parts of learning process that influence quality of goal-seeking behavior.

one lives the more facts and skills one must learn to be able to have a comfortable level of physical and mental balance. The "getting of some goods" may be more difficult or complicated in highly stylized societies. An individual must develop his processes of learning to meet the demands of his culture. The learning processes consist of the perceptual systems, including the visual, auditory, and tactile modalities of learning, language, reasoning or cognitive processes, and creative processes (Fig. 1-4). What a person learns are facts, skills and habits, attitudes or interests (affect), and behavior patterns. He learns these things by the processes of trial and error, conditioning, or associative insight (developed reasoning ability). He makes use of them in adjustive, adaptive, or coping behavior.

Man has a freedom of choice in initiating behavior and in making decisions. He can choose an action that will be correct or one that will be wrong. Perhaps the action will be neutral and produce no results. Once a behavior is initiated, however, its actions are taken over by the cause-and-effect element inherent within all physical and some psychological laws. The outcomes of many actions can be predicted if one could only know all the principles and laws of nature involved. It behooves an individual to develop a value judgment system, a life philosophy of good and bad, better or worse, desirable or undesirable, to enable him to make decisions in keeping with what he considers to be most important in his life. A psychological behaviorist would ask that he learn to stress learning controls; a psychological existentialist or humanist would suggest that he learn how to achieve self-actualization.

Behavior can be learned or innate. Reflexes are an example of unlearned behavior. Most behavior, by far, is learned or initiated on the basis of learned elements. Adaptive behavior is any modification or change in structure or behavior that helps the organism to meet environmental demands. The term is sometimes used more loosely to imply any beneficial change to meet environmental demands. Coping or adjustive behavior is a learned action that permits an individual to live with extenuating or unwanted circumstances. It enables an individual to adjust to the circumstances so that he can get things done. Adaptive behavior may be behavior in which physiological changes take place for the individual to survive, such as learning to live with contaminated water that is needed for drinking or living with air pollution in larger cities. Coping behavior may be learning to live with a handicap or with the loss of a loved one. Each individual has the capacity and the potential for self-fulfillment. He also has the adaptive power to overcome obstacles of his own or of his environment's making.[7]

PHYSIOLOGICAL BASIS OF DEVELOPMENT

The physiological basis for growth and development includes the genetic foundation, the neural system, the glandular system, and the maturation process. The presentations given here will be short and slanted toward the way in which they influence growth and development. The mechanics of these influences will be discussed in a cursory way. Readers are encouraged to seek other texts dealing specifically with these topics for more detailed information on the mechanics of the processes.

Genetic foundations

The study of genetics (heredity) is a fascinating field of biology in which the causative factors of different characteristics and their means of transmission from one generation to another are introduced. There are two categories of cells found in the body—somatic cells and germ cells. Although all cells contain the same combination of chromosomes, only the germ cells, which are the reproductive cells, are transmitted at the time of conception. The somatic cells make up the organs, the brain, the body itself. These cells are the ones that respond to learning. They develop acquired traits. Since the somatic cells are not transmitted in the reproductive process, the acquired learning is not passed on to the offspring. Only the characteristics contained in the germ cells will be passed on by heredity.

Some of the qualities subject to inheritance include such things as physical features, sensitivity of the sense organs, vigor and strength of tissues, early or late puberty, a vulnerability to certain diseases such as heart disease and diabetes due to inherited bodily weaknesses, level of maintenance function in the storage of energy, the rate at which energy can be released and restored, and the degree of femaleness or maleness that an individual exhibits. Although mental ability, per se, is not inherited, the physical characteristics of the brain and the nervous system that respond to intellectual development are inherited.

The elements of heredity constitute a highly complicated process. Chemical substances combine and recombine to make long strands of molecules, which are responsible for most of the physical characteristics of man. Some molecules have the responsibility of carrying the "code of life." Others carry the "building code or blueprint" to the building sites in the developing individual. These molecules turn and twist and exchange parts, enabling man to have a multitude of characteristics.

Deoxyribonucleic acid (DNA) is responsible for the characteristics, metabolism, and variety in man.[8] DNA is composed of molecules of sugar, phosphate, and four bases that combine in different sequences. The bases are the chemicals adenine, guanine, cytosine, and thymine. Within the DNA molecule the pattern of the chromosomes is in the shape of a twisted ladder, called a *helix*. A sugar molecule alternates with phosphate to form the sides of the ladder. The rungs of the ladder are formed by combinations of either cytosine and guanine or adenine and thymine. The order of the chemical combinations on the rungs of the ladder carry the code for the characteristic to be inherited. Thus a sequence of CG, GC, AT, CG, TA may indicate a color of hair, whereas AT, AT, GC, TA may indicate the shape of eyes. This illustration is an oversimplification, of course. The genetic code for a characteristic may consist of a hundred "rungs" of the bases to produce a characteristic. A difference in a characteristic may occur if only one arrangement within the DNA changes. Sickle cell anemia (characterized by the presence of an abnormal red blood cell of crescent shape), for example, is the result of only one change in the 574 amino acid sequence that makes up the protein hemoglobin.

DNA is found only in the chromosomes within the nucleus of a cell. During the fertilization process, fraternal and maternal chromosomes intermingle and interchange genes, which results in the evolution of a totally new and different individual. The process responsible for the mixing of characteristics causing variation is called *meiosis*.

For development to occur the vital message concerning what tissue or organ is to be built must be delivered to the site of growth. This information is transmitted by ribonucleic acid (RNA). Basically, there are three kinds of RNA molecules that aid in the transfer. One is called the messenger RNA. Produced by DNA, this molecule will eventually move out of the nucleus and into the cytoplasm, carrying with it important instructions for protein synthesis.[9] A second kind of RNA is ribosomal RNA. Its function is believed to be associated with the regulation of enzymes involved in protein synthesis—the bringing together of types of amino acids in the proper sequence. Transfer RNA is thought to deliver amino acids to the templates formed by messenger RNA or the ribosomes so that the proper tissues and organs can be built. A summary of the protein-building process is presented below.

In considering genetic characteristics, two terms that often appear are *chromosomal aberration* and *gene mutation*. These processes are responsible for most of the

---

How the genetic code by means of DNA and RNA molecules produces body cell proteins from amino acid

1	2	3
DNA code contains genetic instructions in form of four basic control chemicals plus sugar and phosphate.	DNA produces messenger RNA in its nucleus to carry out orders of the DNA blueprint.	Messenger RNAs travel from nucleus to cell where transfer RNAs and twenty different amino acids are found.

4	5	6
Transfer RNAs are coded to attract specific kinds of amino acids; messenger RNAs activate appropriate transfer RNAs.	Transfer RNAs with proper amino acids attached approach and match the sequential pattern set up by messenger RNAs.	Amino acids, now in correct sequence, produce proteins at that site as requested by the DNA initially.

abnormal organic development in humans. Gene mutation refers to a change in the gene's chemical structure. This change can be in the form of being unable to function chemically or of being destroyed or a change in the base coding of DNA. One of the most frequent causes of mutations is exposure to high-energy radiation. A daily bombardment of cosmic rays on the body may cause natural mutations. Certain chemicals can cause abnormalities in a child's development. Chemicals that produce mutations are formaldehyde, nitrous acid, peroxide, and mustard gas.[10] One particular drug that had a drastic effect on normal development in children was thalidomide. In 1961 and 1962 European physicians were reporting the births of a large number of deformed children. After searching the past records of the mothers, almost all reportedly had taken thalidomide during pregnancy. There were numerous deformities of limbs, absence of fingers, arms, and legs, webbed fingers, undersized ears, dislocation of hips, absence of kidneys or gallbladders, and abnormal livers.[11]

In chromosomal aberrations there is an alteration in the structure of the chromosome or in the number of chromosomes. For example, Down's syndrome, also known as mongolism, is produced when three molecules instead of two get together to form a pair (Fig. 1-5). Down's syndrome is characterized by a short stature, slightly slanted

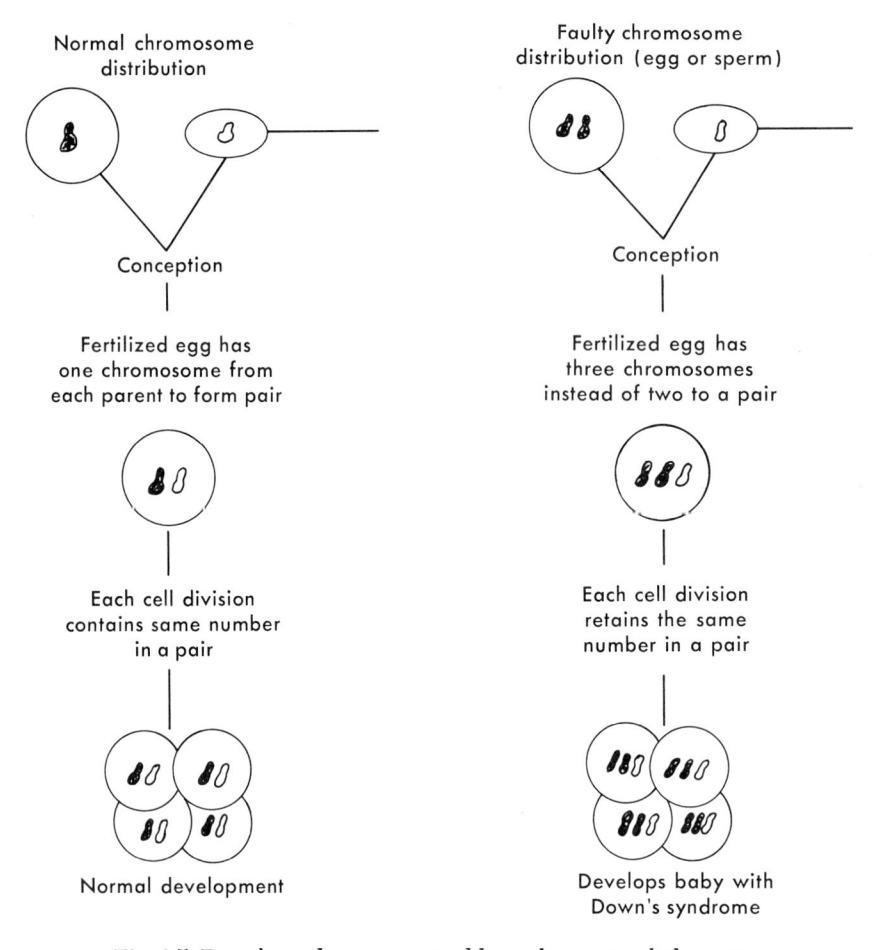

Fig. 1-5. Down's syndrome as caused by a chromosomal aberration.

eyes, and mental retardation. It occurs with greater frequency in children born to older women than to younger women, which may be due to the different types of chemical balance and hormonal secretion in older women. Other aberrations include Turner's syndrome and Klinefelter's syndrome, each produced by an abnormal number of sex chromosomes. In Turner's syndrome there is only one sex chromosome, whereas in Klinefelter's syndrome there are three instead of the normal two chromosomes. (See Glossary for definitions.)

There are reasons for knowing more about DNA, RNA, and the genetic code. First, DNA, RNA, and enzymes are related in some ways to intelligence and memory. It may be possible some day to determine how to improve intelligence and memory chemically. Second, we should know about chromosomal aberrations and the fact that some of these aberrations are hereditary in nature. If aberrations exist in a family, it may be desirable for the children, at the time of marriage or adulthood, to have genetic counseling to determine if they are carriers of the chromosomal deviation. Third, we should be aware of the genetic code and the social implications of seeking to change, influence, or tamper with it. Changing the genetic code to bring about desirable characteristics and eliminate undesirable ones may be significant, but where and how to draw the line at influencing the genetic code for social or political purposes must be considered.

Nervous system

Of all of the systems of the body the nervous system is one of the most important systems. Everything that takes place, consciously or unconsciously, voluntarily or automatically, has its primary genesis within the nervous system. Death comes when the brain, not the heart or the lungs, dies. The quality of response is greatly influenced by the quality and capability of the nervous system and the part of the brain related to that response. It is important to know the parts of the nervous system and how they function, but it is equally important to know how the nervous system reacts to stimuli, what it does to interpret those stimuli, and how it gets meaning and makes appropriate responses. This procedure refers to the perceptual process and the sensory-motor arc. The arc refers to the mechanical pathway; the perceptual process refers to how meaning is derived from impulses traveling along the pathways.

The sensory-motor arc pertains to the transmission of nerve impulses from receptor tissues or sense organs, to the central nervous system, and to the effector tissues of the muscles and glands. The nerve impulses are triggered by external or internal stimuli. Receptors such as the ears, eyes, skin, and taste buds are exteroceptors. Nerves in the muscles or tendons, the so-called muscle sense, are proprioceptors. The nerves in the inner membranes, in the body organs, are interoceptors. Receptors merely transmit the stimulus signals to the spinal cord and brain where meanings are attached to them. For a nerve impulse to be activated the stimulus must be powerful enough to overcome the threshold of stimulation and trigger the impulse. Not all stimuli are that strong.

If the stimulus has immediate survival or protection value, it may only travel to the spinal cord, where a quick estimate of its value is made. If the situation is harmful, such as the fingers touching something extremely hot, the spinal cord will react with a reflex and jerk the hand from the hot object. If a reflex action is not involved, the nerve impulses are sent to the brain, where they are studied, interpreted, and given meaning. That meaning is scrutinized and a judgment value attached to it. That judgment will determine what action should take place, and the brain will program for the next step. The programmed information will activate the appropriate muscles (motor areas) or glands for a response. The muscles involved may be the striped, or striate, muscles of the skeleton, the cardiac muscles of the heart, or the smooth, internal muscles of the organs. The glands will be either the duct glands (sweat and tears) or the endocrine glands, which constitute a complicated chemical system of hormones that regulate and integrate the whole organism.

The nervous system has two major divisions, a central nervous system (CNS) consisting of the spinal cord and the brain, and a peripheral nervous system (PNS) made up of (1) the nerves related to the skin and muscles (somatic or voluntary) and (2) the nerves found in the organs and glands (visceral or autonomic). The main subdivisions of the central nervous system and their functions are noted in Table 1-1. Note that some parts, such as the spinal cord, medulla, and cerebellum, are primarily interested in physiological functions, whereas the thalamus, hypothalamus, and cerebrum are concerned with more complex physiological functions and with cognitive processes.

The PNS has one function that is especially worthy of note. It contains the mechanism that regulates the normal func-

Table 1-1. Major structures of the nervous system

I. Central nervous system		
A. Brain		
Forebrain { 1. Cerebrum		Sense perception; voluntary movements; learning, remembering, thinking; emotion; consciousness; personality integration
2. Thalamus		Sensory relay station on way to cerebral cortex
3. Hypothalamus		Control of visceral and somatic function, such as temperature, metabolism, and endocrine balance
Midbrain { 4. Corpus callosum		Fibers connecting two cerebral hemispheres
5. Midbrain		Conduction and switching center; pupillary light reflex, etc.
6. Reticular formation		Arousal system that activates wide regions of cerebral cortex
Hindbrain { 7. Cerebellum		Muscle tone; body balance; coordination of voluntary movement, as of fingers and thumb
8. Medulla		Via cranial nerves exerts important control over breathing, swallowing, digestion, heartbeat
9. Pons		Fibers connecting two hemispheres of cerebellum
B. Spinal cord		Conduction paths for motor and sensory impulses; local reflexes
II. Peripheral nervous system		
A. Autonomic nervous system		Autonomous or self-regulating mechanism
1. Parasympathetic division		Operates and controls vital life functions at normal level
2. Sympathetic division		Takes over vital life functions in stress or emergency situation; increases functions of those necessary to meet threat and decreases function of those not necessary for survival
B. Craniosacral nerves		Controls sensory nerves, motor and somatic nerves, and vagus nerve

tioning of the body in such things as rate of heartbeat, breathing, digestion, and so forth. It also has a means of moving from normal operations to emergency operations. Whenever the body or the mind is under great stress or is in physical or psychological danger, the sympathetic division of the autonomic system takes over and tries to help the body and mind to survive as best it can by enabling it to perform better to overcome the emergency threat. Operations unnecessary to survival are slowed down or stopped. Body functions that can help are speeded up. The nostrils of the nose enlarge, and the person breathes more quickly to take in more oxygen. Epinephrine and sugar are secreted into the bloodstream. The heart beats faster to pump blood, with its additional fuel, to all parts of the body. The body is geared to meet the threat. When the emergency is over, the body functions settle down, and the normal, parasympathetic division takes over again. The manner by which the body responds to emergencies is known as the general adaptation syndrome and was hypothesized by Hans Selye.[12]

The perceptual process refers to how the brain deals with the nerve impulses it receives so that it can interpret and give meaning to the stimuli that triggered the impulses (Fig. 1-6). The stimuli are picked up by the sense organ as sensations, and the impulses are transmitted to the central nervous system. The signals are directed to the proper places in the brain for interpretation. The brain may or may not recall having dealt with signals before. A scanning procedure is utilized to bring forth any information that would help the brain to make interpretations. The interpretations would include such things as developing concepts or generalizations, gaining insight, formulation of language, or putting the stimuli sensations into a proper sequence. A decision is made as to what to do with the material, and programming for some form of response is done.

Taking in the pattern of the stimulus would be a receptive action, producing a

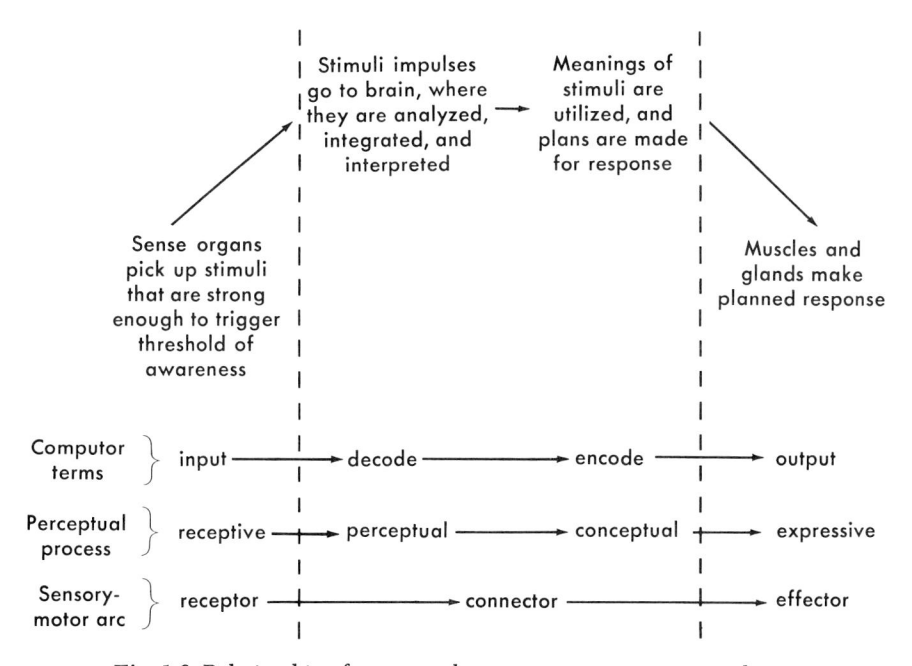

Fig. 1-6. Relationship of perceptual process to sensory-motor pathways.

sensation of some type. Dealing with the sensations and giving meaning to them would be cognitive or perceptive action. Expressive action would be the response. Using computer terms, reception would be input; cognition would first have decoding, then encoding; finally, expressive action would be the output. There is always feedback to indicate the adequacy of the perceptual act. Difficulty in understanding or learning may occur at any point in the perceptual process due to lesions, scars, tumors, poor synaptic transmission, cerebral hemorrhage, or maturational lag in neurological development. Thought does not always have to start with a receptive act; it could begin in the brain in the cognitive part of the perceptual process. In this case the activity is known as ideomotor action, indicating an operational sequence in which a motor response is elicited by an idea. Of course it is possible for thinking to take place without any response in the motor area.

Endocrine glandular system

Within the human body there exists a group of small capsules of tissue, the endocrine glands. These glands are distributed widely throughout the body; they differ from one another in their structure and in the nature of their secretions. The endocrine glands secrete directly into the bloodstream and are therefore called ductless glands or glands of internal secretion. They include the pituitary, thyroid, parathyroids, adrenals, pancreas, ovaries, testes, thymus, and pineal body.

Table 1-2. Principal endocrine glands

GLAND	HORMONES SECRETED	FUNCTION	OVERSECRETION	UNDERSECRETION
Pituitary				
Anterior lobe	Growth hormone	Growth; regulates other glands; water metabolism	Acromegaly; gigantism	Dwarfism; Simmonds' disease; diabetes insipidus
Posterior lobe	Gonadotrophic Antidiuretic Oxytocin			
Thyroid	Thyroxin	Regulates basal metabolic rate, activity; fatigue; body weight	Toxic goiter; Graves' disease	Cretinism; simple goiter; Gull's disease; myxedema
Parathyroid	Parathormone	Regulates calcium and phosphorus; normal excitability of nervous system	Osteitis fibrosa; sluggishness; loss of weight	Splitting headaches; tetany
Adrenals				
Cortex	Cortisone	Salt, water balance; body changes in emotions; carbohydrate metabolism	Virilism; sexual precocity; Cushing's syndrome	Addison's disease; anemia; low blood pressure
Medulla	Epinephrine			
Pancreas (islets of Langerhans)	Insulin Glucagon	Controls blood sugar level and carbohydrate	Hyperinsulinism stupor	Diabetes mellitus
Gonads				
Ovaries	Androgens	Regulate sexual development and functioning	Menstrual disturbance	Failure of sexual maturation; menopause symptoms
Testes	Estrogens Progesterone			

The endocrines are intrinsic regulators of development. They affect health and development through the secretion of complicated chemical substances called *hormones*. Hormones are liberated directly into the bloodstream and are carried to all parts of the body, where they have special functions of initiating, regulating, and controlling some of the activities of organs and tissues. Although the amount of the secretions of these glands may be almost imperceptibly small, they have incredible potency.

The functions of these hormones are diversified. They range from influencing the rate and pattern of growth and maturation to regulating the amount of water excreted by the kidneys. They control the processes by which humans digest foods and rebuild them into blood, bone, muscle, and brain tissue. They largely determine the length of bones, the deposition of fat, and whether an individual shall be short, stout, tall, or thin. They pace the beating of the heart and supervise the working of the liver and kidneys. They time the onset of puberty, control the menstrual cycle, and govern the many staged processes of reproduction, from the first ripening of an egg cell to the final muscle contractions that propel an infant toward independent life.[13] They even regulate one another. The activity of one gland is affected by the secretion of another, and thus the performance of one gland reflects the activity of another. (See Table 1-2 for their functions.)

When the endocrine glands function in perfect concert, the individual is well and happy. When their delicate balance is upset, the individual may suffer from a host of disease processes or emotional disturbances. They are as indispensable to physical welfare as are food, air, and water. Diseases of the endocrine glands are usually associated with their hyperactivity (oversecretion) or hypoactivity (undersecretion). These changes from normal activity may even exist before the birth of a child. In some cases glandular dysfunction of women during pregnancy may retard fetal development.

The endocrine glands appear to be the bridge between the organic constitution of the body and the mental, moral, and esthetic capacities of humanity. The importance of these glands as creative forces shaping both the outer form and inner experience of every human individual is becoming ever more manifest and irrefutable.

Maturation

Occasionally students have difficulty understanding the term *maturation*. Maturation always and exclusively, as a principle of growth and development, refers to physiological maturation. Organisms mature through the maturational process. Maturation does not refer to the development of emotional, social, mental, or spiritual maturity. There are several reasons why it is important to know about the physical maturation process. First, it suggests the sequence of physiological maturity and its behavior. By knowing the sequence the level of development that a child has achieved can be determined. By comparing this level to the proper norms, it is possible to tell if development is at a normal rate or not. Second, knowledge of physiological maturation enables detection if a child is skipping any stages of development or moving through them too quickly or too slowly. These factors are deemed to have some significance in the development of the perceptual learning processes of the child.[14] Third, approximately one fourth of all children ages 5 to 8 years have a maturational lag in neurological development of the perceptual processes. It would behoove parents and teachers to be aware of this lag and its implications.

Maturation is the unfolding of innate organic patterns in an ordered sequence through the growth of the organisms. Prenatal and some postnatal developments of behavior result from the unfolding of potentialities resident within the genes and are thus inherited. However, this growth process results from an integral relation of genes and their constantly changing surroundings. In light of the great amount of work in experimental embryology, development cannot be regarded as potential within the genes alone, neither can it be regarded as essentially determined by environment. It is a product of these two sets of conditions.[15] The universality of the reflex responses is presumptive evidence for the generalization that early fetal behavior is dependent on maturation of sensory, neural, and motor structures. Once the structures have attained a certain degree of functional maturity, exercise may determine some part of further development. On the basis of evidence at present available it is difficult to provide a clear-cut distinction between maturation and learning and between heredity and environment.[16]

There are several implications of the principle of maturation for growth and development. First, implicit in the principle of maturation is the concept of readiness. It is impossible to teach a child, in spite of any amount of practice, any task for which the innate disposition or readiness for learning is not already present. Capacities such as walking, talking, and even doing multiplication depend on natural, innate aptitudes that have reached their "teachable moment" and not on training. The lack of practice in natural functions does not check the development of a maturing pattern, however. Although some capacities are innate and will inevitably emerge irrespective of teaching, practice and training can make all the difference between a skilled or a mediocre or clumsy performance. For some activities there is an optimum time for development that, if it could be determined, is the best time for giving training and practice. For example, it appears that the age for establishing the foundations for a good muscle structure and motor coordination system is about 2½ or 3 years of age.

Environmental conditions play an important part in encouraging or retarding the process of maturation. An environment of some kind is necessary for the expression of a child's capacities. The environment is the arena in which his potentialities are expressed. The more suitable the environment the better will be the development. The child learns to walk, but he walks "somewhere." What he finds and experiences in the places where he walks will have much to do with the development of his other attributes. The environment determines which of a child's native potentialities are developed and which ones are left undeveloped. It is hardly likely that a child born and raised in the arctic north will ever learn to be a great swimmer.

PSYCHOSOCIAL INFLUENCES ON DEVELOPMENT

No child is born with a ready-made "human behavior." All children learn to behave like human beings through associating with other humans. All babies are pretty much alike when they are born. They have the same needs, go through the same sequence in developing locomotion and speech, and have a need to relate to people. Children become different because of the culture in which they grow, the experiences that they have, and the genetic uniqueness of their individual differences. The process of socialization teaches them how to be like their compatriots.

Socialization

All human beings experience socialization. A child is born in a specific culture and is thus subjected to the socializing forces found in that culture. The brief period of childhood, during which human beings are most malleable, is the period when the whole process of socialization, the shaping the person into a socially acceptable form, must occur.[17] The perpetuation of a culture requires that each new generation acquire the patterns of living inherent in their culture.

Becoming socialized means that the individual behaves in such a way so as to be acceptable to the social group with which he wishes to identify. He develops the social attitudes common to that particular social group and will consciously employ these attitudes so as to regulate and control his behavior.

A social role is a pattern of behavior that is expected of fellow members by the members of a social group. For example, there are roles for teachers, pupils, ministers, etc. Their behavior or role is prescribed to them by the other members of their social group, and they must generally act in accordance with these specified patterns of behavior. Every social group has its own recognized patterns of behavior for its members.

Socialization imposes the attitudes, appreciations, social roles, and skills of a culture on the individual. Societies vary in the means used to achieve these goals. Much of the socialization process is implemented by agents—people (or groups) who interpret the culture to the child. They guide and reinforce his learning of the appropriate behavior patterns for his sex, age, and social class, and they inhibit the learning of inappropriate behavior. Fig. 1-7 gives an overall effect that these social agents have on the process of socialization.

Family. The family is the socializing agent most directly responsible for the transmission of the cultural content of the society to the growing child. The socialization process begins in the home. The family passes on its attitudes, prejudices, and points of view to the child. The family also determines the social class, ethnic origin, race, and usually the religion of the child. The family, through the experiences they offer the child, will teach him concepts concerning the world—real and un-

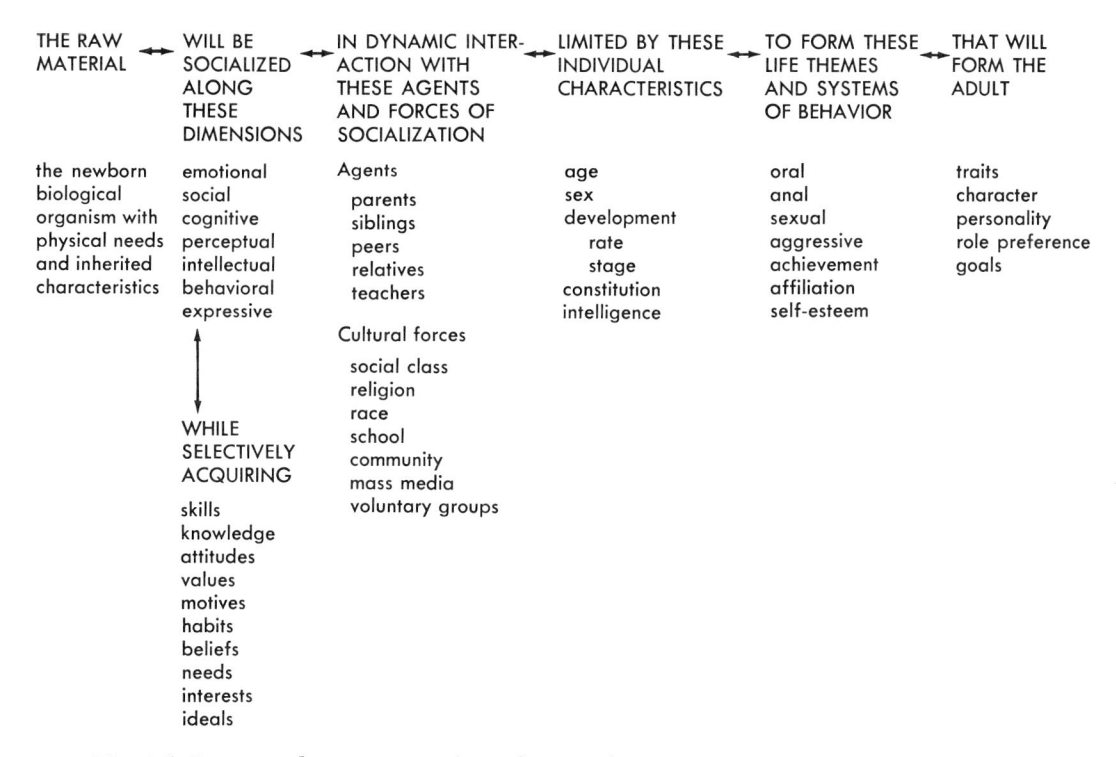

THE RAW MATERIAL	WILL BE SOCIALIZED ALONG THESE DIMENSIONS	IN DYNAMIC INTERACTION WITH THESE AGENTS AND FORCES OF SOCIALIZATION	LIMITED BY THESE INDIVIDUAL CHARACTERISTICS	TO FORM THESE LIFE THEMES AND SYSTEMS OF BEHAVIOR	THAT WILL FORM THE ADULT
the newborn biological organism with physical needs and inherited characteristics	emotional social cognitive perceptual intellectual behavioral expressive ↑↓ WHILE SELECTIVELY ACQUIRING skills knowledge attitudes values motives habits beliefs needs interests ideals	Agents parents siblings peers relatives teachers Cultural forces social class religion race school community mass media voluntary groups	age sex development rate stage constitution intelligence	oral anal sexual aggressive achievement affiliation self-esteem	traits character personality role preference goals

Fig. 1-7. Process and components of socialization. (From Human socialization, by E. B. McNeil. Copyright 1969 by Wadsworth Publishing Co., Inc. Reprinted by permission of the publisher, Brooks/Cole Publishing Co., Monterey, Calif.)

real. This information is given to the child through the use of words. Therefore one of the most important roles of the family is to teach the child language.

The parent-child relationship is a factor that has great influence on the social development of the child. The type of discipline used and how the parent reacts to the child is important, as is the life style of the home. The democratic home life seems to produce an active, aggressive, fearless, and playful child who has leadership characteristics, who tends to be curious and nonconforming. The controlled home, on the other hand, produces a quiet, nonrestricted, well-behaved, and unaggressive child with restricted curiosity, originality, and fancifulness. (See Fig. 1-8.)

The way in which the parent views the child and the circumstances under which the child was born will also affect the parent-child relationship. Such circumstances as, for example, the arrival of a long-awaited baby to older parents, an unwanted child to an unmarried woman, an unwanted child to quarreling parents, or the first child of a young, happy couple will surely have some effect on how the parents feel toward the child, their treatment of the child, and the child's adjustment and social development.

The presence of brothers and sisters within the family also has an effect on the development of the child. The number of siblings, their ages, and birth order help to determine the socialization practices found in the home. For example, a study done by Elder and Bowerman[18] reveals that in large families the mechanics of managing several children dictates parental authoritarianism. The birth order within the family may have an effect on the social adjustment of the individual. Schachter[19] has found that the first-born child receives more attention, is more likely to be exposed to psychological discipline, and is more anxious and dependent, whereas later-born children are more aggressive and self-confident.

Peer group. The peer group consists of individuals who are approximately of the same age and of the same social class. In childhood the peer group is more like a play group, whereas in adolescence the peer group takes on the appearance of a clique or gang.

The peer group projects a pattern of conformity. The members reinforce responses that conform to their expectations. These responses will be reinforced, adopted, and strengthened by the peer group. Responses that are nonconforming will be discouraged.

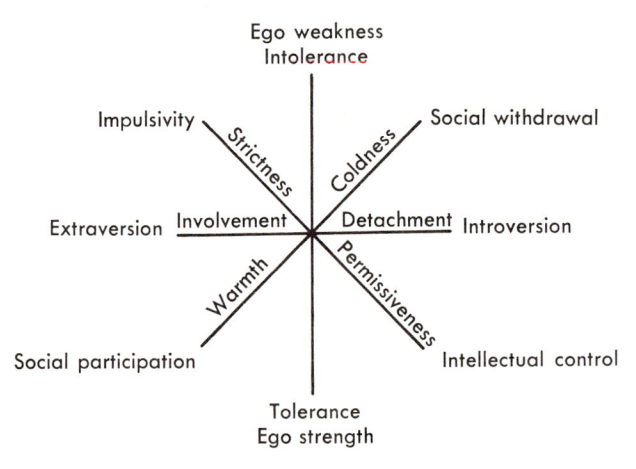

Fig. 1-8. Effects of family relationships on the child's developing personality. (Modified from Slater, P. E.: J. Genet. Psychol. **101**:53-68, Sept., 1962.)

The concept of impersonal authority is introduced to the child through the peer group. Even though in the childhood peer group no one child is the leader, there are certain unwritten rules of the game to which the child must conform. Through his peers the child comes in contact with various attitudes toward himself, toward adults, and toward those things that are to be valued or disregarded.[20]

The child soon learns how to secure the recognition of his group, how to participate as one of its members, and how to avoid the group's displeasure. The child learns patterns of behavior from the peer group that cannot be learned from adults. Concepts of cooperation, sharing, and participation are also transmitted by the peer group to the individual. The child's peer group is one way by which he can become independent of his parents and other authorities. This is particularly apparent during adolescence, when the child identifies with new models and develops new emotional ties.

Society. In the society of today there are numerous opportunities to interact. Mass transportation has provided the ability to reach out and communicate beyond the community. By widening his environment the individual perceives and learns about differences in customs and mores. Society also provides certain rules by which to live, some of which have been written into law and must be adhered to or punishment results.

The community is the first large social structure that provides a framework for socioeconomic life. The community is involved with the individual at every level of development. In comparing one community with another vast differences in their characteristics can be recognized. In many large cities there are communities where the population is constantly on the move. There are few ties between the people. The family receives little assistance in developing a child's civic and interpersonal obligations. The morale of the people is negligible and disorganized; cultural values and expectations appear confused. In more stable communities there is more interaction between the family and school, business people, civic leaders, and clergy, helping to provide a basis for community concern.

The school is the first socializing agent within the community that the child encounters outside of the family. One of the aims of education is to complete the socialization process begun in the family. Educational institutions transmit the knowledge, beliefs, customs, and skills of the society. Organized education is the tool that society employs to civilize its young citizens. The school reaches all the children in the community who are physically and mentally able to attend. The effect of the school on the individual and the community is widespread.

The emerging self

Growth and development is a total process. There is a great interaction of forces that influence the growth process. Intrinsic and extrinsic, internal and external elements are at work contributing their share in manipulating and shaping the individual. Certainly the individual should have something to say about what is happening to him. He cannot control all the forces that are at work on him, but he can make some choices and determine some directions that his life will take through elements that make up his personality. These elements are referred to as "self-determinants," dynamic forces within the individual that make up his "ego," or "conscious self."

Each individual develops a "self-structure"—a pattern of interacting inner forces that serves as reference points around which experiences are organized and behavior patterns formed. The inner forces are psychophysical systems that will provide dynamics that will influence the direction and the intensity that behavior responses take. Since psychophysical systems differ somewhat from individual to individual, behavioral responses will tend to differ. When a person develops his value judgment system, his value considerations of what is important, good, or interesting will also influence his behavior and the goals he will seek.

There is within the individual at birth a series of primitive impulses and reflexes that are intended to help the newborn child survive. They are responsible for most of the child's behavior in the first 2 years. Although an individual never loses these primitive drives, he does gain control of them and lessens their influence as he becomes socialized. If survival is ever seriously threatened, the primitive impulses can emerge again to perform their assigned tasks. However, as a child grows into manhood, he develops other means by which he can promote his well-being.

One of the first steps in gaining control of the primitive impulses and drives is when the child develops an image of self and a self-identity. When the child becomes conscious of self, "to know I exist, to know what I am like and who I am," he is taking giant steps toward becoming a conscious being. This stage occurs initially, in a gross manner, about the age of 2 years. It is at this point that a child can exert a conscious force to get what he wants. However, getting what he wants is not always what others in power or authority over him think he should have. The forces of society go to work to make the individual conform to the expectations that society has of the age level of the child.

The child learns. He begins to realize that some behaviors are more acceptable than others. Furthermore, he comes to develop some likes and dislikes of his own. He develops a "self-ideal," an image of what he wants to be like and of what he needs to do to be accepted by those important to him. He can do some of this by 4 years of age. With a self-ideal to guide him and to remind him of what is important to him, he is now in a position to control and direct his behavior in accordance with his intentions and desires, which in turn are acceptable to society. He develops a life-style, a way of living and thinking. In addition, he learns ways of responding to frustrating times when he does not get what he wants. As he gets older, he modifies his action patterns to be in keeping with society's expectations of his new age levels. If he satisfies the demands of society, he feels accepted; if he does not, he feels rejected. The intensity of his needs and the pattern of inner controls that he has developed will determine how he will respond, how well-adjusted he is, and how accepted he feels.

Ultimately, the degree of a child's feeling of acceptance or rejection will have something to do with his development. He can develop a negativistic attitude toward those who seek to direct his growth. He may withdraw, lose interest, or seek to escape. He may become belligerent and rebellious so that he cannot be reached to be taught. One way or another his emerging self and personality style will largely determine what he will permit to happen to him. He will have something to say about how he develops mentally, socially, emotionally, and spiritually. He may even have something to say about how he will develop physically.

STUDY GUIDE

1. What are the definitions of individuality and universality, and what are their implications for the growth and development of individuals?
2. State the three principles related to directions of growth and development and define them.
3. Five specific developmental principles are mentioned. What are they?
4. Define "developmental task."
5. Look at Fig. 1-2 on homeostasis. Think of the meaning of homeostasis, then

follow the diagram to review how homeostasis strives for a balance within the individual.
6. How does motivation and learning influence behavior (Figs. 1-3 and 1-4)?
7. How do DNA and RNA carry out genetic plans for growth and development?
8. The nervous system is fundamental to all development and behavior. What is the sensory motor arc? What are the parts and functions of the two major divisions of the nervous system? How is the perceptual system related to the nervous system and the sensory motor arc?
9. Identify the glands of the endocrine system and give the function of each gland.
10. What is physiological maturation, and what implications does it have for growth and development?
11. Socialization is said to occur through the influences of the family, the peer group, and society on the developing individual. Which of these three forces do you think is influential in total development? Cite your reasons, even if you conclude that it is difficult or impossible to say which is most important or influential.
12. Describe the emerging self. Can you relate aspects of the emerging self to your own growth and development and behavior? In what ways?

REFERENCES

1. Gesell, A.: The ontogenesis of infant behavior. In Carmichael, L. editor: Manual of child psychology, ed. 2, New York, 1954, John Wiley & Sons, Inc.
2. Kagan, J., and Moss, H. A.: Birth to maturity: a study in psychological development, New York, 1962, John Wiley & Sons, Inc.
3. Barr, J. A., and Hoover, K. H.: Home conditions and influences associated with the development of high school leaders, Educ. Adm. Sup. 43:271-279, 1957.
4. Zaccaria, J. S.: Developmental tasks: implications for the goals of guidance, Personnel Guid. J. 44:372-375, 1965.
5. Havighurst, R. J.: Human development and education, New York, 1953, Longmans, Green & Co., Inc. p. 2.
6. Hess, E. H.: Ethology and developmental psychology. In Mussen, P. H., editor: Carmichael's manual of child psychology, ed. 3, New York, 1970, John Wiley & Sons, Inc., p. 1.
7. Grams, A.: Facilitating learning and individual development, St. Paul, Minn., 1966, Minnesota Department of Education, p. 18.
8. Otto, J. H., and Towle, A.: Modern biology, New York, 1963, Holt, Rinehart & Winston, Inc., p. 142.
9. Burdette, W. J.: Methodology in basic genetics, San Francisco, 1963, Holden-Day, Inc., p. 32.
10. Otto and Towle, op. cit., p. 148.
11. Deformed babies born as a result of sedative, Sci. News, p. 22, July, 1962.
12. Selye, H.: The stress of life, New York, 1956, McGraw-Hill Book Co.
13. Morrison, T., Cornett, F., Tether, J. E., and Gratz, P.: Human physiology, New York, 1967, Holt, Rinehart & Winston, Inc., pp. 348-400.
14. Kaluger, G., and Kolson, C. J.: Reading and learning disabilities, Columbus, Ohio, 1969, Charles E. Merrill Publishing Co., p. 30.
15. Munn, N. L.: The evolution and growth of human behavior, ed. 2, Boston, 1965, Houghton Mifflin Co., pp. 201-202.
16. Ibid., p. 203.
17. McNeil, E. B.: Human socialization, Belmont, Calif., 1969, Brooks/Cole Publishing Co., p. 2.
18. Elder, G. H., and Bowerman, C. E.: Family structure and child rearing patterns: the effect of family size and sex composition, Am. Sociol. Rev. 28:891-905, 1963.
19. Schachter, S.: The psychology of affiliation, Stanford, Calif., 1959, Stanford University Press, p. 174.
20. Levine, L. S.: Personal and social development: the psychology of effective behavior, New York, 1963, Holt, Rinehart & Winston, Inc., p. 187.

2 Prenatal development

The greatest miracle of this age, or of any age, is not the knowledge explosion brought on by electronic technology, or the transplanting of organs from one human being to another, or the landing of men on the moon. The greatest miracle of all is the creation and birth of a new life. When one considers the intricate and complex processes involved in creating, developing, and maintaining life, how a human being is formed from a ball-shaped cell smaller in size than the period at the end of this sentence, and how human development takes place in such an orderly, sequential manner, one has to be impressed by the wonder and marvel of it all.

LIFE BEGINS

Living things have the power to reproduce themselves. The simplest kinds of animals and plants reproduce by the splitting of one cell in half, thus making two separate organisms. Animals and plants that are more complex in development have special cells that are designated for the purpose of reproduction. In human beings, as in other vertebrates, the union of two of these distinctive cells called gametes, one from the male and the other from the female, is necessary to create new life.

Before gamete, or sperm or egg, production can take place the male and the female must reach puberty. Puberty is the period during which the internal reproductive organs become functional. In the female the onset of puberty is marked by the beginning of menstruation. In the male, puberty is indicated by sperm found in the urine. The average age of completion of pubertal development is 12½ years for girls and 14 years for boys. However, there is a wide variation in the ages at which normal boys and girls attain puberty.

Sex cells

The sex cells (gametes, or germ cells) are the egg, or ovum (plural, ova) in the female and the sperm, or spermatozoon (plural, spermatozoa) in the male. The ovum is one of the largest cells in the human body, whereas the spermatozoon is one of the smallest. The spermatozoon is approximately 0.05 mm in diameter or 1/6,000 inch. It has either an oval-shaped head or a smaller, round-shaped head, plus a fine, hairlike tail about ten times as long as its head. The tail lashes back and forth, enabling the spermatozoon to swim through the semen in which it is found. The ovum is a single, ball-shaped cell approximately 0.1

mm or 1/200 inch in diameter and has no means of locomotion within itself. Its movement is dependent on the contractions of the tissues by which it is surrounded.[1] The ovum is a tiny speck barely visible to the naked eye. However, it is still some 85,000 times greater in volume than the sperm.[2]

Female gametes and organs (Fig. 2-1)

The human female has in her ovaries at birth over 400,000 rudimentary ova. Many of these will atrophy before she reaches puberty. Of the 150,000 ova remaining at puberty, approximately 400 will mature, one at a time usually, prior to the menopause.[3] The ovum is yellowish in color because it contains yolk that will be used to nourish a new individual should the ovum be fertilized. In its nucleus the ovum contains 46 chromosomes in 23 pairs. Chromosomes direct the cells they occupy to grow in certain ways, perform certain functions, and transmit hereditary traits. When the ovum ripens, the pairs of chromosomes split by a process known as oogenesis. Half of the chromosomes remain at the center of the ovum; the other half migrate to the outer portion of the ovum and eventually disappear.[4] When the ovum is fertilized, it will receive 23 chromosomes from the sperm, thus again having a total of 46.

The uterus (womb) is a hollow, pear-shaped organ with strong but elastic muscular walls. It is within the uterus that the

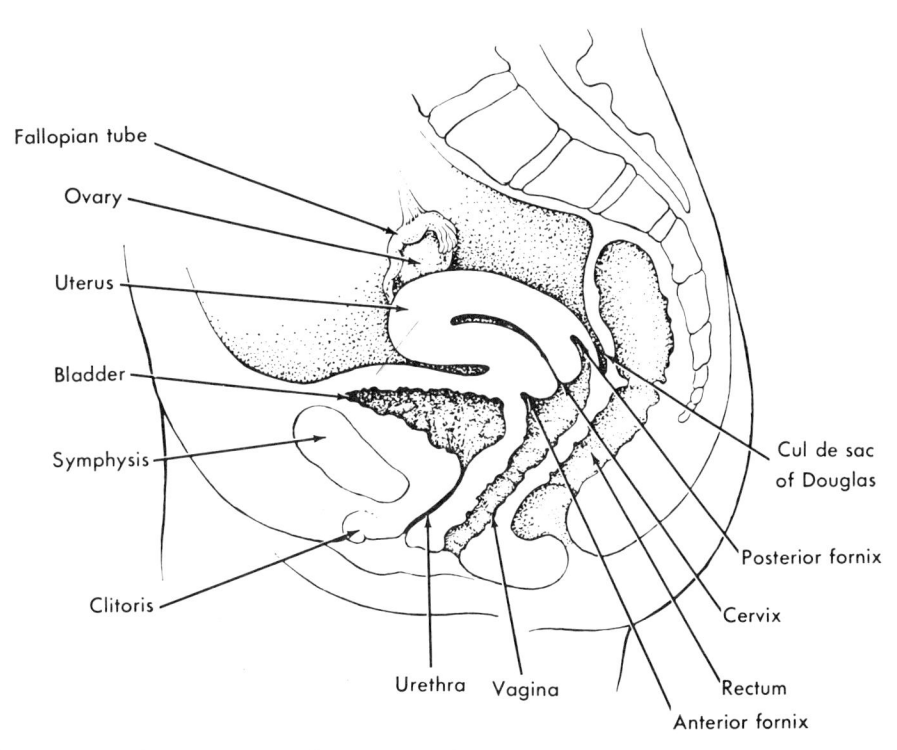

Fig. 2-1. Female sex organs and gamete production. The ovary releases one ovum (egg) a month. The egg travels through the Fallopian tube, where fertilization occurs if sperms are present. If the egg is not fertilized, the wall of the uterus breaks down, and blood cells and disintegrated egg are discharged through the vagina by the process of menstruation. The female system prepares itself for motherhood each month. (From Iorio, J.: Principles of obstetrics and gynecology for nurses, ed. 2, St. Louis, 1971, The C. V. Mosby Co.)

baby will develop. The lower end of the uterus is called the *cervix,* which extends into the vagina. The cervix has an opening through which the sperms will make their way from the vagina into the uterus. When the baby is being born, the cervix will dilate and the baby will pass through this enlarged opening into the vagina and be discharged into the external world.

During a woman's childbearing years, the uterus is normally prepared each month for fertilization and pregnancy. If no pregnancy occurs, menstruation takes place. The menstrual "cycle" begins with the flow of mucus and blood that had accumulated during the previous cycle. The discharge will continue for four or five days. At the end of this time the uterine wall is relatively thin. In the postmenstrual phase the uterus will come under the influence of an estrogen hormone that seeks to increase sexual excitability—and also influences thickening of the endometrium (uterus wall lining). At the time of ovulation the hormone progesterone takes over and prepares the endometrium with thin layers of cells for the reception and development of the fertilized ovum. The lining inside the uterus continues to thicken. If fertilization of the ovum does not take place, the level of progesterone begins to drop about the twenty-fifth day, resulting in a degeneration of the thickened uterine lining. The surface layer of cells passes out with the flow of mucus and blood during the next menstrual phase. The content is normally about 6 to 8 tablespoons. A menstrual cycle lasts for an average of twenty-eight days, paralleling the time of a lunar month.[5]

Ovulation is the process by which a mature ovum is discharged from one of the two ovaries. The ovaries are glands about the size and shape of almonds that lie about 3 inches on either side of the midway point between the vaginal opening and the navel. They are located on each side of the outer uterine wall at the end of the Fallopian tubes. There is a tube for each ovary. Generally, the ovaries alternate in releasing one ripe ovum on or about the fourteenth day of the menstrual cycle. The usual cycle is counted from the beginning of one menstrual flow to the beginning of the next. Therefore ovulation—the time when pregnancy can most likely take place in a woman with a normal menstrual cycle—occurs just about midway between the periods of menstrual flow.

The ovum within the ovary is surrounded by a small sac known as a Graafian follicle. The follicle holding the ovum works its way to the surface of the ovary and there forms a blisterlike swelling. This blister, containing estrogen fluid, ruptures and releases the ovum at the open end of the nearest Fallopian tube. The tiny round egg finds its way into the tube and is propelled through the tube by hairlike cilia cells on the sides of the tube, by the estrogen fluid and by rhythmic contractions of the walls of the tube.[6] The Fallopian tube is about 4 inches long and connects to the uterus. The ovum will survive for three or four days or longer, although it is fertile only during the first part of that time. If the ovum is not fertilized, it deteriorates, and its remains will then be discharged along with other menstrual materials and blood from the uterine lining.

Male gametes and organs (Fig. 2-2)

Whereas only one ovum is ripened every menstrual cycle, several hundred million spermatozoa are developed every four or five days.[7] The implication is that the man is capable of providing sperms for the purpose of conception at almost anytime, whereas the woman produces a mature ovum on the average of only once every twenty-eight days. Furthermore, spermatozoa are formed well into old age, even though the sperms may not always be capable of fertilizing an egg. In the woman, production of the sex cells will cease with the completion of menopause.

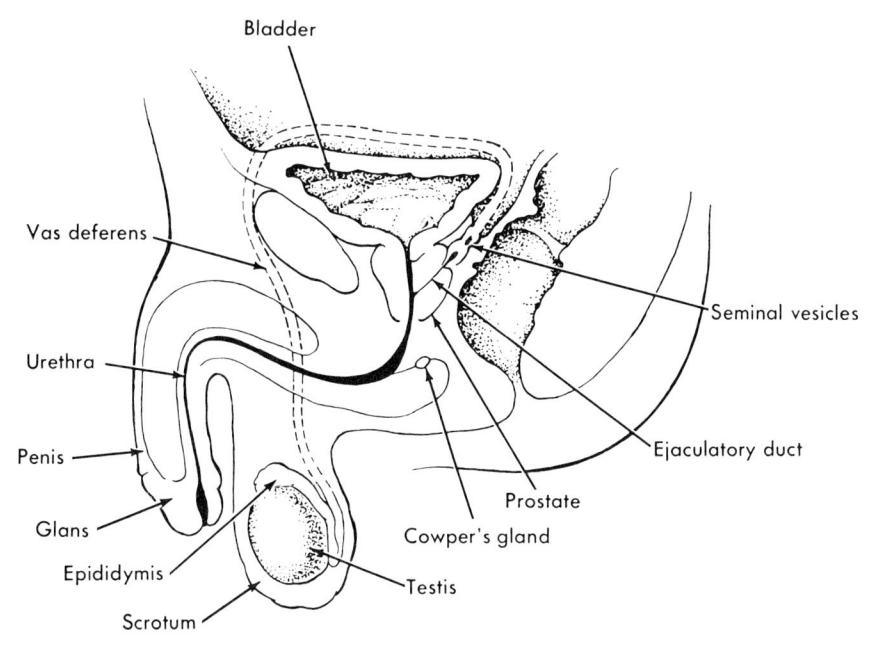

Fig. 2-2. Male sex organs and gamete production. The sperm cells are produced in the testes and are temporarily stored in the seminal vesicles. Male sex organs constantly make and deliver active sperm cells capable of fertilizing the ovum in the body of the female. (From Iorio, J.: Principles of obstetrics and gynecology for nurses, ed. 2, St. Louis, 1971, The C. V. Mosby Co.)

Spermatozoa are formed in the two testes (testicles or male gonads) suspended in the scrotum, a thin-walled sac of skin. The sperm-making cells within the testicles are extremely sensitive to heat. They must have a temperature several degrees below that of the interior of the body; otherwise, they rapidly degenerate and cease producing the male sex cells. The scrotum has a large area of skin surface for the purpose of heat evaporation. The sac will pull close to the body when cold to get more heat and will hang loose when warm to become cooler.[8]

The process by which sperms are produced is called spermatogenesis. Spermatogenesis involves the reduction of the 46 chromosomes by several cell divisions into a sperm that will eventually contain only half that number. The mature sperm has 22 chromosomes plus a sex determination chromosome (X or Y). These 23 chromosomes will pair with the 23 chromosomes found in the female sex cell at the time of conception. From the testes the mature spermatozoa will pass through a long, narrow, much coiled tube called the *epididymis*, where they mix with a fluid. The spermatozoa will then move through other long tubes called the *vas deferens* to the seminal vesicles, where the sperm is temporarily stored. Located near the seminal vesicles is the prostate gland. At the time of ejaculation the fluid carrying the sex cells passes the prostate gland, where a milky secretion is added to make semen. Up to the time of ejaculation the spermatozoa have been relatively motionless. With the addition of the fluids from the prostate gland they become very vigorous. After ejaculation, spermatozoa remain actively motile in the seminal fluid for as long as

36 to 48 hours in the upper portions of the female reproductive tract.[9] Since spermatozoa can live as long as two or three days within the uterus of the woman, the depositing of sperm in the vagina as much as 72 hours prior to ovulation can lead to pregnancy. Spermatozoa that do not enter the uterus from the vagina usually die within a few hours because of the toxic environment of the vagina.

Fertilization (Fig. 2-3)

It is the act of mating, or sexual intercourse, that brings sperm cells and ovum together. The stimulating effect of intercourse on the penis causes the male to ejaculate about a teaspoonful of semen containing about 300 to 400 million spermatozoa into the vagina near the cervix. Only a small number of the spermatozoa succeed in working their way through the cervical opening into the uterus. Even fewer find their way into the Fallopian tubes. The journey takes about 1 to 2 hours. If a viable ovum is present in the tube, the spermatozoa that have made their way into the tube will be drawn to the egg and will cover it. Sperm cells make an enzyme that helps to break down the rather tough outer membrane of the egg cell. Once a sperm does pierce the cell wall, it still has to find its way to the nucleus of the egg. Considering that the ovum is 85,000 times larger than the sperm, the little sperm still has a comparatively long way to go. When a sperm does reach the nucleus, the other sperms cease their activities.

The nucleus of the sperm and the nucleus of the ovum will merge, and their contents will combine. The 23 chromosomes of the ovum's nucleus will pair off with the 23 chromosomes from the nucleus of the sperm to make 23 pairs of chromosomes with thousands of genes. In that fraction of a second when the chromosomes form pairs, the sex of the new child will be de-

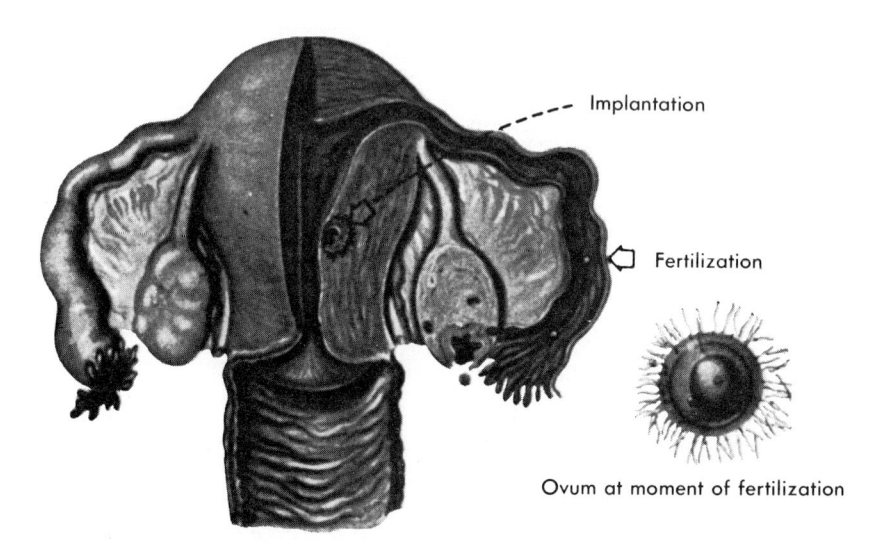

Fig. 2-3. Process of fertilization. Sperm cells enter the uterus and Fallopian tube about the time the ovum is released from the ovary and enters the Fallopian tube. The sperm and egg cell meet and unite in the tube. The sperm fertilizes the egg by entering its nucleus. The fertilized egg cell begins to divide as it travels to the uterus, where it attaches itself to the uterine wall and begins to form into an embryo. (Drawing courtesy Carnation Co.)

termined, hereditary characteristics received from each parent will be set, and a new life will have begun.

Several conditions might exist that prevent conception from taking place. Some of these conditions are an inability of the male to produce healthy sperm; an inability of the male to transfer the sperm to the genital tract because of injury, psychological trouble, or inability to achieve erection; poor female environment for the fertilized eggs; failure of ovulation due to endocrine or metabolic imbalance; Fallopian tubes that are blocked; fear of sex by male or female; or physical obstacles to having children. Out of 600 consecutive private patients investigated for infertility, Payne and Skeels[10] found that major factors were located in both partners in 41% of the cases, in the wife only in 33% of the cases, and in the husband only in 26% of the cases.

PREGNANCY

The moment that a new life is conceived is not immediately evident to the woman. The fertilized egg, however, will probably begin within the hour of conception to divide and to develop into a baby. The woman may not learn of her pregnancy for some days to come.

Diagnosis of pregnancy

A diagnosis of pregnancy can be determined from three types of information: the symptoms of the woman, specific laboratory tests, and certain bodily changes found by the physician on his physical examination of the woman. Failure to menstruate is usually the earliest evidence of pregnancy. However, failure to menstruate may also result from illness or anxiety. Likewise, occasionally a woman may be pregnant and still have signs of menstruation. As a result, laboratory tests for pregnancy provide more definite information. Most laboratory tests seek to determine whether a substance known as human chorionic gonadotropin (CGH) is present in the urine. This hormone is secreted by the trophoblasts and is always present nine to ten days after the first missed menstrual period.

Aschheim and Zondek[11] in 1928 did the research that lead to the first methods by which pregnancy could be indicated with at least 95% accuracy. A small quantity of the woman's urine is injected into a female mouse or rabbit. If the woman is pregnant, a hormone in her urine will cause changes in the animal's ovaries within 48 to 72 hours. Another test using frogs provides results in 2 to 10 hours. More recently, tests have been devised that can give results within minutes. One test consists of a chemical analysis for color change of the woman's urine when mixed with a special reagent. In another test two preparations are placed on a glass slide, and a drop of urine is put on the preparations. If the preparations do not clump together in particles, the urine contains HCG and the woman is pregnant.[12] Pregnancy frequently can be confirmed as early as three weeks after conception, although more time is generally required for certainty.

The most positive signs of pregnancy include hearing and counting of fetal heart tones after the eighteenth to twentieth week of pregnancy, spontaneous fetal movement as felt by the physician, x-ray evidence after the fifth month, and evidence of fetal bones after the fourth month of pregnancy. Commonly experienced physical signs in a woman include (1) cessation of menstruation, (2) nausea and vomiting (morning sickness) from shortly after the first missed period to the end of the first trimester, (3) fatigue, requiring 10 to 12 hours of sleep, (4) tenderness and gradual enlargement of breasts and deeper color in the area around the nipples about the third month, (5) increased frequency of urination, and (6) the feeling of fetal movements (quickening) about the seventeenth or eighteenth week of pregnancy.[13]

Boy or girl?

Of the 46 chromosomes found in germ cells, two are sex determination chromosomes. In the female these two sex determination chromosomes are identical and so are given the letter designation of X and X. In the male, however, these chromosomes are different and so are designated as X and Y. By the process of meiosis, or sex cell production, the ovum will always have 22 chromosomes (called *autosomes*) plus an X sex determination cell. The sperm will also have 22 autosomes plus a sex determination cell, but that cell may be either an X cell or a Y cell. Should it be an X cell from the male that pairs with the X cell from the female, the result will be a girl. A Y cell from the male that pairs with an X cell from the female will produce a boy. It is from the germ cells of the father that the sex of the child is determined (Fig. 2-4).

There have been numerous theories and methods advocated throughout the ages in an effort to choose the sex of a child. The research of Shettles[14] (1960) indicates that some basic principles regarding sex selection may have been found.

Using a phase-contrast microscope and carbon dioxide gas to slow down the movement of living sperm cells, Shettles noticed that sperm came in two distinct sizes and shapes. He eventually concluded that the small, round-headed sperms carry the male-producing Y chromosomes. The larger, oval-shaped type carry the female-producing X chromosomes. The male-producing type he calls *androsperms* and the female-producing type he calls *gynosperms*. He further postulated that the male sperms are weaker and less viable than those carrying the trait for a female. The male sperms are also highly sensitive to the type of acid that is found in the vaginal tract and do not survive long in that environment. In the female, alkaline secretions generally appear only during the 24 hours before ovulation. It also appeared that the relative percentage of androsperms to gynosperms decreases after repeated intercourse and ejaculations.

Based on these findings Shettles prescribes the following practices for couples who desire a child of a particular sex. One suggestion is to promote a chem-

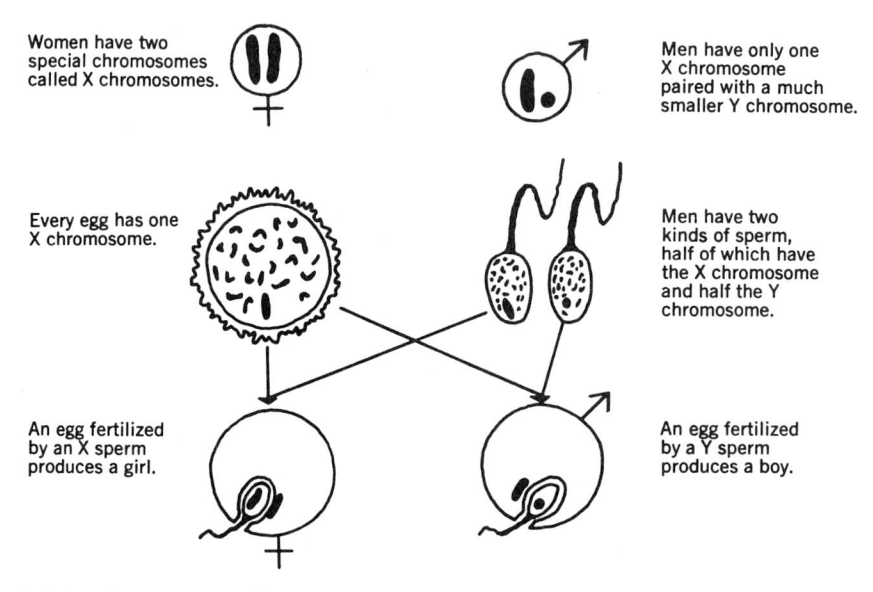

Fig. 2-4. Sex determination. (From Morgan, C., and King, R. A.: Introduction to psychology, ed. 3, New York, copyright 1966, McGraw-Hill Book Co. Used with permission of the publishers.)

ical environment favorable to the sperm preferred. Medical advice and examination should be sought before attempting douching for this purpose. Since the male sperms are not strong enough to resist a highly acidic vaginal environment, Shettles suggests that for couples who desire a boy the wife should douche with a basic alkaline solution (2 tablespoons baking soda to 1 quart water) to neutralize the vaginal acids prior to intercourse. This vaginal environment will permit the male sperm to travel more swiftly as well as to survive better. For couples desiring a girl a white vinegar douche of 2 tablespoons vinegar to 1 quart water is recommended to increase the acidity of the vagina to destroy or weaken the male sperms. Thus the female sperms will have a greater opportunity to be the first to reach the ovum. Couples desiring a boy should also avoid intercourse until the time of ovulation (as previously determined by temperature studies) to assure a higher concentration of male sperms in the semen. Clinical results show at least 80% success. If the couple are conscientious with the douche and the timing, the researchers claim that choosing the sex of the child is successful 85% to 90% of the time.[15] It is important to note that the use of a douche to maximize the probability of a certain sex is still considered highly questionable by many recognized authorities.

More than one

Normally the human female produces only one ripe ovum every menstrual cycle. Occasionally, however, some women will release two or more mature ova at the same time. If more than one ovum are in the Fallopian tube at the same time, there is a good chance that more than one will be fertilized. Sometimes only one egg is fertilized in a tube, but certain conditions exist which cause that egg to split, thus producing two embryos. Either way more than one life has been conceived.

Twins and "supertwins" (more than two) may be of two types, identical or fraternal. The term *identical* is misleading because no two people are alike in every way. For this reason geneticists prefer to use terms that refer to the origin of the twin types. Identical twins are referred to as *monozygotic* (MZ), or one-egg twins, and fraternal twins are *dizygotic* (DZ), or two-egg twins. MZ twins or supertwins originate from a single fertilized ovum that divided into two or more parts at an early stage of development. DZ twins or supertwins occur when two or more eggs are present in the Fallopian tubes (oviducts) and two or more are fertilized by different sperm cells. Since DZ twins originate from different ova as well as different sperm cells, the genetic relationships between these twins is no greater than that of ordinary siblings.[16] Thus DZ twins can be two girls, two boys, or one girl and one boy. MZ twins will always be of the same sex. One third of all twins are identical. Twins occur in one out of eighty-seven births; triplets occur in one out of 7,564 births.[17]

During the development of twins or supertwins, several factors are present that are not as common in single child pregnancies. Both DZ and MZ conceptions must deal with crowding factors, especially if they have a common placenta. In MZ twins the fertilized egg had enough food stored within it for only one baby. Of course, when the egg splits, the food is divided. Food may be lacking for the zygotes to survive. The chance of a premature birth is greater among multiple births than for single births. Koch[18] studied sixty-two sets of twins and found (1) the incidence of prematurity was about 5% higher for twins, (2) most early births occurred in the lowest class families, (3) prematurity rate is higher for girl twins, (4) prematurity rate is higher for MZ twins, (5) chances for American black mothers to have twins are one third higher than for whites, but for Japanese and Chinese mothers it is one third less, and (6) chances for twins increase with the age of the mother and the number of previous births.

Whatever is true about twins applies in extended ways to triplets, quadruplets, and other "twin plus" sets. These supertwins are produced by basically the same process as twins. Normally, five or six sets of quadruplets are born in the United States every year, but few intact sets manage to survive so that there are probably only about a dozen complete sets in the United States at any one time. Quintuplets are even more rare. The Dionne quintuplets, born in 1934, all of whom survived, were the only all-identical set on record. In 1964 all-surviving quintuplets were born in South Dakota and in Venezuela, but they were mixed sets, combining both identicals and fraternals.

Since the mid-1960s, certain hormones have been administered to previously sterile women to induce ovulation and conception. These procedures often trigger the release of more than one egg at a time and have resulted in twins and supertwins. Using hormones, four women conceived quadruplets; three sets are surviving and healthy. Two sets of quintuplets were born, with all five surviving in one set but only one surviving in the other.[19] Sextuplets were born in Denver, Colorado, in 1973 and all survived to the time this book was published. In 1971 nine children were born to a woman in South America, but all of them died within ten days. All of these were fraternal supertwins, since they resulted from more than one egg. The statistics on the number of twins or supertwins born may be upset by a wider use of the hormone procedures with sterile women.

PRENATAL DEVELOPMENT AND BEHAVIOR

Once the fertilization of an ovum has taken place, nature appears to be in a fantastic hurry to move on with the developmental processes. Within an hour or two the fertilized egg will divide to form new cells. Cell division continues until the young embryo is implanted in the uterus; then structures begin to appear. By the time the woman misses her first menstrual period the baby's heart, nervous system, and intestines are already developing. The woman, at this point, may not even know that she is pregnant.

Embryologists usually divide prenatal development into three periods. Each period has its own growth characteristics. First is the period of the ovum, also called the period of the zygote or the germinal period, during which the fertilized egg makes its way to the uterus. Second is the embryonic period, at which time the round ball, the fertilized egg, changes to a recognizable human fetus. The third stage is the fetal period, during which the fetus enhances and refines the structures developed during the previous period. The miracle of growth, the wonder of life, and the marvel of the laws of nature are perhaps most perfectly illustrated during these three periods in which the child develops from two minute cells that came together into a baby boy or girl, the newest member of mankind.

Period of the zygote

Once conception has taken place, two things occur simultaneously; the fertilized egg (zygote) begins to divide, and at the same time it makes its way down the Fallopian tube to the uterus. The zygote will divide, perhaps within 30 minutes, certainly within an hour or two after conception. Ten hours later these two cells divide to make four cells, then the four to make eight cells, then sixteen cells and so on. The cells are related to one another in accordance to the master blueprint plan as prescribed for the total organic structure in the DNA molecules. The entire sphere made up of cells is called a *blastocyst*, or a zygote. Although the cells increase in number, they do not increase the overall size of the zygote.[20]

During the first two weeks after fertilization, the important job is not the development of the actual form of the child but the making of clusters of cells that have special functions. Not all of the blastocyst cells become the human being. Imagine a drawing of the fertilized egg. The outer surface of the fertilized egg does not change into the shape of the child but eventually becomes part of the chorion (an extraembryonic membrane) and, later, the placenta. Cells begin to form within the cell wall of the fertilized egg. The outer layer of cells of the zygote is known as the *trophoblast*. It will develop roots with which to attach itself to the uterus and will eventually become the chorion. An inner mass of cells will develop at one end or side of the interior of the sphere. Within this inner cell mass two hollow areas will be formed with a wall of cells separating the two. The hollow area next to the outer wall will eventually become the amnion (water sac), and the other cavity will become the yolk sac.

The thick wall of cells between the two cavities is called the embryonic, or germinal, disc. This disc becomes the child.

The amniotic sac (amnion) will enclose the embryo in a protective bag of fluid. The fetus will be able to move in this fluid and also to swallow it. This sac will serve to cushion the fetus against possible bumps, shocks, and injuries and will help to regulate its temperature. The yolk sac has a temporary function of making blood cells for the embryo; however, it will soon shrink and gradually disappear when the liver takes over this function. The amniotic sac, the yolk sac, and the embryonic disc will become separated from the outer layer of cells by the formation of a short connecting stalk that becomes the umbilical cord.[21]

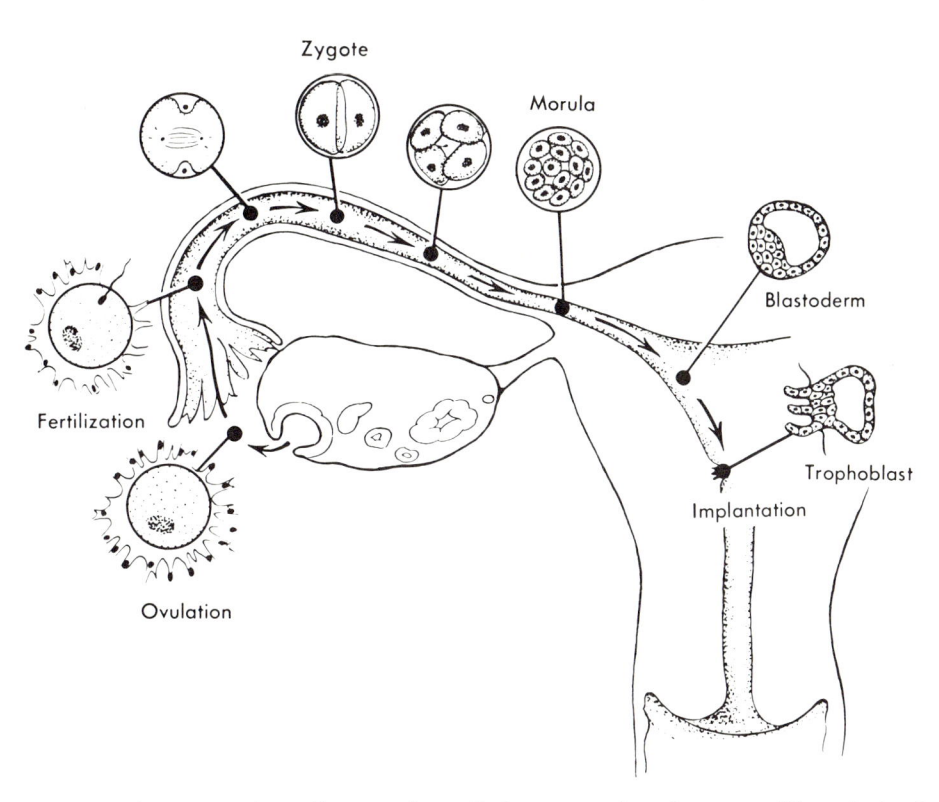

Fig. 2-5. Fertilization in the Fallopian tube, cell division, and implantation. (From Iorio, J.: Principles of obstetrics and gynecology for nurses, ed. 2, St. Louis, 1971, The C. V. Mosby Co.)

The journey down the Fallopian tube to the uterus takes three to five days. Once in the uterus (womb), the fertilized ovum floats in a fluid for a few days before it attaches itself to the uterus. (See Fig. 2-5.) The uterus, meanwhile, has prepared itself —as it does every month—for the reception of the fertilized egg. At this time its lining is at its thickest state and has considerable nourishment in its cells.

The trophoblast of the zygote has roots that will act on the uterine lining once the zygote comes to rest.[22] Enzymes enable the trophoblast to digest or liquefy the tissue of the uterus. At implantation it will burrow into the uterine lining and form a nest for the zygote. Now the chorion begins to develop a network of fine roots, called *villi*, which spread into the lining of the uterus. They are important because they contain blood vessels that are connected with the fetus. They are the sole means by which oxygen and nourishment are received from the mother. There is no gross intermingling of the blood of the mother with that of the fetus, however. The placenta will not be completed until the third month of pregnancy.[23]

The free zygote begins to attach itself to the uterine wall about the sixth or seventh day after conception. By the tenth day it will usually be completely covered, and implantation will have taken place. Implantation marks the end of the period of the ovum. During this time period the zygote remains at about the size of a pin head.

There are certain hazards to the survival of the fertilized egg during the period of the ovum. The ovum must survive largely on its own food until it is implanted. If it does not receive enough nourishment, either because of the minimal amount of food supply or because the zygote takes too long to become implanted, it dies. It will be shed during the next menstrual period without the woman ever realizing that conception had taken place. Occasionally there will be interference with the migration of the ovum down the Fallopian tubes.

Again, the ovum will die if it does not reach the uterus in time to become implanted. If the ovum degenerates in the tube, an ectopic pregnancy, which is the implantation of the fertilized ovum outside the uterine cavity, will take place.

Embryonic period

The embryonic period is one of rapid change. It covers that period of pregnancy from the time of implantation of the ball-shaped zygote in the uterine wall to the time that the embryo becomes a recognizable human fetus. Embryologists say that this time span extends to the eighth week after conception. It is difficult to be precise about the time span because knowledge of this growth period is limited. The science of human embryology cannot be studied experimentally as is the case with infrahuman embryology. Knowledge of the subject for the most part has been derived from the study of embryos that had to be surgically removed because the life and health of the mother were endangered.

During the early part of the embryonic period, the placenta, the umbilical cord, and the amniotic sac are developed to the point where they can protect and nourish the embryo until the time of birth. At maturity the pancakelike placenta will measure about 8 inches in diameter and 1 inch in thickness and will weigh about 1 pound. Although the developing placenta is much too small to be seen at the time of implantation, it does begin to alter the hormonal pattern of the mother.[24]

The umbilical cord is developed from the body stock that connects the placenta to the embryo. Nourishment in the form of minerals, proteins, and oxygen from the mother is passed through the placenta to the embryo by way of the umbilical cord, and waste products from the embryo are filtered back. The cord contains two arteries and one vein but no nerves. It eventually becomes about ¾ inch thick, about 22 inches in length, and looks like a whitish, rubbery tube. It is filled with a substance called Wharton's jelly. The jelly and the pressure of the blood rushing through the blood vessels keep the umbilical cord somewhat stiff, like a soft garden hose. The cord tends to straighten itself automatically when bent. Because of these factors, the danger of the umbilical cord choking a baby are very slim, even though it is not uncommon for it to pass around the baby's neck. The baby is enclosed in the double-walled membrane of the chorion and the amniotic sac. The sac contains a fluid in which the baby floats and moves around, thus giving the umbilical cord a chance to straighten out.[25]

By 2½ weeks the embryo has already begun to take shape. Its head-to-feet and top-to-bottom directions have been determined. The nervous system has begun to develop with the start of a longitudinal neural plate and a groove that will eventually form into a tube with two protrusions for the brain at the upper end. The heart, at first a single tube, may beat haltingly as early as the eighteenth day, even though there is no blood for it to circulate. The heart will pump more confidently by 3½ weeks, but it will not be regular for some weeks to come.[26]

It is during the second and third weeks after conception that the inner mass of cells begins to differentiate into three layers. The outer layer, the ectoderm, will become the skin, hair, nails, sensory and skin glands, and all nerve tissues. From the middle layer, the mesoderm, will come the bones, muscle, and circulatory organs, and part of the excretory organs. From the inner layer, the endoderm, will develop the digestive organs, liver, alimentary tract, lungs, and some of the endocrine glands.[27]

The 28-day embryo still does not look like a baby, but it does have an oval body, a differentiated head region that takes up one third of its length, and at the lower end of the body, a short, slim, tail-like protrusion that will become the last bone in the spine. There is a brain and a primitive spinal cord. The heart is becoming well developed, although it is still only a C-shaped bulge in the body wall. The embryo has developed simple kidneys, a primitive liver, and a simple digestive tract extending from the mouth area to the lower end. The head has rudimentary eyes, ears, and a nose. The first limb buds of the arms and legs appear about this time. Although all these body systems are being developed, the embryo is only about ⅕ inch long—about half the size of a pea. The mother is two weeks overdue for her menstrual cycle. She may not realize she is pregnant as yet because the embryo is so small and causes her no discomfort.

In the beginning the brain and spinal cord grow more quickly than the other structures. Almost all the functions of the body depend on an adequate nervous system. Thus nature in its wise way prepares the nervous system first so that all the other systems can develop and function as they should. Development starts with the brain and head area and then works down the body, the feet developing last. This progression is the cephalocaudal direction of growth.

During the second month, the main features of the human form rapidly appear. The nose, mouth, and tongue emerge more clearly. The developing eye appears as a dark circle. The black pigment layer of the eye is plainly visible, as is the fainter inner circle that is the lens. What looks like a mouth beneath the eye is actually the ear, still quite low on the head. The limbs grow longer; saddles and ridges appear on the end of them, later forming the fingers and toes. The development of the baby teeth begins about six weeks after conception. By the tenth week the rudiments of all twenty teeth are present. The stomach, intestines, pharynx, lungs, and rudiments of the rectum, bladder, and external genital organs all grow from enlargements of the digestive tract. The endocrine system takes shape, the adrenal medulla secretes epinephrine, and the testes in the male begins to secrete androgens.

At the end of the second month the embryo will measure about 1 inch from the top of its head to the buttocks. It will weigh approximately ⅔ ounce.[28] The embryo now represents a miniature individual in its development. The principles indicating the completion of the embryonic period are the formation of the first real bone cells that begin to replace the cartilage and the completion of features that resemble a human being. The embryo looks like a human being and not a monkey, a puppy, or a cat. Human likeness is clearly imprinted on it.

The most crucial time when the embryo's development can be most seriously affected is the first eight to nine weeks of pregnancy, which is precisely the time when most women pay little attention to their new condition. There is a sequence of physical development taking place during the embryonic stage that is systematic and regular. There is a particular time for the emergence of each of the organs and their systems. Any disturbance or interruption with this sequence can be disastrous. If the delicate chemical balance of the mother is upset seriously, permanent damage can occur. Rubella (German measles) and certain drugs are especially serious during the first three months of pregnancy, since they can cause damage to whatever structures are being formed at the time. The brain, too, is susceptible to damage.

It has been estimated that one out of every three fertilized ova does not survive, the most critical time being the embryonic period.[29] Miscarriages are nature's way of getting rid of an abnormally developing embryo or fetus. It could also mean that the uterine environment was not conducive to survival. About 75% of all miscarriages occur by the third month. Falls, malnutrition, or hormone imbalance are among the causes of spontaneous abortion. There are three boy miscarriages for every two girl miscarriages (160 to 100), indicating that in some respects the female has better survival capability than the male.[30] This point will also be noted at other stages in the developmental process.

Period of the fetus

The fetal period of development (Fig. 2-6) is from about the eighth week, when the embryo becomes a recognizable human being, to the time of birth. Having passed the critical embryonic stage, the chances for survival of the fetus are greatly increased. The organs, which have all been started by now, continue to develop and become functional. It is about this time that women usually make an appointment with their physician to find out if they are pregnant. Many expectant mothers would be surprised to learn that by the time they first see their physician their child has already been completely formed and is simply growing and preparing for his entrance into this world.

During the ninth week, the eyelids grow rapidly, and their gluey edges soon fuse and seal the eyes shut. The eyes will now be protected during the final, more delicate stages of their formation and will stay shut until the sixth or seventh lunar month.[31] The first muscle movements of the baby probably occur in the mouth and jaw muscles because they are the first ones to develop. As early as the sixth week, a reflex action can be stimulated in these muscles. By the ninth week the muscles of arms and legs are capable of responding to tactile (touch) stimulation.[32] During the tenth week, the genitals are clearly defined, and it is possible for the first time to determine the sex of the baby by external inspection.

By the end of the third month the buds for the twenty temporary teeth will have appeared. Bones are beginning to replace the cartilage around the cheek, jaw, and nose, giving a more definite shape to the head. Although the fetus gets its oxygen through the umbilical cord from the chorion, it will swallow, inhale, and exhale the fluid in the amniotic sac, as if it were practicing breathing. The fetus becomes more active and vigorous, with much smoother movements than before. It can turn its head, bend its elbows, make a fist, move its hips, and fan its toes. However, these movements are too minute and weak to be felt by the mother. It may even get the hiccups. If it does, the mother will feel every one. For every woman the experience of feeling life for the first time is an unforgettable moment. The fetus is now 3 inches long and weighs ¾ ounce.

The fourth month is a growth month. The fetus will increase its length two or three times and its weight five or six times. By the end of the month it will be 6 inches long and will weigh about 4 ounces. As a result, the fetus is more crowded than be-

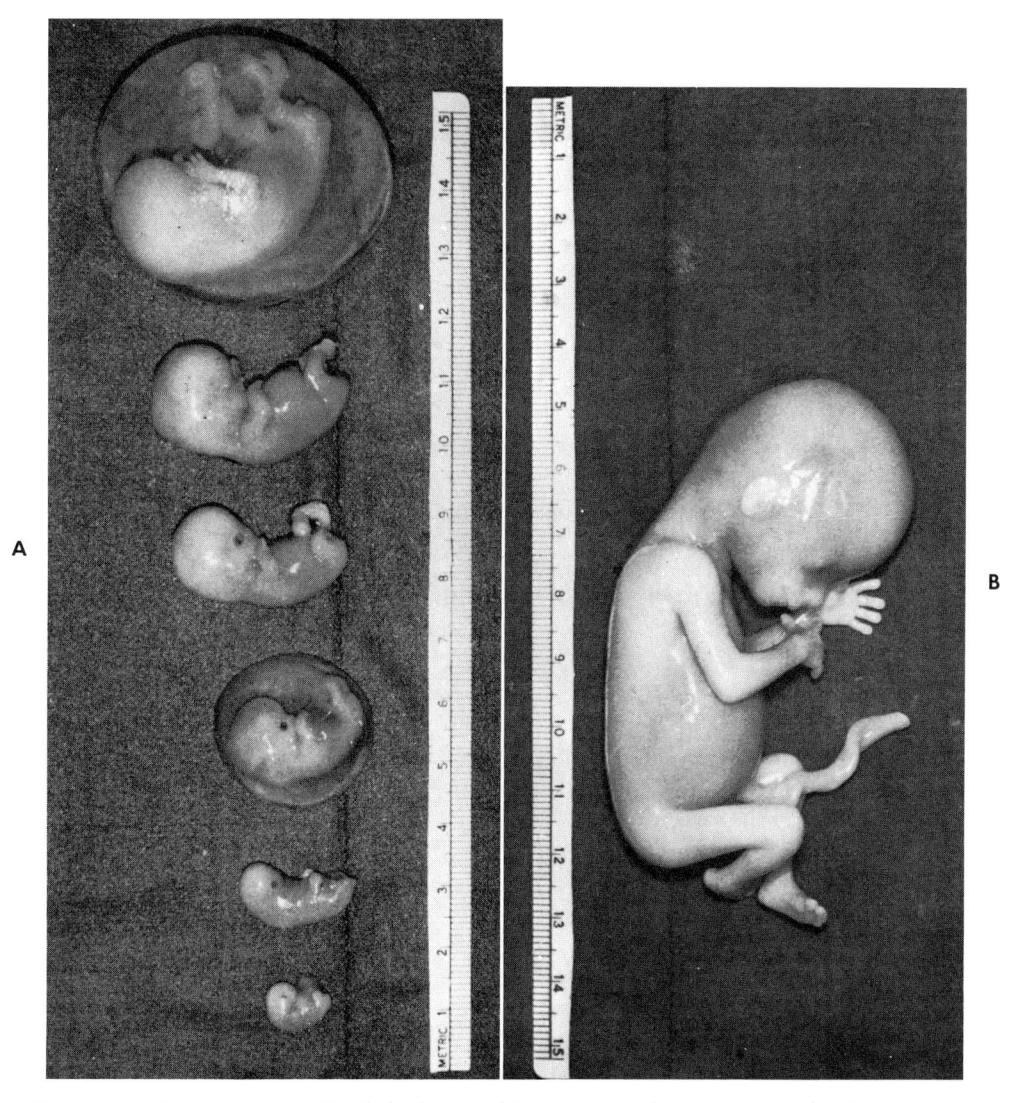

Fig. 2-6. **A**, Progressive growth of the human fetus (measured in centimeters). Two amniotic sacs are shown still intact. **B**, Fetus approximately 7.5 cm. (3 inches) long at almost 3 months' gestation. (From Ingalls, A. J., and Salerno, M. C.: Maternal and child health nursing, ed. 2, St. Louis, 1971, The C. V. Mosby Co.)

fore, and the placenta becomes stretched tightly. The toes and fingers have separated, and fingerprint patterns emerge on the fingertips. Uniqueness and individuality are established at this very early age. The baby gains in strength, and his movements become stronger. About the middle of the month the mother begins to feel the baby stirring. At first it is very soft, like the fluttering of butterfly wings. As the baby develops, the movements become more strenuous, and the mother begins to feel the sharp kicks and thrusts of the arms and legs. Some spontaneous movements of the fetus can be detected by stethoscope by the fourteenth week, although the "quickening" movements felt by the mother are not noticed until the seventeenth week. As the fourth month comes to a close, the mother's abdomen begins to protrude, and she begins to gain weight. Her pregnancy will be noticed by others at about four and a half months, the midpoint of pregnancy. Any morning sickness will probably be past, and she will be in the most comfortable period of pregnancy.

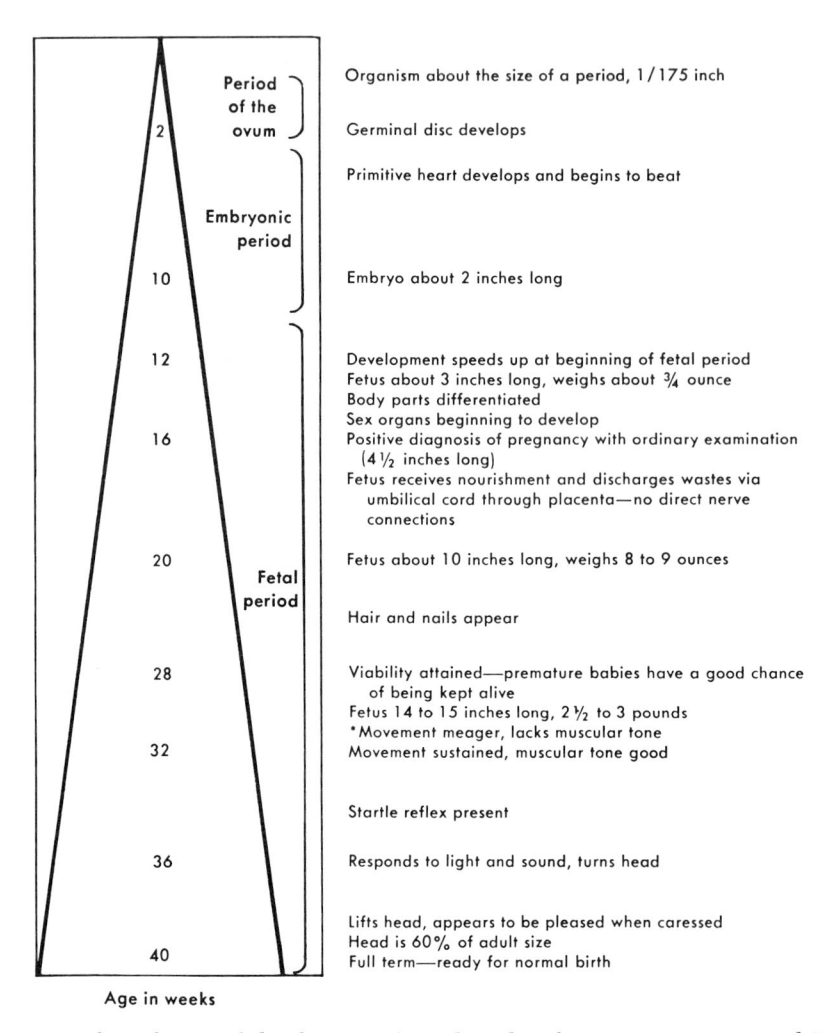

Age in weeks	Period	Description
2	Period of the ovum	Organism about the size of a period, 1/175 inch
		Germinal disc develops
	Embryonic period	Primitive heart develops and begins to beat
10		Embryo about 2 inches long
12	Fetal period	Development speeds up at beginning of fetal period Fetus about 3 inches long, weighs about ¾ ounce Body parts differentiated Sex organs beginning to develop
16		Positive diagnosis of pregnancy with ordinary examination (4½ inches long) Fetus receives nourishment and discharges wastes via umbilical cord through placenta—no direct nerve connections
20		Fetus about 10 inches long, weighs 8 to 9 ounces Hair and nails appear
28		Viability attained—premature babies have a good chance of being kept alive Fetus 14 to 15 inches long, 2½ to 3 pounds *Movement meager, lacks muscular tone
32		Movement sustained, muscular tone good Startle reflex present
36		Responds to light and sound, turns head
40		Lifts head, appears to be pleased when caressed Head is 60% of adult size Full term—ready for normal birth

Fig. 2-7. Time line of prenatal development. (Based on data from Watson, E. H., and Lowrey, G. H.: Growth and development of children, Chicago, 1954, Year Book Medical Publishers, Inc.; redrawn from Bernard, H. W.: Human development in western culture, ed. 3, copyright 1970 by Allyn & Bacon, Inc., used with permission.)

Movements of the fetus continue to get stronger during the fifth month. The baby can turn all the way around from side to side and even turn somersaults. He gives the impression of being an astronaut moving weightlessly in space. He sleeps and wakes at regular times. When sleeping, he has a favorite resting position called a "lie." He may put his thumb in his mouth as if to suck it. The sucking reflex is present. Fingernails reach the tips of the fingers. The heartbeat becomes regular between the fourteenth and sixteenth weeks. By the middle of the fifth month the heartbeat is strong enough for a physician to hear it through a stethoscope placed on the abdomen of the mother, maybe even hearing two beats if there are twins. By the end of the fifth calendar month the fetus weighs over 1 pound and is about 1 foot long.

The sixth month of pregnancy is the time when the skin changes from a thin, transparent layer through which blood vessels can be seen to one that has a layer of fat and some accumulation of hair. In addition, the skin becomes covered with whitish oily, fatty substance, vernix caseosa, that protects the skin from the long immersion in fluid. During the previous month, a soft, fine hair called *lanugo* began to grow on the body. The sixth month there is an accumulation of this hair above the eyes and on the upper lip. The vernix caseosa accumulates on the lanugo and gives the fetus an aged appearance. Hair on the scalp begins to grow heavier and longer than in other places. The eyes are developed, and the eyelids may separate so that the fetus can now open and close its eyes. If the baby should be born at the end of this month, he would probably breathe for a few minutes to a few hours, but seldom would he survive. The fetus is now 14 inches long and weighs a little over 2 pounds.

The chance for survival of a baby born after twenty-eight weeks of pregnancy is fairly good. It actually depends on the capability of the nervous system to operate effectively the organs and vital functions of the body. If born during the seventh month, the infant will need special care in terms of oxygen, prevention of blindness associated with retrolental fibroplasia (treatment nowadays is good), and protection against infections. Some time will have to be spent in an incubator. The fetus is about 16 inches and weighs about 2½ pounds.

The eighth and ninth months are "fattening-up" months. The fetus gains about ½ pound a week for a total of 5 pounds on the average. The body is becoming more rounded, and fatty layers are developing that will help to nourish the baby and keep him warm after he is born. The rapid growth of the baby may cause stretch marks on the mother's abdomen. The finer lanugo hair is being shed and has largely disappeared. The skin is less reddish looking than before, becoming lighter or pinkish in color even if the baby is black. Fingernails are firm and protrude beyond the end of the fingers. Sometimes nails are so long at birth that the nurse will need to trim them. The baby still moves, but his living quarters are getting more and more crowded. The mother's abdomen stops enlarging about the end of the eighth month, and there is a slowing down of fetal movements. About two weeks before birth the fetus will settle or "drop" into the pelvic cavity. See Fig. 2-7 for time line summary.

When the fetus stops its frequent movements and lightening occurs, it will usually take up a more-or-less fixed position. Frequently this position is with the head down, as has been its commonest position during most of the pregnancy. However, the lie assumed could be with feet or bottom downward, or it could be across the opening of the uterus in a traverse lie. Birth through the vagina from a traverse lie is impossible, and the baby's position will need to be changed. The most advantageous presentation is head first.

The total gestation period is 266 days on the average. Since it is difficult, if not impossible, to date conception exactly, pregnancy is generally reckoned from the

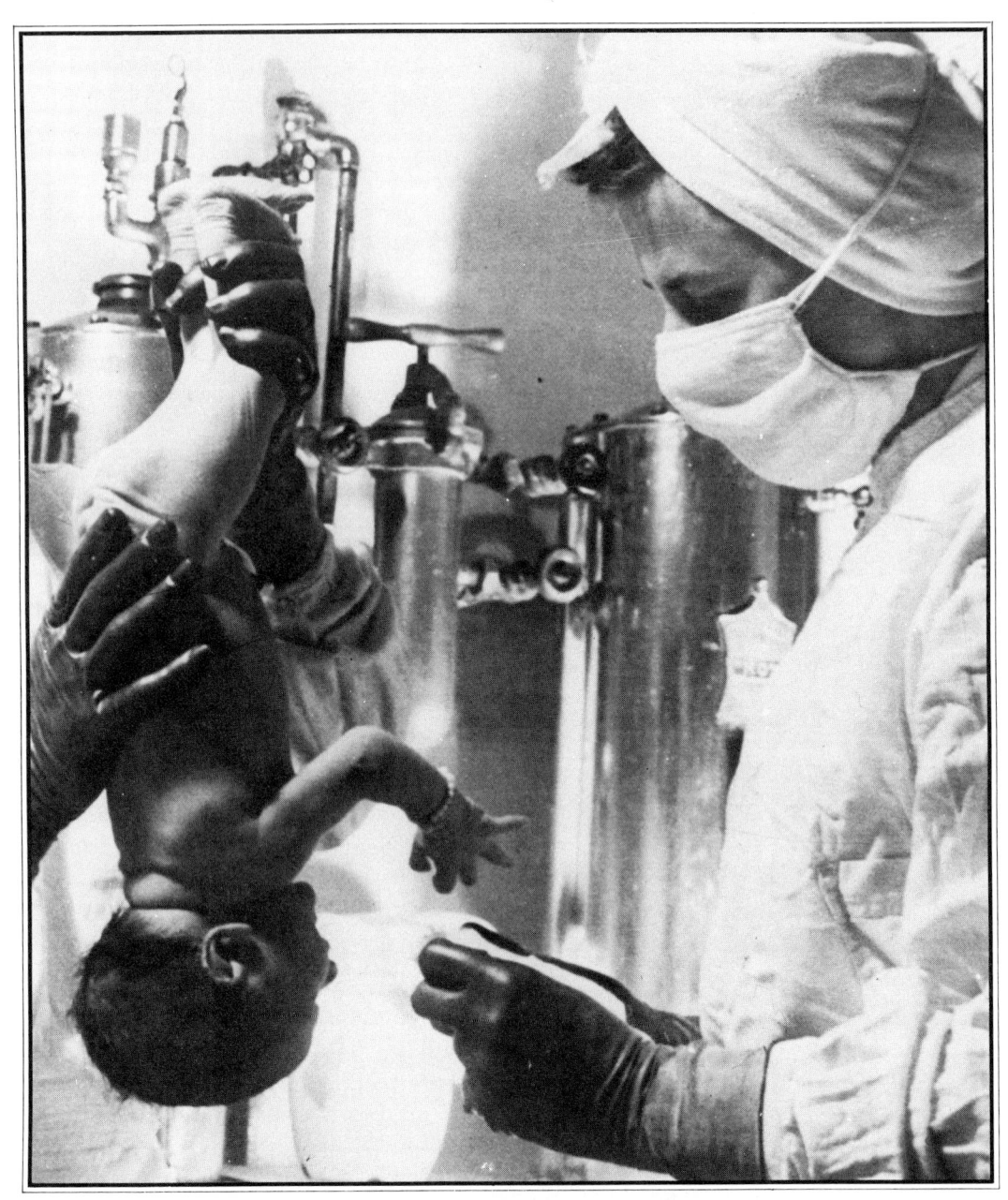

40 *Human development: the span of life*

Frederic Lewis, Inc., New York City.

7 1/2 lbs. - ave. weight of babies born in U.S.

beginning of the last menstrual period. The normal term is then set at 280 days, or ten lunar months. About 75% of all babies are born within one week, either way, of this date.[33]

Up to this point babies the world over develop the same way. All human beings have this part of their growth processes in common. The stage has now been set. The drama of birth is ready to begin—that magic moment when an unknown entity becomes known.

STUDY GUIDE

1. Compare the characteristics of female gametes and male gametes.
2. What is the uterus, and what changes occur to it during the menstrual cycle?
3. Describe the ovulation process and the fertilization process.
4. List the various methods or ways by which pregnancy can be diagnosed.
5. What is the difference between monozygotic (MZ) and dizygotic (DZ) twins? What factors are more common for multiple births than for single births?
6. Discuss the growth and development characteristics of the period of the zygote.
7. Discuss the growth and development characteristics of the embryonic period.
8. Discuss the growth and development characteristics of the period of the fetus.

REFERENCES

1. Guttmacher, A. F.: Pregnancy and birth, New York, 1962, The New American Library, Inc.
2. Stone, L. J., and Church, J.: Childhood and adolescence, New York, 1968, Random House, Inc.
3. Reid, D.: A textbook of obstetrics, Philadelphia, 1962, W. B. Saunders Co.
4. LIFE Educational Report: The moment life begins, Life, p. 3, Sept. 10, 1965.
5. Montague, A.: Human heredity, New York, 1959, Harcourt, Brace & World, Inc.
6. Fitzpatrick, E. A., and Eastman, N. I.: Zabriskie's obstetrics for nurses, Philadelphia, 1960, J. B. Lippincott Co.
7. Scheinfeld, A.: Your heredity and environment, Philadelphia, 1965, J. B. Lippincott Co.
8. Guttmacher, op. cit., p. 19.
9. Bernard, H. W.: Human development in western culture, ed. 2, Boston, 1966, Allyn & Bacon, Inc.
10. Payne, S., and Skeels, R. F.: Fertility as evaluated by artificial insemination, Fertil. Steril. 5:32-39, 1954.
11. Aschheim, S., and Zondek, B.: Die Schwangerschaftsdiagnose aus dem Harn durch Nachweis des Hypophysenvorderlappenhormons, Wchnschr. Klin. 7:1404, 1928.
12. Willson, J. R., Beecham, C. T., and Carrington, E. R.: Obstetrics and gynecology, ed. 4, St. Louis, 1971, The C. V. Mosby Co.
13. Ullery, J. C., and Hollenbeck, Z. J. R.: Textbook of obstetrics, St. Louis, 1965, The C. V. Mosby Co.
14. Shettles, L. B.: Nuclear morphology of human spermatozoa, Nature (Lond.) 186:648, 1960.
15. Rorvik, D. M., and Shettles, L. B.: Your baby's sex—now you can choose, New York, 1970, Dodd, Mead & Co.
16. Lerner, M.: Heredity, evolution, and society, San Francisco, 1968, W. H. Freeman & Co., Publishers.
17. Montague, A.: Prenatal influences, Springfield, Ill., 1962, Charles C Thomas, Publisher.
18. Koch, H.: Twins, Chicago, 1966, University of Chicago Press.
19. Milham, S., Jr.: Hormonal induction of human twinning, Lancet, p. 566, 1964.
20. Hall, R. E.: Nine months reading, Garden City, N. Y., 1969, Doubleday & Co., Inc.
21. Life filmstrip: Life before birth, part I, New York, 1966, Time, Inc.
22. Fitzpatrick, op. cit., p. 75.
23. Ibid., p. 79.
24. Nilsson, L., Ingelman-Sundberg, A., and Wirsen, C.: A child is born, New York, 1965, Delacorte Press.
25. Guttmacher, op. cit., p. 54.
26. LIFE Educational Report: Life before birth, New York, 1965, Time, Inc.
27. Gesell, A.: The embryology of behavior, New York, 1945, Harper & Row, Publishers.
28. Castallo, M. A.: Getting ready for parenthood, New York, 1957, The Macmillan Co.
29. Spencer, W. P.: Heredity: facts and fallacies. In Fishbein, M., and Kennedy, R. J. R., editors: Modern marriage and family living, New York, 1957, Oxford University Press, Inc.
30. Potter, E. L.: Pregnancy. In Fishbein, M., and Kennedy, R. J. R., editors: Modern marriage and family living, New York, 1957, Oxford University Press, Inc.
31. LIFE filmstrip: Life before birth, part II, New York, 1966, Time, Inc.
32. Rand, W., Sweeny, M., and Vincent, E. L.: Growth and development of the growing child, Philadelphia, 1946, W. B. Saunders Co.
33. Schifferes, J. J.: Healthier living, New York, 1965, John Wiley & Sons, Inc.

3 Birth of the baby

BIRTH: MY FIRSTBORN

As we were celebrating our first wedding anniversary, my husband and I were aware of the possibility of my being pregnant. I must admit that this was not a "planned" child. Oh yes, we wanted children, but I did not think that I was ready or prepared to be a mother, not just yet anyway. When the laboratory test showed a positive reaction and the doctor told me that I was very much pregnant, I had mixed emotions. My immediate thought concerned how the baby would affect our lives. Could I ever learn how to properly take care of a baby? I had not been around smaller children like some friends of mine who seemed to know what to do. I suppose part of my deep apprehension was due to a gynecologist who had examined me during my high school days and told me that there was a possibility that, physically, I might never be able to have children. Naturally these thoughts raced through my mind. Yet no doctor had ever cautioned me *not* to have any children. I tried to look at it this way; if this was what God planned for us, then there would be a way and I should have faith and trust.

During my months of pregnancy I had very few complications. In fact, I seemed to enjoy better health during those nine months than I did at other times. I believe this fact is true for most women. What a thrill to have the baby kick me internally at night while I was lying in bed. The baby appeared to kick at one side of my stomach and then jump to the opposite side. We marveled at this experience. So much activity made my husband almost sure it was going to be a boy.

The night I went to the hospital I was more calm than I thought I would be. My husband was very comforting to me in the labor room. We talked and he held my hand. I would squeeze his hand very tightly when an extra hard contraction came. Then wouldn't you know it, he had to leave before the baby came. It was one of those days when his work was such that his presence was practically mandatory. It would not have been fair to delay the work of many other people just because he did not appear. I understood, but I hoped that he could be back at the hospital in time to share our big moment together.

I remember that the delivery room was a large, spotless place full of utensils, an overhead mirror, and beaming with sunlight. As the nurse told me to put on those funny-looking stockings that I thought were very hot and uncomfortable, I began to feel that my baby was on the threshold of being born. The pain increased, and the nurse told me to try to relax and to hold her hand. The problem the gynecologist told me about years before was causing trouble. Then the nurse covered part of my face with a mask and told me to start counting very slowly. I got very sleepy. That is all I remember until in the far distance I heard the doctor say, "You have a baby girl!" My immediate response was "Are you sure?" Everyone had said I was going to have a baby boy. "Is she all right?" I asked. The answer came loud and clear that she was a healthy baby girl. I said a prayer out loud to thank the Lord for that. The next think I knew was that they were wheeling me out of the delivery room so that another expectant mother could take my place. I did not get to see my baby! The nurse had taken my baby to bathe her before I could even get a look at her. The delivery room was in great demand that morning. The doctor called the school and told Dale, my husband, that he was a father. Dale came to the hospital within the hour. He saw our baby before I did! I was the one to give birth to her, but he saw her first!

Dale told me that she was a beautiful baby: no redness at all, round, rosy cheeks, little fists, a dimple in her chin, a short, stubby nose like mine, and she looked a lot like him, too! How thrilled we were with our new baby!

Waiting in my room until I could see my baby, I could not get over the "flat" stomach that I now had since the baby was born. When the nurse brought Denise to my bed for the first time, I remember the wonderful feeling I had as I held that tiny 7-pound 9-ounce bundle. I carefully examined her to see if she had developed properly and had the correct number of fingers and toes and that there were no noticeable birthmarks or defects of any kind. Here was truly a bundle from Heaven. This miracle of birth that I had taken part in was a blessing for which I was indeed grateful.

I could not sleep well that night because of the excitement of having my first baby. You see, she was also the first grandchild on both sides of the family, and the first great-grandchild on both sides also. So she was a *first* in many ways.

When we came home from the hospital, it suddenly dawned upon me that I and I *alone* would be responsible for taking complete charge of Denise. No more dependence upon the nurse to feed and bathe her. This was my duty now.

I remember the first bath that I gave her. I was worn out by the time I was finished. It took me nearly all morning, counting the time of preparation and cleaning up afterward, to give her the bath. My main problem was in knowing how to hold her. Dale said, "She won't come apart, you know." The way I turned her over I was not so sure that she would not do just that—come apart. I was afraid of hurting her. She seemed so small on the blanket without her clothes on. I was so tired after that venture of the first bath that I had to rest before I could do anything else. Each bath that I gave her went a little better, until finally I got the feel of it and I enjoyed the experience. There is nothing so delightful as a clean, sweet-smelling baby.

As I got Denise on her own self-demand schedule, my husband and I began to relax and enjoy her more and more. Each day there would be something new that she would do that was a little different from the day before. The joy of being parents and watching a child grow is a privilege that we cherish. This experience of being a parent is difficult to explain, but it is truly wonderful.

The last few weeks before a baby is born are spent by the baby and the mother getting ready for the birth. The baby has assumed its birth position, usually with the head pushing against the cervix. The uterus sinks downward and forward. The mother's profile changes, making her clothes fit differently. The pressure against her upper abdomen is eased, and she breathes more freely. These changes are called the "lightening" by some; others say that the baby has "dropped." The indications are that the baby is getting ready to be born. Lightening may occur as early as four weeks before birth or as late as the onset of labor. The usual time for lightening to occur is ten to fourteen days before delivery.[1] It may be accompanied by some discomfort and intermittent pain. When this occurs, first-time anxious mothers may think that labor has started and call the physician, only to learn later that nothing eventful is about to happen.

BIRTH PROCESS

True labor is characterized by one or more of the following. The most usual sign of real labor is the onset of contractions, which have a definite rhythm, gradually increasing in frequency, duration, and intensity. They may be 10, 15, or 20 minutes apart at first, lasting about 45 seconds each. Within an hour or two the contractions occur closer together. A characteristic of the true contractions is that they begin in the lower back and then travel to the front of the abdomen. The muscles of the abdomen become stiffer with subsequent contractions. The sharpness of the contractions increases as the uterine muscles prepare to ease the baby out of the uterus. False labor is characterized by contractions that are far apart, with no rhythmic regularity, and with no muscular hardening of the abdomen. Nevertheless, occasionally false labor is difficult to distinguish from real labor. Many a would-be mother has rushed to the hospital only to return home.

A second sign of real labor is the appearance of a blood-tinged mucuslike discharge called *show*. During pregnancy the opening of the uterus is sealed shut by mucus, which acts like a plug. When labor is about to begin, the mucus is eased out and discharged.

A third sign of labor is the "bursting of the water bag." The amniotic fluid that has been cushioning the baby is released before the baby is born, and either a gush of clear fluid or a slow leaking of clear fluid from the vagina may occur. Usually the bag ruptures toward the end of labor. However, it is not unusual for a bag to break a day or more before the child is delivered.

Stages of labor

Obstetricians generally recognize three stages of labor in the birth process. The first and longest phase is the period of rhythmic and regular labor contractions. During this time, the cervix will dilate or "ripen" so that the birth canal can be stretched or widened enough for the baby to pass through. Physicians usually prefer to be called when the contractions are 10 to 15 minutes apart or when the water bag has ruptured, regardless of "show" or contractions. Contractions come closer together as the cervix dilates to its full width of about 4 inches in diameter. The length of this first stage of labor can vary considerably in time. For a first baby the average length of total labor is about 14 hours. For later babies labor lasts an average of 8 hours. Ideally, the labor should not last too long or take place too quickly, since a slow delivery will exhaust both the mother and the baby and a quick delivery may mean that the baby is unable to make the quick physiological adjustment required. Many such children have marginal perceptual problems in learning when they enter school.

When contractions are about 2 or 3 minutes apart and last 60 to 70 seconds, the second stage of labor begins. The baby is born during this period (Fig. 3-1). The actual birth may take about 20 to 70 minutes. With each contraction the baby moves downward through the cervix, through the vagina, and out. The mother can "bear down" (push) to help these movements once the head has passed between the bones forming the pelvic outlet. Unless a woman has participated in a natural child birth education program, she will be given either a local anesthetic, such as a saddle block, a caudal, or a spinal anesthetic, or a general anesthetic if she requires it. If there is danger of the vaginal or surrounding tissues being torn, the doctor may make a small incision called an *episiotomy* to relieve the strain on the tissues and to make a larger opening. Stitches, which will later dissolve, are made after the delivery.[2]

The "crowning" of the head occurs when the widest diameter of the baby's head is at the mother's vulva, the outer entrance to her vagina. The physician will grasp the emerged head beneath the chin with one hand and gently draw on the baby, helping it out. The rest of the body will usually be delivered with one or two more contractions after the head is out. The baby, as he

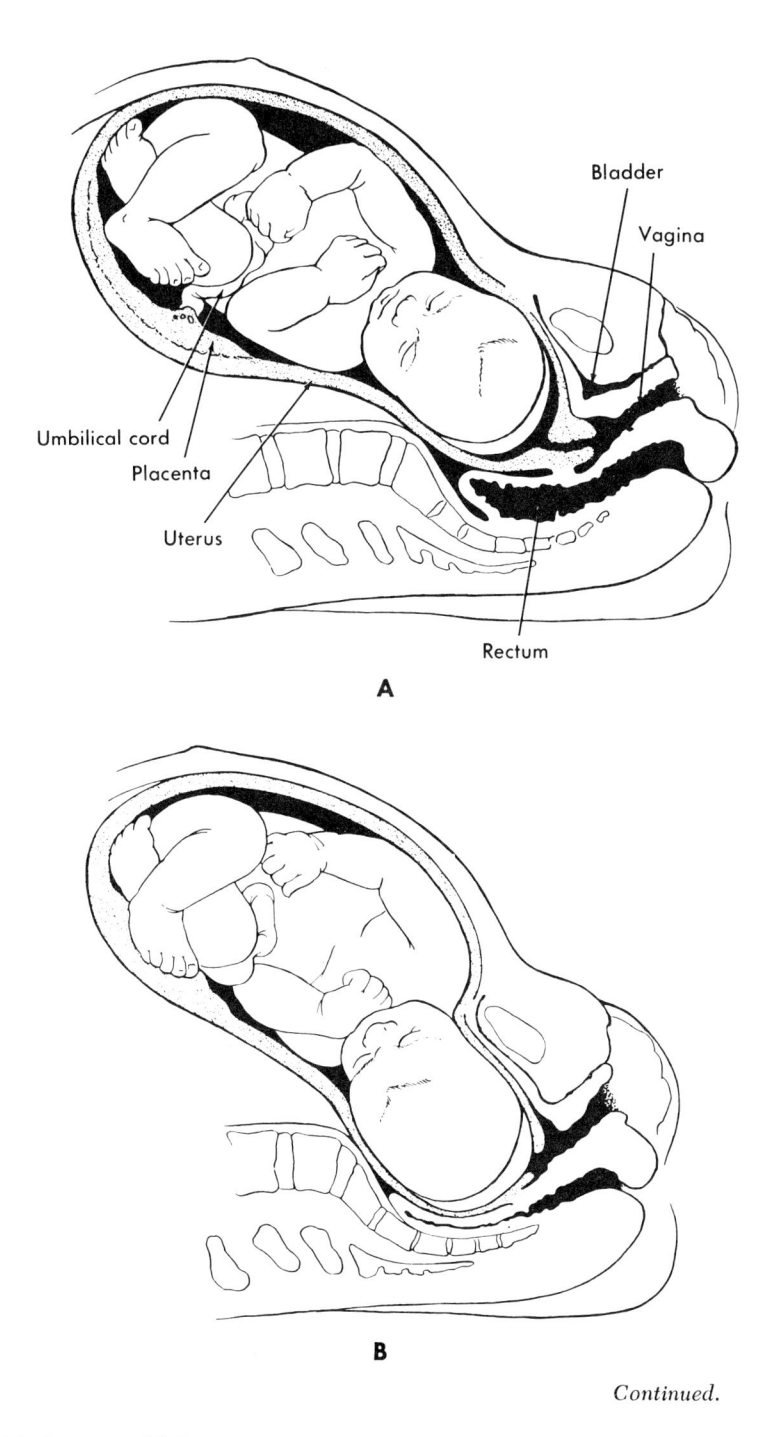

Fig. 3-1. Mechanisms of labor. **A**, Engagement. **B**, Descent with flexion. **C**, Internal rotation. **D**, Extension. **E**, External rotation. **F**, Delivery of the anterior shoulder. **G**, Lateral flexion. (From Iorio, J.: Principles of obstetrics and gynecology for nurses, ed. 2, St. Louis, 1971, The C. V. Mosby Co.)

C

D

E

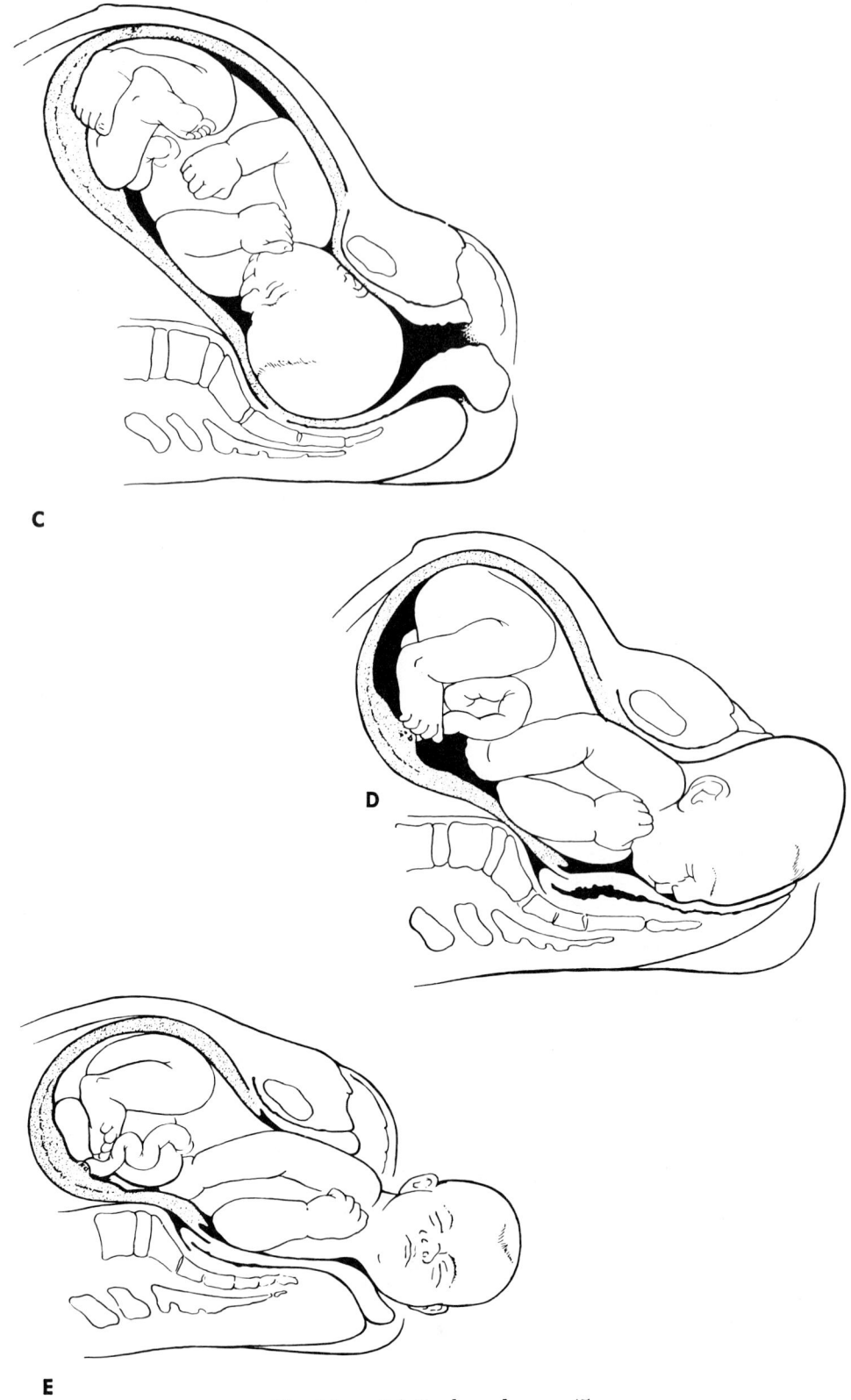

Fig. 3-1, cont'd. For legend see p. 45.

Birth of the baby 47

F

G

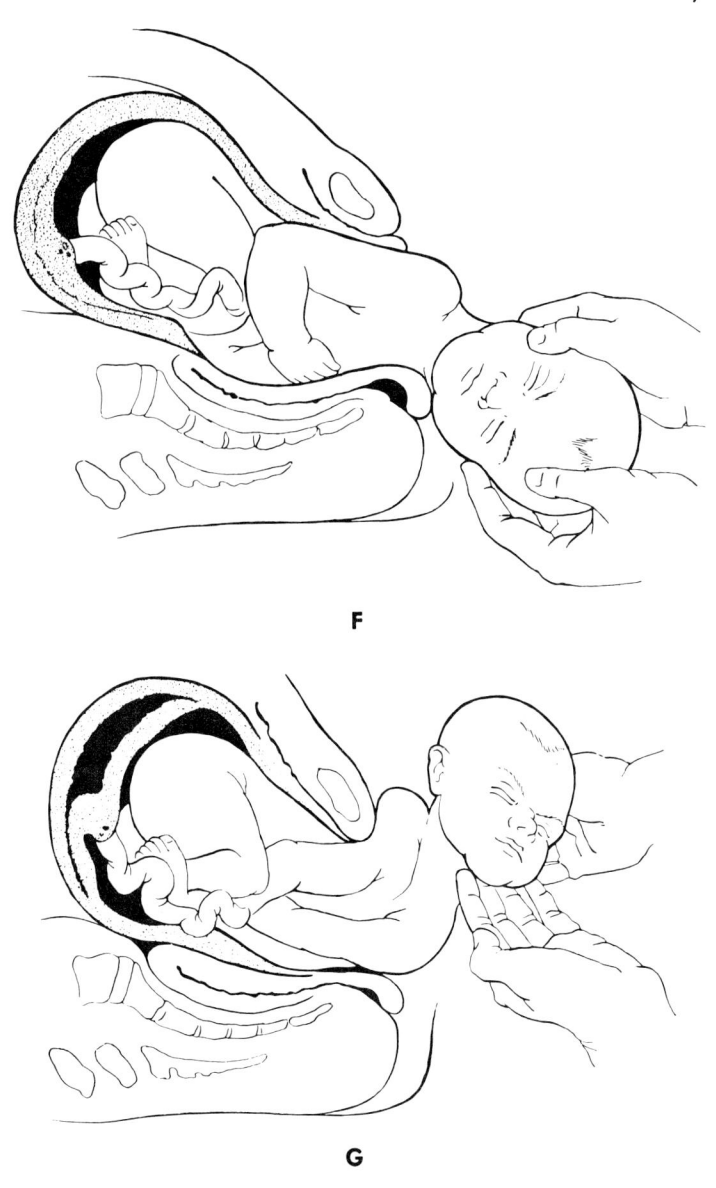

Fig. 3-1, cont'd. For legend see p. 45.

now appears, has a whitish look from the protective vernix coating with which it was covered while in the amnionic sac. He may also have some blood on him from the mucus and tissues. The head may be a little misshapen because of the contraction pressure exerted on it while in the birth canal, but it is pliable and quickly resumes its normal shape. Nature wisely sees to it that the bones of the head are among the last ones to be formed.

When delivery is completed, the baby is held by the heels with his head down. Mucus and other amniotic residue is quickly sucked from the mouth and nose. The buttocks or the soles of the baby's feet may be given a mild tap to get the baby to inhale enough air to inflate all the tiny air sacs in his lungs, which have never been used before. As the baby exhales, he utters his first audible wail. His crying forces the breath through faster. As the baby takes in oxygen, his body color changes to a pinkish hue. The umbilical cord is tied off, cut, and sterilized to prevent infection. The baby is now completely on its own in terms of bodily functions. Drops are put in each of the baby's eyes to prevent eye infection or blindness, which could be due to a gonorrheal infection of the mother. The baby is cleaned, identified with a name bracelet or band, usually footprinted or thumbprinted, weighed, measured, and put to bed in a warm blanket. The baby is fine.

The final stage of labor consists of the delivery of the afterbirth—the placenta with the attached amniotic and chorionic membranes and the remainder of the cord. This process takes about 20 minutes and is virtually painless. The physician will quickly examine the mother and the afterbirth to make certain that no abnormalities exist. The mother will lose a pint of blood, more or less, in giving birth. The physician may knead her abdomen to help restore tone to the uterine muscles. For the next ten to fourteen days the uterine lining will disintegrate and will be shed in a process resembling menstruation.[3]

Kinds of births and deliveries

Ninety-five percent of all babies are born with their heads emerging first in what is called a vertex presentation.[4] This type of birth is the normal spontaneous delivery. No instruments are necessary. Things progress according to the plans prescribed by nature in its wonderful wisdom for the birth of a baby.

About 3% of all babies assume a lie just before birth in which the buttocks instead of the head are positioned in the lower pelvic area. As a result, the buttocks and feet emerge first in birth, with the head appearing last. This type of delivery is a breech presentation. Such births, which physicians can usually detect before they happen, may require special attention by the physicians because they generally are more difficult. However, in most cases there is a satisfactory delivery.

In cases in which the baby is disproportionately large or where his head is larger than the mother's pelvic opening, the physician may advise a cesarean birth. Such a birth is especially necessary if the fetus has assumed a transverse lie and the position cannot be changed. A cesarean section is a surgical delivery through an incision in the abdominal wall and the uterus. The child is removed through the slits, and then both incisions are carefully sewn. This delivery is considered major surgery, but the risks are minimal with modern medical technique. About one baby in fifty is delivered this way.[5] It used to be a common belief that once a woman had a cesarean section, the uterus and abdominal wall were weakened. It is now known that a woman may have several cesarean births satisfactorily.

A forceps or instrument delivery is suggested if the uterine contractions weaken or stop during delivery or when some physiological condition makes it difficult for the baby to push through the birth canal. The forceps are a curved, tonglike instrument shaped to fit on each side of the baby's head. As an emergency procedure, a high-forceps delivery may be made during the first stage of labor or early in the second stage. This procedure is somewhat uncertain because an accurate placement of the forceps may be difficult. A low-forceps delivery is made at the stage of actual delivery and involves less risk. The forceps will occasionally make a bluish mark on each side of the infant's head where the tongs touched, but these disappear after several days. Although the technique of using forceps has improved tremendously because of better training, there is a wide variance in the use of forceps from hospital to hospital and physician to physician.

A growing number of obstetricians believe in inducing labor when a woman is at the end of term. The end of term is determined by a drop in the level of progesterone in the mother's blood. A tiny sensor, in the form of a microballoon, is inserted between the wall of the uterus and the membranes that surround the baby before birth. The hormone oxytocin is injected intravenously into the patient. The balloon sensor, linked to a pressure recorder, tells the physician the magnitude and character of the uterine contractions and exactly how much oxytocin should be given to create the "ideal" level of labor. Ninety-two percent of the women give birth on the day they receive the oxytocin.[6] The advantage of induced labor is that a woman can have her baby on a chosen day when the hospital is fully staffed.

The normalcy of the baby's condition and survival chances at birth have been systematized in the Apgar score (Table 3-1), developed by Virginia Apgar.[7] The scale gives a sum of ratings, scored from 0 to 10, in five conditions: breathing effort, heart rate, muscle tone, reflex irritability, and skin color. Large-scale research studies show that the scores are good gross predictors in identifying babies who need special care.

INFLUENCES ON PRENATAL DEVELOPMENT

There are a variety of conditions that can affect the normal development of an unborn baby. Some of these influences occur during the prenatal period when the fetus is being developed, whereas others take place at the time of birth or just after. Fortunately, 97% of all babies are born without any serious defect.[8] Of the other 3%, there is a wide range of type and severity of defects. On a related matter Pasamanick and Knobloch[9] postulate that there is a "continuum of reproductive casualty, consisting of brain damage incurred during the prenatal and perinatal periods as a result of abnormalities during these periods." Such damage may result in conditions extending from death "through cerebral palsy, epilepsy, mental deficiency, reading disability, and behavioral disorder."

Nutrition of the mother

Studies show that an inadequate maternal diet is probably the most frequently encountered hazard of intrauterine life. It affects not only the infant's well-being at birth but also the physical and mental health of the mother. Burke[10] found that stillbirths, prematurity, rickets, severe

Table 3-1. Apgar score for condition of the newborn baby*

SIGN	0	1	2	SCORE
Heart rate	Absent	Slow (below 100)	Over 100	
Respiratory effort	Absent	Slow, irregular	Good, crying	
Muscle tone	Limp	Some flexion of extremities	Active motion	
Reflex irritability (response to catheter in nostril)	No response	Grimace	Cough or sneeze	
Color	Blue, pale	Body pink, extremities blue	Completely pink	
			Total score	

*From Apgar, V.: Proposal for new method of evaluation of newborn infant, Anesth. & Analg. 32:260, 1953.
Scores are given by physician or anesthetist 60 seconds after complete birth. Nearly all normal infants receive a score of 7 to 9 or 10. A score of 5 to 10 usually indicates no need for treatment; a score of 4 or below indicates need for prompt diagnosis and treatment.

anemia, and tuberculosis were somewhat higher for babies whose mothers were malnourished than for infants from well-nourished mothers. Scientists at the 1967 International Conference on Malnutrition, Learning and Behavior reported findings from South American and Central American countries that strongly suggest that malnutrition can bring about physical and mental impairment.[11] Studies have shown that the myelin sheath that covers the nerve fibers is impaired in animals if the fetus is malnourished during the period when the myelin is being formed.[12] If the same is true in humans, it would be awesome to consider its significance when one realizes the worldwide incidence of malnutrition.

Maternal infections

One of the prime functions of the placenta is to safeguard the embryo by keeping out bacteria and bringing in antibodies that produce an immunity to a variety of diseases. The placenta, however, cannot screen out everything that might be injurious. Certain viruses manage to slip through the barrier and cause defects.

German measles, or rubella, if contracted by the mother in the first eight to ten weeks of pregnancy, will cause visual, auditory, mental, or heart abnormalities in one out of three babies.[13] From 1963 to 1965 an epidemic of rubella centered on the eastern seaboard of the United States approached the level of a national disaster. Fifty thousand women were infected during the first trimester of pregnancy. The total result was 30,000 miscarriages and stillbirths. Even more disturbing were the 20,000 children who were born with defects ranging from mental retardation and heart disorders to blindness and deafness. The most common birth defect is a loss of hearing. Affected children may also develop cataracts. Many of these children will be small for their age.

Rubella is characterized by a rash the first few days but no pronounced cold symptoms. Within 24 hours, pink spots appear, which tend to fade and run together. The overall appearance is a flushed effect. Other noticeable symptoms of rubella are swollen lymph glands in the neck, a slight body temperature rise to 100° F., and a scratchy throat. The incubation period is fourteen to twenty-one days, and the disease is contagious.[14] The mother gets over the effects of rubella in a short period of time. Her unborn child, however, may never get over them.

A vaccine has been developed for preventing rubella. Public health officials hope to stamp out rubella by giving the vaccine to the reservoir of susceptible subjects who can spread the infection. Mass inoculation programs have been conducted in many countries. Immunization is usually started in the earliest grades of school, since this age group is the main source of virus dissemination in a community. The main purpose of vaccination, however, is to protect pregnant women for the sake of their unborn.

Undetected syphilis in the mother frequently attacks the nervous system of the fetus and may result in congenital weakness. Syphilis may cause stillbirth, miscarriage, deafness, blindness, or congenital mental deficiency. In some cases the child may not show any signs of syphilitic symptoms until several years later. One known case in which a child was born with syphilis resulted in senility at the age of 14 years because the syphilitic spirochetes had destroyed so many of the brain cells.

Rh factor

Human blood is not interchangeable. Blood from a donor must be matched with the blood of the recipient to ensure that they are compatible. Although the blood of the mother does not mix with that of the fetus, a problem of compatibility could arise if both the mother and the father have a blood type from the Rh blood group. If both parents are Rh negative or if both are Rh positive, there is no problem because the fetus will inherit a blood type that will be compatible with that of the mother. If the parents differ in their Rh factor and the baby inherits an Rh-positive blood type from the father, there could be a problem if the mother is Rh negative. In about 10% of the cases some blood from the fetus can be diffused through the placenta into the bloodstream of the mother.[15] Since the blood types are incompatible, the Rh-negative mother will produce antibodies to resist the "invasion of foreign bodies." If the antibodies are passed back to the fetus by diffusion, the antibodies will attack the fetal red cells, causing the fetus to become anemic. Usually the fetus can make red cells fast enough for the needs, but if it cannot, it will either die or be born with a severe anemic condition called *erythroblastosis fetalis*. If the child lives, he is highly susceptible to jaundice, which in severe cases can cause some brain damage.[16] Successive pregnancies of the mother with fetuses having Rh-positive blood will raise the level of antibodies in the mother's blood to a critical level and will be more dangerous to these fetuses. Only Rh-negative mothers are affected.

The following outline provides the reaction of Rh factors.

1. Rh compatibility
    Father Rh+ and mother Rh+ = baby Rh+
    Father Rh− and mother Rh− = baby Rh−
    Father Rh+ and mother Rh− = baby Rh−
2. Rh incompatibility
    If father Rh+ and mother Rh− = baby Rh+, then Rh− mother and Rh+ baby are incompatible
    a. Blood antigens from Rh+ baby enter mother's Rh− blood.
    b. Mother's Rh− blood produces antibodies to fight off foreign antigens.
    c. Some of mother's antibodies enter baby's blood by diffusion.
    d. Mother's antibodies in baby's blood attack red corpuscles causing anemia, edema, and/or jaundice.
    e. With successive pregnancies mother's supply of antibodies can increase to a dangerous level for the fetus.

Seventeen percent of mothers in western societies are Rh negative.[17] Striking advances have taken place in the treatment of Rh incompatibility. A serum, RhoGAM, has been developed to prevent the production of antibodies in mothers who have not already formed antibodies. If a child with Rh factors is born anemic, an exchange transfusion can be given to remove sensitized blood. In 1963 the first intrauterine transfusion was attempted with considerable success by a New Zealand physician.[18] This treatment is used if the fetus is in danger of death and is too immature to risk premature delivery.

Drugs and medication

The effect of drugs on the unborn can be most pronounced. The category "drugs" includes medicines that physicians prescribe such as antibiotics; over-the-counter remedies like aspirin, cold tablets, vitamins, and nose drops; and abused or illegal drugs such as heroin, LSD, and marijuana. The full meaning of the influence of medication and drugs on prenatal development is still being investigated. The evidence, however, appears to indicate that women of reproductive age should be careful of taking medications that are not prescribed.

In the early 1960s a sedative drug named thalidomide appeared on the European market. Not realizing the consequences of its effects on pregnant women, physicians prescribed it for those who were tense due to their new condition. Many babies born to these women had flipperlike arms or no arms or legs at all. Deafness of some children can be traced to the mother's use of quinine.[19]

Addictive narcotics are carried in the bloodstream of the mother and are transmitted to the fetus. Less than a day after birth the baby shows the classic signs of withdrawal, which may be so violent that the infant may die. Premature births are higher among women addicted to narcotics than among the general population.

Although there is still much to be learned about the relationship of drugs and narcotics to birth defects, there is more known about the effects on newborn babies of sedative medication given to mothers during the birth process. These drugs do affect the baby, although only temporarily. The more anesthetic given to the mother, the longer the adjustment period of the newborn to postnatal life. Babies of mothers who were heavily medicated showed disorganized behavior for three or four days after birth as compared to one or two days for babies of nonmedicated mothers.[20] What is significant in these cases is that at the time of birth, just when a baby's systems have to be at the peak level of performance to make a smooth transition to the outer world, they are in a state of sedation and may not have that extra push needed to overcome difficulties that may arise.

Toxemia of pregnancy

Toxemia refers to a large group of undesirable physical conditions that may occur in the mother after the twenty-fourth week of pregnancy or soon after giving birth. The signs or symptoms that these conditions have in common are (1) edema, a rapid or excessive weight gain during the third trimester due to an accumulation of fluid in the body; (2) hypertension, a rise in blood pressure; and (3) the presence of albumin, a protein product, in the urine.[21] Acute toxemia is known as preeclampsia. Treatment of preeclampsia is usually effective. If the toxemia becomes severe (eclampsia), convulsions and finally coma will occur. It is estimated that 6% to 10% of all pregnancies are complicated by one of the many toxemias of pregnancy—mostly preeclampsia. With the inception of blood banks and antibiotics, toxemia of pregnancy has replaced hemorrhage and infection as the leading cause of maternal mortality. Infant mortality in all toxemias is about 10% to 25%.[22]

Other factors

The age of the mother when she gives birth to a child appears to have some bearing on the ease of the birth process, the mental ability level of the child, and the physical well-being of the child. Mothers under 15 and over 40 years of age tend to have a higher proportion of retarded children than do mothers who are between these ages.[23] Women who have their first baby when they are 35 years old or over are more likely than younger women to experience illnesses during pregnancy and have a more difficult labor. The optimum age for childbearing appears to be between 20 and 28 years of age.[24] However, advances in obstetrics have made pregnancy and birth at any age much less dangerous and complicated than previously.

A relationship between the weight of a newborn baby and the amount of smoking done by the mother (Fig. 3-2) is suggested by several studies. The National Institutes of Health report that the size of a newborn baby is affected by the mother's smoking somewhat in proportion to the number of cigarettes she smokes per day. The heavy cigarette smoker will have smaller babies than a nonsmoker. In addition, there will also be a significantly greater number of premature deliveries among heavy smokers.[25]

Some anxiety in a pregnant woman is inevitable and seldom harmful. However, excessive emotional stress is known to be transferred to the developing fetus by hormones and chemical factors in the bloodstream. As a result, the infant may be born with a physiological defect or weakness, a slight decrease in bodily weight, or undesirable behavior characteristics. The infant's behavior pattern after birth may take the form of excessive crying, irritability, difficulties in digestion, vomiting, and sometimes diarrhea.[26] Be-

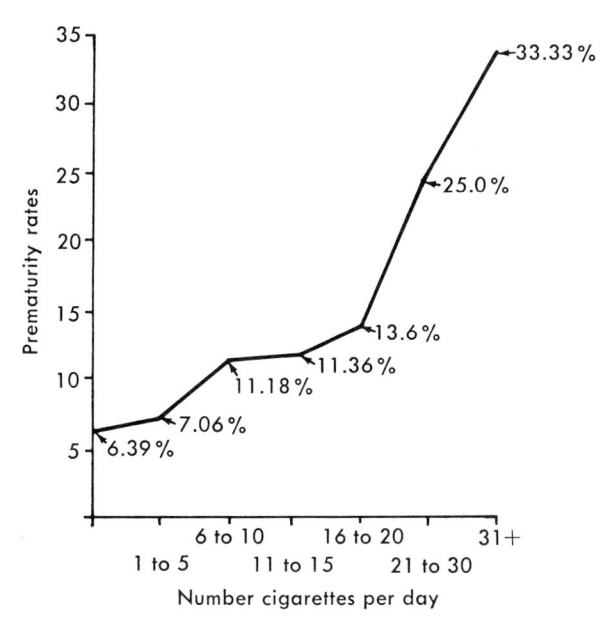

Fig. 3-2. Relationship between number of cigarettes smoked per day by the mother and prematurity rates of infants. (From Simpson, W. J.: Am. J. Obstet. Gynecol. 73:808-815, 1957.)

fore birth there is increased movement by the fetus whenever the mother is undergoing emotional stress. The longer the period of stress, the greater will be the increase of the baby's activity.[27] A case illustrating the effect of great emotional stress on prenatal development is that of an 11-year-old girl who developed ulcerative colitis (ulcer of the colon), which is an uncommon condition in persons so young. The prenatal developmental history revealed that during the second month of pregnancy, the girl's mother was subjected to intense emotional stress when both her parents were in a serious accident and were not expected to live. The medical report on the 11-year-old reasoned that this event occurred at the time when the digestive system, including the colon, was being formed. It was assumed that the stress of the moment produced a chemical change in the mother's blood and affected the development of the colon in the fetus, producing a weakness that made it more susceptible to colitis.

CONDITIONS AT BIRTH AFFECTING DEVELOPMENT
Phenylketonuria

Phenylketonuria, known as PKU, is a hereditary defect in an enzyme of the liver. The child needs the enzyme to metabolize the common protein food product phenylalanine. If the enzyme abnormality is not found and treated soon after birth, certain substances accumulate in the blood and bring about mental retardation by causing damage to the brain. PKU appears about once in 10,000 births. The condition can often be detected by a simple blood test given before the baby leaves the hospital. The infant's heel is pricked, and a few drops of blood are obtained on filter paper and then tested. A urine test can be done after the infant is 3 weeks old.[28] Treatment consists of a scientifically controlled diet, which is begun within the first few weeks of life. If the diet is continued, the child will grow and develop normally. In some cases PKU children can be given normal diets after a few years.

Text continued on p. 58.

Table 3-2. Types of birth defects, estimates, description, and treatment*

TYPE OF DEFECT	NUMBERS AFFECTED ANNUALLY	DESCRIPTION	CAUSES AND TREATMENT
Birthmarks	Very common	There are many unimportant birthmarks. The disfiguring ones are reddish or wine-colored patches consisting of numerous small dilated blood vessels. True blood vessel tumors are rarer. These are elevated and may occur on any part of the body.	Cause unknown. Skilled plastic surgeons can remove many marks. Skin grafts are often used. A new technique for large marks is to tattoo normal skin colors right over the purple area.
Cleft lip (harelip)	About 1 in every 1,000 babies in white populations is born with a cleft lip. Seventy percent of these also have cleft palates. The frequency appears higher in Japanese and lower in black populations.	When the embryo is about 6 weeks, swellings that will become the upper lip have not yet met. If they do not fuse at the proper time, the gap will remain and the baby will have a cleft lip.	These conditions are sometimes related to genetic defects. In experiments with animals it appears that the environment in the uterus, such as the position of the embryo or the blood supply, may be a factor, and some drugs given during pregnancy are also under suspicion. There are now many new operative techniques for repairing the defects. Harelip can be repaired in the first few weeks after birth, and cleft palate before the child is 14 months old in most cases.
Cleft palate	About 1 in every 2,500 babies has a cleft palate without a cleft lip. The two conditions are not genetically related.	A cleft palate is a hole in the roof of the mouth. More boys than girls have a harelip, and more girls have a cleft palate.	
Clubfoot	1 in 250	The foot turns inward (usually) or outward and is fixed in a tiptoe position.	Possibly due to the position of the child in the uterus, although maldevelopment of the limb bud may also be the cause. Mild deformities respond well to shoe splints worn at night. Simple braces and corrective shoes may be needed. More serious clubfoot often will be associated with other defects as well. Treatment must begin early and is prolonged because the condition tends to recur. The muscles and ligaments must be stretched and the bones realigned. Plaster casts can often correct the condition. Surgery is sometimes necessary.
Congenital heart disease	1 in 160	There are many known types of congenital heart defects. Some are so slight as to cause little strain on the heart; others are fatal. In some of the abnormalities, the baby appears blue.	Few causes are known, but German measles during pregnancy is one. An ever-increasing number of heart conditions can be repaired by surgery, saving lives and preventing invalidism.

Congenital urinary tract defects	1 in 250	There are many different types, involving the kidneys, ureters, bladder, and genitalia. Organs may be absent, fused, or obstructed.	Some causes are known, such as certain hormones given during pregnancy. There is some hereditary tendency. Most conditions can be corrected by surgery.
Diabetes	Very common. About 1 in 4 carries the trait. Clinical diabetes, or actual cases, seen in about 1 in 2,500 persons between ages 1 and 20; in 1 in 50 persons over 60 years of age.	Metabolic disorder in which there is a shortage of insulin hormone. Glucose, which comes from carbohydrates, accumulates in the blood and is excreted through the kidneys instead of being stored in the body as glycogen. Possibility of manifestation increases with age. Patient may be susceptible to infection of cuts and bruises. Among older persons serious involvement could lead to hardening of the arteries, gangrene in legs, and blindness.	Cause unknown; possible enzyme defect. Marked hereditary tendency. Persons with family history of diabetes should seek periodic checkups. Physicians can recognize symptoms, make positive diagnosis, and prescribe specific treatment. Special diets, oral medication, and injections of insulin are measures that will usually keep condition under control and permit normal activity.
Erythroblastosis	About 10% of the babies born to Rh-negative mothers married to Rh-positive fathers have this condition. One in 7 of total American population has Rh-negative blood. Among Orientals the figure is 1 in 20.	The baby is often yellow in color soon after birth. Anemia is another symptom. Mental retardation may be severe. Erythroblastosis is a common cause of stillbirth.	Rh blood factor is inherited. Physicians should know Rh factor of both parents. Rh problem exists only if father is Rh positive (baby inherits Rh-positive gene from his father) and mother is Rh negative. Red blood cells of fetus reach mother's blood, causing her blood to form antibodies that pass back through the placenta to the baby and destroy his red cells in varying degrees. First pregnancy is usually uneventful. Cure can now be effected if condition is detected early. Infant mortality used to be 45% but is now 5%. Exchange transfusion, replacing baby's blood with compatible blood right after birth, is the cure. Several transfusions are sometimes necessary.
Extra fingers and toes (polydactyly)	Extra digits are twice as frequent as fused digits. The incidence is 1 in 100 among the black population; 1 in 600 in the white population.	Extra fingers or toes.	Cause unknown; frequently hereditary. Cure is simple amputation of the extra digits. This can often be done at birth or at about 3 years of age.
Fused fingers and toes (syndactyly)	Fused digits do not have such racial variation.	Too few digits.	In syndactyly surgery can improve the function and appearance of the hand or foot. Occasionally artificial limbs are necessary.

*From Apgar, V.: With best wishes for a happy birth day, New York, 1963, The National Foundation–March of Dimes, pp. 4-8.

Continued.

Table 3-2. Types of birth defects, estimates, description, and treatment—cont'd

TYPE OF DEFECT	NUMBERS AFFECTED ANNUALLY	DESCRIPTION	CAUSES AND TREATMENT
Fibrocystic disease (cystic fibrosis)	About 1 in 1,000 births. Rare among black populations; found very infrequently in Orientals.	A recently identified disease, now separated from a vast group of conditions producing a sickly, malnourished child with persistent intestinal difficulties. Victims have chronic respiratory problems, and death is usually due to pneumonia or other lung complications. One clue to disease is perspiration with high-salt content.	Hereditary. Due to a metabolic error. Manifests self soon after birth. Mucous material blocks the exit of the digestive juices from the pancreas into the intestinal tract. Excess mucus is also secreted by lungs. Formerly death was expected before age 2. Now antibiotics, chemical substitutions for enzymes, and other treatments have extended life expectancy. Increasing numbers of adults are found to have a mild form of the disease.
Galactosemia	Somewhat more rare than phenylketonuria	A disorder causing eye cataracts and severe damage to the liver and the brain, resulting in mental retardation.	Hereditary. Caused by the absence of an enzyme required to convert galactose to glucose, important in digestion of milk sugar. Formerly led to many early deaths, but experiments now show that early recognition and dietary treatment can arrest the disease. Diagnosis can be made at birth.
Hydrocephaly (water on brain)	1 in 500	Enlargement of the head due to excessive fluid within the brain. Most cases result from obstruction to circulation of cerebrospinal fluid. In others fluid is produced in excess or is not absorbed fast enough. Pressure from fluid often causes compression of the brain with resulting mental retardation.	Obstruction to flow may result from prenatal infection or abnormality in development. Cause of excess fluid not known. Treatment is "shunt" operation to relieve pressure on the brain. A tube with a one-way valve is inserted surgically to lead fluid from the brain directly into the bloodstream or into some other body cavity. Condition frequently fatal if not treated.
Missing limbs	Very rare	Congenital amputees are born with one to four limbs missing or seriously deformed.	Cause unknown. Recently an international outbreak of this defect was traced to the drug thalidomide used by pregnant mothers. Great strides have been made in prosthetic, or artificial, devices. Emotional problems of the affected parents and children are great but are being overcome to a large extent in many families.

Mongolism	1 in 600. Women 25 years of age have about 1 chance in 2,000 of producing a mongoloid child. For women of 45 the average expectation is about 1 in 50.	Mongolism, mongoloid idiocy, or the Langdon-Down syndrome is characterized by short stature, slightly slanted eyes, and varying degrees of mental retardation.	All patients have chromosomal error. Causes can be hereditary or environmental. Whereas the normal human cell has 46 chromosomes, cells of those afflicted by this defect have 47 or the equivalent. No known cure, although IQ can be improved by special training.
Open spine (spina bifida)	Approximately 1 in every 500 births. It is more common among white children than among black. About half the patients are also victims of hydrocephaly.	Failure of the spine to close permits the protrusion of spinal cord or nerves. This often leads to total dysfunction of the legs, bladder, and rectum. Often the child has other serious defects.	Cause unknown. In some cases surgery in the first 3 months of child's life can either correct or arrest the condition so that other complications do not occur. In the more serious cases, several new surgical techniques are being used on the bladder, rectum, and spinal cord.
Phenylketonuria (PKU)	Approximately 1 in 10,000	Chemical imbalance, resulting in a form of mental deficiency, inherited from apparently normal parents, each of whom has one defective gene. The child appears normal at birth, but his mind stops developing during the first year of life. Retardation is severe. One third never learn to walk, and two thirds never learn to talk. The pigment of skin and hair is decreased.	Caused by a hereditary defect in an enzyme of the liver. In normal metabolism, phenylalanine, a compound making up one twentieth of the weight of proteins in the diet, is changed to tyrosine. In PKU the enzyme responsible for this step is inactive or absent, and phenylalanine accumulates. PKU can be detected between the fifth and seventh day of life. Treatment is dietary; specifically manufactured food with low-phenylalanine content is fed to the infant. The treatment does not cure retardation already present but can prevent it from developing. Therefore treatment should begin soon after birth. Some experiments show that after a few years PKU children can be fed normal diets.
Sickle-cell trait	Low among white populations. Very high (about 40%) in black populations in Africa and high (10%) among American blacks.	When red blood cells of people with the sickle-cell trait are exposed to low-oxygen atmosphere, the cells lose normal form and become crescent or sickle shaped. When accompanied by severe anemia, the condition is usually fatal. The sickle-cell trait carries some immunity to malaria.	Hereditary condition. Severe anemia results if the child receives the abnormal trait from both parents.

Anoxia

The ease or difficulty with which the newborn infant starts to breathe after birth is critical to his future development. If breathing is not established soon, enabling oxygen to reach the brain, serious consequences may occur. If oxygen deprivation (anoxia) is severe, the infant may die. Less severe deprivation may result in enough damage to brain cells to cause cerebral palsy or similar conditions. A lesser degree of anoxia may cause disturbances in cognitive functioning, such as in mental processes related to verbal, conceptual, and perceptual development. Visual-motor coordination may be affected.[29] In preschool and early school years special sensory development and teaching techniques may be needed to help the child develop the various cognitive and perceptual processes. The effects of anoxia on learning ability may be temporary or permanent.

Oxygen deprivation may result from a prolonged or difficult birth or by birth in the breech position. Occasionally, infants born by cesarean section will develop a hyaline membrane, a glossylike condition in the lungs, shortly after birth that causes difficulty in breathing and possibly death. Babies born with a congenital heart defect that bars normal circulation of blood can also be oxygen starved. These so-called "blue babies" are placed in incubators to enable them to survive without producing any damage to the brain. Once their problem has been corrected, they respond adequately.

Also serious in establishing respiration is too rapid a birth. Precipitate labor, which is labor of less than 2 hours duration, may introduce the baby too suddenly to his new environment, with the consequence that he is not yet ready to breathe. Oxygen deprivation occurs in these cases also. The degree of brain damage and the permanence of its effects will depend largely on how quickly the infant can start breathing.

Birth defects

An understandable concern of parents is whether the baby is born free of congenital defects. Fortunately, the large majority of babies are born without serious abnormalities that cause disfigurement or a physical or mental handicap. Yet some children are born with defects, some of which are presented in Table 3-2. About 20% of birth defects are due to heredity; another 20% are caused by environmental factors, such as drugs, medicine, viral infections, and vitamin deficiencies. Another 60% result from an interaction of some environmental factor and a genetic predisposition.[30]

One child in 500 will be born with an open spine (spina bifida). Failure of the spine to close permits some nerves of the spinal cord to protrude. Sometimes surgery in the first three months of the child's life can correct the condition so that other complications do not occur. Clinical cases of mental retardation such as Down's syndrome (mongolism) appear once in 600 births (one in fifty for women over 45 years of age) and as hydrocephaly (water on the brain) in one in 500 births. Mongolism is caused by a chromosomal error, whereas hydrocephaly usually is due to an obstruction of the flow of cerebrospinal fluid. Fibrocystic disease, cystic fibrosis, occurs once in 1,000 births. Children with this condition have chronic respiratory problems and persistent intestinal difficulties. The cause is usually hereditary and involves a metabolic error.

The significant point to be remembered is that most births produce normal, healthy babies. If the mother takes care of herself, especially during the first three months of pregnancy, chances are considerably greater that the baby will be normal.

Prematurity and low birth weight

In the past the term *premature* was applied to the newborn baby who had a gestation age of less than 37 weeks or weighed less than 5½ pounds (2,500 grams) at birth. Several studies have indicated that this "either-or" criterion was inadequate because babies of the same weight spend varied lengths of time within the womb. About 30% of babies born after thirty-seven completed weeks of pregnancy weigh less than 5½ pounds, whereas the truly premature newborn baby of, for example, a diabetic mother, may weigh considerably more.

The term *premature* relates to the length of the gestation period and applies to an infant born before thirty-seven completed weeks of pregnancy. The term *low birth weight* is applied to any newborn, regardless of gestation age, who weighs less than 2,500 grams at birth. Recognition of the different groups of premature babies is important because they differ greatly in terms of the kind of care they may need.

Premature birth is the biggest single problem facing those responsible for the care of the newborn. Although most body organs can function fairly adequately by the twenty-eighth week, the brain is still insufficiently developed to control behavior. The cerebral cortex has little, if any, control over the behavior patterns of either a 7- or an 8-month-old term baby.[31] Special attention must be given to the physical needs of the newborn. The premature infant requires nearly three times as much oxygen as a full-term infant. He is often anemic and may require a blood transfusion. Furthermore, he is more subject to infection and will require careful medical supervision. The use of an incubator helps with these problems while at the same time providing a temperature and humidity climate that seeks to duplicate conditions of the intrauterine environment.

There are many reasons why a mother may have a baby of low birth weight or a premature delivery. Some of the factors are toxemia, a multiple birth, accidental hemorrhage during pregnancy, a placenta previa (a misplaced placenta covering the opening of the womb instead of lying in the proper place), hypertensive cardiovascular disease, diabetes, glandular disturbance, nutritional deficiency, undue emotional stress, or a number of other factors. About 7% of all births are premature. Prematurity is more common among first-born babies and among boys than among girls. It is more frequent in the lower socioeconomic class and more frequent among nonwhites than among whites.[32] Of the babies who die within four weeks of birth, over half are born prematurely, which is the greatest cause of neonatal death in the United States; respiratory distress is second and congenital anomalies third as causes of death.

Studies of the development of premature children reveal that these infants do differ from the normal, at least up to about the ages of 6, 7, or 8 years. By then most premature children catch up in weight, height, and functional mental ability. At the beginning of school a greater percentage of premature children are distractable and excessively active or restless. They obtain slightly lower scores on tests of motor and cognitive development. More premature children have difficulty in learning to read than do other children. The extent of the lag in maturation and functional ability is related to the degree of deviation in low birth weight or prematurity of birth. Most children, however, have an amazing ability to adapt or compensate for any deficiencies they may have. One should look for positive attributes in children rather than focus or dwell on limitations or deficiencies. Children progress to the degree that they are free to do so, and that includes freedom from overprotectiveness by parents, who frequently underestimate the capabilities of children who are born prematurely.

STUDY GUIDE

1. Compare the characteristics of true or real labor at the time of birth with those of false labor.

2. What are the three stages of labor?
3. Describe a normal delivery.
4. Rubella, or German measles, is a serious matter when a mother is infected during the first twelve weeks of pregnancy. What are its symptoms, and in what ways can it affect the unborn child?
5. Discuss the implications of incompatible Rh factors and of toxemia in pregnancy.
6. What is anoxia? How can it affect a child?
7. How do premature babies frequently differ from normal term babies?

REFERENCES
1. Biskind, L.: Having your baby, New York, 1951, Random House, Inc.
2. Story of life, part 4, London, 1970, Marshall Cavendish Books, Ltd.
3. Stone, L. J., and Church, J.: Childhood and adolescence, New York, 1968, Random House, Inc.
4. Birch, W. G.: A doctor discusses pregnancy, Chicago, 1963, Budlong Press Co.
5. Ibid., p. 86.
6. Chevalies, L. R.: New developments in medicine that may affect your health, Woman's Day 34:124, Oct., 1970.
7. Apgar, V.: Perinatal problems and the central nervous system. In United States Department of Health, Education, and Welfare: The child with central nervous system deficit, Washington, D. C., 1965, Government Printing Office, pp. 75-76.
8. Fishbein, M., editor: Birth defects, Philadelphia, 1963, J. B. Lippincott Co.
9. Pasamanick, B., and Knobloch, H.: Retrospective studies on the epidemiology of reproductive casualty: old and new, Merrill-Palmer Q. 12:7-23, 1966.
10. Burke, B. S.: Maternal nutrition during pregnancy. In Stuart, H. C., and Prugh, D. G., editors: The healthy child, Cambridge, Mass., 1960, Harvard University Press.
11. Scrimshaw, N. S.: Infant malnutrition and adult learning, Sat. Rev. 50:64ff, March 16, 1968.
12. Benton, J. W., Moser, H. W., Dodge, P. R., and Carr, S.: Modification of the schedule of myelinization in the rat by early nutritional deprivation, Pediatrics 38:801-804, 1966.
13. Stuart, H. C., and Ingalls, T. H.: Fetal development and congenital malformations. In Stuart, H. C., and Prugh, D. G., editors: The healthy child, Cambridge, Mass., 1960, Harvard University Press.
14. Rubella vaccines, Time 92:60, Nov. 1, 1968.
15. Guttmacher, A. F.: Pregnancy and birth, New York, 1962, The New American Library, Inc.
16. Allen, F. H., and Diamond, L. K.: Erythroblastosis fetalis, Boston, 1958, Little, Brown & Co.
17. Montague, M. F. A.: Constitutional and prenatal factors in infant and child health. In Lenn, M. J. E., editor: Symposium on the Healthy Personality, New York, 1950, Josiah Macy, Jr., Foundation Publications.
18. Liley, A. W.: Intrauterine transfusion of foetus in haemolytic disease, Br. Med. J. 2:1107, 1963.
19. Stuart and Ingalls, op. cit., pp. 55-59.
20. Apgar, V., Holaday, D. A., James, L. S., Weisbrot, I. M., and Berrien, C.: Evaluation of the newborn—second report, J.A.M.A. 168:1985-1988, 1958.
21. Ullery, J. C., and Hollenbeck, Z. J. R.: Textbook of obstetrics, St. Louis, 1965, The C. V. Mosby Co.
22. Iorio, J.: Principles of obstetrics and gynecology for nurses, St. Louis, 1967, The C. V. Mosby Co.
23. Pasamanick, B., and Lilienfeld, A. M.: Association of maternal and fetal factors with development of mental deficiency. I. Abnormalities in the prenatal and paranatal periods, J.A.M.A. 159:155-160, 1955.
24. Montague, op. cit., p. 83.
25. Surgeon General's Committee on Smoking and Health, Washington, D. C., 1962, United States Public Health Service.
26. Ottinger, D. R., and Simons, J. E.: Behavior of human neonates and prenatal maternal anxiety, Psychol. Rep. 14:391-394, 1964.
27. Sontag, L. W.: Maternal anxiety during pregnancy and fetal behavior; physical and behavioral growth, Report of the 26th Ross Pediatric Research Conference, Columbus, Ohio, 1958, Ross Laboratories.
28. Iorio, op. cit., p. 231.
29. Corah, N. L.: Perceptual and cognitive deficits in children as related to perinatal anoxia and level of intelligence, J. Consult. Clin. Psychol. 30:87, 1966.
30. Brody, J. E.: How a mother affects her unborn baby, Woman's Day 33:12, July, 1970.
31. Thompson, G. G.: Child psychology, ed. 2, Boston, 1962, Houghton Mifflin Co., p. 64.
32. Eichenlaub, J. E.: The premature, Today's Health 46:38-39, 1956.

4 Infant motor and cognitive development

INFANCY: ME TO 3 YEARS

Once upon a time, the world (at least a small part of it) was awaiting a monumental event, when all of a sudden, "All systems go! Countdown! 5-4-3-2-1, hello world! Here I am at last." What a trip for a member of the so-called weaker sex.

This is how it was about thirty-five months ago when I first ventured into the world of Playtex nursers, Johnson's baby powder, Pampers, and Q-Tips. For the next few minutes "this is my world and welcome to it."

The way I figure it, my journey began about nine and one-half months before I made my grand entrance. Someone told me that my trip should have lasted nine months, but either someone miscalculated or else I was a little slow in my development because my anxious mommy was ready two weeks before I was. I finally did reach my destination on August 31 at 11:44 P.M., with the most beautiful set of dimples on my cheeks that you ever saw. Baggage and all, I was weighed in at 8 pounds, which wasn't too bad since I was 21 inches tall.

I worried my mommy and daddy at first because I was placed in an isolette. During my arrival a lot of mucus accumulated to hinder my breathing. Nothing to really worry about, though, but you know how first-time parents are.

After seven days in the hospital I entered the unsterile world of people, machines, and pollution. My trip home was relatively uneventful except for Mother Nature helping me remove certain liquid elements from my body, much to my relief but to my mommy's chagrin.

I don't remember much about the next three or four weeks, but according to my mommy and daddy, nighttime feeding was sometimes hectic when my formula would come up faster than it went down. I wasn't sick or anything dramatic—I was just in a hurry to fill my ever-demanding stomach.

During the next three months I learned to tell the difference between my mommy and daddy and the countless number of visitors to my peaceful abode. Did I ever get the attention! No wonder, I was the first baby around my family in twenty years. Some people said I would be spoiled by all this attention, but the way I look at it—what's a baby for if you can't spoil her?

Within my first nine months I gained nine teeth, 14 pounds, 7 inches, and many holes in my posterior because of inoculations for many diseases. I even received a permanent mark, commonly known as a vaccination, on my arm.

My seventh and eighth months were very busy. I learned to sit, I began to crawl and to creep (everywhere to my mommy's dismay), I pulled myself up to a standing position, and I said "Da-Da" and "Mom-Mom." During the ninth month I learned to say, "teddy," "car go," "cow," "doggie," "kitty," and "toe."

I celebrated the month of July (my eleventh month) by asserting my independence by standing without support. When I was about a year old, I began to walk steadily. Since I was chubby (to say the least), I considered this a great feat. I now weighed 25 pounds and was 31½ inches tall.

During my second year I really began to get around. I also improved my talking ability. Because of my association with adults, I suppose my conversation seemed more grown-up than my age would indicate. Once I ran across the road to my neighbor's house. I thought it was a natural thing to do, but nonetheless it must have been frightening to my mommy. I never did it again because my mommy thwarted my adventurous spirit with a swat on my you-know-what.

During my second year I was a big help to my mommy by putting doll clothes in the commode to wash them. My own private washing machine! I also enjoyed sitting on end tables, standing on chairs, and climbing up on tables. Another time I rearranged my mommy's pots and pans in the cupboards. I don't think she appreciated that very much. My favorite friend was an object called a pacifier, or a fooler, but which I called a plug. My mommy often said that she wished she would have never given me my plug. I had it since I was 9 days old, so you couldn't expect me to get rid of it just like that. However, I no longer use it anymore. My mommy said the vacuum cleaner swallowed it, but I wonder.

Now during my third year I learned a few numbers, some letters, and many colors. I can also tell the difference between the sun and moon, hill and mountain, cow and horse, puppy and dog, and a great variety of other animals. One of my favorite pastimes is talking on my toy telephone to Herman, my imaginary boyfriend. Mommy says I'm too little to have a boyfriend, but she must realize "the times they are a-changing."

When I was 2½ years old, I was potty trained, whatever that means. Mommy used to sit by me in the bathroom and teach me songs while I was being "trained." As a result, I can now sing "How Much Is That Doggie in the Window," "Here Comes Peter Cottontail," "Jesus Loves Me," "Do Lord," and a host of other songs. It took a lot of training!

Right now I want to be like my mommy simply "because I want to be." I help mommy sweep, dust, and wash dishes. Although my mommy praises me for this, I hear her tell others that it takes twice as long now. I am very affectionate and free with my hugs and kisses. I figure it can't hurt me, and some day the experience may come in handy. I like people "little" all the time, and many times I like them "big." (In other words, "little" means some, and "big" means a lot.)

Mommy and daddy are teaching me good manners such as saying "please," "thank you," "you're welcome," and also saying prayers at mealtime and bedtime. One of my greatest verbal accomplishments is reciting the Pledge of Allegiance, but who knows what it means? I learned it from Romper Room. A few weeks ago I said a recitation for Children's Day, which made my mommy and daddy very happy. I got an ice-cream cone for doing such a nice job.

I like playing by myself mainly because I have no little friends nearby to play with. However, when my little cousin, Suzy, and I are together, we really have a good time and don't even fight much. I like to be read to, and I also make up a lot of stories, usually about a bear. For some reason I think a lot about bears. Sometimes I even have to sleep with mommy and daddy because I get awake and am afraid a bear will get after me.

Now that I am almost 3, I weigh 34 pounds and am about 38 inches tall. I guess I'm a pretty big girl because I eat almost anything. I especially like to feed myself with my own spoon and fork.

There are a lot of other things I could tell you about myself, but I'm afraid I don't have any more time right now. I must go out and ride my tricycle and help mommy water the flowers. I would be very glad to finish my story, but you will have to come around a little later. Good-bye.

The newborn baby is not really new at all. By the time the baby's day of birth arrives he is already a distinct and accomplished person with characteristics that are peculiarly his own. He is about 280 days old, and he carries the developmental traits that will influence his future growth characteristics. His birth does not alter the basic patterns of his nervous system. Although his weight has increased 2 billion times from what it was at conception, he is still small enough to curl comfortably in a shoebox. By the time he leaves the hospital he has a name, and his life history is well underway.

During infancy, the baby must accomplish certain developmental tasks that will be important to his overall well-being. As he learns the tasks necessary for his growth and development at his present age level, he makes it easier for himself to learn developmental tasks that he must attain at later stages of life. With each task learned the individual becomes a more competent person, preparing for independent living. According to Havighurst,[1] the developmental tasks for infancy are (1) to learn to eat solid foods, (2) to walk and to use fine muscles, (3) to gain at least partial control of the processes of elimination, (4) to acquire the foundations of speech and begin to communicate, (5) to achieve reasonable physiological stability, especially in the coordination of eyes, hunger rhythm, and sleep, and (6) to begin to relate emotionally to their parents and siblings instead of remaining self-bound.

THE NEONATE

Although being born is a natural process, it is not always an easy one. The infant will usually require a few days just to overcome the birth experience. The more difficult the birth, the longer is the period for stabilization or recovery. Since so many features of this stage of life are different from the other stages, a special name is given to the newborn child—he is called a neonate. The neonatal period generally lasts for about two weeks but may extend to three or four weeks, depending on how much difficulty the child is having adjusting physiologically to his new environment.

Physical characteristics (Fig. 4-1)

Even the fondest of mothers may be somewhat shocked at the sight of her newborn, especially if it is her first child. The infant is tiny, his skin is wrinkled or shriveled looking, and his body seems out of proportion. Fat cheeks, a short flat nose, and a receding chin give the newborn a useful facial profile for the purpose of sucking but do not always make the baby attractive initially. The baby's wobbly head is about one fourth the size of his body and may be strangely lopsided due to pressures caused by his passage through the birth canal. The shape of the head will soon become normal in appearance, however. His neck seems to be no more than a fold of skin separating his head from his narrow shoulders. The milky blue eyes that most new arrivals have are about one half their adult size. Since the body is only about one twentieth of its adult size, the baby appears to have an unusually large head and eyes. The legs are extremely short in relation to the trunk.

The average weight of a newborn is about 7½ pounds, and the average height is 20 to 20½ inches. Girl babies, on the average, weigh slightly less than boy babies and are not quite as tall. During the first four or five days, the neonate may lose 6 to 7 ounces. This loss of weight results from inadequate nutrition while the process of digestion is being established and from the evaporation of moisture from the tissues. Once the body is stabilized, usually in seven to nine days, the child begins to gain weight. The weight will generally double in six months and triple to about 21 pounds in twelve months. The height increases by 30% to 50% to about 30 inches in twelve months.

The newborn baby has a coating or protective layer of vernix over his skin that dries and rubs off in a few days; peeling hands and feet are therefore usual. Rose pink or purplish, mottled skin is common with the new baby. The fingers and toes often look blue and will be cold until the baby's circulation pattern is regulated. The bones are soft and cartilaginous, and total muscular equipment of the newborn weighs less than one fourth of its entire body.[2]

Behavioral characteristics

The most common behavior noted in newborn babies is sleep. For the first few days they seem to exist in a nearly continuous twilight state of being. The neonate sleeps or dozes approximately 80% of the time. By the fourth day this figure drops to about 68%.[3] Neonatal sleep is broken by short waking periods, which occur every 2 or 3 hours,

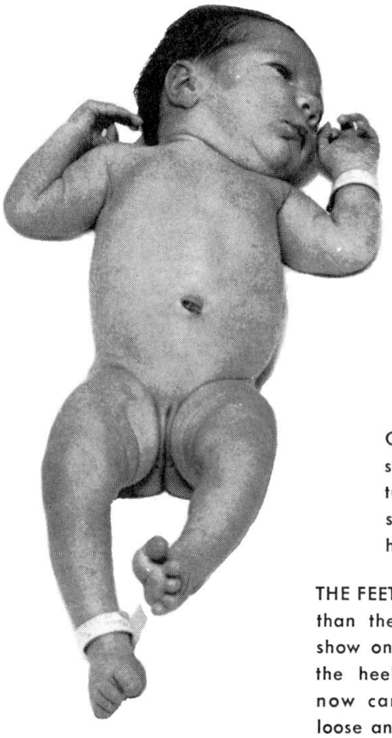

HEAD usually strikes you as being too big for the body. (Immediately after birth it may be temporarily out of shape—lopsided or elongated—due to pressure before or during birth.)

ON THE SKULL you will see or feel the two most obvious soft spots, or fontanels. One is above the brow, the other close to crown of head in back.

EYES appear dark blue, have a blank stary gaze. You may catch one or both turning or turned to crossed or wall-eyed position.

A DEEP FLUSH spreads over the entire body if baby cries hard. Veins on head swell and throb. You will notice no tears because tear ducts do not function as yet.

THE FACE will disappoint you unless you expect to see pudgy cheeks, a broad, flat nose with mere hint of a bridge, receding chin, undersized lower jaw.

THE TRUNK may startle you in some normal detail: short neck, small sloping shoulders, swollen breasts, large rounded abdomen, umbilical stump (future navel), slender, narrow pelvis and hips.

THE HANDS, if you open them out flat from their characteristic fist position, have finely lined palms, tissue-paper thin nails, dry, loose-fitting skin, and deep bracelet creases at wrist.

GENITALS of both sexes will seem large (especially scrotum) in comparison with the scale of, for example, the hands to adult size.

THE LEGS are most often seen drawn up against the abdomen in prebirth position. Extended legs measure shorter than you would expect compared to the arms. The knees stay slightly bent, and legs are more or less bowed.

THE FEET look more complete than they are. X-ray would show only one real bone of the heel. Other bones are now cartilage. Skin often loose and wrinkly.

WEIGHT unless well above the average of 6 or 7 pounds will not prepare you for how really tiny newborn is. Top-to-toe measure: anywhere between 18 and 21 inches.

THE SKIN is thin and dry. You may see veins through it. Fair skin may be rosy red temporarily. Downy hair is not unusual.

Fig. 4-1. What a healthy week-old baby looks like. (Photograph from Ingalls, A. J., and Salerno, M. C.: Maternal and child health nursing, ed. 2, St. Louis, 1971, The C. V. Mosby Co.; description from Birch, W. G.: A doctor discusses pregnancy, Chicago, 1963, Budlong Press Co.)

with fewer and shorter waking periods during the night than during the day. As an infant, the child will sleep as much as is necessary and when necessary. Later he will learn the culturally approved patterns of sleep and wakefulness.

A new baby sleeps best directly after eating. He quickly becomes used to familiar household noises. He should have a room of his own for sleeping or an undisturbed corner away from family traffic. He sleeps best on a flat firm mattress without a pillow. New babies generally waken once or twice during the night for a feeding, but they grow and mature so quickly that they can soon sleep until breakfast time.

During the neonatal period, stimulation of any part of the body tends to activate the entire body. Stimuli such as pain, hunger, or physical discomfort seem to arouse the greatest activity. A wide-awake, hungry neonate is capable of making as many as fifty movements per minute.[4] Newborns need exercise to strengthen their muscles. In their brief wakeful periods they will wave their arms and legs, and before a feeding they become exceedingly active.

Although there is little control of the head movements at birth, early movements of the head and shoulders are basic to the later development of manipulation, posture, and perception. Placed on his abdomen on a flat surface, the newborn quickly learns to lift his head and turn it from side to side. Supported in water, he will make swimminglike movements.

The neonate makes throaty sounds, and he can purse his lips. He has an amazing variety of grunts, mews, and sighs. He cries but has no tears at this age. He sneezes to clear his nose of lint, and he yawns when he needs extra oxygen. The accomplished young baby can scowl, grimace with his mouth, and "smile" in a funny uncertain way.

At birth the child has a ready-made capability for learning. This condition is evident in the way an infant can adapt himself to a feeding schedule. The healthy newborn averages seven to eight feedings in 24 hours and takes 20 to 30 minutes to complete his meal. The interrelationship established between the mother and the child during the first weeks after birth will often determine the type of response the child will have toward eating. If an infant feels maternal impatience or hostility, he will have more anxiety than the child whose mother is patient. The newborn who is held lovingly every feeding, and especially if he is breastfed, will have a better psychological and physiological start in life. The satisfactions and pleasures a baby gets from his feeding affect his sense of well-being. Frequent changes in the type of food or manner in which it is given may create problems in learning because the newborn benefits most from some structure, similarity, and routine. It takes the infant two or three weeks to form a hunger rhythm and to adjust to a regular feeding schedule.[5]

Sensory abilities

During the embryonic and fetal stages of life, the sensory mechanisms gradually develop. By the time of birth the senses can function to the extent that they possess survival value. The infant can use the senses to enhance his physiological and cognitive well-being.

At birth the neonate can see. It is not known, however, how clearly he can see. Researchers had assumed that the newborn could not focus his eyes until he was 3 or 4 weeks old. Until then, the baby would only see things as a blur. Recently, some studies on the vision of neonates question this assumption, although no definite findings have been reported as far as is known by the authors. It is known that soon after birth a baby can respond with his eyes to a moving light. Even on the first day of life a momentary fixation on a near, approaching object can be observed. Sustained fixation on a near object is noted by the end of the first week and on a more distant object by the end of the month. Gesell[6] was led to conclude that the infant "takes hold of the physical world ocularly long before he grasps it manually." This observation may have important meaning, as noted later, for the development of the cognitive processes.

It is not certain whether the newborn can distinguish between colors. The cones in the fovea of the eye are poorly developed at birth, suggesting that the neonate can only see shades of gray and black. The pupillary reflex, in which the size of the opening of the pupil of the eye reacts to the brightness of light, is well established shortly after birth, as are the protective responses of moving the head, closing the eyelids, and crying.[7] Eye movements generally make use of the gross muscular patterns but not the finer ones. Some children have immature eye muscle development so that one or both eyes may rotate outwardly or inwardly. Eye muscle control is usually gained by 4 weeks of age.

While still in the womb, normal babies have been known to respond to musical tones by a speeding up of their heartbeats.[8] Of all the senses at birth, however, hearing is the least functional because the passages of the ear are not completely open. In some infants hearing acuity is completely lacking because the middle ear is filled with amniotic fluid. It may take several hours to several days for the fluid to drain out. Only then can hearing function normally. With normal hearing the neonate can discriminate between loud and soft sounds but does not respond to variations in pitch.[9] The newborn is startled by loud noises, but he is soothed by a soft, gentle voice or low auditory stimuli.

The senses of touch, taste, and smell are all better developed at birth than is sight or hearing. Once the passages of the head are dry, after having been submerged in the prenatal liquid environment, the senses of smell and taste respond fairly well to gross differences in stimuli. Infants can distinguish between different odors such as acetic acid, phenylethyl alcohol, and anise oil and may even try to escape from unpleasant odors by turning their bodies.[10] Most infants react with a feeling of satisfaction to the taste of milk. A sugar solution will cause a sucking that is maintained. The neonate will usually react negatively to unpleasant taste stimuli such as sour, bitter, and salt solutions.[11] It requires a much greater amount of bitterness or sweetness to elicit a discriminatory response in infants than is the case with adults.

The skin of the newborn is sensitive to touch, pressure, temperature, and some pain. At the time of birth, sensitivity to pain is lessened so that the baby will not feel its effects while passing through the birth canal. Responses to pain increase about two days after birth. Certain parts of the body, namely the lips, eyelashes, soles of the feet, skin of the forehead, and the mucous membrane of the nose are more sensitive than are other parts.[12] The neonate can react to differences in temperature, as is shown by differentiated sucking reactions to changes of temperature of its milk. Cold stimuli produce quicker and more pronounced reactions than do heat stimuli.[13] Infants also respond with signs of discomfort to temperatures above or below normal, and especially to extremes of cold.

Body movements and reflexes

Motor development is not a process that begins at the time of birth, but rather, it has its origins in the prenatal period. During the second month of prenatal development, the muscles begin to take shape. By the end of the third month they are developed to the degree that spontaneous movements of arms, legs, shoulders, and fingers are possible. By the fourteenth week the human fetus is capable of producing almost all the reflex responses of a newborn infant.[14] Some reflexes will be vital for survival; other reflexes will function merely as

Table 4-1. Reflexes of the newborn baby*

EFFECTIVE STIMULUS	REFLEX
Tap upper lips sharply	Lips protrude
Tap bridge of nose	Eyes close tightly
Show bright light suddenly to eyes	Eyelids close
Clap hands about 18 inches from infant's head	Eyelids close
Touch cornea with light piece of cotton	Eyes close
With baby held on back turn face slowly to right side	Jaw and right arm on side of face extended out; left arm flexes
Extend forearms at elbow	Arms flex briskly
Put fingers into infant's hand and press his palms	Infant's fingers flex and enclose finger
Press thumbs against the ball of infant's feet	Toes flex
Scratch sole of foot starting from toes toward the heels	Big toe bends upward and small toes spread
Prick soles of feet with pin	Infant's knee and foot flex
Tickle area of corner of mouth	Head turns toward side of stimulation
Put index finger into mouth	Sucks
Hold infant in air, stomach down	Infant attempts to lift head and extends legs

*From Mussen, P. H., Conger, J. J., and Kagan, J.: Child development and personality, ed. 4, New York, 1974, Harper & Row, Publishers, p. 137.

general protective measures. The remainder of the prenatal period is spent in perfecting these movements. Initial diffused mass activities of the organism become more integrated and specific with maturation. Reflexes of the newborn baby are listed in Table 4-1.

Just as in the fetus during prenatal life, the development of the neonate during postnatal life largely follows the cephalocaudal direction and the proximodistal direction of growth. Functions appear and develop earliest in the infant's head and neck, then in the shoulders and upper trunk, and later in the lower trunk and legs. The direction of this sequence is obvious to the observer and is a result of maturation. The newborn baby lacks voluntary coordinated motor control. Neonatal reflex activity is subcortical in origin and so is not voluntary.

A newborn baby in his crib seems to exhibit little activity or movement. However, if a constant vigil is kept, one would find that there is a great deal of active movement going on even in the earliest days. Irwin[15] made a study using a stabilimeter that demonstrated the amount of activity in the newborn child by recording each movement on a moving tape. One child made more than 2,000 movements on the first day after birth, whereas the average for four infants was more than 1,700 movements. Most of the movement was mass activity that was undifferentiated and diffused.

Mouth and throat response. From birth the neonate is capable of opening and closing his mouth. One of the earliest of the various lip movements is sucking. The sucking response can be elicited by light pressure on the cheeks or by touching above or below the side of the lips. Swallowing usually follows the sucking movements. Infants less than 2 weeks old show that they are able to discriminate between the intake of milk or air. When sucking milk, the neonate swallows it; when sucking air, there is no swallowing movement.

When the newborn infant cries, there is much mass body activity such as rolling the head, opening the mouth wide, jerking and twisting the body, throwing the arms about, and kicking the legs. Other mouth and throat responses present in the neonate are sneezing, coughing, yawning, thumb-sucking, hiccoughing, vomiting, holding the breath, and rejecting things from his mouth.[16]

Head and arm movements. A neonate has the ability to move his head up and down as well as to the left and right. He cannot hold the head in midposition, however. He moves his arms a great deal. He flexes them, extends them, randomly moves them about in different directions, throws them over his chest, and moves the hands and fingers. The newborn baby can also grasp a rod or a finger placed in his hand and hold on to it. Many babies are able to support their weight by the grasping reflex when holding onto a rod. This grasping reflex, also known as the Darwinian reflex, later diminishes and is replaced in about three months by the voluntary grasp.

Trunk and leg movements. The newborn baby is only capable of a few trunk movements, since his back is lacking in muscular support. He is able to arch his back and twist his body, but only to a slight degree. The movements in the neonate's legs, feet, and toes are characterized by flexing, extending, kicking, jerking, rotating, rolling, or trembling. The Babinski reflex, the upward and fanning movement of the toes, is observed when the bottoms of the neonate's feet are stroked. The knee jerk is a characteristic of the newborn. When the infant is in a resting or sleeping position, he will usually have his legs flexed, fists closed, upper arms out straight from his shoulders with the forearms flexed at right angles parallel to the head. When the infant is frightened by a loud noise, such as that caused by someone hitting a table top with his hand, the neonate will throw his arms apart, spread his fingers, extend his legs, and throw his head back. This reaction is the Moro, or startle, reflex. The response is basically symmetrical. It will disappear by the age of 3 or 4 months.[17] Persistence of the entire Moro response beyond 3 or 4 months is considered a sign of delay in neurological development.

A summary[*] of the responses of a newborn baby follows:
1. Eyelid and pupillary reflexes: opening and closing the eyes. Adequate stimuli for these responses, particularly for closing the eyes, are numerous, for example, blasts of air, bright light, touching the face near the eye. The size of the pupil changes in response to variations in intensity of light to which the eyes are exposed.
2. Ocular reflexes: pursuit movements, saccadic movements, coordinated compensatory eye movements. When the head is jerked quickly around, the eyes move in a compensatory direction. This has been observed in infants as early as the second day of life.
3. Facial and mouth responses: opening and closing the mouth, sucking, grimacing, yawning, pushing objects from the mouth, frowning, smiling, upper and lower lip responses to touch.
4. Throat responses: crying, cooing, sobbing, sneezing, coughing, gagging, swallowing, holding breath, hiccoughing, and vomiting.
5. Head movements: upward and downward, turning face to side, balancing in response to change of bodily position (appears at 2 days of age).
6. Hand and arm reflexes: closing hand, arm flexion, rubbing of face, startle response of arms and legs, grasp reflex, and "random" movements.
7. Trunk reactions: arching the back, twisting, drawing in of the stomach (abdominal reflex).
8. Genital organ reflexes: cremasteric reflex (raising the testes), penis erection.
9. Foot and leg reflexes: the knee jerk

---
[*]Modified from Dennis, W.: A description and classification of the responses of the newborn infant, Psychol. Bull. 31:5-22, 1934.

and the Achilles tendon reflexes have been observed in some infants; flexion and extension of the legs, kicking, fanning the toes in response to stroking the sole, stepping movement when the child is held upright with feet touching a surface.

10. Coordinated responses of many body parts: resting and sleeping position (legs flexed, fists closed, upper arms out straight from shoulder with forearms flexed at right angles parallel to the head), springing position (infant held upright and inclined forward, the arms extend forward and legs are brought up), stretching, shivering, trembling, unrest with crying, creeping, bodily jerk, Moro reflex (throwing arms apart, spreading of fingers, extension of legs, and throwing head back).

MOTOR DEVELOPMENT DURING INFANCY

The period of infancy is one of tremendous motor development. The word *motor* refers to muscular movements. The general mass activity and reflex actions of the neonate gradually change to specific muscle control, permitting voluntary, coordinated motor responses to take place. In addition to muscle development motor control also makes use of sensory acuity and awareness, perceptual discrimination ability, and adequate sensory-motor integration and coordination. Accurate perception of sensory stimuli is needed to perfect the motor skills.

During the first year of life, maturational forces are of primary importance in the development of motor coordination. Maturation determines the rate, the level of readiness, and the pattern of the early motor responses. Progress in motor development can be influenced, however, by factors such as a lack of opportunity to practice the motor skills, the child's attitude toward learning the skills, and psychological and physiological inhibitions to learning.[18] The process of development is sequential in nature unless interfered with by abnormal conditions within or outside the infant. Thus movements begun during the prenatal stage are basic to the later development of posture, locomotion, prehension, and cognition.

Table 4-2. Motor developmental norms of young children*

AGE ZONE	MOTOR DEVELOPMENT
4-week	Lacks head control
	Asymmetrical in supine position
16-week	Head erect, slight bobbing
	Symmetrical supine postures
28-week	Sits, leaning forward
	Turns from supine to prone position
40-week	Sits well, creeps
	Pulls self to feet by holding playpen or chair
52-week	Walks, one hand held
15-month	Walks alone, toddles
18-month	Walks well alone
	Seats self in small chair
2-year	Runs
	Climbs up and down stairs alone
3-year	Rides tricycle
	Stands on one foot momentarily

*Modified from Latham, H. C., and Heckel, R. V.: Pediatric nursing, ed. 2, St. Louis, 1972, The C. V. Mosby Co., p. 65.

The following two complex motor tasks must be learned during infancy: (1) upright postural control and locomotion and (2) manipulability and prehension—the ability to reach with the hand, grasp, and manipulate objects.

Postural control and locomotion

There is a basic sequence that leads to walking (Fig. 4-2). This sequence will vary as to time of occurrence from infant to infant, but there is a progressive regularity in the development. The five basic stages are (1) postural control as in sitting with support, (2) postural control as in sitting alone, (3) active efforts toward locomotion,

Birth Keeps his legs tucked up under him and bears his weight on his knees, abdomen, chest, and head.	**2-3 months** Extends his legs and lifts his chest and head to look around.
5-6 months Can sit up with support, hold his head up, and is alert to surroundings.	**6½-7½ months** Sits up alone and steadily without support. Legs are bowed to help balance.
8-9 months Creeping; the trunk is carried free from floor. With practice, rhythm appears and only one limb moves at a time.	**9-11 months** Pulls himself up and stands holding onto furniture. Feet far apart, head and upper trunk carried forward.
11-12 months Stands alone, can walk with help.	**12-14 months** Walks alone on wide base with legs far apart.

Fig. 4-2. Development of posture and locomotion in infants. (From Ingalls, A. J., and Salerno, M. C.: Maternal and child health nursing, ed. 2, St. Louis, 1971, The C. V. Mosby Co.)

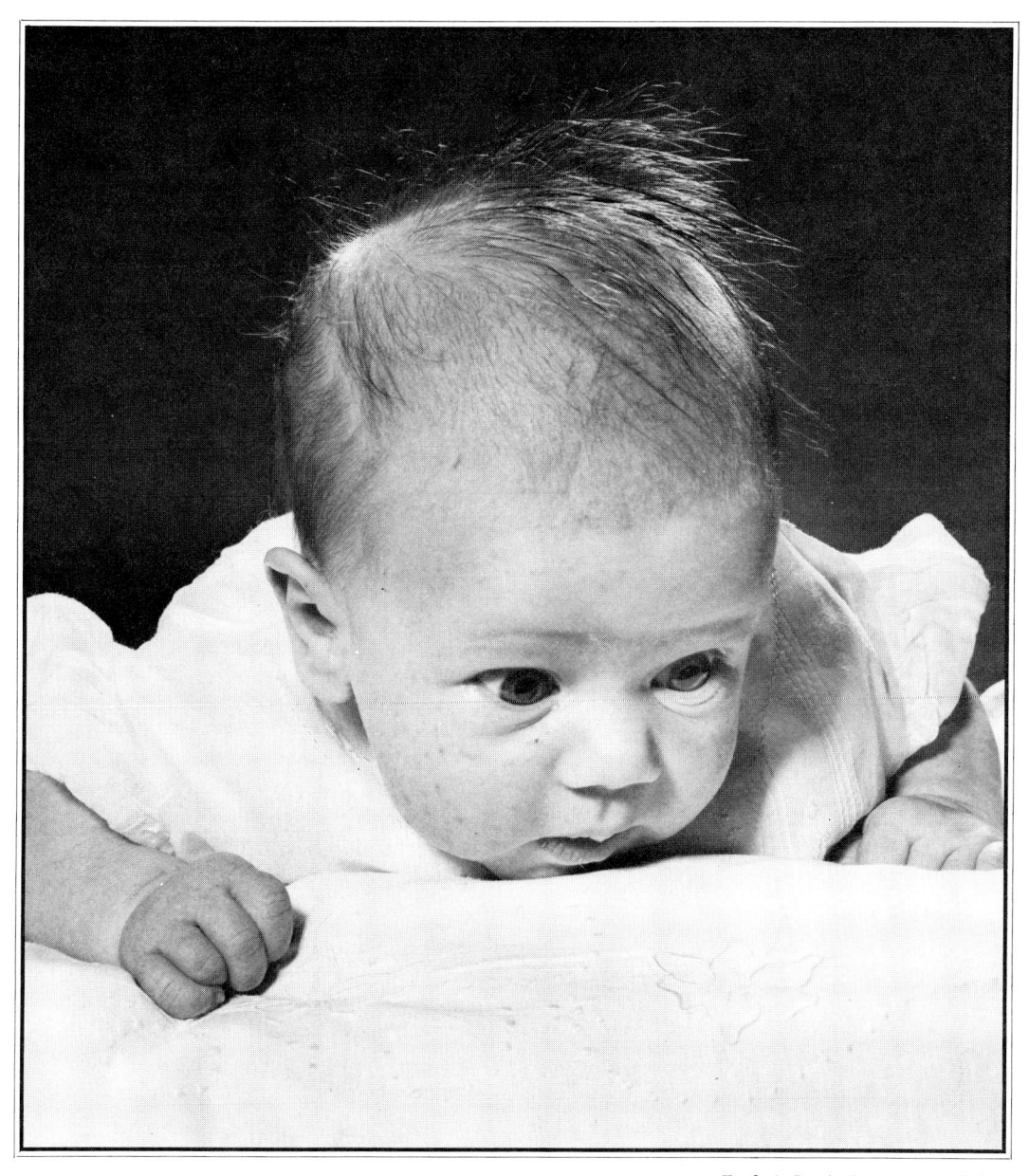

Frederic Lewis, Inc., New York City.

(4) creeping and walking with support, and (5) walking alone.[19]

The newborn infant is normally unable to hold his head erect when lying prone or when being held in a sitting position. At the age of 1 month the infant can hold his head straight out in a horizontal plane when supported in the prone position. By the age of 2 months he can hold his head above the horizontal plane at an angle of as much as 30 degrees.[20] By the time an infant is 4 months old he nearly always lifts his head and upper trunk when placed prone on a table. He is no longer content to lie on his back. However, the infant must develop a certain amount of rigidity of the spine before he will be able to sit up unsupported. This rigidity is usually developed about the seventh month; then the infant sits alone.[21]

Crawling is attained about the fifth month. Crawling refers to various forms of progression in which the infant does not lift his body from the floor while moving on all fours. In crawling the infant may even move about in a sitting position, using one leg to push himself along. In creeping the infant's body is lifted off the floor and he propels himself on all fours.

Shirley[22] has observed the following stages in the development of creeping: (1) lifting the head and chin free when on the stomach, (2) lifting the head and chest free when on the stomach, (3) knee pushing or swimming, (4) rolling, (5) rocking, pivoting, and worming along, (6) scooting backward by using the hands, and (7) creeping forward.

When a child first begins to walk, his movements are awkward. He walks in a stiff-legged manner, with his legs far apart, toes turned outward, and arms close to the body or held out like a tightrope walker. If the infant watches the floor, he cannot maintain balance. To keep from falling he holds his head erect and slightly forward. His steps are high off the floor and uneven. At first he may move one foot forward, shift his weight to it, and then bring the second foot about even with the front foot. Next he may shift his weight back to the second foot and move the first foot forward again. Gradually, as his movements become coordinated, he begins stepping forward by alternating his feet.

By 14 months of age two thirds of the babies can walk without support, and by the age of 18 months the average baby walks like an adult.[23]

The infant will be able to creep up stairs about the thirteenth month. At 18 months he will be able to walk up the stairs if his hand is held, climb into an adult chair, and throw a ball but not with much accuracy. When he reaches the twenty-first month, he will squat while playing, walk upstairs while holding the railing, and kick a large ball. By 24 months of age he can run well without falling and walk up and down the steps alone.[24]

Prehension or grasping

The infant's grasping reflex and his uncoordinated arm movements are the starting points for a sequence that eventually leads to highly skilled manual activities of the adult. Prehension is not merely a function of motor control but, rather, a function of sensorimotor control. Kinesthesis and vision are the two chief sensory activities involved in the coordination of arm-hand movements. (See Table 4-3.)

The reflex grasp that is present at birth is different from the voluntary grasp of later life in that it is a digital grasp rather than a palmar grasp. The thumb is not used in opposition to the forefinger but, rather, is placed in the palm under the rod. The reflex grasp begins to decline about the second month, and the voluntary grasp, which is well established by the ninth month, begins to develop.[25]

Investigations by Halverson[26] and Castner[27] of infant's reaching and grasping behavior illustrated the sequence of development for this type of motor skill. According to their findings, very young infants made no effort to grasp the cube placed before them on the table. At 16 weeks of age the infants looked at the cube for approximately 5 seconds but made no effort to grasp it. By 24 weeks of age one half of the children reached for and touched the cube. The time that the infants spent gazing at the cube also increased.

The infant's grasping movements undergo a series of developmental changes as he grows older. These changes are influenced by maturation and experimentation. His movements progress from a whole hand closure to a scissors-type of closure and finally to a pincer prehension. Between 4

Table 4-3. Development of arm-hand control in young children*

AGE ZONE	ADAPTIVE DEVELOPMENT
4-week	Brief eye following
	Drops toy immediately
16-week	Incipient approach, rattle
	Regards rattle in hand
28-week	Reaches and grasps toy
	Transfers toy
40-week	Combines two toys
	Picks pellet, using thumb and index fingers
52-week	Puts cube into cup
	Tries to tower two cubes
15-month	Towers two cubes
	Puts six cubes into cup
18-month	Towers three to four cubes
	Imitates a stroke
2-year	Towers six to seven cubes
	Imitates circular scribble
3-year	Imitates "house" of cubes
	Imitates cross +

*Modified from Latham, H. C., and Heckel, R. V.: Pediatric nursing, ed. 2, St. Louis, 1972, The C. V. Mosby Co., p. 65.

and 7 months of age a backhand sweep characterizes his grasping. At 5 months of age the infant does not grasp the block but, instead, corrals it with his hand and presses it against his body or other hand. By the seventh month he reaches the hand-grasp stage where his fingers encircle the block. The palm grasp, in which position the thumb and fingers cooperate in holding the cube against the palm of the hand, is usually evident by 8 months of age. By 1 year of age the more mature pincer movement is well established. The child grips the cube between the thumb and the ends of the fingers. He is now able to hold a crayon. In six more months he will be able to scribble with considerable enthusiasm. By 2½ years of age he will be able to copy a vertical or horizontal line.[28]

Profile: learning to walk

Observing my daughter Audrey learning to walk was a most fascinating experience. The process of "locomotion" actually started when she was in her crib. She would crawl from one end to the other. Soon she yearned for more room and tried to crawl through the posts of the crib. Eventually she was allowed to crawl on the living-room floor. With much struggle and strain she could sometimes traverse the living room in the amazing time of 2 minutes. She started out by using a method that made her look like a frog in water. It was a completely uncoordinated attempt at locomotion. Soon she graduated to kneeling and leaning on her palms, and thus she would creep. This seemed like a most efficacious way to get across the room and pleased her greatly. After each successful venture I tried to give her some kind of reinforcement, be it a kiss or some other type of reinforcer.

Eventually her creeping became a means to an end. Before she was content to creep for the sake of creeping, but now her creeping was goal directed. When she set out on an expedition, her purpose was usually to crawl over to a small coffee table that she could grasp onto. Like an acrobat she would, without hesitation, pull herself up until she was standing. Of course, once she got up she did not know what to do for an encore. She just stood there for a few moments and then realized that she was in trouble. She was too scared to leave the table, but she did not know how to get back down. In a few moments she would beckon our help by a loud wail.

After a few weeks she simply let herself drop to the floor. On hitting the floor, she immediately began to laugh. I had all kinds of visions of her breaking a leg or something by this method of descent. Often I wanted to stop her, but my wife always intervened. She thought that this was natural and that we should not stop her. Deferring to my wife's sagacity, I reluctantly watched my daughter time after time bounce off the floor. Of course there were no injuries, and she soon graduated to her next level of development. When she would get adjacent to the table, instead of dropping down she would gradually descend. Slowly her knees would bend, and she would lower herself onto the floor. From this point on, dropping to the floor was old hat. After all, she was becoming a big girl now and growing up called for more sophisticated actions.

This up-and-down activity lasted for about a month; then something happened. On certain occasions she would get herself up and then release her grip on the table. With great timidity she would stand about 6 inches away from the table. After about 30 seconds of this she grabbed the table and descended. In no time at all she was taking a step or two away from the table. After a few steps she would lower herself to the floor. The next great achievement occurred when she would take a few additional steps and then fall down. All these precursors of actual walking lasted until about the thirteenth month.

Then it happened! Without any fanfare she just started to walk. It was one of life's greatest moments for me—one that is indelibly marked in my mind. I was talking on the telephone while Audrey was holding onto a chair in the kitchen. Always liking telephones, she apparently wanted to play with the telephone that I was using. Without any hesitation she let go of her support and started to cross the kitchen, a distance of about 20 feet. At first I thought that she would take a few steps and fall to the ground as she had been doing. Holding her hands out for balance, like an acrobat on a high wire, she started to cross the room. Wavering from side to side, but regaining her balance each time, she actually crossed the room. I must have been in a state of shock as I saw her walking for the first time because no words came out of my mouth. The person to whom I was talking on the phone must have thought that I had dropped dead because my silence lasted at least 30 seconds. Finally I was able to shout, "She's walking, Audrey is walking." I dropped the phone and hugged my daughter as she grabbed hold of my leg. Audrey did not walk like this again for some time. Apparently she had reached a plateau or was scared when she finally realized what she had done. In about another month she began to walk freely. As walking ability increased, so did her confidence.

DEVELOPMENT OF INTELLIGENCE

Consider the newborn baby at birth. How much "intelligence" does he have? What is his "intellectual potential"? These questions are difficult to answer because the true nature of intelligence is not yet known. Most of the definitions of intelligence tell what intelligence "does" rather than what intelligence "is." Generally, the definitions speak of (1) the ability to deal effectively with tasks involving abstractions, (2) the ability to learn, and/or (3) the ability to deal with new situations. How much of these three concepts can the newborn or the infant do? Obviously, little or none of them. Would it be correct to say, then, that the newborn has no intelligence at all? That does not seem right either. So, the newborn baby is said to have a "potential" but that he must develop or "mature" into that potential. Something must happen within the neurological system of the infant to enable him to make use of cognitive processes that affect his potentialities.

The implications of intellectual growth, as we see them, are as follows. First, the infant must be born with certain innate features and physical characteristics that operate in accordance with principles and laws of nature related to how the intellect is to develop. Second, intellectual attributes will develop only to the extent or limit to which these innate elements have the potentiality to develop. Third, the potentiality of intellectual growth can be influenced by factors or forces outside the child, such as nutritional adequacy, sensory stimulation, perceptual activities, verbal and language development, learning experiences, and opportunity to learn. Fourth, some kind of physical or psychic change must take place within the neurological system when the intellect is developing. Fifth, since the intellect "develops," it must start from a meager "reflexive-cognitive" beginning and grow to an accumulative, integrated, cognitive, and perceptual pattern or "mental computer" kind of thing that can be used to do abstractions, learning, and problem solving in new situations. The origins of intelligence are to be found in the central nervous system and in its capability to perceive, retain, recall, integrate, and reorganize cognitive components. Both the maturational process and the functioning of the perceptual processes in a stimulating and responsive environment aid in intellectual development. The word *cognition* and its derivatives refer to any process whereby an organism (the brain) becomes aware or obtains knowledge of an object. It includes perceiving, recognizing, conceiving, judging, reasoning, and sensing.

Piaget's system of cognitive development

Jean Piaget, the noted Swiss child psychologist, has developed a significant theory concerning cognitive development based on his research and observations. Piaget believes that cognitive development is a coherent process whereby the individual develops stages of cognitive structures called *schema* (plural, schemata). Each successive schema is derived logically and inevitably from the processes of assimilation, accommodation, and intellectual adaptation. Assimilation describes the capability of the organism to meet and respond to new situations and new problems with its present mechanisms. In so doing the organism "assimilates" new knowledge, skills, and insights from its interaction with the world. Accommodation describes the process of change through which the organism becomes able to handle situations that were too difficult to handle before. It is a process by which the cognitive process, because of the new material assimilated, has matured to the point that it can now "accommodate" or solve a more difficult task than it could before. (See Fig. 4-3.)

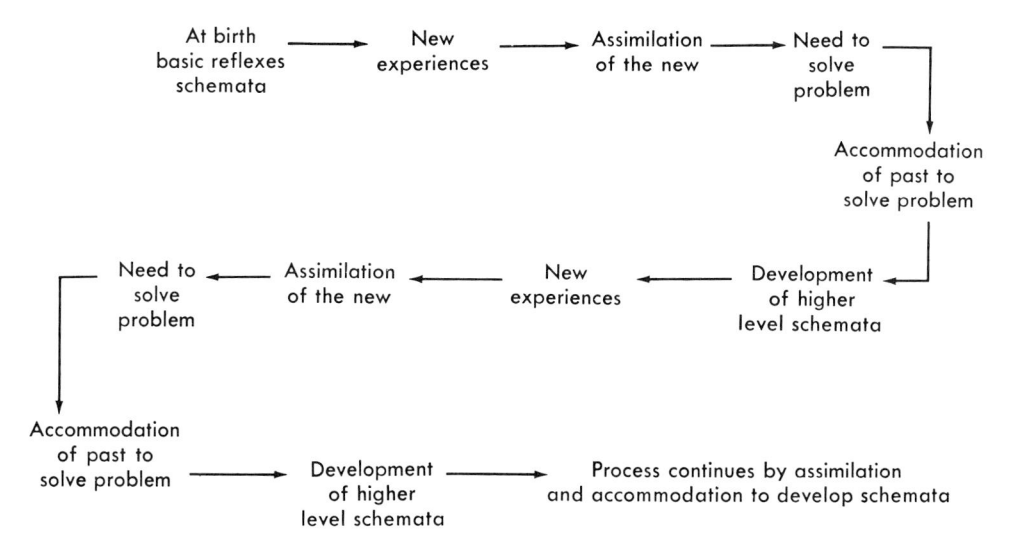

Fig. 4-3. Piaget's development of schemata using assimilation and accommodation.

Adaptation occurs when the organism has improved its ability to meet new environmental demands. This change is also called coping behavior. One form of adaptation is coping with the environment by organizing and reorganizing thought patterns to the extent that the new cognitive capability becomes a higher level schema. Intelligence, according to Piaget, is a process of adaptation by which higher cognitive levels are attained. Piaget tries to identify the cognitive structures of schemata of each age level and seeks to show how individuals adapt to environmental demands and to one another.[29]

Piaget's theory divides the intellectual development process into four main chronological periods or stages, which are further divided into phases. The order of succession of these steplike patterns is constant, although the ages at which different stages are attained may vary somewhat, depending on the child's maturation, innate capacity, practice, and environmental differences. The four periods are (1) sensorimotor stage covering ages 0 to 2 years, (2) preoperational stage, ages 3 to 7 years, (3) concrete operations stage, 7 to 11 or 12 years of age, and (4) formal operations period, ages 11 to 15 or 16 years. The word *operations* in the foregoing stages refers to intellectual functions or performance. The four stages will be presented separately in the chapters dealing with the appropriate age levels. Only the sensorimotor stage will be presented in this chapter.

Piaget's sensorimotor stage of cognitive development

The sensorimotor stage of development, according to Piaget, encompasses the period in a child's life from birth to about 2 years of age (Table 4-4). This period is essentially preverbal, since the child's adaptations to his new environment do not involve extensive use of symbols or language.

The child has several intellectual developmental tasks that he must achieve during this period. He must learn to coordinate and organize simple motor actions and incoming perceptions (sensory) so that they can be converted into adaptive behavior. He must come to realize that information concerning one object or event can be reaching him through different senses and that the information must be coordinated and integrated instead of being considered as being unrelated. The infant must also

Table 4-4. Piaget's sensorimotor period of cognitive development

STAGE	BEHAVIOR	EXAMPLES
1. Reflexive schemata (0 to 1 month)	Use of reflexes	Sucking is most salient reflex
2. Primary circular reactions (1 to 4 months)	Extension of reflexes	Sucks fingers; puts out tongue
3. Secondary circular reactions (4 to 8 months)	Earliest stage at which "intention" is distinguished	Moves in crib to make toys on crib shake
4. Coordination of secondary schemata (8 to 12 months)	Application of familiar means to new situations; "means" differentiated from "ends"	Holds a block in each hand and drops one, picking up a third one just presented to him
5. Tertiary circular reactions (12 to 18 months)	Discovery through active experimentation	Devises different ways of making something fall or slide "to see what happens"
6. Invention of new means through mental combinations (18 to 24 months)	Emergence of capacity to respond to or think about things not immediately observable	Uses a stick to reach out beyond arm length to pull something closer

come to think of the world as existing as an independent, permanent place and existing even when he does not perceive it. The same thing is true of the existence of objects in that he must develop an "object reality," which involves learning to differentiate between object and self.[30] The child must learn to combine individual actions into a coordinated effort and sequence to reach a goal. By the end of the sensorimotor period the child should be able to use simple tools to obtain what he wants by anticipating the consequences of his actions. Although this cause-and-effect principle is not completely comprehended during infancy, its recognition is enhanced by repeating certain actions and observing the results.

Piaget has divided the sensorimotor period into six phases: (1) the use of reflexes, (2) primary circular reactions, (3) secondary circular reactions, (4) coordination of secondary circular reactions, (5) tertiary circular reactions, and (6) invention of new means by mental combinations.

The first phase, the use of reflexes, begins at birth and lasts until the end of the first month. The child repeatedly uses the reflexes with which he was endowed. The reflex behaviors that Piaget believes are most important are sucking, grasping, eye movements and visual accommodations, and reflexes associated with hearing and phonation.[31] The reflexes mostly used shortly after birth include sucking, tongue movements, swallowing, crying, and gross bodily movements. The child does not perceive his accomplishments because he exists in a state of complete bodily egocentrism, unaffected by his contacts with a shadowy, outer reality. There is an absence of genuine intelligent behavior. Nonetheless, this phase is an extremely important one, since it is from behavior established during this period that subsequent intelligence will emerge.[32] The reflexes are the building blocks of the perceptual-motor receptive and expressive patterns.

The second phase, that of primary circular reactions, begins after the first month and lasts until the fourth month. Circular reaction refers to a behavior that provides the stimulus either for its own repetition or for the continuation of the initiating behavior. During this period the neonatal reflexes undergo numerous changes due to the interaction of the baby with his environment. The infant is continuously bringing about, prolonging, and repeating some forms of adaptive behavior that have not previously occurred. The simple reflexes are slowly being replaced by systematic, sequential combinations of reflexes and, in some cases, by voluntary movements. For example, sucking is an innate reflex, but systematic thumb and finger sucking is only acquired as the infant develops hand-to-mouth coordination. The infant's vision also becomes more developed during the second and third months. He begins to "look" at objects within his visual field; he learns to focus on stationary objects; then he learns to follow moving objects as well. During this phase, a differentiation is noted in the cries of the infant in that he begins to cry in different ways for different needs. He also begins to differentiate other vocalizations and to repeat some sounds for their own sake. Prehension, which requires a coordination of grasping and vision, also develops according to a systematic, sequential pattern. By the end of the second developmental phase the child is beginning to lose some of his egocentrism and to respond to the world around him.

The behavior patterns of the third phase of sensorimotor development, ages 4 to 8 months, consist of secondary circular reactions that are concerned with the external (secondary) environment rather than with the infant's body, as in primary reactions. The *beginnings* of "intentional" adaptations are noted; that is, a desire, intention, or a purpose can be associated to the movement. Thus the child kicks his legs to shake his crib and make a hanging mobile or toy move. He will shake a rattle to produce a sound. He begins to show a greater awareness of the world surrounding him. Although he is not yet interested in particular objects in his environment, he likes to use them and enjoys the resultant actions. He also begins to recognize objects and people that are familiar to him. His conception of a stable external world has begun. He still does not have an idea of the permanence of objects, nor does he have enough intelligence to reverse a feeding bottle that has been presented to him the wrong way.[33] However, when an object vanishes, he will look for it. The child has attained some idea of the world around him when he looks for objects that no longer can be seen.

There are two principal areas of intellectual accomplishment during the fourth developmental phase, from the eighth to the twelfth month. The secondary circular reactions of phase three become coordinated to form new behavior totalities that are now unquestionably intentional. The child also begins to exhibit anticipatory behavior by using signs or signals to anticipate coming events. He indulges in such activities as removing a lid from a box to find a ball inside. He can now reverse a feeding bottle that has been given to him the wrong way. He can use new schemata in different situations to solve problems. For the first time the child's actions correspond to a definition of intelligence from a functional point of view. This phase marks the beginning of the permanence of things and of objective spatial groups.

The fifth phase, 12 to 18 months of age, deals with tertiary circular reactions and the discovery of new means. These reactions refer to the repetitive behavior that fascinates a child of about 1 year of age when he repeats an action many times but does not repeat it in a stereotyped form. The child not only acts on the objects in his environment but also varies his action on them or tries out new responses to reach the same goal. This is the beginning of trial-and-error experimentation and problem solving. The child also becomes extremely interested in pursuing new experiences. He tries to produce new actions that create a pleasing effect for himself. Every situation has numerous possibilities that seem to need further exploration, explanation, or modification. The adaptive reactions of this phase have all the characteristics of true intelligence.

The final phase begins about the eighteenth month and continues to the twenty-fourth month. The most significant sensorimotor skill developed during this phase involves the child's ability to solve problems without physically exploring their possibilities or solutions as he did in phase five. This is called the invention of new means through deduction or mental combinations. The child is now able, by use of symbolic or visual imagining, to "invent" or "figure out" the solutions internally. He can solve some simple problems, can remember, can plan, and can imagine. For example, a child playing next to a fence takes hold of an object on the other side. The object is too big to be brought in between the slats. At this stage of development he is able to raise the object to the top of the fence (if not too high) and bring it over the top. The child was able to picture the events to himself and follow them through mentally. He is doing thinking and primitive problem solving.

DEVELOPMENT OF THE PERCEPTUAL PROCESSES

Although the newborn child has about all the brain cells he will ever have, his central nervous system is not developed or organized to the point that it can provide meaning to stimuli. In fact, the neonate will have only the grossest type of awareness of stimuli that are outside of the body. The child will need to develop a perceptual-conceptual process by which it can receive stimuli, get meaning from them, develop concepts, and make appropriate responses. This sequence approximates the function of the sensory-motor arc, which is basic to the way in which man neurologically comes to know his world.

Perception is the cognitive process by which the various senses (1) become aware of stimuli, within or outside the body, and (2) refer the stimuli to the central nervous system (CNS), where some meaningful interpretation is attached to them. The central nervous system then seeks to make an appropriate response. The word *perceptual* pertains to the process and the function of perception. *Conceptual* refers to concept, idea, or general meaning that has evolved from perception. The perceptual-conceptual process refers to the means by which an individual becomes aware of something, attaches meaning to it, and changes the meaning in to a "memory bit" or apperceptive knowledge that can be used at another time. Learning and the cognitive processes are involved in the perceptual-conceptual process.[34] The development of intelligence, it is believed, hinges on the nature and development of the perceptual-conceptual process.

At birth the neonate responds almost completely on the basis of reflexes and primitive reaction behavior. His perceptual pattern for receptive and expressive behavior is meager. However, he does possess the beginnings of the elements that will make up his perceptual process. Among the things that a newborn child can do but does not have to do are (1) observe a very elemental figure on ground perception that will develop into visual perception; (2) perform various motor acts, such as flexing and extending limbs, moving the eyes, turning the head, and grasping objects by reflex; (3) demonstrate a primitive auditory perceptive ability that is aware of loud and soft sounds; (4) produce crying and single noncrying vowels and consonant sounds that will develop into vocal and speech patterns; (5) exhibit a primitive memory ability that can retain impressions gained through simple conditioning acts of learning; and (6) demonstrate the beginning of an ability to integrate and coordinate behavior. All of these fundamental "beginnings" or "primitive patterns" will be further developed into a viable perceptual-conceptual process by the maturational process and by learning gained through interaction with the environment.

Many authorities working in the realm of intellectual development, including Piaget,[35] Gesell and Ilg,[36] Gibson,[37] and Smith and Henry,[38] suggest that the basis for the development of the cognitive processes is to be found in the perceptual-motor aspects of development at birth or shortly thereafter. A child is able to make use of primitive sensory and motor reactions as well as the reflexes mentioned in the previous paragraph. It is on these basic sensory and motor response patterns that the perceptual-conceptual processes are developed through learning and maturation. Our work with school-age children who were having difficulty in learning, although they had average or better mental ability, revealed that most of these children lacked the ability to execute basic motor patterns that are normally developed in the first year of life. These children lacked proper body symmetry, posture control, and balance. They were also deficient in the use of one or more of the sensory or perceptual modalities.

The theoretical position of Kaluger and Heil[39] is that a child must develop symmetry in his posture mechanism and adequate weight-shift mechanism for balance before he can develop efficient and effective perceptual and motor skills. The time period in which an infant generally learns these body adaptations is from the third to the ninth or tenth month of age, that is, from the time he can lift his chest and hold his head erect at midline position while lying supine to the time he begins to increase his sitting-up or standing activity. This is the period when the infant is developing hand-eye coordination because most of the motor activity he is using is from the waist up. He is developing a sensory-motor match by learning to reach to a spot where he is looking. With a symmetrical posture the child can better shift his body weight to obtain good balance. With consistent balance the child will have a stable base from which he can perceptually move into the outer world. Furthermore, the world will appear the same way to him each time rather than changing because of inconsistent body positions.

An implication of Kaluger and Heil is that babies from the age of 3 months to the time they are sitting unsupported or beginning to walk should be permitted to spend as much of their time as possible in a horizontal prone position. Preferably, they should be placed toward the middle of the room during the time they are awake so they can react to stimuli coming at them from varied directions. If they are lying awake in a crib next to a wall, most of the visual and auditory stimuli will be coming from the same side of the child. Extensive use of infant seats, jump seats, and the like is not recommended for use before a child is ready to sit up unsupported and is capable of crawling and creeping.

STUDY GUIDE

1. Review the developmental tasks of this age level. Do they make sense to you?
2. Who or what is a neonate?
3. List the physical, behavioral, and sensory characteristics of a neonate.
4. Review the summary of motor responses on pp. 68 and 69 and become aware of the body and limb movements that a baby can make.
5. Trace the basic motor development of locomotion of an infant during the first twelve months of life.
6. How does grasping develop?
7. Jean Piaget is internationally known and accepted for his work on cognition. Answer the following questions according to his theories.
    a. What does he mean by schema or schemata, assimilation, accommodation, and operations?
    b. What are the four periods of cognitive development? Give their age ranges.
    c. At what stage of the sensorimotor period of cognitive development does the infant appear to be using his intellect in a manner that can be observed by another person?
    d. Relate the use of the simple reflexes listed in Table 4-1 and the sequence of motor development in Fig. 4-2 to Piaget's sensorimotor period in cognitive development.
8. The perceptual process is mentioned in Chapter 1 in the discussion of the nervous system. Combine that information with what is found in Chapter 4. Then look ahead to Chapter 6 for a preview of a more sophisticated interpretation of the function of the perceptual process as it relates to learning. Can you tie all of this information together?

REFERENCES

1. Havighurst, R. J.: Human development and education, New York, 1953, Longmans, Green & Co., Inc.
2. Brisbane, H. E., and Riker, A. P.: The developing child, Peoria, Ill., 1965, Chas. A. Bennett Co., Inc.
3. Brown, J. L.: States in newborn infants, Merrill-Palmer Q. 10:313-326, 1964.
4. Crow, L. D., and Crow, A.: Child development and adjustment, New York, 1962, The Macmillan Co.
5. Olmstead, R. W., and Jackson, E. B.: Self demand feeding in the first week of life, Pediatrics 15:396-401, 1950.
6. Gesell, A.: The ontogenesis of infant behavior. In Carmichael, L., editor: Manual of child psychology, ed. 2, New York, 1954, John Wiley & Sons, Inc.
7. Pratt, K. C.: The neonate. In Carmichael, L., editor: Manual of child psychology, ed. 2, New York, 1954, John Wiley & Sons, Inc.
8. Brisbane, op. cit., p. 63.
9. Leventhal, A. S., and Lipsitt, L. P.: Adaptation, pitch discrimination and sound localization in the neonate, Child Dev. 35:759-767, 1964.

10. Engen, T., Lipsitt, L. P., and Kaye, H.: Olfactory responses and adaptation in the human neonate, J. Comp. Physiol. Psychol. 56:73-77, 1963.
11. Bell, R. Q.: Relations between behavior manifestations in the human neonate, Child Dev. 31:463-477, 1960.
12. Well, G. M., and Bell, R. Q.: Basal skin conductance and neonatal state, Child Dev. 36:647-657, 1965.
13. Ibid., p. 653.
14. Hooker, D.: Early fetal activity in mammals, Yale J. Biol. Med. 8:579-602, 1936.
15. Irwin, O. C.: The amount and nature of activities of newborn infants under constant conditions during the first ten days of life. Genet. Psychol. Monogr. 8:1-92, 1930.
16. Dennis, W.: A description and classification of the responses of the newborn, Psychol. Bull. 31:5-22, 1934.
17. Hughes, J. G.: Synopsis of pediatrics, ed. 3, St. Louis, 1971, The C. V. Mosby Co.
18. Bayley, N., and Espenshade, A. S.: Motor development from birth to maturity, Rev. Educ. Res. 11:562-572, 1941.
19. Watson, R.: Psychology of the child, ed. 2, New York, 1965, John Wiley & Sons, Inc.
20. Bryan, E. S.: Variations in the responses of infants during the first ten days of postnatal life, Child. Dev. 1:56-77, 1930.
21. McGraw, M. B.: The neuromuscular maturation of the human infant, New York, 1943, Columbia University Press.
22. Shirley, M.: The first two years, Minneapolis, 1931, University of Minnesota Press.
23. Carmichael, L.: Onset and early development of behavior. In Mussen, P. H., editor: Carmichael's manual of child psychology, ed. 3, New York, 1970, John Wiley & Sons, Inc.
24. Gesell, A., and Amatruda, C. S.: Developmental diagnosis, ed. 2, New York, 1947, Harper & Row, Publishers.
25. Skinner, C., and Harriaman, P.: Child psychology, New York, 1941, The Macmillan Co.
26. Halverson, H. M.: An experimental study of prehension in infants by means of systematic cinema reports, Genet. Psychol. Monogr. 10:107-286, 1931.
27. Castner, B.: The development of fine prehension in infancy, Genet. Psychol. Monogr. 12:105-193, 1932.
28. Ibid., p. 158.
29. Piaget, J.: The origins of intelligence in children, New York, 1952, International Universities Press.
30. Inhelder, B., and Piaget, J.: The early growth of logic in the child, New York, 1964, Harper & Row, Publishers.
31. Baldwin, A. L.: Theories of child development, New York, 1967, John Wiley & Sons, Inc.
32. Flavell, J. H.: The developmental psychology of Jean Piaget, Princeton, N. J., 1963, D. Van Nostrand Co., Inc.
33. Piaget, J., and Inhelder, B.: The child's conception of space, New York, 1956, Humanities Press, Inc.
34. Kaluger, G., and Kolson, C. J.: Reading and learning disabilities, Columbus, Ohio, 1969, Charles E. Merrill Publishing Co.
35. Piaget, op. cit.
36. Gesell, A., and Ilg, F. L.: Child development: an introduction to the study of human development, New York, 1949, Harper & Row, Publishers.
37. Gibson, J. L.: The senses considered as perceptual systems, Boston, 1966, Houghton Mifflin Co.
38. Smith, C. V., and Henry, J. P.: Cybernetic foundations of rehabilitation, Am. J. Phys. Med. 46:379-467, 1967.
39. Kaluger, G., and Heil, C. L.: Basic symmetry and balance: their relationship to perceptual-motor development, Progr. Phys. Ther. 1:132-137, 1970.

5 Psychosocial development in infancy

INFANCY: A PEACEFUL SUNDAY MORNING WITH RUTH

Ruth Annette Baily was born a year and a half ago and is the youngest of our children. The other children are 17, 11, and 10 years old. This report is a record of her behavior for one half day.

At 4:45 A.M. I heard Ruth cry out. I listened for a while, but there were no more sounds. Ruth had gone back to sleep, and so could I. "Da-Da, Ma-Ma, Da-Da, Ma-Ma." These sounds repeated over and over wakened me the second time. About 7:00 A.M. she said in a loud voice. "Ma-Ma." When she gets to this stage in her talking, I know she is not just rambling but is ready for me to go to her.

I went into her room, and she was waiting as always at the foot of her crib with her empty bottle in her hand. With a twisting motion of her wrist and a musical sound like "allee-allee," she indicates that her bottle is empty. She enjoys getting the blankets out of her crib every morning; so as she hands them to me, I hang them over the side rail. I raised the shade. Ruth saw the "brrr" (trucks) on the highway nearby and made a panting sound, which is her word (sound) for our dog. I yawned. Ruth imitated me and laughed. We did this three times, and Ruth loved it. She imitates many sounds that people make such as coughing, sneezing, gargling, etc.

She asked about "Ba-Ba" (Bobby), "Da-Da" (Daddy), "Ka-Ka" (Kathy), and "Pa" (Patty). I told her that they were still sleeping. She put her finger to her lips and said, "Shhh." I wanted to take off her sleeping outfit and get her out of the crib, but she rebelled and went to the crib corner. I sat down and started writing some of the things she had done so far. She changed her mind then and wanted to get out. She called my name, but I just kept on writing. She said, "Ma-Ma" over and over in a very stern tone. Finally, I got her up before she woke everyone else.

During the past two months, getting dressed or changing diapers was sometimes a difficult chore. She often cries and sometimes kicks while I'm working with her. This morning we picked out her red pantsuit with a white ruffled front. She is particularly fond of this, and we "oh" and "ah" about how pretty she looks while I'm dressing her. (She seems typically feminine even at this age.) Since the appropriate remarks were made, dressing went very smoothly this morning. Ruth was playing with an empty plastic bottle. She dropped it, making a noise, so I said, "Shhh, you will wake Daddy." I gave the bottle back to her, and about a minute later she threw it down again. She listened for the noise. Nothing happened. She had to sit up and look over the side of the counter to see what happened to the noise. The bottle had fallen into the open clothes hamper this time. Ruth looked around and started talking about "Da-Da's" toothbrush on the other side of the counter.

Now Ruth was dressed and ran into our bedroom to get praise from Daddy about her outfit. Pretty soon she came back into the bathroom. The Vicks jar lid had not been tight, so Ruth had Vicks on her hands. I wanted to wipe them quickly before she got some in her eye, but she objected. They were wiped anyway.

Next we went to the kitchen to unload the dishwasher and put on the coffee water. Ruth kept fussing and pushing at my legs, wanting me to take her. I scooted her away. She went over to the waste can, found the bottom of a dress I had cut off, placed this around her neck for a necklace, and went off to show Daddy.

Daddy and Ruth came out for breakfast. I fed her baby food cereal, then put presweetened cereal on her tray for her to eat with her fingers. She saw a bag of cheese twists on the counter and wanted some.

Ruth got down from her high chair. I no sooner had it pushed to its proper place, when Ruth wanted to be at the table again. She climbed up on a kitchen chair; when she tried to get from her knees to her rump, she almost fell. This chair climbing just started a few days ago. She had been climbing up on a bench behind the table, and there she had more turning-around room. She seems to judge her area fairly well.

When she heard the girls aged 11 and 10 years going to the bathroom, she beat it down from the chair, grabbed a cheese twist from the bag, and joined them in their room. All three of them then went to our bedroom and got into our bed.

After this novelty wore off, Ruth headed back to me in the kitchen. On the way she saw the two cats sitting outside the window. She said, "Meow," went to their food dishes, and brought the milk dish to me to be filled.

She went to the girls' room, and soon she was crying. She can only play with them for a short while before becoming discontented. They seem to be too possessive of her. I yelled for them to just let her play her own way, but it wasn't long before she was wanting their attention again.

Breakfast time for the rest of the family. Ruth wanted her chair again, so Kathy pushed it over and wanted to lift her up. She refused and ran over to her Daddy because she wanted to sit on the bench between her Daddy and me. She ate some more cereal and drank juice from her lidded cup.

Everyone but Ruth and me got ready for Sunday School and Church. Ruth kissed everyone good-by. She went to kiss Bob, our eldest; but he would not bend over as the others had. He had to tease her. She fussed and made a sort of deep-knee bend motion with her legs until finally he picked her up and kissed her.

After everyone left I turned on some music and made my bed. Ruth wanted me to listen to a song, so she kept tapping me on the legs until I paid attention. She started dancing by pivoting on one foot, round and round, stopping every once in a while to see if I was still watching.

When the bed was made, I put some things away. Ruth had climbed onto my bed, and just as I told her she would fall because of the way she was prancing around, she fell bumping her head on the headboard of the bed. She really cried hard so I knew she was hurt. To distract her I carried her out to the living room to look out at our dog. This seemed to take her mind off her now-raised bump. Some birds were flying near the window, and that really thrilled her.

She enjoys putting one thing into another thing. I gave her a small plastic cup, several pencils, a straw, etc., and this kept her happy for about 15 minutes. She started to act tired as if her teeth were bothering her. She had just cut one new tooth through, and her gums have several other swollen places. As of now, she only has five teeth.

At 11:00 A.M. I fed her lunch. She enjoys looking at the Sears' Christmas catalog while she is eating. We discuss things on every page. We just finished when the family came home.

At noon she said, "Good-night" to everyone and was anxious for her bottle and wanted to go to her bed, but then she fussed. This is also a new thing. Until just a few days ago we could just lay her down, give her a blanket she likes to feel, and she would soon be asleep. This no longer works.

This has been a morning with a 17-month-old. What will this afternoon bring?

Although the emergence of motor skills is the most noted and obvious element of development in infancy, there are other aspects of growth that are just as important, if not more so. Psychosocial development is fundamental to the mental well-being of each person throughout life. Speech and language, social and emotional characteristics, and the origins of personality all have their beginnings in infancy.

INFANT SPEECH AND LANGUAGE

The foundations of language development begin as soon as the infant is born. When the baby cries and his mother responds to this cry, the first step in communication has been taken.

The infant makes his needs and feelings known by using simple forms of communication consisting of body movements, facial expressions, and emotionally charged vocalizations such as whimpers, urgent screams, gentle coos, attention-seeking calls, and laughter. A mother quickly learns to interpret these prelinguistic communications and reinforces them by responding to his calls. As mother and child interact, speech, language, and thought are developed. Prelinguistic communication reaches a peak at about 16 to 20 months of age. As the child's spoken language and vocabulary improve, he has less need to communicate in nonverbal ways. (See Table 5-1.)

True language development, that is, interpersonal linguistic communication with understanding, begins when the infant is about 2 years old. Much speech development must have taken place in the meanwhile. According to Berry and Eisenson,[1] the infant must progress through five essential developmental stages before he can speak conventional, adultlike words. These stages are (1) reflexive vocalization, (2) babbling, (3) lalling, (4) echolalia, and (5) true speech.

Reflexive vocalization

The first sound that a newborn baby makes is the birth cry, which is produced by a reflexive inhalation and exhalation of air across the vocal cords, which were tightened by the trauma associated with the air pressure and temperature change of the extrauterine environment. Almost no noncrying vocalization is heard until after breathing, sucking, and swallowing are well established.[2] The reflexive period of speech development is one of nondescript sounds or speechlessness.

By the end of the first two or three weeks the mother can usually detect differences in the cries of the infant. He has matured enough, physically and mentally, to react with differentiation to varying stimuli and conditions. The baby has one kind of cry that he makes when he is hungry, another kind when he has a sharp pain, and still another kind when he has a dull, aching pain or a fever. He has different cries to indicate when he is uncomfortable, wet, tired, or wants attention. At this early age the child is seeking to communicate to others to make his needs known.

Table 5-1. Development of language in young children*

AGE ZONE	LANGUAGE
4-week	Impassive face
	Small throaty sounds
16-week	Coos, responds to adult by vocalization
	Laughs aloud
28-week	Squeals
	M-m sound
40-week	Da-Da-Ma-Ma
	One other "word"
52-week	Two other "words"
	Responds to "give it to me"
15-month	Four to six words
18-month	Ten words
	Jargon
2-year	Joins two to three words
	Names three to five pictures
3-year	Sentences
	Gives full name, sex

*Modified from Latham, H. C., and Heckel, R. V.: Pediatric nursing, ed. 2, St. Louis, 1972, The C. V. Mosby Co., p. 65.

The shrill cries of hunger or discomfort are quite different from sounds made when the baby is comfortable and happy. This is due to the contractions of the facial muscles when a child is experiencing discomfort and to the more relaxed muscle tone when the baby is comfortable. It is with these shrill cries and comfort sounds that the infant begins to form many consonant and vowel sounds.[3] A child makes vowel sounds before making consonant sounds because when the mouth is opened and air is expelled, a vowel-like sound is made. To make a consonant sound the lips or the tongue must be used.

Babbling and lalling

At about 6 or 7 weeks of age the infant shows by his behavior that he is aware that he is making sounds. Thus reflexive vocalization becomes babbling. He usually makes sounds when he is enjoying himself, and one can tell that he delights in producing or repeating sounds. These sounds are different from the comfort sounds or the discomfort cries. Although he may only be making about seven different phonemes (the smallest unit of speech sounds), the sounds are phonetically diversified. It is usually around the fourth month that the infant learns to manipulate his tongue and lips along with his throat and voice. At that time he may experiment with the sounds he can make.

During the babbling period, which usually lasts until about the sixth month, the sounds produced are still mainly reflexive in nature. As a result, all babies everywhere, the Occidental babies as well as the Oriental babies, make the same sounds. For the same reason babies who are born deaf can babble and make the same sounds that are made by children with normal hearing. For the first 3 months of age the quality of the sounds produced by deaf and hearing children is virtually identical.[4]

The earliest signs of a child's response to language are naturally his responses to his mother's voice. The mother is the center of the child's life. She satisfies his needs, so her voice becomes part of the whole experience. As young as 4 or 5 weeks old, an infant can be comforted solely by the sound of his mother's voice. A little later he may smile on hearing her voice, and soon after that he may smile and make comfort sounds and excited bodily movements. At about 4 or 5 months of age an infant usually begins to differentiate his responses on the basis of the tone or manner of the voice. He still does not understand specific words, but he can respond to intonation of voice.[5] This is shown by babies who respond differently to the same word spoken in different tones of voice.

Babbling is vocalization that the baby makes for his own pleasure. While lying in his crib, he is practicing self-initiated sounds that he will need to use in the more advanced stages of articulation and speech development. About the sixth or seventh month it becomes apparent that the baby is beginning to repeat sounds that he has picked up from his environment. He is now lalling, which is the repetition of sounds or sound combinations that the child has heard.[6] For the first time hearing and sound production are associated. Hearing comprehension is taking place. Vocalization also becomes more socialized as the baby begins making squeals or shouts of delight at the approach of a familiar person.

At about 7 or 8 months of age the baby begins to join his vocalized syllables into repetitive sequences, such as ma-ma-ma or ba-ba-ba-ba. It is usually about this time that the mother or father says that the baby first said "ma-ma" or "da-da." As the parents constantly work with the child to bring about more words, the baby will increasingly use the words of his culture and will drop from his repertoire sounds not used in his environment. The child who is born deaf may increase the number of sound combinations that he makes, but these sounds will be mostly of the reflexive type that he was making earlier in life.

Echolalia and true speech

At about 9 or 10 months of age the infant begins to repeat, by imitation, sounds that he has heard around him. There is a definite acoustic awareness of the sounds made by others. Frequently, the sounds just made by the baby are repeated by someone near him. This repetition by others and the consequent echolalia (imitative repetition or "echoing" of sounds or words just spoken by another) by the baby stimulate even more speech activity. In other words language and speech development go along at a faster pace if the parents repeat the baby's sounds. The baby, in turn, will echo the parents' sounds. The feel of his tongue, lips, and throat, the sounds he makes and hears, the association of other people's voices with lip and facial movements all play an important part in the development of speech. Soon he will be producing elaborate reduplication of two or more syllable combinations. Although there is no comprehension of the sounds, the baby is developing a repertoire of sounds of the language he is to learn. Children who have a remarkable ability to echo sound combinations and speech inflections may develop an "expressive jargon" that has all the mannerisms of conversational adult speech.

When the child is 10 to 12 months of age, he begins to pay attention to a few familiar words. He also seems to have more interest in some words than in others. By his first birthday he can stop when told "no" and, sometimes, can follow very simple directions. The infant is demonstrating a passive understanding of the language. The active use of it will come later. He recognizes his name and usually those of his family and household pets. He will turn to look for them if they are mentioned.

True speech takes place when a child intentionally and correctly uses a conventional sound pattern (a word) and anticipates a response appropriate to the word he has just uttered. Verbal understanding is necessary on the part of the child for him to use and to respond to true speech. The average child begins to use true speech between 12 and 18 months of age, although the first word spoken may have been said at the age of 10 or 11 months. By 15 months of age he usually speaks four intelligible words even though his understanding vocabulary is much larger. At about 18 months of age his speaking vocabular consists of ten spoken words. He can respond to "give me that" and can point to his nose or eyes on command. The child understands the language of others before he is able to use the same words.[7] The average child of 2 years of age uses more than fifty words, and he can put two distinct words together into a sentence. Complete speech comes when the child can use differentiated speech communication in sentences with grammatical structure.

Egocentric and socialized speech (Piaget)

Piaget[8] divides the conversation or talk of children into two categories—egocentric speech and socialized speech. In egocentric speech the child does not direct his speech to anyone in particular nor does he bother to learn if anyone is listening to him. He talks either for himself or for the pleasure of associating anyone who happens to be there with his activity of the moment. He is merely talking in the presence of others. Although the child is not actually speaking to anyone, the speech is related to his own actions and thoughts. This particular kind of egocentricity is a product of the child's intellectual limitations. Egocentric speech aids in the development of his cognitive processes.

Socialized speech is subdivided by Piaget into (1) adapted information, involving an exchange of thought or ideas; (2) criticism of the behavior or work of others; (3) commands, requests, and threats; (4) questions;

and (5) answers. At this stage in the development of speech the child speaks "from the point of view of his audience." He speaks now to communicate his thoughts to other people.

EMOTIONAL AND SOCIAL DEVELOPMENT

As with all areas of development in the newborn and infant, the psychosocial aspects of development are either nonexistent at birth or they exist in a primitive form. It is only after the infant has adjusted to the "outer" world and survival is more ensured that he begins to differentiate his behavior to develop emotional, social, and personality patterns.

Emotional development

The word *emotion* is sometimes used to describe certain behavior, such as fear, anger, joy, disgust, affection, or pity. It is also used, however, to imply a system of feelings, such as sentiment, instead of a single feeling. Most psychologists agree that (1) emotion is affective and there is a feeling element or awareness present; (2) the central nervous system and the autonomic system are involved in producing characteristic motor, glandular, and visceral activities; (3) emotion is related in some way to motivation as an energizer of behavior; and (4) emotions can be classified into types of phenomena such as fear, anger, and affection. The problem in applying all of these factors of emotions to the young infant is in knowing how to determine if he does have such a complex feeling state and, if so, how he manifests this state into a behavior. Because development, in all areas, evolves from mass or general behavior to specific activity, this principle will be used in the approach to discussing emotional behavior.

A baby's emotional life is relatively simple and spontaneous. The child places no restraint on a free expression of his emotions, which come and go depending on the extent to which his desires and needs are satisfied or frustrated and on the amount of understanding he possesses of his relationship to others and to his environmental makeup. The baby's emotions are brief and transitory, although expressed more frequently than in adults.[9] As soon as the emotion is past, it is forgotten and the baby is free from stress and strain until new conditions arise that require an emotional response.

The infant is an egocentric little human being with most of his desires and needs coming from within. There is a definite relationship between emotional states and personal organismic needs. Needs are simple at birth and so are emotions. When the baby has a strong need, such as for food, his emotional response will be one of crying and fairly intense physical movements. If the child is hungry and his mother makes him wait beyond the point of physical endurance, the baby's whole body will reflect his displeasure. Likewise, when he has been fed and is satisfied, his movements will subside and he appears to no longer have an emotional condition.

The mother is the first emotional climate to which the infant is exposed. The way in which the mother feels about the baby is consequently extremely important. Warmth, softness, and bodily satisfaction become the equivalent of love of the mother for the baby. If the mother is gentle and loving and makes the infant comfortable while being fed, the infant feels physically (and possibly psychologically) secure and develops a positive, friendly response to people.[10]

The reward value of a mother's touch was demonstrated by Harlow[11] in his experimentation with newborn monkeys. He placed each monkey into a booth with two surrogate mothers. One mother substitute was made of wire mesh, which gave it a hard surface. The other surrogate, made of wire mesh also, was covered with foam and terry cloth and made soft. The monkeys consistently preferred the soft mother, even when the only food given to the monkeys was placed by the hard mother. When frightened, the monkeys would run to the terry cloth mother for security. Similar studies done with babies reflect the same types of preferences. Early mother-child relationships influence both immediate behavior and long-term adjustment.

Considering single emotions, the first emotion that is evident in the newborn is a general, gross, undifferentiated type of response that can best be described by the word *excitement*. This undifferentiated behavior soon changes to some specific types of emotional responses. An oft-quoted study by Bridges,[12] done on the basis of intensive observation of about sixty infants over a period of several months, indicates the ages at which successive differentiations are made. The first emotion to be detected after excitement is distress, which is observed by the end of the first month. By the end of the second month the feeling of delight can be noted. Between the third and sixth months anger, disgust, and fear are reflected. The only two fears that seem to be present at birth are a sudden withdrawal of support of the body and a reaction to loud, harsh noise. All other fears are learned.

Changes that occur in the emotional responses of the infant during middle infancy and the beginning of late infancy are products of complex interactions of maturation and learning. Maturation of the nervous system and muscles provides the potential for differentiated reactions, whereas learning has a determining effect on the manner in which the emotion will be expressed. Learning by conditioning occurs easily during the early years because the child lacks the reasoning ability and experience to realize how irrational or insignificant many of his emotional experiences are.

By 18 months of age the infant shows evidence of discrimination among people by smiling at those he knows and reacting with fear to strangers, whereas at 6 months of age he would smile indiscriminately in response to a nodding face or mask, regardless of facial expression.[13] This development in perceptual discrimination in the ages from 6 to 18 months demonstrates the role of maturation in emotional and perceptual development.

By the end of the first year the mother should modify her role. She must still provide care but must train the infant according to the demands of our particular society. In the process of this training she should wait until the child is ready before expecting him to take part in processes such as toilet training. With personal emotional participation in learning the infant integrates the experience into his whole being and takes over personal responsibility earlier. The care that the mother provides and the example she sets is of greater influence on him than any other in the establishment of his temperament, character, and personality traits for later years. Some child psychologists go so far as to say that a child's level of emotional stability is well determined by the end of his first year and that his mother had much to do with this development.

Social development

Every infant, like every adult, depends on other people for existence. Not only is the child dependent on a social group, but the social group also helps to determine what kind of individual he will become. The first or primary social group of a child is his family. This group plays an important part in establishing his attitudes and habits. As the child grows into adolescence, he relies less on the family and more on his friends and other social companions. Table 5-2 outlines eight stages of psychosocial development.

Berkowitz[14] has found that there have been changes in the overall practice of child rearing and, as a result, so has there

Table 5-2. Eight stages of psychosocial development*

STAGES (AGES ARE APPROXIMATE)	PSYCHOSOCIAL CRISES	RADIUS OF SIGNIFICANT RELATIONS	PSYCHOSOCIAL MODALITIES	FAVORABLE OUTCOME
1. Birth through first year	Trust versus mistrust	Maternal person	To get To give in return	Drive and hope
2. Second year	Autonomy versus shame, doubt	Parental persons	To hold (on) To let (go)	Self-control and willpower
3. Third year through fifth year	Initiative versus guilt	Basic family	To make (going after) To "make like" (playing)	Direction and purpose
4. Sixth year to onset of puberty	Industry versus inferiority	Neighborhood; school	To make things (competing) To make things together	Method and competence
5. Adolescence	Identity and repudiation versus identity diffusion	Peer groups and outgroups; models of leadership	To be oneself (or not to be) To share being oneself	Devotion and fidelity
6. Early adulthood	Intimacy and solidarity versus isolation	Partners in friendship, sex, competition, cooperation	To lose and find oneself in another	Affiliation and love
7. Young and middle adulthood	Generativity versus self-absorption	Divided labor and shared household	To make be To take care of	Production and care
8. Later adulthood	Integrity versus despair	"Mankind" "My kind"	To be, through having been To face not being	Renunciation and wisdom

*Modified from Erikson, E. H.: Childhood and society, ed. 2, New York, 1963, W. W. Norton & Co., Inc.

been a change of influence on social development. Between the two world wars it was believed that parents had to be extremely rigid in their discipline of the child from the time of birth. In the 1940s a much freer type of child care was pursued, but in the 1950s the shift went back to more parental restraints on the child. With the 1960s parents sought to follow love and some training in addition to gratifying the child's needs. Parental restraint was less than in the past decade.

Social development follows a pattern. Every child usually passes through certain phases of becoming socialized at about the same age that other children do. Children must learn social skills and how to make adjustments to others.

At birth the baby has a complete lack of interest in people. He does not care for companionship of others as long as his bodily needs are taken care of. The baby will stop crying when lifted or touched.

Social behavior begins when the baby first distinguishes between objects and persons. The first social responses of the baby are to adults. Although at 4 weeks of age he is not ready for real social stimulation, his behavior patterns are undergoing organization. He stares at faces that are close by, and he seems to enjoy following the

Frederic Lewis, Inc., New York City.

movements of objects and people.[15] He babbles and coos.

In the second month the infant gives evidence that he is actively aware of adults who care for him but unaware of other babies in the same room. He gradually begins to respond to smiles of those around him and also to differentiate among the individuals in his home. He babbles and coos.

By the end of the third month the child may turn his head or eyes in response to a voice and may follow his mother's movements. His social presence is beginning to be felt. A smile can be evoked by an adult exhibiting a smile, an angry face, distorted facial expressions, tones, or gestures. Incidentally, a child born blind knows how to smile. A baby's first response to people is a positive one.

There is an increased demand for sociability at 4 months of age. The infant now likes to have people pay attention to him by talking or singing to him or just moving him about. Usually this demand for social attention is stronger toward the end of the day. Beginning at the age of 5 months he may even begin to cry when people leave the room or his presence.

At 5 months of age the child smiles in reply to another's smile, and he may cry at other social stimuli. His powers of perception are developing rapidly, and he begins to interact with the various forces of his immediate environment. His interest in his father and siblings increases.

At 7 months of age the child may join in a game of peek-a-boo or "hide your face." He follows any object that is placed in motion and will smile when a person uses his hands to cut off the view from his face. His interest in people and things is increasing. He can respond to more than one person at a time. He enjoys the attention of others but is becoming a little doubtful of strangers; he prefers familiar faces.

The baby displays more aggressive behavior toward adults between the eighth and tenth months. He will pull an adult's hair, grab his nose, tug at his clothes or other personal features. He is also able to imitate some vocal sounds. He now shows an awareness of another child placed close by him, although he is not able to share toys at this point.

At 10 months of age the baby will not play by himself for long periods of time and is quick to show his desire for a shift of company or toys. When shown a mirror, he makes a sort of playful response to it. Although he stays in the crib for specific periods of time, he likes to be with the family group.

Social give and take is greatly enjoyed at the 1-year-age level. If he has been alone in his playpen during the morning, his sociality occurs in the afternoon. He learns that others besides his family are friendly. His attention is no longer held by playthings because he now loves being chased while he is creeping. He throws things to the floor with the hope that they will be restored to him.

It seems that at the fifteenth-month level the child is getting into everything. He seems to enjoy pulling things out of place and, less often, putting them back. At this age the child wants to be attending to his own business of walking, bending, and stooping, instead of bothering with people. He does, however, cooperate in being dressed.

At eighteen months the child is still getting into everything, never seeming to stay in one place for any period of time. Now he likes to be on his feet to go exploring. He is beginning to know where things are kept because of his interest in the activities of the household, and he knows what belongs to different people. At this age he is more responsive to adults and is conscious of social approval.

Moral behavior

The baby is neither moral nor immoral in his actions but nonmoral in the sense that his behavior is not guided by moral standards. Before the baby can behave in a moral way he must learn what the group to which he belongs believes to be right or wrong. He will acquire morals from the teachings, attitudes, and experiences of his parents, peers, teachers, and others.

At first the baby's moral behavior is guided by impulse. He judges right and wrong in relation to the pleasure or pain the act affords him rather than in terms of good or harm done to others. The baby is too young intellectually to realize that an act is wrong unless ill effects follow. He thinks only of his behavior and how it affects him personally, doing what pleases him, regardless of the effect on others. He feels no obligation to modify his behavior because of others unless his behavior is accompanied by unpleasant consequences. A "guilty conscience" from doing wrong is unknown at a young age because it requires the development of definite standards of right and wrong. The baby acts on the basis of his primitive needs, impulses, and the pleasure principle.

No child can be expected to build up a moral code of his own. He must be taught the universal standards of mankind of right and wrong as they are handed down. He must also learn concepts that his social group has found to be useful.

Toilet training

Toilet training is a major area of concern for many parents and some psychologists. The toddler is faced with reality when he is asked to give up the pleasure of doing what he wants to gain his mother's approval. The age for beginning this process is a matter of individual growth. However, by the end of the first year, he should be physiologically and psychologically ready. When the child can stand alone, his nerve pathways have developed to the extent that he can physically control his anal and urethral sphincters.[16] However, if the child does not understand what is expected of him, the mother should wait until later to start. Bowel training begins before bladder training, since the number of stools a day is fewer than the number of times the child urinates. Usually it is wise to wait at least a month after bowel training has been established to begin bladder training.

The method of toilet training begins with observing the time of day when the child has bowel movements. He is then placed on a seat that is comfortable for him a little before the time he usually defecates. The child should not be given toys to play with, since he would be distracted from his purpose. After the mother has indicated to the child by some gesture or words what is expected of him, she should keep him on the toilet chair for 10 to 15 minutes. It is good to teach the child an acceptable and easily understood word to use when he must eliminate so that strangers can understand his desire. He should be praised when he succeeds in his task, but disapproval should *not* be shown when he does not. When children are old enough to go to the toilet alone, their clothes should be easy to manage. Bowel control is established by one third of the infants at 18 months of age, daytime bladder control by 2 years of age, and night control by 3 years of age.[17]

Problems in maintaining elimination control are often encountered and should not be upsetting to parents. Sometimes children revert to wetting themselves because they do not want to interrupt their play or do not allow enough time to get to the toilet. Teething, illness, and excessive intake of liquids are reasons for wetting. Any emotional strain or upset may cause a relapse. The arrival of a new baby in the family and going to school are situations that commonly cause strain.

Fecal smearing is a problem that arises with some children. Although this practice is offensive to adults, it is not abnormal for the child. He has not acquired the distaste for his excretions and enjoys the odor, regarding it as a gift from himself. He created it so he may not hesitate to manipulate it and smear it on the floor. The adult should not show strong disapproval, but he should provide a more acceptable means for the child to gratify this desire to smear. Playing with clay or sand are good methods at first. Later, finger painting may be used as a substitute for fecal smearing. Cleaning the child promptly or pinning the diaper securely are ways of preventing access to the feces. Sometimes flushing the toilet can be a helpful diversion by allowing the child to pull the handle.

There have been many evaluations of the effects of toilet training on the child. If training is begun too early before the child can learn control himself, he can become frustrated and insecure. The child often has ambivalence toward his mother during this period. He loves her but feels antagonistic when she asks him to comply with her wishes. She must have patience and show love and friendliness toward her child. Psychoanalysts traditionally postulate that severe pressure on the child during this period will cause the child to be tight-lipped, stingy, meticulous, and punitive in later life.[18] No pressure at all, however, may cause the child to develop a permissive attitude toward any kind of controls. The modern trend of thought as expressed by many authorities is that there is no significant effect of toilet training itself on the child's personality. Rather, it is the dominating influence of the type of parent who puts pressure on the child that affects his development.

NATURE AND ORIGINS OF PERSONALITY

The distinctness of a human being as a "person" includes the concept of an individual who performs both physiological and psychological functions. This individual, although unique, self-contained, and striving for goals, is also receptive to the world around him and is capable of having experiences.[19] The physiological part of a person is readily observed and accepted. The psychological side is not as easily known or observable. Thus personality, which is basically psychological in nature, is difficult to ascertain with any degree of accuracy or ease.

Nature of personality

The term *personality* embodies two root ideas in definitions. First, it may refer to the outer distinguishing qualities or characteristics of the individual that can be observed by others. Second, personality may also refer to the inner being, which is made up of psychophysical systems and forces that are part of a dynamic intrapersonal organization. The inner self is usually considered to have conscious and unconscious elements of being. Both outer and inner manifestations of personality must develop.

Many psychologists and psychiatrists believe that, in addition to the individual's organic systems, such as the cardiovascular, neuromuscular, hepatic, cerebral, endocrinal systems, a person also possesses a psyche system. The psyche is that part of a person that is the performer of psychological functions and activities. It is the mind, yet more than the mind—it is the personification of the life principle.[20]

Most psychologists accept a schematization of the psyche, such as the one postulated by Freud and various psychoanalytical theories. Some believe it neither necessary nor desirable to apply terms to psychological abstractions that are, for all intents and purposes, unknowable and possibly nonexistent. The authors of this text will make use of a schematization because they believe that by this approach the abstract concepts of personality development can be made more understandable. The schematization will make use of some of the more widely accepted concepts of psychoanalytical theory. Other ideas, however, will also be presented.

Emergence of personality structure

Newborn and very young infants are not considered to have a differentiated conscious awareness of self or even of existence. The stimuli of the external world will force themselves on the infant. As the maturing central nervous system, memory, and perceptual systems absorb and accumulate more and more of these experiences, an organized psychic structure called the ego, or self, is formed.

The ego is the conscious part of the psychic structure. The prime functions of the ego are the perception of reality and the learning to deal rationally and effectively with reality. Eventually, the tasks of the mature ego will include such processes as perception; adaptation to reality; use of the reality principle and the mechanism of anxiety to ensure safety and self-preservation; motor control; reason and making judgments; storing knowledge and solving problems; and overcoming the demands and discharges of the primitive, primary forces and impulses of the self by using the secondary psychic processes of judgment, logic, and intellect to regulate and control them.

The concepts of primary and secondary psychic processes are pertinent to this discussion. All children are born with certain basic, innate processes, drives, and demands that are necessary for self-maintenance and survival. These forces are universal in nature. Babies the world over have the same needs for food, water, air, sleep, comfortable temperature, release of bowel and bladder tension, rest, and avoidance of pain. In addition, they also have certain psychological needs such as those provided for by comfort contact, assertiveness, curiosity, affection, and security. Whenever any of the biological or psychological needs is not fulfilled to a satisfactory degree (satisfactory for physical or mental survival), the infant will try in every way it can to make its survival wants known. The behavior pattern that he develops in making his wants known becomes identified as part of his personality.

For the first two years or so of life the primitive biological urges necessary for survival and development emerge. These urges are survival-reaction behavior, egocentric in nature and nonsocial. After the child has learned to do the first developmental tasks necessary for survival, the secondary psychic processes of value judgment and intellect begin to emerge and develop. They will seek to control the intense primitive impulses so that the child can become less egocentric. Development of the ego begins to take place as the cognitive system gains control over the primary forces and permits their expression only in keeping with socially acceptable behavior. The foundations of personality are being formed as the primary and secondary forces compromise and develop behavior patterns. The first two years are spent in permitting the primary psychic forces to express themselves so that these forces can provide survival drive for the child. Then for the next two years or so the secondary psychic processes seek to gain control by developing a behavior control pattern that comes to be recognized as part of the child's unique personality.

The ideas presented here on personality development are theoretical and should not be considered as proved fact. Although we are not psychoanalytically oriented, we do find in psychoanalytical theories some worthwhile ideas concerning the early development of personality. Some of these concepts are based on the modified psychoanalytical teachings of Hadfield,[21] a British child and consultant psychologist, who in turn based much of his thinking on the developmental concepts of Gesell.[22] Hadfield[23] suggested the sequence of personality development described on the following pages.

We believe a substantial part of a child's personality is related to innate behavioral elements that emerge as part of the unfolding maturational process. These behaviors have physical, psychological, and social survival values. They are the foundation of personality growth. Uniqueness and deviations in personality come from differences in the way these behavioral expressions are treated by persons working with the child and by the artifacts and mentifacts of his environment.

During the first three or four years of life, there are certain behaviors exhibited by the child that appear to be found in children everywhere. These behaviors apparently are universal in the sense that they are part of nature's plan by which human beings mature. Although several types of behaviors can be noted at any one time, there does seem to be one behavior that is emphasized or at least predominates in influence at that period or phase.

The infant and the child, then, do go through phases. Furthermore, each phase has a special learning task, purpose, or function that needs to be accomplished during that phase. If the task is not learned, the demands of that task continue into the next phase and cause some confusion and conflicts. The environment, especially the one involving the parents and siblings, will have a great influence on the nature, direction, and type of personality that a baby develops by determining how well the developmental tasks are accomplished.

Physiological stability. Consider the newborn child. He is born in a state of helplessness. His only responses are reflexes and gross motor reactions. He needs care and help to survive. The first dominant characteristic behavior of the newborn is one of physiological stability and physical dependency. The infant is dependent on others for food, warmth, protection, and security. He is only interested in his own well-being and is so egocentric that he is not even aware at first of the fact that others are tending to him. His self-centered concern is shown during the first month by the fact that he sleeps for 60% of the time and dozes much of the rest of the time. He has a need to have close contact with his mother; he will snuggle close and wants to be nursed and cuddled. This contact gives him a sense of protection and security. He has a cry of distress, and he uses a clinging or embracing movement. This feeling of dependence never completely disappears. It does, however, later in life change its form from physical to psychic, to social dependency, and finally, to interdependency.

Control of body movements. Developing body and motor control is another dominant feature of the first year of life. At about the third month the infant will have sufficiently matured neurologically so that he can now coordinate some of his reflexes and movements; he now has some motor control. His control will start with his eyes, moving down the body from head to foot in sequential order, according to the cephalocaudal direction of growth principle. During the first year he will kick, twist, jerk his head, move his arms, and make many motions that appear to have no purpose. Actually, this period is one of physical preparedness. He is getting ready for the time when he will put his muscles to good use. The maturational process is at work. Motor development, in conjunction with perceptual development, is thought to provide a foundation for the development of the cognitive processes. Certainly personality development in some measure will be related to the ability to have adequate voluntary control of the body. As a person can move, so can he act. When he acts, he makes choices and decisions that reflect his personality pattern.

Physical satisfaction. During the latter half of the first year, the infant appears to be performing several motor actions for the fun he gets out of them. He derives pleasure from shaking things, touching things, and reaching for and trying to grasp objects. And, of course, anything that he can pick up he brings to his mouth, which

Table 5-3. Emerging physiological and behavioral characteristics and personality development

AGE LEVEL	CHARACTERISTIC PHASE	MAIN EMPHASIS
0 to 14 months	Physiological stability	Vital life systems stabilize
	Motor development	Sitting, reaching, locomotion
	Physiological satisfaction	Oral and motor pleasures
15 to 30 months	Attention seeking	Calls attention to self
	Exploration and curiosity	Investigates surroundings
	Verbal imitation	Speech and language development
	Self-assertiveness	Exerts his will
31 to 48 months	Behavior imitation	Copies actions of others
	Suggestibility to feelings	Reflects attitudes and moods
	Identification prone	Personality identification
	Emerging self-ideal	Start of self-judgment

has been his major source of pleasure. So many of his satisfactions and pleasures up to this time have come to him through his mouth; for instance, consider the number of times he has been fed during the first year alone. Thus it gives him pleasure to suck. He has pleasure in moving his limbs. He is thrilled with his accomplishments in learning to move about. During this phase, he is experiencing pleasure in physiological activities and bodily function. He seeks to enhance those activities that give him pleasure. The child who is permitted to find pleasure in these early physical activities by not being unduly restricted tends to develop a joyous attitude toward life. The happy child is a healthy child, and the healthy child will be a good child because he is contented.

Attention seeking. Once the child begins to walk or to get around fairly well, he is now ready to move out of his egocentric shell and take a more active interest in the world around him. He has had a year of protectiveness and close watching. But now he has accomplished some of the personal developmental tasks necessary for his survival, and he is ready to begin emphasizing some of the other primary innate behavioral responses that are necessary for his pursuit of living. He is ready to explore his environment, but he does not have the confidence to feel secure enough to move freely into the environment. So he seeks to call attention to himself to make sure others are watching out after him. This phase of self-display is often brought about because he is left alone in a room more frequently than before. The mother has got used to the baby, and she does have a "million" things to do around the house. The baby, however, wants to make sure that his mother is still near, so he calls out to her. He is reassured when he hears her voice answering. At this age of 12 to 14 months the baby does enjoy being the center of attention. Everybody loves a baby who is socially responsive. The baby of this age can jibber-jabber, wave bye-bye, play peek-a-boo, and enjoy having someone play "this little piggy went to market" with his toes. He is developing social contacts, and he is discovering what behavior pleases people.[24] All of this attention, plus the recognition that his mother is still around even when he cannot see her, helps the infant move from the strong need for direct care and protection of the first year to a freedom to explore in the second year.

Exploration and curiosity. As the baby feels more secure, he begins to use his facilities for moving around. He is now making use of his innate curiosity, exploring at first close to his mother, then allowing himself to move further away. He learns to discriminate between the various objects that he examines. Soon he is going by himself into other rooms and getting into things. This is about the time the baby discovers the bottom cabinets and drawers in the kitchen where his mother keeps her pots and pans. Sooner or later he wants to see what his mother keeps in these cabinets, and so he takes out all the pots and pans and puts them in the middle of the kitchen floor. Soon he wonders how his mother got all of those pots and pans into that small cabinet. When she tries to get all of them back into the cabinet, she wonders the same thing! Most parents can recall some similar experience that their child had at this phase of life.

Verbal imitation. Since speech and language are the major adaptive behaviors that are being emphasized during the second year, it is only natural that the innate capacity of imitation should emerge about this time. Imitation, like the reflexes, enables an infant to acquire adaptations to life for which there are no innate or hereditary responses.[25] One of the most valuable acquisitions gained by imitation is speech and language. With speech the child takes a major step in the direction of personal independency and adaptation to life. Verbal communication not only permits the child to make his needs known more readily but it also will serve as a mediator for his thought processes. Thinking usually involves the use of words. Thus the greater the comprehension vocabulary that a child has, the further afield he can go by way of his cognitive processes. As the baby imitates his mother or father, direct learning takes place in behavior, attitudes, and the social graces in addition to language.

Self-assertiveness. By the age of 2 or 2½ years the toddler has learned to do the developmental tasks that are basically required of him to survive. He can eat solid food; he can communicate; he can comprehend verbal responses; he can walk and make coordinated movements of all sorts; and he can generally exercise some control of his bodily processes. The primary processes that nature has given him to help him with self-maintenance and self-preservation have served him well. What else is left for him to do but seek to assert his will upon the world? Assertiveness and aggressiveness become the characteristic behavior of this age. The time of the "terrible twos" and temper tantrums has arrived for most children.

As the child pushes to make his wants known, he is not trying to be a "bad" child. He is only emphasizing a concept and behavior pattern that he has learned in the first two years of life. Right or wrong, he has come to believe that the "world revolves around him," and he can pretty much have what he wants. During his first year of life, any time that he ever needed or wanted anything someone provided it for him. The pattern did not change much during the second year. Whenever he wanted anything, he simply cried or asked for it. Sometimes he had to be persistent, but he usually got what he wanted.

However, his parents have now reached the point where they have decided that their child must learn that he cannot always have what he asks for, and certainly he must learn that the crying "has got to stop"! Unfortunately, the parents do not fully realize just how embedded the baby's idea is of how he is supposed to let his parents know when he wants something. He has always cried or made some kind of fuss when he wanted something. This was standard procedure. All of a sudden this approach no longer works because his parents have decided to put a stop to it, but the baby does not know how else he can make his needs known. So he intensifies his crying and fussing. He may even begin to bang his head on the floor or hold his breath until he turns blue to let his parents know how desperately he wants something. He does not realize, as yet, that he is going to have to curb his primary "pleasure-seeking" impulses and that his wishes are not "commands." He will continue his temper-tantrum behavior until he realizes that this approach no longer works. It is at this point that the child is ready to seek new ways of getting what he wants.

Temper tantrums can be considered as ways by which a child is practicing asserting himself. In life there are times when a person must be assertive for his own good. However, one cannot or should not be assertive in all situations. The give and take of social interaction and of compromise must also be learned. Parents can help a child who is having a temper tantrum by diverting his attention from what he is crying about to something else that is interesting, such as looking out a window, or introducing a new object, toy, or idea. The golden rules for the parent are calmness, fairness, firmness, and consistency. A quiet firmness on the part of the parent may enable the child to be quiet and firm with himself. An occasional smack on the bottom is acceptable if it says, "that's enough of that—it's time for you to learn that there are better ways of asking for what you want and also realize that no one can ever get everything he asks for." In the meanwhile the child should be encouraged to learn more acceptable behavior patterns and control. The parents should set good examples by their actions and attitudes. The child will learn by imitation and identification. The secondary psychic processes are now being developed.

STUDY GUIDE

1. Study Table 5-1. Consider the relationship between language development and speech development.
2. What are the identifying characteristics of the five stages of speech development?
3. According to Piaget, what is the difference between egocentric speech and socialized speech?
4. In terms of emotions and emotional behavior, what are the four points that most psychologists accept as being true.
5. Discuss the implications of Harlow's studies with monkeys for the rearing of infants.
6. Trace social development in infants by citing the types of social behavior manifested at different age levels.
7. Toilet training is said by many psychologists to have an effect on the child's developing personality characteristics. According to these psychologists, how are toilet training and various aspects of behavior related?
8. What are the two basic categories or root ideas used in defining the term *personality*?
9. Discuss the nature of the ego, or the self, and its relationship to innate, primary psychic processes.
10. What is the main thrust, direction, or purpose of personality development during the first two years?
11. Review the phases of personality development as presented in Table 5-3.

REFERENCES

1. Berry, M. F., and Eisenson, J.: Speech disorders: principles and practices of therapy, New York, 1956, Appleton-Century-Crofts.
2. McCarthy, D.: Language development. In Wood, N. E., editor: Language development and language disorders; a compendium of lectures, Monogr. Soc. Res. Child Dev. **25**(3):7, 1960.
3. Lewis, M. M.: How children learn to speak, New York, 1959, Basic Books, Inc., Publishers.
4. Lenneberg, E. H.: Speech as a motor skill with special reference to nonaphasic disorders. In Bellugi, V., and Brown, R., editors: The acquisition of language, Monogr. Soc. Res. Child Dev. **29**:162, 1964.
5. Lewis, op. cit., p. 34.
6. Berry and Eisenson, op. cit., p. 20.
7. Miller, G. A.: Language and communication, New York, 1951, McGraw-Hill Book Co.

8. Piaget, J.: The language and thought of the child, London, 1952, Routledge & Kegan Paul, Ltd.
9. Gesell, A., and Thompson, H.: The psychology of early growth, New York, 1938, The Macmillan Co.
10. Gruenberg, S. M., editor: Our children today, New York, 1952, The Viking Press, Inc.
11. Harlow, H., and Harlow, M. H.: Learning to love, Am. Sci. **54:**244-272, 1966.
12. Bridges, K. M. B.: Emotional development in early infancy, Child Dev. **3:**324-341, 1932.
13. McCall, R. B., and Kogan, J.: Attention in the infant: effects of complexity, contour, perimeter and familiarity, Child Dev. **38:**939-952, 1967.
14. Berkowitz, L.: The development of motives and values in the child, New York, 1964, Basic Books, Inc., Publishers.
15. Gesell, A., and Ilg, F. L.: Infant and child in the culture today, New York, 1943, Harper & Row, Publishers.
16. Marlow, D. R., and Sellew, G.: Pediatric nursing, Philadelphia, 1961, W. B. Saunders Co.
17. Ibid., pp. 398-399.
18. Hoffman, M. L., and Hoffman, C. W., editors: Child development research, New York, 1964, Russell Sage Foundation.
19. English, H. B., and English, A. C.: A comprehensive dictionary of psychological and psychoanalytical terms, New York, 1958, David McKay Co.
20. Hensie, L. E., and Campbell, R. J.: Psychiatric dictionary, New York, 1960, Oxford University Press.
21. Hadfield, J. A.: Childhood and adolescence, Baltimore, 1962, Penguin Books.
22. Gesell, A., and others: The first five years of life, New York, 1940, Harper & Row, Publishers.
23. Hadfield, J. A., op. cit., p. 84.
24. Ibid., p. 89.
25. Ibid., p. 97.

6 Early childhood
3 to 5 years of age

EARLY CHILDHOOD: LIFE WITH A 4-YEAR-OLD

Four-year-old Keith is usually awake and full of vigor before the alarm goes off. He comes into our room and says "good morning" to me a few times. If he doesn't get a response, he tries this on his father. He knows this always works. While I am getting up and oriented for the day, Keith and his father play "tent" in our bed and, as he states, "talk things over." Then father and shadow are off to the bathroom to shave while I am fixing breakfast and feeding our 10-month-old daughter. When they come back to the bedrooms to dress, Keith chooses his own clothes for the day, as I've placed his things in drawers that he can open and decide for himself. Sometimes his combinations are ill matched, but at least he has made the selection by himself. Keith dresses himself and usually engages in a race with his daddy to see who is dressed first. He always is. He must also place his father's belt through the loops of his trousers and try to fasten the buckle.

They are then ready to come to the breakfast table. Each morning it's always a hard decision for Keith to select the cereal he would like to eat. He usually picks the box that has a present pictured on the front of the box. When he shops with me in the grocery store, he paces up and down studying the boxes of cereal to see which ones have pictures of toys and puppets. Therefore he knows at breakfast he will have a surprise in the box. After the box has been opened, though, he is disappointed on the second day to find there is no give-away inside.

After he kisses his daddy good-bye, I turn on the television so Keith can watch "Captain Kangaroo." While he is engrossed in his show, I get dressed and try to wash the dishes. I'm always being interrupted when I'm doing my tasks because Keith is calling me to come and see a new animal Captain is showing the boys and girls. The show holds his attention fairly well, and he enjoys the stories and songs presented each day.

Making the beds is one job that Keith likes to help me do. We end up having a tug-of-war because he thinks I have more than my share of linens on the side I am making. After he has come around the bed to check, he is satisfied and leaves to continue watching Captain. Sometimes he will come into the kitchen and dry the dishes for me, but mostly he likes to take the saturated sponge to wipe the table and everything in sight. He will, however, get a towel to dry things off.

At 8:30 A.M. we leave to go to nursery school. On our 15-minute ride he calls to my attention the trucks and billboards along the highway. Sometimes we see one of my husband's company trucks. He always screams in my ear, "There's Daddy's work truck!" We like to count the vehicles we see and especially the flags when the men are painting new lines on the expressway. We also talk about the color of each car we see. Keith is an incessant talker and must explain to me everything that comes into his mind. Most of the time these are events, stories, or conversations we've had, sometimes weeks ago. Then we have to talk these things out all over again. He never tires of recalling incidents to me and giving me the same explanations I've given him previously. At the end of the expressway we reach a traffic light. He knows that we must stop on red and go on green, but if I go through a yellow light, I receive quite a lecture on how bad I've been. I must then apologize before I've been excused for my unpardonable sin.

This past school year I was employed at Keith's nursery school. At first he was very possessive of me and was quite the show-off because his mommy was one of the teachers. After he was put into another class, he simmered down a bit. Then he would simply say "Hi" to me as he raced by on a tricycle on the playground. All the children participate in pledging the flag and singing "America" in our morning exercises. When we make a circle to sing and do our exercises, Keith is adamant to the point of bossiness in making sure the children raise their hands when making their particular requests. He has learned the alphabet, knows many, many rhymes and stories, can count independently to 31, and knows basic shapes and colors. He gets along relatively well with the other children, but at times he fights with them over toys or special chores that the children must take turns doing. His sister sleeps in an adjacent room while we are at school. Keith is very protective and proud of her as we enter and leave school. We go home at 11:30 A.M., and sometimes he isn't ready to leave. By the time we're on the expressway again and looking at the trucks and tractors he has forgotten the tears shed over leaving school before he was ready to go home.

When we arrive home, Keith races me to the front door to get the mail. Since he says he's my helper, he holds the door while I balance the baby, books, and pocketbook to unlock the front door. Once inside, he positions himself on the top step to wait for daddy to come home for lunch. He likes to fix his own peanut butter and jelly sandwich and insists on getting his own knife, bread, and jars. He usually spreads his jelly from the bread to the tablecloth, but at least he has made his own lunch. He also insists on measuring the teaspoon of Ovaltine for his milk and replacing the cap himself. After lunch Keith goes to his room for an afternoon nap. He must have a blanket, any blanket will do, to finger the edge in falling asleep. We've let him take a blanket to bed with him since his sister was born because we feel he needs this bit of security. He also wants his blanket to comfort him when he falls or at other anxious moments. Usually a bit of discussion about the crisis will suffice, but not always.

When Keith and Beth Anne have wakened from their naps, we put Beth Anne in her stroller and walk a few blocks. Sometimes we go shopping or to the nearby recreation park. There he tries out all the equipment and chases the squirrels. He likes to push his sister's stroller because he's "a big boy" now, and I am supposed to follow behind them. When we return home, Keith sometimes sets the table. He knows the placement of the silver and napkins. He likes to help me cook. He enjoys stirring Jello and licking the beaters on the mixer. We make cookies and he decorates them. At Christmas baking time we ended up with more decoration than cookie!

After dinner Keith and his daddy go for a walk or mow the lawn. He has a little lawn mower of his own and follows on his daddy's heels the whole time they are cutting the grass. Sometimes he'll pick some flowers for me, and I must put the clover and dandelions in water immediately. When his daddy gets out his toolbox and tinkers with the cars, Keith must also get out his workbench tools Santa brought him and work on his pedaling car.

At bedtime we take turns reading stories to him. We must both accompany him to bed to kiss and tuck him in. He tells us whose turn it is each night to do the tucking. Keith is lots of fun and full of questions right now. Everything is "why," and even after each explanation he still asks why. We enjoy taking him to parks and the zoo. He has been to only one museum but can remember details of our trips long after the adventures and wants to talk about them time and time again. Four is a frustrating age for him and us at times, but it's fun and exciting all the same!

The child of early childhood age is a complex individual with important tasks to accomplish. Developmentally, he is about to begin the steepest ascent of his life. Between the ages of 2½ and 5 years the child will be transformed from a baby who is just beginning to be aware of the concrete world around him to an individual who is ready to delve into the abstract world of books. Life at this age moves extremely rapidly. Many significant events and achievements take place. The adult of the future is truly being formed.

The infant of the first two years matured and enhanced his physical self to accomplish the developmental tasks for his age. The preschool child will need to make a more solid contact with the world of people and objects to accomplish his goals. Basically, most of the developmental tasks of early childhood are extensions of tasks that were being learned in infancy. Certain tasks must now be developed to a higher level of proficiency or sophistication. Some new tasks will be added. Life is a combination of continuity and change.

Developmental tasks emphasized during early childhood include the following: (1) achieving integrated motor and perceptual control; (2) completing control of the elimination of bodily wastes; (3) achieving physiological stability; (4) improving ability to communicate and to comprehend what others say; (5) achieving independence in self-care areas such as eating, dressing, and bathing; (6) learning sex differences and sexual modesty; (7) forming simple concepts of social and physical reality and learning how to behave toward persons and things; (8) learning to relate oneself emotionally to parents, siblings, and other people; and (9) learning to distinguish right and wrong and developing a conscience (value judgment system).

PHYSICAL CHARACTERISTICS AND MOTOR SKILLS

Stages of maturational development always follow a particular order. The child does not stand before he sits, nor can he draw a square before he can draw a circle. However, this orderly progression of events moves forward at different rates of speed, some children growing and developing at a faster rate than others. Therefore some 3-year-olds may be able to do some tasks normally expected of 5-year-olds, and some 5-year-olds can do only the tasks usually expected of 3-year-olds. There is a wide range of individual differences, and each child must be treated as a unique person. It is established, however, that girls pass through the periods of development more rapidly than boys. Adults, as well as the children themselves, should realize that many different patterns of growth are normal.

The plan of physical growth is so well coordinated that the successful emergence and development of each stage is dependent on the level of mastery attained on the previous stage. The growth rates of four major types of organs and tissues, however, do change. General body tissue, including most of the internal organs, muscles, and bones, grows rapidly during the first two years of life. After the third birthday body growth increases at a slow but steady pace until the age of puberty, when a growth spurt takes place. Neural development takes place so rapidly in the early years that by the age of 2 years, neurological development is 60% complete, and by the age of 6 years the brain is close to 90% complete. Nature has provided for this rapid neural growth because it is so important and fundamental to all other aspects of growth. Genital development, however, is slow because reproductive organs need not be functional until after puberty.

Lymphoid development is interesting. It has the second most rapid rate of growth. By the age of 4 years it is 60% complete; by the age of 8 years it is 90% complete. Note the rapid increase in the next three years to a peak, at the age of 11 years, of 195% of what will be total development of the lymphoid masses at maturity. Lymphoid masses fight infections and help ward off illnesses. As compared to any other age level, fewer 11-year-olds die of diseases, and more 11-year-olds die from accidents.

Physical characteristics

The average increase in weight during the second and third years is from 3 to 5 pounds annually. The typical 2-year-old weighs between 25 and 28 pounds. The 3-year-old weighs 3 to 5 pounds more. The average 4-year-old weighs about 36 pounds, and the 5-year-old about 41 pounds. There is no significant difference in weight between boys and girls, although boys do tend to be slightly heavier.[1] The height for a 2-year-old is, on the average, approximately 32 to 36 inches. For a 3-year-old the average height is about 3 inches more. At the age of 4 years the child is about 40 inches tall, and at 5 years the average height is 43 inches. The child's stature at the age of 5 years is a moderately good predictor of his adult height, since the correlation between heights at these two ages is close to .70.[2]

One major change that all children go through is the "lengthening out" process, during which the child's build changes from a baby look to a proportioned "little adult" look. He gradually becomes slimmer, taller, and more solid looking. The protruding abdomen flattens, and the shoulders become broader. These changes in baby proportions are due mainly to an increase in the length of the legs. By the second year the length of the arms and legs has increased 60% to 75% from what they were at birth. The lower part of the head still appears small and underdeveloped, but this appearance is due to the smallness of the baby teeth.[3] However, the set of temporary teeth is generally complete, and the child is equipped to eat solid foods. During early childhood, eyes look oversized. Because of the shape and developmental status of the eyes, most young children are farsighted.

Up to the age of 4 years, growth in the muscular system is roughly proportional to the growth of the body as a whole. Thereafter the muscles develop at a faster pace. During the fifth year, 75% of the child's weight can be attributed to muscular development.[4] Throughout this period the larger muscles remain better developed than the small fine muscles. For this reason the young child is more skillful in activities involving large movements than in those involving fine coordination.

Motor characteristics

Because of his limited physical development, the 2-year-old is still geared to gross motor activity. He likes to run and romp, but his coordination is still slow in improving. His fine motor control is not much better. The 2½-year-old is at the crossroads stage in the growth of his action system. His capacity for determining the proper amount of muscle control to use in a certain action is poor because his nerve cell organization is still immature and incompletely developed.[5] This limitation shows itself in such actions as grasping and releasing. He tends to grasp too strongly and to release with overextension. He has not learned to let go. Limitations of his action system account for his inability to modulate his behavior.

By the time the child is 3 years old he has much more motor control. He is more sure on his feet, walks erect, and can stand on one foot. He can go upstairs alternating feet. His whole motor set is more evenly balanced, and he no longer walks with arms outstretched but, rather, swings them in an alternating pattern somewhat like an adult. He likes to hurry up and down stairs, but he also enjoys sedentary pastimes that involve finer motor coordination. He can build a block tower of nine or ten blocks. The 3-year-old now has an eye for form, which suggests that the small muscles which operate his eyes are more facile than they were before. This is also the year when sphincter muscles of bladder and bowel come under rather complete voluntary control.

A 4-year-old is able to run smoothly and quickly with confidence. He can swerve to avoid obstacles and turn corners at an angle. He can gallop, but not well. He can steer his tricycle at full speed. The art of learning to catch a ball is gradually developing, and he can now throw the ball overhand. His eye-hand coordination, which involves the smaller muscles, is developing. He can now pour water from one container to another without spilling it. He can wash his hands and face, brush his teeth (fairly well), dress himself, button his front buttons, and comb his hair. Although he will work at it, tying his shoelaces is still a difficult task.[6]

The 4-year-old draws objects with few details. He enjoys painting, but he shifts his ideas frequently. His designs and letters are crude. He enjoys having his name put on his drawings. He likes to copy his name but usually copies only the first few letters, making marks for the rest of the letters in his name. He attempts to use scissors and can cut a crude straight line.

The 5-year-old is more agile than the 4-year-old and in greater control of his bodily activity. He is closely knit. His arms are held near his body. His stance is more narrow. He still has more control over his large muscles than over his small ones. He is beginning to use his hands more in catching a ball, but he still has some trouble catching it. His alternating mechanism is put to practice in much of his behavior. He alternates his feet when descending stairs, he can usually skip, and he will try to jump rope. He can march to music with good rhythm. He will experiment with roller skates and perhaps stilts, although he cannot sustain a performance for long. The 5-year-old is an active child but without the restlessness that he may have at the age of 4 years. He plays in one location for longer periods of time. He responds to his growth needs by enjoying games in which there is plenty of action. His activity has definite direction.

Handedness is usually well established by 5 years of age (Table 6-1); the 5-year-old can identify the hand that he wants to use for writing. His initial approach is with the dominant hand, and he does not transfer the pencil or crayon to the free hand. The hand and eye do not yet work with complete coordination. The child may still have difficulty when he tries to reach for things beyond arm's length and may sometimes spill or knock them over.

For a child to develop normally he must have adequate nutrition, exercise, rest, and sleep. Children inherit their potential for

Table 6-1. Schematic sequence of major forms of handedness*

AGE ZONE	HANDEDNESS
16 to 20 weeks	Contact unilateral and, in general, tends to be with left hand
24 weeks	Definite shift to bilaterality
28 weeks	Shift to unilaterality; most often right hand is used
32 weeks	Shift again to bilaterality
36 weeks	Bilaterality dropping out; unilaterality coming in; behavior usually characterized "right or left"; left predominates in majority
40 to 44 weeks	Same type of behavior, unilateral, "right or left," but now right predominates in majority
48 weeks	In some a temporary and in many a last shift to use of left hand (as well as use of right), either used unilaterally
52 to 56 weeks	Shift to clear unilateral dominance of right hand
80 weeks	Shift from rather clearcut unilateral behavior to considerable interchangeable confusion; much bilaterality and use of nondominant hand
2 years	Relatively clearcut unilateral use of right hand
2½ to 3½ years	Significant shift to bilaterality
4 years	Unilateral, right-handed behavior predominates

*Modified from Gesell, A., and Ames, L. B.: The development of handedness, J. Genet. Psychol. **70:** 155-175, 1947.

Early childhood 105

growth from their parents and grandparents, but environmental factors such as physical care, nutritional adequacy, and parents' attitude toward health and safety have a great bearing on the physical growth of the child. Children who are undernourished and lack good sleeping habits are low in energy and will not be mentally alert. A 4- or 5-year-old cannot develop his physical being and motor skills to their fullest potential if he is the victim of poor health.

PERCEPTUAL-MOTOR PROCESSES FOR LEARNING (Fig. 6-1)

What happens internally when a child is learning to learn? Something has to occur in the neurological processes because it is only there that any kind of cognitive consciousness can take place. As the advertisement used to say, "If it hasn't got it there, it hasn't got it." The young infant is busy maturing his motor areas so he can begin to make coordinated movements that will

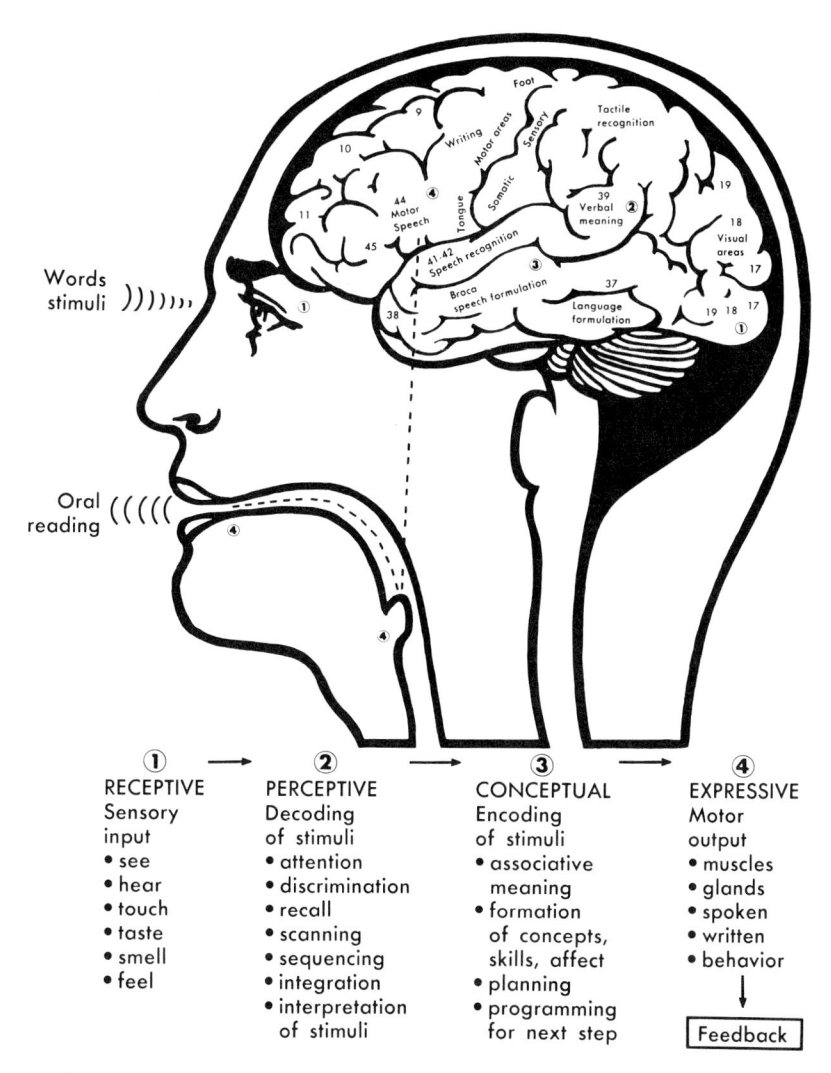

Fig. 6-1. The perceptual pattern for receiving, interpreting, learning, and responding. The drawing illustrates the processes and neural areas involved in oral reading; 1, receives stimuli and transmits to visual area; 2 and 3, interpret and prepare responses; 4, produce the responses.

enhance his survival level. Soon his sensory systems combine with the motor systems to develop the perceptual-motor processes. Eventually the child reaches a point when he must develop his skills for learning so that he can make better use of his intellect. Although he is born with all the brain cells and nerves that he will ever have, he is not born with an innate, ready-made neurological organization that will automatically begin to "learn" when the time is right. It is true that the infant can be "taught" through the use of conditioning techniques and also that he makes use of his capacity for imitation and identification to pick up new skills and attitudes. But when it comes to problem-solving ability and cognitive learning, a neurological organization of some type must be developed if the child is to attain a high level of functional effectiveness and efficiency in the use of the intellectual processes.

Rationale

We believe that the perceptual-motor processes must be adequately developed if a child is to be able to learn to read, work with symbols, or develop abstract concepts. The only means by which an individual can pick up information from his environment is through his senses (the perceptual receptors). The more abstract, intricate, and complex the stimuli the more efficient must be the perceptual processes to be able to perceive these complicated stimuli, discriminate differences, and attach meanings to them. The work of developmental specialists and neurologists such as Gesell and Amatruda,[7] Piaget,[8] Penfield and Roberts,[9] Hebb,[10] and Smith and Henry[11] leaves little doubt concerning the importance of combined perceptual and motor experiences in developing a neurological (mental) structure, organization, or pattern (whatever you wish to call it) that can learn, retain, recall, and respond.

It is our theoretical point of view that the basic neural system for learning consists of (1) a pattern of reflexes, including primitive motor, visual, auditory, vocal, and kinesthetic reflexes; (2) a motor response capability including a postural weight-shift mechanism that provides symmetry and balance; (3) a memory endowment to retain and recall bits of information learned; and (4) after a period of maturation, the ability to imitate certain behavior. The infant is bombarded by stimuli from the world around him. To keep the brain from becoming overloaded nature apparently helps him to shut out many of these stimuli by making it possible for him to receive and perceive initially only the grossest of them. As he becomes more capable of handling these stimuli (by maturational development and experience), he becomes aware of finer, more precise stimuli. Soon he is able to reach out into the world of stimuli and select those that are of more significance to himself. To do this, however, he will need to develop his perceptual processes.

There are four adaptive processes related to the perceptual pattern for learning that are developing within the child during the first six years of life that are germane to this topic. Although all four processes are operating and developing at the same time, they differ as to the degree to which they are emphasized at any one age level. These developmental processes related to the perceptual pattern for learning are (1) gross sensorimotor processes, (2) auditory-verbal development, (3) visual perception and fine visual-motor coordination, and (4) the cognitive processes.[12]

Sensorimotor processes (Table 6-2)

Of all the processes the gross sensorimotor processes receive the most developmental emphasis during the first two years of life. The infant first learns to control his eyes, then to hold his head in the midline position. The sequential maturational process of motor development soon has him sitting up, reaching out, and grasping as

Table 6-2. Theoretical concept of development of motor and perceptual processes and relationship to each other

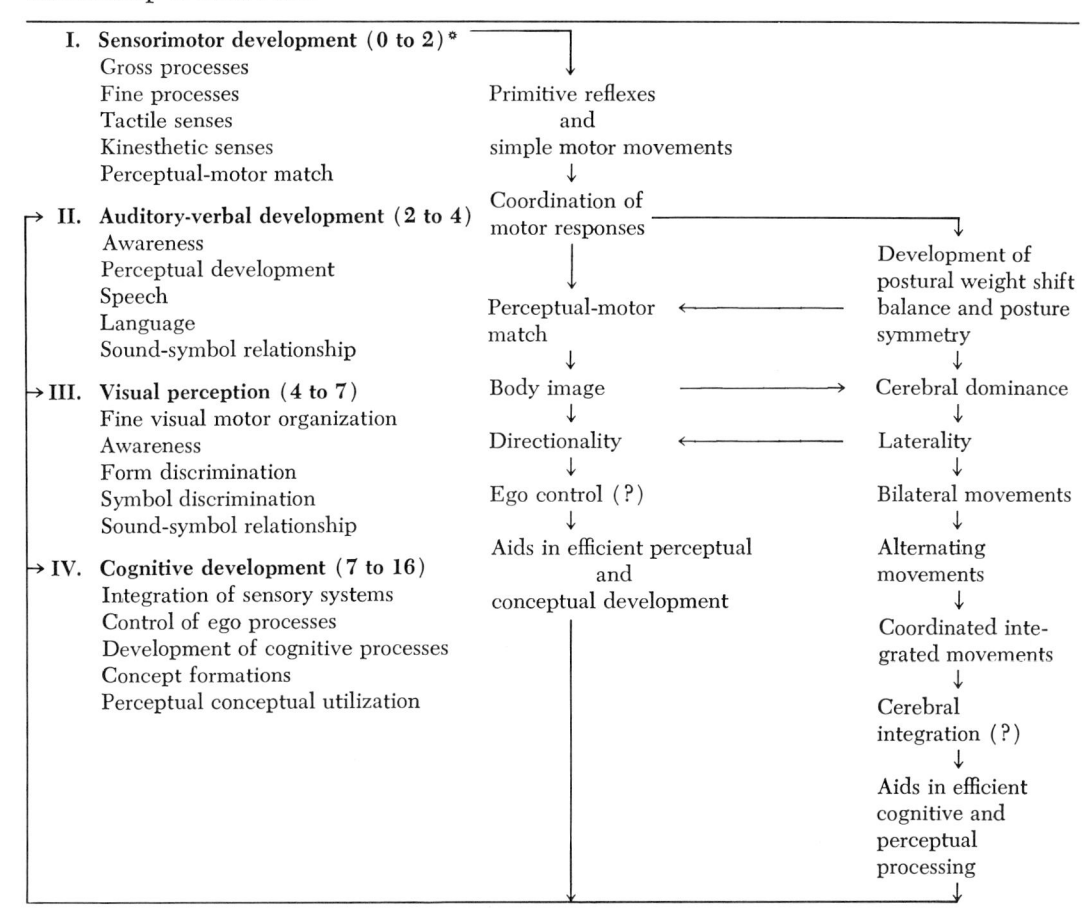

I. Sensorimotor development (0 to 2)* Gross processes Fine processes Tactile senses Kinesthetic senses Perceptual-motor match	↓ Primitive reflexes and simple motor movements ↓ Coordination of motor responses ↓	
II. Auditory-verbal development (2 to 4) Awareness Perceptual development Speech Language Sound-symbol relationship	↓ Perceptual-motor ← match ↓	Development of postural weight shift balance and posture symmetry ↓
III. Visual perception (4 to 7) Fine visual motor organization Awareness Form discrimination Symbol discrimination Sound-symbol relationship	Body image → ↓ Directionality ← ↓ Ego control (?) ↓ Aids in efficient perceptual and conceptual development	Cerebral dominance ↓ Laterality ↓ Bilateral movements ↓ Alternating movements ↓
IV. Cognitive development (7 to 16) Integration of sensory systems Control of ego processes Development of cognitive processes Concept formations Perceptual conceptual utilization		Coordinated integrated movements ↓ Cerebral integration (?) ↓ Aids in efficient cognitive and perceptual processing ↓

*Numbers refer to mental ages when development has priority. Left column presents the major process being emphasized for development in each age span. The two columns to the right are interrelated. They show the details of sensorimotor development and how ego control and cerebral integration are cognate to the efficient development of auditory-verbal, visual, and cognitive processes.

prehension develops. After creeping and crawling the infant is walking. These are the more obvious gross perceptual-motor tasks learned. In a more subtle way the infant is actually developing a motor pattern that will enable him eventually to control and to work better with incoming stimuli. The goal of motor development is not only to learn to use all the muscles in a coordinated fashion but also to form a balanced, stable base or body platform; from this base the child can perceptually receive stimuli in such a way that he can depend on his accurately perceiving the stimulus as it actually is. What is needed is perceptual constancy and certainty in terms of the perceptual input of symbols. He should reach a point where he can count on his perceptual system telling him every time he looks at a "b" that it is a "b" and not a "d," "p," or "q."

If the child is to accurately receive and organize information from the world about him, he himself must be organized or structured internally. Evidence of this internal structure is noted when the child can perform integrated motor movements and retain his postural balance in so doing.[13] This ability level may not be reached until the child is 5 years old. Constancy (accurate perception) of sensory input is needed if the child is to build an apperceptive mass and mental content that has any degree of efficiency and certainty of its accuracy. In addition, an accurate perceptual-motor match is needed to be able to do the motor movement that he perceptually realizes he should do; for example, he should be able to control the movement of his hand and fingers to copy a design accurately with a pencil.

It is our belief that basic body symmetry in terms of postural control is usually acquired by the age of 6 months. Symmetry and postural weight-shift ability are fundamental to developing an adequate motor base on which perceptual input and information can be structured. The first level of gross motor coordination is the bilateral level, where both sides of the body do approximately the same thing at the same time. This movement can be seen in the baby who moves both arms or both legs at the same time. A more complicated bilateral movement performed by a child 3 to 4 years old is the side-straddle hop or jumping jacks exercise. Alternating laterality occurs when the two-sided movement is broken down into the ability to control movement on one side of the body at a time and, also, to alternate or transfer that movement to the other side of the body. Creeping and crawling are alternating lateral movements, as are marching, hopscotch, and hopping games in older children. The integrated laterality level is reached when the two sides of the body can either do different things at the same time or work together and help each other. Skipping is an integrated movement, as are using scissors to cut out a pattern on paper held by the opposite hand, stringing beads, and other manipulatory activities.

Laterality refers to the neurologically preferred sidedness, such as being right handed, right footed, and right eyed. It is an internal preference of handedness, footedness, and eyedness and not merely a knowledge of "rights" and "lefts." It entails the preferential use of one side of the body in tasks demanding the use of only one hand, one foot, or one eye. This type of sidedness is thought to be conducive to establishing cerebral dominance, which in turn, is thought to be needed for an efficient processing of the neural structures related to cognition.

Directionality, or left-right orientation ability, is an inner awareness of outer directional movements and locations in space. It is also the ease with which the individual can project the conscious self into space, relating to rights and lefts and other directional verbalisms. It includes the ability to be able to move one's self in the appropriate direction. For example, it is necessary to develop directionality to keep from reading such words as *was, on,* and *but* backward.

Body image, the identification of size, shape, and parts of the body, comes about the age of 2½ years. Laterality develops during the next three years so that handedness is usually well established in a 4-year-old. Directionality stems from good laterality, maturing and increasing in sophisticated use as laterality also matures. The child of 6 years of age should be able to tell his left and right sides of the body. The 7-year-old should be able to cross the midline of his body and perform in the proper manner when directed to "touch your left knee with your right hand."

Auditory-verbal development

The infant makes distinct vocal sounds early in life, but it is not until he begins to listen to sounds and seeks to repeat them

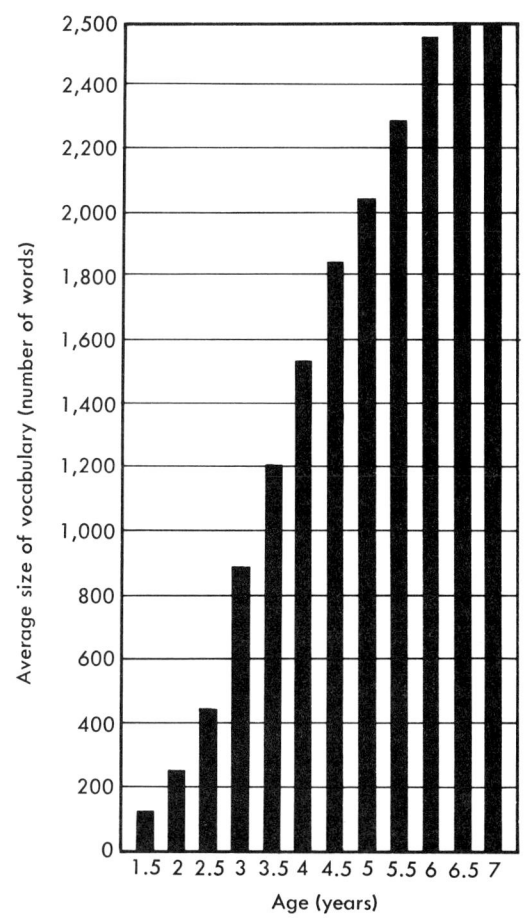

Fig. 6-2. Average vocabulary size at various ages. Ten sample groups of children were used in the study. (Modified from Lenneberg, E. H.: The biological foundations of language, New York, 1967, John Wiley & Sons, Inc.)

that he is ready to get meaning from them. At the age of 1½ to 2 years the child can make, understand, and discriminate between many but not all sounds. More significantly, he says and uses words to communicate. Between the ages of 2 and 4 or 5 years language develops at a rapid pace, and vocabulary building is an important activity (Fig. 6-2). The 2-year-old asks, "What is that?" He wants to know what do you call that, what is its name? The 4-year-old asks, "Why is that?" He is now seeking to improve his cognition level by gaining more understanding about how things work.

Lack of auditory stimulation or verbal development during this age period will have dire effects on the child when he is taught how to read at school. He will have difficulty in discriminating between letter sounds and so will have trouble with phonics. Faulty hearing, even a marginal loss of 15 decibels in the middle and higher frequencies, can also cause a deficiency in learning to read. It is necessary for a child to develop auditory awareness (listening), auditory memory to remember what he heard, auditory discrimination to be able to tell differences in sounds, auditory perception to know what the sounds mean, and sound-symbol relationships or auditory-visual integration to be able to relate and connect what he sees with what he hears.

Fine visual-motor organization and perception

The neonate is believed to be able visually to discriminate enough to separate what he sees into individual objects or figures rather than to consider them as one mass. This ability to perceive figures from ground is especially true if the objects are moving. The infant has this capability even though his eyes do not appear to focus. Gross visual and motor-coordinated movements occur when the infant begins to reach out to grasp objects. By the age of 2 years the child has fairly good gross control, but his finer visual-motor coordination patterns still need to be developed.

Between the ages of 3½ and 7 years the child emphasizes the development of visual perception and visual-motor coordination and dexterity. The 2-year-old can match a circle, square, and triangle to similar holes in a form board, provided the forms are lined up, such as having the circle next to the cutout hole of the circle in the form board. The average child of 3 years should easily match the forms to the holes, even if the form board has been turned around. The 4-year-old should be able to discriminate among a larger number of shapes, and the 5-year-old should have little difficulty picking out the item that is different in a series of pictures or symbols, such as letters.

Finer visual-motor coordination begins to develop when the infant learns to make use of his finger and thumb to pick up a small object that he is observing. He can do this at about 10 months of age. When it comes to controlling and guiding a crayon over paper, however, he still has much maturing to do before he can make effective use of it. At the age of 18 months the average infant will just make a haphazard line or mark on the paper—there is no rhyme or reason to it. The marking is mostly accidental. By 2 years old the child can control the crayon enough to scribble predominately in an up-and-down (vertical) direction. At 2½ years he can scribble in a side-to-side (horizontal) direction. He can copy a single vertical line at the age of 3 years. In fact, the average 3-year-old can control the crayon enough to move it in a circular movement and bring the ends together. It is not until the child is 5 years old that he can copy right angles and draw a square. He should be able to stay within narrow lines with a pencil. The average 5-year-old can print his name, but he usually "draws" each letter instead of writing or printing it smoothly. The average 6-year-old cannot copy a diamond; it takes a mental age of 7 years before a child has enough motor control to make acute angles and reverse directions. (See Fig. 6-3.)

Ocular control is a developmental area that we believe should receive more attention than it does from parents, educators, and psychologists. Complex form perception and discrimination require a high level of coordination because tiny muscles are involved. Eyes (through the brain) must learn to see visual intricacies of form just as legs and body must learn the intricacies of walking. Children who have eyes that are not working together often learn to suppress the vision in one eye so that an image is not double. The problem is that visual input may then become sporadic, since the child intermittently makes use of the suppressed eye and visual perception becomes inconsistent.

Children 6 years of age and under are generally farsighted. As a result, much of what they see at near point, such as reading material, may be seen indistinctly. A 5-year-old should be able to track a moving target, up and down, side to side, in a circle, and diagonally. The child should be able to fixate on a target and visually hold on to it as it is moved. If his eyes dart ahead, lag behind, or lose contact completely, he is in visual trouble.

Concluding thought

There can be no cognitive development without sensory input. There can be no efficient, effective perceptual development to provide the sensory input to the brain without a stable, balanced body position from which the senses can pick up stimuli with any degree of accuracy. There can be no stable point of reference within the body from which perceptual constancy can take place without a sound motor structure on which perceptual systems can develop. Gesell points out the sequence by which this development takes place; Hebb suggests what happens neurologically; and Piaget provides the theory that suggests how cognitive development starts with the sensorimotor period. Piaget's ideas are presented in the next section.

COGNITIVE DEVELOPMENT

The dominant mental activity of the child during the sensorimotor period is one of overt actions as evidenced by his outward behavior and his direct interaction with the environment. Apparently little internal intellectualizing is done until close

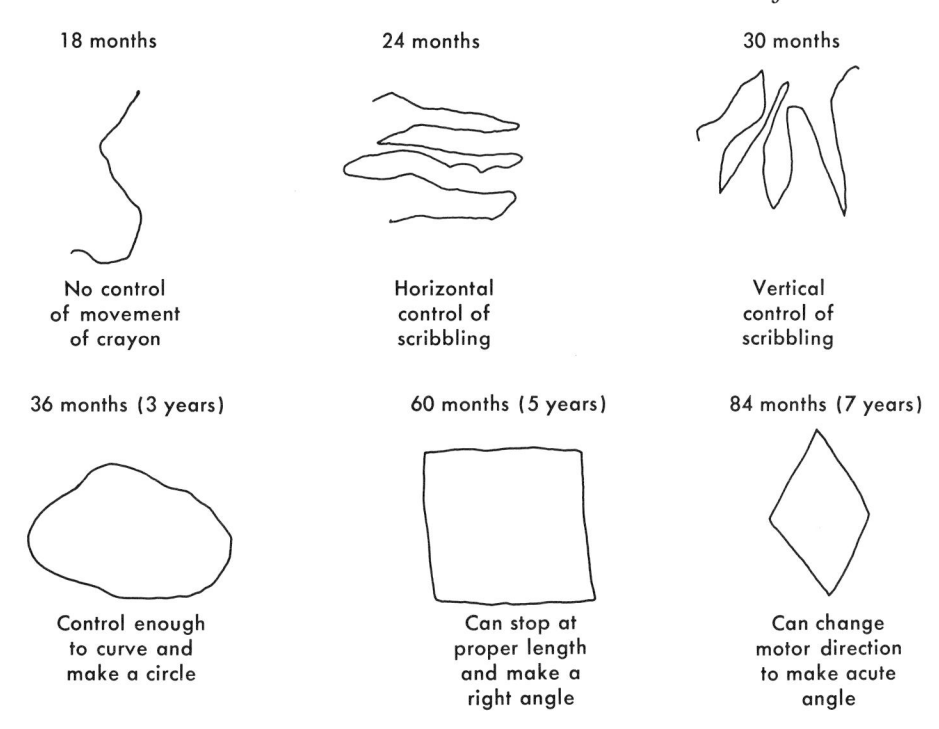

18 months	24 months	30 months
No control of movement of crayon	Horizontal control of scribbling	Vertical control of scribbling
36 months (3 years)	60 months (5 years)	84 months (7 years)
Control enough to curve and make a circle	Can stop at proper length and make a right angle	Can change motor direction to make acute angle

Fig. 6-3. Development of perceptual-motor control in children. Ages refer to mental ages.

to the end of the sensorimotor period. During the second period of cognitive development, the *preoperational stage*, it will be noted that the dominant mental activities of the child change from overt actions to perceptions whereby symbols are used to represent the environment. During this preoperational period there will be increasingly differentiating internalization of verbal and nonverbal symbols.[14] The child will be able to make internal responses (mediations) that represent objects or events, even if they are not present.

Preoperational thought

The second broad period of cognitive development begins at approximately 2 years of age and is known as the period of *preoperational thought*. It lasts until approximately the age of 7 years. The most significant characteristic associated with this period is egocentrism, which refers to the child's inability to realize the point of view of another person on the same problem. His thoughts are centered within himself and his own ideas.

The first two years of this period (until about the age of 4 years) are known as the *preconceptual stage*, during which the child begins to associate certain objects as being representative of other objects. He begins to indulge in symbolic play. He thinks of his toy gun or even a stick as a real gun and of his tricycle as a racing car or fire engine. He frequently talks to himself or to his toys, even in the presence of others. His conversations are associated with his immediate activity, such as asking his truck, "Did you haul in that load of logs that you were supposed to bring?" Physical cause-and-effect relationships or conceptions of the world and nature are of little interest to him at this age.[15]

From approximately 4 to 7 years of age the child progresses through the next phase of preoperational thought, which is known as the period of *intuitive thought*. During this time he begins to think more complexly and he elaborates his concepts more. His egocentrism tends to be replaced by social interaction and social signs. He becomes more flexible in the use of language and begins to use the word "because" spontaneously, thus making simple associations between ideas.[16] He is now able to group objects together into classes according to his own perception of their aspects of similarity. He refrains from talking aloud to himself to any degree and, instead, resorts to covert speech while manipulating an object or a toy. The function of language begins to take on the purpose of communicating his thought to other people as he strives to make his hearers listen and contrives to influence them.

As for his perception of the world about him, Piaget noticed that in earlier stages the child had no image either of himself or of the external world as such. However, with the emergence of symbolic thinking, his egocentricity induces him to draw for himself highly specific images of himself and of environmental objects. He is likely to ask many questions concerning various phenomena. He begins to have definite perceptions of various situations but can only take into account one idea or dimension at a time. This characteristic is called *centering* and implies that the child's attention is centered on one detail of the event. He cannot see variations, but a single, salient part of an event can be influential. This child cannot cope intellectually with problems concerning time, space, causality, measurement, numbers, quantity, movement, and velocity.[17] He merely understands these things in simple, concrete situations. He is certain that everything is just as it appears.

Preoperational thought tends to be animistic and artificialistic. Consequently, the child of this age thinks of inanimate objects as having human powers such as thinking, feeling with emotion, and desiring. His observations are allied somewhat in terms of movement. Hence any object that to him seems to have movement is considered to be conscious or alive. In this respect the sun, moon, stars, clouds, rivers, winds, fire, carts, and so on are all regarded as conscious.[18] The words "because" and "since" increase in his vocabulary. If he is asked to give a reason for a certain happening, he will give some coincidentally occurring characteristic such as "The sun sets because people want to go to bed." This example illustrates *intuitive thought*. The child is becoming aware of the cause-and-effect relationship principle.

As for discerning his right hand from his left, tests have indicated that a child is usually able to do this at the age of 5 years. At this age right and left are only names for him; the age of correct orientation for himself is approximately 6 years.[19] The concept of relativity of left and right in connection with other objects, including lefts and rights of another person, does not emerge until the age of 8 years.

Concept formations

According to Piaget's theory of cognitive development, a child does not begin to internalize verbal images until sometime after the age of 2 years. After that age his language development provides him with words that will represent objects and events in his environment. At first these words apparently have no other use than merely to provide a means or way of indicating "What is that?" The child is learning the labels (words) by asking, "How do you call that?" Later, about the age of 4 years, he is more interested in "What makes it go?" and "Why?" Thus he indicates that he is beginning to use words as mediators for reasoning. As a result of this gradual development of understanding, many concepts learned by the child before the age of 5 years have only "surface" meanings, with no depth of insight or relationships to other concepts.

Concepts of time are rather vague in early childhood. The child cannot tell time by a clock much before the age of 6 or 7 years, and he has no idea of the length of time in terms of minutes, hours, days, weeks, and so forth. By associating specific activities such as "Daddy comes home after my TV program," he can make some estimates if he has been told the time involved. By the age of 4 or 5 years, most children can learn what day of the week it is. They will not know the month, season, or year before the age of 6 years unless they were specifically taught that concept.[20]

Numbers mean little to young children. At first they learn the concept "one." For a good while afterward any amount or quantity more than one is always "two." A person can usually tell when the child has learned "half" because when asked his age, he will often say, "Four and a half" if he is past his fourth birthday. Children ages 3 to 5 years can be taught the meanings of the numbers one to five, but they will have only vague concepts about numbers above that.[21]

Concepts of space and size develop more readily. At a mental age of 3 years a child can select the largest and the smallest objects from a group of objects of varying sizes. Selecting middle-sized objects or in-between variations of size in sequential order does not occur until the age of 5 years.[22] When shown two lines of different length, the 3-year-old can also select correctly in answer to, "Which one is shorter?" This child can also answer the question, "Which one has more?" but he cannot do such a simple intellectual task as realizing that the liquid poured from a wide, squatty glass into a narrow tall glass is the same amount. Until the child learns that different materials have different weights, he is likely to estimate weight in terms of size. The 5-year-old can make some differentiations.

Profile: concepts of a 4-year-old

It is at about the age of 4 and 5 years that a child no longer completely relies on sensory equipment to learn about things. He can now use his language to satisfy his curiosity by asking question upon question. Sometimes the questions may be asked to get attention, but soon enough he really wants to know.

Questions about life and death are frequent. Although he cannot fully understand the meaning of death, it is necessary to try and answer his questions within his experience and level of understanding. Our 4-year-old son accepted the death of his pet goldfish easily because he felt the fish was old and ready to die. When it comes to the thought of himself dying or someone close to him dying, he becomes very disturbed. The sooner he is given short and practical answers that he can understand, the less disturbed he is.

Our son reacts to those things that have meaning for him. However, he needs an experience to develop realistic concepts. Since his experiences are limited, he will create experiences to relate to a realistic concept. Apparently our boy feels the need to create an experience in his imaginary play dealing with birth. He has a toy horse that he can ride and crawl under. He loves to pretend the horse is his mother and that he is the baby horse that came from the mother's belly. While he is trying to provide a realistic experience about birth to gain a realistic concept, he may also be relieving some of the tension he must be feeling because he cannot understand the whole complicated idea of birth. His reasoning tends to explain things by "magical" or mysterious forces.

His spatial relationships are just now beginning to have meaning for him. He understands that adults are taller than he. He knows he cannot reach the sky. He likes to make himself bigger by standing on a chair or sitting on an adult's shoulders. Touching the ceiling is a great feat.

Although he can say his numbers up to nine and recognize their symbols, he still cannot relate a number to a set of objects consisting of that number. He does not understand the sixness of six or the fiveness of five. In fact, he cannot count to nine while touching successive objects up to nine.

Another interesting factor about the 4- and 5-year-old's intellectual development is his sense of time. At this particular age his time sense is just beginning to develop. Our son knows that after he eats lunch he must rest. He knows that during suppertime "Lassie" is on the television. He can tell you that he was born on the eighth of March. He does not know how long he will rest or how long the "Lassie" program will last. He does not make any connection between his birthday and other happenings or holidays in the year. Any important event, such as a tonsillectomy in our son's case, that occurred in the past week or so may seem ages ago to him. In fact, when we asked him how long ago it was that he was in the hospital, he said it was not a real long time ago, only three months ago. Actually, it was only one week ago.

DEVELOPMENT OF LANGUAGE

During the early childhood years, the development of language and thought is one of the child's most important accomplishments. The development of true language ability (Table 6-3) begins when the child is about 2 years old. By the time he is 5 years old he is usually proficient in his speech and is capable of using an amazing number of words. This time of life can be a bit trying for parents, since the child seems to ask an inexhaustible number of questions; the child wants to know "what?" and "why?" about everything. Later development of language is related, almost inseparably, to the child's ability to think. Language makes it possible for a child to put thoughts and feelings into words. The better his language ability the better he can make clear to himself what he knows.

By 2 years of age a child may know as many as 100 words. By 2½ years most children use twice as many words as they did at 2 years, and by 3 years they can generally use twice as many as at 2½ years. Although this rate of learning does slow down somewhat, the child often learns fifty new words a month until he is 4½ years old.[23] A child may spend a good amount of time whispering words to himself. He seems to do this for the pure enjoyment of making and using the sounds he has just learned.

By the time a child is 3 years old he starts using the vocabulary and language skills that he has been developing. The 3-year-old may often seem to talk continuously with hardly a pause for a breath! This gives the child practice, and usually by the time he is 3½ years old articulation has greatly improved. The mispronunciations used in baby talk are generally gone; however, grammatical constructions still leave much to be desired. A sentence such as, "I'm busy, I'm the mostest busy" is typical of this age.[24]

Initially a child's vocabulary consists mainly of nouns, although he will use a few verbs, adjectives, or adverbs. In the beginning the child hardly ever uses pronouns, conjunctions, and prepositions. The relativism of pronouns may cause problems for the young child. He may call himself "you" and someone else "I." Much of his vocabulary is learned by hearing words in context. Along with an increase in vocabulary he is also learning grammar and syntax. His grammar is anything but flawless, however. It is not uncommon to hear him say things like "I bringed" or "I walk homed."

The child's language is now a social skill. He learns how to communicate his complex feelings and motivations to others. He uses language to solve problems he formerly solved by physical means. He remembers, generalizes, and reproduces former experiences through words and applies them in the context of the present situation.

Questions at 5 years of age are fewer and more relevant than they were at 4 years. He now asks questions for information and not merely for practice in the art of speaking. Parents tend to be less annoyed by his

Table 6-3. Pattern of normal language development in expressive speech and comprehension of speech*

AGE	EXPRESSION	COMPREHENSION
1 to 2 years	Uses 1 to 3 words at 12 months, 10 to 15 at 15 months, 15 to 20 at 18 months, about 100 to 200 by 2 years. Knows names of most objects he uses. Names few people, uses verbs but not correctly with subjects. Jargon and echolalia. Names 1 to 3 pictures.	Begins to relate symbol and object meaning. Adjusts to comments. Inhibits on command. Responds correctly to "give me that," "sit down," "stand up," with gestures. Puts watch to ear on command. Understands simple questions. Recognizes 120 to 275 words.
2 to 3 years	Vocabulary increases to 300 to 500 words. Says "where kitty" "ball all gone," "want cookie," "go bye bye car." Jargon mostly gone, vocalizing increases. Has fluency trouble. Speech not adequate for communication needs.	Rapid increase in comprehension vocabulary to 400 at 2½ years, 800 at 3 years. Responds to commands using "on," "under," "up," "down," "over there," "bye," "run," "walk," "jump up," "throw," "run fast," "be quiet," and commands containing two related actions.
3 to 4 years	Uses 600 to 1,000 words; becomes conscious of speech. Uses 3 to 4 words per speech response. Personal pronouns, some adjectives, adverbs, and prepositions appear. Mostly simple sentences, but some complex. Speech more useful.	Understands up to 1,500 words by age 4 years. Recognizes plurals, sex difference, pronouns, adjectives. Comprehends complex and compound sentences. Answers simple questions.
4 to 5 years	Increase in vocabulary to 1,100 to 1,600 words. More 3- to 4-syllable words, more adjectives, adverbs, prepositions, and conjunctions. Articles appear. Uses 4-, 5-, and 6-word sentences; syntax quite good. Uses plurals. Fluency improves. Proper nouns decrease, pronouns increase.	Comprehends from 1,500 to 2,000 words. Carries out more complex commands, with 2 to 3 actions. Understands dependent clause, "if," "because," "when," "why."
5 to 6 years	Increase in vocabulary to 1,500 to 2,100 words. Complete 5- to 6-word sentences, compound, complex, with some dependent clauses. Syntax near normal. Quite fluent. More multisyllable words.	Understands vocabulary of 2,500 to 2,800 words. Responds correctly to more complicated sentences but is still confused at times by involved sentences.

*Modified from Miller, G. A.: Language and communication, New York, 1951, McGraw-Hill Book Co., pp. 140-157.

questions because they are more meaningful than they were at the age of 4 years.

PSYCHOSOCIAL DEVELOPMENT

As with the other aspects of growth and development in the early childhood, social and emotional maturity are still in a beginning budding stage. The 2-year-old receives considerable attention from those around him. However, he has been so busy learning how to control his motor processes and how to make his needs known that he has not had time to learn the social and emotional skills necessary for smooth interaction with others.

Social development and play (Table 6-4)

The 2-year-old child is an egocentric person. At this stage he takes, others give. He is possessive and believes himself to be the most important person in the universe because that is how he is treated by those close to him. He will become concerned with others, learn his limitations, and de-

Table 6-4. Developmental sequences of play activities from 15 months to 5 years*

AGE	PLAY ACTIVITIES
15 months	Endless exercise of walking activities Throws and picks up objects Puts objects in and out of receptacles
18 months	Rapid shifts in attention; moves actively and "gets into" everything Pulls toy Carries or hugs doll or teddy bear Imitates many things as reading paper, dusting, etc. Solitary or onlooker play
2 years	Less rapid attention shifts; manipulates play material by patting, pounding Interest in dolls and teddy bears (domestic mimicry), strings beads, transports blocks in wagon Imitates things and events present to his senses Parallel play although he obviously enjoys being with other children Little social give-and-take Does not ask for help; adult must be constantly watchful and ready to assist without waiting to be asked
3 years	Dramatization and imagination begin to enter into play Interest in combining playthings such as blocks and cars Increasing interest in playing with other children; may play in groups of two or three but these are always shifting in makeup and activity Will put away toys with some supervision
4 years	Considerable increase in constructive use of materials and in manipulation and dramatization of play Has very complicated ideas but is unable to carry them out in detail and has no carry-over from day to day Prefers to play in groups of two or three Suggests turns but is often bossy Puts away toys by himself Likes to dress up
5 years	Very fond of cutting out and pasting Likes to work on specific project that is carried over from day to day Plays in groups of two to five Friendships are becoming stronger Spurred on in activity by rivalry

*Modified from Gesell, A., et al.: The first five years of life, New York, 1940, Harper & Row, Publishers, p. 251.

velop into a socialized person, but only after he has received some training and has had more social experiences with other children.

The child's companions at this time are usually adults of the family, brothers and sisters, and a few children from the immediate neighborhood. His social world is that of his immediate environment. Because the first social group for a child is his family, that group plays an important role in establishing his attitudes and habits. It also influences his approach to the other groups with which he will come in contact as he grows older. With each succeeding year his interest in playmates of his own age increases, and with this comes a decrease in interest in adult associations.

Negativism is a form of behavior by which the child shows his resistance to adult authority by being self-assertive and independent. The child is said to be "stubborn and quite difficult to manage." This behavior reaches a peak at 2½ to 3 years. It

Table 6-5. Development of social play and concept of possession

AGE	TYPE OF SOCIAL PLAY	CONCEPT OF POSSESSION
2 years	Isolated or solitary play	"What's mine is mine; what's yours is mine"
3 years	Parallel play alongside	"What's mine is mine; what's yours is yours"
4 years	Begins associative group play (50% to 60%)	"What's mine is mine; but you can play with it sometimes"
5 years	Cooperative socialized play (75% to 80%)	"What's mine is mine; you can have it anytime I don't want it"

is so common at this age that it may be regarded as normal. Negativism may result from aggressive use of discipline, intolerant attitudes on the part of adults, or aggressive behavior by a child who has not learned to curb his primitive, self-assertive impulses.

The 2-year-old also becomes increasingly aware of people and at the same time goes through a period of being shy with strangers, especially adults. There is the desire to hide from them by burying the head in the mother's lap, hiding behind a piece of furniture, or refusing to speak. How pronounced this will be depends on the opportunities that the child has had to come into contact with different people and environments.

At the beginning of the second year the child prefers solitary play to parallel play (playing alongside another child) and seldom plays cooperatively. He is in the precooperative stage, watching what others are doing rather than participating. By the age of 2½ years, however, most children enjoy parallel play with another child. They may be together, but each plays or does whatever he likes. There is no interaction with other children even when their activity is the same. The 2-year-old has not learned to share or take turns yet, and problems arise when the two children want to play with the same toy. This is the period of everything being "mine" and little understanding of "yours." It is a good idea for an adult to stay close by when the children are playing because kicking, pulling hair, and snatching of toys from one another may take place (Table 6-5).

The 3-year-old has become a bit more mature in his play activity. There is an increase in social play because this child has increased his ability to control his body movements, to handle objects, and to talk. He is now beginning to understand what it means to take turns and he likes to play simple games with others. By the end of this year children begin to impersonate adults near and dear to them.

When a child reaches 4 years of age, he wants to become involved in associative play. He is more mature mentally and physically and can participate in cooperative activities. Furthermore, he is ready to learn social patterns. He gets satisfaction from playing with other children and in many cases is rewarded for having friendly and outgoing responses. Four-year-olds will play with others for about half their playtime.

When children encounter frustrating experiences with one another, they will argue. Boys tend to be more violent and participate in more physical attacks than girls. On the whole, however, 4- and 5-year-olds are more friendly and cooperative than uncooperative. Competitiveness appears around the age of 3 to 4 years. By the time the child is 5 years old he is competing vigorously with other children.

The young child who has no real playmates will often create an imaginary playmate or pet. The child derives much pleasure from playing with his imaginary playmates, since this relationship fills a gap in his social development. Parents may have to go along with this imaginary playmate even to the extent of setting an extra plate at the table "for my friend, Charlie." This interest in imaginative playmates can begin as early as 2½ years of age. Imagination and imaginary play reach a peak at about 3½ or 4 years, but it is not unusual for a 5-year-old to have an imaginary playmate. Probably all imaginative life in the child satisfies some inner need for companionship, someone to look up to, or someone to boss.[25]

The 5-year-old is very good at playing. It is one of the things he can do best. His imagination is not used as much as it was previously because his play activity is more practical in nature. He will want to play with others about 80% of the time. The 5-year-old is greatly interested in his home and acts out this interest by playing "house," being mother or father, playing "doctor," or "going to the store." Both boys and girls enter into this home-centered dramatic play. A 5-year-old boy has not yet established his definite sex role and does not mind this type of activity. He will be willing to be mother, baby, or any other character. He, like most 5-year-olds, has an interest in babies and dolls.

The age of 5 years is that delightful stage when one takes life as it comes. The child's life problems are restricted in scope and easy for him to handle. His parents find him a joy to have around the house. He is extremely helpful; he is usually within earshot; and he keeps his parents posted about his activities by asking permission.

Under normal circumstances a 5-year-old boy will display a particularly warm attachment to his mother.[26] He is most concerned if he cannot find her when he comes in from play. He wants a close working relationship with her and constant assurance of her approval. When things go wrong, he wants her physical and spiritual medication. He likes her to talk with him, to explain things, and to tell him about the exciting and mysterious things in life.

All this may be disturbing to a father, but it is only a characteristic of the age. The attachment to the mother will lessen in a year or so. The love of a 5-year-old son for his father can be perfectly normal, and still he will call on his mother when trouble arises. A girl will also depend rather heavily on her mother at this age, but she will also display a warm attachment to her father.

Emotions and behavior

Emotions seen in a simple form in infants change by the age of 2 years, when significant conditioning begins to take place. The infant is egocentric, but the early childhood child shows more responsiveness to the environment. With this involvement comes a change of emphasis from the child's inner world, with its sensations and desires, to an outer world. The eventual outcome is a transfiguration in personality. New contacts and experiences increase the child's chances of emotional stimulation. As the child's awareness of his surroundings increases, so does his capacity for emotional response. Not only is the child influenced by his immediate environment but also by his anticipation of future events. Even though emotional development of the 3-, 4-, or 5-year-old has extended far beyond infancy, it is important to remember that this child is still a baby in many respects. He still depends highly on his parents for emotional support.

At the preschool level children's fears are associated more with imaginary, anticipated, and supernatural dangers rather than with fears of actual objects or unusual stimuli, as is the case in infants. For the most part the frequency and intensity of overt signs of fear decrease with age. Crying reactions diminish, although characteristic facial expressions remain.

Frederic Lewis, Inc., New York City.

Early childhood is the time when personal-social experience, such as the addition of a member to the family, begins to have an influence on the child's emotional responses. When the new baby comes, jealousy builds up in the preschooler because he feels deprived of attention and affection. This reaction does not always occur, but it is a common characteristic when the child is the firstborn and has been accustomed to having the full attention of his parents. Because the new baby is showered with so much attention, the older child feels neglected. The young child is too immature to comprehend the need for changes in his life that the arrival of a new baby will bring. It must be realized that a certain amount of jealousy in any child is normal, whether it is jealousy of the baby, older brothers or sisters, or even of the mother or father. Love and affection freely given to the 4- and 5-year-old can go far in counteracting the negative effects of deep-seated jealousy.

Anger is a complex emotion because it takes different forms at different age levels. The child of 4 and 5 years outgrows the tantrums of kicking, pounding, and screaming because he can now translate his anger and frustration into words. He often begins to threaten and yell at other children at this age. The 4-year-old usually directs his anger to the object causing the frustration. For example, a boy may blame a chair for causing him to trip and spill his milk rather than put the blame on his own clumsiness. Children of this age tend to remain frustrated and angry for longer periods of time now, but they begin to find ways to keep from showing their anger to other persons. If they are not given the opportunity to get rid of their fears and angers, they may become cruel and hostile to someone else. They may want to inflict self-punishment or pain and finally develop psychosomatic and neurotic tendencies.[27] One of the best ways for a child to get rid of frustration, fear, anger, and guilty feelings is by creative art work such as painting, using clay, or pounding wood and by playing out the fears that are real and imaginary.

ORGANIZATION OF PERSONALITY

Up to the age of 2½ years the personality of the infant has been a natural development with the emergence of behavior characteristics that nature provides for the child to help him promote his own well-being and survival. The infant developed through stages where he sequentially emphasized physical dependence, control of body movements, physiological pleasures, self-display, curiosity and exploration, imitation of verbalisms, and, by 2½ years, self-assertiveness.

During the phase of self-assertiveness the infant is reminded in many ways by his parents that "this is not the way you are supposed to act." The child becomes amenable and is willing to learn new ways of behaving. Between the ages of 2½ to 4 years or so the child learns to control his primary nature forces, drives, and impulses. He also develops a behavior pattern that will reflect the influence of secondary external elements on his personality development. The social and emotional atmosphere and environment of the 3- to 5-year-olds are extremely important because both overt and covert aspects of personality are being crystallized.

Duplication of behavior

The temper tantrums of the twos and the general conflict that exists between parent and child at this time give way to a child who now says, "Maybe I really wasn't ready to be on my own yet. I guess there is more to be learned." So as he approaches being a 3-year-old, he reverts to a learning technique that he had used earlier. He makes use of imitation again. However, this time instead of imitating speech and language, he replicates the behavior and actions of others. In a way he is saying, "If my behavior wasn't correct when I was two, then I'll copy yours so I can learn the right way to behave." He is taking over the behavior of others, especially of his parents. The actions of his parents, for better or worse, will become his actions. He is developing standards of behavior that will be based on the actions of others who are important to him.[28]

Suggestibility of feelings

As the child moves into the "trusting threes," he allows himself not only to imitate the behavior of others but also to begin to reflect their moods, attitudes, and ideas. The child is in the phase of suggestibility. In some ways he is becoming dependent on others for the development of his mental and emotional responses. He is unconsciously absorbing their feelings and outlooks. The child tends to copy his mother or his father. If his mother is calm, cheerful, and happy, the child can become the same way; if the child responds more to the father, let us hope that he is not irritable, cynical, or selfish. Politeness, friendliness, consideration for others, patience, and moral conduct in general are all suggestible traits.

The child is not aware that he is taking over the moods and feelings of others because suggestibility is an unconscious process. If the suggestions were to be made openly and deliberately taught, the child would probably reject them. To illustrate: At a state park the swimming area was away from the bathhouses where swimmers could change clothes. To get to the lake it was necessary to walk across a road covered with gravel. A father and his boy started barefooted across the road. As he stepped on the small bits of gravel, the boy winced and said, "That hurts." "Yes, it does," replied the father and kept on walking. The little boy made a real effort to be brave like his daddy as he walked across. Another father and his boy started across the graveled road. "That hurts," cried the boy. "Oh, nonsense," said the father, "It doesn't hurt at all." As this boy stepped gingerly over the stones, you could tell by the expression on his face that he was thinking, "That does *so* hurt!" Which father provided a better example for his son? You can imagine the second boy thinking about his father, "He's either lying or else he's some kind of a superman. Either way, can I ever hope to be like him? Can I really trust him to know how I feel?"

Personality identification

The phase of suggestibility gives way to identification, in which the child takes over the entire personality of another, with all of its strengths and attributes. Personality identification is the process of accepting another person emotionally so completely that his characteristics and abilities are adopted as a person's own. The child no longer is just pretending that he is doing things "like my daddy does," but for all intents and purposes he acts as if his daddy's traits and abilities are also his own traits and abilities. The child impersonates another so completely that for the moment he *is* that person.

We know of children who identified so completely with "Superman" or "Batman" in their play that when they received costumes of these characters, the children believed that they could do what Superman and Batman did. Two children, playing in Batman costumes, jumped from the railing of a porch as they pretended to be chasing the "bad guys." Each child broke his right arm. Identification is a behavior mechanism used by people of all ages. Have you ever cried during a movie or felt "choked up inside" while reading a story or observing an event? You were identifying with an individual or a situation, and for the moment his or her circumstances were yours.

During the identification phase, the child generally responds to people whom he loves or who possess some trait or power that he admires.[29] The child gains a sense of security by identifying with an older person whom he loves, in whom he has complete confidence and trust. The older person is loved because he is lovable to the child. There is no hesitancy on the part of the child to become like that person because "he is so nice to me, and I want to be like him." When a child identifies with a person or a characterization because of the traits that individual or character possesses, the child is beginning to reach out into the world for personal characteristics that he wishes to make his own. He likes the idea of the power or ability implicit in the brave act or performance of another, and he does not mind becoming that way. With either the identification motive of love or power the child is developing a characteristic behavior or attitude that can be instrumental in setting the direction that his personality development will take. He is on the threshold of developing his own character, with behavior and attitudes that will have a tremendous influence on all of his future actions.

Beginnings of a value judgment system

As the child matures, the impact of the identification process as a motivator of behavior is lessened to the degree that the child will eliminate the personal attachment to the individual as an object of identification, although still retaining the characteristics of that person. It is no longer, "I want to be brave like my daddy." Now it is simply, "I want to be a brave boy." The traits and ideals of the person become part of the child's emerging self-ideal. A self-ideal is an integration of the values that one holds for oneself and that one seeks to realize.[30] The self-ideal becomes sort of an inner standard of behavior that is considered important enough to strive for and live by.

The self-ideal is also called the superego, the ego ideal, and the conscience. We like to consider it as a value judgment system that will eventually be highly instrumental in influencing the decisions that an individual makes as well as regulating his behavior. "I want to be brave. Brave boys don't cry, so I'll try very hard not to cry." We can imagine a 4-year-old boy with his eyes filled with tears, biting his lips as he tries so hard not to cry.

As the child incorporates a self-ideal into his personality, several things happen. He now has an "other self," which he can consider when he is making decisions about what is good or bad, important or unimportant, of interest or of no interest. He becomes more conscious and critical of his behavior in terms of its appropriateness and, as a result, seeks to control his behavior so it will be more acceptable. This function of self-criticism concerning one's behavior constitutes the essence of a conscience. It should be realized that not all children develop an adequate value system. Some children will identify with adults who have values and ideals that are too strict and severe, others with adults who tend to be too easygoing and undisciplined. Either way, these models can induce unhealthy mental patterns in children who identify with them.

The self-ideal should be such that it (1) can control the innate survival drives and impulses of the early years of life while still enabling use of their energy output and (2) makes use of an integrated, well-developed value judgment system to give direction to one's behavior. It will take many years before an individual will have an effective, competent value system, but when he does develop it, he will be considered a "mature person."

With the beginnings of a self-ideal the 4-year-old develops more self-assurance and more independence. He feels more capable because he is acting more like a "little adult." After all, he is copying their behavior; he has an organized personality that, along with his budding intellect, is enabling him to ask better questions and to make better decisions than before. He feels more independent. He likes to show off, and he asks others to watch him while he demonstrates how capable he is. He is noisy at times and is constantly into something. At Christmas time, several years ago, a mother became aware of an unusual quietness in her house. She decided she had better check on her 4-year-old to see what he was up to. She found him sitting in a chair in the living room. "What are you doing?" she asked. "Nothing," he replied, "What can I do, what with you, God, and Santa Claus watching me all the time!"

CONCEPTS OF MORALITY

At this point a concept regarding the meaning of morality and the development of a moral sense in a child will be introduced. It will be important to realize that the term *morality* has two dramatically different meanings. These meanings stem from what philosophers consider to be the two basic sources of principles, standards, or rules that indicate "right" and "wrong" in behavior.

One source of right and wrong is the individual himself or the group with whom he identifies. This source of moral standards states that right and wrong are determined by the people, individually, collectively, or in some combination of the two. Each social structure develops its own moral code. Morality, in this context, implies a conformity to the mores, customs, and rules of the particular group of people if one wants to get along with them. When in Rome, do as the Romans do! Since each group creates or determines its own values of right and wrong, each society can have its own standards of morality. This point of view concerning morality indicates that moral values can change and can differ from group to group and that there is no constant truth. Philosophically, this interpretation of morality is known as relativism.

The other source of morality is believed by some philosophers to be inherent in the very nature of the universe itself. Just as there are physical (scientific) laws that are the same the world over, so are there behavioral (moral) laws that are universal and eternal. All men everywhere are subjected to these laws, whether they agree with them or not, whether they are even aware of them or not, just as they are bound to the cause-and-effect relationships of the scientific laws. Man does not create these laws; he discovers them. Just as science reveals physical laws, so do philosophy and theology reveal moral laws. Man's social experiences throughout the ages of history may make him aware of certain standards of conduct that are intrinsically good. This awareness may come in the form of social evolution, but ultimately man learns that these principles always were good for men everywhere, at any time, under any condition. As such, the principles are universal and eternal. Philosophically, this interpretation of morality as universal principles is known as absolutism.

As early as 18 months of age, a child will drop and run away from an object that he should not have taken. He is inhibited in his behavior by his mother's "no, no." At 2 years of age he associates being good with routine duties well performed, and at 3 years of age he tries to please and conform by asking, "Do it this way?" By the age of 4 years he begins to understand about "rules," although he is not always capable of following them. He may begin to have a considerable interest in God but may ask many inappropriate questions about Him. The 5-year-old often believes that God is responsible for everything, yet the child's sense of goodness and badness is pretty much limited to things the parents permit or forbid.[31]

The development of a moral sense of some sort in the child is inevitable. The elements of imitation, suggestibility, and identification indicate that the child will pick up some kind of a moral consciousness. The nature of that moral sense, whether it be heavily loaded in the direction of relativism or absolutism, will be largely determined by the child's models and environment. Moral insight of an abstract nature will not come to the child for several years yet, however.

It is possible that a child may constantly be placed on his own in a highly unstructured situation where he is given no clues as to what he should think in terms of right and wrong. Some parents want their child to "decide for himself what he wants to believe." Such a child may eventually develop a morality or identity crisis because he has few or no guidelines to follow.

STUDY GUIDE

1. Review the developmental tasks for this age level. Compare them to the developmental tasks of the infant as mentioned in Chapter 4. What advancements in development and behavior are required?
2. Trace motor development from the age of 2½ to 5 years. Note how gross motor and fine motor skills improve in a relatively few years.
3. The ages of 2 to 5 years are extremely important years for the development of perceptual processes of learning. Consider the following:
   a. Review the information on the perceptual process as it was presented in Chapter 1 in the discussion of the central nervous system and in Chapter 4 in the discussion of cognitive development. Relate all of that information to development of the perceptual pattern for learning as presented in this chapter.
   b. Can you relate any of Piaget's ideas, as presented in Chapter 4 on the sensorimotor operations period, to the sensorimotor processes discussed in this chapter?
   c. Why is auditory-verbal development at this age level so crucial in terms

of future learning ability and potential?
   d. Consider a child who is 5 years of age. What would be his fine visual-motor capabilities? What would he normally be able to do?
4. Discuss the characteristics of Piaget's preoperational thought period and its manifestations in concepts formulated during that age bracket.
5. What are the social characteristics of the 3- to 5-year-old?
6. Make a chart showing in one column the stages of personality development found in ages 3 to 5 years, and in a second column, present the features or characteristics of each stage of personality development. When finished, compare your chart to Table 5-3 to note the different emphasis in the type of personality being developed.
7. Define the two basic sources of moral principles or standards. Give illustrations of each type as you note them in today's society and within your age group in particular. What do you think?

REFERENCES

1. Gardner, D. B.: Development in early childhood, New York, 1969, Harper & Row, Publishers.
2. Watson, E. J., and Lowrey, G. J.: Growth and development of children, Chicago, 1958, Year Book Medical Publishers, Inc.
3. Hurlock, E. B.: Child development, New York, 1950, McGraw-Hill Book Co.
4. Tanner, J. M.: Physical growth. In Mussen, P. H., editor: Carmichael's manual of child psychology, ed. 3, New York, 1970, John Wiley & Sons, Inc.
5. Gesell, A., and Ilg, F. L.: Infant and child in the culture today, New York, 1943, Harper & Row, Publishers.
6. Woodward, O. M.: The earliest years, New York, 1966, Pergamon Press, Inc.
7. Gesell, A., and Amatruda, C. S.: Developmental diagnosis: normal and abnormal child development, New York, 1941, Paul B. Hoeber, Medical Division of Harper & Row, Publishers.
8. Piaget, J.: The origins of intelligence in children, New York, 1952, International Universities Press.
9. Penfield, W., and Roberts, L.: Speech and brain mechanisms, Princeton, N. J., 1958, Princeton University Press.
10. Hebb, D. O.: The organization of behavior, New York, 1949, John Wiley & Sons, Inc.
11. Smith, O. U., and Henry, J. P.: Cybernetic foundations of rehabilitation, J. Phys. Med. 46:379-467, 1967.
12. Kaluger, G., and Kolson, C. J.: Reading and learning disabilities, Columbus, Ohio, 1969, Charles E. Merrill Publishing Co.
13. Kephart, N. C.: The slow learner in the classroom, Columbus, Ohio, 1960, Charles E. Merrill Publishing Co.
14. Phillips, J. L.: The origins of intellect: Piaget's theory, San Francisco, 1969, W. H. Freeman & Co., Publishers.
15. Piaget, J.: The child's conception of the world, Paterson, N. J., 1960, Littlefield, Adams & Co.
16. Piaget, J.: Judgment and reasoning in the child, Paterson, N. J., 1959, Littlefield, Adams & Co.
17. Piaget, J.: The language and thought of the child, New York, 1955, Meridian Books, Inc.
18. Piaget, The child's conception of the world, op. cit., p. 179.
19. Piaget, Judgment and reasoning in the child, op. cit., p. 10.
20. Cohen, J., Hansel, C. E. M., and Sylvester, J.: An experimental study of comparative judgments of time, Br. J. Psychol. 45:108-114, 1954.
21. Wohlwill, J. F., and Wiener, M.: Discrimination of form orientation in young children, Child Dev. 35:1113-1125, 1964.
22. Terman, L. M., and Merrill, M. A.: Stanford-Binet intelligence scale, ed. 3, Boston, 1960, Houghton Mifflin Co.
23. Greene, M. C. L.: Learning to talk, New York, 1960, Harper & Row, Publishers.
24. Almy, M., Chittenden, E., and Miller, P.: Young children's thinking, New York, 1966, Teachers College Press.
25. Gesell and Ilg, op. cit., p. 211.
26. Skonsen, W. C.: So you want to raise a boy, New York, 1962, Doubleday & Co., Inc.
27. Gardner, op. cit., pp. 233-234.
28. Hadfield, J. A.: Childhood and adolescence, Baltimore, 1962, Penguin Books, Inc.
29. Ibid., p. 128.
30. English, H. B., and English, A. C.: A comprehensive dictionary of psychological and psychoanalytical terms, New York, 1958, David McKay Co., Inc.
31. Gesell and Ilg, op. cit., p. 416.

7 Middle childhood
6 to 8 years of age

MIDDLE CHILDHOOD:
WHAT IS A FIRST GRADER?

What do you see when you look at a first grader? You may see a front-toothless, squirmy, 5-, 6-, or 7-year-old jumping rope, swinging, or tumbling on the grass. You may see a clean pair of trousers become grass stained before the blink of an eye. You may see imagination and personality bubbling forth as in no other time in life. But to be sure, you will see a group of individuals so unique, and yet so unbelievably alike.

As a first-grade teacher, I never cease to marvel at my "charges." They come to school knowing so little, and they leave, having learned a vast amount of information ranging from reading, to social relationships with others, to a discovery of what school is really all about.

A first grader has usually developed his large muscle movements quite well. Small muscle coordination is another story. A pencil surely is a strange and horrible creation during those first few weeks, and to have to sit still for more than 10 minutes at a time! Unheard of! Often it takes a whole year before some first graders learn to control their small muscles and their huge bursts of energy.

Cognitive development during this age is truly amazing. Imagine looking at all those strange-looking symbols called the alphabet, being told that each symbol is a letter, that each has its own sound, and that combinations of these funny looking things will form something called words. How frightening and overwhelming it must seem in those first few weeks of school. Often I am amazed at how fast these little bundles of energy can learn—not only reading but arithmetic as well. More strange symbols with unique meanings! I feel that in no other grade do the children begin with so little and learn so much. So much progress can be seen in all pupils. Yet for some a sense of frustration is encountered when others begin to pull away, leaving them behind. Learning is harder for some, and these children come to know that "Steve is a good reader," but that "I can't read so good."

Individual differences begin to show through in other areas as well. Social relationships concern every first grader. Whereas some children have companions and best friends, others become isolates and encounter social problems. No one wants to be friends with a child who always wants his own way, who does not play fairly, or who cannot keep up in games because of intellectual or physical limitations. Here children must learn to cope with the "different" children and help them to become accepted and adjusted.

Influence by peers increases greatly in first grade. Previously, ideas fostered at home were supreme. Now the realization begins that other ideas and beliefs might not be so bad after all. Maybe everything Mommy and Daddy say isn't right! "But my friend Jimmy said . . ." becomes a new phrase. First graders want to go to their friends' homes. They want to call them on the telephone. They delight in seeing each other in the grocery store or at the shopping center. They desire to have the toys their friends have and to wear the same types of clothing. This was the year of the bell bottoms, of "whizzers" (toys utilizing the principle of gravity to make them spin), and of dinosaurs. One boy's interest became the fuse that ignited the fires of his classmates' intellect. One coloring book is shown and is followed by ten more like it the next day. Interests truly are dictated by peer group influence.

Emotional developments are great in 5- to 7-year-olds. Many first graders are quick to cry, whereas others brood and pout. The first day of school is an emotional trauma—the strange bus ride, the new building, meeting a new teacher, and just being taken away from Mommy is enough to set the tears in motion, not to mention being thrown in with twenty-six other children undergoing a similar trauma. But luckily, fears and tears soon disappear as the days go on. Emotional adjustment continues throughout the year, and vast improvements can be seen by the end of school.

First graders love competition. Whether they are racing on the playground or trying to see who will get his work done first, these children are in their glory when competing. They delight in playing games, as long as they do not lose all the time. Spelling bees and arithmetic competitions are a source of enjoyment, even for the slower pupils who manage to win often enough to keep them interested.

A typical day might begin with two children forgetting their lunch money, a common problem. (My Mother forgot to give it to me!) The day continues with a few tattles ("Donnie pulled my hair," "Mark is copying from my paper") and some comments by the teacher: "Michele, put that away," "Robert, don't you ever stop talking?" As an aside, first graders love to talk. They begin when they come in the morning and are still talking as they walk up the hall to their buses when school is over for the day. Recess is enjoyed, since it is a time for running and playing. After lunch the afternoon begins with settling an argument about whose turn it really was to take the ball out at noon recess or determining whose superball Roger really has—his or David's! The afternoon concludes with the usual race of the children riding Bus 51 to see who can get his chair up the fastest and get in line first.

First graders are an interesting and rewarding age group with whom to work. They are dependent, yet independent; serious, yet comical; aggravating, yet satisfying. Their teacher is their mother away from home, their helper, referee, friend, and aid to learning. If one were to look at a first grader, just what *would* he see?

The 6- to 8-year-old child is a fascinating person. For the parent he is full of surprises, new and different each day; for his siblings he is someone to love, someone to tolerate, or someone to have nothing to do with; for his teacher he is an individual, eager to learn in any way he can. As the child goes through these years, different growth characteristics appear. There is no clear-cut line or age, however, where one stage of development ends and the next begins. Generally, the child goes from one phase to another without any earth-shattering experience to tell people of the change. Most of the time he proceeds without any trouble. Parents, teachers, and friends will be able to see differences, however, between the child at 6 years of age and at 8 years. Up to the age of 5 or 6 years children all over the world grow, develop, and act similarly. Throughout the ages, babies everywhere have been much the same. The principles of growth and development are eternal and universal in nature. By the age of 5 or 6 years, however, the distinctive cultures of each society are imprinted on its children. Little Ivan, little Joe, and little Wang-Ti start the same, but the man-made influences of their respective cultures begin to have a different impact on the growth and development of each child, creating differences in attitudes, behavior, and even

Frederic Lewis, Inc., New York City.

in certain physical characteristics that are unique to the culture.

The developmental tasks of middle childhood are centered about "three great outward pushes." Socially, the child makes his way out of his family environs into a peer group society. Physically, he moves into a world of games and activities requiring neuromuscular skill. Mentally, there is a thrust into school and the world of concepts, symbols, logics, and communication. Specifically, the developmental tasks are as follows: (1) acquiring social and physical skills necessary for ordinary games, (2) learning to get along with peers, (3) building a wholesome concept of self, (4) learning an appropriate sex role, (5) developing fundamental skills in reading, writing, and arithmetic, (6) breaking family ties and developing a growing independence by entering school, and (7) developing conscience, morality, and a value judgment system.[1] These developmental tasks will be paramount in importance until the child reaches puberty and adolescence.

PHYSICAL DEVELOPMENT

The middle childhood years are characterized by a relatively slow, but steady growth rate as compared to the years of infancy or puberty. This age level is one of the most comfortable periods of physical adjustment. The developmental pace is sufficiently slow so that under normal conditions the child can meet the physical and psychological demands made on him.

Body growth

By 6 years of age the child has usually lost most of his baby contours. His legs and arms are lengthening, and he is gaining in height and weight, although growth is less rapid than before. Girls at this age are generally more physically mature than boys in terms of ultimate level of physical development. However, boys do tend to be slightly taller and heavier than girls up to the age of 10 years. The average child of 6 years in North America stands 46 inches tall and weighs about 48 pounds. The annual expected growth is 2 to 3 inches in height and 3 to 6 pounds in weight.[2] Each child has his own growth rate, however, and there are a few 6-year-olds who are as tall and heavy as some 10-year-olds.

There is a change in the structure of the face that is noticeable in comparing a 4- or 5-year-old with a 6-year-old. The face begins to look more slim and lean because the child is beginning to lose his "baby fat." It is during this sixth year, also, that he loses his first tooth. Being more physiologically mature, girls shed their teeth a bit earlier than boys. As permanent teeth replace baby teeth and as new molars come in, the jaw lengthens and the face changes in shape. The "toothless gap era" declines at about the age of 8 years, when the permanent teeth appear, starting at the front and developing to the back. Permanent teeth will continue to arrive until about the age of 11 or 12 years.

The eyes of a 6-year-old are still immature in size and shape. There is a strong tendency to farsightedness, a situation usually corrected naturally between the ages of 8 and 10 years when the child's eyes attain adult size and shape.[3] The younger child should be provided with books that have larger than normal print. At this age it is important for the child to be tested for near-point vision. Most visual screening charts test a child's vision at far point, but it is near-point vision that a child must use in reading.

Motor skills

The child can take fairly good care of himself at 6 years of age. He can hop, skip, jump, dress and undress, tie a bow, and use scissors. He no longer grasps a pencil with a fist hold but, rather, uses a finger hold. The 6-year-old's larger muscles are more advanced in development than his smaller ones. Because of this condition, his small muscles do not permit him to do precise writing, sewing, or drawing. Tying shoelaces will be an effort for some at this age. He still becomes frustrated by his lack of fine motor skill development.

Six years is an age of activity. Running, jumping, climbing, bike riding, and "cleanup" jobs at school make use of the child's large muscles. Although he enjoys finer motor activities, he becomes restless after sitting for a short period of time. He wriggles on a chair and sits on the edge. Frequent bangs or thumps can be heard in the classroom—he has fallen off his chair. Six-year-olds seem to use their whole body in everything they do. There is a good deal of oral activity such as blowing through the lips, extending the tongue, and making all kinds of mouthing noises.[4] When they write, they screw up their faces, bite their lips, and pull themselves back and forth in their chairs. They are easily distracted by the environment.

Although his large muscles are still better developed than his small ones, the 7-year-old is gradually becoming more skillful in using his small muscles in eye-hand coordination activities. Indication of improved small muscle control is shown by the Stanford-Binet test of tying a bowknot. Only 35% of the 6-year-olds could pass this test as compared to 69% of the 7-year-olds and 94% of the 9-year-olds.[5] It is during the second grade in the United States that most children learn to do cursive writing, which requires a different kind of control over their hand motions than was needed for manuscript writing. Advancing from the gross approach to activities of the 6-year-olds, the 7-year-olds combine thought with activity. They are more inclined to "think before jumping." They are more cautious in new performances and show a new awareness of heights. They will play vigorously in one activity but will quickly drop it for another, although they do not change from loud to quiet types of activities as frequently as do the 6-year-olds. Girls have somewhat poorer visual acuity than boys, but their color discrimination is superior on the average to that of boys. Auditory acuity is as good at 7 years of age as it will ever be. The ability to discriminate pitch, however, will continue to improve for the next three or four years.[6] Nervous habits begin to appear in 7-year-olds. The commonest habits are nail biting, tongue sucking, or scratching and pulling at the ear. These are more frequently found among girls than among boys. Some of these habits may disappear within a couple of months or years, whereas others, such as nail biting, may persist until adulthood.

The 8-year-old is continuing to develop steadily and slowly. Active play is most characteristic of this age. The 8-year-old has achieved equilibrium in body balance and can move freely with fluidity because of improved small muscle development. He does not drop his pencil as frequently as he did when he was 7 years old, nor lose it as often as when he was 6 years old. In writing he spaces words and sentences well and can control his hand movements so that slanting letters can be achieved easily. Nearsightedness may develop at this age so that visual care must be maintained. He is quicker in his responses, mentally and physically. His attention span is longer; this is helpful to the teacher since she will not have the multitude of activities to react to that the first-grade teacher has.

In summary, with the development of large muscles to the point that they can be used effectively in producing alternating movements, the 6- to 8-year-olds now seek to try out a variety of physical skills that they could not do before. They delight in doing the physically unusual or different such as walking on ledges or balancing on fences rather than walking on the sidewalks. A ball becomes an indispensable toy because the child can now take aim and make the ball go where or do what he wants it to. Kicking skills become important because the repertoire of games in middle childhood includes many involving kicking, running, and jumping. Children in this age group will kick cans, rocks, anything that can be moved. A favorite playground game is kick ball.

A significant developmental point to be noted at this time is that making one's way into the peer group begins to depend on the child's skills for playing the approved games of the group. The importance of these skills increases as the child reaches the ages of 10 to 12 years. This factor is more important for boys than for girls because their sex role includes more physical activities. Many children, boys in particular, become misfits when unfortunate circumstances make them meagerly equipped to play games with their peers. Many delinquent boys have been found to be unskilled in playing games of the group. Most children learn the skills needed for games without help from the school. It is the wise teacher or parent who tries to find ways for a child to learn the skills if he does not possess them.

SOCIAL GROWTH

The ages of 6 to 8 are years when the child's social environment expands rapidly. The life of the child begins to center around the school and the children and activities that are found there. The child now has authority figures other than the mother and father who seek to guide him. Peers take on greater importance, and the group phenomena begin to influence the child's behavior and growth. Family influences lessen as the external socialization process makes its impact. Since his whole being evolves around his friends and peers, the child must learn social skills and communication skills that will enable him to maintain successful relationships. Learning to get along well with others is often difficult, and lack of social experiences or of good teaching models (mothers, fathers, and other acceptable adults) can be handicapping.

Social characteristics

The social behavior of the 6-year-old develops more rapidly than previously because he is away from home more and is with children his own age. His social maturity and stability is highly inconsistent, however. His behavior often regresses in maturity, especially when he is tired. Group activities help to develop the social maturity of the child. He learns new ascribed roles for his age, develops social interaction and communicative skills, and begins to understand the needs and rights of others. Through maturation and learning the child acquires the more refined social behavior of adults.

The 6-year-old is often trying to his parents. One minute he is agreeable and loving, and the next minute he dislikes everybody and everything. Six years is just not old enough to be reliable and stable. He craves help but refuses to accept it. He wants to play with others, but if things do not go his way, he may threaten to go home or engage in name-calling. Six-year-olds cannot handle a younger brother or sister well without considerable direction and attention on the part of the parent. At times he can be bossy with a younger sibling. Despite all of these problems, there are times when he has a very close relationship with his parents. The 6-year-old is sensitive to parental moods and tensions, and he can be most sympathetic when his mother is sick. Not only may the child show anxieties concerning the well-being of the mother and father but of his teacher as well.

A highly important aspect of social development at this age pertains to ethnic identification. The 6-year-old is unaware of ethnic identification of the children with whom he plays.[7] He picks his playmates more on qualities of age and size rather than sex and color. As children mature, they respond more to the prejudice of others, often as a result of the influence of their home atmosphere. The child views the opinions and ideas of his parents and teacher as most important because to him they are the smartest people in the world.

A social concern both at home and at school is manners. The child of 6 years of age has considerable difficulty in formal social situations because he has not learned the social skills as yet. He does not know how to speak or act properly. He is not good at shaking hands with strangers and saying "How do you do" or "Good-by"; likewise he has difficulty in responding to "How are you?" He often forgets to say "Please," "Thank-you," and "Good-by." The child opens the door to people he knows and says with enthusiasm "Come in," but it is a different situation with strangers. If parents give the child the exact words to use in a social situation, he may be able to repeat them; but on his own he may be at a loss to know what to say or do.

All of the ups and downs of a 6-year-old are a part of his growing up and his search for autonomy. He thought he was ready for independence when he was 2 years old and had learned all of the developmental tasks that were necessary for his basic survival. Again, when he was 4 years old, he thought that he was ready for the world because he was developing a consciousness of good and bad actions. Now, at 6 years of age he is in a new world; surely he must be ready for independence. His past experience and his intellectual insights, however, raise some uncertainties in his mind.

The 7-year-old is becoming more aware of the social differences around him but not to any great extent that it will change his thinking. The choice of friends at this level is still uninfluenced by the social and economic status of the child or his home. However, the awareness of differences between his home and that of his friends is increasing.

The child of 7 years of age is learning to be self-critical; he likes to do things well. This self-insight is leading toward a state of autonomy. He likes to assume some responsibility. The child is also very talkative, often fighting verbally rather than physically. Frequently when he is angry at his parents, he toys with the idea that he is not their child or gets a notion about running away from home. Stealing is not unusual at this age.

He can now greet people with "Hello" while looking straight at them, but "Goodby" may not be as easy. He may be able to shake hands but not comfortably. Many 7-year-olds will say "Excuse me" spontaneously if things go wrong. One point difficult for many older people, especially grandparents, to understand is that children may initially behave well when company is present but are likely to withdraw to their own activities before too long. Oftentimes one hears "Why won't Jimmy stay in the room with us when he comes for a visit?" Usually it is because he does not understand what is going on and wants to do something that is of interest to him.

At home the 7-year-old is a more cooperative member of the family than he was at 6 years. Although he likes to help around the house, his performance does not always match his good intentions. He does get along better with his mother and is developing a closer relationship with his father. He will play with his younger brothers and sisters and will look after them, although jealousy will still occur at times.

At play the 7-year-old does fairly well with others, but he will spend some time in solitary activity as well. There is less chance that he will use direct physical and verbal attack if things go badly in play. He is more concerned than previously about his place in the group and about being well liked. It is not unusual for 7-year-olds to develop "love affairs." In fact, boys may have more than one girl friend, and girls may like more than one boy. If one friend stops liking you, you simply find another. The loss of a boy or girl friend is usually taken as a matter of course, although some children cannot move this readily from one friend to another. This kind of a child can become upset, and tears may result when they have lost their "one and only." In spite of these relationships, the peer culture is beginning to separate the sexes in play activities.

Most 8-year-olds will have completed the transition to their peer culture. They now accept and prefer the activities, fads, and associations of their peers rather than those of adults. They generally give their allegiance to other children instead of to adults in case of a conflict.

Eight-year-olds gain security from being accepted by the group. They are responsive to group activities, and they hate playing alone. Whatever they do they want to do with other persons. The 8-year-old is fond of team games, comics, television, movies, adventure stories, and collections. His best friends are those of the same sex.

He is often careless and argumentative, but at the same time he is alert, friendly, and interested in people. His self-concept is affected as he learns what other people are like and how they behave. The 8-year-old is sensitive to criticism. However, he is a growing individual, and his contacts with others will modify his personality for better or for worse.

The 8-year-old recognizes property rights if his training has been sound. There is evidence of increasing modesty and self-control. Social pressures, especially by his peers, are influential in this respect. The child has a new awareness of individual differences and of what to do about them.

The social manners of the 8-year-old are better than they were, but they still need some improvement. Most 8-year-olds verbalize proper greetings and goodbys.

Some can carry on excellent social conversations with adults; many have good company and table manners—away from home.[8]

The 8-year-old gets along well with his parents, but he gets along better with his friends. His relationship with his mother can be demanding, complicated, and subtle. He expects her to do certain things and is annoyed when she does not do them. He often demands her complete attention and companionship. Although he expresses a preference for his mother, his father is coming in for an increased share of affection if he is available and reachable. The 8-year-old can be strict with his younger siblings; he may become upset if he is forced to follow the same home rules, such as the time he has to go to bed, as are required of the younger children. In terms of chores and work around the house he likes to be paid for his help; often parents become dismayed by this sudden "money-mad interest."

Peer and play culture

There is something both universal and eternal about the nature, purpose, and semblance of play in children. Children have been playing as long as there has been history. Toys, play materials, and drawings of children playing games have been found in the pyramids of Egypt and in the ruins of Pompeii. Blind-man's buff, hide-and-seek, and tug-of-war were enjoyed by children in Plato's Greece.[9] Ancient Rome knew the finger-flashing game of paper-scissors-stone, still played around the world and not only by youngsters. We were "taught" the game at a geisha party in Kyoto, Japan, on a visit there. There are drawings in the ancient tombs of noblemen and pharaohs buried in Luxor showing children at play, and on the pavements of old Jerusalem there are stone carvings that were used by the Roman soldiers to play adult games. The interesting observation is the similarity of the types of games played by children throughout the ages in all types of cultures.

The nature, and perhaps the purpose, of play changes as the child gets older (Table 7-1). The center ingredient of play undergoes three separate, although somewhat overlapping stages of evolution.[10] During the first two or three years of life, the most noticeable feature of play is physical activity involving sensorimotor recognition of objects and happenings. At about the ages of 3 or 4 years to about 6 or 7 years fantasy is added to physical activity, thereby permitting certain gestures, objects, or behavior to indicate or "stand for" other things or situations. Emotions are experienced more intensely at these ages than at any other time in life. The third stage involves much physical activity and fantasy but now includes a greater emphasis on being with children of one's own age group. The children begin to see the need for rules. They may make up their own rules and once agreed on, the demand to abide by them is vigorous.

At all age levels the play of children can be divided into four categories: imitative, exploratory, testing, and model building play.[11] Imitative play reaches a peak when 4- to 6-year-olds play "house," "policeman," "school," or circular group singing and rhythmic games such as "ring-around-the-rosy," "mulberry bush," or "Sally Waters." Exploratory play increases with cognitive development and the discovery of manipulative objects, such as blocks, clays, toy models, and even riddles. Most children ages 6 to 12 years engage in testing play, whereby a child tests his own ability, agility, and capability. Physical contests such as dodge ball or kick ball become important. Games involving memory, impulse and physical control, choice, or decision are also popular. Five- to 6-year-olds play "hide-and-seek" or tag games, which will continue for many years. Seven- to 8-year-olds play "release," "ring-a-lievo," and "kick the can," which involves some harassment of the person who is "it" (or "he" in Great Britain). On rainy days or in the evenings

Middle childhood

Table 7-1. General play interests from ages 5 to 10 years*

AGE ZONE	GENERAL PLAY INTERESTS
5 years	More independent play
	Much play centers around a house
	Plays with dolls
	Runs, climbs, swings, skips, dances
	Rides tricycle
	Uses sand in making roads
	Imitative play: house, store, hospital
	Paints, draws, colors, cuts, pastes
	Copies letters and numbers
	Builds with blocks
6 years	Elaborates and expands 5-year play interests
	Mud, sand, water play
	Games of tag, hide-and-seek
	Ball playing: tossing, bouncing
	Rough-and-tumble play
	Roller skates, ice skates
	Simple carpentry
	Table games with cards
	Paints, colors, draws, uses clay
	Collects odds and ends
	Imaginative play
	Builds with blocks
7 years	More intense interest in some activities, fewer new ventures
	Has "mania" for certain activities
	Bicycles
	Puzzles, magic, tricks
	Collecting and swapping
	Swimming
	Rudiments of ball play
8 years	Variety of play interests; prefers companionship in play
	Games of all kinds
	Dramatic play of giving shows
	Collecting and arranging of collections
	Beginning interest in group games
	Unorganized group play of wild running, chasing
	Beginning of secret clubs
	Boys and girls begin to separate in play
9 years	Variety of play interests
	Works hard at his play
	Individual differences become stronger
	Baseball, skating, swimming, sports
	Collecting of stamps, minerals, etc.
	Hikes
	Complicated table games

*Modified from Gesell, A., and Ilg, F.: The child from five to ten, New York, 1946, Harper & Row, Publishers, pp. 367-370.

8-year-olds and older can be enthusiastic about table games such as Monopoly, Parcheesi, rummy, and hearts. Red rover and run-sheep-run are popular with 9- to 10-year-olds, whereas 11- to 12-year-olds play the more complex game of prisoner's base. Model building in a primitive way becomes explicit by about the age of 4 years and reaches a peak at 10 to 12 years of age. The commercial world of today provides so many model toys such as trains, dolls, cars, and even monsters that they may be interfering with the advantages gained by some of the constructive, solitary play of children who used to make their own models.

As children of 6 years and older grow, individual differences become stronger. Some children read more and enjoy sedentary activities, whereas others head for the out-of-doors at the first chance. The sex role as emphasized by the family, neighborhood, and culture will have some influence on games played and types of interests displayed. A 5-year-old boy will not particularly hesitate to play the part of the mother in playing house; a 9-year-old boy would not be "caught dead" playing that part. Sex differences vary slightly in games and activities for the 5- to 7-year-old, but as the children grow older the more they tend to drift apart in interests and play activities.

At all ages girls generally like to play with boys. Their advanced physical maturity enables them to hold their own in games, but the influence of what it is "to be a man" begins to show in boys. The mores of the peer culture take over, and the gulf between boys and girls begins to widen. As an illustration, at the age of 5 years the girl tells the boy what games they will play and the boy plays them. At 6 years of age the girl tells the boy what games they will play and the boy says "No, I want to play this game," and the girl plays it. At the age of 7 years the boy tells the girl what games they will play, and she plays them. At the age of 8 years the boy says, "I don't know if I want to play with you; you're a girl." The 9-year-old boy is likely to say to the girl "Get out of here!"

INTELLIGENCE, LANGUAGE, AND THOUGHT

The 6-year-old is on the threshold of a new world. He can control his muscle movements so that he can do more precise physical activities than ever before. Socially he is becoming a member of a society consisting largely of others of his own age. Intellectually, he is on the verge of answering his own "why" questions. It is important to understand that the child is only at the starting point of all of these ventures, but he is at that point, and the school will seek to help him make the most of his newly developed abilities and interests.

Piaget's stage of concrete operations (ages 7 to 11 or 12 years)

Briefly summarizing the development of cognitive ability from birth to 7 years of age, according to Piaget (Table 7-2), the early months of life consist of disorganized, unrelated, and diffused perceptions. The later months of the sensorimotor period involve egocentric experiences wherein the infant becomes aware of his involvement in actions. During the preoperational thought period, the child gradually becomes aware of his thoughts, although his reasoning is restricted to immediately observable circumstances. He cannot reason beyond the observable. Generalizations and

Table 7-2. Piaget's stages of intellectual development*

STAGE	APPROXIMATE AGES	CHARACTERIZATION
I. Sensorimotor period	Birth to 2 years	Infant differentiates himself from objects; seeks stimulation and makes interesting spectacles last; prior to language, meanings defined by manipulations so that object remains "the same object" with changes in location and point of view
II. Preoperational thought period		
Preconceptual phase	2 to 4 years	Child is egocentric, unable to take viewpoint of other people; classifies by single salient features: if A is like B in one respect, must be like B in other respects
Intuitive phase	4 to 7 years	Child is now able to think in terms of classes, to see relationships, to handle number concepts, but is "intuitive" because he may be unaware of his classification. Gradual development of *conservation* in this order: mass (age 5), weight (age 6), and volume (age 7).
III. Period of concrete operations	7 to 11 years	Child is able now to use logical operations such as *reversibility* (in arithmetic), *classification* (organizing objects into hierarchies of classes), and *seriation* (organizing objects into ordered series, such as increasing size)
IV. Period of formal operations	11 to 15 years	Final steps toward abstract thinking and conceptualization; capable of hypothesis testing

*Modified from Piaget, J.: The origins of intelligence in children, New York, 1952, International Universities Press.

ability to follow through with sustained deductions or successive judgment are lacking. A significant change in intellectual behavior emerges during the preoperational thought period, when the child develops symbolic schemata that permit representative or symbolic behavior, in either verbal or nonverbal form. During this stage, the child will also progress from making judgments formed from a perceptual basis (what he sees) to making judgments from a conceptual basis (what he reasons). Decentering is the process by which a child develops more than one point of view about a particular subject or by which he can understand the many features or essentials of a group rather than isolated elements. Decentering has its beginning in the preoperational stage, but it becomes a major factor of cognitive functioning in the concrete operations stage.

The period of concrete operations begins at about the age of 7 years and lasts until ages 11 or 12 years. This period is characterized by the child's ability to solve concrete problems—problems that he can manipulate or "see" in a concrete fashion. He begins to understand relationships between classes and sizes of objects, something he found difficult to do in his preschool years. He also begins to understand conceptions of time, space, and, eventually, logic. As the child grows older, he becomes more adept at solving concrete problems so that by the end of this period he begins to attack abstract problems.[12]

During the concrete operations period, the child reaches a level where he understands equality relations, uses arithmetic and measurements, understands the notion of right and left as applied to objects in themselves, and understands the concept of number. Piaget hypothesizes that the child's conception of numbers goes hand in hand with the development of logic.[13]

It is during this stage that the child realizes that other people see things differently from the way he does. Through repeated and often frustrating interchanges with his peers he has come to cognitive grips with other viewpoints and perspectives that differ from his own. At the same time the necessity of maintaining an original premise in an argument is also being developed.

During the concrete operations period, the child's conception of the world definitely changes. The idea that nature is made by man disappears entirely toward the age of 9 or 10 years. By this time all of nature is imbued with purpose (i.e., the sun has been made for the purpose of giving us warmth and light, and the clouds for the purpose of bringing us rain).[14] As for his conception of physical causality, this third broad stage of cognitive development has produced a new parallelism between logic and the real categories—in other words at approximately the age of 10 years, when logical thought becomes deductive, one's interpretation of reality breaks away from forms of primitive realism, such as "seeing is believing," and becomes a logical or reasoning necessity.[15]

Piaget states that the value system and social interaction of children fit into the nine groupings that make up the concrete operations period. (The nine groups are not presented in this text.) A child must interact socially to grow intellectually because without social life he would never succeed in understanding the reciprocity of viewpoints. Consequently he would not develop adequate perspectives, geometrical or logical.

Mental characteristics

Most 6-year-olds operate on a precausal level of reasoning. The child has not firmly established a concept of "cause and effect" or the idea that a person can sometimes reason what the cause or the result might be. However, the child does ask "Why?" and "What for?" and "How?" He begins to realize that objects and events serve certain purposes that he wants to know. The 6-

year-old is still in the preoperational stage of conceptual development, however. Therefore his reasoning process will be largely governed by the appearance of things, and he can form only rudimentary generalizations.

When given two objects, the 6-year-old can more easily see the differences that exist between the objects than the similarities. Differences can be seen or experienced directly, but similarities must be abstracted from generalizations, an ability not developed until about 9 years of age. The 6-year-old also has difficulty in making decisions, even about such things as what flavor of ice cream he would like to have or what color of a balloon to buy. His memory is such that he can repeat sentences of ten or twelve words or repeat four digits in order. He knows number combinations up to ten.

The experience of school has helped the 7-year-old in developing his mental powers. His activities are becoming more specialized; they are not as general as they have been up to this point. He now has the mental ability that enables him to count by ones, twos, fives, and tens. He now grasps the basic idea of addition and subtraction. However, many times the work done along these lines is the result of memorizing addition and subtraction tables. Modern math seeks to teach how to reason by sets and groups.

The 7-year-old does little abstract thinking. He learns best in concrete terms and when he can be active while learning. He prefers to participate rather than to be just a spectator. His speech is no longer egocentric but is now sociocentric—others centered.

He has a rudimentary understanding of time and monetary values. He can tell time and make some small purchases. Allowing the child to make these purchases on his own gives him a feeling that his parents trust him to handle money, even if they are standing by and watching him.

At this age curiosity begins to arise as to the difference between the sexes and where babies come from. These ideas show an interest in reality and indicate the importance of giving truthful information. Sex information may well be given at this age —not to be taught in great detail but enough to satisfy the 7-year-old's curiosity.

The 7-year-old child is entering Piaget's stage of concrete operations. He now begins to use elementary logic and to reason about size, space, weight, volume, number, and time. He can group objects according to a given attribute, such as color, and still realize that they can be regrouped according to another attribute, such as size. He can also order things into a series, such as from larger to smaller. He is able to apply the principle of conservation, which states that certain properties remain constant and invariant regardless of changes in their appearance. For example, he understands that the water from a beaker remains the same when poured into a shallow dish.

Almy and associates[16] investigated children's ability to apply the principle of conservation. She used a longitudinal approach to test and retest youngsters on their conservational ability in three tasks, two involving number and one involving quantity of liquid. One of her findings was that 76% of the 7-year-olds from a middle socioeconomic background conserved on all three tasks. This was in agreement with Piaget's theory.

The 8-year-old shows an interest in causal relationships. He is curious about all types of changes and happenings and wants to know about cause and effects. This level of thinking represents the scientific dimension of recognition and is proceeding from concrete to abstract and metaphysical relations.

The 8-year-old's memory span is increasing. His memory span for words will, of course, vary greatly according to their familiarity, interest, and meaning for the child. He can answer five out of six simple questions on a story about 100 words long and can repeat without errors a sentence of about sixteen words after hearing it once.

Mentally the 8-year-old is still developing through experience. He likes to take field trips and questions all he sees. He still sees the teacher as the authority. The child is much interested in the past. He likes to talk about Indians and their ways. He can now tell the day of the month and the year. Far-off places and ways of communication now have real meaning. As a result of all this experience the child is starting to use some abstract thinking.

Language and logical thought

By the time a child is 6 years old he has an oral vocabulary of approximately 2,500 words. He uses sentences averaging about five words in length, and he makes use of all the various parts of speech. He knows some of the letters of the alphabet and can give their names on seeing their visual form. He may even be able to recognize the printed form of a few words. During the elementary school years, the child refines and extends the language he has developed up to that point. His speech becomes more socialized. He begins to put his thoughts and feelings into words more easily and soon begins logical thought. He begins to understand more abstract forms of language such as puns and figures of speech.

The 2- to 3-year-old asks the question "What is that?" He wants to increase his vocabulary by asking for a word or a name for an object. The 4- to 5-year-old asks "Who is that . . .?" "What is he doing . . .?" and "Why does . . . ?" and other similar questions. The child is reflecting his awareness of the world around him, especially of the actions of humans. He is usually satisfied by almost any positive response, as compared to one which merely suggests that he be quiet. The implication is that the child is reflecting his curious and inquisitive nature, but he is not yet aware of logic and reasoning. To some degree his questioning may also indicate the type of communicative skill he has developed for carrying on a conversation with adults. He may not know of any other way by which he can talk to older people. Most 6- to 7-year-olds, however, have reached the precausal level of reasoning, and so their questions of "Why?" and "What for?" and "How?" indicate that they are beginning to know that objects, actions, and events serve certain purposes; they want to know what they are.

During the preschool years, speech is mainly egocentric in the forms of (1) repetition of words, syllables, or rhythmic phrases that the child enjoys saying, (2) a monologue whereby the child converses with himself as if he were thinking out loud, or (3) a dual or collective monologue that concerns another person or persons but in which the child does not make a strong effort to communicate with them.[17] By the time a child enters school, however, his speech is proceeding toward more socialized speech. Piaget[18] divides socialized speech into (1) adapted information that involves an exchange of information between two or more people; (2) criticism, by which the child is making some sort of a subjective value judgment, not just stating a fact as in adaptive information; (3) commands, requests, and threats, representing the minimum interchange of speech necessary for communication; and (4) questions and answers. Socialization of thought and speech comes to a child between his seventh and eighth year, partly because he now has a more extensive social life as he begins to work and play with a larger, more stable peer group.

Verbal understanding increases, and the child can now communicate his own thoughts more objectively. The 7- to 8-year-old is more likely than the younger child to be able to arrange stories of explanations logically. The 8-year-old's growth in vocabulary is shown not only in an increased number of words but also in his ability to give more precise definitions than previously. A 6-year-old will define an orange as "You eat it," and a puddle as "You step in it." The 8-year-old responds with "It's a color or a fruit," and "A little pool of water made by rain."

PERSONALITY, SELF-CONCEPT, AND SEX ROLE

A major influence on the child's developing personality and self-concept is his entrance into a school situation that stresses learning of the basic academic skills. There is a cultural significance attached to "going to school" that may make the child see himself differently in terms of his capabilities (or lack of them) and of what he perceives is expected of him by others.

Personality development

Individual differences in basic personality attributes are fairly well established by the age of 6 years.[19] However, the basic traits are not completely formed by this age, and three significant changes in personal makeup usually occur. First, the child learns some degree of self-control. As such, he learns to live and cope with frustrations. He finds ways of avoiding trouble and of achieving success through his own decisions. Second, there is an increase in the independence of children between the ages of 6 and 9 years. They make friends away from home, become interested in external events and experiences, and begin to demand decision-making prerogatives in keeping with what they learn other children have. Third, a feeling of self-worth is either enhanced or decreased, depending on the ease with which they acquire the basic skills of reading, writing, and arithmetic. The way in which a child reacts to his specific situation greatly affects his future personality, patterns of adjustment, and degree of self-acceptance.

During middle childhood, a child's social and communicative skills must expand rapidly or he risks the possible rejection or aggression of his peers. The teacher becomes a major socializing agent. At least in the initial school environment she assumes the role of the surrogate parent. In this role the teacher is in a position to influence both the social and the personality development of the child. She can teach social and communicative skills as they are needed. By her actions, attitudes, and words she is instrumental in shaping the pliable, developing self-image of the child.

For the first time he is away from the constant supervision of his mother. As a result, he is in a position where he can make some value judgments and simple decisions of his own, such as which way to walk home from school and whom to talk and play with in the meanwhile. With this increase in freedom a more realistic self-concept develops. Instead of relying on his parents and family for an appraisal of his behavior, he can now look to his teacher and peers for such impressions. As he gets older, more and more will the peer group be influential in determining which personality traits he will develop. The personality of the child is affected by people and how they react to him. He is especially vulnerable to labels or characteristics that others apply to him, such as lazy, stupid, happy, friendly, neat, or careless. As the child strives for an identity that he can recognize and accept, he will often feel insecure and lonely. Parents and teachers need to show their confidence in the child until he gains a satisfactory self-impression.

Self-concept

When a child recognizes and identifies with his ways of growing, behaving, and thinking, he is strengthening his awareness of himself. This awareness of self-attributes, as he sees and believes them to be, constitutes his self-concept. The self-concept is developed from comments made by others and from inferences from experiences the child has had in his life space. Only as cognitive ability increases to the stage that the child is able to conceptualize will he have a concept of self and his particular physical, social, and emotional characteristics. His reasoning ability has to develop to the concrete operations stage, as conceived by Piaget, before he has an opportunity to ascertain a more realistic concept of self.

The child reaches middle childhood with a self-concept derived through his parents, immediate family, and a limited number of peers. His self-concept is likely to be distorted or incomplete. As he is subject to the approval or disapproval of teachers, other adults, and peers, he may begin to question the validity of his view of his attributes and abilities. Between the ages of 6 and 9 years the child more than once will be concerned about his capability and acceptibility. Negative concerns such as "I'm no good" and "Nobody cares about me" may arise. These thoughts will not be easily dispelled. As the child grows more insightful, he is more likely to wonder about himself. Unfortunately, some children get little or no support or direction from others they consider important to help them keep negative thoughts in proper perspective. In fact some parents unknowingly nurture a negative self-concept in children by (1) teasing or never being satisfied; (2) usually doing for the child what the child could do for himself, thus making him feel inadequate and helpless; (3) being so dominant that the child feels that he is not being completely trusted and loved; or (4) being more concerned with something other than the child and thus neglecting him. A negative self-concept may also come from a type of discipline by parents or teachers that embarasses and humiliates (Table 7-3).[20]

A positive self-concept enables a person to feel adequate, likeable, intrinsically worthy, and free.[21] These feelings lead to self-respect, self-confidence, and eventually, happiness. Children must be considered as individuals with characteristics all their own. They must be brought up in an atmosphere of trust, respect, and good regard if they are to emerge as happy, well-adjusted persons. The middle years is a time when the self-concept needs to be carefully nur-

Table 7-3. Relationships between the home and child behavior*

TYPES OF HOME	TYPE OF CHILD BEHAVIOR ASSOCIATED WITH IT
Rejective	Submissive, aggressive, adjustment difficulties, feelings of insecurity, sadistic, nervous, shy, stubborn, noncompliant
Overprotective, "babying"	Infantile and withdrawing, submissive, feelings of insecurity, aggressive, jealous, difficult adjustment, nervous
Dominating parent	Dependable, shy, submissive, polite, self-conscious, uncooperative, tense, bold, quarrelsome, disinterested
Submissive parent	Aggressive, careless, disobedient, independent, self-confident, forward in making friends, noncompliant
Inharmonious	Aggressive, neurotic, jealous, delinquent, uncooperative
Defective discipline	Poor adjustment, aggressive, rebellious, jealous, delinquent, neurotic
Harmonious, well adjusted	Submissive, good adjustment
Calm, happy, compatible	Cooperative, superior adjustment, independent
Child accepted	Socially acceptable, faces future confidently
Parents play with child	Security feelings, self-reliant
Logical, scientific approach	Self-reliant, cooperative, responsible
Consistent, strict discipline	Good adjustment
Giving child responsibilities	Good adjustment, self-reliant, security feelings

*From Radke, M. J.: The relation of parental authority to children's behavior and attitudes, Child Welfare Monograph No. 22, University of Minnesota Press, Minneapolis. Copyright 1964 by the publisher.

tured and developed into a stable, acceptable image.

Sex roles and sex typing

Sex role development refers to the identification of the individual with culturally assigned physiological, sociological, and psychological characteristics and concepts of what constitutes maleness and femaleness. The implication is that a boy should take on and aspire to the male characteristics and girls to the female characteristics.

Until the child reaches the middle childhood years, there is no extensive striving or concern for assuming the appropriate sex role. As mentioned previously, at the age of 5 years a boy will play the part of either the father or the mother in a make-believe situation. However, by the age of 9 years the boy would absolutely reject the idea of playing a female part. This change suggests the degree to which sex roles are strengthened during middle childhood. Table 7-4 indicates stages of ego development and conceptions of sex role.

The sex role phenomenon is one that generally takes place in the home and family setting. Boys find it natural to pattern themselves after their fathers and girls after

Table 7-4. Loevinger's milestones of ego development and extrapolations to sex role development*

STAGE	IMPULSE CONTROL	INTERPERSONAL STYLE	CONSCIOUS CONCERNS	CONCEPTIONS OF SEX ROLE
Presocial/symbiotic		Autistic, symbiotic	Self versus nonself	
Impulse ridden	Impulse ridden, fear of retaliation	Exploitive, dependent	Sexual and aggressive bodily feelings	Development of gender identity, self-assertion, self-expression, self-interest
Self-protective (formerly opportunistic)	Expedient, fear of being caught	Exploitive, manipulative, wary	Advantage, control, protection of self	Extension of self, self-extension, self-enhancement
Conformity	Conformity to external rule	Reciprocal, superficial	Things, appearance, reputation, self-acceptance	Conformity to external role, development of sex role stereotypes, bifurcation of sex roles
Conscientious	Internalized rules, guilt	Intensive, responsive	Differentiated inner feelings, motives, self-respect	Examination of self as sex role exemplar vis-à-vis internalized values
Autonomous	Coping with conflict, toleration of differences	Intensive, concern for autonomy	Differentiated inner feelings, role concepts, self-fulfillment	Differentiation of sex role, coping with conflicting masculine–feminine aspects of self
Integrated	Reconciling inner conflicts, renunciation of unattainable	Cherishing of individuality	All of the above plus identity	Achievement of individually defined sex role, integration of both masculine and feminine aspects of self, androgynous sex role definition

*From Block, J. H.: Conception of sex role, Am. Psychol. 28:513-514, 1973; modified from Loevinger, J., and Wessler, R.: Measuring ego development, vol. 1, San Francisco, 1970, Jossey-Bass, Inc., Publishers.

their mothers. The parents find this responsiveness gratifying. When chronic antagonism and disharmony exist between the parents, problems arise. The boy may find it hard to identify with his father because he is afraid of losing his mother's love. Likewise, he is also fearful of identifying with his mother because he may incur his father's anger. However, if emotional circumstances are such that the boy rejects the father completely, he may overidentify with the mother.

A case in point regards a boy in a kindergarten class who was brought to our attention. When the boy was 3 years old, his baby brother died. He witnessed his mother's hysteria and his father's sternness in trying to help his wife gain control of herself by slapping her. Unfortunately, for a long period of time afterward the father showed no love for his wife or for the surviving son. The boy only remembered that his father slapped his mother and that during that period of life his father was rather mean and short-tempered with him. The mother was the child's only adult source of love and protection. He became afraid to go near his father and began to identify with his mother and his two sisters, who were nice to him. The boy became obsessed with the idea of being a girl. He had gone as far as asking the other children to call him Janie. During playtime, he preferred to play house, at times dressing up in women's clothes and pretending to do the shopping or take care of the baby. It was only through skillful handling by his teacher that he began to work at a workbench and finally became interested in working with tools.

If the mother or father is missing from the home and no model is there with whom to identify, the child may identify with the teacher at school. In the case of boys, researchers have concluded that some male teachers are needed in elementary schools. One study of the effects of a man teacher showed an improvement in the behavior of hostile boys, and mothers of boys in the study reported that their sons were easier to handle at home.[21] In another study it was determined that the male elementary school teacher was especially significant in the inner city. The conclusion was that boys from low-income families needed an effective male figure with whom they could associate and identify to learn their appropriate sex role.[22]

In the past, sex roles were rather clearly defined. Today the characteristics of the sex roles are not as readily ascertained; in fact the nature of the roles may be changing. A research study involving 105 white, middle-class, urban children sought to answer the question, "Are children of varying family backgrounds, defined in terms of the modern-type family and the traditional-type family, developing different sex role concepts?" The results showed that 85% of all children chose their own sex as the one they liked better. This result was in keeping with other studies. It was also determined that girls from modern families were the most likely to depart from sex-typed expectations. Traditional families produced the most highly aggressive boys and the most highly dependent girls. The study indicated that sex typing was more the result of family experiences than school experiences.[23]

EMOTIONAL AND MORAL DEVELOPMENT

The innate excitement of the newborn is the beginning of emotions. Gradually, distress and delight appear and eventually other emotions, most of which are learned through experience. During the preschool years the child displays his emotions rather openly. As he enters school and gets older, he tends to use more subtle expressions of emotions. Emotional development is shaped by the experiences of the child and the forms of emotional expression or behavior he has learned to apply to the affective experience. Moral development also partly depends on the types of events, attitudes, and verbal experiences to which the child has been exposed. Unlike emotional development that is related to affective responses, moral development depends on cognitive development, knowledge, and awareness.

Emotional characteristics

Although there is a decrease in the number of emotional explosions during the age of 6 years, the child is still in a more-or-less constant state of emotional tension and agitation. In some respects a 5-year-old seems to be more emotionally stable than the 6-year-old. The intense activity of the 6-year-old is partly due to new social and scholastic demands and partly to his desire to take a giant step forward in asserting independence, but he is fearful because of his lack of success in doing so at ages 2 and 4 years. In a sense he is now trying to act on his own even though it may be by defiance, and he is beset with uncertainties and fearfulness. Sibling jealousy may still persist, especially if there is a younger sibling at home that the child believes may be getting more attention now that he is away at school all day. At 6 years of age the child is very fearful, especially of sounds such as are made by thunder, rain, and wind. Man-made noises, such as static, telephone, or flushing of toilet may induce fear until they are identified. There exists some fear of ghosts and witches. Fears of someone hiding under his bed or of someone in the closet are common.

The 7-year-old is less stubborn, more polite, responsive, and sensitive than he was at 6 years. He shows less aggression and has fewer outbursts. The child of 7 years of age is his own main concern. He worries that things will be too difficult for him, that second grade may be too hard, that people may not like him, that something might happen to him. This child has a tendency to withdraw from situations or at least is hesitant before acting. He often lacks confidence to the point of not wanting even to try. The 6-year-old jumps right in only to find he cannot handle the situation. The 7-year-old is more protective of himself, possibly because his cognitive development has reached a point where he is just a little more aware of consequences and cause and effect than he was previously. He accepts some form of discipline, although grudgingly. He is conscientious and tries to take his responsibilities seriously, although he is not old enough to be completely reliable. He is beginning to be able to put himself in another's place, so much so that he is moved by sad stories. Thus fears can be stimulated by television programs, movies, or reading. He still has fears of ghosts and of "someone hiding in the cellar" but is learning to control some fears such as swimming with his face under water and having his hair washed. There is a more common understanding regarding fear between children and their peers than between most children and their parents.[24] Parents are likely to recognize and agree with fears related to objective conditions but may be ignorant of subjective situations. For example, some 7-year-olds report a fear of being an adopted child, whereas most mothers are not aware of this fear in their child.

The 8-year-old is less likely to withdraw than the 7-year-old. In fact he may be full of impatience and wanting to get things done at once. He seeks to display courage and often will not admit his fears even to himself. However, he may still be afraid of fighting, failing in school, or of others finding fault with him. Often he may attack a feared experience, directly or indirectly, or compulsively dwell on it to resolve it. Children who tend to cling to the past and who have difficulty coming smoothly into the future may become worriers.[25] The 8-year-old cries less than others from inner confusion, but he may burst into tears, especially when tired, for many overt reasons such as having his feelings hurt by being criticized or not receiving or being able to do something that he wanted. Sometimes this child begins to think of himself as a martyr and rationalizes to himself, "They'll be sorry they treated me so mean when they see how bad I've been hurt (or am gone or when I'm sick in bed because of what they did)." The 8-year-old is often bossy, rude, and argumentative, even with his mother, but he is also affectionate and friendly. For the first time the child thinks of giving something to his mother and father. He is developing a feeling of being able to create love by initiating an activity on his own.[26]

Moral judgment and character development

Children develop their basic philosophical orientation to life at home. The family is the workshop, where for better or for worse the child develops an internal pattern of attitudes and beliefs that shape his character and influence his behavior. The community exerts a major modifying influence, to be sure. However, the home determines the initial strength and nature of the moral character of the child, and this strength, in turn, determines the degree to which the influences of the community can change the character.

The child learns early in childhood that there are some forms of behavior that are acceptable and some that are not. They come to associate "good" with a reward for approved behavior and "bad" with a punishment for unacceptable behavior. Eventually the child conceptualizes the thought that there are certain rules and regulations that must be followed to receive the acceptance and approval of others (society). By the age of 6 or 7 years children have internalized the concept of rules and the idea of right and wrong. As the 6-year-old enters the classroom world, he becomes aware of forces outside the home that relate to his concepts of "good," "bad," "right," and "wrong." For the next few years he considers making adjustments to his moral consciousness that he now recognizes must be more extensive, insightful, and judgmental than the family-oriented code of conduct that he had developed up to this time. Turner, Peck, and Havighurst, as cited by Rains and Morris,[27] suggest that there is little reason to expect significant changes in a person's basic character after the ages of 9 or 10 years. It could be, then, that the primary teacher may be the last person who could be responsible for or capable of helping to determine the basic character of the child.

The 6- to 8-year-old is still egocentric, a characteristic that greatly affects his own concept of moral behavior. As a result, his inclination is to justify his behavior by some rationalization, which to him is perfectly logical and acceptable. If this approach does not work, he may seek to protect himself by lying or cheating. The 7-year-old is quick to demand honesty from others and recognizes the moral implications of not lying to his friends. The 8-year-old becomes conscious of the effect of his wrongdoing on his status among his peers. Older primary children have a strong sense of fair play for themselves. The cry "That's not fair!" is often heard. The child may be right, but sometimes he is trying to avoid the fact that he is in the wrong. By the age of 9 years "being fair" tends to apply to all who are playing the game.

Taking things belonging to others is rather common among the 6- and 7-year-olds. The 6-year-old does this openly and if confronted with the fact, will deny the stealing or will say "But he gave it to me." The 7-year-old is more subtle, and the 8-year-old is more careful. A conscience, or a moral judgment, is slowly developing in the child. This development started at the age of 4 years, when the child began to develop a self-ideal. By the age of 8 years the conscience will serve as a source of self-control or, if overdeveloped, as a cause for feelings of guilt. However, the conscience of an 8-year-old will tolerate some stretching of the truth but will have some control over impulses of the moment which suggest that something be stolen. The 8-year-old may become proficient at alibiing or at placing the blame for a misconduct on something or someone else. A third grader who wanted to stay at a friend's house longer to play turned his watch back an hour. When he got home late, he acted surprised, saying that something must be wrong with his watch.

There is an expanding awareness of moral conduct in society as children mature. As they get older, they differentiate between what is acceptable conduct within their peer group and what is acceptable to the adult world. They recognize, but do not necessarily understand, the ambiguities that they observe between what adults tell them is the "right" thing to do and what the adults themselves do under the same circumstances.

A child's spiritual interests appear to develop through experience. The philosopher Kant and some others state that man is born with some basic moral "imperatives" that relate to man's consciousness of what is moral. For example, Kant says that man knows—he does not have to be taught—that it is right "to be good" and that "he ought to be good" (quotation marks are ours). Yet Kant recognizes the influence of the external world on the child's "natural morality" and his spiritual growth.

By middle childhood God becomes important to the child who has been exposed to the concept of God (or of Buddha, Allah, or Shiva). As the child develops reasoning ability, however, he will ask questions such as "How can God be everywhere at one time?" and "How can God see everybody in the world?" Although there is a slight wonderment, if not skepticism, children of these years (who have been exposed to the idea of God) believe that God will help them and may influence what happens to them. They will pray to Him fervently for many things.

Piaget studied the moral development of children and concluded that, in many respects, moral judgment was related to level of cognitive development and to the degree of interaction with other children, especially in learning rules of games.[28] To study children's moral judgments Piaget used pairs of stories in which children were involved in misdeeds of various kinds.[29] The children between 6 and 8 years of age had to decide which story depicted the worst misdeed. In one pair of stories the first was about a boy who broke twelve cups while helping his mother set the table, whereas the second story was about a boy who broke one cup while trying to get some jam that he had been forbidden to have. The children judged the boy who broke the twelve cups to have been most at fault.

Another story involved the telling of falsehoods. A boy came home from school and told his mother, to amuse her, that he had seen an elephant in the street. Another boy tried to deceive his mother and stated that he had received a better grade than he had actually received. In this case the children stated that the boy who told the elephant story was most at fault. Children at this age judge actions on the quantitative basis rather than on intentions.

Piaget studied the games of children to discover their "natural morality." He believed that in simple childhood games the morality or rules are taught by older children to the younger. In this manner the rules are passed down from generation to generation with little or no influence or change by adults. Based on his studies Piaget divides the child's morality into (1) the practice of the rules and (2) the consciousness of rules. The practice of the rules evolved through four stages from (1) a purely motor and individual character in which the child was learning to play the game, to (2) the egocentric stage in which the child plays largely by himself but knows that rules exist, to (3) the cooperation on the rules for the games in which children play together, to (4) the codification of the rules, in which the rules are fixed and everyone knows them. Consciousness of the rules develops at the same time that the practice of the rules evolves. Consciousness evolves from the level (1) at which the rules are not coercive in nature or believed to be mandatory, to (2) at which the rules are sacred and must not be broken, to the last stage (3) at which the rules must be respected but may be changed by common consent.

Piaget is challenged by some researchers on his theory concerning development of moral judgment.[30] In general, two observations are made. First, although moral judgment of children is affected somewhat by age, it is more strongly affected by sociocultural influences. Piaget did not place enough emphasis on this point say the dissident researchers. Second, although Piaget believed that reactions at one given stage tend to be uniform, others found that there seem to be different levels and types of development within a given stage. The researchers challenging Piaget believe that learning experiences are more important than maturational processes in forming character. Significant learning experiences encompass such areas as social class attitudes and learning conditions, cultural and traditional behavior, parental emphasis and attitudes, and type of disciplinary measures to which the child was subjected.

STUDY GUIDE

1. Review the developmental tasks of this age group. Think of a child whom you know who has recently or will soon enter the first or second year of school. Can you see these tasks as being reflected in the needs, behavior, and goals of these children? How?
2. What advancements in motor skills have the 6- to 8-year-olds made as compared to the 3- to 5-year-olds?
3. How does the play culture of the 6- to 8-year-olds relate to their levels of social development? Do you see any carryover or relationships?
4. Describe Piaget's stage of concrete operations. Compare its level of development in a child with the cognitive developmental features of the preoperational thought stage presented in Chapter 6.
5. How are language, speech development, and logical thought related?
6. It is important that you know the definitions, the details, and the implications of the term *self-concept*. After you study the meaning of self-concept, seek to identify the various aspects and characteristics of your own self-concept. How do you see yourself? How do others see you? Are your notions about yourself correct? Are theirs?
7. The concept of sex roles and sex typing is being challenged by some psychologists and some liberation movement advocates who claim that sex roles are no longer as rigidly defined as they used to be and certainly no longer as applicable and influential as they used to be. As you consider growing boys and girls of today, what do you think influences boys to "act like boys" and girls to "act like girls," or do you think there are few directions or influences guiding them into sex roles? Who will do the cooking, the laundry, and care for the baby when you raise your own family?
8. Which age level has a greater sense of morality, the 6-year-old or the 8-year-old? Is it possible to say? Justify your position.

REFERENCES

1. Havighurst, R.: Human development and education, New York, 1953, Longmans, Green & Co., Inc.
2. Watson, E. H., and Lowry, G. H.: Growth and development in children, ed. 5, Chicago, 1967, Year Book Medical Publishers, Inc.
3. Jenkins, D. G., Shacter, H. S., and Bower, W. B.: These are your children, ed. 3, Glenview, Ill., 1966, Scott, Foresman & Co.

4. Gesell, A., and Ilg, F. L.: The child from five to ten, New York, 1946, Harper & Row, Publishers, p. 100.
5. Strang, R.: An introduction to child study, ed. 4, New York, 1959, The Macmillan Co., p. 273.
6. Burt, C. L.: Child psychology, vol. V, Chicago, 1969, Encyclopaedia Britannica, Inc., pp. 503-508.
7. Hutt, M. L., and Gilby, R. G.: The child: development and adjustment, Boston, 1959, Allyn & Bacon, Inc., pp. 227-277.
8. Ilg, F., and Ames, L.: Parents ask, New York, 1962, Harper & Row, Publishers, pp. 204-206.
9. Opie, P., and Opie, I.: Children's games in street and playground, New York, 1969, Oxford University Press, Inc.
10. Pickard, P. M.: The activity of children, London, 1965, Longmans, Green & Co., Ltd., pp. 67-68.
11. Sutton-Smith, B.: Children at play, Nat. Hist. 80:54-59, Dec., 1971.
12. Flavell, J. H.: The developmental psychology of Jean Piaget, Princeton, N. J., 1963, D. Van Nostrand Co., p. 82.
13. Piaget, J.: The child's conception of number, New York, 1965, W. W. Norton & Co., Inc., p. viii.
14. Piaget, J.: The child's conception of the world, Paterson, N. J., 1960, Littlefield, Adams & Co., pp. 374-375.
15. Piaget, J.: The child's conception of physical causality, London, 1966, Routledge & Kegan Paul, Ltd., p. 305.
16. Almy, M., Chittenden, E., and Miller, P.: Young children's thinking: studies of some aspects of Piaget's thinking, New York, 1966, Teachers College Press, p. 515.
17. Piaget, J.: The language and thought of the child, New York, 1959, The Humanities Press, Inc., p. 10.
18. Ibid., pp. 20-27.
19. Emmerich, W.: Stability and change in early personality development, Young Child. 21:233-243, 1966.
20. Hogan, E. O., and Green, R. L.: Can teachers modify children's self-concepts? Teach. Col. Rec. 62:423-426, Feb., 1971.
21. Burtt, M.: The effect of a man teacher, Young Child. 21:92-97, Nov., 1965.
22. Hogan and Green, op. cit., p. 425.
23. Minuchin, P.: Sex-role concepts and sex-typing in childhood as a function of school and home environments, Child Dev. 36:1033-1048, 1965.
24. Lazar, E. A.: Children's perception of other children's fears, Ph.D. dissertation, New York, 1963, Teachers College, Columbia University.
25. Grollman, E. A.: Explaining death to children, Boston, 1968, Beacon Press, p. 16.
26. Fromm, E.: Love between parent and child, Psychol. Today 1: Feb., 1968.
27. Rains, S., and Morris, R.: The role of the primary teacher in character education, Young Child. 25:105, Dec., 1969.
28. Piaget, J.: The moral judgment of the child, New York, 1948, The Free Press, p. 1.
29. Elkind, D.: Children and adolescents: interpretive essays on Jean Piaget, New York, 1970, Oxford University Press, Inc., pp. 59-60.
30. Bandura, A., and McDonald, F. J.: The influences of social reinforcement and the behavior of models in shaping children's moral judgment, J. Abnorm. Soc. Psychol. 67:274-281, 1963.

8 Late childhood
9 to 11 years of age

PREADOLESCENCE: OUR GANG

As I look back over the years when I was 11 and 12 years old, I now wonder how I survived it all! And for my peace of mind I luckily remember only some of the many traumas I experienced.

Some things I remember were so exciting, especially learning about certain new things. Seventh grade and learning about Greek and Roman mythology and about Norsemen and medieval castles was really interesting. My mind felt like a sponge absorbing all that "good stuff." One particular instance is vivid in my mind. These years were years of isolation—boys stayed away from girls and vice versa, but the competition was for mental achievement. Teams were formed, boys against the girls, of course. We had contests and played the learning baseball game to see who knew more about the geography of Europe. I may be prejudiced, but the girls were usually the champs. Mainly this was because Lonny was the only boy on their team who studied for the contests. That didn't keep the boys from trying to win, but then again that didn't get them to study either.

Top that fact off with the situation that the girls were physically larger than most of the boys. The girls were sometimes larger in two directions, not only taller but wider. I was one of the lucky "chunky" ones, or as my mother kindly put it, "You are solid." I had a horrible nickname to go with my "solidness." The male cafeteria partner I had named me Sixteen Tons, to go along with Frankie Lane's song. All the way to the cafeteria he teased, while a red-faced girl walked beside him.

I may have been chunky, but my physical skill at sports was nothing to tease about. My best—very best—friend, Peggy, and I beat the only boys on our block, Ronnie and his brother, in baseball, hit-the-can, and marbles almost every evening in the summer. Peggy could hit good home runs all the way down the road. I can still see Ronnie hunting for the ball in the high weeds while I cheered for our side. The score? 19 to 4—our favor, of course!

Emotionally it was a trying time. What would I have done if I had not had a best friend to confide in! My mother didn't understand me! Then, too, there were the inevitable discussions about Peggy's heroine, Clara Barton. (Peggy wanted to become a nurse.) My favorite book was *Little Women*. I would sit there and cry for everyone in that family.

Socially, I remember the age of 11 and 12 years as a time of cruelty, according to my adult standards. How inconsiderate we were, but that was our gang.

Our girls' gang had a leader. Meggie had very little going for her academically, but she was one of the biggest girls in our class. She also had red hair, a fiery temper, and could verbalize some of the choicest, vulgar words we girls had ever heard. Of course, we had our home and neighborhood groups, but since we traveled by bus to school, this primary gang was Meggie's private domain. She certainly was cruel to others, but we would not break the solidarity of the gang. Meggie always batted first for her team. If the recess bell rang, all normal sixth graders would go inside the building, but not Meggie. She would stay on the base until everyone was afraid to stay out to tag her out. Then when everyone went tearing in because we were late, Meggie would run to home plate fast and claim another run for her team. She still could run into school fast enough to not be in trouble. How exasperating when you were on the other team!

Meggie also set the intellectual tone for the sixth grade room. If she did a math problem wrong on the chalkboard, most girls would not offer to correct it because Meggie would let the words fly at recess and also make faces at you during class. The intellectual corrector could also be sure she would be ostracized from the group at recess—the pressure of the group made conformists of us all. Just to belong to the group was most important.

The nasty notes that Meggie passed to her "enemies" were group pressures, too. The words were overwhelming and the spelling was poor, but no one ever bothered to correct Meggie.

We seldom considered telling an adult about our gang's situation. I can remember going home upset by some of Meggie's antics, but if it had not been for a highly perceptive parent who gave me the option. "You seem upset, want to talk about it?" I think those emotions may have overwhelmed me.

By seventh grade and age 12 years the tone of the group had changed considerably. We formed new gangs, usually excluding Meggie. She was in another homeroom (luckily for us), and she was also separated from her best friend and partner in crime. Divide and conquer seemed to be the best cure for Meggie's actions. At lunch the new gang often sat on a bench and just gossiped about teachers, friends out of the group, and clothes. I still remember the fact that one girl owned fourteen pairs of shoes. Tremendous!

Our notes were now friendlier and sometimes just for fun. Of course we always wrote our notes in pig-Latin code. One dear little teacher intercepted a note of mine en route. Terror! She read it (I guess she could interpret pig Latin), then discreetly tore it up and put it in the paper can.

Even in seventh grade the boys did not bother us much. They played running games a lot; often we just sat on the sidelines and talked. Occasionally, we watched team games.

The most traumatic social experience in seventh grade involved us in a moral issue as well as in pressure of the gang. You might guess that it involved Meggie, and by my standards of today it was quite cruel. One girl in our class was a Jehovah's Witness. No one had ever taken time to explain why she wouldn't salute the flag or participate in some of our group activities, but we weren't bothered about it. Our group accepted Lynda, and things went smoothly. However, Meg's group noticed Lynda's differences and began a campaign for exclusion. Lynda did not give in easily, and since Meggie's power over the group had diminished, the group was on Lynda's side this time. For some time the group was under tremendous pressure, but it ended Meggie's ultimate power over us and helped us to learn about tolerance.

We had our problems, we formed our own solutions, and we tried to go it alone without adult intervention. As I look backward, I see that I gained a great sensitivity to the needs of others from all that cruelty.

The ages of 9 to 12 years are interesting because they depict childhood at its highest form of development. Soon the youngsters will leave childhood and move on to the next major phase of growth and development—adolescence. They will never be children again. There is no universal rule as to when children take on the characteristics of late childhood, or preadolescence. (We use the two terms interchangeably in this text.) Generally, the first psychological signs are detected in 9-year-olds; the signs are clearly evident in the 11- and 12-year-olds.

The preadolescent stage is one of the least studied age groups. There are volumes of research material available for the middle childhood years and for adolescence, but research on late childhood is meager by comparison. A major reason for this lack of emphasis in studying late childhood is the overlapping of similarities that exist between middle childhood and late childhood and between late childhood and adolescence. Late childhood is a strong continuation of developmental characteristics started in middle childhood, especially of the 8-year-olds. A study of puberty and early adolescence usually covers the 11- and 12-year-olds of late childhood. However, we submit that the years of 9 to 12 have differences from the middle childhood and adolescent years that are significant and unique enough to deserve special attention.

Preadolescence is a trying period for parents and teachers as well as for the child. The child is trying to grow out of his dependence on his parents for guidance and direction. He enjoys separating himself from the family in his interests and activities, and so family relationships and interactions change from what they used to be. He frequently challenges his parents and other authority, although his judgment is often erroneous and immature. The child's interest in acquiring knowledge is a wholesome development, but it also creates problems at times. The child can no longer be "fooled" by his parents or teachers. Yet he does not have enough information and insight to produce good perspectives on his own. The preadolescent is highly competent, as a child, but he still lacks the development necessary to make him completely reliable, effective, and resourceful.

The developmental tasks of late childhood are somewhat clouded because there is such a strong continuum of life experiences that pass on from middle childhood into the adolescent period. The developmental tasks begun in middle childhood continue to be faced in late childhood. The difference is that in late childhood the tasks require a higher level of proficiency for attainment. The developmental tasks for preadolescence are (1) gaining freedom from a primary identification with adults by learning to become self-reliant, (2) developing social competency in forming and maintaining friendships with peers, (3) learning to live in the adult world by getting a clearer perspective of one's peer group role or place in that world, (4) developing a moral code of conduct based on principles rather than specifics, (5) consolidating the identification made with one's sex role, (6) integrating and refining motor patterns to a higher level of efficiency, (7) learning realistic ways of studying and controlling the physical world, (8) developing appropriate symbol systems and conceptual abilities for learning, communicating, and reasoning, and (9) evolving an understanding of self and the world (society and cosmos).[1]

PHYSICAL GROWTH AND MOTOR DEVELOPMENT

Although the preadolescent is somewhat of a mystery to adults in regard to his internal makeup, external data concerning this age group are available. The preadolescent years are transitional years. For some children, particularly girls, this period is the beginning of pubescence. For others, particularly boys, it is a time of steady growth in height and weight. For all it is the most healthy period of their lives. During these few short years, they will enjoy a pause between childhood diseases and the diseases of adulthood. However, it is important to watch out for accidents because these are "daring" years.

Physical characteristics

Physical growth during late childhood is characterized by a gradual steady gain in bodily measurements. The various parts of the body not only increase in size but also become more functional. In other words, physical development improves in quality as well as quantity. The skeletal frame becomes larger, the trunk increases moderately in length, and the extremities become proportionately longer. The trunk broadens and deepens, with shoulders and hips developing similarly in each sex. The muscles accelerate their rate of growth, and the ligamentous structures become firmer and stronger. As a result, body posture is improved over that found in the young child. Body stance and balance are more appropriate for efficient erectness, for locomotion, and for strength in the use of arms and trunk. At 12 or 13 years of age girls are about a year ahead of boys in the development of the bones of the wrist (carpal bones), which is one of the best single measurements of physical maturity.[2]

Boys at the age of 9 years will have an average height of 53.3 inches and at 11 years, 57 inches. There is an increase in height of 1.1 inch per year. Nine-year-old girls will have an average height of 52.3 inches and 11-year-olds, 58.3 inches. There is an average increase of 2 inches a year.[3] From third to fifth grade, boys are slightly taller than girls, but in sixth grade the average girl is taller than the boy. Progress in height is closely correlated with approaching sexual maturity. The most rapid growth period in height for girls precedes menarche usually by two years. Growth in height for boys appears linked to genital development.[4] A positive correlation also exists between tallness in preadolescence and tallness later in adulthood. Children who grow rapidly during this period tend to be taller as adults.[5]

In weight boys at 9 years of age will weigh an average of 66 pounds and at 11 years, 77.2 pounds. Increase in weight for boys per year is 3.7 pounds. Girls will weigh an average of 63.8 pounds at 9 years of age and 78.3 pounds at 11 years. The increase in weight for girls is about 4.8 pounds per year. During late childhood, girls mature faster physically than boys and tend to be larger than boys during the latter part of this developmental stage. Progress in weight tends to be less regular than height, since weight is greatly influenced by environmental factors. Weight, like height, seems related to advent of sexual maturity. The greatest increase in weight for girls occurs about three months before menarche, around 12 years of age. The greatest growing period for weight for boys is around the age of 14 years. (See Table 8-1.)

From birth until the age of 4 years rapid growth development takes place in the heart. There is rather slow growth of the heart during early and middle childhood, but it speeds up during the latter part of preadolescence. The greatest rate of growth of the heart occurs at the time of the child's greatest growth in weight. By 12 years of age the heart has gained seven times in weight as compared to its birth weight, and it will increase its size by twelve times by adulthood.[6] The rate of heart growth during childhood does not seem to keep pace with overall body growth, especially at the ages of 9 and 10 years. The relationship of the size of the arteries and the heart is especially critical. The typical size of the arteries and heart during childhood leads one to question the advisability of extended, intense physical exertion for some children, especially when accompanied by the stress of competition.

Extreme deviations and disturbances in physical growth can affect mental health adjustment of preadolescent children. Very tall girls feel especially self-conscious. Boys are particularly disturbed at being undersized and often worry about whether they will ever grow up. Uneven growth may create problems of awkwardness and self-consciousness. Inappropriate growth, such as a boy who develops feminine features, presents still more problems of adjustment. Personality difficulties and emotional conflicts often arise out of fears of physical inadequacy.[7] Parents and teachers should be particularly understanding of these possibilities and help the child through this period of adjustment.

Table 8-1. Height and weight gains for boys and girls ages 9 to 12 years*

	PERCENTILES (BOYS)				PERCENTILES (GIRLS)		
	10	50	90		10	50	90
9 years				**9 years**			
Weight in pounds	56.3	66.0	81.0	Weight in pounds	52.6	63.8	79.1
Weight in kilograms	25.54	29.94	36.74	Weight in kilograms	23.86	28.94	35.88
Height in inches	50.5	53.3	56.1	Height in inches	50.0	52.3	55.3
Height in centimeters	128.3	135.5	142.6	Height in centimeters	127.0	132.9	140.4
9½ years				**9½ years**			
Weight in pounds	58.7	69.0	85.5	Weight in pounds	54.9	67.1	84.4
Weight in kilograms	26.63	31.3	38.78	Weight in kilograms	24.9	30.44	38.28
Height in inches	51.4	54.3	57.1	Height in inches	50.9	53.5	56.4
Height in centimeters	130.6	137.9	145.1	Height in centimeters	129.4	135.8	143.2
10 years				**10 years**			
Weight in pounds	61.1	71.9	89.9	Weight in pounds	57.1	70.3	89.7
Weight in kilograms	27.71	32.61	40.78	Weight in kilograms	25.9	31.89	40.69
Height in inches	52.3	55.2	58.1	Height in inches	51.8	54.6	57.5
Height in centimeters	132.8	140.3	147.5	Height in centimeters	131.7	138.6	146.0
10½ years				**10½ years**			
Weight in pounds	63.7	74.8	94.6	Weight in pounds	59.9	74.6	95.1
Weight in kilograms	28.89	33.93	42.91	Weight in kilograms	27.17	33.79	43.14
Height in inches	53.2	56.0	58.9	Height in inches	52.9	55.8	58.9
Height in centimeters	135.1	142.3	149.7	Height in centimeters	134.4	141.7	149.7
11 years				**11 years**			
Weight in pounds	66.3	77.6	99.3	Weight in pounds	62.6	78.8	100.4
Weight in kilograms	30.07	35.2	45.04	Weight in kilograms	28.4	35.74	45.54
Height in inches	54.0	56.8	59.8	Height in inches	53.9	57.0	60.4
Height in centimeters	137.3	144.2	151.8	Height in centimeters	137.0	144.7	153.4
11½ years				**11½ years**			
Weight in pounds	69.2	81.0	104.5	Weight in pounds	66.1	83.2	106.0
Weight in kilograms	31.39	36.74	47.4	Weight in kilograms	29.98	37.74	48.08
Height in inches	55.0	57.8	60.9	Height in inches	55.0	58.3	61.8
Height in centimeters	139.8	146.9	154.8	Height in centimeters	139.8	148.1	157.0
12 years				**12 years**			
Weight in pounds	72.0	84.4	109.6	Weight in pounds	69.5	87.6	111.5
Weight in kilograms	32.66	38.28	49.71	Weight in kilograms	31.52	39.74	50.58
Height in inches	56.1	58.9	62.2	Height in inches	56.1	59.8	63.2
Height in centimeters	142.4	149.6	157.9	Height in centimeters	142.6	151.9	160.6

*From Latham, H. C., and Heckel, R. V.: Pediatric nursing, ed. 2, St. Louis, 1972, The C. V. Mosby Co.

Late childhood is the time when the permanent teeth appear. Girls are more advanced than boys in dentition at any age in childhood. In the following statements the sequence of the appearance of teeth is more significant than the age at which they are said to appear. Major individual differences occur in the age of appearance. At 8 years of age the first permanent back teeth (first molars) and the center front teeth (central incisors) appear. Between 8 and 9 years of age the eye teeth on the lower jaw (canines) emerge. The upper canines may not appear for at least two more years. Between the ages of 10 and 12 years the two teeth (bicuspids) on the sides behind each canine appear.[8] Most children have all their permanent teeth except wisdom teeth by the age of 12 or 13 years.

Health

The ages from 9 to 12 are usually the healthiest years of a child's life. A major reason is that the lymphoid masses which help to fight infections are at their highest point of development in quantity. The average 11-year-old has almost twice the lymphoid masses that he will have as an adult, and before and after the age of 11 years his body will have well above the amount of a 20-year-old. Mother Nature must have known how difficult it would be to keep preadolescents out of the rain and to have them button their coats to keep warm in the winter, so she wisely gave this age group some extra protection to ward off colds and other diseases. A more likely explanation for the extra lymphoid masses is that if the child has survived to this stage in life, nature wanted to do what it could to increase survival potential to adulthood when the individual can help to perpetuate the species, which is one of the basic aims of life. Another reason for the good health of this age group is that most children have already been exposed to the communicable diseases of childhood or have in some manner become immune. They have an interest in outdoor games that gives them sufficient physical exercise to maintain good muscle tone and good intake of oxygen. For the most part they get 9 to 10 hours of sleep a night. They are not as tempted to stay up late as they will be when they are older. They have enormous appetites so that they generally get enough food. Fresh air, rest, exercise, good nutrition, plus an innate ability to ward off diseases all contribute to a healthy life. However, imaginary illnesses are not uncommon. This youngster soon learns that he is not expected to carry on his usual activities when he is ill. Pressures at school, such as tests or difficulties with his peers, may put him to bed for a day or two. Most, however, miss less school than formerly.

Motor ability and activities

During late childhood, children gain in vigor and balance in sensorimotor control and coordination. They generally improve in manual dexterity, increase their resistance to fatigue, and develop greater muscular strength. These factors allow for finer motor usage of small muscles over longer periods of time, resulting in a rapid improvement in the ability of these children to control their bodies and to manipulate objects with which they play. They improve in agility, accuracy, and endurance. They run faster, throw and catch much better, and can jump and climb with ease and assurance. By the age of 9 years eye-hand coordination is good. The child is ready for crafts and shop work. His eyes are almost adult size, and he is ready to do close work with less strain.

This is a period when children have so much energy that they do not know when to stop. Their constant drive, inability to be quiet, and concentration on the game are enough to drive the most understanding adult supervisor to distraction. Parents often become concerned with so much physical play and roughhousing. Popular physical activities at this stage are playing ball, riding a bicycle, jumping rope, ice and roller skating, hiking in the woods, hopscotch, swimming, and running. Team games are popular. Vigorous bodily activities are preferred to finer motor skills. Children usually devote more time to the use of their body than to tools or toys. It is an unhappy youngster who does not possess the physical skills needed to play the games of his peer group.

At this age children, boys especially, are constantly pushing themselves into new activities that require new skills or courage. "I dare you" is an often-used phrase. Playing "follow the leader" or taking a dare to walk along the top of a narrow fence improves motor skills and balance. Thus children develop more versatility, speed of movement, physical strength, and control of their bodies.

Frederic Lewis, Inc., New York City.

Lack of success is rarely frustrating to the young preschool child. However, elementary grade youngsters become easily frustrated when they fail to grasp immediately the technique of an activity such as dribbling a large rubber ball. They need freedom from overdemanding standards of control while learning simple coordinations. Exposure to fellow classmates and the scrutiny of the teacher when learning a new skill are particularly upsetting. A child is conscious of what he thinks is a disapproving glance from the teacher and the titters of his classmates. Usually the titters come from the classmates who themselves are inadequate in this particular skill. If at all possible, a teacher should arrange a time or way for the child to experiment and practice motor skills in an accepting atmosphere. It is unwise to push a child into a game or test situation until he has adequate chance to learn the particular skill or skills needed.

Prelude to puberty

The earliest ages at which puberty normally occurs are 10 years for girls and 12 years for boys. As will be noted in the next chapter, there are indications that there is an increase in the number of girls who reach puberty at 9 years of age. In general, the average age of puberty for girls is about 12 years, and for boys it is about 14 years. Before puberty occurs, however, there are some physiological changes that take place in both sexes, in girls before boys.

With the approach of puberty general

body proportions change in both sexes. In girls an overall rounding and softening of the body features begins. At 11 years of age noticeable individual differences are apparent between slow and fast physically maturing girls. Heavier, taller girls generally begin the pubertal period before thinner, shorter girls. The pelvic area of the prepubescent girl broadens, whereas the shoulder width remains about the same. An adipose (fatty) tissue is formed on the hips and chest. The face is fuller. The legs become more shapely as they lose their long, thin, toothpick look. The breast buds appear, and the nipples begin to darken. Most 10- to 11-year-old girls are greatly aware of their breast development and may be concerned if there is no evidence of this. Some become concerned because they believe the development is evident to others. The spurt in height growth starts a year or two before the climax of puberty. For girls the fastest growth in height and weight, on the average, is during the twelfth year. They may gain 2 to 4 inches in height and 8 to 10 pounds in weight during their peak year.

Boys do little sexual maturing until the end of preadolescence, when the genital organs begin to grow. At the age of 10 years a smaller proportion of adult height is achieved than in previous years. Eleven years of age is known as the "fat period" because a general overall adding of fatty tissues occurs. Body proportions of the boys become more solid, and rounding of the contours around the neck and chin becomes noticeable. There is an increase in the bone structure, bringing the skeletal structure into prominence, especially in the chest area. The peak year for gains in height and weight, on the average, is 14 years of age, when boys gain 4 to 5 inches in height and 12 to 14 pounds in weight. At about 11 or 12 years of age boys usually begin to mature sexually. There is a rapid development of the primary sex characteristics. Secondary sex characteristics usually do not appear until the ages of 13 or 14 years.

There is a change in body chemistry in prepubescence. The pituitary gland pours hormones into the bloodstream that have potent effects on growth. Other hormones produce emotional effects on the children. In some cases personality traits change or behavior patterns become different. Children may withdraw temporarily from their family, they may react with irritation over little things that never bothered them before, and they have some strong rebellious feelings that manifest themselves in unexpected ways. They have a growing awareness of sex and sex differences. They are concerned about the appearance of their changing bodies. Not all children mature at the same rate—physical growth proceeds unevenly. Natural developments may alarm some youngsters if they do not understand what is happening. They need information and reassurance from a competent adult they can trust.

SEXUAL AWARENESS AND SEX INFORMATION

One of the characteristics of the so-called permissive society of recent years has been a liberal, less restricted, uninhibited social and cultural mass media approach to sex and sexuality. The availability of pictorial and printed material on the topic of sex, the open display of nudity and sexual behavior in films and on the stage, and the loose, sometimes completely lacking, moral considerations of such matters have subjected individuals of all ages to behaviors, suggestions, and attitudes that in the past were treated, at least in the open marketplaces of society, with more restraint. What effect this exposure has or will have on today's children is open to speculation. Characteristics related to sex and sexuality in children and adults in the world of tomorrow are yet to be determined because of life-space influences of today. As far as we are concerned, we can only report the results of research on this topic as they are available at this time.

Psychosexual development and awareness

Sexual awareness begins long before puberty. In a general way it may be said that in earliest infancy a child is exposed to environmental stimuli that affect the development of sexuality. The baby's body is washed, examined, dressed, and caressed. He is picked up, fed, and rocked. Almost all his feelings of pleasure and security come from some form of physical contact. It is reasonable to assume that the infant will soon associate contentment, well-being, and love with the pleasant physical and sensory stimulations provided by the persons taking care of him. Before long the infant enjoys physical stimulation that he provides for himself. He plays with his hands, explores his feet and toes, moves his arms and legs, and eventually puts almost everything he picks up into his mouth. Love, pleasure, and physical stimulation go together. The importance of the quality of physical contact provided by mothers is indicated by the studies of Harlow[9] with infant monkeys. Monkeys exposed to a "hard-surface" surrogate mother made of chicken wire did not develop as healthy a sexuality in adulthood as did the monkeys exposed to a soft mother.

In early childhood, between the ages of 3 and 5 years, there is a growing concept in the child that his physical sexual characteristics differ from those of some other people. The degree and appearance of this awareness depend on the age and the sex of the child, the presence or absence of brothers and sisters, and the bathroom and dressing practices of the home in which he is reared.[10] Physical responses between preschool children are not unusual. They will hug and kiss each other without giving any indication that one sex is preferred over another. Sexual awareness enters the life of a preschool or school child when a new arrival is expected in the family. Depending on the age of the child, questions concerning the physical change in the mother are asked, and curiosity is expressed regarding preparations being made for the arrival of the new baby.

It is when the child enters school that he learns the true meaning of sex differences and sex roles. The boys belong to one group, and the girls belong to another. A number of activities and situations, such as separate lavatory facilities, increase the awareness of differences. Feelings of modesty develop in earnest. The child from 5 to 8 years of age has many questions that are related to sex.[11] Questions such as "How does a baby get inside the mother?" and "Does the mother's egg ever go into the father?" and "How does the baby breathe inside the mother?" are often asked. Six-year-olds are usually satisfied with a simple explanation, but an 8-year-old may need a more detailed answer. Mild forms of sex play between members of the same sex or with the opposite sex are not unusual because they are curious and interested in each other's bodies. By 8 years of age there is some interest in peeping, provocative giggling, and in writing or whispering words dealing with sex or elimination functions.[12] This interest and activity increases during late childhood.

The late childhood youngster socializes with his or her own sex. This is a period when emotional identification is with the peers of one's own sex and the opposite sex is rejected. Just because there is little connection between the two sexes at this time, it does not mean that they are not aware of each other. It is during the preadolescent years that boys draw the female anatomy, looking through mail-order catalogues in the section showing pictures of women modeling panties, brassieres, and lingerie, and trying hard to get their hands on pornographic literature. Girls are not all innocent. Some of them also draw pictures, read and write notes with sexual implications, and engage in double-meaning talk among themselves.

Preadolescent girls show an absorbed interest in their new physical developments, not only of their own but also of other girls their age. Many look ahead to the day when their breasts will be advanced enough to wear a brassiere. Fortunately, manufacturers have recognized the desire and need for a very small brassiere so that even small-breasted girls can qualify when contemporaries check on which ones are wearing brassieres. Not all girls, however, are pleased or proud of their breast development. Some are embarrassed and hunch their shoulders in an effort to hide their development. For most girls, however, this initial embarrassment will be alleviated by 12 or 13 years of age, and they will exchange their loose blouses for sweaters and T-shirts. By 11 years of age most girls have some knowledge about menstruation, intercourse, and reproduction.

Most preadolescent boys, especially at the age of 9 or 10 years, do not feel free to discuss sex matters with their parents. If they do ask questions, they do so at inopportune times for discussion, indicating their immaturity in such matters. Some 10-year-olds will still think that being married is essential for having babies. They still have to learn about the functions of marriage and the importance of the family for the birth and rearing of a baby.[13] An 11-year-old is starting to realize that marriage involves personal relationships which go beyond mating and that someone does not have to be married to have a baby. Spontaneous erections occur among many 11-year-olds, caused by such things as physical movements, conversations, pictures, daydreams, and general excitement of any kind, not necessarily sexual in nature. As at all ages, boys are more likely than girls to tell smutty jokes and write four-letter words in public places. They do not completely understand why these words and jokes are emotionally loaded, but they do know that "it sure gets adults."

Sexuality and sexual learning

There is evidence to support the claim that many children experience some type of sex play during or before the preadolescent years. Children are experimentalists and curious. The sex play is incidental and transitory in nature. It is not due to love relationships or to a sex urge, since organic development has not yet begun. It is play and not lovemaking. Whether or not emotional scars or guilt feelings result depends a great deal on how the behavior is handled by the parents if such play has been discovered or if the child views his actions as something wrong in the eyes of his parents or God.

Elias and Gebhard[14] did a study on sex and sexuality in 1969 with a sample population of 305 boys and 127 girls, ages 8 to 12 years, grouped by occupational class of the parents. Part of the research was related to sex play engaged in before reaching puberty. The study reported that sex play before puberty involving more than oneself had been experienced by 52% of the boys with other boys and 34% of the boys with girls. In the sample of girls 35% had sex play with other girls, and 37% had heterosexual experiences. The average age for some sex play among boys was 9.2 years and for heterosexual play was 8.8 years. The same study revealed that although boys and girls from blue-collar homes learn at an earlier age about intercourse, abortions, and prostitution (average age range 8 to 10 years), children from white-collar homes (middle-class socioeconomic status) surpass the others in total knowledge in all categories of sex knowledge surveyed. The girls from the lower-class homes were pathetically lacking about some extremely vital information. For example, more of these girls knew more about coitus than they did about the cause of pregnancy; many were unaware of "where babies come from."

Schofield[15] cites a study of 934 boys and 939 girls designed to determine when they first found out about the facts of life. The research indicated that 67% of the boys and 76% of the girls had such information by the age of 12 or 13 years. The implication is that the time for giving sex information should be no later than late childhood, since after that age period there would be a need for reeducation because of incomplete facts or misinformation learned previously. Most sex learning during this period comes from the peer group and often brings with it many misconceptions. Eighty-eight percent of the boys in the blue-collar group and 70% of the boys in the middle-class group received their sex knowledge from their peer group.[16]

SOCIAL BEHAVIOR

By the age of 9 years most children will have made the change from being family oriented in activities and control to being members of their own age group. The group begins to have a tremendous influence on the attitudes, desires, and behavior of the child—an influence that increases as the child grows older and becomes an adolescent. Late childhood is a transitional period, during which the social patterns and behavioral characteristics of childhood change to those that are considered more typical of adolescence. Specifically, the social behavior characteristics of preadolescence stem from three basic attitudes. First, there is strong desire to be with age mates of one's own sex. Second, there is a loyalty to a gang or group composed of other children similar in age, sex, size, and interests. Third, there is a change in regard to authority, expressed largely by a seeming rejection of adult standards.

Social structure in preadolescence

Social development and change take place rapidly in late childhood. The child no longer wants to play at home alone or do things with members of the family. One or two friends are not enough. He wants to be with the "gang," his play group. The gang gives him a feeling of belonging and of being liked. Learning to live in the social world, however, is hard for a child, especially if he has not received preparatory training for it at home during his earlier years. The gang members will work it out and help each other. Unfortunately, there is a survival element in the give-and-take of group interaction, and some "hurts" will be encountered. Some children will not make the grade and will have to go into adolescence socially unprepared or as misfits.

During late childhood, boys develop a social structure separate from that of girls. Girls do not care for this arrangement, but they have little control over the matter. Boys are more interested in developing and asserting their masculinity than they are in being friendly with girls. To be a "he-man" means to be tough, strong, and daring, and girls are none of these things. Nicknames may crop up among the boys, such as Rocky, Speedy, or Alligator. Their toughness and adventurousness are expressed by the television programs they watch, the books they read, and the "I dare you" schemes they concoct.

This period is also the secret clubhouse age, where boys seek to have their own hideaway. The clubhouse may be a tree house, a garage, an abandoned shack, or an outdoor spot difficult to get to or find. It is their way of saying to others, "I belong here and you belong elsewhere." Gangs made up of 9- and 10-year-olds often have a name and sign for the club, such as the one in our neighborhood, "The Bachelors Club—No Girls Allowed!" Secret codes, special passwords and handshakes, even club rituals may all be part of the picture. In spite of all this atmosphere of mystery and intrigue, the gang is rather loosely knit with no strong organizational structure and probably even without a recognized leader, except for special activities. As the boys approach the ages of 11 and 12 years, their relationships take on a more organized appearance and become more activity oriented, such as organizing a sports team or joining the Boy Scouts or the YMCA.

Boys have an interest in the gang stage longer than do girls.

Girls are not particularly happy in being rejected by boys. They would still like to play with them and be around them. In fact, there does not seem to be any age when girls are not interested in boys. However, in late childhood the boys set the social pace, and girls have little choice but to form their own groups. Girls groups tend to be more tightly knit than are those of boys. They are also more exclusive and autocratic about who can belong and who cannot. They place more demands on themselves as to how to act toward each other and what to do in certain situations. They keep in touch with each other by incessantly writing notes in school; note writing is one of their favorite pastimes. Girls usually meet in the home of a member where there is a minimum of interference. If they form a club, there are two things that most girl groups do almost immediately. The first is to draw up a constitution, which is usually a list of do's and don'ts such as "You will always speak to your friends when you see them" and "You will never tell secrets of the club to anyone in the whole, wide world." The second thing is to collect dues. They are not sure what they will do with the money, but they know it is important. A male looking at this setup gets an uneasy feeling that there may be a universal conspiracy among women to conquer and rule the world, and they start at an early age to learn how to run it. It is unlikely that women, or men for that matter, will ever gain control of the world, however, because unbeknownst to any of us, cats already rule the world and they are not about to give up the nice, easy living that they enjoy!

Joking aside, girls and boys do travel different social routes during late childhood. Furthermore, there is some bickering or antagonism toward each other. Boys seem to work harder at this with their aloofness and teasing than do girls. Boys and girls set up differing values and standards, too. The most admired qualities in boys at 11 and 12 years of age are competence in group games, ability to lead or keep a game going, and fearlessness and readiness to take a chance. It is much more desirable for a boy to be rough, tough, and a degree unkempt than to be quiet, withdrawn, and too clean. In girls, aggressive behavior is strongly disapproved, unless it might be in a game against the boys. Some girls, however, do become tomboys and try to imitate the boy sex role. Disturbances in the classroom are frowned on by girls. Hence in a classroom it is usually the boys who start a mischief and usually a girl who tells. For girls, prestige demands such qualities as being friendly, attractive, tidy, quietly gracious and considerate, and more "grown up." They are taught to control aggression, including assertion and extension, while being encouraged to regard the familial world as the proper sphere of their interest.[17] Differing value patterns for boys and girls can, in part, be attributed to an earlier maturity status in girls during these years of growth.

Friendships in later childhood

In addition to the gang or group phenomenon personal friendships are important to preadolescents. The behavior of "friends" might seem strange to onlookers. The more boys like one another the more frequently they seem to get into fights. Actually, they are developing loyalty and the capacity to stand up for each other. Girls tend to have an on-again off-again relationship. They get angry at each other over little things and then make up again. Both boys and girls have long talks on the telephone, calling each other often. To fathers it sometimes seems as if their daughters are forever on the telephone. The youngsters are mostly seeking support and security from each other while going through the growing-up process. A child chooses friends who are much like himself.

The reasons given for choosing friends are primarily personal. They choose friends who are cheerful, kind, agreeable, even tempered, and loyal.[18] As children grow older, they show a preference for responsibility in their friends and for children of their own socioeconomic and racial groups.[19] Frequent associations, such as the same grade in school or the same neighborhood, and similarity of interest, age, and social maturity are other factors frequently found among friends.

A statement should be made concerning boy-girl relationships in fifth and sixth grades. Not all prepubertal boys and girls reject members of the opposite sex. In some communities and subcultures there are children of these grades or ages who are interested in the opposite sex because it seems to be the fashionable thing to do. Some are even dating before entering junior high school. Cultural and social influences have been stressing boy-girl relationships, albeit on an older age level, through television, movies, comics dealing with romance, and books. Some parents consider boy-girl relationships a sign of growing up and often will push their children into early dating before the youngsters really want it or are ready for it. If dating and pairing off are encouraged during preadolescence, it is our belief that many children will be deprived of time needed to develop social and communicative skills necessary for social adequacy in junior high school. We also believe that early dating patterns will promote a faster pace and a greater diversity of social life in adolescence. The outcome will result in social experiences and behavior that could be inappropriate and possibly harmful to the child in terms of what his adolescent level of social and emotional maturity can accept.

Emerging social independence and the family

Even though the home and family will continue to be a major emotional focus for years to come, the preadolescent child is taking increasing interest in people outside the home. Consequently, contacts with family members become fewer, less influential, and less meaningful than contacts with persons outside the family unit.

As early as the age of 6 years, when he enters school, the child becomes more independent than previously by virtue of being on his own and by making more independent decisions. By the age of 8 years he makes an important discovery—he suddenly realizes that adults can make mistakes, that they do not know everything, and that they can be criticized. This knowledge provides a giant step toward self-autonomy. Because of increasing intellectual development, the 9- to 12-year-old reaches a point where he can see more clearly the shortcomings of adults. They challenge the thinking and decisions of persons in positions of authority. Soon they reject or question many of the standards of their parents and of adults in general. This characteristic does not imply that the children become discipline and behavior problems, but it does mean that they are not as ready to accept rules and standards unquestioningly as they did at an earlier age. Clashes may result, overtly or covertly.

Children from 8 through 11 years tend to be irritable toward adults, willful, critical, easily discouraged, and rejecting of rules and standards that they previously respected.[20] They begin to wonder about adult intellectual and behavioral competency. A sixth grader was asked to write an essay for his English lesson on the subject of "Parents." His comment: "We get our parents when they are so old it is very hard to change their habits or to educate them." Piaget,[21] in discussing the moral judgment of the child, suggests that a change takes place in the child's relationship to authority at ages 9 or 10 years. He suggests that at the age of 8 or 9 years the child begins to respond to the standards of his peers. It is at that age that Piaget finds children beginning to reject adult standards.

Although friction within family relationships is on an increase, the family is still a most significant part of the child's social life. Members of the family can help or hinder the child in his social adjustment process by the way in which he is treated, respected, trusted, loved, and permitted to grow. Personality and adjustment of the parents, parental expectations, methods of child training used, socioeconomic status, parental occupations, and solidarity of the family are all factors that influence the type of relationship the preadolescent child has with different family members. These are critical years in adult-child relationships. If the child breaks away from his family, he will have only the judgment and influence of his gang to guide him. Rejecting attitudes of this period will only become more intensified during the adolescent years.

Children's perspective of their parents changes at this age. Whereas their concept of "mother" is still primarily in terms of what she does for them, they recognize that she has less authority in the world than they thought she did when they were younger. The concept of "father" depends on how the father has been relating to his children. If he has delegated the job of raising the children to the mother and has been more-or-less an outsider providing for the material needs of the family, the children may never develop a close relationship with him because of the distance between them in past years. In fact, he may even be rejected if the child had an image of what the ideal father should be like and his father failed to live up to it. On the other hand, if the father has been responsive to his children during their developing years, he may now assume a greater role of importance in their eyes. Father, to the children of this age, represents the "outside world"—the world they associate with independence. He does all the things they want to do some day. He leaves the home and goes out into the world to work. He is free to come and go. He earns money and makes big decisions. He becomes a model that they want to copy. The mother is still good and nice, but she represents one who stays at home and takes care of little children. To both boys and girls the father can now become an important influence.

COGNITIVE DEVELOPMENT AND SCHOOL LEARNING

As children grow from the ages of 9 to 12 years there is major improvement in their ability to do more complicated intellectual tasks. This cognitive development is illustrated (1) by an increased ability to see significant details in a situation and to detect absurdities, (2) by more sensible answers to questions, (3) by using words more correctly and defining abstract words more precisely, (4) by making generalizations from verbal and mathematical relationships, and (5) by exhibiting a larger fund of general information. They are better able to use information they already know to make judgments or deductions in areas that are only indirectly related to the information.[22] Development of cognitive abilities during the concrete operations stage (ages 7 to 12 years) of Piaget was presented in Chapter 7. The reader is referred to that chapter for a theoretical interpretation of cognitive development for this age level.

Mental characteristics

The 9-year-old is fairly responsible and dependable. He understands explanations and tries to do things well. He has some original ideas and interests and is capable of carrying them out, although not always. He does have many interests and will often drop a project when his attention wanes. He may go on to another project or activity, never finishing the original project. However, his attention is somewhat longer than that of an 8-year-old, and he is capable of concentrating on a particular subject for a longer period of time. Girls may spend longer on a task than do boys. At 9 years of age the child is becoming critical of his performance and may work hard to perfect a skill. He wants and needs to be good at physical and mental skills so that he can get the admiration of other children.

The 10-year-old is less enthusiastic about rote learning and drill exercises as compared to the 9-year-old. At 10 years he is developing a growing capacity for abstract thinking. He asks many searching questions and wants thoughtful answers. He is now aware that people have many varying opinions and that different adults, even among those he admires, have different standards of right and wrong, good and bad. He is sensitive to lying, cheating, and unfairness and may turn on anyone with indignation if he suspects this kind of behavior. He is becoming aware of differences among people and of social problems. His ideas are broadening, and his attitudes and prejudices are being formed. He cannot understand why there are hungry people and criminals. Why doesn't somebody do something about it? In an elementary way he is interested in discussing social concerns.

Eleven- and 12-year-olds are rounding out their childhood years and are alert to what it means to grow up. They often seem to be looking curiously and eagerly, but with some apprehension, to adulthood. They are concerned about their own physical and mental development as they approach puberty. These preadolescents are intensely realistic—even imaginative activities are applied in concrete ways. It is a time for eager absorption of information and accumulation of ideas. They ask many questions. Almost two fifths of their questions are scientific in nature, dealing with the physical world. About half their questions concern social studies, and area into which they are just now beginning to gain some insight. They understand the significance of the natural laws of science, but they are just beginning to feel their way with the social realm.

School learning

Children of this age are seeking reality in social and physical relationships. Not only are they interested in the immediate but also in matters well removed from them in time and place. Their sense of time and space has developed sufficiently so that their thinking reaches backward into ancient lands and times and forward into the world of tomorrow. They are fascinated by faraway places and distant times. They are collectors of facts as well as of baseball pictures, international dolls, and seashells.

A child's oral or spoken vocabulary is about 3,600 words at the age of 8 years, 5,400 words at 10 years, and 7,200 words at 12 years. By sixth grade his reading vocabulary will average 50,000 words.[23] Words with special meaning and limited use, such as a science, social studies, or health vocabulary, are learned at this time. Sixth graders should know how to use a dictionary, an encyclopedia, a card catalogue, and an atlas. They should understand the use of footnotes and index. Slang and swear words become part of the vocabulary, more so for boys than for girls. A new form of language, a secret language, may be developed at this time for use in communication with intimate friends. The language may be in written form using a code, in verbal form using "pig Latin" or clicking tongue sounds, or in kinetic form using fingers or gestures.

Girls as a group are superior to boys in word building, sentence completion tests, and rote memory. They write longer compositions and use longer sentences. Generally, girls make higher marks in language arts. Boys and girls, as a group, like to read books about travel, biography, science, nature, home, and school. Girls specifically like books about heroines and some romance. Boys like books about adventure, explorations, the Wild West, mysteries, and tall tales. There is a great range of reading ability in late childhood. A range of reading achievement of two years above and two years below the grade level is usual within the class. In a heterogeneous classroom of sixth graders the reading ability can range from third to tenth grade.

Boys excel in abilities involving number manipulation and in arithmetical reasoning. A boy's ability to reason in the fourth, fifth, and sixth grades seems to be better than that of girls. Numbers take on new meaning. Schoolwork in math helps this age level to formulate more definite ideas of space and distance. Children can estimate short intervals of time more accurately at the age of 12 than at 6 years. Boys do better than girls in childhood in this sort of perception.

Most children show the onset of permanent memory by 4 years of age. For some, however, it comes as late as the eighth year. Memory span for digits increases to six digits between fourth and sixth grade. Children remember longer what they see than what they hear. Words need to be reinforced by pictures. Memorizing is impeded by boredom, worry, a scolding, or daydreaming. It is not unusual for a boy in this age bracket to remember batting averages, completed passes, or the make, model, and year of most cars on the road, but it is difficult for him to remember how much is eight times nine. Power of attention gradually increases. Many of an adult's complaints about a child's inability to give attention is a wrong appraisal. The child is probably not interested in the thing he is asked to learn or attend to. He is more interested in learning what he wants to know than in what the teacher may want to teach. A boy is curious and loves to manipulate objects. He is a creative thinker. He is a questioner. A girl is more likely to remember the details of such things as a presidential campaign. A boy is more likely to question its purpose. Boys outclass girls in mathematics, science, and creative thinking.

Between 7 and 11 years of age the child is still not capable of formal logical thought. He tries to justify his judgments, yet he is often unable to share the point of view of the person with whom he is conversing. By the age of 12 years this special condition of childhood has faded. The child is now able to see the point of view of the person with whom he is talking. No longer does he ask questions as if answers are always possible and as if unforeseen circumstances never intervene in the course of events.

AFFECTIVE AND MORAL DEVELOPMENT

The affective and moral development of the child is closely integrated with cognitive and social development. The child at this stage is greatly influenced by the way others react to him. He has the basic emotional needs of love, belonging, security, success, new experiences, and independence. Although he exhibits less open expression of love to his parents, he still is greatly concerned about the amount of love his parents have for him. He wants to be independent and expresses his desires in the form of rebellion, back talk, disobedience, and discourtesy. Many parents at this stage feel they must have brought their child up wrongly.

Preadolescents often daydream of wild conquests or adventures they will undertake and often engage in a fantasy life. By contrast they often go through long periods of empty daydreaming or staring into space. When asked what they are thinking about, they reply, "Nothing." And nothing may be actually what they are thinking about. Occasionally, a child of this age may revert to an infantile form of behavior such as bedwetting, constant moving of legs, arms, and head, or of fingernail biting. It is all too frustrating to adults. Although these types of actions are irritating to parents, what angers and troubles them most is the seeming breakdown of the solid relationship they enjoyed with their child during earlier childhood.

One reason given for the resurfacing of regressive or infantile characteristics is that the childhood personality is becoming disorganized and loose to permit the child to develop a new personality for adolescence and adulthood.[24] It is essential that the child leave behind many of his childhood attitudes, behaviors, and habits. Internal emotional and personality changes are taking place, resulting in conflict and stress. These emotional factors, in turn, express themselves in fears, suspicion, and a withdrawal from parents and other adults. Peer standards take on significant meaning and importance for the prepubescent child.

Emotional characteristics

The emotional characteristics of late childhood are both pleasant and unpleasant. They are pleasant to the children when they are releasing pent-up spirits by giggling, squirming, and general body activity. They are unpleasant when they involve tempers, anxiety, and feelings of frustration. The emotions found at this age are the same as those found in early childhood. The only difference is in the circumstances that give rise to the emotions and in the form of expression. Experiences and learning are responsible for the changes. Girls cry and have temper outbursts, and boys are sullen and sulky, but they both learn that violent expressions of unpleasant emotions are not acceptable to their contemporaries so they try to control their outward expression of emotions. There is an increase in the fear of imaginary, fanciful, or supernatural things. This age group is afraid of being "different" or of being called "chicken" or " 'fraidy cat." The most common worries are about the family, school, personal and social adjustment, and health. School worries are more common than out-of-school worries. Girls worry more about school and safety than boys do. Generalized anxiety is more common than any one specific worry.[25] This anxiety is greater in the child who is unpopular and, as a rule, is greater in girls. It increases in intensity for girls as they grow older. Anxiety can be strong enough in late childhood to handicap a child in learning, especially in reading and arithmetic. Errors tend to increase their feelings of insecurity and, as a result, the level of anxiety is increased, causing more errors or else inhibiting responses or attempts to learn.

The 10-year-old is easygoing and balanced. He seldom cries and does not anger easily. When he gets angry, it is physically and emotionally violent and immediate, but it soon becomes resolved. He may plot revenge, but he seldom remembers to carry it out. He seems to enjoy noise—at least he makes enough of it. He has fewer worries than he does fears. His worries center around school, such as homework, grades, and being late. He is scared of blood, ghosts, dead bodies of animals, criminals, wild animals, high places, and the dark. During the fourth and fifth grades, children may have the feeling that no one—teachers, friends, or parents—likes them, and this may result in crying sessions with the mother. No matter how much is said to allay these fears, the children remain or pretend to be adamant on the subject. They need their ego nurtured and bolstered.

The age of 11 years is one of the most worried and fearful ages for the child. He worries about school, money, his parents' welfare, and his own health. Some children even worry about their father's driving, family relations, and world conditions. Some of these concerns may be due to an advanced level of cognitive development but with no knowledge or insight to back up the interpretations of what is seen or experienced. Strange animals are feared most, although the child still has a great fear of being in the dark and of high places.

Anger is aroused more frequently than at the age of 10 years. Physical violence is the most common response, although violent verbal retorts are also common. By this time, however, he has developed enough behavior control so that he can suppress laughter where it is inappropriate, such as in church or on a solemn occasion. Instead of laughing, he expresses his joviality by a twinkle of the eye, a smile through tightly compressed lips, or a meaningful clearing of the throat.

The 12-year-old has fewer worries than he did at 11 years. School is still the main source of worries, but social and personal worries are on an increase. He fears being alone, being in the dark, snakes, crowds, and high places. Twelve years is the last age when immediate physical violence is more common than verbal responses to anger. The child of this age level gossips, makes disparaging remarks, uses retaliatory behavior, and gets jealous over prestige in games, achievement in school, honors, and family reputation. Feats of strength and skills give boys great satisfactions. Although he has reached an age when he can be reasoned with, the 12-year-old can be overcritical, changeable, and uncooperative. However, he can also be decisive, responsible, and dependable when he feels more secure and confident. Also, he either loves or hates—there is no middle ground.

Moral and spiritual development

The child in late childhood makes substantial gains in his understanding of and feelings toward right and wrong. He does have conflicts, however, between the morality of adult authority, including the home, and that of the gang. Although preteen children assert themselves against authority, this is a period when conscience develops more fully. The home will have the most influence in religion, racial attitudes, and general ideology. The gang will have the most influence in manners, speech, and general behavior.[26] They will make all kinds of rules of conduct for themselves, for what to wear, for the way to talk and act, and for playing games. Children of 11 and 12 years commonly believe in justice and fair play. To this point in age the key to moral development in an individual has been his interaction with others in his environment. Intellectual speculating about right and wrong has been minimal up to now due to an inability to do much abstract reasoning. Now the child is on the verge of being able to do formal logic and reasoning, and the next few years will bring about some pointed questions concerning morality and spiritual concerns.

The growth of spiritual and ethical concepts is related to cognitive development, experience, and social interaction. The following sequence of spiritual and ethical growth was determined by Gesell and his co-workers.[27,28] The 12-month-old may be inhibited by "no, no"; the 18-month-old drops an object he should not have taken and runs away when he hears someone coming. The 2-year-old associates "good boy" with routine duties well performed. At 3 years of age he tries to please and asks "Do it this way?" The 4-year-old begins to understand about rules and shows a considerable interest in God if he is taken to Sunday School or church by his parents, although he will ask inappropriate questions about God. The 5-year-old thinks of God being a man like his father; he may believe that God is responsible for everything, including pushing him when he falls. At the age of 6 years the child grasps the idea of God as Creator of the world, the animals, and nature. Prayers are important, and he expects them to be answered. The 7-year-old asks more appropriate questions about God, has continued interest in Sunday School, and Bible stories, but he has a slight skepticism when he distinguishes what he now knows from what he was told in the past. For the 8-year-old good and bad are no longer only what parents permit or forbid. He is interested in the information that the soul only, and not the body, goes to heaven.

The 9-year-old does not have a strong interest in God and religious matters, but he may pray spontaneously on occasion if in great need or danger. Bible story interest shifts to portions of the Old Testament. He may begin an interest in "fairness." The 10-year-old may think of God as an invisible man. He may seek God's help to find something and does not always blame Him for misfortunes. At 11 years of age he may regard God as a spirit. He vaguely begins to feel that what happens to you is determined by your acts. The 12-year-old does a lot of thinking about God and religion. Belief in God becomes more important than attending Sunday School or church. God is defined as "half spirit and half man." The 13-year-old may be more skeptical about the existence of God than at any other age. He may be shocked at his own disbelief. However, the practice of religion is important to him, and he may pray every night. At the age of 14 years he has more definite beliefs, and for many this is a peak year of enthusiasm for religious youth program activities. God is more abstract, such as a "power over us." The 15-year-old is more searching rather than reaching. At this age they are uncertain about ideas of the Deity —"kind of hard to say." Church service may be preferred, but often they do not want to sit with their parents. The 16-year-old shows more belief in God than at any preceding age but still has not built up a continuing personal relationship with God. He thinks of God as a divine power or guiding ruler. A mental age of 17 years is needed before deeper meanings of God can be recognized, and a mental age of 20 years is needed to perceive profound spiritual insights.

STUDY GUIDE

1. Review the developmental tasks of late childhood. Compare these tasks to those of middle childhood and of early adolescence. What common threads do you find connecting these three stages of growth?
2. Compare height and weight gain of boys and girls by consulting Table 8-1. How do extreme deviations in physical growth affect the mental health of preadolescents?
3. What physical changes take place in the period preceding the peak of pubertal development? Why do you suppose most girls reach puberty before boys?
4. Read the section on psychosexual development and awareness. Think of when you were 6 to 10 years old. How did you and your young friends learn about sex? You are not being asked to share this personal information with others.
5. What does the research say about the source of sex information and the age at which it was obtained?
6. In what ways do girls and boys differ in their social patterns during preadolescence? To your knowledge, do the groups of boys and girls of this age with whom you are familiar act this way? Does a boy act differently when he is by himself compared to when he is with a group?
7. What steps do many children of late childhood years take toward independence or self-autonomy?
8. What are the major characteristics of cognitive development during late adolescence? How are these characteristics manifested in school?
9. Late adolescents have their emotional problems. What do they worry about? What are they anxious about?
10. The moral consciousness of many preadolescents is highly pragmatic, concrete, and narrow in expression and related strongly to the situation at hand. Is this point of view much different from that held by adults with whom you are acquainted? How? Do you find it difficult to identify the

moral beliefs of others? How about identifying your own beliefs?

REFERENCES

1. Bernard, H. W.: Human development in western culture, ed. 2, Boston, 1966, Allyn & Bacon, Inc., pp. 278-293.
2. Greulich, W. W., and Pyls, S. I.: A radiographic atlas of skeletal development of the hand and wrist, Stanford, Calif., 1959, Stanford University Press.
3. Britton, E. C., and Winaus, J. M.: Growing from infancy to adulthood, New York, 1958, Appleton-Century-Crofts, pp. 46-56.
4. Hawkes, G. R., and Pease, D.: Behavior and development from 5 to 12, New York, 1962, Harper & Row, Publishers, p. 146.
5. Dearborn, W. F., and Rothney, J. W.: Predicting the child's development, Cambridge, Mass., 1941, Sci-Art Publishers, p. 147.
6. Sontag, L. W., and Reynolds, E. L.: The Fels Composite Sheet. I, J. Pediatr. 26:327-335, 1945.
7. Strang, R.: An introduction to child study, ed. 4, New York, 1959, The Macmillan Co., p. 377.
8. How a child develops, ages seven to twelve, Good Housekeeping, p. 187, May, 1968.
9. Harlow, H. F.: The nature of love, Am. Psychol. 13:673-685, 1958.
10. Katcher, A.: The discrimination of sex differences in young children, J. Genet. Psychol. 37:363-378, 1966.
11. Suehsdorf, A., editor: Facts of life for children, Indianapolis, 1954, The Bobbs-Merrill Co., Inc., pp. 93-94.
12. Ilg, F. L., and Ames, L. B.: The Gesell Institute's child behavior, New York, 1955, Dell Publishing Co., Inc.
13. Gesell, A., Ilg, F. L., and Ames, L. B.: Youth—the years from ten to sixteen, New York, 1956, Harper & Row, Publishers, p. 78.
14. Elias, J., and Gebhard, P.: Sexuality and sexual learning in childhood, Phi Delta Kappa 50:401-405, 1969.
15. Schofield, M.: The sexual behavior of young people, Boston, 1965, Little, Brown & Co., pp. 93-96.
16. Elias and Gebhard, op. cit., p. 403.
17. Block, J. H.: Conceptions of sex roles: some cross-cultural and longitudinal perspectives, Am. Psychol. 28:512-526, 1973.
18. Strang, op. cit., p. 410.
19. Kanous, L., Daugherty, R. A., and Cohn, T. S.: Relation between heterosexual friendship choices and socioeconomic level, Child Dev. 33:251-255, 1962.
20. Bossard, J. H., and Boll, E. S.: The sociology of child development, ed. 4, New York, 1966, Harper & Row, Publishers.
21. Piaget, J.: The moral judgment of the child, New York, 1932, Harcourt, Brace & World, Inc., p. 52.
22. Bruner, J.: Course of cognitive growth, Am. Psychol. 19:8, 1964.
23. Wolman, R. N., and Barker, E. N.: A developmental study of word definitions, J. Genet. Psychol. 107:159-166, 1965.
24. Redl, F.: Pre-adolescents—what makes them tick, Child Study 21:47, 1954.
25. Hurlock, E. B.: Developmental psychology, ed. 3, New York, 1968, McGraw-Hill Book Co., p. 279.
26. Britton and Winaus, op. cit., p. 55.
27. Gesell, A., and Ilg, F. L.: Youth from five to ten, New York, 1946, Harper & Row Publishers, pp. 403-410.
28. Gesell, Ilg, and Ames, op. cit., p. 389.

9 Puberty and early adolescence
12 to 14 years of age

EARLY ADOLESCENCE: IS AGE 12 THAT DIFFERENT FROM AGE 14?

Bobby and Mike are friends. Bobby is 12 years old; Mike is 14 years old. They do not see each other often, just on occasion. Saturday was one of those occasions.

Bobby will enter eighth grade in the fall. His mother, 30 years old, and his father, the same age, are divorced. He sees his father occasionally on weekends and sometimes spends a week with him in the summer. He enjoys being with his father, and he has mentioned that he would maybe like to live with him. Bobby's home is a second-floor apartment on the edge of a small city. His mother works, so that during the school months Bobby has to go to a babysitter until his mother gets home at 5:30 P.M. During the summer he spends all day at the babysitter's, except when his mother has a vacation or when he goes to stay with his father. When I say he stays at the babysitter's, I mean that he is to be there when his mother comes to get him. He usually spends his time on his bike and with his friends. He does not attend Sunday School regularly, but he has been attending summer Bible School.

I would describe Bobby as a friendly but pensive child. He is about 5 feet 4 inches and weighs 107 pounds. He is very good looking and well groomed and will probably develop into a handsome teen-ager.

Mike, on the other hand, is from a tightly knit family. In the fall he will enter tenth grade. He has three older brothers. The two oldest are 26 and 23 years old, both of whom are married. The other brother is 19 years old, unmarried, and will be a sophomore in college. Mike is the only son living at home. His home is three miles from a small city. It is a nice-sized, two-story home with plenty of lawn and garden. Mike's mother is 51 years old, and his father is 52 years old. He attends Sunday School and church regularly. Individuality is considered important by the parents; each child therefore has been able to develop his own interests and be accepted into the family for himself. However, the one emphasis that does run high in the family is athletics. Mike's father was an outstanding athlete as a boy, and all three of his brothers have excelled in high school sports. His 19-year-old brother is receiving a great deal of praise due to his excellent baseball season during his freshman year at college. There definitely is pressure on Mike to succeed in some area of sports.

I would describe Mike as a very outgoing, friendly, talkative teen-ager. He is a good-looking and well-built boy who usually dresses neatly. He has a great personality and is just an all-around nice guy.

My husband, Mike, and I went to pick up Bobby and his sister early last Saturday morning. Bobby, who was sitting on the porch, started making joking comments to Mike who was in the car. Mike just laughed at Bobby's wisecracks. As soon as the two got together in the back seat, there were punches exchanged, started by Bobby. Soon Mike decided to display his strength and make Bobby promise to behave. He promised but it didn't last long. There was, of course, an occasional spat between Bobby and his 6-year-old sister.

When we got to our destination, which was an air show at the local airport, Bobby and Mike were content to spend their money on food and just pal around together, never staying in one place for long. The conversation seldom turned to anything serious, except when discussing which was the "neatest" airplane.

That evening at the local fair they went off on their own, budgeting their money between rides and food. Bobby apparently was quite impressed by Mike's many girlfriends. When leaving the fair, both boys boasted about how well they had budgeted their money. They were proud that they still had some money left. They said goodbye and briefly talked of what they would do the next time Bobby came to visit.

Later I asked both Bobby and Mike the same ten questions to get a better idea of what they think about. I found it difficult to learn much about their inner selves by just observing them because they do so much joking and "putting on." Following are the questions and answers given by Bobby and Mike.

1. How much have you grown physically this year?
   BOBBY: About 2 inches.
   MIKE: Three to 4 inches taller, 10 to 13 pounds heavier.
2. How many special friends do you have?
   BOBBY: Girls, 5; boys, 11.
   MIKE: Girls, 3; boys, 2.
3. Describe your favorite boyfriend.
   BOBBY: He is taller than me, a little older than me, and a little stronger than me.
   MIKE: Physically he is about 5 feet 11 inches with brown hair, brown eyes, and weighs 145 pounds. He has some interests such as mine and likes basically the same kind of music. He is not as athletically minded as I am, though he is out for track. He is cool headed and a guy who believes in fun but not trouble. He is friendly, likes to laugh, and one can talk to him easily.
4. Describe your favorite girlfriend.
   BOBBY: She is smaller than me, same age as me, nice looking, and is pretty nice.
   MIKE: She is short and slightly chubby. She is a very cheery girl who has a fine sense of humor and a good personality; she doesn't mind being kidded. She enjoys sports, is a cheerleader, and gets involved in things she thinks are important.
5. What is something that happened this year that made you the happiest?
   BOBBY: When school let out.
   MIKE: My brother's baseball season.
6. What is something that happened this year that made you the saddest?
   BOBBY: When my grandfather died.
   MIKE: The deaths of a relative and of a close friend to our family.
7. What are you most interested in? Why?
   BOBBY: Motorcycles because I plan on having one some day.
   MIKE: Sports: football, baseball, basketball, particularly football.
8. When you daydream, what do you dream about?
   BOBBY: What I plan on doing in the future, what I would like to do, and girls.
   MIKE: Running through a huge clover field very happily. The field has a small spring running through it. I believe this daydream has reason behind it. I think it's a dream of no pollution, no population problem, and no food problem in the world along with freedom.
9. Have you ever really lost your temper? If so, when and why? If not, why?
   BOBBY: Yes, about a year ago, when the boy down the street kept picking on the dog.
   MIKE: No, basically because I don't like to get hurt, but mostly I don't want to harm anyone else.
10. What would you like to know more about?
    BOBBY: Motorcycles and cars.
    MIKE: People because I feel in order to stop pollution, overpopulation, wars, the hunger problem, and other world problems one must get to the bottom of the problem, which is peo-

ple. If people understand each other, maybe these problems can be solved.

Bobby and Mike are alike in some ways. They enjoy many of the same activities. They both like to help and please those people who are their friends. When blamed for starting a fight or doing something wrong, they each in their own way become defensive. They both shout at times when something goes wrong. Girls are beginning to appeal to them; however, Mike has been looking at girls for over a year, whereas Bobby has just started looking.

Bobby and Mike are also very different. Whereas Mike talks almost constantly and has ideas about everything, Bobby often has periods of complete silence. I wonder often what he is thinking. When I ask, he answers, "Nothing." Bobby has always been made to put things away. His room and his appearance are always neat. Mike's room always looks a mess, but his appearance is nice.

Mike can adjust amazingly well to people of any age. He gets along well with Bobby, who is two years younger than he. One of his favorite friends is going to be a freshman at college this fall. He likes to go many places with his 19-year-old brother. Bobby is also friendly toward almost anyone, but responds more slowly.

Bobby and Mike, although similar in some ways, are also definitely individual personalities, each at his own stage of development.

Early adolescence is a time of growing, learning, adventuring, scorning, and dreaming. It is a time of anxieties and problems, but these are outweighed by joy, innocence, excitement, and gladness. The term *adolescence* comes from the Latin verb *adolescere*, meaning "to grow into maturity." As such it is a transitional period—a time of physical, social, and emotional metamorphosis. As someone has said, it is a time when the individual is "neither man nor child, nor fish nor fowl." In some ways adolescents are like squirming, wiggling caterpillars engaged in the agonizing fight to escape childhood's cocoon and enter into adulthood's full flight. Each adolescent views the adult world as full of beautiful butterflies free of everything restrictive. He cannot wait to break out and fly. Unfortunately, nature prefers that this be done in an orderly, maturing fashion.

The early adolescent is no longer a child, yet he is not an adult. He is at an in-between stage, when it is difficult to know how he should be considered. If he is treated as a child, he resents it bitterly. If he is treated as an adult, his lack of maturity becomes evident and he is embarrassed. What should be recognized is that adolescence is more than a period, or stage, of human development. It is a way of life with its own culture, values, characteristics, activities, demands, situations, and problems. Adults must not be too quick to make the child a man. In a primitive society in a less intricate world it might have been possible to move from childhood to adulthood with a minimum of complications. Today's world with its computerized systems approach to the business of life requires more cognitive, communicative, and collective competencies on the part of the individual before he can become an independent, self-supporting adult. A longer period of time is required to learn the skills needed for competent adult living. This extended length of time makes it possible for the adolescent of today to reveal his uniqueness and to develop and demonstrate characteristics that are typically adolescent in nature but that in another day and age would not have had the time to be expressed. In a less complex society youth went about doing the work of an adult world soon after they left the period of childhood. Youth of today have the time to be adolescents.

No sharp age lines separate the stages of growth at any level. Especially is this statement true when one works with narrow developmental divisions as in this text. As long as we talk about the characteristics of the group, we are reasonably accurate. If we think in terms of an individual, then we must definitely keep in mind the broad range of normal differences that exist within the group. The reader must make allowances for these individual differences when making application of characteristics mentioned in this book to a specific person. In addition, one must recognize and accept the fact that there will always be an overlapping of characteristics of successive developmental stages in individuals.

During the total span of adolescence, the individual is working harder than ever before on two primary developmental tasks: (1) to establish independence from adults, and parents in particular, in self-identification and emotional independence, and (2) to develop social, intellectual, language, and motor skills that are essential for individual and group participation in heterosexual activities. Other developmental tasks include (1) accepting changes taking place in one's body and physical appearance and learning good grooming practices, (2) achieving appropriate relationships with age mates of both sexes, (3) accepting a masculine or feminine role that is appropriate for the age level, and (4) acquiring moral concepts, values, and attitudes that contribute something to life in family, school, church, and peer group activities. Adolescents see this period as beset with problems, but they generally enjoy themselves as they make their way to adulthood.

PUBERTAL AND PHYSICAL DEVELOPMENT

Early adolescence is a time of physical growth and change. Many physiological changes occur rather suddenly and are frequently a striking contrast to characteristics that existed earlier. Such changes are disquieting to the young person, but adults often think of them as humorous, if not wonderful. Physical changes, as at any age, mean that the fairly well-formulated body image of the preadolescent must now be changed. The new bodily form at least must be reconciled to the existing self-concept. Neither alternative is easy. Many individuals find that adjusting to the realities of their new physical selves is an exceedingly difficult thing to do. This adjustment must be made by the teen-ager, the middle-aged person, and the individual in senescence. The teen-ager is confronted with the problem more quickly because changes occur in such a short span of time, almost "overnight."

Onset of puberty

The early stage of adolescent development is referred to as the pubertal period. The term *puberty* is derived from the Latin word *pubertos,* which means "the age of manhood." The implication is that a person who has gone through the pubertal period has entered adulthood and is now physically able to participate in the reproduction of the human species. Manhood or womanhood is not achieved suddenly or completely at puberty. The changes taking place at this stage are part of a developing process that began early in the life of the individual and that will continue to be active for some years to come.

The pubertal stage consists of the following three periods of development: pubescence, puberty, and postpubescence. The entire stage usually lasts for four years. Pubescence, called *prepuberty,* or *preadolescence,* by some writers, refers to the period of about two years before puberty when the child is developing preliminary characteristics of sexual maturity. It is characterized by a spurt in physical growth, changes in body proportion, and the beginning of primary and secondary sex characteristics. The peak, or climax, of the pubertal stage is called puberty, the period during which the generative (reproductive) organs become capable of functioning and the secondary sex characteristics become highly evident. The initial appearance of these characteristics does not mean that the boy or girl is immediately capable of reproduction, however. In the postpubescence period there is a one- to two-year span of adolescent sterility. During this time, most of the skeletal growth is completed and the new biological functions become fairly well established. The age of nubility or fertility has now arrived. It should be noted that in England the term *puberty* is sometimes used in a legal rather than a biological sense. In the eyes of British law, girls reach puberty at the age of 12 years and boys at 14 years.

At this point it would be well to define the terms *primary sex characteristics* and *secondary sex characteristics*. The external and internal organs that carry on the reproductive functions are known as the primary sex organs. During infancy and childhood, the sex organs are small and do not produce cells for reproduction. The pubescent stage, when functional maturity takes place in these organs, is the dividing line between the sexually immature and sexually mature person. The primary sex organs were discussed in an earlier chapter on prenatal development.

The secondary sex characteristics are those that distinguish the sexes from each other but play no direct part in reproduction. In boys these include pubic hair, which becomes curly, darker, and coarser with adolescent age; facial hair, first above the upper lip, then on other parts of the face, necessitating shaving at about the age of 16 years; body hair on the arms, chest, legs, and armpits; coarser skin with enlarged pores; changes in voice; increased length of the shoulders, depth of the chest, and size of the neck; and slight enlargements or breast knots around the mammary glands, lasting only a few weeks.

Secondary sex characteristics in girls include an increase in the width and roundness of the hips; more shapely legs and arms; menarche; thicker, coarser skin with enlarged glands; the appearance of facial hair on the upper lip and cheeks; development of breasts through four stages, starting with the papilla stage (nipple of early childhood), the bud stage about 10 or 11 years of age when there is an elevation of the nipple and surrounding areola, the primary breast stage where fatty tissue develops under and around nipple and areola, and the secondary breast stage of maturity; appearance of pubic hair, first as straight, then as kinky hair (pubic hair appears in a large amount only after the breasts develop); and changes of voice from a high-pitched tone to a more mature tone because of a slight growth of the larynx.

Several criteria are used to determine the climax of puberty. Menarche (pronounced "men-AR-kee"), which is the occurrence of the first menstruation, is usually a valid sign of puberty in girls. At the same time the secondary sex characteristics appear.[1] The average age at which most North American girls experience their first menses is 12.5 years old. The normal age range is considered to be 10 to 15 years. About 3% to 4% of all girls have menarche before the age of 10 years. Some school nurses report an increase in this percentage in their districts. Few begin menses after the age of 16½ years.[2] Evidence from many parts of the world indicates that the average age of menarche has dropped by at least two years and perhaps by as many as five years in the last century.[3] In 1820 working girls in Manchester, England, reached menarche on the average at 15.7 years. Studies done in the late sixties in England and in many other parts of the world show averages at about midway between 12 and 13 years. In New York City in 1934 the average age of menarche was 13.5 years; in 1964 it was 12.5 years.[4] Better nutrition and better living conditions are generally cited as the reasons for the lowering age of first menses. There is some indication, however, that the drop in the age of menarche may be leveling off in the more affluent populations.

The classic view that menarche occurs earlier in hot, humid climates has been largely discredited. The mean age of menarche for girls in Nigeria has been found to be 14.22 years, and for Alaskan Eskimos it is 14.42 years. Tanner reports that Chinese girls in Hong Kong and Cuban girls experience menarche as early as European girls on the highest living standard.[5] Girls who are city dwellers, live in low altitudes, or are totally blind appear to reach menarche earlier than their counterparts. An interesting effect of altitude on menarche has been found in the high Andes of Peru by Jean McClung of the Harvard Medical School. Menarche is reported so delayed there that it is difficult to find a girl in the high Andes who has borne children before the age of 18 years.[6]

In boys there is no striking change to indicate puberty. One of the more reliable indicators of puberty in boys is the presence of live spermatozoa in their urine. The presence of the gonadotrophic hormone, or androgen, in the urine is also an indication of puberty. An overt sign in boys is the beginning of nocturnal emissions. When the boy is sleeping, the penis becomes erect, and semen, which is fluid with sperms, spurts out or is released. Spontaneous nocturnal emissions will persist into adulthood and will occur whenever the reproductive organ has an excess of semen. After puberty this action is frequently accompanied by a dream of short duration whose content has sexual connotations. At puberty the male gonadal hormones also stimulate the growth of the male sexual apparatus, including the penis, the prostate gland, seminal vesicles,

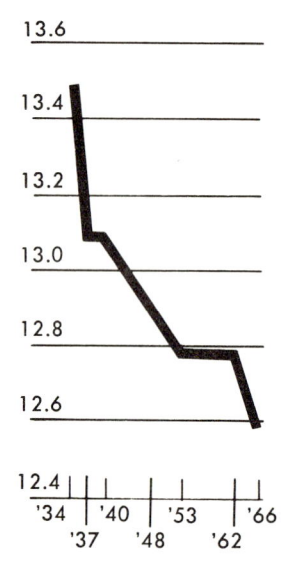

Fig. 9-1. Lowering age of first menses in American girls.

Table 9-1. Normal maturation sequence in girls*

PHASE	APPEARANCE OF SEXUAL CHARACTERISTICS	AVERAGE AGE	AGE RANGE
Childhood through preadolescence	No pubic hair; breasts are flat; growth in height is constant		
Early adolescence	Rounding of hips; breasts and nipples are elevated to form bud stage; no true pubic hair	10 to 11 years	9 to 14 years
Middle adolescence	Appearance of pubic hair; increment in height to 18 months before menarche; with menarche, labia become enlarged, vaginal secretions become acid, areola and nipple elevate to form "primary breast"	11 to 14 years	10 to 16 years
Late adolescence	Pubic hair fully developed; breast fills out to adult form; menstruation is well established; growth in height decelerates between 16¼ and 17¼ years	14 to 16 years	13 to 18 years
Post-adolescence	Breasts fully developed; height increases stop	16 to 18 years	15 to 19 years

*From Caplan, G., and Lebovici, S., editors: Adolescence: psychosocial perspectives, New York, 1969, Basic Books, Inc., Publishers, p. 33.

and scrotum. These hormones bring about the development of male secondary sexual characteristics. (See Table 9-1.) The average age at which boys reach puberty is 14.5 years. Two thirds of all boys attain puberty between 12.5 and 16.5 years of age.[7] We have not been able to find research since 1935 indicating that the average age of puberty in boys has lowered the same as it has for girls.

Physical changes at puberty

Among the earliest physical signs of puberty are obvious gains in weight and height. The growth spurt begins one to two years before the child becomes sexually mature and continues for six months to a year afterward. The growth spurt in girls begins at between 8.5 and 11.5 years of age. After the spurt, growth continues until the age of 17 or 18 years, when height is fairly well established. As indicated in the last chapter, girls will grow 2 to 4 inches a year during the growth spurt and gain 8 to 10 pounds or so. Gains of 5 or 6 inches are not unusual. Boys begin the accelerated growth pattern between 10.5 and 14.5 years of age and reach a peak between 14.5 and 15.5 years. This period is followed by a gradual decline until 18 or 20 years of age, when the average adult height is attained. On the average, boys gain 12 to 14 pounds and grow 4 to 5 inches in the peak year.[8] As a teacher of ninth graders, whose average age was 14 years, one of us (G. K.) had his homeroom group of thirty-eight pupils mark their height on a wallboard during their first week of school in September and again during the last week in May at the end of school. Every youngster in that room grew at least 2 inches during the school year; most grew 3 to 4 inches. One boy grew 7 inches in nine months! Increases in height and weight in either sex generally result in a greater intake of food. Appetite becomes ravenous and will be so for three

Table 9-2. Normal maturation sequence in boys*

PHASE	APPEARANCE OF SEXUAL CHARACTERISTICS	AVERAGE AGE	AGE RANGE
Childhood through preadolescence	No pubic hair; no growth in testes and penis since infancy; growth in height constant		
Early adolescence	Testes increase in size; scrotum grows; penis follows with growth in length and circumference; no true pubic hair	12 to 13 years	10 to 15 years
Middle adolescence	Pubic hair becomes apparent; penis, testes, and scrotum continue growing and become larger; significant spurt of growth in height; prostate seminal vesicles mature; spontaneous or induced emissions occur; voice begins to change as larynx thickens	13 to 16 years	11 to 18 years
Late adolescence	Facial and body hair appear and spread; pubic hair becomes denser; voice deepens; testes and penis continue to grow; growth in height decreases; 98% of mature stature between 17¾ and 18½ years; indentation of frontal hair line	16 to 18 years	14 to 20 years
Post-adolescence	Mature and full development of primary and secondary sex characteristics; muscles may continue increasing[15]	Onset 18 to 21 years	Onset 16 to 21 years

*From Caplan, G., and Lebovici, S., editors: Adolescence: psychosocial perspectives, New York, 1969, Basic Books, Inc., Publishers, p. 30.

Table 9-3. Height and weight tables for adolescent boys and girls*

	PERCENTILES (BOYS) 10	50	90		PERCENTILES (GIRLS) 10	50	90
12½ years				12½ years			
Weight in pounds	74.6	88.7	116.4	Weight in pounds	74.7	93.4	118.0
Weight in kilograms	33.84	40.23	52.8	Weight in kilograms	33.88	42.37	53.52
Height in inches	56.9	60.0	63.6	Height in inches	57.4	60.7	64.0
Height in centimeters	144.5	152.3	161.6	Height in centimeters	145.9	154.3	162.7
13 years				13 years			
Weight in pounds	77.1	93.0	123.2	Weight in pounds	79.9	99.1	124.5
Weight in kilograms	34.97	42.18	55.88	Weight in kilograms	36.24	44.95	56.47
Height in inches	57.7	61.0	64.1	Height in inches	58.7	61.8	64.9
Height in centimeters	146.6	155.0	165.3	Height in centimeters	149.1	157.1	164.8
13½ years				13½ years			
Weight in pounds	82.2	100.3	130.1	Weight in pounds	85.5	103.7	128.9
Weight in kilograms	37.29	45.5	59.01	Weight in kilograms	38.78	47.04	58.47
Height in inches	58.8	62.6	66.5	Height in inches	59.5	62.4	65.3
Height in centimeters	149.4	158.9	168.9	Height in centimeters	151.1	158.4	165.9
14 years				14 years			
Weight in pounds	87.2	107.6	136.9	Weight in pounds	91.0	108.4	133.3
Weight in kilograms	39.55	48.81	62.1	Weight in kilograms	41.28	49.17	60.46
Height in inches	59.9	64.0	67.9	Height in inches	60.2	62.8	65.7
Height in centimeters	152.1	162.7	172.4	Height in centimeters	153.0	159.6	167.0
14½ years				14½ years			
Weight in pounds	93.3	113.9	142.4	Weight in pounds	94.2	111.0	135.7
Weight in kilograms	42.32	51.66	64.59	Weight in kilograms	42.73	50.35	61.55
Height in inches	61.0	65.1	68.7	Height in inches	60.7	63.1	66.0
Height in centimeters	155.0	165.3	174.6	Height in centimeters	154.1	160.4	167.6
15 years				15 years			
Weight in pounds	99.4	120.1	147.8	Weight in pounds	97.4	113.5	138.1
Weight in kilograms	45.09	54.48	67.04	Weight in kilograms	44.18	51.48	62.64
Height in inches	62.1	66.1	69.6	Height in inches	61.1	63.4	66.2
Height in centimeters	157.8	167.8	176.7	Height in centimeters	155.2	161.1	168.1
15½ years				15½ years			
Weight in pounds	105.2	124.9	152.6	Weight in pounds	99.2	115.3	139.6
Weight in kilograms	47.72	56.65	69.22	Weight in kilograms	45.0	52.3	63.32
Height in inches	63.1	66.8	70.2	Height in inches	61.3	63.7	66.4
Height in centimeters	160.3	169.7	178.2	Height in centimeters	155.7	161.7	168.6
16 years				16 years			
Weight in pounds	111.0	129.7	157.3	Weight in pounds	100.9	117.0	141.1
Weight in kilograms	50.35	58.83	71.35	Weight in kilograms	45.77	53.07	64.0
Height in inches	64.1	67.8	70.7	Height in inches	61.5	63.9	66.5
Height in centimeters	162.8	171.6	179.7	Height in centimeters	156.1	162.2	169.0
16½ years				16½ years			
Weight in pounds	114.3	133.0	161.0	Weight in pounds	101.9	118.1	142.2
Weight in kilograms	51.85	60.33	73.03	Weight in kilograms	46.22	53.57	64.5
Height in inches	64.6	68.0	71.1	Height in inches	61.5	63.9	66.6
Height in centimeters	164.2	172.7	180.7	Height in centimeters	156.2	162.4	169.2
17 years				17 years			
Weight in pounds	117.5	136.2	164.6	Weight in pounds	102.8	119.1	143.3
Weight in kilograms	53.3	61.78	74.66	Weight in kilograms	46.63	54.02	65.0
Height in inches	65.2	68.4	71.5	Height in inches	61.5	64.0	66.7
Height in centimeters	165.2	173.7	181.6	Height in centimeters	156.3	162.5	169.4

*From Latham, H. C., and Heckel, R. V.: Pediatric nursing, ed. 2, St. Louis, 1972, The C. V. Mosby Co.

Table 9-3. Height and weight tables for adolescent boys and girls—cont'd

	PERCENTILES (BOYS) 10	50	90		PERCENTILES (GIRLS) 10	50	90
17½ years				17½ years			
Weight in pounds	118.8	137.6	166.8	Weight in pounds	103.2	119.5	143.9
Weight in kilograms	53.89	62.41	75.66	Weight in kilograms	46.81	54.2	65.27
Height in inches	65.3	68.5	71.6	Height in inches	61.5	64.0	66.7
Height in centimeters	165.9	174.1	182.0	Height in centimeters	156.3	162.5	169.4
18 years				18 years			
Weight in pounds	120.0	139.0	169.0	Weight in pounds	103.5	119.9	144.5
Weight in kilograms	54.43	63.05	76.66	Weight in kilograms	46.95	54.39	65.54
Height in inches	65.5	68.7	71.8	Height in inches	61.5	64.0	66.7
Height in centimeters	166.3	174.5	182.4	Height in centimeters	156.3	162.5	169.4

or four years, necessitating frequent and more costly trips to the supermarket.

Table 9-3 summarizes the growth in height and weight for both sexes.

Psychological reactions to being too tall or too short are prevalent among early adolescents. It is no problem for the boy if he is taller than his classmates and is coordinated enough to use the height to his advantage, especially in sports. Shortness in boys, however, is incompatible with their ideal of maleness. Short boys often seek to compensate for their lack of height by swearing, smoking, boisterousness, or being overdaring. Being tall may be a problem for the early adolescent girl, however, because she dreads being different from the other girls. Furthermore, few boys want to date or go with a girl who is much taller than themselves. Many women vividly recall the embarrassment they felt as shy teen-agers as they towered over their partner's head on the dance floor at a school party. Many postures have suffered as a consequence. In late childhood boys are taller and huskier than girls. From ages 11 to 14 years girls have the advantage. Thereafter boys are again physically taller and heavier than girls.

Statistical studies show a worldwide tendency in the last century toward an increase of stature.[9] The average 14-year-old boy in the United States is 5 inches taller than a boy of the same age in 1880. This increase is proportional for most other countries in the world. The average height at maturity for American women today is 65 to 66 inches. The average American boy at 18 years of age is 69.5 inches with little growth beyond that age. The average American woman today weighs 135 pounds, whereas the average American man weighs 165 pounds. American adults weigh more than those of twenty-five years ago. Women weigh, on the average, 6 pounds more and men 10 pounds more than the preceding generation.[10]

There are sex differences in the distribution of fat during puberty due to hormonal changes and an increase in appetite. About half of all boys and girls go through this fat period. The thickness of the skin in the neck, thorax, and abdomen increases more in boys than in girls. Just before puberty in boys there is an increase in fat around the nipples and over the stomach, hips, and thighs. Fatty tissue in boys decreases after puberty. With the beginning of puberty girls develop fat over the abdomen and hips. The adolescent fat in girls will be present for about two years or so until their bodies gain some physical stability. The way girls react to their chubby appearance varies according to their past experiences of behaving under stress. Some girls withdraw to their room, away from people. Other girls resort to wearing loose-fitting, matronly clothing. Some girls go on "crash" or starvation diets, often encouraged by well-meaning mothers, whereas other girls go to a "fat camp," where a prescribed routine for losing weight is followed. Some accept their weight gain as being normal.

Significant changes in body proportions and contours are characteristic of this age group. The early adolescent boy's form usually is characterized by straight leg lines, slender hips, wide shoulders, broadened chest, and accentuated muscle development in shoulders, arms, and thighs. The girl's leg lines become curved, her breasts fill, and her hips become wider. There is a deposit of fat in the buttocks, thighs, and upper arms. Disproportionate facial features are noticeable in either sex when the face lengthens. The forehead becomes higher and wider. The nose looks large because it grows before puberty and is nearly completed at puberty. Later the mouth and lips become fuller. The jaw is the last part to reach adult size. A high waistline develops in early adolescence as the trunk lengthens, but it drops as adult proportions are reached. Just before puberty the legs become longer than the trunk, and the arms increase in length. Hands and feet look disproportionate because they reach their mature size before the arms and legs.[11] Most children will have some obvious uneven features during these years.

Motor awkwardness in early adolescence is often partly caused by uneven growth of muscles and bones. If the bones grow faster than the muscles, the muscles become taut on the bones, making them respond with a quick, jerky motion. If the muscles grow faster than the bones, the muscles become loose and sluggish. The brain has been programmed during late childhood to provide the muscles with a certain amount of energy to move the limbs of the body to a certain position in space. In early adolescence the ratio of the bones and muscles changes, but the brain still operates on the programming pattern of an earlier age; it will continue to do so until it has been reprogrammed. As a result, when a certain movement is needed, such as reaching out with the arm and hand to catch a ball, the brain sends the same amount of energy to the muscles as it did for the bone-muscle ratio of the younger age. The energy applied now to taut muscles causes the arm to move too fast to catch the ball; applied to loose muscles, the energy is not enough to get the hand up in time to catch the ball. A clumsy-appearing performance results. This awkwardness in arm and leg movements will continue until the growth of bones and muscles reaches a stable condition and the brain can be reprogrammed for the new bone-muscle ratio. It must also be stated that the emotional response of the early adolescent to various motor activities may also have something to do with the degree of awkward motor responses that a child may make.

It is almost certain that the physical changes which occur at puberty will have psychological implications. Boys who are awkward in motor skills necessary to play sports or the games of their peers will believe that they are not acceptable. Embarrassment among boys is often caused by their changing, uncontrollable voices. The growth of hair, especially on the face, may create emotional concern. A boy may be as sensitive about his first shaving experience as a girl is about wearing her first brassiere. Some girls attempt to hide their developing breasts, whereas others are delighted with their bust development and wear tight-fitting sweaters to accentuate it. In cultures where breasts are considered sexually attractive—and they are not considered so in all cultures—a flat-chested female may feel inferior. Menstruation can be a traumatic experience because of its sudden onset, especially if the girl was not taught what to expect. The way in which a girl accepts menstruation depends a great deal on the strength of her female identity and her acceptance of the inevitable. Boys may be concerned about the size of their genitalia and may be upset about having to shower and change clothes for gym class. Skin eruptions, clogged pores, perspiration, and body odors bother most teen-agers. Learning good grooming habits becomes a major task.

Some psychological reactions, such as changes in interests and attitudes, are desirable and mentally healthy. Other reactions, such as fear, guilt, and shame brought about by the development of the sex organs, should be avoided. The extent and depth of psychological responses to puberty are predicated partly on the adequacy of the preparations for these changes that the early adolescent has received. If the youngster has been adequately prepared or if the changes occur slowly, the transition may take place without psychological disturbance. One way or another the teen-ager will have to accept the changes that have occurred in his body. His parents can do much to help him develop pride in his new status.

EMOTIONAL CHARACTERISTICS

The change in physical appearance brought on by puberty is accompanied by a change in emotional control and response. In late childhood the youngster was a rather stable individual. He had reached the peak of childhood development. He knew and understood what his body could do. He was satisfied with his peer and family relationships. His pattern of behavior was acceptable to him; he knew what he could get away with and how to manipulate situations to his advantage. In short, he was in control of his life pattern. All of a sudden puberty comes along and upsets his well-structured approach to the world. His body changes rapidly, and he is bewildered. He no longer looks like a child, but he is not ready for adulthood and its demands. His emotional approach to handling frustrating or conflicting situations is undermined and no longer appropriate. He is uncertain as to how to act, what to do, or what to think. It looks like he is going to have to start all over again, building a new self-image, adapting to a new social pattern, and developing new emotional responses and mental health mechanisms. In addition to all these changes, the instability of the chemical balance in his bloodstream hinders him from making quick adjustments simply because his hormones will not permit him to do so.

In the early years of adolescence feelings and emotions vary considerably. The origin of most of these feelings is within the teen-ager rather than his environment. There is a great increase in moods and sentiments. Emotions vacillate up and down; one moment he is up on cloud nine, and the next moment he is down in pit five. Ambivalent feelings are prevalent. Control or balance of affective experiences seems lost; emotions frequently get out of proportion. Little things can cause an emotional upheaval and can mean a lot, depending on how the teen-ager interprets what he encounters. Emotional responses and feelings, such as enthusiasm for a project, cannot be counted on from day to day. Heightened emotionality often causes overreaction of response. Transfer of affection and love from parents to peers and eventually to members of the opposite sex is a major change. New mental defense mechanisms must be developed. In the meanwhile the mechanisms that are used may be taken to extremes. Daydreaming may be so intense that adolescents may not hear a person talking to them (withdrawal mechanism), or they become hostile and ready to fight, complain, or resist everything (aggressive mechanisms). And when an adult seeks to be compassionate, he may get the reply, "Just because I'm a teen-ager you don't have to be so understanding!"

Twelve-year-olds are happy most of the time because the majority are not well into the puberty period. They can still use their preadolescent behavior in acceptable ways. They are becoming funnier from an adult point of view, but their humor is biting, and they use it to criticize actions of their parents and to insult their friends. "If I couldn't do better than that, I'd go and hide my head in the sand." "Oh yeah, you think you're smart—how about the time you . . ." And so it goes. Twelve-year-olds try to keep their moods and feelings a secret. However, when their feelings are hurt, they will react with talking back, name calling, or saying something mean rather than leaving the scene.

Although the 13-year-old is moderately calm, he will sulk and cry and make faces at people. Generally, he will simply ignore the situation or the person who hurt his feelings. He will confide in certain friends while hiding his hurts from others. This is an age when many youngsters worry about their schoolwork. It can be particularly upsetting for some if they have to take a course from a teacher who has a reputation for being tough and strict, but a good teacher. One eighth grade teacher, a big hulk of a woman, with such a reputation, told us of a telephone call she received from a parent, "I think you should know that my son is learning a lot in your class, but he is petrified every day he goes to your room. If he ever does anything wrong in your class, instead of bawling him out, pick on the child next to him. This will frighten my child so much so that he'll stop whatever he shouldn't be doing. If you pick on him, he'll collapse and be a nervous wreck!"

Fourteen-year-olds are more adept at controlling their anger in front of people. They may lock themselves in their room and occasionally slam doors or make harsh verbal responses later on to show their discontent. Humor, mostly of the insulting or teasing variety, is often used against teachers and parents. They are practical jokers, which can make them rather irritating at times. Generally, they are more happy than not. They do not cry much and when they do, it is usually caused by anger.[12]

Early adolescents need to develop ego strength and to experience acceptance and love. They need to be able to give as well as to receive these qualities. It is important that they be able to display tenderness, admiration, and appreciation. Deprivation only leads to exaggerated, often unacceptable behavior. The following excerpt is from a nun who was a student in one of our classes in human development.

The lack of love and the inability to express love can lead to the saddest of consequences. This I have observed while working in a protectory, a home for boys staffed by our sisters. The need to be deeply and uniquely loved and accepted was of paramount importance to these boys. The lack of these responses worked havoc with most of them. Yet, more detrimental to them was the fact that they were not able to display any beautiful emotions. They had already experienced deep rejection at home and did not want to be rejected by the boys with whom they were now living. In order to be accepted, they had to conform to the standards set by the other boys. The first standard was to refuse to be emotional, appreciative or affectionate toward anyone. They developed an almost hostile reaction toward adults when they were in the presence of the other boys. However, when they were in their own cubicle at bedtime, and I went to say good night to them, they responded beautifully to a pat on the head or a touch on their shoulder. On occasion they would try to display their affection by saying small simple phrases such as "You're O.K." or "You really understand." It hurt to see the boys looking in all four directions to make sure that no one could see them saying "thanks." Even more painful was the experience of watching the difficulty these boys had trying to understand how anyone could really care for them. How often have I heard them say, "How can you really love me when even my own parents don't?" Sad to say, they were convinced that this rejection by their parents was due not to parental neglect or indifference, but rather to their own imagined unlovableness.

Even under the best of family conditions there is anxiety, uneasiness, and uncertainty in the early adolescent. There is a great discrepancy between what he is and what he knows he has to become. But how do you get there? "There is so much to learn, and I don't even know where or how to begin." Fears of ridicule, of personal failure, and of inadequacy persist. Becoming an adolescent does not alleviate personal concerns and fears, many of which were started in childhood.

SOCIAL DEVELOPMENT

Just as physical changes at puberty have an effect on emotions, so do they have an effect on social development and relationships. There is no chemical factor involved to influence social development as there is to modify emotional development, but the changes in physical characteristics are great enough to create attitudes and concerns regarding social relationships. The early-maturing child feels different from the others and may want to withdraw. However, the other children may look to the early-maturing individual for leadership and direction. The late maturer has social problems because he seems to be "too far behind" everybody else and is not "grown-up" enough.

On another point the appearance of adult physical characteristics often brings a demand from adults for the teen-ager to be more responsible and to act more "grown-up." The early teen-ager does not possess the social and cognitive skills necessary to be competent as an adult. Their physical maturity belies their social maturity. Finally, the physical discrepancies in weight and height between girls and boys, especially at the age of 13 years, is enough to make boys cringe. Many girls in the eighth grade look sufficiently physically mature to be mothers of the boys. That is a slight exaggeration, but there is a gap to be bridged. Can the girls wait for the boys to catch up?

Peer group influence

Although the early adolescent is struggling for independence, strong dependency needs arise as he attempts to find himself and identify his role in society. Peer groups play a major part in the gratification of these needs. Through frequent contacts with his peers plus an increasing absence of parents from the home—or at least fewer hours of contact with parents—the peer group becomes the important socializing agent. Group pressures are beginning to have tremendous effects on behavior. Values and attitudes are being created and reinforced by the group phenomena. Conformity demanded by the group may discourage individualism and self-assertion. However, as the adolescent matures, he tends to regain his individual characteristics.[13]

The adolescent measures his whole being by the reaction of his peers. It is they who accept him and encourage him to keep on behaving as he is. If he is ignored or criticized by his peers, he may develop feelings of inferiority, inadequacy, and incompetency. The peer group is greatly responsible for the modification of behavior and for providing a forum by which the teen-ager sees himself for better or for worse.

Teaching how to get along with others is a socializing value of the peer group. Within the group he must learn to be considerate of the feelings of others and must be able to listen to their views. The first groups in early adolescence are usually made up of one sex. This situation is merely a continuation of the group makeup in late childhood. Girls congregate in the intimacy of someone's bedroom to talk about boys, clothes, boys, makeup, and boys. The activities of boys revolve around sports, hobby activities, and rough games. There is some comfort and advantage in being with one's own kind at this time. Give and take are more acceptable. There is more freedom to discuss any and all subjects. They can give each other support in learning about themselves and, eventually, about the opposite sex. Ego development, increased self-reliance, and establishing self-esteem through contributions made to the group are all possible by group association.

By the age of 13 years girls have begun to form definite cliques based on personal likes, dislikes, interests, similarities in socioeconomic background, and proximity of residence. They exclude others on the basis of irrelevant factors. The peer group may begin to shift from one sex to both, often in imitation of older teens. It must be kept in mind that early adolescents are less concerned with expressing heterosexual feelings than with the questions of growing up, their social status in the group, and their comparative standing with others of their own sex. Here is an opportunity to associate with others having similar growing problems.

Although early adolescence is a gregarious, social stage, it is also one in which youngsters tend to select a "best" friend of the same sex with whom confidences are exchanged. Some parents become concerned when they note such a strong relationship between their child and another. Parents wonder if good heterosexual relationships with others will ever develop. Parents need not worry about this type of association. As children grow older, they tend to widen their circle of acquaintances and may eventually drift apart from earlier friends. People often talk about this happening by saying "When they were in junior high school, they were as close as two peas in a pod. No one ever thought that anything could separate them. Now they hardly ever see each other."

Parent–teen-ager relationships

A major developmental task in early adolescence is the attempt to achieve emancipation from the home. As a result, early adolescence emerges as a period of intense rejection of adults, and especially of parents. This rejection is not consistent, however, because it varies from mood to mood of the teen-ager. Sometimes the young person feels highly competent and demands his "rights." At other times, after he has been hurt in his battles with the world, he becomes compliant and accepts parental guidance. The adolescent issues his "declaration of independence," but the problem is that he needs to be independent in a dependent type of way. Children who come from families in which the mother and father have helped the child in the growing-up process by providing opportunities to learn responsibility, self-reliance, necessary skills, and self-respect make a much smoother transition from childhood dependency to adulthood competency. Parents who have been liberal, overly permissive, or uninterested about their child's behavior may have more difficulty with their child because he lacks a structure or system of standards or values by which he can determine whether his behavior is suitable and his decisions appropriate. Overprotective parents never give their child an opportunity to learn how to make important decisions and how to assume responsibilities.

Many parents have ambivalent feelings about their growing child. Some parents are among the last to accept the fact that he is growing. It is alarming, to some fathers in particular, to learn that their "little girl" is going out on her first date with a boy. When teen-agers assert their right to be more grown-up, they often create tensions within the home. They resist family control; they resent being treated like a child. This is the age of "You don't understand me" and "You always treat me like a baby." If really pressed, the child may think, if not say, "It's not my fault I was born. You have to put up with me."

Parents sometimes feel hurt at this lack of gratitude or appreciation. "This is the kind of thanks I get for staying up late at night with you when you were sick? This is the way you treat me after all I have sacrificed for you so that you could have nice things to wear and good food to eat?" It is necessary to recognize that it is difficult for parents to change as quickly as the child is changing at puberty. For the past twelve or thirteen years the parents

Puberty and early adolescence 181

Frederic Lewis, Inc., New York City.

have been making decisions for their child; the child was dependent on them. How can parents change these relationships overnight, especially when they are struggling with their own problems and life? The most important thing for parents to keep in mind, at any time or any age of the child, is not to do or say anything that will break down or cut off the lines of communication between parent and child. All teen-agers need help, even if they do not recognize this need or seem grateful for it. They must feel comfortable and free to seek that help from their parents or loved ones. If teen-agers cannot talk to their parents or to other acceptable adults, they only have their peers and friends to turn to. How much good advice and information on serious matters can one 13-year-old or 15-year-old give to another?

Conflict areas between parents and children include use of the telephone, table manners, homework, disrespectful behavior, hours for coming in from activities or for going to bed, readiness for adult responsibilities, money, grooming habits, and dress. The teen-ager's room and its cleanliness are always a source of friction, especially if it's a girl's room. Concerning good grooming and dress, conflict in these areas is high before the age of 14 years. According to current indications, this conflict may be continuing throughout later adolescence —either that or the parents simply say "I give up!" Parental disapproval is often based on a rationale of "It isn't right." More likely, parental objections are really related to tradition, status quo, or the sin of disobedience toward one who has their best interest at heart.[14] Adolescence is a period of experimentation during which identity is sought. Since manner of dress usually means conformity to the peer group, the adolescent is willing to defy parental authority, sometimes in a nice way and sometimes more violently, to be acceptable to their group.

Teen-agers want to complain or talk about schools, but they do not want their parents to fight their battles for them, to visit the school, or to attend the parent-teacher organization (secondary level). In fact, teen-agers often are embarrassed by being seen with their parents, especially by their friends. Some say that when a child becomes an adolescent, he no longer wants to sit with his parents in church or go to the movies with them. When he returns to sit voluntarily with his parents, he has outgrown his early adolescent stage.

Developing heterosexuality

Early adolescence begins with gangs or groups made up of members of the same sex and ends with a coming together of the two sexes in crowd activities and possibly with some dating (Fig. 9-2). There is a gradual mixing together of the sexes, starting with parties in sixth and seventh grades. By the ninth grade most boys are willing to tolerate or seek girls just for the fun they get from being around them.

As social development takes place in early adolescence, teen-agers begin to reconstruct their value systems and interest patterns regarding the opposite sex. They change according to their interpretation of what are considered by their peers, parents, and community to be accepted heterosexual practices and activities. The age at which heterosexual interests begin is largely determined by these forces. If there is a conflict of thinking among these forces, the teen-ager responds to the force that has the greatest meaning and influence to him personally.

In some areas heterosexual activities begin on a noticeable scale among 11- and 12-year-olds. In other communities heterosexual involvements are not widely noted until the ages of 14 or 15 years. Two points relevant to our statements concerning age level heterosexual interests and practices will be emphasized. First, there are age level differences in social practices in various com-

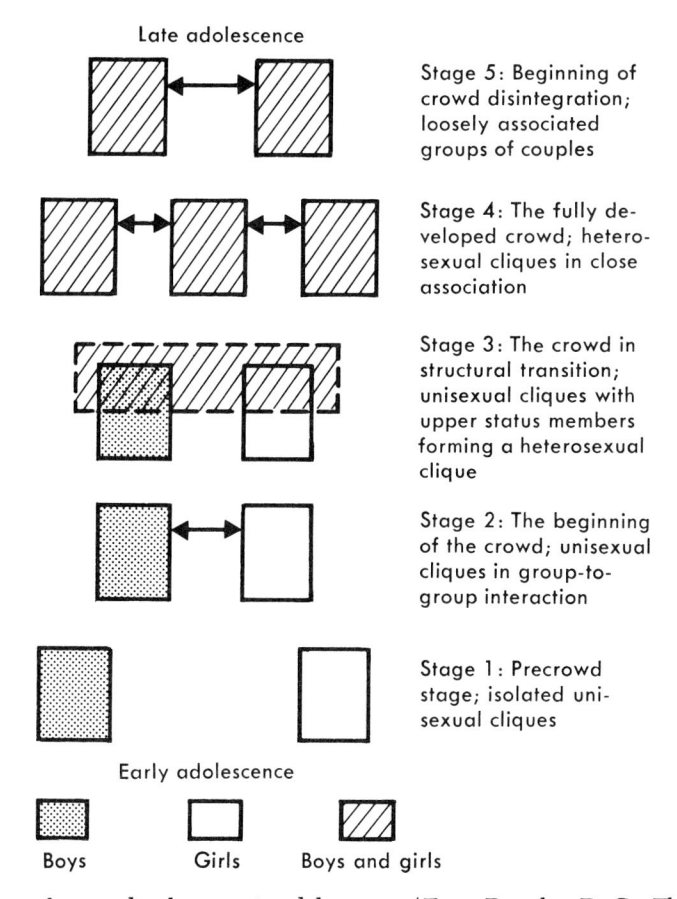

Fig. 9-2. Stages of group development in adolescence. (From Dunphy, D. C.: The social structure of urban adolescent peer groups, Sociometry 26:236, 1963.)

munities, social groups, and subcultures. Children in different communal areas are exposed to differences in accepted mores, customs, roles, and degrees of permissiveness in social relationships. In some communities it is proper for a 13-year-old girl to go out on a single date. In other communities this action is deeply frowned on, and all kinds of social restrictions are imposed to hinder such dating. Second, regardless of the community, there will always be individuals who do not follow the generally accepted practices. People do not fit neat, rigid categories, and some persons will not abide by the customs. These statements are intended to refer to "commonly observed practices" and not to "the exception to the rule" or to the few who are the forerunners of a change in social behavior.

Early adolescent years include a considerable number of heterosexual contacts, most of which are related to school affairs or to community activities provided for young people. Group contacts are desirable because they give opportunities to practice social skills, such as conversation, courtesy, and cooperation. Usually the first heterosexual activities are "group" or "crowd" affairs. Pairing off by couples is not the usual relationship. A group or the "crowd" is invited to a party. The girls will dance together while the boys watch. Some special activity, such as a mixer game, will be needed to bring the two sexes together.

However, at a party in a home, it would not be unusual for the group to play kissing games such as "post office" or "spin the bottle." Boys go along with such games because the products of the games are "daring"—something like "forbidden fruit." Boys get a feeling of pleasant amazement "to think that someone likes me well enough to call *my* number to go to the post office for a stamp!" It is not that the kiss means so much; it is the idea that "someone likes me enough to ask for a kiss." Of course girls have their own reasons for enjoying playing kissing games. They have been waiting for such opportunities for a long time.

There is less antagonism toward the opposite sex, an ever-widening circle of friends of both sexes, and a broader range of social experiences in early adolescence. The barriers set up by the same sex groups are tumbling down. There will be a few holdouts, especially among the boys. As far as unwillingness to engage in heterosexual activities is concerned, these cases will be rare by the age of 14 years. Dating activities will begin when shyness, timidity, and antipathy toward the opposite sex decrease and a desire to be like older teen-agers increases.

In seventh grade most boys are still embarrassed enough of girls to consider it a major threat to their self-esteem to be seated between two girls. Girls at this age (12 years) tend to be more mature, and they do not mind boys. If given a chance at a party or school dance, girls will seek to dance with boys even though the boys are usually shorter. By the eighth grade boys are more interested in girls than before, and fewer would feel threatened by being placed between two girls. In fact, some boys would be highly pleased to be forced to sit next to a girl, but they would try not to show it. They may protest loud and long but don't try to change their places! They are still unsure of themselves but do mingle more freely. As for eighth grade girls, they may be more aggressive and more openly "boy crazy" than at any other age. They are desperate—that may be too strong a word—but they are certainly interested in boys. The problem they have, however, is that they have not learned the subtle, social skills necessary to know how to show an interest in boys without appearing too eager, too forward, or too bold. One eighth grade girl was asked by a teasing adult, "Jack McDonald says he likes you, do you like him?" "Yes," replied the girl, "Who is he?" "You mean you don't know him and you say you like him?" "Sure," replied the quick-thinking girl, "if he likes me, he has good taste, and that's all that matters!" The summer between the eighth and ninth grades seems to bring about unbelievable changes in heterosexual development as a number of boy-girl relationships blossom and begin to be longer lasting. Many boys are now taller than their girl classmates. They are more sure of themselves and less embarrassed about seeking female companionship. Ninth grade girls are definitely interested in male companions. The more mature girls may be dating fellows who are several years older than themselves.

Observation on early heterosexuality

There may be a risk in having too many older or adult-type social experiences at too young an age. An emphasis placed on "earliness" in developing social relationships, especially involving dating, could be undesirable. A rationale for such beliefs is not proved scientifically, but our associations and work with young people lead us to certain premises and hypotheses.

It would seem that many young people do not develop the social stability, judgment, and control necessary to overcome the dominant influence of peer demands, attitudes, and pressures concerning social relationships and activities until they are about 19 or 20 years old. Up to this age the adolescent responds to group domination. His dress, talk, attitudes, and actions are determined largely by his peer group or the prevalent social moods and thoughts of the time. He is unsure of himself and too inexperienced to know what decisions to make or what behavior to pursue. The world knows best, and he is willing to follow the world. As a result, he will continue to be group oriented and to involve himself in a variety of interpersonal experiences. Not until he reaches a point of social stability or maturity will he feel competent enough to break away from group thought and emphasis and to judge and decide for himself what behavior is important to his well-being.

A second premise is that each society has within its social framework a body of skills and knowledge which is learned by most of the adolescents of that culture as part of their heterosexual development. This core is somewhat sequential in nature, going from global social activities at first to more mature, individualized activities later on. Movement in social development is step by step; the young person moves from one level of competency to another. There is a point in development, however, at which he is considered to have attained the information and skills necessary to operate effectively in everyday adult behavior. The rapidity with which an individual acquires this level depends on (1) the initial age at which the needed experiences were encountered, (2) the amount of practice he had in developing the social skills related to those experiences, and (3) the degree to which he assimilated or internalized the lessons and emotions of those experiences. Some individuals go through these basic social learnings much sooner than others. For example, some girls begin to date when they are 12 or 13 years old. Some may have their first cigarette, drink, or sex involvement at that age. Other girls may have none of these experiences until they are much older. The basic point of the second premise is that there is a hierarchy of skills and information, learned by different activities and experiences, culminating in an acceptable level of social competency. Earliness of social experiences within the hierarchy is a crucial factor in determining the age at which that level of competency is reached.

A third and last premise is that the adolescent who has not attained personal dominance in social judgment and control will continue to place a great emphasis on social experiences and activities in his daily life, even though he has learned all the skills he needs to know. Once a certain skill has been mastered or a desired activity has been experienced to a satisfying degree, the adolescent rarely wants to stay on that level of development. He will seek new social experiences. He still has a great need for social contact, participation, and acceptance. This need is a major dominating force in his rational life. It is at this stage that he is most susceptible to involvement in a wide range of unusual, unacceptable, and often dangerous experiences. He has already had the usual social experiences. He wants something different. Not until he places a different value on the importance of social acceptance or on social activities in his life will he change his focus of emphasis in daily behavior. Our experience seems to indicate that most individuals do not reach this level of personal control and change of philosophy until they are 19 to 20 years old.

The conclusion would seem to be that too much social sophistication too soon makes it easier for adolescents to engage in practices that they would have rejected or avoided had they not had the more typical social activities too early in life. Emotional growth cannot take place as rapidly in early adolescence as can social growth. Even though a 12-year-old may be superior in worldly social know-how, he still has only the natural emotional needs of a 12-year-old. This level of emotional development is hardly adequate for an adult world.

Sexual awareness

The typical preadolescent appears to be relatively unconfused about sexuality. However, with the onset of puberty and adolescence, even the most well-adjusted child will have some uncertainties and confusion.

Even when the child has received most of his sex education at home in an anxiety-free atmosphere, he may still be perplexed. He is at an age when adult authority is not respected and accepted as it once was. The parents of the 12-year-old may find their child far more inclined to believe in the teaching of his peers. Discrepancies between what the peers say and what the parents say add to the uncertainty. If the peers provide a more extensive, in-depth discussion concerning sex, the child may wonder whether the parents may be hiding some facts from him and "treating him like a baby." He begins to look for answers of his own. The parents applaud his desire to look for information relating to a history project but may show no enthusiasm when he seeks answers to sex questions. The youngster is further confused by this inconsistency.

Television and magazine advertisements bombard the young teen-ager during his free moments. The glowing reports of what happens when you use a certain mouthwash, hair cream, toothpaste, or underarm deodorant make heterosexual activities of a romantic nature seem so possible. Girls tend to be more influenced by these pressures than boys, but boys are definitely influenced by the glamorous portrayal of the virile male. They may begin smoking under the impression that "it is manly." They disdain the "bookworm" and the "sissy." Their vocabularies are expanded to include such terms as *queer, gay,* and *homo.* At about 14 years of age, boys appear to begin worrying about their own ability to perform the sex act. They do not usually seek to experiment to find out, but they do show a greater curiosity about the sex act. Their interests are no longer just in their own maleness but in their ability to become part of a heterosexual society.

Adolescents show some concern about their secondary sex characteristics. Boys are conscious of the formation of their sex structure and concerned if they believe there are any deviations. They are troubled by nocturnal emissions and wonder if anyone, especially their mother who usually washes the pajamas and bed sheets, might find out. Girls are concerned mostly with breast development and whether or not anyone can tell when they are having their monthly periods. Most adolescents of this age level experience something akin to masturbation, boys more so than girls. There are questions such as why is there an erection, what causes it, why does it feel different to "do it," will it hurt anything, is it sinful or bad, does it mean that I'm oversexed, and does anyone else do this too? Most adolescents probably engage in self-stimulation because of sexual responses that are stirred and the emotional tone experience that is felt.[15] Sex attraction begins in the middle adolescent years. The sensory experience of just looking at or touching that certain person, or their picture, is enough to bring about a sexual response. Boys may be extremely upset over trying to hide the fact that they are having an erection in daylight, in public, and often for no apparent reason.

Petting, attachments to others of the opposite sex, and masturbation are the most frequent methods of sexual release during this period. Our counseling work with young teen-agers has indicated that there is more sexual involvement taking place among girls of this age than most adults realize. The involvement is generally of the initial necking and petting variety. Almost always this activity involves an older boy. Our counseling experiences indicate that whenever a girl of junior high age (13 or 14 years) goes steady for at least three months with a boy who is two or three years older, there is invariably some extensive petting taking place (not necessarily the sex act). Petting takes place sooner if an automobile is used extensively by the couple. Among junior high school couples who go steady for more than a three-month period, there may be necking and some light petting taking place but seldom much heavy petting. We are less concerned about a junior high school girl if she is going steady with a boy of her own age than if she is a steady dater of a boy two or three years older than herself.

TEEN CULTURE AND INTERESTS

The development of interests during early adolescence can offer many positive rewards. Interests open gateways to the mind and usually make a person more receptive and eager to learn. Interests help to establish channels of communication with others. Sharing ideas on the professional football players and exchanging records provides a bond of mutuality among teenagers. The development of interests can lead to constructive use of leisure time and may help to crystallize a vocational pattern for later years.

Interests

Boys like to spend a great deal of time in active outdoor sports and just "going out with the guys." They also spend time on hobbies of a mechanical nature. Watching television comprises a good bit of their time. Being with girls does not constitute a large part of their leisure activity, although it does occupy more time as they enter the freshman year of high school.

Girls' leisure activities show a sharp contrast. Their activities include fewer outdoor pursuits than those of boys. More time is spent in "just being with the girls," listening to records, and experimenting with makeup. Their more active pursuits include one that never exists for boys—dancing among themselves.[16]

The early adolescent girl shows a keen interest in boys, even though they may not be interested in her at this age. She enjoys writing notes to and about boys, and this topic is always on her mind. Due to her increased awareness of the feminine role, she now is highly conscious of her personal appearance. Exploration of the female world seems to be a natural inclination. Lipstick and powder may appear on girls as early as the age of 9 years. Clothing of the latest style is a must for her. She likes to go shopping for clothes, but she and her mother seldom agree on fads, colors, and skirt lengths.

Other interests include listening to new records and loud music. Being able to recite the most popular hit records is part of this pattern. Watching movies, especially sentimental ones, is another pastime. Any movie, book, or television program dealing with romance will be of interest to her at this level. Also typical for this stage is keeping a diary. Daydreams, events, and emotions that cannot be shared with real people are confessed to a diary. The diary affords role playing and fantasy without involving action in reality.

The young adolescent and preadolescent may become an active community participant as a member of Girl Scouts, Boy Scouts, Boys' Clubs, or Campfire Girls because it is at this time that the young person is greatly interested in forming gangs and groups and joining social clubs. For boys, gangs are a spontaneous effort to create a society for themselves and get the thrill of participating in common interests, fighting, hunting, and the like. Girls may be even more organizationally oriented than boys. They are more mature in seeking friendships with others and are more interested in social activities. However, girls' club activities do not include any participation on an organized team as do boys' clubs. Approximately 60% of girls and 11% of boys want social activities to be included in a club.[17] Girls are more interested in homemaking activities, whereas boys are interested in sports, games, and outdoor activities. Forty-one percent of 13-year-old boys and 44% of 13-year-old girls wanted both boys and girls in their clubs.[18]

Much of the leisure time of early adolescents at home is spent watching television, reading, working at hobbies, playing games, caring for animals, doing chores, eating, and sleeping. Little time is spent in studying at home. Young adolescents may watch television because it is something they can do together. Reading may satisfy their demands for adventure, boys preferring stories about animals, adventure, and sports of all kinds, girls enjoying biographies about women, mysteries, stories of home life, and love stories. In early adolescence there is usually a great interest in movies for the same reason adolescents have an interest in television—because they can go together. Movies catering to youth, often relating to differences in generations, draw many junior high students on weekends. Girls prefer movies over athletics, whereas boys do not. Boys who go to the movies would prefer to see a sports, mystery, or adventure story or a movie with excitement, realism, humor, or violence. Girls enjoy a romance story or something sentimental.

Whereas a movie is not something a junior high student can enjoy all the time, a radio is. Many young adolescents carry around transistor radios and combine the music with studying, walking, and many other activities. In study halls it is not uncommon to see a boy or girl with a transistor radio hidden in his lap and a listener's plug in his ear. Rock and roll or popular music is preferred at all grade levels. Girls at early adolescence prefer music on television or the radio to a greater degree than boys. Rock and roll is one of the surest ways to the heart and wallet of the adolescent, creating a ritualized world of dances, slang, the charts, and fan magazines.[19]

When young adolescents are not going to the movies, reading, or listening to music, they are probably talking. They find it easy and desirable to talk to their friends in "gab sessions," which is their main out-of-school activity. Boys may spend hours talking about sports figures, athletics, and cars; girls talk about parties, dates, clothes, and social happenings at school. These conversations may take place on the telephone, exasperating parents and the person on the party line alike. However, this conversation with friends is helpful to the young adolescent, building up his self-confidence and ability to converse with others.

Fads and fashion

A form of interest that seems most characteristic of early adolescence is the "fad." A fad is a short-term fashion or practice pursued with exaggerated zeal and bordering on a cult. It is usually temporary and unpredictable. Young adolescents are extremely concerned with being accepted by their peers. This intense desire for acceptance is part of the reason why fads catch on so quickly during adolescent years. They help to give each individual a feeling of belonging while saying to adults "We're different from you." It seems that junior high schools can expect at least one major fad to hit the school each year. Teachers often wonder, "What will they think of next!" A perennial fad in some areas is the use of water pistols by the boys.

One junior high school teacher writes concerning her experiences with fads in her school:

One group of our junior high girls went around for days braless in tee-shirts and jeans. The fellows all wore headbands. Girls used curling irons so their hair was in ringlets. (Two years ago I spent hours trying to straighten mine.) When I was in junior high we wore sneakers in the spring to be "in." When my sister reached her junior high school years, a dime in each loafer was the thing to do. I also spent hours making a chain with gum wrappers as tall as my boyfriend at the time, then burning it; if it burned all the way to the end, our "love" would last. Strange as it may seem, none of mine ever made it to the end. Fads, of course, can change overnight as do the interests of early adolescents; but they allow the adolescent to feel he is truly like his peer group.

Other fads include the wearing of certain clothing, such as Bermuda shorts, beanie caps, Ivy League clothes, sweatshirts, or certain colors, usually wild. Stockings and socks have gone the route from white ankle socks, to ribbed white socks half-way up the calf and knee socks, to flesh-colored nylon hose, to colored hose, to textured or patterned hose, to hose and long-line girdles, to colored panty hose and leotards. Hair styles among boys have included crew cuts, skin heads, Mohawk Indian cuts, flat tops, duck style, brush cuts, shaggy hair, and no cuts. Girls would bleach streaks of their hair, use food dye to color their hair green, blue, or red, or let their hair grow stringy and long, giving them an intellectual, unwashed look. In some schools students would speak in an imitation "Chinese language" by beginning the words with the "y" sound. A recent fad was the use of psychedelic-colored flower posters and stickers on textbooks, clothing, or bedroom walls. Can you recall what fads were popular in your crowd when you were 13 to 15 years old?

Various attempts have been made to explain the reason why adolescents' fads take hold. According to Rand,[20] the strongest motive is a combination of the desire to receive attention, the desire to assert independence from adults, and the desire to be one of the gang. Rejected by adults, adolescents feel a comfort in being like others their age. Apparently the most important factor in understanding teen fads is recognizing the "herd" instinct, to look alike, to feel part of a group by wearing the same clothes, using the same language, or developing the same mannerisms.

At the same time fads permit adolescents to express their individuality by wearing more and crazier charms on their bracelets or by being the first to hear and use a new slang phrase. Fads such as a current dance style may also produce enjoyable tension. Fads may compensate for boredom and low morale—especially for the adolescent who is patiently waiting for the time until he becomes an adult. They can represent a pioneer spirit and a yearning for freedom from regimentation. In fact, food fads and idiosyncrasies in language, manner, and clothes may be subtle expressions of the rebellion typical of this age.

Another related and familiar phenomenon is simply fashion—the very latest in dressing, writing, behaving, etc. This usually involves a socially approved variation of dress, furniture, music, art, speech, and other areas of culture. Each age group has its own varieties of fashion, reflecting certain characteristics of that age.

At times, being in fashion is a question of keeping tabs on changing sizes, knowing, for example, that sunglasses are growing larger, hair is longer and curlier, and boys' ties are getting broader. Girls have put away their too-long, leg-hiding skirts (with the exception of the Granny dress) and are taking satisfaction in the most comfortable, although revealing, clothes in years, the hot pants, micromini skirts, and pant suits. Who knows, tomorrow may see a return to skirts that are longer than ever! Whatever their cause or result, fads and fashions are a part of modern society.

PERSONAL PROBLEMS AND CONCERNS

The personal problems of adolescents are fairly well documented. At this point, we merely wish to present some personal statements written in a free-response, permissive situation by junior high school pupils. The intent of personalizing the problems of teen-agers is to show the degree of intensification these young people have concerning their problems and the implications of these problems for a need on the part of the adolescent to reconstruct and reorganize his personality from what it was in childhood. The child of 9, 10, or 11 years was a fairly stable individual. With the coming of puberty every single avenue of growth and development undergoes extensive changes, making the personality of the younger child inadequate for the emerging new individual.

Problems of adolescents can be grouped under the following categories: (1) physical problems, such as facial problems, uneven growth, late maturing, early maturing, and sex problems; (2) personal problems involving self-identity, self-concept, and personality; (3) social problems relating to home and family, peer group, and social status; (4) scholastic problems of the school, including study, tests, homework, and teachers; (5) religion, moral values, and development of a personal philosophy; and (6) future problems concerning vocations and alienation from society.

The following personal concerns were written by seventh, eighth, and ninth graders in response to the query: "What problems or difficulties do you have for which you would like help? In other words, what is bothering you in relation to people, your family, money, friends, or any other part of your life? (Your name is not needed.)" The problems are presented as they were written. They are some of the more common problems and concerns.

Girl, 12 years, seventh grade
I don't have any problems other than not getting enough allowance and having pimples. My pimples are getting better, thank goodness.

Girl, 12 years, seventh grade
Do you think I am old enough to let a boy kiss me? He tried to do it a few times, but I covered my face. He asked me to go to the football game, but my mother would not let me go; she said I was too young. I know he will ask me to go some place else. How can I get my mother to let me go? The trouble is I want to go but I would rather pay my own way.

Boy, 12 years, seventh grade
How will I know what to say to a girl so I won't get my head knocked off?

Boy, 13 years, eighth grade
My father left my mother, my sister, and me when I was 12 years old. If I were younger, it wouldn't have meant much to me, but I wasn't and I have felt strong resentment toward him. It bothers me in school and in other places. If I could overcome my resentment toward him, I could get along better with other people.

Boy, 13 years, eighth grade
I don't know when I have time to study, since I work to help support the family because my father is sick. I do not get very much sleep in the evenings. So, when I don't have any written work in class, I sort of doze off.

Girl, 13 years, eighth grade
I have learned to be happy most of the time, and I am very contented with my life. But, when I act happy, people think I am nuts.

Boy, 13 years, eighth grade
Parents are pests. They're always nagging me and will not let me outside past 8 o'clock.

Girl, 13 years, eighth grade
How old do you think I should be before I should be allowed to date? Some of the girls my age are already dating. Do you think this is the right age or should I wait till I'm older?

Girl, 13 years, eighth grade
Last week in geography class I had to collect the homework papers. As I went to collect one of the girl's papers, she told me not to tell the teacher because she didn't have her homework finished. As I went up to tell the teacher I just couldn't figure out whether to tell the teacher or leave it go because I was afraid the girl would be mad at me. Would you please tell me if I should have told the teacher?

Girl, 14 years, eighth grade
I am worried about someone grabbing me in a car coming home after dark.

Boy, 13 years, eighth grade
What should you do when your parents always seem to be arguing and you don't even want to go home? It seems I'm always trying to figure out a different excuse for going some-

where. The family seems to be growing further apart.

Girl, 14 years, ninth grade
My father is under the impression that no boys are good enough for me, and therefore I'm not permitted to associate with them. But this is not true. It's just that I may not be good enough for the boys and they do not seem interested in me.

Boy, 14 years, ninth grade
Should I wait to get drafted or enlist when I graduate from high school?

Boy, 14 years, ninth grade
The school—it stinks! I hate school. I like young teachers, not old, grouchy teachers. School is all right if you don't have too many lessons.

Girl, 14 years, ninth grade
I don't know what course to take in high school. It is hard for me to make up my mind as to what I want to do and what subjects to take.

Boy, 14 years, ninth grade
The main question in my mind is sex education. I wouldn't want anybody to think I am immoral or indecent but rather just trying to receive a good education. When you receive any advice on this matter from another youth, you never get it straight. It is always told to you the wrong way. I have gathered that sex is a thing to be hidden and whispered about. The movies and magazines play it up but that is not sex information. I cannot help but think that educated people should take this open-mindedly and straightforward. I would like some advice or help on this question. Maybe I'm too young; I don't know. But if I am, I wish someone that is qualified to say would tell me.

Boy, 14 years, ninth grade
My father and I aren't together enough. I would like to get closer acquainted with him and have more activities together when he is not working.

Boy, 15 years, ninth grade
I live 13 miles from high school. I have to get up at 5 o'clock in the morning so I can do my barn work. Then I leave for school at 7:30 to catch a bus. I don't get home until 5:30 in the evening. After I get my barn work done and eat supper it is time to go to bed. And the teachers want us to work at least two hours at home on our lessons. We should have shorter school days or fewer unimportant subjects.

Girl, 15 years, ninth grade
How can I learn to study at home with a lot of kids playing in the hallways, television sets blaring out all over the apartment house, and people yelling at the top of their voices?

Girl, 14 years, ninth grade
I would like to get along with my sisters and brothers, but they don't seem to like me for some reason.

Girl, 16 years, special education class
I don't have much interest in school. But my parents want me to go to school. I try to get my work but can't get it too well. I would like to know of a way that might interest me in school. I feel so selfconscious because I am only in eighth grade (special education). I was thinking about quitting school, but then I took the second thought about it. What can you do without an education? My parents don't want me to quit, but I don't seem to have any interest in school.

It was difficult to pick out representative problems as they were written by early adolescents because there were so many good ones from which to choose. We have conducted this study over a five-year period and have over a thousand papers. The first time I (G. K.) collected papers from the students I could not wait to read what they had written. So I read a number of the papers before I left school to go home. I will never forget the depressed, heavy feeling that overcame me. My shoulders and head actually felt the weight of the burden of their problems. I thought that they were such happy-go-lucky kids, but, instead, they were immersed in deep, often unresolvable problems. Here were children worrying about their mothers and fathers separating, about when they would get something decent to eat, or how to avoid the clutches of criminal elements and drugs, and we teachers were trying to teach them something about ancient Rome, binomial theorems, and dangling participles!

AWAKENING OF REASONING

Approximately one year after the beginning of puberty the individual begins to feel confident in his intellectual abilities. There is a growing insistence on submitting all things to the test of one's own reason. It is at this time that he thinks he knows everything. Despite this attitude, which certainly may get him into trouble with adults, he is beginning to show interest in thinking, experimenting, and generalizing. Often these interests are directed to science. The act of formulating a hypothesis and actually testing it gives him great satisfaction. Prior to this time he has used the method of trial and error to reach his learning goals. He will now spend some of his time thinking of a solution rather than immediately acting and then having to make corrections. Piaget's explanation of this stage will be given in Chapter 10.

A tendency to insist on one's own judgment and reason increases throughout early and middle adolescence. In childhood many things were accepted on the authoritative statement of parents or teachers, but in adolescence all authority may be questioned and criticized. Childhood was generally marked by unquestioning belief and acceptance of what was said by parent or teacher or Bible or textbook, but adolescence is an age of doubt.

Many parents and teachers are disturbed by this natural appearance of a tendency to question matters that are accepted implicitly by children and considered authoritative by adults. There is, however, a kind of good fortune in this adolescent trait. Were it not for the adolescent tendency to criticize and doubt, they would all come to adulthood with a fixed confidence in the status quo, and progress would not exist.[21]

Since the mental functions grow in an orderly sequence, memory, reasoning, imagination, and interpreting ability develop to their highest peak during late adolescence. Mental growth curves show an increase in mental development from childhood through early adolescence to a gradual increase in late adolescence. Social interaction gives the adolescent many experiences and opportunities to help develop his mental functions fully while in the adolescent stage of life.

Daydreaming

Early adolescence is marked by an exuberant imagination that is not yet under control. The mind is awakening to a deeper intuition of the meaning of things but has not yet learned how to regulate by use of reason this unraveling of insight.

Early adolescence is the period of daydreams and extravagant imagination and hence is peculiarly exasperating to the unsympathetic adult whose youthful visions have long faded. The boy or girl who goes through the day sluggishly and absentmindedly may be lost in a world of daydreams. Of course, such a person must be recalled to realities of life, but it should be done with sympathy and understanding. Many boys and girls who have been harshly treated on this score, their youthful ideals meeting no sympathetic response from older people, have built a wall of defensive reserve and behind this have lived a dream life that is quite isolated from everyday experiences.

Socioeconomic influence on intelligence

Functional intelligence is traditionally measured by an "intelligence" test. Items on such tests generally include measurements of general information, vocabulary or word usage, the ability to reason, arithmetical reasoning, memory, commonsense judgment, and aspects of visual-motor performance. Many of these items are related or influenced by life-space culture.

Socioeconomic relationships play an important part in the mental development of the early adolescent. On intelligence tests Billy, who comes from a middle-class white home, as an example, often outscores Harvey, who comes from an economically deprived black home. We dare not conclude that Harvey is less intelligent than Billy, however. Billy perhaps has had more verbal and sensory experiences than Harvey. Also important in this situation is the adolescent's relationship with his parents and the motivating atmosphere of the home environment. Harvey has learned to put value on immediate, extrinsic results that he can partake of today rather than on something of an elusive, intellectual nature because the latter is not tangible to him. Billy, on the other hand, thinks about his future, his learning, and further education because he has been guided by parents and siblings and has been influenced by the accepted thinking of his immediate environment, which stresses the future.

Moral awakening

The early adolescent's moral development depends on his parents, his peer group, and his own experiences of resolving right from wrong. He usually adopts the accepted behavior of the group that is most significant to him. He must feel a relatedness to someone or some group to feel free to accept and develop a strong moral code. Right and wrong must be presented in tangible terms. Groups set norms for their members, and enforcement of the norms results in conforming behavior. Groups also relate to other groups. As a result, group behavior can be influenced in directions that involve status-earning achievements.

The influence may be positive, as in the case of a group seeking to excel in sports or some other form of healthy competition, or it may be negative, as in the case of aggressive behavior, gang wars, or disruptive activities.

The child entering adolescence has no difficulty in being able to identify the truth. He has developed the power to reason and easily recognizes the truthful manner. However, he is also governed by his peers, and this calls for ability to know when to and when not to lie in preservation of the self.

The adolescent soon discovers that what people say and what they do may be two entirely different things in certain situations. This inconsistency results in much misunderstanding and questioning in his mind. At this stage in life the teen-ager is highly idealistic, and when these ideals are shattered by adult hypocrisy, detrimental effects may result if he is not strong enough to accept the fact of fallacy.

As the adolescent gains experience, he also gains responsibility. He wants to follow common sense on issues that require a decision of right or wrong, and he is always ready to take a stand on what he believes. Drinking, smoking, cheating, stealing, and drugs are very tangible issues in the life of an adolescent. Not being fully committed to such practices, the adolescent may casually attempt these activities, or he may decide to participate fully in one or more of them. The dominant alter influence in his life will determine if he will accept or reject these behaviors.

STUDY GUIDE

1. Review the developmental tasks of early adolescence. Can you recognize how they are heading down the pathway leading to adulthood?
2. Define the terms *primary sex characteristics* and *secondary sex characteristics*.
3. What is considered to be evidence of

the climax of puberty in boys and in girls?
4. Physical changes are abundant during the pubertal and early adolescent period. Make a list of what you would consider to be the more dramatic or outstanding changes in boys and in girls.
5. Most early adolescents lack emotional control. Why is this so?
6. Parent–teen-ager relationships often become strained during early and middle adolescence. What are some of the more common sources of conflict? When you were an early adolescent, did you have any adjustment problems with your parents? Did the problems seem insurmountable or all-important then? As you look back, were the problems of that moment as demanding and as gigantic as you thought them to be? How were they finally resolved?
7. When you were 12 to 15 years of age, what were some of the fads or fashions that you or your classmates followed? Consider clothing, activities, slang expressions, or food. What fads or fashions are you responding to now that you are older?

REFERENCES

1. Tanner, J. M.: Growth and endocrinology in the adolescent. In Gardner, L. I., editor: Endocrine and genetic diseases in childhood, Philadelphia, 1969, W. B. Saunders Co.
2. Daniel, W. A.: The adolescent patient, St. Louis, 1970, The C. V. Mosby Co.
3. Sullivan, W.: Boys and girls are now maturing earlier, The New York Times, p. 36, Jan. 24, 1971.
4. Zacharias, L., Wurtman, R. J., and Schatzoff, M.: Sexual maturation in contemporary American girls, Am. J. Obstet. Gynecol. **108**:833-846, 1970.
5. Tanner, J. M.: Growth and physique in different populations of mankind. In Baker, P. T., and Weiner, J. S., editors: The biology of human adaptability, London, 1966, Clarendon Press.
6. Alexander, W. M.: The emergent middle school, New York, 1969, Holt, Rinehart & Winston, Inc., p. 76.
7. Bayley, N.: Growth curves of height and weight by age for boys and girls scaled according to physical maturity, J. Pediatr. **48:** 187-194, 1956.
8. Lidz, T.: The person, New York, 1968, Basic Books, Inc., Publishers, pp. 305-306.
9. Krogman, W. M.: The physical growth of the child, New York, 1957, Oxford University Press, Inc., pp. 417-425.
10. Bernard, H.: Human development in western culture, Boston, 1968, Allyn & Bacon, Inc., p. 267.
11. Crize, W. W.: Adolescent psychology and development, New York, 1953, The Ronald Press Co., p. 79.
12. Gesell, A., Ilg, F. L., and Ames, L. B.: Youth: The years ten to sixteen, New York, 1956, Harper & Row, Publishers, pp. 339-352.
13. Wagner, H.: Increasing impact of the peer group during adolescence, Adolescence **2**:52-53, 1971.
14. Weimberger, M. J.: Dress codes—we forget our own advice, Clearing House **44**:471-475, 1970.
15. Strain, F. B.: The normal sex interests of children, New York, 1948, Appleton-Century-Crofts, pp. 168-184.
16. Coleman, J. S.: The adolescent society, New York, 1961, The Free Press, pp. 12-15.
17. A study of boys becoming adolescents, Ann Arbor, Mich., 1957, Institute for Social Research, University of Michigan, p. 239.
18. Douvan, E., and Kaye, C.: Adolescent girls, Ann Arbor, Mich., 1957, Institute for Social Research, University of Michigan, p. 239.
19. Lyndon, M.: Rock for sale, Ramparts **137:** 19-20, June, 1969.
20. Rand, L.: Kaleidoscope of teen-age fads, New York Times Magazine, Oct. 17, 1954.
21. Dunbar, F.: Your teen-ager's mind and body, New York, 1962, Hawthorn Books, Inc., pp. 20-22.

10 Middle and later adolescence
15 to 18 years of age

LATER ADOLESCENCE: STAN, TYPICAL OR ATYPICAL IN TODAY'S WORLD?

Stan is 16 years old. He is the elder of two boys belonging to an upper middle-class family. In appearance he is handsome, slim, 5 feet 8 inches tall, has beautiful white teeth, and is very tan from his job as a lifeguard. Since hair is often a bone of contention between some parents and sons, I feel I should mention that Stan's hair is fashionably long, but he keeps it carefully trimmed so that neither teachers nor parents could object.

As typical of most boys his age, he is concerned about his appearance. He had the beginnings of an acne problem about two years ago. This was expected because both of his parents had bad acne problems when they were teen-agers. Stan, however, watched his diet meticulously and would not eat anything that could possibly cause a bad complexion. He exercised the same self-control when he was on his high school wrestling team and needed to maintain a particular weight.

Stan's grades are high average. His grades in algebra, science, and physical education have always been "A," but he has had some trouble in the past in English and geography. At one time he was in an accelerated class, but he did not believe that it was important enough to do the necessary extra work to maintain the standards. He will be a senior this year and has already been accepted at the college of his choice. He will be a liberal arts major because his career decision has not been made. Neither of his parents had any college education.

Stan was not allowed to date until the tenth grade, even though girls were calling him on the telephone a couple of years before that. His dating pattern now is to date one girl exclusively for several weeks and then switch to another partner. His parents always know where he is going and with whom. Over Memorial Day weekend he took a carload of his friends to the all-night drive-in movies. His parents were not too happy about this but did not think that it was a legitimate battleground.

Stan's parents bought him a car this summer primarily to let him drive back and forth to work. He is a cautious driver. Stan never seemed to have to learn how to drive. As a very young child, he would go everywhere with his father, and driving seemed like a natural thing for him to do. Most of his summers' earnings are going for dates, car upkeep, records, and some clothes. His parents were more concerned with his having a constructive way of spending his summer than with his making much money.

The one time that Stan really upset his parents, primarily his father, was when he seemed to be searching for answers, as teen-agers will, and decided to investigate another religion. He had been brought up as a Protestant and attended church every Sunday with both of his parents. Stan's parents had a mixed marriage. His mother was Jewish, and he had been exposed to Judaism through her family. Completely on his own, Stan began attending a Conservative Jewish Temple every Friday night and had private talks with the Rabbi. This continued for several months and then abruptly stopped. Whether or not Stan found his answers in his original church or whether he decided the answers he was looking for were not to be found at all is uncertain. I believe that the interesting aspect was that he sought answers not through drugs, the use of which is prevalent at his high school, but, rather, through religion. This is indicative that at this point in his life he is seeking answers and values in a healthy manner, at least so far. The fact that college contacts will shortly be exposing him to different moral and value judgments cannot help but make us wonder how much longer he can maintain his conservatism. It will be interesting to note in two or three years what going away to college can do to an unsophisticated young man.

Stan is a well-mannered person and has good rapport with his parents. He compliments his mother when appropriate, but recently he drove her "up a tree" until she gave up her nineteen-year-habit of smoking a pack of cigarettes a day. He explained to her that she could not expect him to respect all her wishes unless she also would listen to reason about something as hazardous to her and thus to her family as smoking. Quite a guy!

It is more appropriate to title this chapter "middle adolescence" rather than "late adolescence" because the ages it intends to cover do not extend to the ages of 20 or 21 years, which are usually cited as the ages at which full maturity and development are attained.

In recent years it has seemed unrealistic to speak of a 19- or 20-year-old as an adolescent, even though there is still some "growing-up" to be done. The level of worldly sophistication of 18- to 21-year-olds is so much higher than that of the same age group of recent generations. Their behavior patterns are more adultlike. To further negate the label of *adolescent* for this older age group, the age at which an individual is legally considered an adult has been changed in most states from the age of 21 to 18 years. Voting privileges in federal elections have been granted to 18-year-olds. However, there are still disquieting questions that ask, "Is an individual matured, in all ways, to adulthood before the age of 21?" "Does a change in laws necessarily produce a change in developmental characteristics?"

People recognize that 18- to 21-year-olds of today are different in many social ways from individuals of the same ages of two or three decades ago. But are they different physically, emotionally, or even morally? Do they make better value judgments? There is no common censensus on these points. Therefore we consider "middle adolescence" in this chapter as dealing with high school youth. Chapter 11 will discuss post–high school youth, or emerging adulthood. There is an overlapping of characteristics of these two groups, even though their behavior patterns may differ. We want to stress the need to consider both chapters as discussing terminal adolescence.

The developmental tasks of this age group are basically an extension of the tasks of early adolescence. Although the physical changes brought about by puberty are now fairly well established, there is still a need to develop a feeling of physical adequacy and acceptability. A greater degree of social and emotional independence must be attained. Heterosexuality must be established on a higher level than previously, and a regard and respect for others in general must become part of one's attitudinal pattern. Progressive growth in the development of a value judgment system is important for middle adolescents, as is the development of ego identity in personality and character structures. The initial skills, interests, and information related to such matters as civic competency, choice of a vocation, post–high school living, and preparation for marriage and family life must be garnered at this time. The ultimate goal of adolescence is that of "identity" as an adult.

ADOLESCENCE AND THE COMING OF AGE

In simple, less complex societies a young person had no difficulty in knowing when he passed from childhood to adulthood. There was an event or ceremony that marked his or her coming of age. In primitive tribal societies the transition was and still is marked by initiation or puberty rites. In ancient Rome this changeover was signaled by the wearing of a toga; in medieval times it occurred when the boy of 14 years, who was not a serf, became a squire and began his apprenticeship for knighthood. All of the ceremonies and status symbols stress the passing from the capricious behavior of childhood to the serious accountability of manhood.

Puberty rites still exist among people such as the Mende of Sierra Leone in Africa, the Hopi Indians of Arizona, the aborigines of Australia, and the Sevaray tribe in the Sahara. The Duna tribe, the Porgaiga tribe, and the "mudmen" from the Asaro River, all from New Guinea, as well as the Amaaiura Indians, also practice puberty rites. The ceremonies of these groups are all different, but a common theme underlies the rites in whatever kind of society they may occur. The theme is that having learned the traditions and the behavior patterns of the tribe, having passed the tests of adulthood, the young person now leaves his childhood behind him forever and socially is accepted as an adult by the other tribal members.

Western societies do not provide a symbolic event, signal, or custom by which the young person knows for sure that he has entered adulthood and is accepted by adults as such. There are ceremonies such as Confirmation, the first Communion, and the celebration of Bar Mitzvah that give a child a sense of identity with an adult group, but these events do not signal a general acceptance of the child into the social world of adults. Western societies of today have increased the amount of knowledge and preparation needed before an individual can be considered ready for adulthood. More education and training is required before an individual is ready for an advanced, technological society. Children no longer go into the job market at the ages of 14 or 16 years. They "are not ready for it." The result has been to extend the period between childhood and adulthood, giving the adolescent stage greater visibility.

Adolescence, as a stage of development, has only received an identity of its own, within our society, in the last thirty years or so. The term *teen-ager* has only gained wide usage in that same time span. It was after World War II that adolescence was recognized and treated by adults as a separate developmental period with needs and characteristics of its own. Times were changing. For the first time these young people did not drop out of school in large numbers at the end of ninth grade to enter the adult job market.

At that time this identifiable group began to emerge as a significant element of society. First were the bobby-soxers of the prewar and war-time era who were popularized by the news media. No doubt the "zoot suits" of the late forties gave the boys a sense of "being different" from younger children and the more conservative adults. Manufacturers of women's clothing found a ready market for "clothes for teens." Terms such as *junior miss, debutante, teens, preteens*, and others appeared on clothing for girls. Department stores added a "teen" section of clothing in addition to their traditional Misses and Children's sections. The news media of the 1950s popularized the term *teen-ager*. Unfortunately, it did so in connection with the term *juvenile delinquency*. The late 1950s saw an emphasis in the news media on the "beat generation" with its beatniks; the 1960s had their hippies; and Pepsi-Cola created a whole new emphasis on youth with its "generation" advertising campaign. Today adolescence is accepted as a stage of growth with an identity of its own. A recognition of young adults or the 18- to 21-year-old group has also been achieved. The lines between the various groups never have been clear-cut, but there are enough characteristics particular to each developmental group—childhood, adolescence, young adult, adulthood—to permit separate categories and classifications of each.

The principal characteristics of adolescence, however, are universal and timeless. Adolescents the world over exhibit the same type of needs. The ways in which these needs are expressed differ, but their implications are the same. Teen-agers have to accomplish the developmental tasks that will prepare them for adulthood in their society. In some societies the transition runs smoothly; in others, with more effort. There is always that criterion of adult maturity, which time alone does not ensure. The demands of the particular society set the standards. If the requirements are meager, such as in primitive societies, there are few problems. If the criteria of maturity are too high, such as in more complex societies, youth will have time to assert itself by revealing its own standards and probably exhibiting immature, inexperienced, and often unwarranted behavior as compared to adult expectations.

Here are three quotations of interest. "I see no hope for the future of our people if they are dependent on the frivolous youth of today, for certainly all youth are reckless beyond words... When I was a boy, we were taught to be discreet and respectful of elders, but the present youth are exceedingly wise and impatient of restraint." A second quotation is as follows, "Our youth now love luxury. They have bad manners, contempt for authority, disrespect for older people. Children nowadays are tyrants. They no longer rise when their elders enter the room. They contradict their parents, chatter before company, gobble their food and tyrannize their teachers." A third quotation: "Could you but take a view of this part of town on a Sunday, you would be shocked indeed for then the streets are filled with multitudes of these wretches who spend their time in riot and noise, cursing and swearing in a manner so horrid as to convey to any serious mind an idea of hell rather than of any other place. Their parents have no idea of instilling into the minds of their children principles to which they themselves are entire strangers." The first quotation was written by Hesiod in the eighth century B.C.; the second quotation is from Socrates, written 2,300 years ago in Plato's *Republic;* and the third quotation is by Robert Raikes, founder of the Sunday School movement, in Gloucester, England, 1783. The least that can be said is that adolescence appears to be consistent throughout the years in the sense that "this generation is going to the dogs."

Adolescence bridges the gap between dependency and adulthood. It is usually an uncertain period for the adolescent because it is a time when parents relax their hold and shift responsibilities to a young person who has not learned how to handle them. This is a time of trials, experimentation, and learning. Three major types of changes are taking place—physical, social, and emotional changes. They constitute growth that is continuous rather than periodic, and more gradual than abrupt. To survive, every society must train its young for responsible adult roles if it wishes to avoid an unsettledness that comes from the uncertainty of youth trying to find its place in the adult world.

PHYSICAL GROWTH AND DEVELOPMENT

Increase in height and weight during middle and later adolescence gradually lessens. This slowdown permits the older adolescent to stabilize the organization and functions of the different muscular patterns. As a result, the awkwardness that was characteristic of early adolescence gradually corrects itself.

The ultimate weight and height of the adolescent when his growth is completed will depend on such factors as hereditary endowment, prenatal and postnatal feeding and health, race, environmental conditions, exercise during infancy and childhood, and general health. The age at which pubertal maturing occurs influences the ultimate size of the individual, with late maturers tending to be somewhat taller than early maturers.[1] According to national averages the average American male is 69½ inches tall and weighs 153 pounds, whereas the average woman is 66 inches tall and weighs 135 pounds.[2] Girls reach mature physical development around the age of 18 years and boys approximately one year later. Differences in height are less noticeable than are differences in weight. No predictable evidence has been discovered which would show that the age of maturing has any permanent effect on weight. The increases in weight during late adolescence are usually found in areas of the body that did not fill out during early adolescence.

The problem of a disproportioned body, which causes great anxiety in the young adolescent, slowly changes as the youngster's body takes on the form of an adult. The oversized nose of early adolescence now assumes a correct adult proportion. The lower jaw grows larger in late adolescence, and the lips become fuller. The trunk elongates and the chest broadens. The "gawky" look of the early adolescent disappears. The breasts and hips of a girl are fully developed by late adolescence so that her body now has the smooth curves of an adult female. Studies show that late-maturing individuals, girls and boys, tend to have thin legs, whereas early-maturing individuals have stocky legs.[3]

Bone measurements show that the skeleton, on the average, stops growing at the age of 18 years.[4] The wisdom teeth usually do not emerge until late adolescence. Despite the fact that secondary sex characteristics are usually mature in size and are functioning late in adolescence, the primary sex organs may not be mature until a year or two later. The oiliness of hair and skin, characteristic of early adolescence, gradually stops, and skin problems like acne usually subside with the onset of late adolescence. The growth of the digestive system also slows, and girls and boys tend to eat less during this growth period than during early adolescence.[5]

A healthy childhood generally indicates that adolescence will be a healthy period. Menstruation during late adolescence is usually much less uncomfortable than during the previous stage of adolescence.[6] Girls have generally adjusted to the menstrual cycle and can continue with their active daily routines.

Imaginary illness is a curious "disease" that occurs in early and late adolescence. Both age groups frequently use illness as an excuse for escaping from unpleasant duties or responsibilities. Small upsets are frequently exaggerated to the point where the youth feels that he is too ill to face his problems. Girls have more imaginary illnesses than boys. Social situations are usually the cause of girls' frustrations.

ACHIEVING INDEPENDENCE FROM HOME

By the age of 16 years most teen-agers will have learned to accept adults in their lives. Parents, if they had been relegated to a minor role during the previous two years, are usually reinstated to their position of prominence within the thinking of the adolescent. If the adolescent is treated with respect and positive regard and if he has been permitted to grow responsibly without undue restraint, he will begin to assume his adult roles and to be comfortable with them. He will think it less necessary to assert his independence with exaggerated, extravagant behavior. Understandings between parent and child still have to be "hammered out," however, but these can be accomplished with less conflict and fewer hurt feelings than previously. Arguments with adolescents should not be interpreted as an indication of an unhappy home. Rather, they are indications that the children are growing up naturally. The time to be concerned is when the child is unusually acquiescent or amenable and does not seek to achieve a spot outside the family.

Problems in seeking independence

The need for a sense of independence from family domination is a requirement for the adolescent if he is to achieve full maturity. There are barriers to be overcome, and there are skills to be attained. Parent-child conflicts during adolescence tend to fall into two main categories: (1) issues involving greater demands for independence by the adolescent than the parents are willing to grant, and (2) issues involving more dependent or childish behavior on the part of the adolescent than the parents feel able to tolerate. The first category would include arguments over such topics as the time the adolescent gets in at night, use of the family car, and freedom to choose his friends among boys and girls. In the second category would fall parental objections to noisiness and untidiness, teasing of siblings, silliness, and shirking of home duties.[7]

A cause of conflict may be due to a need for experiences by the adolescent to mature his thinking and the refusal by the parents to grant the adolescent ample experimental opportunity to prepare for adulthood. The young person may feel psychologically ready to assert himself as a grown-up, but his efforts to act as one may be thwarted by a lack of money to carry out his plans or by the parents ignoring his wishes or ideas. Depriving an adolescent of his attempt to enter or to contribute to adult society may frustrate him into retaliatory action. Dejected, the adolescent may sever communications with his parents and set out on his own to prove he is an independent individual.

Frequently an adolescent will aggressively demand adult prerogatives but strenuously resist the rights of others to control or limit his use of them. The fact that he appears to be uncompromising in his determination to impose his terms on the adult culture leaves the parent in a quandry. A conflict of interests or wishes between the parents and the youth leads to an unfortunate struggle for domination.

It is difficult for parents to know when they are overprotective or overrestrictive with their children. Children have different limits of tolerance due to differences in their personalities. They also have different degrees of need for security. Independence does not come overnight for any child. It is a gradual process, taking place over a number of years. Wise parents and teachers will provide opportunities to learn responsibilities at a rate that can be tolerated by the adolescent and will not be too demanding, too restrictive, or too permissive during the learning process. Some semblance of direction, structure, and limits is needed. Communication channels must also be kept open at all costs.

Conflicts within the family

The telephone is a constant source of irritation between parents and adolescents in the home. Teen-agers spend a great deal of their time talking to friends and neighbors on the telephone, discussing dates, experiences, fads, school—just about anything. Since their social relationships have greatly increased with adolescence, it is understandable why so much time is consumed conversing on the telephone. Parents, unfortunately, do not always view the problem sympathetically. To some parents it seems that the son or daughter is always tying up the telephone. Thus restrictions and rules regarding its use must be made and enforced, much to the protests of the youngsters.

Some parents demand to know the thoughts and activities of their teen-agers. They want to know where they are going, where they have been, whom they are with, and why they are late. These kinds of parents may also go through their child's possessions and then justify this action by saying that they were only trying to find out what their son or daughter was doing, since they never talk about themselves. Parents will establish trust only when they respect the adolescent's privacy and when they show an honest and sincere interest in what the adolescent believes and feels.[8] In his quest for privacy the adolescent may ask for his or her own bedroom and telephone.

Another sensitive area of conflict centers around use of the family automobile. This is primarily a problem with boys, usually at the age of 16 years, when they have received their driver's license. Heated arguments often result over the amount of time the teen-ager will use the car, where he plans to go, when he will return, and why he needs a car in the first place!

A car is a sign of security and independence to the adolescent boy; it may also serve as a status element among his peers. To deny him access to the family automobile would imply that he is not yet mature enough to accept the responsibilities of an adult. "You don't trust me." This merely increases the tension. Fear of not being accepted as one of the group may also trouble the adolescent if everyone but him has a car. Since he cannot afford his own car, the frustrations he develops while waiting for that moment to arrive often cause hostile feelings toward parents. A deeper understanding of the adolescent's needs, a concern for him as an individual, and a sense of sharing the family items can do much to eliminate such stress.

Some adolescents lack respect for and trust in their parents. They have been taught to believe in their mother and father and to honor them, yet they often have difficulty in explaining inconsistencies that they see between what their parents say is the right thing to do and the behavior their parents exhibit. At a time when so many values, judgments, and adjustments have overwhelmed the adolescent's thinking, his struggle for an understanding of himself is further complicated by a breakdown in regard for parental sanctification. A disinterested adult society also adds to the bewilderment. Who can you trust? What can you believe?

Conflicts between parents and adolescent over the young person's social activities reach a peak in middle adolescence. Disagreements are usually centered around dating and choice of friends. Often parents are guilty of a superficial "popularity syndrome" in which they involve their children. The adolescent is pressured into social circles for the purpose of gaining the title of "personality plus." This status is measured not only in terms of the number of friends the youngster has but also of the social status they hold in the community and the type of prominent social activities in which they engage. A popular son or daughter is often a source of social prestige for some parents—something to talk about over the telephone or to brag about over the bridge table. An adolescent in this situation will question his own value as well as the true meaning of friendship. In addition, he may see himself as an object being used by his parents for their own gratification and not a person of intrinsic worth.

Control as opposed to autonomy in parent-child relationships

A study on the topic of parental variations in child-rearing techniques involving 7,400 adolescents revealed seven parental structures along a continuum of authority and control as opposed to freedom and autonomy.[9] These seven parental types are as follows: (1) autocratic—youth is not permitted to express his views on decisions related to himself; (2) authoritarian—youth may express views, but parents make decisions based on their judgment; (3) democratic—youth contributes freely and may make a decision, but parents reserve the right to approve the decision or change it; (4) equalitarian—parents and child are involved to an equal degree in decision making; (5) permissive—adolescent is more active and influential than parents in making decisions; (6) laissez-faire—youth is in a position to either accept or reject parental wishes in making decisions; and (7) ignoring—parents do not involve themselves at all in directing the adolescent's behavior or decision making.

Results of the study indicate that autocratic or authoritarian parents tend to suppress the orderly development in the adolescent of independence from the domination of the parents. Laissez-faire, ignoring, and completely permissive parents may fail to encourage the development of responsibility. The parent who retains an interest in and some responsibility for the adolescent's decisions, whereas encouraging autonomy as he grows, is likely to develop both responsibility and independence in the youth. The study also revealed that (1) children exposed to democratic practices consider their parents more fair (85%) as compared to autocratic parents (50%), (2) fathers are more likely to be considered autocratic (35%) than are mothers (22%), (3) parents of larger families tend to be more autocratic regardless of social class, (4) fathers are considered more fair if they at least listen, even though they make all the final decisions, (5) permissiveness is considered a more acceptable role for mothers than for fathers, and (6) by far, the largest percentage of adolescents who felt unwanted were those with autocratic (40%) or laissez-faire or ignoring parents (58%), as compared to democratic parents (8%).

It appears that a feeling of independence occurs more frequently among adolescents whose parents listen, who frequently explain their reasons for decisions and expectations, and who are less autocratic in their exercise of parental powers.[10]

ESTABLISHING HETEROSEXUAL RELATIONSHIPS

Fifteen- to 18-year-olds have developed rather specific perceptions of their sex roles. Now they are seeking opportunities to play out their roles in adult ways. Boys become more interested in social activities, although sports remain a close second in their interests. A gathering place, or a hangout, usually becomes a focal point where young people gather to practice their social skills and to engage in heterosexual activities. Adolescents are tremendously sensitive to social approval, acceptance, and demands. No other problem seems to them as important as the establishment of themselves in their own society. They react faster and more deeply to the influence of their age mates than to that of adults, including parents.

Peer acceptance

The adolescent has a need to be recognized and accepted by someone. This is most readily done through friends and acquaintances who are his peer mates. Being of the same age, they share his feelings, experiences, goals, and doubts in a way that his parents cannot do. In a peer group situation the adolescent can find belonging, affiliation, acceptance, and status as the independent person that he so strongly desires to be.

Most adolescents are not sufficiently secure or confident so that they can tolerate differences between themselves and their colleagues. As a result, conformity becomes a rule within the primary group of friends.[11] This conformity extends to appearance, dress, fads, fashion, hair style, makeup, activities, and attitudes. As a result, an adolescent often finds that his personal values clash with those of his friends in such matters, for example, as starting to smoke, drink, or engage in questionable behavior. Threatened by a possible loss of friends or his popularity, he generally gives in rather than stand by his beliefs. The fear of losing his friends is too powerful a threat. This action, in turn, may cause mental anxieties and concerns, since he is not being true to himself. This is one conflict that can only be resolved by adopting the behavior of his group or else by leaving these friends and seeking new ones. Group pressures are hard to overcome.

There are several reasons for lack of acceptance by a group. Shyness is one of the causes of not finding social acceptance. If an individual does not have confidence in himself, the group has none in him. Social ineptness may be a stumbling block, since the social skills that provide access to the group have never been learned. A person who seems emotionally unstable is actively rejected by the group because they cannot afford to have such a person identified with their group. Social, economic, or ethnic background provides another reason for a person not being accepted. Social distance is a relative matter for many individuals, but in certain localities ethnic, racial, and social differences are magnified and are causes for exclusion, rejection, or ignoring.

Sequential pattern of dating

The sequence by which the dating pattern emerges is fairly certain; the time and rapidity with which it emerges are dependent on many cultural variables. The general attitude and philosophy of the community (or locale), the general wishes of the parents of the children involved, the customs, traditions, and folkways of the area, and the thinking of the young people themselves have a great influence on the age at which different levels of the dating sequence take place. Some communities may be two or three years ahead of others in the time at which girls and boys begin to date. In some communities, steps within the dating sequence are compressed within a short time span, whereas other steps persist for a long period. There are differences in dating practices. The time sequence presented here is typical of the country as a whole rather than of specific regions.

The 12-year-old boy and girl are still in a period of social development in which they cling to friends of their own sex. There may have been some group activities and heterosexual interests as early as the fifth grade, but these are not the typically sought-after activities or choices of the youngsters. The nature of most school programs and organizations, including the junior high school grades, is such that there are more opportunities for mixed group activities than previously. Sports and music programs of the school, club organizations, and exposure to more classes and teachers broaden social possibilities.

The more typical dating activities, the first in the dating sequence, are "crowd" dates, usually at organized school functions in the seventh and eighth grades. A group of girls just happens to be around a certain group of boys at a football or basketball game. What is interesting is that the same group of girls seems to be around the same group of boys at most of the activities. Seldom is there any pairing off within the groups. By the ninth grade crowd dates are still popular, but now there is some pairing off of couples. It is not unusual in the seventh grade to notice a few boys and girls who are seeing each other frequently on a paired-off basis. It will be obvious that some eighth grade couples are going steady, but as we said earlier, this is not typical or expected of the majority of the seventh and eighth graders. Steady couples are more common in the ninth grade than in earlier grades.

In the tenth grade there will be paired crowd dates. Some boys and girls will come to the activity as a couple and join the crowd. Four, five, or more couples will make up the crowd, although there may still be some unattached friends within the group. Double dating is a common practice in eleventh grade and single dates or double dates in twelfth grade. Going steady takes a big jump in numbers during the junior year. By the end of the freshman year about half of the freshman boys in urban or suburban areas will have dated a girl. By the end of the junior year about three fourths will have dated, and by their senior year 95% are dating to some degree.[12] Might there be some single dates in seventh or even sixth grade? Yes, but it probably would not be the common practice. Each community and social group has its own features. What was typical of dating practices when you were 12 to 16 years old?

We would like to illustrate boy-girl relationships from our experiences. We had the extraordinary opportunity of being with the same group of boys from the time they were in seventh grade until they graduated from high school. Of twenty-nine boys who started with us in a seventh grade Junior Hi-Y, twenty-four boys were still with us when they graduated. This was a most unusual group of boys—service minded and extremely active. They adopted an 84-year-old man and kept him in food, tobacco, and company for over three years. They collected two panel truck loads of comic books, while in eighth grade, and gave them to be used at a veterans' hospital nearby. In ninth grade they sponsored a "Have-a-Heart Week" during the week of St. Valentine's Day as a campaign to improve courtesy within the school. Any young person seen by a teacher or club member doing a courteous act or a good deed had his name turned in to a central point that evening. The next morning when the pupils returned to school, they found a small paper heart on their desk for each time their names were turned in. The students proudly wore these hearts. At the end of the week a prize was given to the boy and girl with the biggest (most) heart, the homeroom with the biggest heart, and several other prizes for "hearts." No one ever saw a group of 12- to 14-year-olds in a school of 900 pupils who were so courteous, not only for that week but for the rest of the year.

Every boy in the club went on to some type of post–high school education (not all college). From that group there are now six engineers, four electronic specialists, three lawyers, several merchants, one physician, one teacher, one YMCA secretary, a Roman Catholic priest who studied at the Vatican for four years, a boy who studied for the Lutheran ministry, a Greek Orthodox priest, and a Jewish Rabbi, who among other things was arrested in one of the early civil rights marches in the South.

Now for the development of the dating pattern. In seventh grade the boys decided they would like to have a hayride. For six weeks they planned whom to contact for the wagons, how to get there, and what to eat. They went on the hayride and had a marvelous time. Nobody mentioned girls, and no one brought a girl. In eighth grade they voted to have another hayride. Someone said, "Let's bring girls." Everyone laughed, but no one brought a girl. In ninth grade they again decided on a hayride. Someone said, "Let's bring girls." Someone else said, "Let's not." They voted, and the girls lost out by two votes. That night, in early October, they voted to bring girls to their Christmas Party. Anyone who did not want to bring a girl could be on the refreshment and clean-up committee. Three boys ended on that committee, two of whom were the first of the group to get married later on. The hayride was a "so-so" affair that year. Everyone was looking forward to the Christmas Party.

While in tenth grade they agreed to have another hayride. The topic of girls was brought up again. Someone said, "Let's vote." The girls won out by a good margin. In the junior year they decided on a hayride. Someone asked, "Are we bringing girls?" Someone replied, "What else?" To continue the tradition of hayrides in twelfth grade they decided to have a final hayride. All the plans for the activity were completed within a half hour. No one mentioned girls, but everyone brought a girl. That was the most eerie hayride by moonlight my wife and I ever went on. For much of the ride we were the only ones who could be seen on the wagons. Laughter, giggling, and singing seemed to be coming from underneath the straw on the wagons. After the hayride we had the biggest problem ever getting the couples off the wagons and out of the haystacks on the farm so they could get back to town by midnight!

Dating differs in types and degrees of seriousness. The first stage of dating, during early adolescence, is of a noncommittal nature. It is extremely mobile in style in that there are few if any deep romantic attachments. The nervous excitement of a novel experience is sufficient to interest a person in another. Playing the field does not produce lasting relationships, and there is a minimum of emotional stress involved. The amount of time spent in this type of dating varies from individual to individual. Interests in love, courtship, and marriage do not reach a peak until late adolescence.

Within western culture it has been the responsibility of the male to select the dating partner. Girls must make sure that they are attractive enough to become selected. There are various ways of doing this. External attributes that many girls consider essential for entry into the dating game are being dressed in the latest fashions, whether they be sweaters and skirts or blue jeans, and good looks. The nonmaterial, idealist point of view of many of today's youth is slowly lessening the emphasis on money, clothes, and social prestige. What a boy seeks are personality, concern for others, looks, and dependability. Girls, on the other hand, seem to want manners, neatness, and an ability to carry on a conversation. These are not the only qualifications, but they provide some idea of what a later adolescent looks for in a dating partner. Similarity in characteristics is also an important factor in date selection. The tendency is to choose someone with similar rather than opposite interests, needs, and appearance. What might be noted is that the qualities being sought are of the type needed for a good life mate. This could indicate the seriousness of dating during this period. Late adolescents are beginning to search for that certain person with whom to spend the rest of their lives.

Early dating and steady dating of adolescents are chief concerns of parents. Parents fear that pairing off on a steady basis leads young adolescents into sexual and emotional intimacies long before they are ready for marriage. Adolescents, on the other hand, believe that steady dating, even as early as 12 or 13 years of age, provides security and acceptance by the group. They cannot understand their parents' reasoning. Many a household is filled with turmoil resulting from conflicting views on dating. The teen-ager who is denied dating privileges may feel rejected, resentful, and deceived. He may increase the friction by sneaking out on dates; some will exceed sexual behavioral limits simply to spite their parents.

Problems related to dating are of two types: namely, "I can't get a date," or else, "Now that I'm dating, how far should I go?" Individuals who have not had the opportunity to develop social skills will have trouble knowing what to do to get to know the opposite sex better. This may also leave them isolated in other group activities. Concerning the second problem, girls are upset by the aggressive behavior of boys who try to see how far they can go. Boys dislike the way girls flaunt their sexuality.[13] Even a nice girl can give the wrong impression. As to "How far should I go in kissing, necking, and petting?" usually the boy tries to get as much as possible, and the girl yields as little as possible. The girl is expected to set the limits, and the boy is expected to conform. Girls may be the aggressors, but that is not considered to be their role. These questions cause considerable anxiety and tension for adolescents.

LOVE RELATIONSHIPS

Early adolescence, marked by the advent of heterosexual relationships, is a critical period in the life of the 13-, 14-, or 15-year-old. He is placed in closer social contact with the opposite sex, thus offering him more opportunity to establish feelings of affection for particular members of the opposite sex. He might very well consider himself in love with a person, yet his strong feelings are too often dismissed by adults as "puppy love," nonsense, or simply a game all teen-agers play. Closer observation reveals this stage to be a trying one for the adolescent, since he has never before felt this way about the opposite sex.[14] In later adolescence the relationships become more involved, hence the problems become more complicated.

A common phase that many adolescents go through is the "crush" stage, in which an adult individual or individuals is the center of the adolescent's affection. This particular phenomenon is also known as hero worshipping. Crushes occur in situations where some important or well-liked person in the youngster's life, perhaps a teacher or friend, embodies the qualities that the youngster regards as being most important or desirable. This leads to strong feelings of attachment and a reaction that the adolescent usually interprets as love. Crushes seem to occur most often between 15 and 19 years of age in boys and between 13 and 18 years in girls.[15] Most of them last from one to six months, some longer. Boys base the attraction on physical and/or mental abilities, whereas girls concentrate mainly on mental and personality qualities.

The crush itself is common and not a problem. The difficulty arises, however, when the adolescent becomes too involved emotionally with the "love object," perhaps to the point where sex interests are implicit in his affection. If the love object fails to recognize the amorous intentions of the adolescent, deeper frustrations resulting in more extreme behavior may set in. It is at this point that many youngsters are torn between their "love" for the individual and their "hatred" at his failure to see it and respond to it effectively. Such tensions may cause erratic behavior in school and at home. Girls with such problems are embarrassed to discuss them at home, fearing being labeled childish or immature.

One cannot ignore the fact that there is substantial evidence supporting the fact that many adolescent love relationships, crushes and otherwise, are legitimate. They necessitate careful consideration and understanding to avoid severe emotional harm to the adolescents involved.

A problem arising from being in love and going steady is early marriage. Many adolescents get married within a couple of years after graduation from high school. Marriage between college students is increasing at a surprising rate. Prolonged association with one person leads to sexual exploration. Many couples who are going steady end up getting married so that their child will have a name. Marriages on this basis are not solid and are a major cause for divorce among those who married during the adolescent years. Overanxious mothers often promote early marriages. They have their daughters in high heels by 12 years, in makeup by 13 years, partying by 14 years, dating by 15 years, "going steady" by 16 years, and ready for marriage by 17 years.

Although the healthy child has always realized that love and sexuality are related, adolescence is a time when this realization is brought most sharply into focus. Most older teen-age boys believe that love and sex can be separated—an attitude that is

Middle and later adolescence

Frederic Lewis, Inc., New York City.

carried often into adulthood. But middle teen-agers, boys and girls alike, believe that one cannot exist without the other. They get crushes on each other. They are certain that they feel real love for each other. They feel strong desires to touch and excite one another.

The feelings of a teen-age girl are further confused by the fact that society gives to her the responsibility of stopping the boy's advances; however, conformity and popularity are key reasons for girls conceding. Boys, even in the so-called "enlightened era," still have a tendency to distinguish between "good" and "bad" girls and to prefer "good" girls for marrying and "bad" girls for satisfying loneliness or lust. Thus no matter how strong the girl's love and desire may be, she has to face a barrage of fears. She has the fear of pregnancy, of being designated as "bad," of venereal disease, and of being considered everybody's pet but no-one's girl. She has, on the other hand, to face the fear of unpopularity if she is a "prude." The boy's fears are much the same. He may fear hurting the girl or causing her to become pregnant. He often fears his own sexual inadequacy or that the girl may expect him to go "farther" than he does.

MATURING INTELLECTUAL OPERATIONS

Middle and late adolescence is a period of steady development in learning how to use the various intellectual functions. These include mental operations such as (1) cognitive thinking, involving discovery, recognition, or awareness of knowledge; (2) memory or the retention of what was cognized; (3) divergent thinking, the ability to produce a large variety of responses by moving apart from the usual opinions, attitudes, and thinking and to come up with new ideas; (4) convergent thinking, the ability to reason or use logic to arrive at the one best answer; and (5) evaluation, or assessment, of how adequate one's reasoning or conclusion is at that moment.[16] The capability to use abstract reasoning starts about the ages of 11 or 12 years. Early adolescence is a time when this capability emerges to a functional level. Middle adolescence is the period when this capability matures to its highest potentiality. Hopefully, the late adolescent learns how to use this potentiality.

The typical 15-year-old can do rational, realistic thinking about himself. He is mainly interested in the present, but he begins to think more about his future. After this age he becomes increasingly open-minded and liberal in his attitudes. He is largely responsible for determining his own behavior and is willing to assume responsibility for his actions. When necessary, he is able to compromise his intellectual behavior according to the challenges and demands of his life situation. However, his collective cognitive ability to make good judgments and to have deep intellectual insights is limited by an inexperienced, underdeveloped, apperceptive mass of knowledge from which he can establish an adequate perspective concerning the problem he is seeking to solve. His idealistic and pseudo-optimistic nature also distorts his perspective.

Mental characteristics

In any large group of adolescents there will be a wide distribution of mental ages. Among the general population of 15-year-olds, for example, almost 23% are likely to have a mental age between 14-6 and 15-11 years; 23%, a mental age between 13-8 and 14-6 years; 18%, a mental age between 16-0 and 17-6 years. About 2% would have a mental age under 10 years, and a little over 4%, a mental age above 19 years, with the rest of the group being distributed between these extremes.[17] Intellectual differences increase during adolescence as the experiences and environments of individuals become more diversified. Individual differences within any group of late adolescents, boys, girls, blacks, whites, high or low socioeconomic level, are much larger than differences between groups.

At one time it was believed that young people stopped growing mentally at about 16 years of age. Now many authorities believe that individuals grow in certain aspects of intelligence beyond the age of 16 years.[18] Some kinds of mental ability increase more than others during the late adolescent years. For example, both boys and girls may be expected to increase in vocabulary. Boys generally show a greater increase in arithmetical scores than do girls. Both sexes show little or no increase in scores on items that primarily involve memory. By the age of 20 years the rate of growth on oral directions, dissected sentences, and arithmetic problems reaches a peak and does not decline until later. On commonsense items, analogies, and numerical completions the peak of performance is reached before 20 years of age, whereas growth in vocabulary and general information continues to a slight degree well into the adult years.[19]

Growth in mental abilities as measured by various intelligence tests is influenced by the kind and amount of schooling the individual has received, the nature of his work and other experiences, and the cultural content and reading level of the test. Those who leave school often lose the intellectual stimulation necessary for the full development of their mental ability, whereas those who continue their education in high school and college may realize undeveloped capacities.[20]

Piaget's period of formal operations

Piaget's theory divides the intellectual development process into four main chronological periods, which are further divided into phases or stages. The order of succession of these steplike patterns is constant, although the ages at which different stages are attained may vary somewhat depending on the child's motivation, practice, and cultural differences. Also, as the child progresses from one stage to the next, early structures become integrated with later ones—they are interdependent and interactive. The first three periods were presented in earlier chapters.

The fourth broad period of cognitive development, known as the period of formal operations, begins early in adolescence (11 to 15 years of age) and it is during this period of development that Piaget characterizes the individual as living in both the present and the nonpresent. He is no longer merely concerned with the real but also is concerned with the possible. In committing himself to possible outcomes of a situation, he thinks beyond the present. In other words "the adolescent begins to build systems or theories, whereas the child does not theorize or build systems."[21]

It is during this period of development that he becomes capable of scientific reasoning and of formal logic in verbal argument; moreover, he reflects about, evaluates, and criticizes the logic and quality of his own thinking. He does not need to center his attention on the immediate situation. He can imagine what might be possible and can consider hypotheses that may or may not be true; he can consider also what would follow if they were true. As he approaches 15 years of age, he is able to use formal logic in an adult manner, and when this is possible, Piaget asserts that he has reached the critical stage of intellectual development. From now on learning how to use the tools of logic and frequent practice in their usage will be necessary to enable the individual to function well within his level of potentiality.

EMOTIONALITY

If the child received abundant love and patient understanding during infancy and early childhood, if the imposition of societal demands reflected an understanding by parents of individual patterns of readiness, and if occasional regressions were accepted as merely a part of growing up and as inevitable, at adolescence there is usually a minimal amount of difficulty and strain in coping with the problems and conflicts of this stage. On the other hand, the child who has been the object of parental rejection, overdominance, or overindulgence is likely to experience an unusually stormy adolescence.[22] Achievement of independence and emotional maturity is hampered by excesses in parental domination, friction between the parents, sibling rivalry, and an unwillingness on the part of the parents to allow adolescents to share in decisions that affect the family.

Emotional characteristics

The older adolescent experiences similar emotions as the child and early adolescent. The differences deal with the amount, intensity, types of responses, and types of stimuli that create the emotions of the late adolescent.

Anger. Anger is the major disruptive emotion found in later adolescence. Moodiness is the commonest nondisruptive emotion. The commonest causes of anger are restraints on the adolescent's desire to do something and interruption of activities that have become routine for the adolescent. Environment is the major stimulus for anger. If the environment of the later adolescent prohibits his desires, anger will usually result. Girls respond more often and more violently to social situations than do boys.

The childish responses to anger of hurting, biting, and throwing objects are no longer found. Name calling and verbal responses are the most common responses of anger in later adolescence.[23] The duration of anger is longer because the older adolescent attempts to conceal his anger, thus making it last longer.

Jealousy. Jealousy displays itself in heterosexual situations in later adolescence more than in any other way. Toward the end of adolescence, interests change from a general regard for members of the opposite sex to one specific person of the opposite sex. In this situation jealousy arises when one member, or both, feels that the other is cheating in their relationship.

Envy. Material possessions and social status have a strong appeal to the later adolescent. Leadership and social status are closely related, and the older adolescent is envious of persons who possess these two items. Most adolescents seek jobs to acquire material goods, but some resort to shoplifting and stealing as their means for achieving social equality with others. The cause of much juvenile delinquency is envy of the possessions of others more fortunate than the delinquent.

Happiness. Happiness comes from four situations. If the adolescent is able to feel at ease in a situation, contentment will usually follow. The adolescent must also be able to understand the comic parts, the humorous aspects of a situation. When the later adolescent has achieved superiority over others, happiness and pride are the result. Finally, situations are needed where the adolescent can release stored-up emotional energy.[24]

Affection. Later adolescence is a period of intense affection because the individual is concentrating his affection on one member of the opposite sex or on a small group of friends. Generally, if the individual is well adjusted, this display of affection will be directed toward a member of the opposite sex.

Fear and worry. Fear is less recognizable in later adolescence than it was in the previous period. Fear of social situations, environment, and people is no longer a problem. The adolescent is capable of avoiding embarrassing situations by planning activities that will enable him to avoid them.

In later adolescence worries take the form of imaginary fears. Feelings of inadequacy is an extremely common occurrence. Problems related to money, jobs, the use of the automobile, physical appearance, social acceptability, sex, and marriage are also causes of worry.

Emotional maturity. An individual has achieved emotional maturity when he is capable of controlling his emotions until a socially proper time and place are available for him to "let off" his feelings. An emotionally mature individual is capable of ignoring stimuli that as a child he would have reacted to emotionally. Heightened emotionality, when expressed, reflects itself through feelings of insecurity, tension, indecision, and exaggerated or sometimes irrational behavior.

Self-identity

Early in the adolescent period the growing child begins to realize that he is an individual and not simply an extension of his parents. It is at this point that he wants to know "Who am I?" This drive for self-assertion becomes one of the prime motivating forces during this period.[25] It is a struggle against "getting lost" and feeling like a stranger to oneself. By the time an individual is ready to leave later adolescence he has probably developed his sense of personal identity and now knows who he is. The struggle to find this identity can be a hard one.

The adolescent achieves his self-identity through his self-concept. The self-concept is developed as he confronts the world and gains an impression of it. He must relate the world to himself and himself to it. At this time he is greatly concerned with his own personal worth. In his struggle to find himself he is afraid that he cannot live up to his own expectations. He may ask "Am I good enough, smart enough, or popular enough?"

NEED FOR A VALUE JUDGMENT SYSTEM

Changing times bring changes in attitudes and in people's beliefs as to what is and what is not important. An activity or a point of view acceptable to one generation may not be equally acceptable to another. It is often difficult for one generation to appreciate the point of view of another generation. It is important for a young person to know the effect of given attitudes or values on himself and on others. It is also important to know ways and means of developing "good" attitudes and of discouraging "bad" ones. The development of a value judgment system is basic not only because of its moral and ethical implications but also because of its influence on the decision-making process.

Value judgment system

A value judgment system consists of an individual's beliefs, values, and attitudes that reflect his views and opinions of what is good or bad, desirable or undesirable, important or unimportant, right or wrong, valuable or not valuable, and that influence his emotional and rational thought processes in the making of decisions and choices. The development of a value judgment system begins when a child learns to inhibit or to direct his behavior according to the wishes of others. It does not become mature until, as an adult, he has overcome external domination of his behavioral and judgmental processes.

Environmental factors such as the peer group, parents, institutions, vicarious experiences, and prevailing social attitudes as revealed by communications media are important in shaping an adolescent's attitudes. Of these, peer group and parental influences and dominant social beliefs are the most significant. In general, the adolescent will tend to be readily influenced by those individuals he likes or loves and by those who possess some attributes or skills that he admires.

Moral and spiritual growth

During adolescence a serious questioning of the moral code begins. Often these codes are questioned as a result of discovering that adults, frequently parents, verbally ascribe to a code but do not adhere to it.

One aspect of morality involves a recognition of the consequences of behavior and the way it affects others. At this stage the adolescent begins to do logic and reasoning. He searches himself and his beliefs. He decides which part of society's moral code is applicable to him in his relationship to others. There is always concern by adults about the lack of morality among the young. There is no need for excessive alarm. Many of the problems of moral behavior in adolescents come from developmental changes in perception and insight. Most, although not all, adolescents recognize their inept behavior and seek to make adjustments. Many will need a point of reference from which they can begin to restructure their moral thinking.

There is a lack of attendance at church. This may be due to their questioning of all authority, including church, to the beginning of a period of investigating religion anew as a possible source of emotional and intellectual satisfaction, to hesitancy of being associated with any pious group or members of the "establishment," or to their busy social calendar.

However, most adolescents are idealistic and basically good. Informal prayer is used frequently by adolescents. The modern adolescent wants to find meaning in life. In spite of a small minority of highly verbal cynics, religion continues to play a part in human existence and is of special value during the adolescent years in formulating ideals and standards of conduct. All churches and moral groups must attempt to meet the needs of the young who really seek a philosophy of life.

In general, adolescents acquire religious attitudes and ideas much as they acquire other types of attitudes and ideas. If the importance of religion and morality is stressed in the daily environment and if it is presented in such a manner that it meets the adolescent's needs, religion and morality are likely to be important forces in his life. If, on the other hand, religion and morality are presented in such a manner that they are foreign to the needs and aspirations of an adolescent, if they are harsh and unreasonable, or if they are ignored by the parents, an individual is likely to reject them or to set them aside as much as he possibly can.

An adolescent who has accepted the religious and moral beliefs of his parents in early years may face fear and guilt feelings if he finds his beliefs and attitudes changing. It becomes particularly difficult for the adolescent to make an adjustment when he first encounters conflicting points of view toward religion and moral behavior, unless he has been so completely indoctrinated that he is unwilling to consider varying points of view. The longer a child has retained his beliefs in religion and morality, the less likely he is to change. A completely new environment providing points of view that are entirely different from those that he had in the past may bring about changes in the individual. Colleges have been pointed to as a source of changes in religious attitudes. The evidence indicating that students become more liberal in their beliefs and attitudes about religion is inconclusive when related to all colleges, however. It is not possible to evaluate the contributions of schools, churches, and other forces outside the home on the moral development of adolescents, but each contact may contribute to their moral development. A religious worker told us recently, "My own experience with adolescents and church has seemed to indicate that young people admit they need God, as we all do, but they are not so certain that they can find Him in formal public worship. It is our task to make them feel a part of our religious community and to make morality meaningful to them especially through our example."

PROBLEMS OF MIDDLE ADOLESCENCE

Middle and later adolescents are still in the process of establishing a new life style and of learning the basic skills and information related to their new pattern of living. Problems, worries, and concerns are to be expected. The intensity of the concerns will be in keeping with the adequacy of the adjustment pattern that the adolescent will have developed in the past. Problem areas include home and family relations, peer status and social development in general, educational planning, adjustment and achievement, emotional stability and personality factors, physical adjustment and sexual maturity, and self-identity, value judgment, and life existence concerns. Inasmuch as some of these problem areas have been discussed in other sections in this chapter, more attention will be given to related areas.

Delinquency and youth

Aggressive, destructive, and antisocial behavior is characteristically a behavior of youth rather than adulthood. The incidence of delinquency rises slowly during the early teens. It gathers momentum at the ages of 14 and 15 years and climbs precipitously until the age of 19 years. During the early twenties the rate of delinquency still increases but at a slower rate. The peak of delinquent and criminal incidence is reached by the age of 25 years and declines rapidly thereafter.[26] To view the problem of adolescent delinquency in its proper perspective one must keep in mind that only a small percentage, perhaps less than 5% of all adolescents, ever are legally classified as delinquents. Few aggressive or destructive acts result in apprehension, formal arrest, and prosecution. Some forms of antisocial behavior violate no existing statutes. The actual amount of delinquency among adolescents may never be completely known.

The probability of delinquency occurring during adolescence is much greater if there is a childhood history of antisocial behavior. In fact, approximately two thirds of adolescent delinquents begin their delinquent careers in preadolescence.[27] The adolescent period is characteristically associated with a more regular, serious, and organized kind of delinquency. Greater freedom of movement and less adult supervision during adolescence also make delinquent behavior more possible.

More important perhaps than greater opportunity and capacity for executing delinquent acts are the developmental task pressures, antiauthority responses, aggressive attitudes, and peer group sanctions that exist during adolescence. Prolonged status deprivation superimposed on other psychosocial and psychobiological problems increases emotional instability and lowers the threshold for aggressive behavior.

Important differences exist between boys and girls in the incidence, age of onset, etiology, and kind of delinquency practiced. Four to seven times as many boys as girls become delinquent, but the ratio of boys to girls has shown a steady decline over the past fifty years.[28] Boys also become involved in delinquency at an earlier age than girls. This difference is partly due to the greater supervision to which younger adolescent girls are subjected and partly to the fact that sex offenses, which constitute the most frequent category of delinquency among girls, do not occur until an older age. However, if these differences between boys and girls are environmentally determined and reflect cultural attitudes toward male and female sex roles, the difference in age of onset of delinquency can be expected to become increasingly less pronounced in the future.

Sex differences in the kinds of offenses committed are striking. Stealing, mischief, traffic violations, truancy, auto thefts, and running away from home are the major misdemeanors of adolescent boys. Delinquent girls, on the other hand, are most frequently charged with ungovernability, sex offenses, and leaving home.[29]

Personal problems of adolescents

The following statements are taken from unpublished research conducted by the authors in which over 1,000 adolescents between 15 and 18 years were sampled.

Male, 15 years, ninth grade
I have trouble with algebra. I don't see why anyone has to take algebra unless they want to be a doctor or an engineer. It's just silly junk. My mother took algebra and it didn't help her. I think I should learn more about how to write a check, how to use interest, and other useful studies.

Female, 15 years, tenth grade
My home is my problem, especially my father. I had to leave my home last year because he beat me and was always threatening me. He has always abused me.

Female, 15 years, eleventh grade
I'm in love! It's real, too! The boy I'm in love with loves me just as much. He's in the service. Every once in a while he gets a weekend pass and comes home. We don't see each other very often and that's really hard when you're in love. We always try to squeeze so much into one evening that things start to happen. We're neither one that kind of person. We just can't help ourselves. So far we've been able to stop before it goes too far. What can we do to keep even this little bit from taking place? It's not what we want, it just happens.

Male, 16 years, eleventh grade
My trouble is money. I have a job and work five nights a week, 4 to 12 o'clock. My parents have very little money so I don't like to ask them for any. But my parents don't want me to work so long. They'd rather I spend more time on my schoolwork.

Male, 16 years, eleventh grade
I seem to find it very hard to get my parents to understand that I have somewhat of a life of my own. They can't understand that I have also grown in age and maturity. They still want me to abide by the privileges they granted me at age 13.

Female, 16 years, eleventh grade
My problem is that I have a very bad inferiority complex. I feel that people are talking about me. When I'm with a group I hardly know what to say. When I leave the group I get the feeling that they talk about me and don't want me.

Male, 16 years, eleventh grade
I have a slight amount of trouble with my mother. It bothers me because I don't want to make her unhappy. I realize she has done many things for me and I want to repay her.

Male, 17 years, twelfth grade
When I finish with high school I want to go to a trade school to study television repair. With the world in such a turmoil at the present time it looks like I will have to go to the service. Should I discontinue my thoughts about going to school and go to the service and get it over with?

Male, 17 years, twelfth grade
Although my parents treat me exceptionally well as far as material things are concerned, I would sooner have a little less of these things and a little more understanding.

Female, 17 years, twelfth grade
My parents object to my marriage to a boy of a different religion. Why should they object when the boy and girl are willing to give up certain things for each other and are sure they can make it work?

Female, 17 years, twelfth grade
Right now I have the problem that I have applied for admission to a very fine college to further my education. However, I wonder sometimes if I really want to go to college. My parents say it is up to me.

Female, 17 years, twelfth grade
I have gone with a fellow for about two years but we have just recently broken up. I can see him going deeper and deeper on drugs and he won't stop. I still want him, but not that way.

Female, 17 years, twelfth grade
> I have been planning to be married in July but the boy is of a different religion than me and is quite a few years older. He is in the Army. My parents don't think it would be good to marry him. I don't agree because he can be depended upon; he is thoughtful and kind and loves me a lot. I'm looking forward to marriage. But there's going to be some trouble because a boy I haven't seen for two years who has been in Germany is coming back. He knows I'm to be married but he says he still loves me.

Female, 18 years, twelfth grade
> I have a problem. My mother and father are separated and getting a divorce. I don't know who to go with if I were asked to pick my home.

Male, 18 years, twelfth grade
> Do you think it is right to always ask Mom or Dad for some cash to spend if you never stay home in evenings to be with them? I usually come in at all hours of the night and a word has never been said. Do you think that your parents should worry?

Male, 18 years, twelfth grade
> With my senior year drawing to a close it won't be long until I will be going away to college. It bothers me to realize that I will be leaving my family and that I will have to depend upon myself.

ADOLESCENCE IN DISADVANTAGED ENVIRONMENTS

Between 15% and 20% of the population of the United States is classified, by federal definition, to be living on the poverty level.[30] Often they are members of a minority group or immigrants who have recently migrated to large northern metropolitan areas. The majority of the urban poor live in highly concentrated depressed areas within large cities. However, there is a large segment of economic and socially disadvantaged families who live in rural areas, geographically isolated parts of the country, such as mountain land or on reservations. For the most part the disadvantaged comprise the economic underworld of American life, including the unemployed, the underemployed, the blue collar workers, the minorities, and the aged. This is the segment of the American population that Michael Harrington refers to as *The Other America*[31] because it has been isolated and removed from the mainstream of American life by various processes, not the least of which is the mass exodus of the middle class to the sanctity of suburbia. Although not as obvious as in previous decades, this hidden portion of American society still suffers the ravages of poor housing, inadequate nutrition, overcrowding, lack of sanitation, and other forms of social and cultural deprivation.

Because the large majority of the disadvantaged class is made up of sporadic laborers, crop followers, and reliefers, there is a tendency for the mainstream of society to look down on these people. Parents in this group are likely to be passive and fatalistic about their status. In general, they work sporadically, move frequently, and live in the poorest dwellings. Because of the meager and often nonexistent earnings of the fathers, the mothers often work as domestics to supplement the family income. Although there is an average of five children per mother, more than half of the homes are broken by separation, desertion, or death. Due to the instability of marriage, common-law marriages and mutual agreement living situations are increasing in number—the poor cannot afford the cost of a divorce.

Perhaps an extreme but realistic study of the lower class social structure is characterized by the deterioration of the black family. The statistical data surrounding the family structure of black society is overwhelming. Nearly one third of the black women living in large metropolitan areas who have ever been married are divorced, separated, or living apart from their husbands. In 1964 over one fourth of all black births were illegitimate. An offshoot of this disproportionately high divorce, separation, and desertion rate is the fact that only a minority of black children reach the age of 18 years having lived all their lives with both parents.[32]

In general terms the black family has the largest number of children and the lowest net income; consequently, many black fathers cannot support their families. The only solutions rest in either the mother going to work or the family applying for welfare assistance. Should the mother choose to work, the dependence on her income tends to undermine the position of the father and deprives the children of maternal attention and care. Should the family apply for welfare assistance, in most cases the father will undergo serious feelings of inadequacy. Also, in view of current welfare rulings, the family can obtain increased aid if the father is not in the home but is receiving separate aid. Thus the family structure is torn apart for the family to seek out a meager subsistence.

Perhaps the individual who suffers the most severe consequences of this disorganization of the basic family structure is the child. Since the discipline and authority of the father figure is lacking in over one third of the familes of the lower echelon of society, the process of young males identifying with their fathers as strong figures so necessary in sex typing is forestalled. Often the mother, who heads the family, is forced to neglect the children, since she must earn their living. Growing up in a family lacking strong traditions and consistent discipline will often produce a child who lacks strong goals for himself and may be characterized as aimless and unambitious. Often the child who has not learned consistent standards of behavior in the home will turn to the streets because there he can find meaning that appears to be consistent and obviously related to his way of life. Since disorganized families tend to be concentrated in the least desirable sections of any city, the codes of conduct that are offered to the child by the street-corner gang are likely to be at best socially disapproved and at worst blatantly antisocial.

During adolescence, social groups such as cliques, crowds, or gangs will be formed. Cliques are small, closely knit groups based on clanishness and exclusion. Crowds are looser, somewhat less personal groups. Gangs, however, have a membership that is highly organized and usually arise out of conflict and outside pressures that bring the members together for mutual assistance and support. They are most frequently found among recent immigrant groups and in neighborhoods where there are racial or national tensions.

Although some gangs are benign, the majority appear to be breeding grounds for juvenile delinquency.[33] The gang member finds the gang a proving ground, a need-fulfilling but fear-inspiring stage on which to strut his nascent manhood and prove his emancipation. The gang sets tasks and standards which he must meet, and there is always the fear that he may not meet these standards, that he may fail the test of gang membership and acceptance. This is especially significant with the disadvantaged adolescent. The motivation to pursue the delinquent act is bolstered by pressure to achieve those things that are of greatest value to the peer or reference groups of the delinquent, rather than by rebellious elements within his personality organization. The compelling elements of gang motivation appear to be adherence to group standards of excitement, toughness, and smartness.

Another segment of disadvantaged adolescents is the school dropout, or as the case may be, the "shove out." But who are the dropouts? They are more frequently males than females. They are young people who have usually endured environmental, social, and personal liabilities that affected their chances to compete equally with others in most phases of life. Most dropouts quit in the tenth grade because this is the transition grade from junior high school to senior high school, and they generally have reached the age whereby they can legally separate from school. Some of the major factors involved in the dropout problem are reading retardation, grade retention, low intelligence, negative self-images, and poor family attitudes. It should be emphasized that the dropout is not synonymous with the juvenile delinquent.

Several generalizations may be made concerning the disadvantaged adolescent. In general he has received inadequate nurturing during his early childhood. He is likely to lack ego skills, to have an extremely poor self-image, and to see the world as a pervasively hostile, inconsistent environment. Although disadvantaged individuals share many of the dominant or conventional values of society, they also show more acceptance of certain unconventional or different values. The value structure of the lower class differs in many ways from that of the middle class, and the child will be affected by these differences. Immediate, extrinsic values such as a big car or flashy clothes are frequently more sought after than are delayed, intrinsic values such as those that are brought about by schooling or long effort.

THE YOUTH MARKET

The youth market has emerged as a powerful influence on national economy in the United States. The purchasing power of young people is felt not only through their direct purchases but also through a significant influence on family purchases.

Significance of youth market

Recognition that teen-agers constitute a separate market segment has occurred during the last twenty-five years. Prior to this time there was a children's market and an adult market; youth was not recognized as a separate market. Even the word, *teen-ager,* was not in the dictionary. The marketers classified teen-agers either as children or as adults, using some age, such as 15 or 16 years, as the dividing line. By the early 1950s most marketers realized that teen-agers were a distinct market segment and that they had their own social rules and their own patterns of buying behavior, as well as product and brand preferences. Furthermore, the teen-age peer group exerted strong influences on individual buying decisions.[34]

The extent of the youth market is significant. It was estimated that during 1959 there were 18 million teen-agers who spent an average of $555 a year each for goods and services, not including the necessities normally supplied by their families. In 1965 there were approximately 20 million teen-agers who spent $10 billion. Girls averaged $9.53 per week, and boys averaged $10.25 per week. In 1967 the teen-age population was still increasing, and the annual income of boys and girls in the 13- to 19-year-old group was estimated at around $600 overall. In 1968 there were 28 million teen-agers who spent $20 billion for an average of $714 each for the year. In 1969 teen-agers spent about $22 billion.[35] One marketer estimates that the population for the age group of 10 to 19 years will increase to over 53 million by 1990. This group includes the teen-agers plus what many people call the preteen group.

Teenage purchases

The teen-ager buys many items and services, but the most common purchases are records, cameras, cosmetics, cars, soft drinks, wristwatches, and clothing. *Sponsor*[36] magazine said that some of the teen-age buying statistics were as follows:

Teens account for 81 percent of all phonograph records, 55 percent of all soft drinks, 53 percent of all movie tickets and 20 percent of all potato chip consumption. Teenage girls account for 23 percent of all cosmetic expenditures and 22 percent of all women's apparel sales. Teenage boys account for

40 percent of all men's slacks and 33 percent of all men's sweater sales.*

It is also estimated that teen-agers buy 24% of the nation's wristwatches, 30% of its low-priced cameras, 45% of its soft drinks, and have a significant say in another $30 billion in family purchases.

In addition to the preceding items teen-agers have been buying more and more appliances such as tape recorders, radios, television sets, and hairsetters. Housewares have also taken on increasing importance because many teen-agers are becoming engaged or married. In 1966 it was estimated that 800,000 girls would be engaged and over half of the women under the age of 20 years would become housewives before reaching that age.[37]

STUDY GUIDE

1. Review the developmental tasks of middle and later adolescence.
2. Physical development is nearly complete during this period. Give a thumbnail sketch of the physical characteristics of late adolescents.
3. Study the section discussing control as opposed to autonomy in parent-child relationships. What do you think this study says as to how parents should treat, raise, or consider their adolescent children?
4. Remember the first time you became interested in someone of the opposite sex? The second time you did? The third time . . . ? How did your experiences fit in with peer group heterosexual behavior and the sequential pattern of dating as presented in this book?
5. What are some of the mental characteristics of this age level? How do they reflect the cognitive characteristics of Piaget's period of normal operations?
6. Define "self-identity." Has this ever been a problem for you? Is it a problem now? Will self-identity ever be recognized and defined to a point where the individual will never have to change his self-concept or identity again?
7. In your opinion is the need for the development of a value judgment system by late adolescents as crucial as the author seems to be suggesting? Could this value judgment system be developed later with no harm done? Need it be developed at all?
8. There have been some changes for the better occurring in many so-called disadvantaged neighborhoods and communities. From your vantage point in time, what do you see happening to the ghetto black, the poor white, the rural poor, the Chicano, the Spanish-speaking Easterners, and the migrant workers? Have conditions changed "all that much" since the civil rights movement started in the middle 1950s? Does each generation require a new effort, bringing with it new problems?
9. What was your allowance when you were a kid? Did you even have one? What did you buy with your money?

REFERENCES

1. Tenner, J. M.: Growth at adolescence, Oxford, England, 1963, Blackwell Scientific Publications, p. 27.
2. Livson, N., McNeill, D., and Thomas, K.: Pooled estimates of parent-child correlations in stature from birth to maturity, Science 138:818-819, 1962.
3. Bayley, N., and Pinneau, S. R.: Tables for predicting adult height from skeletal age, J. Pediatr. 40:423-441, 1952.
4. Merry, F. K., and Merry, R. V.: The first two decades of life, New York, 1958, Harper & Row, Publishers, p. 143.
5. Peckos, P. S., and Heald, F. F.: Nutrition of adolescents, Children 11:27-30, 1964.
6. Rose, A. A.: Menstrual pain and personal adjustment, J. Personal. 17:287-300, 1949.
7. Mussen, P. H., Conger, J. J., and Kagan, J.: Child development and personality, ed. 3, New York, 1969, Harper & Row, Publishers, pp. 626-627.
8. Schmuck, R.: Concern of contemporary adolescents, Nat. Assoc. Sec. Sch. Prin. Bull. 49: 20-21, April, 1965.

---

*From The U. S. teen market, Sponsor 22:25-26, Jan., 1968.

9. Elder, G. H., Jr.: Structural variations in the child rearing relationship, Sociometry **52**:241-262, 1962.
10. Elder, G. H., Jr.: Parental power legitimation and its effect on the adolescent, Sociometry **26**:50-65, 1963.
11. Jones, D. R.: Pressure and adolescents, Educ. Lead. **23**:209, 1965.
12. Shearer, L.: Youth and sex, Parade, p. 4, Jan. 29, 1967.
13. Leidy, T. R., and Starry, A. P.: The American adolescent—a bewildering amalgam, Natl. Educ. Assoc. J. **5**:11, Oct., 1967.
14. Schneiders, A. A.: Personality development and adjustment in adolescence, Milwaukee, 1960, The Bruce Publishing Co., pp. 122-123.
15. Ibid., pp. 123-128.
16. Guilford, J. P.: The nature of intelligence, New York, 1967, McGraw-Hill Book Co.
17. Terman, L. M., and Merrill, M. A.: Stanford-Binet intelligence scale: manual for the third revision, Boston, 1960, Houghton Mifflin Co., p. 18.
18. Bayley, N.: On the growth of intelligence, Am. Psychol. **10**:805-818, 1955.
19. Strang, op. cit., p. 276.
20. Vernon, P. E.: The psychology of intelligence and G. Q. Bull. Br. Psychol. Soc. **31**:11, 1955.
21. Inhelder, B., and Piaget, J.: The growth of logical thinking from childhood to adolescence, New York, 1958, Basic Books, Inc., Publishers, pp. 338-339.
22. Hountras, P. T.: Mental hygiene, Columbus, Ohio, 1961, Charles E. Merrill Publishing Co., pp. 191-194.
23. Cruze, W. W.: Adolescent psychology and development, New York, 1953, The Ronald Press Co., pp. 207-208.
24. Hurlock, E.: Adolescent development, ed. 3, New York, 1967, McGraw-Hill Book Co., pp. 95-98.
25. Wittenberg, R. M.: The troubled generation, New York, 1967, Association Press, p. 89.
26. Conger, J. J., and Miller, W. E.: Personality, social class and delinquency, New York, 1966, John Wiley & Sons, Inc., p. 4.
27. Kvaraceus, W. C.: Anxious youth: dynamics of delinquency, Columbus, Ohio, 1966, Charles E. Merrill Publishing Co.
28. Glaser, D.: Social disorganization and delinquent subcultures. In Quay, H. C., editor: Juvenile delinquency, New York, 1965, D. Van Nostrand Co., Inc., pp. 30-36.
29. Gold, M.: Juvenile delinquency as a symptom of alienation, J. Soc. Issues **25**:130, Spring, 1969.
30. Keyserling, L. H.: Progress or poverty, Washington, D. C., 1964, Office of Economic Opportunity, Government Printing Office, p. 10.
31. Harrington, M.: The other America, New York, 1962, The Macmillan Co., pp. 10-13.
32. United States Department of Labor: The case for national action; the Negro family, Washington, D. C., 1965, Office of Planning and Research, Government Printing Office, pp. 5-27.
33. Goldenson, R. M.: The encyclopedia of human behavior, Garden City, N. Y., Doubleday & Co., Inc., p. 23.
34. Cundeff, E. W., and Still, R. R.: Basic marketing: concepts, environment and decisions, Englewood Cliffs, N. J., 1964, Prentice-Hall, Inc., p. 28.
35. Teen spending still soaring, Rand Bureau says: per capita youth cigarette spending wanes, Advert. Age **41**:67, April 13, 1970.
36. The U. S. Teen Market, Sponsor **22**:25-26, Jan., 1968.
37. MacLeod, A.: I am curious (teen-ager) should be the marketer's motto, Media/Scope **13**:33-34, Sept., 1969.

11 Emerging adulthood
The awakening years

EMERGING ADULTHOOD: FROM TEENS TO TWENTIES

I spent my late teen-age years and early twenties, like thousands of other young people, in college preparing for my future occupation. But unlike many others my presence in college was not the result of years of planning, preparation, and parental guidance. Because of my background, I was not really expected to pursue higher education. In fact, I became the first in the history of my family line to receive a college degree. I was reared in a small town, went to a small high school, and was seemingly destined to remain in that locale doing an insignificant, but responsible job, except for perhaps a brief hitch in the army.

For the most part I had resigned myself to this, my destiny, and therefore spent my last years in high school devoted to having a good time. I gave little thought to my future, which I was sure would take care of itself. From time to time someone would ask me if I had given any thought to the idea of going to college, but I would quickly reply that since I was one of nine children, it would be a financial impossibility. Although I was envious of my classmates who were preparing for college, I resolutely accepted the notion that this was not part of my future. Besides, I had something else on my mind—I was in love!

Most of my last year in high school was spent involved with three concerns: my girlfriend, school sports, and my weekend job in the supermarket. When the school year ended, I was offered a full-time job, which I accepted without hesitation, and began to discuss the possibility of getting married within a year.

After a few months of working and saving as much money as possible I began to go through a period of transition in my life. I became dissatisfied with the plan that my life had been following. I realized that I needed to broaden my horizons, to branch out, to see something of the outside world, to find out who I was and what I really wanted out of life. I became particularly interested in spiritual values at this time. I was concerned with being of service to God and man. I decided to try college.

My girlfriend also shared these sentiments, and as I prepared to go to college, she prepared to enter nurse's training. This was an exciting decision, but I had mixed emotions. I was reluctant to leave the only life I had ever known, to step into a strange world—a world I was not prepared to enter, but one that I knew I had to delve into to find my rightful place in life.

I traveled over 600 miles away from home to enter a church college. My brother, who was 22 years old and who had traveled widely while in the air force, drove me out to the school. I was 19 years old and had many fears of the unknown as we made our way across several states to enter a school that I had only read about in our church magazine.

Up until this time I had not been away from my girlfriend for more than two days at a time, and the prospect of going for several weeks without seeing her was very disheartening. Nevertheless, I convinced myself that it was the best thing for us, and I somehow endured the agony.

The first days on campus were very exciting. Meeting my roommates and fellow students from all over the United States and from several foreign countries showed me that college life would offer some unique experiences not to be had in my former life. The excitement of the first few days gave me little time to think about home, but the loneliness of those first nights in this strange place began to take its toll as that indescribable illness called homesickness began to show its symptoms.

The first nine weeks moved slowly and heavily. During this time I discovered that I had never learned how to do concentrated study. At first I thought college work would be similar to that in high school, just a bit more rigorous. I found, however, that high school requirements had been only child's play when compared with those of college. When I received a report of my progress after nine weeks, I was utterly shocked and disappointed. It did not take me long to snap out of my despair, because I realized that my grades would have to improve if I was to remain in college. After this experience I learned to budget my time and improve my study habits, but I soon realized that my next obstacle was not to be an academic one but a financial one.

With no financial backing it was necessary to obtain jobs on campus. With the help of three different jobs, yard crew, night watch, and usher, and an additional government loan, I managed to survive the costs of the first year of college.

During the first year I spent much of my free time involved in intramural athletics. I believed then, and still do, that without this diversion from the routine of studying I might have become discouraged enough about college, especially because of the financial hazards, to consider dropping out after the first year.

When the year was completed, I felt a great deal of self-satisfaction. I was extremely proud when I arrived home and my parents complimented me on my achievement. I also had a feeling of exhaustion—mental exhaustion. I felt as though I had already completed my entire education rather than one fourth of it. I had worked so hard at being a freshman that I was not sure there was enough energy left for three more years of the same.

The summer vacation was just what was needed. It gave me time to get a new perspective concerning my future. I am not sure, but I think it was about this time that I began to consider the possibility of becoming a teacher. My girlfriend had had a successful year in nurse's training, and hence our futures began to become a little more clear after the unsurety of the year before. I celebrated my twentieth birthday late that summer with a surprise visit by my girlfriend who had come home unexpectedly. We discovered that the months apart had really strengthened our relationship, rather than severed it. I actually began to look forward to my second year of college. I wanted to rush the future.

The second year was much like the first. With studies, sports, and extra jobs my schedule was hectic. My grades improved as I was able to adjust to the routine of college life. By the end of that year college became a way of life to me. I felt constrained to carry on with my education no matter what.

Between the second and third years it became necessary for me to drop out of school for one semester to earn some money. By the time I returned to school several changes had occurred: I transferred to a college nearer home, I reached the age of 21, and I became engaged to be married. With my fiancee's planning to graduate from nurse's training and my taking teacher education courses, my future seemed all the more definite.

From this point on my education began to take on its greatest meaning. I developed a philosophy of life which has changed little since that time. Working as a laborer on construction jobs during the summers before graduation helped me to appreciate the problems and satisfactions of the average working man. I was able to make comparisons and contrasts between these men, some of whom were practically illiterate, and the members of the academic community with whom I had become associated.

By the time I graduated from college I was

married and had a child. I entered college as an immature, unsure teen-ager with lots of energy and no future plans. I left college a married man with three dependents, a good outlook on life, and a definite plan for the future.

Although the transition from teens to twenties for me was not exactly a smooth one, it was a rewarding one. I was ushered into adulthood by experiencing what life had to offer—the good and the bad. I can only be thankful for my experiences and at the same time sympathetic toward those young people, who for some reason have difficulty making this transition and therefore miss some of the happiness of the early twenties.

Society in America changed its concept of "when a person becomes an adult" when legislation was passed granting 18-year-olds the right to vote. Before that time the age of 21 years was considered to be the time when a person "legally" became an adult. Laws, however, cannot dictate or change developmental patterns decreed by nature. The question still remains, "Developmentally, when does a person become an adult?"

Late adolescence, postadolescence, and *young adulthood* are terms used by developmental psychologists to indicate the age range of 18 to 21 or 22 years of age. Labels (terms) as they are applied to human beings are seldom satisfactory categorical descriptive devices because there are so many exceptions to the rule. In adulthood, in particular, it is better to describe developmental stages by a criterion rather than by a label, phrase, or certain age.

The late adolescent is in the final stages of making the transition from being a teenager to being an adult. He will have some adultlike characteristics but not all of them. He will also have some characteristics that are peculiar to the 18- to 22-year age level. A general criterion for suggesting when an individual is more of an adult than a late adolescent would be that point in time when an individual assumes the role of an adult by taking on the responsibilities, obligations, and characteristics of adulthood.

Specifically, adulthood is attained when an individual achieves a competent level of emotional, social, and economic independence, establishes a career or family pattern, and maintains a degree of personal, behavioral, and conceptual maturity that enables him to live with some measure of satisfaction within a social milieu. Late adolescence is a stage of transition wherein the individual is approaching the attainment of several developmental goals related to adulthood but has not yet completed them.

Attitudinal and behavioral characteristics common in late adolescence generally result from an idealistic view of the world, its people, and the means by which progress is accomplished, from a recently developed ability to do abstract reasoning about ways of men, the course of things, and life in general, and from a tendency to intensify on a problem or issue to a degree beyond its worth. Since this postadolescent period generally provides some time free from the all-encompassing responsibility of making one's living and providing for one's family, the individual at this stage of growth will think about those things in which he is interested and finds important. He may be swept up in the current issues and social fads of the times. If so, he generally brings his idealism and power of reasoning and self-answering to bear on these issues. He is influenced by statements or clichés that to him seem so obviously true. Assertions such as, "There are answers and solutions for the problems of the world if you look at them in their simplest details, devoid of the encumbrances imposed on them by the past, and study them," and, "All things are possible through love, hard work, and smart thinking if only you can separate yourself from traditional ideas that have you trapped."

In recent years emphasis on the social issues of the times has led many young adults to the conclusion that there is much about governmental, social, and institutional structures that is inadequate, incompetent, and inappropriate, that the adult world and its pattern of living is inept, indifferent, and not at all what it could or should be, and that "the system" had things bound in such a way that freedom of thought, of choice, and of movement are unduly and unnecessarily restricted. Not all young people had these ideas, of course. Some individuals were not particularly interested in the social issues, some were less aggressive by nature and preferred a spectator role rather than a participant role, some had their own concerns and problems to worry about, and some had insights and guidance that made them less susceptible to group domination of their thoughts and behavior.

What is not recognized or fully realized by this age group is that their capacity to make good, valid judgments is restricted because they are limited in the effective use of their reasoning powers by their limited experiences, depth and breadth of knowledge, and inadequately developed foresight. Their idealism further influences their decision-making processes. As a result, their perspective concerning total reality is extremely narrow, restricted, and sometimes even distorted. There is no question that they do have a glimpse of the truth of reality, but often they are unprepared to see the whole picture. There is an old proverb that says, "He who has seen little, amazes much." One might add, "He who makes major pronouncements based on the little he has seen, will find himself at odds with those who have been around a lot longer."

There is a universal timeless characteristic typical of those who are at the stage of emerging adulthood. Young people seek to assert themselves in different ways to let others know (and perhaps to convince themselves) that they are of age, that they know something too, and that they possess an intellectual and social power which must be recognized and accepted. The world over, youth at this age show agitation and confusion that they reveal by their protests. In America the Vietnam war and the draft were attacked. In Japan, where there was a national commitment to peace and anti-militarism, the students were among the most determined of all young radicals. French students had none of the American causes to protest against and none of the Japanese causes, yet protests occurred. Even in Venezuela student behavior followed the same pattern, and their protests were perhaps the most violent of all. There appears to be a universal tendency for

Table 11-1. Students' and fathers' attitudes on recent issues*

ISSUE	ACTIVISTS STUDENTS	ACTIVISTS FATHERS	NONACTIVISTS STUDENTS	NONACTIVISTS FATHERS
Percent who approve:				
Bombing of North Vietnam	9	27	73	80
American troops in Dominican Republic	6	33	65	50
Student participation in protest demonstrations	100	80	61	37
Civil disobedience in civil rights protests	97	57	28	23
Congressional investigations of "un-American activities"	3	7	73	57
Lyndon Johnson	35	77	81	83
Barry Goldwater	0	7	35	20
Full socialization of industry	62	23	5	10
Socialization of the medical profession	94	43	30	27

*From Flacks, R.: The liberated generation: an exploration of the roots of student protest, J. Soc. Issues 23(3):67, 1967.

young people to want to improve or to reject the life style imposed on them by their elders. They want to "improve things." They must find some issue or authority against which they can protest. The "protest" is the characteristic; the issue is secondary (Table 11-1).

Consider the statement: "Youth is disintegrating. The youngsters of the land have a disrespect for authority of every form. Vandalism is rife, and crime of all kinds is rampant among our youth. The nation is in peril!" This quotation was not written by an adult of this generation. It was written by an Egyptian priest about 4,000 years ago when his country was undergoing one of its periodic transitions.

DEVELOPMENTAL SELF

The gradual emergence of the adolescent's independence from the family and the confrontation with new responsibilities, new abilities, new values, and new freedoms make it necessary for the postadolescent to restructure his image of self and his potential and worth for the world. There are new things to be learned at this new stage of life; there are new dimensions to be added to one's personality and value judgment system.[1]

Developmental tasks

Primarily, late adolescents define their values in terms of relationships with age mates. Together they display a high degree of conformity to the norms of that particular peer group. In spite of a high degree of conformity to peer norms, adolescents are aware of adult expectations at this developmental stage. Most realize that they are expected to "settle down" and make many adjustments and decisions about the future. Such decisions as choice of vocation, choice of college, and personal code of conduct are imminent, and the adolescent responds to societal demands by conforming or withdrawing.

The idealism that characterizes this period results in a closer evaluation of principles in terms of "real" behavior—his own and others. Often the result is disillusionment because people often fail to live up to their expressed ideals. Negative reactions to this feeling result in maladaptive behavior, at times, and are observable in such ways as campus unrest, withdrawal from the social order, and the drug-laden "hippie" culture.

Positive reactions might be expressed in a desire to change the culture by becoming involved in pursuits that serve mankind such as service as a volunteer in Vista, Peace Corps, or peace groups. At worst an inability to correlate ideals with life tasks may result in a feeling of meaninglessness, currently called "the existential vacuum," which is expressed in apathy or in extreme manifestations of exaggerated behavior. The existence of such attitudes appears to be characteristic of times of great social and technological change, when the culture fails to "provide definitive models for identification."[2] Moreover, lacking models who base conduct on inner convictions, young people may require a longer period of experimentation to consolidate an adult system of values. The nature of the task demands that it be resolved by the individual himself. It has been suggested that a mature acceptance of religious values may provide an organizing principle for this whole process, since it identifies the goals and relationships of the individual during the present life and relates them to a life of happiness hereafter.[3]

Specifically, the developmental tasks of emerging adulthood are (1) selecting and preparing for an initial occupation or career pattern; (2) desiring and achieving socially responsible behavior; (3) developing concepts for civic competency in terms of moral, ethical, social, economic, and political aspects of life; (4) building sound personality traits, social and communications skills, and healthy attitudes in preparation for marriage and family life; and (5) acquiring a set of values by the formation of an identity and a concept of one's place in the world as a human being.

Physical and intellectual self

Although social development in the youth stage is transitional, physical and intellectual growth is essentially coming to a state of completion.

The height of the late adolescent has reached its peak for adult life and will remain stable until a person reaches old age. The weight spurts of the adolescent years level off near the end of the second decade of life, increasing gradually until the middle fifties, much to the dismay of many individuals. By the age of 17 years muscle growth has reached adult proportions, but muscular strength continues to grow, reaching its peak in the late twenties.

The brain has reached full size by the age of 16 years, but the adolescent has not developed sufficiently neurologically to use all brain parts adequately. Brain waves reach adult patterns in all cortical areas around the ages of 19 or 20 years, although this range of maturity may extend to 30 years of age.[4]

Most of the glandular development in the youth stage has reached its peak. The glandular processes level off for adulthood, although certain glands continue to develop. From puberty to the age of 17 to 18 years the heart size doubles, primarily because of the increase in muscular development around the heart. Blood pressure reaches a normal level for adults. The heartbeat stabilizes at about 72 beats per minute. At about the age of 17 years the lung capacity of girls has reached adult proportions; male lung capacity is reached several years later.

Bone growth ends when bone fusion takes place. The ossification of bone parts begins in the hands at the age of 17 years with girls and 19 years with boys. Continual bone fusion takes place over the next few years. In general, there is modification of body proportions between the ages of 18 and 22 years, changing the appearance of the oversized limbs and facial features of earlier adolescence.

The development of intellectual potentials is also reaching its peak when a person is 18 to 22 years old. As was noted previously, full brain use occurs around the age of 19 to 20 years, which may well account for the mental aggressiveness displayed during this period.

The individual of this age has approximately 85% of his logical reasoning abilities developed. Studies done by Welford[5] on subjects ranging in age from approximately 6 to 60 years investigated a person's capacity to understand and to apply a fresh method of thinking. He concluded that between 15 and 25 years of age the person tends to draw logical deductions based strictly on the statements as given in the test, whereas older adults sought to introduce supplementary premises based on their broader backgrounds or to confine themselves to comments on statements. Younger persons confine their logical reasoning to the question and knowledge at hand, whereas older persons operate from a broader perspective. On the other hand, young subjects can easily shift their thinking processes if they have additional problems to solve, whereas the older group has difficulty with mental flexibility.

Emotional self

The prolonged task of achieving emotional independence actually begins many years before adolescence when the child enters school, expands his contacts with peers, and widens his sphere of autonomous activities. Unless the importance and difficulty of the task are realized by parents, some young people will be facing problems of achieving emotional independence from parents. The task of achieving emotional independence is made particularly difficult in American society by prolonged education, which forces the young person to be financially dependent on his parents for many years, by delay in work opportunities brought about by child labor laws, by mechanization and automation, and by continuous family contacts, which render it difficult for parents to perceive the growth changes that are slowly but steadily pushing the young person toward maturity.

The growth and development of the child in adolescence are accompanied by glandular changes that are closely related to emotional control. The heightened emotional states during this period of life have been recognized as a part of the nature of adolescents. However, there is also an expansion of the emotions into the social realm. Fears and angers related to social situations become important. Self-conscious feelings about one's own inadequacy appear. The adolescent is concerned over the approval of his peers. This increased fear is observed in connection with classroom situations. Fear of reciting in class, fear of failure, and fear of ridicule are common, although less common than at 14 to 16 years of age.

One of the most noticeable characteristics of late adolescence is an increase in stability and control. Interests, friendships, career choices, and relations with parents are all more stable and predictable than they were in early adolescence. Opinions tend to be based on fact and are less liable to be affected by the generalities of propaganda than they were during the more "impressionable" period of adolescence. Their opinions can and do change under planned study and from the impact of interpersonal relationships. Current experiences still have an impact on the responses of the late adolescent, however.

IDENTITY AND SELF

The question of identity has two aspects. On one hand it is a question of self-image, "Who am I?", on the other hand it is a plea, "Don't lose my individuality in the mass of technology and overpopulation." Until the end of formal schooling the individual has been "role playing" the image of an adolescent. He is not sure how he should act or what he should be so he acts out his role as he perceives it from watching his peers. The postadolescent realizes that role playing is no longer adequate. He must accept the fact that he is making some decisions which will affect his life for years to come. He is also taking on some characteristics that will identify him with certain values and life styles. Self-image conflicts pervade the transition between adolescence and adulthood and seldom permit the individual to be at rest emotionally.[6]

Self-image

The postadolescent must have a positive self-image if he is to function properly. This is a large part of his search during postadolescence. He is looking for a stable, balanced self-image, a reliable view of himself that remains more or less steady throughout life. This image may come about through the values of community, of family, or from conflicting groups among his contemporaries. In earlier adolescence the self-image was not much of a problem. The adolescent could do as his parents told him or do the opposite. He could live with his self-image by doing either of these because either form of behavior was expected and accepted.

In today's society it is becoming increasingly difficult for the young adult to find his self-image. He stands rather alone in an unstructured moral climate. He is not given guidelines or standards to contemplate and by which to pattern his life. Emphasis is on being free and "doing your own thing." With a lack of background, how can he know what is most desirable for him? He proceeds, timidly, by trial and error or by imitating those who seem to know what they are doing. Some writers believe that a counterculture is needed to provide a climate of intimacy in which the individual can come to a sufficient sense of self so that the process of self-image integration can begin.[7]

Identity

The struggle for an identity is like a struggle against getting lost. Often it is a feeling of depersonalization, frequently brought on by some distinct change in the life of the postadolescent from a known, familiar environment to an unknown, impersonal world. It may be starting a job, entering college and living in a dormitory, or being drafted into the Army. There is an uncertainty as to how one fits into the new world. Then there is a fear that the new world might not recognize and appreciate the individual's uniqueness and competencies. There may be serious questions raised as to whether the individual is as capable or as ready as he thought he was. "What am I doing here?" "Is this really what I want?" "Save me from getting lost in this maze of life!" Much of adolescents' anger results from frustrations encountered in defining goals and being accepted for what they can produce.[8]

Identities are easily lost to the student at the big university, where he is dehumanized to the extent that he begins to think of himself as a number on a class card or an anonymous unit in a statistics population. At a large university, for example, a student is bound to feel like a nonentity when he picks up the undergraduate catalogue and reads the impressive list of emeriti assigned to teach his courses and then reports to class to find it being taught by a succession of underqualified graduate students, filling in for the Big Name while he does research or takes sabbaticals. Treatment of this sort can easily cause a student to question the system and even to grow hostile toward the institution itself.

The mass media, another sprawling institution so influential in American culture, provide young people with multiple and often-conflicting reflections of his identity. The individual sees student uprisings, and at the same time he sees his contemporaries cleaning up the environment. He is faced with making decisions about his own identity while being bombarded with many images of what he could be like. The mass media have kept him so well informed that, unlike any previous generation, there are a myriad of choices at his disposal but no clues as to which image is better for him.

Identity in minority groups

Perhaps the most difficult of all identity crises are endured by members of minority groups and disadvantaged youth from poverty pockets. The tendency is for such young people to cling fiercely to their minority status, claiming pride in their origins, and to lash out in violent resentment against those in authority on whom they blame their present plight. They feel trapped by their situation and react aggressively. The city street becomes the medium of expression for these young people. It is the common ground and liaison between all minorities in a poverty area, lending them a sense of belonging and unity. It gives birth to gangs of young people who because of class, society's ostracism, or perhaps a police record, have been snubbed or discriminated against. Gangs offer youngsters an escape from the boredom that stalks impoverished areas. They provide a certain amount of security, as do most groups, and a sense of importance when intimidating a rival gang. Young people involved in gangs find heroes among themselves to emulate, generally the gang leaders, and these become a sort of father figure to the boys. Gang dynamics have been extensively analyzed as an extremely important facet of minority and poverty culture.[9] They provide a kind of instant identity for underprivileged young people.

Responsibility is a key word in today's identity crisis. Young people long to be able to respect themselves as adults, and self-respect is generally a product of learning to handle responsibility capably. Today's young person wants to take credit for his successes; *just as much* he wants to pay the penalty for his own mistakes. This youngster knows he has done wrong and is ready to atone for it. When he does not get the discipline he needs, he feels frustrated and resentful. Young people are ready for responsibility well before their twenty-first birthdays. They are ready to prove that they can pay the price, both in successes and in failures, for this load. Perhaps the current legislation lowering the voting age nationwide in America will allow postadolescents all the privileges and penalties of adulthood at an earlier age and thus take some of the edge off the identity crisis.

MORAL AND RELIGIOUS UNCERTAINTY

Accepting values to live by is a major developmental task for the later adolescent. The behavioral guidelines of childhood and early adolescence are no longer tenable as standards of behavior, and neither is a value system based on a concept of rewards or punishment adequate, nor a moral code structured on a list of "do's" and "don'ts" or the "either-or" criteria. The adolescent realizes that the system which enabled him to make judgments in the past is not applicable to his newly acquired growth status in society. Unfortunately, society of today does not seem to have a frame of reference concerning right or wrong, good or bad, whereby youth can begin to build a more adequate value judgment system for himself. Too much uncertainty, too much hesitancy, and the lack of positive guidance seem to exist in all nations of the world, wherein the individual rather than society is placed in the exalted position of having a freedom of choice in the determination of physical, social, and cognitive behavior.

Commentary on moral uncertainty

In the United States the history of the 1930s and 1940s seems to provide some insight into the problem. What we are about to present is all speculative, of course. Consider the adults of the 1970s. They are the children and the young adolescents of the depression years of the 1930s—hard times when jobs, money, food, and adequate clothing were scarce. During the 1940s they were personally involved in wartime activities and its aftermath. The 1950s were years of personal building and of getting one's feet on the ground. An entire generation grew into adulthood from a background that stressed security and survival. As adults, this generation concentrated on supplying the material goods that were missing in their youth and on advancing technology, which it believed to be the key to future survival. As a result, the world experienced a knowledge and technological explosion such as had never been experienced before in the history of mankind. One of its most laudable achievements was the landing of man on the moon. Unfortunately, the technological sciences far surpassed advancements in the social sciences, with the result that man did not learn how to live in his new world of computers, electronics, and instant communication. A balanced life was lacking. Youth of today is faced with the moral and cultural vacuum that was permitted to develop during the past thirty to forty years.

A second factor instrumental in creating an image of moral uncertainty has been the inconsistent, ambiguous, indefinite, sometimes lacking responses by adults to the social and moral issues of the day. The abundance of pornographic-type literature for sale on the magazine stands and the wide distribution of films featuring nudity, sex, and violence make young people ask, "If you don't believe it is right or good, why don't you do something about it?" There is a great cry concerning crime in the streets, and the country has witnessed three assassinations of national figures. A gun control law was passed, only to be watered-down to the point of making it meaningless.

Young people have keen minds and time in which to use them. They have time to examine what is taking place, and they conclude that adults have much uncertainty in the realms of morality and religion. Adults offer little in these areas that young people can hold on to.

A third factor contributing to a moral uncertainty has been the attitudes and acceptance of adults concerning the need for changes in society. As young adults, they saw and were revolted by violations of civil rights in various parts of the country. They could not understand acts of prejudice against different religious and major political groups within the nation. They were the ones who pleaded with educational leaders to "make education more practical (relevant)." The pressures of the times, however, demanded that the young people of those years devote their energies to the business of making a living and making up for lost years. In turn, however, they did create an affluent society that gave more time and money to its youth. Young people could now afford to devote more time to right the wrongs of society. Adults were predisposed to permit changes to take place, and they were permissive with their children when they sought to do something about it. Some activities got out of hand because young people lack a social and political perspective, but many good changes were brought about.

Religious uncertainty

Religious uncertainty developed much in the same way. Mothers and fathers placed great stress on producing and gathering the material goods of life. Moral development was left to the church and school. There was one brief flare-up during the 1950s wherein attention was paid to the importance of spiritual, moral, and patriotic development. The movement quickly subsided, however, because of a lack of knowledge of how to promote spiritual and moral values. Regardless, the time had come to enter the race for space. The emphasis on science and mathematics overshadowed all else in the schools. Parents somehow hoped that spiritual values would be absorbed by their children.

For a period of time church membership soared from 30% of the prewar population to 65% in the late 1950s. Increased church membership, however, was not the answer. The church could not seem to meet the social problems of racial prejudice, poverty, and war in the 1960s. The church failed, the schools failed, and the parents failed. Young people grew up in a spiritual vacuum with no guidelines, no structure, no pressures "to conform." The stage was set for a "permissive point of view." Much of the mass communications media began to emphasize "the new morality" and "the permissive society." The United States Supreme Court at one time seemed to promote permissiveness by its rulings on obscenity, pornography, and criminal actions. Of course, the Supreme Court sought to stress "due process" and "the rights and freedom of the individual." But the public read the other side of the coin, which said, "permissiveness"!

In the late 1960s there was a strong movement among young people that had religious overtones. Having gone through unrest, violence, sex, drugs, flowers, and hippie communes, young people began to seek something more meaningful and more permanent than these things. Many were beginning to say "I believe in God, but not in the church."

In a survey of 2,000 youths in 1969, Bienvenu[10] found that most of them believed in God, that they wanted more religious activities involving the family, and, most important, that they wanted better lines of communication. It seems that most parents were upset at the young people rebelling against childhood practices such as attending Sunday School or church services. The young people said that they still believed but wanted to do it their way. The time had come for the church once again, as it had done periodically throughout the centuries, to upgrade its level of thinking and restructure its program to meet the demands of a more sophisticated society.

Stages of moral development

A look at the various developmental stages of moral judgment in individuals may give some insight into the levels of moral judgment pursued by societies. Kohlberg and Turiel[11] have formulated and validated a conception of moral development based on the core assumptions of the "cognitive-developmental" theory of moral education (Table 11-2). A key assumption of this theory is that the stimulation of moral development rests on the stimulation of thinking and problem solving by the child. The theory claims that morality represents a set of rational principles of judgment concerning human welfare and justice which are valid for every culture. Individuals acquire and refine the sense of justice through a sequence of invariant developmental stages as follows:

1. Orientation to punishment and reward and to physical and material

Table 11-2. Stages of moral development according to Kohlberg*

I. Preconventional level	Behavior abides by cultural rules because of punishment or reward consequences.
Stage 1: The punishment and obedience orientation	Good and bad, right and wrong are thought of in terms of consequences of action. Avoidance of punishment.
Stage 2: The instrumental realistic orientation	Right action is whatever satisfies one's own needs and occasionally needs of others. Exchange of favors. "Do for me and I do for you."
II. Conventional level	Behavior is self-controlled due to expectations of others and desire to conform and accept social expectations.
Stage 3: Interpersonal acceptance of "good boy, nice girl" social concept	Good behavior is what pleases and is approved by others. Response to stereotype. Social units are loose and flexible.
Stage 4: The "law and order" orientation	Right behavior accepts and shows respect for authority. Doing one's duty for the good of the social order. Laws are permanent and not likely to change.
III. Postconventional, autonomous, or principled level	Effort to define moral values and principles that are valid beyond the authority of the group and even beyond the self.
Stage 5: The social contract, utilitarian orientation	Adherence to legal rights commonly agreed upon by society but with laws subject to interpretation and change in terms of rational consideration for the rights of the individual while maintaining respect of self and others.
Stage 6: The universal ethical principle orientation	Right behavior is defined in terms of ethical principles based on logical comprehensiveness, universality, and consistency, and which respects the inherent dignity of human beings as individuals.

*Based on data from Kohlberg, L.: Stage and sequence: the cognitive-development approach to socialization. In Goslin, D., editor: Handbook of socialization: theory and research, Chicago, 1969, Rand McNally & Co.

power. Social power is diffused. Moral thought is based largely on doing good to avoid punishment.
2. Right action consists of that which satisfies one's own needs and occasionally the needs of others. Beginning notions of reciprocity. "You be nice to me and I'll be nice to you."
3. Moral behavior is that which is approved by others. There is much conformity to stereotypical images of what is "majority behavior." Morality is defined by individual ties of relationships.
4. Orientation toward authority, fixed rules, duty, and maintenance of the social order. "Law and order" is important. Whether the order is social or religious depends on which is considered of primary value.
5. Right action tends to be defined in terms of (a) general individual rights and (b) standards such as the American Constitution, that have been examined and agreed on. This is a "social-contract" orientation with emphasis on equality and mutual obligation.
6. Morality consists of self-chosen abstract ethical principles that have logical comprehensiveness, universality, and consistency. These are principles of justice and equality of human rights and of respect for the dignity of human beings as individual persons. Life is inherently worthwhile in itself.

The stages are not defined by opinions or judgments but by ways of thinking about moral matters and bases of choice. Stages 1 and 2, which are typical of children and delinquents, are described as "premoral," since moral decisions are based on self-interest and material considerations. The group-oriented stages 3 and 4 are the conventional ones at which most adult population operates. Stages 5 and 6 are "principles" stages, with only 5% to 10% of the population ever reaching stage 6. Why do some people reach higher levels of moral development than others? Much depends on the value judgment system and philosophy developed by the individual. That development depends on the type of reasoning and problem-solving experience an individual had and the type of knowledge and information he uses in his thinking. The individual who receives little or no information develops a moral and religious uncertainty because he has to work out so many answers for himself. In addition to suffering from a "kindergarten theology," which is of no use in solving problems in an "adult world of reality," people also suffer from being too busy making a living and just getting along in the daily world to be able to take time to deal with weighty moral problems. Some help is needed.

YOUTH AND SOCIETY

The appearance and actions of youth are often so dramatic that it is easy for adults to be diverted or misled from the universal principles which truly interpret this age group. To emphasize such things as hair styles, daily behavior, language usage, the "natural look," or the whole area of fads and fashions that we group under the heading of the "blue jeans syndrome" (named after a widely accepted dress style) is to overlook the true nature of this age group. Fads and fashions change. Popular social behavior, music, and clothing styles change. But the basic needs of youth are universal and eternal. This point must not be forgotten when adults look at today's youth.

The social dropout

From a society that has a long-standing commitment to a stress on individualism and on an intellective mode of consciousness, the young are moving toward a sense of identity that is communal and nonintellective in nature. Youth's very desire to experiment with drugs, sex, and alcohol has had a prominent and provocative effect on society. Their actions seem appalling and rebellious to older members of society. A gap of acceptability was created between the generations. This dissent in young people began in the late 1950s, when they began to question the American ideal of the "self-made" man and the importance of "material success." When youth questions society's values and systems, change or conflict is not far off.[12]

Young people often express resentment against their parents' generation in two ways: by aggressive rebellion or by apathetic escape. Present society has chosen to label these two groups as "hoodlums" and "hippies," respectively. By far the greatest amount of attention has been to the latter category—hippies. These are young people who have "dropped out" of the mainstream of society and banded together to form a subculture of their own. Their habitats have ranged from sections of cities, such as the famous Haight-Ashbury district of San Francisco, to whole towns, such as Taos, New Mexico, to abandoned farms and ranches, such as the Manson family's Spahn Ranch. Urban areas often cater to their hippie groups with special shops displaying the psychedelic themes. Soup kitchens have sprung up in hippie districts, offering hot lunches to young people who, having dropped out of society, have dropped out of employment as well. Syndicated newspapers in the jargon of the cult pepper urban newsstands and provide the hippies with a kind of cultural cohesion.[13]

Hippies are characterized as a passive, not active, group. They are plagued by pessimism, poverty, and insecurity, which tends to make them avoid all thought of the future. They have no real identity of their own so that they hide in the relative comfort of their group and together snatch at whatever they can to draw attention to themselves and give themselves a pseudo-identity (such as their attachment to flowers and finger signs meaning "peace"). Hippies band together to eschew responsibility. To forget more easily that which they cannot face, they assimilate drugs into their culture.

The hippie is generally from an affluent home and has had little responsibility or discipline given to him. When one looks at the overloaded job market and the competition and pressures a young prospect is up against, the idea of the unfettered "free" life could be rather attractive. An interesting point is that most hippies do not remain hippies for a long time. Eventually, tired of crowded flats and accomplishing nothing, the hippie filters back into the established society, where he becomes a productive worker and is lost to surveys and the press.

The other social dropout, the hoodlum, also aligns himself with a peculiar subculture, although less easily defined than that of the hippie. Hoodlums band together because society has shunned them, not because they have shunned society. A postadolescent becomes a criminal (or hoodlum) through a much more gradual series of events than his dropout counterpart— from misdemeanors to major crimes. He is generally a product of a disadvantaged environment, as opposed to the hippies' affluence and, being active instead of passive, he is by far the greater threat to society.[14] The reasons for young people turning to crime are highly complex, but in general they refer back to the postadolescent identity crisis once again. This is most easily illustrated in the case of prostitution. A young girl may choose to associate with a gang of boys for protection and often hero worship. The price for the protection, of course, is her body. After the novelty of her sexuality has worn off she is rejected by the gang and is forced to become a "pro." At the age of 21 years a former "gang's girl," and an aging prostitute, her life is behind her; she is physically and mentally worn out. Drugs, alcohol, anxiety, and depression make up the essence of her life.

A high percentage of these unfortunates are never rehabilitated. Unlike the hippie, the hoodlum often does not have the opportunity to tune himself back in to the established society. He has been subjected to legal discipline and often has a police record, which may mark him as an undesirable for life.

Basic motivation for any social dropout is identity. The search for a viable identity produces any number of effects in youngsters, and "cop-outs" is one of these effects. There is a current feeling among today's young people that there is little in mass society with which to identify. Current standards, to them, are meaningless. Appearance, class, school grades, athletic ability, and ambition represent success in establishment terms, but postadolescents find these criteria too shallow. They want respect, and they want to be credited with the ability to choose their own frame of reference and be held responsible for their own mistakes. The mass society is notably reticent about giving its respect to the next generation, primarily because adults notice in it a deviation from their own set of standards. It is this lack of respect that many dropouts are rebelling against and running away from. They take the negative course from that of their parents, aligning themselves with marijuana and other drugs. Sex is openly discussed and experimented with among young people rather than treated as a "hang-up," as it is among older people. Above all, youth is concerned with the realistic and moral issues rather than the romantic and material issues of their parents. When they find no tolerance for their views among those in authority, there is bound to be a reaction.[15]

The drug scene

In the last fifty years an obvious shift in drug use, from the middle-aged adult to the emerging adult, has taken place. According to studies by the California Rehabilitation Center,[16] the median age of drug use introduction is 16.4 years of age for both males and females, and the use of "hard" narcotics centered around the age of 19.9 years for males and 20.6 years for females. Thus emerging adulthood appears to be a critical period in drug use.

Most of today's youthful drug users are from middle class or upper middle class homes, usually have higher-than-average intelligence, and have some degree of affluence. They are free from worry about providing for themselves; they are well fed, clothed, housed, and educated. Thus they have more than ample time to contemplate their precepts of the weakness and hypocrisy of society, their own future, and the failure of the presiding generation.

As the adolescent casts his judicious view at his cultural environment and its values, he sees that gain is the gross national product, without all people having access to its rewards. A man is landed on the moon, but the earthly environment continues to deteriorate with its air too foul for breathing, its aquatic life dying, and man drowning in the midst of junked used cars and tin cans. He sees "cheating, lying, stealing, adultery, and even premeditated murder (in Vietnam) conditionally and situationally identified and approved, while honesty, fidelity, and virtue are situationally disapproved."[17]

In the adolescent's attempt to realize the "adult pattern of life" he is highly affected by his interaction with his cultural environment. From a mass of diversified societal and cultural interaction he must develop a set of moral values that he perceives to be acceptable to himself and to his society. Often confused, upset, and frustrated by the unpredictable and contradictory morality of his cultural environment, youth seeks immediate relief and escape from a futile situation. He may become aggressive, and he strikes out at an unfair, unhappy world filled with nothing but despair and failure for him. He may avoid or postpone the responsibilities of a threatening adulthood by withdrawing into an aura of drugs, which offers immediate relief to this threat. Many young people neither strike out nor seek to escape the world. They work out a moral code by which they can live in peaceful coexistence with society, in spite of its shortcomings.

Youth culture

The mentifacts and artifacts of a particular time in history reflect the cultural taste of the bulk of society at that moment. Acceptance of these modes of thought and objects, including fashion paraphernalia, makes one part of the majority in society. Occasionally a group, consciously or unconsciously, seeks to advance its own thoughts, fashions, and objects. This movement becomes a counterculture, which appeals to youth who are seeking recognition or wish to express their resentment or rejection of society's cultural interests. How long should a point of view last? How long should people continue to wear certain clothing styles? How long should they continue to believe that Guy Lombardo's music is the "sweetest music this side of heaven?" Change in taste and styles must come. Man on the move is that kind of a being. He must have variety; he must seek improvement to satisfy his need for self-assertion and for achievement. Youth seeks to promote change through their fads and fashions. At the very least, even if they are not promoting change, they are encouraging styles of thought and living that are unique to their age group.

It was the mass media of television, radio, newspapers, and magazines that woke up the youth of America in the 1950s and united them into a highly important part of the culture. Ever since that September evening in 1956, when Elvis Presley appeared on nationwide television with the bottom half of the television screen masked so that his pelvic movements could not be seen, society has awakened to the realization that youth were a force on the move and had to be reckoned with. His tight pants and his hip gyrations were objected to by many parents, but his songs and style of dance started to rock and roll the very foundations of the values system that parents supposed would always be acceptable for their children.[18]

In the western countries like the United States the arts and humanities are the means by which youth can create a new communal sense of taste. This is the type of approval that youth prefers, rather than going through a process of psychosocial maturing.[19] To find alternatives to mass society values in music young musicians constantly reevaluate and adjust their style to what might be termed the *avant-garde*. One of the reasons that the Beatles managed to maintain their long-time high standing in the young music world, for example, is because their style changed almost drastically from album to album. Their early records consisted almost exclusively of simple melodies in 4/4 time, easy to dance to, and designed to coincide with the introduction of the current dance rage. They popularized hard rock music. As drug cultures among young people expanded, the Beatles reflected the trend in their lyrics: "Lucy in the Sky With Diamonds" standing for L.S.D. They were quick to add sitar music to their repertoire when Ravi Shankar appeared on the scene from India. Finally, when the wave of nostalgia hit the youngsters, old-time honky-tonk turned up in the Beatles' "When I'm Sixty-four" and "Rocky Raccoon." The group quickly anticipated the trend and acted on it.

Music, important to the postadolescent because a certain area of it belongs exclusively to his age group, is a medium of intense involvement for him. It yields escape from his detached life. This is particularly true of psychedelic and electronic music.

Soul music reveals youth's disaffection for the affluent way of life. Many middle class youngsters believe that there is no soul in their own economic stratum. There is a spontaneity, depth of feeling, and vibrancy in soul music that was unknown in the tunes of the 1950s, and it is underscored by intense, highly dramatic performances of these numbers. Soul music originates in the part of society where ideals and character can express themselves without being molded by the mass society, such as among minorities and in ghettos. Its blues lyrics and somewhat repetitious melodies challenge establishment notions about such things as male-female roles, marriage, and steady jobs.

Indian music also negates middle class values and embraces eastern (as opposed to western) thought. It offers the most coherent complete alternative to the mode of thinking dictated by the mass society. Indian music is traditional rather than technical, introspective rather than demonstrative. Its acceptance among young people has led to an acceptance and following of the philosophy and religious ideals of the East. Zen Buddhism, for example, took the United States by storm in almost every facet of youth culture from the arts to the act of religious conversion.[20]

With time the young person expects more excellence in the music designed for his generation. The 18- to 21-year-old will look at a development in rock music, such as "Bubble Gum Music," with the same disdain that he would reserve for the music of the late 1950s.[21] Even though "bubble gum" is a form of rock, it is popular with the preteen and early teen and is not up to the level of sophistication that postadolescents demand from music. Rock, jazz, country, folk music, and the big band sounds are often heard in the popular band groups of college-aged people.

Youth's contribution to the field of art has not been as highly productive as their contribution to music. Except for the contributions made by the serious art student, the art form peculiar to youth is the poster. Photography has come into its own with today's postadolescent, partly because of his insistence on reality and partly because of a flagrant desire to exhibit shocking life styles to a disapproving establishment. Subjects of photographic posters are most often sensual—nudes or couples making love. One senses a bold defiance among the youngsters who throw these posters in the face of the previous generation, to whom these subjects are verboten. Gimmicks also attract youthful art fanciers, often reflecting the pop-art approach of the Campbell soup can.[22]

Fashion is the one area of culture most affected by the postadolescent. No matter whom the clothes are for, the accent is on youth: It is fashionable to be young! This attitude is reflected in most department stores, who give their moderately priced departments names like "The Casual Look" or "Youth Circle." These are designed to entice the older woman. The same philosophy applies to advertising. The older woman is virtually nonexistent in department-store clothing advertisements, even though the older woman has more money to spend. Youth affects style for the whole society. Most new fashions have that "far-out" look that brand them as a product of hippie influence. Colors, prints, and trims are outspoken, and one gets the feeling that "anything goes" in fashion—much the same feeling as one gets when watching the behavior of youngsters. Clothes for men, previously a rather conservative area, have become an area of concentration for designers. Oldsters respond to youth worship where fashion is concerned; older businessmen are wearing longer hair and wider neckties, and middle-aged mothers have given in to "hot pants" and peasant dresses. There is no question but that the youth culture in music, art, and fashions has influenced the living styles of all generations of the day. See question 5 in the Study Guide.

Youth and government

There are many postadolescents taking an active interest in politics today, and nearly all of them are characterized by a deep concern with the moral and psychological implications of the political process. As in many other areas, they seek honesty in politics—genuine noncorruption must be evident on the human side of a candidate, and his convictions must not be altered when political aspirations step in. Young radicals especially believe that psychological change must precede or accompany political change. The demands of activists reflect these attitudes as shown by their radicalism.[23] In general, youth views the government as seemingly dishonest and compromising, existing more for personal gain and the furthering of personal ends than to better serve the interests of the American people. Young people are extremely idealistic in their views on government, and when attacking its institutions as they so often do, they come armed with stringent moral principles that may not be strayed from.

A distrust for mass society is supported by an intrinsic emotional dislike for the conformity it demands. This reaction generally leads the postadolescent against specific institutions like selective service, bureaucratic education, and outmoded churches because these bulwarks against the onslaught of change seem the most imposing, and therefore the most attractive, to young people's quixotic goals. Dissent is most often the result of such a reaction.

Implicit in the term *liberal* is the essence of the goals set by young people for *their* adult society. They want freedom assured to them and their contemporaries—freedom to conduct individual life styles in any manner of choosing, freedom to decide moral as opposed to immoral issues in government, freedom to change what is unjust in law, freedom to enter or refuse induction into the military, and many more specific freedoms. They are asking for their dissenting voices to be considered by society as constructive rather than subversive in nature, and they ask only to be respected rather than ridiculed.

A FINAL WORD

Alfred North Whitehead[24] made an interesting observation relative to the need of the generations to get together. He writes to the effect that youth is imaginative, and if his imagination can be strengthened by discipline, this energy of imagination can be preserved for life. The tragedy of the world, as he sees it, is that those who are imaginative have slight experience and those who are experienced have feeble imaginations. Fools act on imagination without knowledge; penchants act on knowledge without imagination. The task of the university, says Whitehead, is to weld together imagination and experience. One must go to those older to learn the past; but one must go to youth to learn the future because they are the only ones native to the new technological age.

In every age, every generation, youth takes bold steps toward adulthood. The style and the clamor of those steps change from period to period. The activism and the apathy of the past decade will give way to a new look. The new look may well be "the new naturalism."[25] Three themes appear to be emerging—the stress on community, the apparent anti-intellectualism, and the search for what is sacred in nature. No one knows what the future holds, but the underlying universal principles pertaining to the movement of emerging adulthood state that youth will make itself known.

STUDY GUIDE

1. Read the beginning section of this chapter, which is our point of view. Do you agree or disagree? Support your position.
2. The developmental tasks as presented in this chapter are not as objectively and precisely presented as in other chapters. Try to list them by identifying the specific task.
3. What is the intellectual competency level of most 18- to 20-year-olds?
4. The section on "commentary on moral uncertainty" takes a rather conservative view on morals and morality. Read the next section on "religious uncertainty."

In your opinion are the positions overstated or distorted? You recognize, we hope, that you are at liberty to take issue with personal views that are not supported directly by research. In your judgment, what would be a suitable moral climate for society today? Compare your judgment with Kohlberg's findings on the stages of moral development.

5. In a description of the fashions and themes of the day, such as in the section on "youth and society," there is the possibility that the fashions, themes, and words will have changed after the book has been in print for a few years. The youth culture is particularly subject to change. Indeed, between the time the authors first wrote that section and the time it appeared in print (about fifteen months), some aspects of the material presented had changed. Recognize this entire section from a historical perspective. How do you see youth and society today?

REFERENCES

1. Keniston, K.: Youth: a "new" stage of life, Am. Schol. 39:631, Autumn, 1970.
2. Committee on Adolescence, Group for the Advancement of Psychiatry: Normal adolescence, New York, 1968, Charles Scribner's Sons, p. 96.
3. Pikunas, J.: Human development: a science of growth, New York, 1969, McGraw-Hill Book Co., p. 266.
4. Zubek, J. P., and Solberg, P. A.: Human development, New York, 1954, McGraw-Hill Book Co., p. 127.
5. Welford, A. T.: Skill and age: an experimental approach, New York, 1951, Oxford University Press, Inc.
6. Wittenberg, R. M.: The troubled generation, New York, 1967, Association Press, p. 85.
7. Pilder, W. F.: Youth: society's hope for love, Theory Into Practice 8:121, April, 1969.
8. Ohlsen, M. M.: Dissident students, Contemp. Educ. 42:157, 1971.
9. Cain, A.: Young people and crime, New York, 1968, The John Day Co., p. 61.
10. Bienvenu, M. J.: Kids want more religion, America, p. 252, Oct. 4, 1969.
11. Kohlberg, L., and Turiel, E.: Research in moral development: the cognitive-developmental approach, New York, 1971, Holt, Rinehart & Winston, Inc.
12. Rosak, T.: Counter culture, Nation, p. 402, March 25, 1968.
13. Gerzon, M.: The whole world is watching, New York, 1969, The Viking Press, Inc.
14. Cain, A.: Young people and crime, New York, 1968, The John Day Co., p. 29.
15. Fletcher, G.: What's right with our young people? New York, 1966, Whiteside Inc., Publishers, p. 57.
16. Duster, T.: The legislation of morality, New York, 1970, The Free Press, p. 46.
17. Elliot, R.: Narcotics: a crucial area of school responsibility, Educ. Digest, pp. 44-47, Sept., 1970.
18. Zalaznick, S.: Youthquakes in pop culture, Fortune, p. 85, Jan., 1969.
19. Arasteth, R.: The rebirth of youth in the age of cultural change, Acta Paedopsychiatr. (Basel) 36:327-345, 1969.
20. Gerzon, op. cit., p. 75.
21. Horowitz, I. L.: Rock on the rocks, or bubble gum, anybody? Psychol. Today, p. 59, Jan., 1971.
22. Canady, J.: The revolution that couldn't, in a show that doesn't, New York Times, p. 23, section D, June 27, 1971.
23. Keniston, K.: The young radicals, New York, 1968, Harcourt, Brace & World, Inc., p. 54.
24. Whitehead, A. N.: Aims of education, New York, 1929, The Macmillan Co. (copyright renewed, 1957, by Evelyn Whitehead).
25. Yankelovich, D.: The changing values on campus, New York, 1972, Pocket Books.

12 Early adulthood
The developing years

EARLY ADULTHOOD: OH, TO BE 24 AND THE MOTHER OF TWO!

There goes that nasty alarm, meaning another busy day lies ahead. As I catch a glimpse of the clock, I see it is 6:30 A.M. Stumbling out of bed, my feet hit the cold bare floor. Quickly I reach for my slippers and then grasp for my glasses. Everything looks a lot brighter now. Since the children are still sleeping, I tiptoe to the bathroom and hurriedly get dressed. Descending to the kitchen, I fix my breakfast, consisting of a glass of milk and two slices of toast. Before the girls awaken I like to get my wash started, so to the laundry room I march. White clothes, dark clothes, towels, baby clothes, and diapers; that should take care of my morning work. As I start the washer with the first load, the cries of a 4-year-old can be heard, "Mommie, Mommie, I want something to eat."

I prepare a fried egg and toast for my little girl, and soon the baby is awake. Cereal, fruit, and milk are quickly heated for her. Having fed both the children, it is time to make the beds. Just then the phone rings. It's a friend of mine saying she'll pick me up in an hour to go to our club meeting. Naturally, the children go along and stay in the nursery. Now the big rush is to get the girls dressed and try to finish some of the wash.

There goes the phone again. This time it is Aunt Hilda, passing on more gossip. Little time do I have, so I quickly make excuses to talk to her later. Next the doorbell rings, and the diaper man is here to collect dirty diapers.

As I try to dress my 4-year-old, she wants to watch cartoons and does not cooperate. Coaxing her by telling her that we are going away, she soon responds to my efforts. Next is the baby, who by now needs a change of diapers and a clean suit. After dressing her completely she proudly opens her mouth and spits up her milk all over her clean suit. Well, I have to try again, and quickly! Carol is due in 5 minutes, and I have to comb my hair and apply a few touches of makeup.

By now a horn is beeping outside, so hastily I get coats and sweaters on all of us. As we are rushing out the door, the phone is ringing again. Too bad, I think; that person will have to wait.

The meeting goes fine, although I am elected to prepare next month's program and to select babysitters. The children are left in the nursery with sitters during the meeting, which is quite a relief. Afterward refreshments are served to the adults and the children.

The meeting is over, and we are on our way home. Then I remember that I need a few things from the store, so my friend stops and we all go in to the grocery store. What a joy this is, "Mommie, get me this," "I want a book," "Let me push the cart," and so on. Quickly I gather my needs and we are on our way again.

By this time my little ones want some lunch. I prepare some leftovers and feed myself and my eldest; then the baby starts to cry until I have a nice warm lunch ready for her. She is still hungry so, in addition, I give her a bottle of milk. Now that she is satisfied, I put her in bed for a nap. Of course, my 4-year-old is at the age of rejecting naps so she stays up and plays. With the record player, the radio, and the television going all at once I can hardly hear myself talk.

My phone is ringing again. It seems that as soon as the phone rings, a green light must flash and tell my daughter to get into trouble. She either opens the refrigerator or tries to wash my dishes.

I want to make spaghetti for supper so I must start my meat sauce. As I'm browning the meat, I suddenly hear a crash. I turn around to find my daughter has broken some glasses while trying to wash them. What a helper! Finishing the sauce, I decide to sit down and sew a little. I'm in the midst of making some spring dresses for my little one. Here, again, she tries to be mother's helper by taking my pins and scissors and cutting up some of the material.

As I finish my sewing for the day, I can hear the baby jabbering away. Joyfully I go up to get her and bring her down to the playpen. Now I quickly dust and vacuum before my shows come on television. Then I sit down and relax a while until it is time for dinner.

My 4-year-old watches "Sesame Street" as I prepare dinner. This is a help. During the commercials she helps me set the table, and I serve the spaghetti, garlic bread, and salad. Now I must feed my baby her dinner and a bottle of milk. Meanwhile, my dishes are waiting in the sink. How nice it would be to have a dishwasher, but good old soap and water does it for me. As I'm doing the dishes, I hear a scream from the playpen. Big sister has climbed in with the baby and is tormenting her.

Tension is building up, and I am thinking of my night out at card club tonight—only 3 hours away. Just then my eldest rushes into the kitchen screaming, "Help, Mommie, Help!" The baby has her hand caught in a toy and can't release it. "I wonder whose fault that was?" I say to big sister.

Someone is knocking at my back door. My neighbor asks me if I could quickly mend a torn shirt. Naturally I say that I can and go to my sewing machine. Not knowing I was going to my card club, she sits and talks for a while. I almost have to ask her to leave, but I'm saved by the bell—my doorbell. The babysitter has arrived a little early, but I am glad. Now I have some help. I take my 4-year-old and give her a bath. Of course, she loves the bath water, so I let her play a while. Suddenly from the other room I hear a big splash. She had jumped and slipped in the tub, splashing half of the water on the floor. Quickly I dry her and put on her pajamas. Number One is now ready for bed. Now to get Number Two ready. The baby loves to have her bath so this is a joy. After the bath and hair wash, I dress her for bed and put her brace on her feet.

I let the babysitter feed the baby her bottle so that I can get myself ready to go. It seems that mothers never have enough time to fix themselves—they always have to rush. At least this is the way it happens to me!

Finally, I put my baby to bed. Both angels are sleeping, and it is time for me to go. I give the sitter instructions in case either one should awaken. Then I leave—on my way to relaxation and fun. If you ever sit in at a ladies' card club, you will discover that there is more chatting done than card playing. But we enjoy it.

The fun is just beginning when the phone rings. It is my babysitter, of course. The baby had awakened and was coughing badly. "What should I do?" the sitter asked. "Give her some cough syrup and put her back in bed." I tell her to call back if she needs any more help.

I return to the gossip table and resume playing. Time goes on, and there is no call. I tell myself that everything is all right. I'm not very good at playing cards, so again I win the booby prize. I enjoy the relaxation and change of atmosphere, but I am soon on my way home. As I say goodbye to the babysitter, someone is asking mommie for a drink of water. I climb the stairs and tuck them both in bed again.

I look at the clock and see that it is 11:30 P.M. Realizing that in 7 hours another busy day will begin, I decide that I had better go to bed. As I lie in bed, I think how wonderful it is to be a mother—to have someone who needs your love, your kindness, your security, the warmth of your body, and your guidance. I also think how nice it would be if John, my husband, didn't have to be out of town much longer on his temporary assignment.

After the turbulent stage of late adolescence the developing individual is faced with yet another major task—that of competent, satisfactory integration into adult society and culture. The challenges and responsibilities that must be met and accepted are varied, and the possible hindrance to satisfactory adjustment and development are many. The time has come to be independent, as well as interdependent. The point in time when a person becomes an adult cannot be designated in years but, rather, at that point when he begins to assume the responsibilities of adulthood and takes on the role of the adult. For most people this time will be in the early twenties.

One fourth of an individual's life is spent growing up. Three fourths of his life is spent in adulthood, growing older. Should we not have more concern than we do with the nature of adulthood and how to enter it, as well as leave it, gracefully and with hope?

Early adulthood, or the period from approximately 20 to 35 or 40 years of age, is a busy and exciting time for most people. It is the "expansion of growing phase" of adulthood. It is that time of life when adults invest enormous amounts of energy in their work, striving for promotions, positions, and raises. They are also extending their social contacts, widening their circle of friends, and seeking to become part of organized social entities. They marry, establish homes, and have children. There is forward movement in watching and helping the children grow. A home, a car, a color television set, and a stereo layout become part of the dimensions of a higher standard of living. For early adults who are striving to get ahead the road stretches into an indefinite future, a goal beyond dreams. The developing period of adulthood is an ever-growing, ever-expanding time of life. It is beautiful but hectic!

Developmental tasks

The early adult finds himself confronted with the role of the adult, which includes that of being a worker, a consumer, a social being, a citizen, a taxpayer, and a family person with children. He is the one who must now and for the rest of his life make decisions, rather than having them made for him. In addition, he is confronted with a number of life-style changes and new experiences. It is in the course of coping with these experiences that he is likely to undergo changes in his personality. No longer a child, the early adult learns to tolerate some frustration and aggravation. He is expected to use some logical reasoning and insight in making decisions. The requirements of the adult role not only contribute to changes of personality and modes of adjustment but also to the need for an updated value-judgment system. Up to the age of 30 years it is common for both men and women to be underdeveloped in some areas of behavior and judgment, whereas at the same time showing considerable maturity in other areas.[1] With new experiences and new expectations by others, however, a more even development on a more mature level begins to take place.

The social and economic roles of early adulthood are so familiar and clearly defined that few early adults have any doubt as to what the expectations of society are. These expectations, indicated as developmental tasks, are (1) selecting a mate, (2) learning to live with a marriage partner, (3) starting a family, (4) rearing children, (5) managing a home, (6) getting started in an occupation, (7) taking on civic responsibility, and (8) finding a congenial social group.[2] Successful achievement of these tasks will do much to bring about a more satisfying middle and late adulthood. Whether or not the ultimate future is in clear focus for the early adult, he is planting the seeds that will bear the crops for harvest in his later years.

Personal independence

"To me, independence and responsibility for a male just out of college or just turning twenty-one means getting out from under parental control and influence and moving into the world of freedom and self-reliance." This opinion typifies the early adult's view of independence and responsibility. Independence is usually demonstrated by the early adult moving out of the parents' home and into an apartment to live on his own. He hopes to prove to his parents and to himself that he can accept and handle the responsibilities of living away from home. As our friend said, "I'm supporting myself and, in a sense, going through a dry run for the later responsibilities of marriage and a family." The early adult is formulating goals and is probing new areas. This is opposed to his earlier years of waiting until he "grew up" to achieve any goals in life. Now it is time for him to be what he is to be.

The task of becoming independent and responsible entails attaining emotional independence, social independence, and economic independence. Emotional independence is the most important, yet the most difficult to achieve. The need is to progress from emotional dependence on parents, or others, to relative autonomy while still being able to maintain close emotional ties. The need is to reach a point where, although the individual has extremely personal feelings for those close to himself, he is still able to be emotionally independent enough so that he is not unduly influenced by the emotional responses of despair, displeasure, or disappointment of others around him. To be self-reliant rather than self-sufficient is the answer. The self-sufficient person draws a circle around himself and says, "I don't need anybody else—I can take care of my needs." Actually, he is often afraid to let anyone into his bubble for fear of being hurt. The insufficient person says, "I need everybody's love, attention, and support. This person needs all kinds of help. The self-reliant person says, "I can stand on my own two feet, emotionally, but I'm willing to share my feelings with others and let them become part of me." The key to emotional independence is the ability to receive, share, and give love, to be interdependent, without becoming overwhelmed and emotionally dominated. The capacity to love someone other than oneself is an integral factor in adult emotional independence. The self-reliant person is such an individual.

Social independence comes more readily because the young adult has been working in this direction ever since he was an early adolescent. Of course, social independence carries with it responsibilities in civic, political, occupational, educational, religious, social, and community affairs. The essence of social independence is not a "cop-out" or denial of social responses; it is not a matter of "doing my own thing"; rather, it is an element of social trust and of self-direction in social thought and decision.

The element of social trust entails the extent to which others (society) can count on the individual to make an effort to contribute to the well-being of others by being socially responsible. As someone in our group of young adults said, "I should be able to count on you to drive on your side of the road, to stop at stop signs when I have the right of way, to pay your share of the taxes for our common welfare, and to trust you to control those primitive impulses of yours that would permit you to strike out at me and to steal and to cheat. In return, you should be able to trust me to do my best to act in accordance to those principles that would enable us to live together amicably."

Self-direction implies being free from group domination in establishing or determining a social pattern of living and of thought. Adolescence is a time when the desire for social acceptance is so great that whatever the group says is what the adolescent does or thinks. At some point the individual must separate himself from the social and emotional domination of others. "To be my own man." A person may subscribe to the views of a group, political, religious, or social in nature, but within that allegiance the individual should still be able to be selective in the social views, ideals, values, and behaviors that he will follow.

Economic independence demands an acceptance of financial responsibility, self-support, and support of family. Knowing the value of money and how to spend it wisely and learning to limit desires to ability to pay are equally important. To be constantly in debt shows poor management and economic immaturity.

Economic independence involves several measures to ensure financial success. First, the early adult should have at least one marketable or saleable vocational skill that he can offer an employer in return for a job that will pay enough to provide for basic needs. Second, there should be some type of career plan involving specific training, apprenticeship, or schooling that can lay a foundation for future training and experience. Third, some money management knowledge is needed in terms of budget making, clothing management, household expenditures, and repair costs. Fourth, some knowledge of credit buying, of interest rates, and of life insurance would be desirable.[3] Economic independence is more than having a job and being on one's own—it includes the whole concept of economics and money management. It begins with decisions that adolescents make when they decide what courses or programs they want to take in school, what interest areas they develop, and what attitudes they adopt toward work.

Career development

Almost every adult devotes a major part of his activity and interest to the occupation in which he earns his living. A successful vocational adjustment is therefore a strong integrative factor in the lives of most men and of many women. Success in a job not only ensures one's economic existence but provides many other satisfactions as well. In the American culture a man's occupation and his achievements in it are major determiners of his social status and of his self-esteem. Emotional needs for approval, preeminence, and security are satisfied by a good vocational adjustment.

Career development in adulthood includes establishment and maintenance of a career and adjustments throughout the years while in the vocation. The individual must first find a place in the occupational world. Successful establishment may involve mobility as much as security and stability in an occupation. Adult vocational identity is largely a function of career movement within occupations and work organizations, although the individual may progress within the same organization.[4]

No special theory of career development for women would be necessary if the portion of their lives that they spend as a mother and homemaker could be regarded as one of the several occupations that they have available to choose from. But such is not the case. Many women have dual careers of homemaker and of some occupational role outside the home. Few would quarrel with the observation that women have a fundamental biological difference from men, manifested in the ability to conceive, bear, and nurse offspring. Woman's role has been traditionally organized around the children and the support of the effort of the family's breadwinner. Neither the biological nor social role of the homemaker is as static as some advocates would have us believe. Women now have an option in childbearing. The feminist-suffragette movement of the nineteenth century and the acceptance of women into the work force in World War II have set in motion challenges to the stereotyped social role for women that, paired with the changes in social expectations for men, may ultimately wipe out distinction between the two.[5]

A large part of a young man's time and energy during young adulthood is spent getting started in an occupation. In the early years of his working life there is much changing of jobs. The skilled and professional workers, however, after spending several years of searching tend to settle into a particular occupation and remain until retirement. In contrast the less skilled workers continue to switch employment and employers for most of their working years. Truck drivers and construction workers sometimes show employment in ten to twenty different jobs before retirement.

Professionals, such as chemists, accountants, teachers, and others, rate the nature of their work as the single greatest source of satisfaction.[6] Industrial workers with less schooling indicate that working in an area of genuine interest is an important factor in job satisfaction. However, they emphasize job security and pay rates as conditions that play the most important part in job satisfaction.

GETTING MARRIED

Vast social changes have been taking place in American and Western society. The change from the rural to urban society, the economic emancipation of women, the increased secularization of social life, the resulting decline in religious sanctions, the individual approach to mate selection and marital expectations have all had their impact on the nature of family life. It is axiomatic that whenever social systems of any type go through change, instability of some type will result. Many professionals see the current crisis in family life as one phase in the process of social change. The alleged current family and marriage crises are viewed as stemming from the fact that whereas the traditional basis of family has apparently been weakened, a new basis for family living has not yet fully emerged. In the meanwhile, young couples will continue to fall in love, some will marry and some will not, and children will be conceived in either case. Some couples will be happy with their situation, others will not.

The why and wherefore of marriage

Marriage, as distinct from mating, is an entirely human relationship. Animals that mate do not marry. Should an animal suddenly feel that a different member of the species is more attractive, it is free to act accordingly. The pattern of life in one animal family, however, is much the same as that of any other mating unit of the same species. Human family patterns, on the other hand, differ according to culture, personality, and geography.

Mating is an inborn drive in man, but marriage is a formal institution. One of the major considerations in instituting the custom of marriage was probably the desire to enjoy the sex drive as fully as possible with a minimum of hazards and anxieties.[7] The natural sexual impulses of man and the aim of procreation needed to be satisfied, and yet some responsible control over it was also necessary. Having the same woman or women at his command would simplify the man's life; having the same man or men possess her would also assure the woman of protection from other men. Historically, general promiscuity has been abandoned in all types of societies for the stability and security of family life. The pattern of control in mating eventually evolved into the marriage ritual.

More important, family living affords a means for the nurture and care of the young child. Two parents are important for the proper rearing of the human infant because he remains helpless for a much longer period than does the offspring of animals. Experience indicates that the emotional needs for growth and development of the child, as well as his physical needs, are best fulfilled by two parents through the stability afforded by the institution of marriage.

Historically, every age had its share of common-law marriages, trial marriages, or "people just living together because there's no hard, fast commitment that way." Yet the interesting observation is that as long as there has been recorded history, regardless of the sophistication or the simplicity of the society, the family was always the basic biological and social unit, and with it there was some aspect of the marriage institution. Society can absorb a goodly number of couples who "live together for as long as we love each other, even without the benefit of a piece of paper indicating marriage." However, when the number of marriageless couples reaches a saturation point, the political fiber of society's structure will alter. Not only will the element of stability deteriorate but so will the pattern of record keeping, on which so much of current, complex societies depend. Obtaining a marriage license is a systematic method by which government can keep track of the status of its adults and give legal sanction to the union.

Reasons for marriage. Over 90% of all Americans will be married at least once before they die. The reasons why people marry are many—love, economic security, desire for a home and children, emotional security, parents' wishes, escape from loneliness or from a parental home situation, money, companionship, sexual attraction, protection, notoriety, social position and prestige, gratitude, pity, spite, adventure, and common interests.[8] The law indirectly plays a part in marriage. The individual is not forced by law to marry, but to enjoy certain rights and privileges he must do so.

A socially induced reason for marriage is conformity. The single person finds himself different because the majority are married. A married couple may tend to play matchmaker for the individual still single by arranging dates or even inviting two "singles" for dinner. The individual in this way may be pressured into marriage. The idea is expounded that to be mature or grown up, the individual must be married.

The individual may marry for satisfaction of his ego needs. To be wanted more than anyone else and to be of value to the other person are important needs for some people. Ego satisfaction plays an important role throughout the individual's entire life, and marriage is one way of achieving this. In general, marriage provides for security, recognition, response, and new experiences. These factors are basic to the emotional needs of man.

We have some "nonscientific" theories as to why people get married. There is the "schoolgirl theory." You get married when you find your "true love." "Somewhere in this world there is a man, just for me. He will be a knight in shining armor, riding on a white horse. He will come dashing down the street and sweep me off my feet." The only problem with this theory is that this knight in shining armor may turn out to be no more than an Ajax salesman. The "name-of-the-game theory" is ageless. The name of the game is "get married," and all plans, all efforts are directed to that end. Indeed there seems to be a conspiracy among the women of the world that "man shall not live by bread alone"—he needs a helpmeet. Then there is the "tom cat theory" of marriage—an individual gets married to stabilize sex relations. The "avoidance theory" is where an individual gets married to avoid some unpleasantry. More serious is the "tender-trap" theory. Love is a tender trap. Love is tender. Love is nice. It appears to be the central ingredient in happiness. From a physiological point of view, however, the main purpose and intent of love is to create new life. It really is not concerned with making people happy. Therefore the idea that love and happiness are synonymous is an illusion, designed and perpetrated by nature for the purpose of propagating the species. After the honeymoon is over and the couple discover the harsh realities of marriage at the breakfast table, only then do they realize they have been hoodwinked and are now trapped; thence the tender trap. The last theory is the "contagious disease theory." We see this on the college campus so often. Let one girl in a dormitory get engaged, and every girl living in her corridor will get the left hand, third finger itch! So much for nonscientific theories. They make interesting conversation but should not be expounded at length in a scholarly treatise!

Marriage and college. Until World War II marriage was generally delayed until education was completed. Before World War II many colleges and universities actually expelled students who married while in school, but with the return in the late 1940s of tens of thousands of veterans who attended schools all over the United States on the GI Bill, the married student ceased to be a statistical rarity. Indeed low-rent housing units for him and his family were quickly provided by the hundreds on campuses. The schools also tried to provide part-time jobs for student husbands and wives. Today one in five undergraduates attending American colleges is married and living with his spouse (United States Bureau of the Census, 1964), and more than half of the graduate students are married.[9]

Perhaps the central reason for this large percentage of student marriage is the increasing stresses associated with the contemporary American mass society. Among the present generation of young people (more than one half of the population is under 25 years old) the need to belong, which translated means the need for emotional support and security, for companionship, for love, and for a permanent paired relation, has become more pressing and significant in the context of an impersonal and materialist society. Marriage is the only primary institution in our society that can reliably and satisfactorily fulfill this need. The need and, in recent times, the expectation for a complete heterosexual life in early adulthood has also contributed to the increasing number of campus marriages.

However, there are disadvantages to marrying while attending school. The husband, for example, who both works and attends classes knows that if he falls behind on his job, he may be fired; if he does not keep up his grades, he may flunk out for the rest of his life. On the other hand, if his wife works to support him and any children they may have, he may feel guilty or ashamed at not fulfilling what he considers to be the traditional breadwinning role of the husband. At the same time the working wife may resent the time her student husband devotes in the evenings and on weekends to his studies and may regret that she, too, cannot experience the social and intellectual stimulation of student life.

If the wife does not work but like her husband is a student, she may feel little incentive to continue with her education, since she has found the security and status of a husband; therefore with the first pregnancy the student wife almost always discontinues full-time class attendance.

Meaning of love

Love is more than just the physical, sexual aspect in marriage, yet a definitive meaning of love is a difficult item to come by, since each source that speaks of love has its own definition. However, one definition which seems to have widespread appeal is that taken from the New Testament of the Bible, I Corinthians 13:4-8, which reads, "Love is patient, it is kind; love does not envy, it is not pretentious nor puffed up; love is not ambitious, nor is it self-seeking; love is not provoked; thinks no evil and does not rejoice over wickedness, but rejoices with the truth; it bears with all things, believes all things, hopes all things, and endures all things. Love never fails, whereas prophecies will disappear, and tongues will cease, and knowledge will be destroyed." From this definition comes the meaning of love that lasts through times of frustration and achievement, sadness and joy, youth and maturity.

Love, then, is a quality that defies exact definition but can mend strained relationships and reestablish lines of communication between the marriage partners when they have been cut off. In her study of fifty-two married couples over a ten-year period beginning in undergraduate years, Rachel Cox[10] found that, except for a very few, the strength and satisfaction of the marriage tie increased as the years went by. She asked her subjects to grade various aspects of love as listed on a rating scale. In analyzing the answers, she found that a hopeful, supportive, and essentially uncritical love characterized thirty-three of the fifty-two marriages. In eighteen marriages love was such that the spouses were more objective about the flaws in the other spouse and in their marriage. Love was found to be a needed element in exploring the reaches of another personality and redefining one's own emerging self in relation to the expectations and needs of that other personality.

People "fall in love" for different reasons. Some fall in love for physical reasons—for physical attraction and sexual response. Others fall in love for social reasons—"It is the thing to do." Among some adolescents, "You're nobody unless you've got a boyfriend (girlfriend) and going steady." An older man, having finished time in the Armed Forces or returning to college from a job, often finds himself quickly married simply because he was heard to express the idea that "Well, I'm older now; it's time for me to settle down." Some people fall in love for emotional reasons. It is a tremendous feeling to have "someone who understands me" or to think "she needs me." To want and to be wanted, and to have emotional needs satisfied is truly a good feeling but hardly enough of a basis for a lifetime relationship.

There is infatuation, artificial love, romantic love, and nature love. Infatuation is exciting and tingling, but it is shallow because the individual is responding to what he or she is getting out of the relationship. "It's real love—she loves *me!*" Artificial love stems from motives, often not even associated with love. Some individuals marry to escape from an unhappy parental relationship or home or from intense feelings of loneliness. Some marry so that they can find meaning in life by living through the accomplishments of their marital partner. Others marry for possessions, a change of scenery, the opportunity to travel to a distant place, or for money. These reasons for marrying are often based on artificial love.

Romantic love is storybook love. "Love means never having to say you're sorry." This kind of love carries with it immature beliefs such as the idea of the one and only, love at first sight, and the thought that love can solve all problems. Romantic love has its place. Some people experience this type of love several times in their lives before marrying. It can serve as a binding or cementing force to help a young couple through their first months, when adjustments are being made toward a more mature outlook on married life.[11] Mature love emerges out of human interaction. It comes about through the process of adjustment and readjustment of the personalities of two people who have a great regard for each other as total personalities and have a desire to do all that they can to make the other person's life meaningful and happy. An individual who is ready for marriage (1) likes the one who is loved, (2) is not merely in love with the idea of love, and (3) is emotionally mature to the point of surviving an adjustment period while still maintaining a high regard for the other person. Love, like a diamond, has many sides or facets to it to make it sparkle. If you experience only one or two facets of the diamond, you may miss a serious flaw in one of its other sides. You could be purchasing a worthless diamond. The same is true with love. You must look at all the different aspects of love before you can be sure you have a good love. Unlike a diamond, however, love can grow if it does not have any serious defects.

Frederic Lewis, Inc., New York City.

Accepting a marriage partner

The young adult is expected by his society to be able to love a person of the opposite sex and to choose a partner whom he will marry and live out his life. Studies of marriage for the past generation have tended to emphasize reasons for mate selection as the principal basis for explaining happy or unhappy outcomes. However, explaining what John sees in Mary or why they choose to marry each other can be complex indeed. Their reasons for selecting their mate will vary greatly. In any society, however, there are factors that generally affect and "partially" explain who marries whom. Certainly laws, religion, age, class, and race are factors that influence the choice of mates.

There are several influential reasons and theories why certain people come together. First, considerable study has centered around the propinquity theory as a major factor in mate choice. Propinquity means nearness or in close proximity. People who usually meet each other in some form of close association, such as at work, school, neighborhood, church, or leisure-time activity tend to gravitate together because of familiarity. A positive reaction to this association can become very meaningful. A second theory is related to the "ideal mate" concept, with traits and characteristics they would like to see in their marriage partner. "She's everything I've ever wanted." A person with this approach can usually make a list of the qualities they desire in a husband or wife. This theory is close to the value theory, which holds that each person possesses a value system that consciously or unconsciously guides them in their mate selection.[12]

The theory of complementary needs states that a person is attracted to another who has the characteristics he has always wished he had himself or who can help him to be the person that he needs and wants to be. Wish fulfillment is the motive for marriage. In people with deep psychological needs opposites do tend to attract, thus complementing the self.

A more widely recognized theory of why certain persons are chosen as marriage partners is the homogamy theory. In general, couples respond readily to each other if they have similar economic, racial, and social characteristics. Even the divorced and widowed tend to marry their kind.

The last theory is that of compatibility, which in all of its forms does much to bring couples together. Couples who can enjoy a variety of activities together and can communicate, understand, and accept each other because they share a common feeling or philosophy respond to each other deeply. They are compatible. It might be desirable to have complementary emotional needs patterns so that a couple can support and strengthen each other, but it would be just as important to have a supplementary or a common interest pattern in some aspects of their lives so that they can share wonderful experiences together. Love is a useful criterion in choosing a marriage partner. However, a more thorough, mutual understanding of the individuals involved is needed to discover the cause-and-effect relationships of why they chose each other.

Predictors of marital happiness

Although love is needed in marriage, it is not the sole requirement. Studies have been made to determine the ingredients of a successful marriage. The studies take on a specific pertinence in view of the increased divorce rate in society today. Unfortunately, there are so many variables involved and the personalities of individuals are so varied that it is difficult to make predictions for individual couples. However, suggestions related to success can be made for the group as a whole (Table 12-1).

One of the most comprehensive studies in the field of marriage was conducted by Stanford psychologist L. M. Terman[13] and his associates. In their project they tested and interviewed several thousand subjects

Table 12-1. Factors in marital happiness*

	FAVORABLE	UNFAVORABLE
Premarital factors		
1. Happiness of parents' marriage (high)	X	
a. Parents divorced		X
b. Parent or parents deceased		X
2. Personal happiness in childhood	X	
3. Ease of premarital contact with the opposite sex	X	
4. Mild, but firm discipline by parents	X	
5. Lack of conflict with parents	X	
6. Courtship		
a. Acquainted under one year		X
b. Acquainted over one year	X	
c. Approval of parents	X	
d. Similarity of age	X	
e. Satisfaction with affection of other	X	
7. Reason for marriage		
a. Love	X	
b. Loneliness		X
c. Escape from one's own family		X
d. Common interests	X	
Postmarital factors		
1. Attitudes		
a. Husband more dominant		X
b. Pair equalitarian	X	
c. Wife more dominant		X
d. Jealous of spouse		X
e. Feels superior to spouse		X
f. Feels more intelligent than spouse		X
2. Good relationships with in-laws	X	
3. Not living with in-laws	X	
4. Community of interest	X	
5. Desire for children	X	

*Based on data from Kirkpatrick, C.: The family: as process and institution, pp. 346-354, 599-617. Copyright 1955, The Ronald Press Co., New York.

and followed their progress. From the analysis of their data some surprising conclusions were drawn. It was found that their most important predictor of a happy marriage was the happiness of the parents in their marriage. Other factors were happiness during childhood and firm and consistent discipline during childhood.

In another area Terman found that adequacy of sex instruction, the amount of "petting" before marriage, the use of contraceptives, varieties and types of sexual techniques, and differences between how often intercourse is desired and the actual number of times it occurs had little or no relationship to marital happiness. Terman determined that marital happiness was more dependent as a whole on family background than on sexual factors. He concluded that "a large proportion of incompatible marriages are so because of a predisposition to unhappiness in one or the other spouse." The key is the type of attitude toward life and marriage that each partner has. An embittered pessimistic one has a poor prognosis.

Burgess and Locke[13a] also did a study on factors related to a successful marriage. Some of the predictors of happiness in marriage that they found were (1) possession of positive personality traits such as an optimistic temperament, emotional balance, and sympathetic attitude, (2) similarity of cultural backgrounds, (3) a socially responsive personality, (4) a harmonious family environment, (5) compatible religious observations, (6) satisfying occupation and working conditions, (7) a love relationship growing out of companionship rather than infatuation, and (8) a wholesome growth of attitudes toward sex relations. In general, Burgess and Locke consider the social environment within the marriage, the personality factors of the people involved, and the patterns and processes of family interaction. The success factors are always relative to the values held by the individuals and the society to which they respond.

Ultimately, the success of a marriage depends on the capacity of the man and woman to make it successful. This capacity involves personal values, personality traits, social characteristics, and ability to adapt, adjust, and change. The key factors are self-insight, self-acceptance, awareness of the needs of one's partner, and the ability to cope, understand, and accept. Expectations are crucial, since they give the individual a point of view that will affect his behavior. Consider these detrimental factors to happiness: intense personal problems, incongruity of main personality traits, inability to meet growing obligations, and poor outlook on life. They all reflect some inadequacy in personality maturity. It is important that the couple learn communicative as well as interpersonal social skills. How do you get along with others, living in a highly personal, close, intimate relationship? The skills required for prolonged, close living are somewhat different from those required for neighborly, occasional social contacts. The success of a marriage will depend largely on the psychological, emotional, and social readiness of the couple, individually and as a pair, to meet the demands of married living.

In addition, covert as well as overt personality and social characteristics are important. A predisposition to unhappiness or pessimism in one or both spouses can lead to unhappiness. No one appreciates or likes to live with a "gloomy gus." An optimistic point of view on life, in general, is desirable. It is interesting to know that all couples, happy and unhappy, have about the same number of grievances and problems in daily living. It turns out that the unhappy couples are the ones who are bothered by them more; they complain longer and more bitterly.

It would also be helpful socially if the couple enjoy some leisure-time activities together and hold some values in common. It is important for the husband and wife to be friends and companions to each other as well as lovers. Companionship has been singled out as being the primary basis for marital satisfaction.[14] It encompasses love, esteem, acceptance, insight, and enjoyment of the other individual, receiving as well as giving. It focuses primarily on the affectional relationship of a man and a woman, a husband and a wife.

BEING MARRIED

Getting married may seem like the biggest job to be done, especially to the one who has not found a marriage partner as yet. However, being married also requires an effort. There is an adjustment period to go through in which two people learn to live as one. Then there is the never-ending task of working with the problems, decisions, and unexpected circumstances that always seem to occur. Do not despair. Life is made up of changes, challenges, and choices. That is what it is all about. Meeting these situations individually and as a couple is what makes life interesting and exciting if you let yourself see it that way.

Developmental tasks of newlyweds

Marriage is a developmental process, and the conditions of the marriage are modified in time as people change and adjust to life's situations. A marriage keeps changing as each partner changes, and a successful marriage comes about through its potential for continued development and adaptation. Adjustment and attainment of the developmental tasks in early married life will do much to bring about desirable adult development and to lay the groundwork for success and happiness in marriage.

Very early in marriage the couple will need to (1) learn to live as a couple instead of singles, (2) work toward integrating their personality traits and styles of living, (3) achieve a satisfying sexual relationship and understanding, (4) become aware of acceptance of the realities of married life, and (5) evolve a marriage development plan that will bring to the couple their desired short-term and long-term goals in life. Some of the developmental tasks to be accomplished before the first child is born are (1) developing competency in decision making, (2) getting and spending the family income, (3) learning to accept and communicate each other's feelings, (4) developing an attitudinal, as well as material, readiness for parenthood, (5) learning social skills and increasing socialization as a couple instead of singles, (6) developing a pattern of cooperation and understanding that permits them to overcome adjustment problems with less friction, and (7) working out routine schedules and chore tasks around the house.[15]

To accommodate one's mate it sometimes is necessary to change some pet habits and develop new ways of doing things. Although one should not expect to "make people over" after marriage, both partners should be reasonable and considerate. Certainly no expectations of major change should be anticipated. The girl who says, "but I know he will not want to do that after we're married" may well be fooling herself and doing wishful thinking. Even simple behavior patterns and habits can be problems that require adjustment—how late one is used to staying up at night, whether one likes to shower in the morning or evening, being accustomed to eating at 5:30 instead of 6:30 P.M., sleeping with a window open, finding it hard to give up the personal privacy of a bathroom, learning how to accept relatives who are overwhelming.

Personal adjustment

The marriage relationship may have either a positive or a destructive influence on the psychological well-being of the husband or wife. It involves many of the most crucial adjustments a person will ever have to make. Each partner brings to marriage the equipment of motives, attitudes, and preferred modes of adjustment that have been learned through previous experiences.

The two personalities are brought into an intimate and pervasive contact that has unusual potentialities for working out emotional responses. Some adjustment problems, such as those of school or employment, can be relieved temporarily by evading or ignoring them, but the adjustments of marriage are less escapable. For a successful outcome the personalities of the partners in marriage must be complementary and harmonious at the outset or sufficiently flexible to make new adjustments without undue anxiety or hostility.

The success or failure of a marriage is popularly attributed to the "good" or "bad" character of the husband or wife. To the psychologists the main determiner of success is the quality of the adjustments that the husband and wife make to each other. The history of their childhoods is significant because the relationships in marriage have much in common with those experienced between a parent and child. A married person who retains either resentful or dependent attitudes toward his parents readily generalizes them to his spouse.[16]

An immature dependent wife may expect the same kind of treatment from her husband that she received from her father. She is therefore anxious and "hurt" when she is called on to assume adult responsibilities. On the other hand, a spouse who has developed rebellious attitudes toward his parents cannot handle the limitations on his freedom that marriage requires. He is always demanding and is angry when his wife's needs prevent the fulfillment of his desires.

If a couple can make the following adjustments, their marriage can be happy, successful, and fun. First, marriage requires a continuous process of adjustment by both members. Second, the couple must have an understanding and acceptance of each other as persons. Third, the couple must be aware of problems and solve them together. Fourth, the couple must learn to accept the insolvable problems. Fifth, the couple must have a desire for success in marriage. Sixth, marriage is not a fifty-fifty situation but, rather, a situation where the one member may give more in a certain aspect than the other.[17] Seventh, it is the interaction of psychological, interpersonal, social, sexual, and financial aspects that makes the marriage a success.

The constructive influence of marriage includes factors other than stable home life and sexual adjustment, although the importance of these primary satisfactions must not be minimized. The well-adjusted husband and wife provide a kind of continuous psychotherapy for one another. This close and confidential relationship aids each partner to gain insight into his or her attitudes and to feel the strength of a united effort against difficulties.

Sex in marriage

The function of sex in marriage is an integral part of the concept of marital oneness. It is so defined by society and culture. Many states have statutes defining legal married sexual intercourse. Religion and customs also influence the sexual attitudes of married couples. In recent years, however, psychologists, marriage experts, and other social scientists have broadened the definition of normal sexual intercourse to include acts that the couple themselves freely and willingly perform in the love-making ritual. One husband and wife may believe particular precopulatory tactile, visual, oral, and other activity a vital necessity. Another pair may regard as desirable anything but direct intromission.[18] The specific drives, attitudes, and outlooks of the married couple determine the nature, frequency, and attitude toward their particular sexual activities. Generally, it is important that the marriage partners understand each other's levels of sexual arousal, length of orgasm, sensitivity to tactile stimuli, and other facets leading up to and following intercourse.

The problem of sexual adjustment usually occurs during the early months of marriage. During this time, sexual relations will need to be followed with considerable care if the couple is to arrive at a fully satisfactory relationship. In a study of approximately 409 couples it was found that only about 65% achieved early satisfaction; 12.5% of couples took up to a year to do so; 10% of couples took from one to twenty years; and the remaining 12.5% of couples never reached a satisfactory relationship.[19] One should recognize that sexual satisfaction does not necessarily have to include consistently reaching orgasm or even that intercourse has to take place each time there is sexual play. The point of view of each partner will determine the nature of sexual satisfaction for themselves.

In situations where satisfaction is clearly far below an average expectancy after a few months of sincere effort, it will do little good merely to wait. Something more definite needs to be done for the couple to reach a satisfactory relationship. A counseling psychologist, marriage counselor, or physician should be consulted. Only in rare cases is such satisfaction impossible.

Sex in marriage provides a sense of mutual gratification between marriage partners. In fact it has been shown that far from becoming bored with the same sexual partner, in the great majority of marriages that have endured, the couple discovered that the exclusive mutuality of their married love was accompanied by increasing capacity to give and receive. Sex is a form of communication, probably the most intimate, in which two people express a oneness of mind and feeling.

Marital problems

Marital conflicts are not necessarily undesirable or harmful to a marriage if they do not involve attacks on the self-worth of the marriage partner. Conflicts can be healthy in exposing areas of dissatisfaction and can lead to their eventual resolution. An overriding need to make the marriage work is essential when a conflict occurs. If there is no attempt at making a successful marriage function under some stress or conflict, any conflict, however mild, will only serve to drive apart the partners of an already shaky marriage relationship.

The dynamics of conflict need to be understood. How does a person react under stress or frustration? Horney[20] has identified one form of reaction as externalization. Things being equal, people are likely to externalize their feelings by finding fault with others when the stresses and tensions that they normally carry become too burdensome. This reaction is frequent among men who work in competitive jobs where there is an emphasis to produce. When the husband returns home, he is irritable and anxious. The family suffers a great deal until the stress is relieved. As far as the wife is concerned, the social and career roles, as well as the husband's expectations of her, may create stress and result in externalization in the form of exaggerated behavior.

Another dynamic of conflict takes the form of concealed discord.[21] In this case the partners suppress their true feelings toward each other; they express them by frustrating the other partner or by dropping subtle remarks designed to hurt the other person. If the conflict is not resolved, ten-

Table 12-2. Analysis of 1,412 help-request letters addressed to the American Association of Marriage Counselors*

CATEGORY	HUSBAND (%)	WIFE (%)	TOTAL (%)
Affectional relations	11.5	31.0	27.6
Spouse cold, unaffectionate			
Spouse is in love with another			
Have no love feelings for spouse			
Spouse is not in love with me			
Spouse attracted to others, flirts			
Excessive, "insane" jealousy			
Sexual relations	42.1	20.6	24.4
Sexual relations "unsatisfactory"			
Orgasm inability; frigidity, impotence			
Sex deprivation; insufficient coitus			
Spouse wants "unnatural" sex relations			
Personality relations	23.4	17.2	18.3
Spouse domineering, selfish			
Own "poor" personality, instability			
Clash of personalities; incompatible			
Spouse's violent temper tantrums			
Spouse withdrawn, moody, "neurotic"			
Spouse quarrelsome, bickering, nagging			
Spouse irresponsible, undependable			
Intercultural relations	11.5	11.4	11.4
In-law relations troublesome			
Religion and religious behavior			
Deviant behavior	7.5	8.7	8.5
Heavy drinking, alcoholism of mate			
Own heavy drinking or alcoholism			
Spouse's "loose" sex behavior			
Own illicit sex behavior			
Compulsive gambling			
Role tasks–responsibilities	0.0	6.0	4.9
Disagreement over "who should do what"			
Spouse's failure to meet material needs			
Situational conditions	4.0	3.4	3.5
Financial difficulties, income lack			
Physical illness, spouse or self			
Parental-role relations	0.0	1.7	1.4
Conflict on child discipline			
Parent-child conflict			

*From De Burger, J. E.: Marital problems, helpseeking, and emotional orientation as revealed in helpseeking letters, J. Marriage Family **29**:712-721, 1967.

sion can build up over a period of time and suddenly explode when one of the partners can no longer contain it. Unresolved conflicts usually have a chronic effect on the marriage and may emerge as sexual unresponsiveness.

Conflict between two people may also be expressed by forms of resistance that make it difficult for the couple to resolve their differences. One form of resistance is a reluctance to admit that a marital problem exists; another form is a lack of communication between partners. Without communication all types of distortions and imagined grievances can occur. Occasionally, a partner will not communicate to avoid hostility and argument, or perhaps he will hold communication in abeyance, to be used strategically at the opportune time. Other dimensions of conflict include (1) dealing with symptoms rather than causes, (2) substituting superficial problems for the real problems, (3) generalizing a problem so that only the surface but none of the nitty-gritty details are recognized, and (4) intellectualizing the problem on a cognitive level to the point that the underlying feelings, which are highly important in conflicts, are ignored.

The areas from which marital problems can arise are numerous, and the problems themselves are complex (Table 12-2). The most often used term to describe an inability to get along is *incompatibility,* but it is only a general term that does not specify the conditions under which marital conflicts arise. Incompatibility, for example, may arise because the ethnic, religious, or cultural backgrounds of the couple are different; thus there may be differences with respect to attitudes, values, and what each partner may wish to achieve in life and marriage. Some conflicts arise simply because people do not know how to handle stress. Sometimes conflicts are intensified because neither partner has learned skills for dealing with conflicts. As a result, it is usually "the problem" that gets the blame and not the individual's inadequately prepared personality for dealing with problems.

What do most married couples quarrel about? What problems lead to separations and divorce? A University of Pennsylvania research team interviewed 300 couples, 200 of whom had once sought marital advice.[22] Husbands and wives, questioned separately, reported that the following problems bothered them most frequently: (1) money, (2) household management, (3) personality clashes, (4) sex, (5) sharing household jobs, (6) children, (7) leisure-time activities, (8) the husband's mother, (9) personal habits, (10) jealousy, (11) husband's occupation, and (12) the wife's mother. Infidelity ranged seventeenth on the list.

Many persons come to physicians with marital problems, even though they are not marital counselors. Herndon and Nash[23] reported the following problems mentioned in physicians' offices. The following problems were cited by men: (1) sex, (2) money, (3) too much or too little affection, (4) inability to discuss problems with wife, (5) in-laws, (6) failure of wife to express appreciation, (7) inability of wife to conceive, and (8) wife's fear of pregnancy. Women brought up problems related to (1) sex, (2) fear of pregnancy, (3) too much or too little affection, (4) money, (5) inability to discuss problems with husband, (6) failure of the husband to express appreciation, (7) inability to conceive, and (8) in-laws. For both men and women half of the first six most-mentioned problems had to do with appreciation and communication.

How important is sex in a marriage? It all depends upon whether you are male or female. Clifford Adams[24] at Pennsylvania State University ranks the importance of sex second with men and sixth with women. After studying 6,000 couples Adams reports that men rank the various ingredients of marriage in the following order: (1) companionship, (2) sex, (3) love-affection, (4) home and family, (5) encouraging helpmate, and (6) security. Women listed (1) love-affection, (2) security, (3) companionship, (4) home and family, (5) community acceptance, and (6) sex. Again social and emotional responses ranked high. Marriages founded on sexual attraction usually have a flimsy foundation on which to build.

We would like to make one last point concerning marital problems. Numerous studies will show that sex and money are most frequently mentioned by couples as their major problems. Experts have long known that these factors may simply be the outer manifestations of more crucial, deeper, underlying conflicts. There is a real need to "get to the root of the problem." Money problems are easy to pick on because so many people simply do not have enough money for everything they want to do. And how can two people feel free to have sexual intercourse with each other when underneath they are heartsick about the problems they are having with their marriage? It is difficult to have a satisfactory sexual relationship with someone who is causing you to have personal problems.

Crises in marriage

A crisis exists when the family faces a complicated state of affairs for which there is no available solution; for example, loss of income, infidelity, bereavement, and divorce. These crises may permanently disable the family involved, especially if the surviving members are incapable of absorbing the duties of the individuals handicapped by the crisis. On the other hand, the family may be drawn closer together by the threat to their cohesion and may emerge from the crisis stronger than ever.[25]

Loss of income. After the depression of 1929-1936 research found that many afflicted families surprisingly absorbed the shock of poverty without demoralization or great personal disorganization. The disorganization that did occur culminated when the family accepted the fact that it could not function by its old buying and living pattern. A period of emotional stress followed the loss of income, but it usually terminated with an adjustment to the situation; otherwise evidence of pathological reactions resulted.

A crisis, because it sweeps away the customary ways of living, tends to expose the resources or deficiencies of the family. The families studied who had refused to face issues in earlier family crises were found to have evaded facing the changes in family life brought about by sudden poverty. This crisis did not seem to cause new reactions, but it did seem to exaggerate family traits previously exhibited. For example, the occasional drinker began to drink excessively; the happy family became more unified and loyal.[26]

Infidelity. Infidelity is symptomatic that something is not as it should be in the marriage. It is hard to know whether it is cause or effect in a crisis. Many men and women turn to another person when they have been deeply hurt by their partner. The Kinsey report states that one fourth of the wives and one half of the husbands studied had at least one extramarital affair during their marriage. For women the incidence before the age of 30 years is low, after which the percentages sharply increase.[27]

A husband's infidelity may be an attempt to prove his manliness; it may be a revolt against his conscience; or it may possibly be a method of solving misunderstood impulses originating during childhood. His other woman may be a sanctuary from an overprotective wife or a means of "getting back" at his wife. Extramarital affairs are usually evidence of emotional immaturity in a marriage. However, in the Kinsey study[28] among 221 cases of infidelity by wives in which the husbands knew of the affair, only 42% created any serious difficulty in the marriage; 58% of the husbands seemed able to tolerate and forgive their wives' infidelity, and wives were even more tolerant of their husbands' infidelity.

It is important to consider the reasons that lie behind the problem. Generally, the problem is due to some need that is not being met by the marriage. Therefore it seems sensible for the couple to consult a professional counselor for help.

Bereavement. Prolonged illness and/or death of a member of a family is both a financial and emotional difficulty. A closely knit family will have more security on which to lean, and they will be more readily able to overcome the crises than the family without close ties.

Two things happen to a member of the family when another member dies: (1) he senses that the circle is broken and that the family is threatened, (2) he senses that a part of himself as a person has been lost. The first reaction is a sense of disbelief and then numbness, which helps to ease the shock.[29]

The routines of the funeral help the family to accept the idea of death, but afterward there is no professional help. This is the most difficult period. Families are supposed to adjust quickly and then carry on in a normal manner. Our personal experiences are that children generally do not manifest a change in their school work patterns until about the third month after the death. Then there is a lowering of grades and sometimes a start of behavior problems.[30]

Divorce. In a study that has long been accepted as classical, Burgess and Cottrell[31] found that men who marry between the ages of 28 and 30 years have the lowest divorce rate. Glick[32] found that girls who marry before they are 18 years old are nearly three times more likely to be divorced than are girls who marry when they are 22 to 24 years old. Why are early marriages generally less stable than later marriages? No one knows for sure, but there are several possible interpretations. Early marriages may simply reflect the socioeconomic pressure of this group. Also, chronologically immature people are likely to be emotionally immature and, in consequence, make unsound mate selections. Often early marriage curtails the husband's education; thus there would be greater economic pressures in early marriages than in later marriages. If the husband does continue his education while his wife works, he may "outgrow" her. Finally, in many young marriages the wife was pregnant before marriage; premarital pregnancy is correlated with a relatively high divorce rate.

The percentage of marriage failures, as reflected in divorce rates, has generally increased in American society since the 1920s. The current estimates based on numbers of marriages and divorces reported by the various states indicate that about one out of every four marriages is terminated by divorce or annulment compared to one out of eight marriages in 1922 and one out of twelve in 1900. In addition to this high rate of divorce 3% of all marriages are termi-

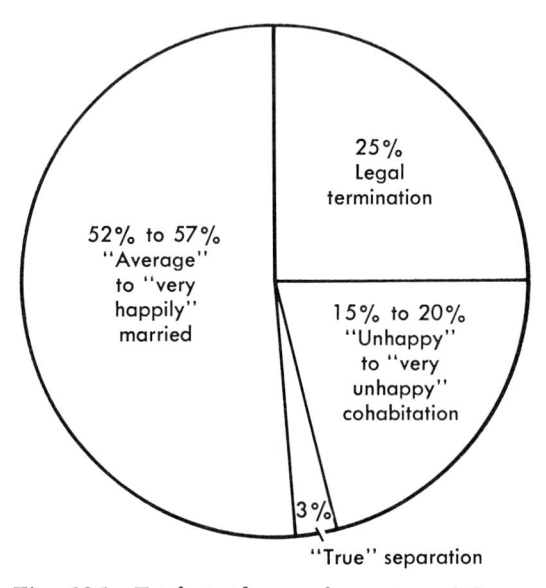

Fig. 12-1. Total incidence of marriage failure. (From Saxton, L.: The individual, marriage, and the family, ed. 2. Copyright 1968, 1972, by Wadsworth Publishing Co., Inc. Belmont, Calif. Reprinted by permission of the publisher.)

nated by "true separation," that is, those couples with legal decrees of separation, those living apart with the intention of obtaining a divorce, and those permanently or temporarily separated because of marital discord. Finally, numerous studies agree that about 15% to 20% of all married couples can be classified as unhappy cohabitants—those whose marriage is considered extremely unhappy, both by the couple themselves and by their friends (Fig. 12-1).[33] With statistics such as these it is little wonder that the young adult faces much trepidation on entering marriage.

According to Glick[34] about two thirds of the women and three fourths of the men who procure a divorce will ultimately remarry. About 20% of marriages involve cases in which one or both parties have been previously married. The time between divorce and remarriage on the average is 2.7 years, as compared with 3.5 years between widowhood and remarriage.

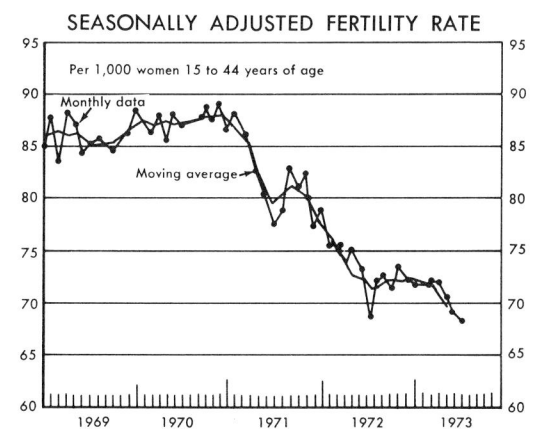

Fig. 12-2. The fertility rate in United States for a twelve-month period ending July, 1973, declined 7% compared to the previous year. Rate of natural increase was 5.9 persons per 1,000 population compared to 6.9 persons for the previous twelve months. Marriage rate in the same period was up 1.4% with 2.2 million marriages; divorce rate was up 9% with 884,000 divorces. (Redrawn from National Center for Health Statistics, Monthly Vital Statistics Report, vol. 22, no. 7, Sept., 1973.)

Parenthood

Among man's basic instincts is the procreation of the species. Starting a family is one of the developmental tasks of early adulthood. The nature of the task is to have a first child successfully. As for the psychological task of starting a family, Havighurst[35] raises the questions of acceptance or rejection of the pregnancy on the part of the woman, confidence in the physician, worry over possible failure to have a normal baby, desire for sexual relations during pregnancy, the uncertainty of breast feeding, and the matter of the reactions of relatives and friends to the pregnancy.

Probably the most crucial task is that of acceptance or rejection on the part of the mother. If she is scared or disgusted at the thought of pregnancy, the task will be difficult for her. The husband's attitude toward the baby must also be considered. An attitude of rejection on his part can have an effect on the woman and the family almost as serious as if the woman had rejected the pregnancy.

Next in order of importance is confidence in the physician. To some extent he will have both lives in his hands during the period of birth. The woman's confidence in her physician can cure many lingering doubts she may have about her pregnancy.

Some women experience little desire for sexual intercourse during pregnancy, whereas others have increased sexual desire. The adjustment of the husband's sexual behavior is important. If he cannot adjust adequately, the woman may not accept another pregnancy.

There can be a deep sense of pride in being pregnant since the mother "makes" the baby. The sense of pride, however, also fills her with concern about the many possible "things that could go wrong." While fathers pace up and down hospital floors waiting for the baby to be born, the mother is afraid of miscarriage, neonatal death, or a deformed baby.

The question of breastfeeding can be answered with a sterilized bottle and enriched milk. Many women in the past decades preferred not to nurse the child. There seems to be a general trend back toward breastfeeding, if only as a reaction to the pollution and contamination that modern society has unwittingly engineered. Some reject breastfeeding. The woman might worry about her figure; her husband might think that breastfeeding will tie his wife to the baby's side and cut down on their social activities.

Finally, the reaction of friends and relatives should be considered. The in-laws especially may express adverse opinions about the entire idea of having a baby or of what to do with him after he is born. This seems to be the least tenuous task.

Once the child is born, the family life revolves around the newborn child for some time. During this period the parents have to adjust to new demands placed on their time and energy. One young couple said, "The baby can be quite demanding of attention and help; often at times it is a real sacrifice to stop whatever you're doing and tend to his needs." The early years of childhood are day-to-day happenings in which the child slowly develops physically, emotionally, socially, morally, and mentally.

THE UNMARRIED YOUNG ADULT

For the adult choosing the single life the anxieties do not lessen. Although the unmarried young adult has more freedom to leave home, to change jobs, and to travel and see the world, he still faces subtle social pressures because of his single status. The longer he waits to get married, the more obvious the pressures become. A man over 30 years of age is often suspect if he is not married. This single status may even affect his chances of getting certain jobs.

Of the men still unmarried at 30 years of age, 70% will ultimately marry; of the girls still unmarried at 30 years, 55% will marry before 50 years of age. Of those still unmarried at 35 years, half the men and about one third of the women will marry. By 40 years of age the men's chances have been reduced to one in four and the women's chances to about one in six.[36]

These statistics may be interesting, but on the whole they are not too reassuring. The young adult cannot tell for certain whether he or she may be that one person out of ten in the United States who goes through life unmarried. By the time a young woman reaches the age of 30 years the chances are still about even that she will never marry. The same is approximately true for the man of 35 years of age. Under such circumstances it would be folly for either of them to ignore the wisdom of making some plans for life adjustment without marriage. Although they ought to keep their eyes open for the possibilities of marriage, they ought to give equal or even greater consideration to the successful management of life as single persons.

There are several things for which the young adult needs to prepare himself if he is to be happy although unmarried. Too many unmarried people develop exaggerated forms of behavior or eccentric personalities because they resigned themselves too soon to a life of isolation, loneliness, and negativism. History reveals many people who, without benefit of marriage, have lived happy, successful, and socially congenial lives.

The young adult should prepare himself for some creative career in life and give himself to it with the same romantic abandon he might have given to love and marriage. The unenthusiastic person is pretty much of a dud, whether single or married. Many a librarian, a nurse, a school teacher, although well past the age when she might expect to attract men, has been discovered by some man looking for a woman who could forget herself in her enthusiasm for her cause.[37]

However, aside from the enhancement of her chances for matrimony, such an attitude toward life and work makes the person interesting. If it cannot be called a substitute for marriage, it certainly is one of the most realistic antidotes for the anguish of loneliness. It is an attitude likely to make friends, and in the long run friends are what count for most in life.

MATURITY AND THE EARLY ADULT

To understand what adult maturity is it is better to think in terms of principles that reflect the nature of maturity rather than to consider a list of specific forms of behavior. One could not possibly cover all the types of "mature behavior" that exist. The first principle is that the mature adult has developed a system of internal and external behavior controls which are acceptable on the adult level. Ever since this individual was an early adolescent, he has been trying to learn how to control his emotions and behavior so they would be acceptable to society at large. As an adult, he should have reached this goal.

The second principle is that the mature individual has developed a value-judgment system which would enable him to live acceptably within a social group. This value-judgment system is a personal philosophy of what is important or unimportant, good or evil, desirable or undesirable. It enables the individual to make choices and decisions that are in keeping with what he considers to be his individuality and his personal well-being. At the same time his value-judgment pattern should permit him to live within a social pattern. He may not necessarily live as others do, but at least he is not offensive to the point that they reject him.

Traits of maturity

The mature individual has perspective. His behavior is based on a good balance of intellectual insights and some emotions and imagination. He learns to live with problems he recognizes as unsolvable and works to find a solution for those that can be solved. He is open to suggestion but is not overly influenced by others. He learns to profit not only by his own experience but also from the experience of others.

He has some knowledge of social life, love and marriage, and the requirements for living in a society. He takes responsibility for his own welfare, does not expect others to make decisions for him, and is willing to work for what he wants. The mature adult lives partly by intelligent compromise, but at the same time he respects his own individuality. Along with this he accepts authority to the point that he knows that the first attempt to improve a situation should be through rational discussion.

The mature individual also takes responsibility for his own behavior. He does not blame his background for mistakes he makes or use it as an excuse for a shortcoming. He does not evade responsibility or put the blame on someone else.

The mature adult realizes the relation of personal gain to personal effort. He is able to endure present discomfort for future gain and satisfaction. His behavior is based on principles. He does things because he considers them as values and not because someone forces him to do so. According to Bell,[38] maturity refers to a person's ability and motivation to accept adult rights and obligations in a variety of adult role relationships. Adult responsibility entails attempting to deal with all contingencies as sincerely as possible.

Individuals in this age group, because of the recency of their exposure to the demands and expectations of a formalized learning environment, are probably more receptive to learning than any other age group. However, young adults, especially those who are married, are plagued by numerous distractions that may constitute barriers in the learning process. Some of these are adjusting to marriage, getting ahead on the job, rearing a family, buying a home, and the like. The degree to which these tasks constitute barriers in the educational process depends on the maturity of the learner.[39]

Heath[40] did a study on maturity that compared definitions of maturity as written by experts and by nonexperts. Definitions of maturity from the writings of thirty-five expert psychologists were collected. These definitions were based on rich and intimate experiences with a wide range of persons or on the results of diffuse and general empirical observations. Forty-three nonexpert college male youths were asked to select the most mature person they knew and in 5 to 10 minutes describe his most central characteristics. A content analysis was made of both sets of definitions.

Without any pretension of having exhausted available expert definitions or of having used the most rigorous of empirical procedures, the most striking result of the study was the essential similarity of the traits selected both by nonexperts (in 5 to 10 minutes of reflection) and by experts (after years of reflection). Both groups of judges agreed on eight of the thirteen trait categories. In both cases the mature person emerges as a judiciously realistic individual with a reflective sense of values and an underlying meaning to his life that he maintains with integrity. However, he is not closed to new experience but is open to continued growth. Such a person can adapt to others and can tolerate and control most of the tensions of living. He has a basic human warmth or compassion and respect for his fellow man. The experts add that he is integrated, basically accepting of himself, self-reliant, capable of tender, loving relationships, and creative. The nonexperts say the mature person has wide interests, is happily married, has close family ties, is generous, empathic, and sensitive to others.

Hierarchy of basic values

Man has values. He tries to reach for his total potentiality. Animals, pretty much, have a "horizontal development." Once they have established their systems for survival and response, they seem to be limited in growth of value insight. Some animals, such as our pet cat Paddy, do seem to have some humanlike qualities, but on examination their value system is greatly restricted in scope and depth. Man, however, is capable of "vertical development." Not only does he learn survival values but he also learns human values and spiritual values.

Maslow's hierarchy of basic needs[41] can be translated readily into a hierarchy of basic values. The level of values and needs closest to survival are the physiological needs of food, water, sex, and other biological needs. Security needs represent a step-up in values, as manifested in the economic needs of man to make money and collect material possessions. The money-hungry person may live most of his life on this level. Some animals also collect materials, in terms of food, to last them over the winter months. Recreation or play needs are a step-up in the ladder of values. To have some fun and to partake in leisure-time activities it is necessary to re-create the body and spirit. (See Table 12-3.)

It is more fun to play with someone, however, so people move up to a category more closely resembling human needs. Belonging to a group, having friends, and being part of an organization have association values. Some people stress these values more than any others. But people also talk about reputation and "being well thought of" so that on a higher level there are character values, which go beyond the individual's need to just be part of a group. A man could live a whole lifetime on the character value level, and when he died, people could say, "He was a good man." Yet he may not have made the most of his potential as a human being. There is a higher category of values on the intrinsic, abstract level.

This same man could have made more use of his intellect in a search for truth, intellectual values, curiosity, or seeking just for the sake of learning. Even beyond that

Table 12-3. Hierarchy of basic needs and values in pursuit of self-realization*

Highest	Spiritual needs and values	Devotion to ideal beyond the self
"Others"	Association needs and values	Beauty, creativeness, nature
	Intellectual needs and values	Understanding, knowledge, curiosity
"We"	Character needs and values	Respect, self-esteem, independence
	Association needs and values	Friends, belongingness, love
"I"	Recreational needs and values	Pleasure, leisure time
	Economic needs and values	Material possessions, comfort
Lowest	Physiological needs and values	Food, drink, sex, security

*Based on data from Maslow, A. H.: Toward a psychology of being, ed. 2, New York, 1968, Van Nostrand Reinhold Co.

are the values of creativity and material beauty. Things that have been created by the hands and minds of man are precious, and so are the things of nature that have been created by wondrous ways. The highest intrinsic level to which man can aspire is the total being or spiritual level—the level of self-actualization wherein man gives of himself in devotion to an ideal beyond himself. On this level personal, material needs are transcended for the common welfare. The self-actualized man, the mature person, according to Maslow,[42] has a realistic orientation, is accepting of self, has spontaneity, is task oriented, has a sense of privacy, independence, appreciativeness, and spirituality, has a sense of identity with mankind, a feeling of intimacy with loved ones, democratic values, philosophical humor, creativeness, and some nonconformity.

All the needs and values on the hierarchy are important; at times some are more important than others. Certainly if a man is starving, his physiological needs must be met. What is crucial, however, all things being equal, is which category or which values does the individual tend to emphasize as his prime motivator of behavior? Does he emphasize the survival values, the social values, or the intrinsic values? What he stresses will determine his basic philosophy of life and his level of maturity in terms of potential as a human being.

To keep a proper perspective on life there are four things that a person ought to do at least once a year. He should visit a museum to see what the creative mind of man has been able to produce throughout the years and to note that modern man does not have a claim to an intellect which is superior to that of ancient man. Cromagnon man was also an intellectual giant. Modern man should use his creative powers just as the cave man did. Second, he should attend a wedding to see and feel the excitement of a couple getting together, prayerfully, for a lifetime together to raise children and to create a home and a family unit. Third, he should go to a hospital to visit some sick friends to see the frailty of man and his body—to be reminded that the physical housing of humans is perishable and destructible and that the individual must take care of it. Finally, he should attend a funeral, at least once a year, to be reminded that this life is limited, that there is an end. This will reinforce a person's awareness that physical things die but that intrinsic, spiritual things continue to live even after the physical death. A proper perspective on life is needed to encourage human beings to seek the better parts of this earthly existence.

STUDY GUIDE

1. What is meant by "the developing years" or "the age of expansion"?

2. Review the developmental tasks of early adulthood. How many of these tasks are you in the process of achieving, have achieved, or will be starting to achieve soon?
3. Personal independence implies emotional independence, social independence, and economic independence. How are these forms of independence interrelated? How do they aid and abet, or possibly interfere with, career development?
4. What are the "whys and wherefores" of marriage? In print and in the news media descriptions have currently appeared about "communal living" with the concept of shared partners, about unmarried couples living together without the confining demands of marital ties, about clubs and apartments for "singles." Several authors suggest that "marriage is on the way out." What do you think? Do you agree or disagree?
5. What is love?
6. What appears to be the central ingredient for a successful, happy marriage? "It all boils down to . . ."
7. Several studies are cited as predictors of marital happiness. Make a composite list of these predictors and compare it to Table 12-1.
8. Review the developmental tasks of a newly married couple.
9. Marital problems are often adjustment problems. Different kinds of adjustment need to be made at different stages of a marriage. Can you think of changes in life style or life patterns that may necessitate a change and an adjustment of the couple in their thinking and behavior toward each other?
10. The section describing the unmarried adult is not intended to suggest that unmarried adults represent a deviant type of behavior. Unmarried adults do constitute a minority, however, in a marriage-oriented society. With the mediam age of marriage getting slightly higher (older) and with the current emphasis on "singles" cultures and living, how do you view the unmarried adult in today's society? How do you see this person ten years from now? Twenty years from now?
11. What constitutes maturity of adults?
12. What do you consider to be your main emphasis, philosophically and pragmatically, in terms of the hierarchy of basic values presented in the last section?
13. What is it like to be an adult 21 to 30 years of age? What are the sociological, psychological, and physiological factors involved?

REFERENCES

1. Hurlock, E. B.: Developmental psychology, ed. 3, New York, 1968, McGraw-Hill Book Co., p. 535.
2. Havighurst, R. J.: Developmental tasks and education, Toronto, 1958, Longmans, Green & Co., Inc., p. 75.
3. Butterfield, O.: Planning for marriage, Princeton, N. J., 1956, D. Van Nostrand Co., Inc., p. 130.
4. Peters, N. J., and Hansen, J. C.: Vocational guidance and career development, New York, 1966, The Macmillan Co., p. 381.
5. Zytowski, D. G.: Toward a theory of career development for women, Personnel Guid. J. 47:660-664, 1967.
6. Hass, K.: Understanding adjustment and behavior, Englewood Cliffs, N. J., 1970, Prentice-Hall, Inc., p. 129.
7. Duvall, E. M.: When you marry, Lexington, Mass., 1953, D. C. Heath & Co., p. 15.
8. Bowman, H. A.: Marriage for moderns, ed. 6, New York, 1970, McGraw-Hill Book Co., p. 317.
9. Saxton, L.: The individual, marriage, and the family, Belmont, Calif., 1968, Wadsworth Publishing Co., Inc., pp. 346-347.
10. Cox, R.: Youth into maturity, New York, 1970, Mental Health Materials Center, p. 180.
11. Boodish, H.: Psychology for today's living. II. Love, romance, and marriage, Soc. Stud. **55:** 143, April, 1964.
12. Landis, P.: Making the most of marriage, New York, 1965, Appleton-Century-Crofts, pp. 259-264.
13. Terman, L. M.: Psychological factors in men-

tal happiness, New York, 1938, McGraw-Hill Book Co., p. 110.
13a. Burgess, E. W., and Locke, H. J.: The family: from institution to companionship, ed. 2, New York, 1953, American Book, pp. 431-437.
14. Hawkins, J. L.: Associations between companionship, hostility, and marital satisfaction, J. Marriage Family 17:282, 1970.
15. Kenkel, W. F.: The family in perspective, New York, 1966, Appleton-Century-Crofts, pp. 19-25.
16. Shaffer, L., and Shohen, E.: The psychology of adjustment, Boston, 1956, Houghton Mifflin Co., pp. 578-584.
17. Duvall, op. cit., pp. 309-315.
18. Hass, op. cit., p. 117.
19. Landis, J., and Landis, M. G.: Building a successful marriage, Englewood Cliffs, N. J., 1952, Prentice-Hall, Inc., p. 239.
20. Horney, K.: Neurosis and human growth, New York, 1950, W. W. Norton & Co., Inc., pp. 178-179.
21. Lantz, H. R., and Snyder, E. C.: Marriage, an examination of the man-woman relationship, Carbondale, Ill., 1962, Southern Illinois University, p. 228.
22. Problems of marriage, Parade, p. 28, Nov. 6, 1966.
23. Herndon, C. N., and Nash, E. M.: Premarriage and marriage counseling: a study of North Carolina physicians, J.A.M.A. 180:395-401, 1962.
24. Sense of values, Parade, p. 12, Nov. 2, 1969.
25. Koos, E. L.: Clan differences in family reactions to crises, Marriage Family Living, pp. 77-78, Summer, 1950.
26. Cavan, R. S., and Ranck, K. H.: The family and the Depression, Chicago, 1958, University of Chicago Press, pp. vii-8.
27. Kinsey, A. C., and others: Sexual behavior in the human female, Philadelphia, 1953, W. B. Saunders Co., pp. 416-417.
28. Ibid., pp. 434-436.
29. Duvall, op. cit., p. 307.
30. Kaluger, G.: Problems of adolescence (unpublished data), 1962.
31. Burgess, E. W., and Cottrell, L. S.: Predicting success or failure in marriage, Englewood Cliffs, N. J., 1939, Prentice-Hall, Inc., p. 37.
32. Glick, P. G.: American families, New York, 1957, John Wiley & Sons, Inc., p. 136.
33. Saxton, op. cit., p. 212.
34. Glick, op. cit., pp. 138-139.
35. Havighurst, op. cit., p. 78ff.
36. Butterfield, op. cit., pp. 315-316.
37. Ibid., p. 317.
38. Bell, R. K.: Marriage and family interaction, Homewood, Ill., 1967, Dorsey Press, p. 122.
39. Vontress, C.: Adult life styles: implications for education, Adult Lead., p. 90, May, 1970.
40. Heath, D.: Explorations of maturity, New York, 1965, Appleton-Century-Crofts, pp. 3-8.
41. Maslow, A. H.: Motivation and personality, New York, 1954, Harper & Row, Publishers, p. 154.
42. Maslow, A. H.: Some basic propositions of a growth and self-actualization psychology. In Perceiving, behavior, becoming: a new focus for education, Washington, D. C., 1962, Yearbook of the Association of Supervision and Curriculum Development, National Education Association.

13 Middle adulthood
The years of stability

MIDDLE ADULTHOOD: ON THE OTHER SIDE OF FORTY

Some years ago, during my undergraduate years in college, I read a book entitled, *The Best Is Yet to Come*. I don't recall the author or much that was written other than, as each stage of life was described, the author developed the theme that when an individual was in a certain stage in life, even though he was contented and happy, the best was yet to come. I remember that in the later stages of life the author believed that then and then only did the individual realize real contentment as he evaluated his life and looked toward death, believing that the best was yet to come. Young at the time, in my early twenties, I remember thinking, "Well, that's his opinion."

Today, on the other side of 40, I am inclined to think that perhaps the author knew what he was talking about. Does life begin at 40? Well, it depends on what you mean concerning "life."

If you mean that physical life begins at 40 years, we all know that isn't so. By that age, after having lived over 45 years—days and nights—physical being is definitely not beginning. Oh, no, physical suffering would be more like it! If you have had a healthy body, prepare for aches and pains of a general nature to creep into your being. Chronic illnesses may emerge at this time so that yearly checkups begin to make sense. Believe me, even the faithful eyes that have always seen everything and never failed begin to sting, water, and even blur everything together. Needles can no longer be threaded. Help is obviously needed.

On the other hand, when you are on the other side of 40, you have begun to accept your limitations. A certain amount of rest is needed so you see that you get it—not because some health book tells you but because you know you have to have it. You also follow a sensible diet because you now know that you alone will suffer the consequences if you don't. It is easier to do the right thing after you are 40 years old. You accept and understand what must be and go on from there.

You don't become so upset over the trivial things of life. By the age of 40 years you have experienced enough really important incidents of life so that energy is not wasted on the unimportant. What once seemed likely to be "the end of the world" is no longer viewed disproportionately. Little things are left to take care of themselves, and activities and problems are kept in their proper place.

When you are young, you have so many dreams and ideals. When you are over 40 years old, you now know that some of these dreams will never come true. Rich? Probably you will never be rich in material things, only in the things that make your life what you want it to be. You no longer plan to conquer or improve the world. You no longer expect the impossible from yourself or from those you love. What a relief! Now you can settle down to do the kind of thing you can do well and be satisfied with the doing of it. Gone is frustration. Now you can be satisfied. Now you can realize self-fulfillment in many facets of life.

If you are a parent, by this time your children are well on their way to adulthood. How nice it is not to wash diapers, observe schedules, and pick up after messy children! How proud you can be of your children and their accomplishments. How great it is to discuss interesting affairs of the world with them. If you are so fortunate as to be the mother of sons, how delightful it is to be "spoiled" by these fast-growing men. I love every minute of it!

Married couples who are over 40 years old have found the person they most want to be married to. Long ago they have given up changing the other member in their marriage. They accept him, limitations, behavior lackings, and all, and are thankful for them. So what if your husband is not the greatest lover of the century. After all, you are no prize package yourself. Positive attributes are appreciated, and negative aspects are either forgotten or overlooked. It is so nice to love and be loved just as one is. Gone are the role playing, games, and lack of communication that characterize a new marriage. Understanding and insight have taken over, and it is marvelous!

The sad part of being on the other side of 40 years is that you begin losing some of your loved ones, especially those parents whom you have loved for so long. Sitting through my own dear mother's funeral and listening to the preacher expound on some of the familiar and beautiful passages from the Bible: "I am the Way and the Life . . . The Lord is my Shepherd," I was suddenly overwhelmed with the feeling that this is what life is all about. Life does go on! Life does have meaning! Wonderful!

When you are over 40, you don't have to keep up with the Joneses any more. In fact, who cares about the Joneses? Let them have or do what pleases them, and we'll find our own satisfaction. How free it is to relax with those of your choosing, those you really enjoy being with, and no longer worry what others will think.

Being on the other side of 40 is nice career-wise, too. By now you hope that you have developed some common sense and learned some valuable lessons from experience which will enable you to do a better job. Some of us have reached our goals or see them in sight. Some of our dreams have been fulfilled.

Intellectually, it is pleasant to know a little bit about a lot of things. It is also good to realize that even though you can't know everything—ever—you can know where to find out what you don't know. This calms down nervous feelings of inferiority. By 40 years of age you know that others are just like you. No one is ever perfect. There is a lot of congenial give-and-take and little pretense at this time.

At 40, or on the other side, you can look at the world, love it; look at yourself, accept it; and feel that it's a great thing to be alive after all. Life is meaningful and fulfilling, and the best is yet to come!

Forty?
Contented, fulfilled,
Facing the future confidently,
*   Enjoying the present.*
The other side is best.

The developmental trend has come to that point in time known as "middle age" or as our Pennsylvania Dutch friends say, "Ve get too soon oldt, und too late schmart." They also say, "Throw the horse over the fence some hay," which does not make much sense. But, then, to many people middle age does not make much sense, yet somehow the message gets across. However, we are not here to condemn middle age. We wish to present it in its proper perspective and place in the total life-span. It can be a beautiful time of life because it ushers in the years of stability and freedom.

Early adulthood comprises the "developing years"—that period when all growth movement is vertical, upward and forward. The expansion phase of adulthood is a fast-moving period in which the young adult strives to achieve mastery over the external world, seeking material gain and approval of others. Sooner or later in each life there comes a time when the expansion phase tapers off. When and how this time occurs varies. It may come when the man finds himself looking over his life situation and saying, "You know, if I can just maintain what I now have and am for the rest of my working days, I would be happy." To maintain the status quo, to just keep pace, to live and let live because life is satisfying at that point is to have arrived at the years of stability, where life will be on a more even keel. Now is the time when a person can turn his interests inward to achieve self-satisfaction and self-mastery. Activities that offer personal satisfaction can now be most important. The children are out of school, many of them are married, and the mother and father now have more time for each other and their own interests.

As with most age levels, it is difficult to cite an age at which middle adulthood begins and ends. When one reads the literature, it is interesting to note that as the lifespan of man lengthens into the upper seventies, the ages cited for different adult levels are shifted upward. Three and four decades ago middle adulthood, or midlife, was indicated as starting at the age of 30 years, and in some cases at 25 years, and extending to 45 and 50 years of age. More recent writings equate the late thirties or the early forties as the beginning of middle age and continuing to the early sixties. There is more agreement on the circumstances that surround these years than on the actual age range itself. Middle age is generalized as the period between the time when the traditional roles of child rearing and becoming established as a provider have been completed and full retirement. The intervening period is one of more personal freedom, less economic stress, greater availability of leisure time, and fewer demands for material growth.

Developmental tasks

The connotation of the years of stability and freedom can be grasped more clearly by examining the developmental tasks of middle adulthood. The tasks are more intrinsic in nature; they relate to interpersonal roles as well as intrapersonal development, and for the first time many of them stress the "comforts" of life.[1]

This is a time for the renewal and full development of the wife-husband relationship. It is a time of cutting through the thick overlay of habits of child-centered days and of nurturing a deep and abiding intimacy as a couple. This renewed awareness of the initial relationship in the marriage partnership will lead to rich and satisfying interaction between husband and wife. The couple will find encouragement, support, and reassurance from each other. There will be the time and desire to do things as a couple again and to find each other after years of struggling with the physical, financial, and emotional strain of parenthood.

The joint responsibility that seems to be most difficult for couples at this time is the finding of each other as individuals again and of redefining or modifying their roles as husband and wife. The ability to meet each other's needs emotionally and sexually at this time is a goal to which the middle-aged couple must address itself if this drawing together is to become a reality. The man and woman need to reassure and fully accept one another as they are at this moment if their individual identity is to be recognized and, with that, their identity as a couple. Learning to share feelings and satisfactions and to recognize and appreciate each other as individuals who have desires, aspirations, and disappointments will lead to a fuller life for both partners.

The "mature" mother responds to the tasks of middle adulthood with the serenity born of a knowledge of "selfhood" that has been nurtured over the years. Her children are free to develop as persons without her being emotionally dependent on them. She feels no threat in sharing the affection of her offspring as their circle of social contacts grows. Standing by to assist their children practically or in an emotionally supportive way is a positive task of the mother and father at this stage in life.

Development of creativity that has perhaps lain dormant during the child-rearing phase can be a highly satisfying task of the woman or man at this point in life. This may take the form of career pursual or resumption, of an active part in civic, social, or religious organizations, and of exploring new hobbies and areas of talent and skill. The satisfactory use of leisure will be a source of contentment and bring feelings of self-worth to the woman of this age group. The use of leisure time is the task that befuddles the male born and brought up in the utilitarian framework of American culture. This task is a "natural" for those who have learned the art of the "minivacation" and the joy of the long weekend, but to many serious, competitive business and professional men this poses a great challenge.

Mature social and civic responsibility is a goal toward which the middle-aged adult must grow. This includes the understanding of one's civic responsibilities and how one can fit into the broad scheme of civic and social betterment of the world. As a rule, at this time the man and the woman have the time and vision to make their mature judgment a source of community, national, and international contribution.

The middle-aged adult also faces the task of developing a wholesome relationship with aging parents. Being aware of their interests and needs without allowing dominance or undue dependence to creep in requires much maturity and compassion. The adult of this age must stand as a bridge between the younger generation and the aging parent, allowing each to understand and value the other.

The middle-aged woman must come to terms with the changes in her physical being. Menopause must be viewed as a normal functional change rather than a threat to youth and desirability. Distress at signs of changes in hair, skin, and energy output tend to rob the woman of the ability to face the task at hand—that of "relishing the bloom and pace of maturity as a woman."[2]

Creation and maintenance of a pleasant home occupies the adult at this stage, meaning the enrichment of the existing home for nine out of ten couples to meet the needs and long unrealized desires of the couple. For the other small percentage of couples this may mean moving to an apartment and giving up what is considered a burdensome house and yard.

Learning to hit a balance between spending money for personal gratification and putting aside funds for future security is another challenge for the family unit. Many couples find great joy in "living it up" without neglecting their future security needs now that their children have been successfully launched. Conversely, some cannot free themselves of their former frugal habits and cannot strike a healthy balance between having some fun and salting away every available cent for the proverbial rainy day.

At this time in life the task of intergenerational adjustment comes to the fore as well. The new in-law and grandparent roles are now part of the middle-aged adult's emotional scope. The way in which each member accepts these new roles, whether enthusiastically or reluctantly, will determine in some measure his contentment at this time. Fragmentation of the whole family unit may result, with its ensuing loneliness and heartache if this task is not successfully met. Middle-aged couples must rise to the occasion and realize the enrichment that these relationships can bring to their lives.

There is an important lesson to be learned in middle age—that all that any of us really has is the moment we are now living. The time has come to be prudent about how much stress should continue to be placed on "saving for a rainy day." The world of economics is different today. Life is also short, and there are no guarantees. Now is the time to enjoy, the time to fulfill dreams.

The youth cult threat: a commentary

For some not entirely clear reason the United States has developed a thought form that places great stress on the desirability of being young, looking young, and feeling young. The emphasis on youth has been overwhelming—so much so that youth fashions dictate mature adult fashions; youth foods dictate the eating and drinking styles of many middle-aged persons; and social pronouncements by youth have been influential in dictating the degree and type of value acceptance by the older generation. The overabundance of "youth-a-mania" has done much to confuse the self-concept image and identity of middle adulthood.

As a group, the middle-age group seems to feel a need for a prestige role in American society. The age group of 40 to 60 years comprises about one fifth of the population, yet it is this group that occupies the seats of power, foots the bills, and makes decisions that affect the other four fifths of the people. It is the "command generation."[3] Nevertheless, this age group needs to feel that its role as the command generation is approved by those around them, rather than to feel defensive or self-conscious. Their chief antagonist is the youth cult in the United States.

The self-concept of the middle-aged is further fragmented by the humorists, who enjoy capitalizing on a reluctance of many people to release their hold on youth and its often-glorified advantages. We saw a cartoon recently in which a man is saying to his wife, who is hiding under the bed, "But, Ethel, everyone has to become 40 some day!" Most oldsters forget how they dreaded becoming 30 years old. And how many people refer to middle age as "fifteen years older than I am"? Humorist Peg Bracken[4] notes the period as "not quite twilight, and certainly not bedtime! Call it the cocktail hour, the happy hour, or high tea if you prefer." She refers to contemporaries who resist the aging process as victims of the "Peter Pan syndrome: everyone else is supposed to grow older but me."

Age needs to be put into its proper perspective without the undue distortions caused by the beating advertising drums from Madison Avenue. It is not that 40 years is so awfully old, it is just that being 20 years old is so awfully young! How much has a 20-year-old really lived and experienced of life? If we are speaking of a person who went to college, he actually has spent almost all his life "going to school." Is this living? Think of what a person does in the second twenty years of his life as compared to the first twenty years. It is in that second twenty-year period that life is lived, loved, lost, laughed at, regained, reconstituted, enhanced! Change is an inevitable aspect of life. The man of 40 years is different in many ways from the youth of 20. The 40-year-old man anticipates change and knows how to bring about desired changes. By this age life has meaning based on having been lived, not on the expectations of what will be. The forties are the old age of youth; the fifties are the youth of old age.

Probably most people associate getting older with a loss of the physical attractiveness of youth. But ask the question, "At what age does a woman reach her highest peak of physical attractiveness?" Pick an age, any age from one to a hundred. Would you believe that the majority of people are their most attractive in their late thirties and early forties? It is at the age of 38 years that the average adult reaches his peak of total development. That could be hard to see if you are in your early twenties, but it is true. There is an essence of beauty and attractiveness that can only come with age. Call it a mellowness, if you wish. It is an inner glow that manifests itself outwardly in beauty. It takes time to mature. For physical beauty we would choose women in their late thirties; for excitement and exuberance in living, the twenties; for volatileness, the teens; for simplicity of life and faith, the little child; for charm, graciousness, and sincerity, old age. On the college campus it is always interesting to visit the various five-year reunion classes on alumni day. Invariably, the most attractive women and men are in the twentieth year reunion class. They know how to dress, how to communicate, and how to be attractive. Each class, however, has its own aura of attractiveness about it, each in its own way.

A final word on attractiveness. Each age level has its own criteria for attractiveness. The important thing for the individual is to learn how to be attractive to people of his or her own age level, not to those who are twenty years younger (or older) than themselves. It is important for adults, women especially, to keep up with changing fashions for their age levels, particularly hair styles. What looked good on the individual in college may continue to be attractive for another five years or so, but at some point a change in clothing or hair style may be needed. Some men were still sporting their GI haircuts twenty-five years after World War II ended. How sad. Will the straight, stringy, long hair on the college girls of the late 1960s and early 1970s still look good on them when they are 40 years old? Long hair gives some girls that "intellectual, unwashed look." What will it look like on them twenty years later?

LIFE IN THE MIDDLE YEARS

The period of life called middle age is a relatively new period of development in American lives. People in the United States have been living longer, and there are many more people. Medical science and technology have increased rapidly, especially since World War II. New industrial techniques are used that prevent people from draining themselves during their younger years. Forced retirement ages are in effect in most businesses, and for the first time people are living long enough and healthily enough to enjoy retirement. In 1975 there will be approximately 65 million people in the United States who are 45 years and older; 44 million of these will be between 45 and 64 years of age.[5]

Since middle age is such a recent phenomenon, there are few guidelines and criteria for living available for this age level. Precedent and tradition, as well as research are noticeably absent. Psychologists and other researchers are just beginning to turn their attention to middle-age development. Most studies have focused on either the very young or the very old. There is a need to study this middle adulthood group who create and manage society for the rest of the population.

Developmental changes during the middle adult years occur slowly, since this period represents a long "plateau" in the lifespan. Furthermore, there is an overlapping of ages at both ends of middle adulthood when some adults are manifesting the changes and characteristics of an earlier or later developmental stage. The point is that changes will take place—sooner in some people and later in others. We must discuss these changes, but some judgment must be used in applying the characteristics too rigidly to ages. It is important to consider the characteristics and changes in the total developmental perspective of the individual. Seen in that manner, changes which seem pessimistic when viewed in isolation, lose some of their harshness when seen in the total framework of developmental age.

Physical characteristics

Generally speaking, the human body is still functioning at almost peak efficiency as a person enters the phase of life that has been labeled the middle years. There are few characteristics to distinguish the "middle adult" from the young adult at the onset of this developmental stage. However, as this phase progresses, gradual

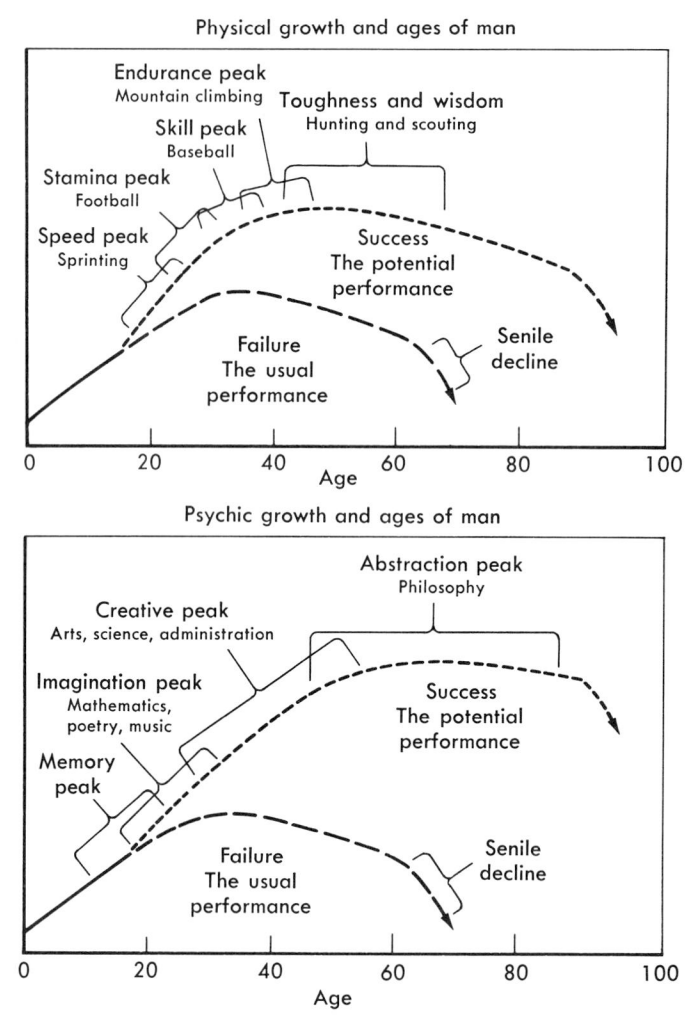

Fig. 13-1. Potential and actual performance. The upper lines indicate the physical and psychological potentials of normal people with peak periods for various activities; the lower lines indicate how most people fail to measure up. (Modified from Still, J. W.: Man's potential and his performance. Copyright 1957 by The New York Times Co. Printed by permission.)

changes can be identified as being peculiar to this time of life. It can be stated, however, that barring disease, physical vigor can be expected to be retained during the middle adult years. (See Fig. 13-1, upper chart.)

Most readily identifiable are the slight and gradual changes beginning to take place in physical appearance that have a tendency to "sneak up" on the individual. One day the "fortyish" adult becomes aware of a few gray hairs beginning to appear. The all-discerning mirror reflects an image of small creases or lines (optimistically referred to as laugh lines rather than wrinkles!). Skin may become dry and begin to show signs of loss of elasticity. There is a redistribution of fatty tissue in both males and females at this time, regardless of lack of change in diet or exercise patterns.

Energy is no longer something that can be expended endlessly. There is a longer period needed to recoup strength after strenuous and extended activity. Few middle-aged adults can work long hours and pursue a taxing and unabated social life without feeling the needs of slowing down. Minor illnesses such as the common cold seem to hang on longer, and there is a decided increase in the length of time necessary to recover from more serious ailments.

Physical fitness has become a middle-aged obsession, especially among men. There are more and more men of this group jogging, running, and working out in gymnasiums. Medical science approves of their physical activities. Some men go to great lengths to convince themselves and others that their bodies are still in good condition. However, they find that after a day of hard physical exercise it takes a few days rather than a few hours to get the weariness out of their joints and muscles. Middle-aged women are also more conscious of health and fitness, but they show more concern with the physical well-being of their husbands than with their own. Women tend to be healthier.

A person employed as a laborer will realize soon after his fortieth birthday that he does not have the vigor that he had formerly. However, his muscles are still as strong. When a person reaches middle age, he is best at tasks that require endurance rather than quick bursts of energy. The middle-aged person must learn his new limitations.

It is a fact that bodies do undergo changes at about the time of middle age. The skeletal muscles increase in bulk until the age of 50 years, but they stay on a plateau until they begin to degenerate at the age of 60 years.[6] Gross motor coordination depends on these muscles, and therefore the peak is at an earlier age. It has been found that the smooth muscles change little with age. Therefore the vital organs can, in reality, be kept healthy until death.

The sense organs of middle-aged people undergo change at an amazing rate of uniformity among individuals. The sense organs are the means by which people keep in contact with the external world. Thus any change in the development of the senses affects people not only in physical but also in psychological ways.

One of the most noticeable changes is in the eyes. Many people feel the shock of realizing that they have hit middle age when they are required to wear bifocals or reading glasses. One of the most common occurrences at approximately 45 years of age is presbyopia, a condition characterized by the reduction in the elasticity of the crystalline lens of the eye that has progressed to the point where the lens can no longer change its curvature sufficiently to allow accommodation for near points of vision.[7] This is the reason why older people start to hold their reading material at arm's length until they are fitted for glasses with convex lenses. Many ophthalmologists are now finding this condition initially at the age of 50 years instead of 45 years. Man's sensory ability level appears to be improving.

The ears also undergo change during middle life. This sensory change especially brings a need for emotional adjustment to the individual, since it is this change that can affect the individual's relations with others. Beginning with middle age there is a gradual deterioration and hardening of the auditory cells and nerves. Thus almost everyone experiences some degree of loss of auditory acuity. The commonest hearing difficulty is identified with age and is not pathological in origin. This is presbycusis, which is the loss of hearing for tones of higher frequency. This decline begins in early adulthood and becomes greater as age increases. There are significant sex differences in auditory sensitivity between men and women of all ages. There are no differences between the sexes up to the middle ranges of frequency, 2,048 cycles, but above this point women of all ages are able to hear much better than men. Deafness for voice-range tones or lower usually does not occur until about the age of 60 years. Most individuals can adjust to these changes unconsciously, but when hearing loss interferes with work or participation in normal activities, a hearing aid of some type is needed.

It is pragmatic to consider that most problems peculiar to geriatrics start at about 40 years of age, the approximate median of life.[8] There is a general slowing down of metabolism in the early forties, causing a weight gain and its undesirable effects on the other systems of the body. There may be signs of diabetes, and the incidence of kidney and gall stones increases. General decrease in the elasticity of the lungs is evident around 45 years of age; chronic bronchitis may develop slowly. The loss of elasticity and changes in appearance and structure of the lining coats of the arteries that can lead to many cardiovascular conditions is an acknowledged fact for people past the age of 45 years. The body systems should be periodically checked as the middle years begin so that physiological vigor can be maintained throughout the middle adult years. It is completely possible for a person to remain in a condition of sound health throughout this time period, despite the general slowing down process (Table 13-1).

It is of interest to note that scientists working with the space program consider the age of 38 years to be the peak year of adult development. The adult of this age can be more mentally alert, physically sound, and emotionally stable than at any other age. Neil Armstrong, first man to step on the moon, was 38 years old. The ages of the moon astronauts ranged from 36 years to Alan Shepard's 45 years. The look of youth may not be present, but the stamp of maturity is indelible.

Social characteristics

Socially speaking, it can be said that middle age is the time when there is an expansion of horizons through friendships, business contacts, and acquaintances made in the community. This is the stage of development in which the individual enjoys the highest social status in adult society.

Active club and organization membership is at its peak during these years. Adults who never before had time become productive and enthusiastic members of the groups that have goals akin to their own. Some aspects of a man's social contacts will be business or professionally related because career advancement still plays a role in his social life. However, there is now time to become involved socially in things that really matter to him as an individual. Wilensky's study[9] demonstrates that there is a positive relationship between amount of social participation in formal associations and job satisfaction. Furthermore, this general curve reflects the number of work-

Table 13-1. Functional capacity of men at various age levels compared to 100% capacity of an average 30-year-old man*

PHYSIOLOGICAL CHARACTERISTIC	AGE					
	30	40	50	60	70	80
Nerve conduction velocity	100%	100%	96%	93%	91%	87%
Basic metabolic rate	100	98	95	92	86	83
Body water content	100	98	94	90	87	81
Work rate	100	94	87	80	74	
Cardiac output (at rest)	100	93	83	58	70	
Filtration rate of kidney	100	98	90	82	77	59
Maximum breathing capacity (voluntary)	100	92	78	61	50	41

*Modified from Shock, N. W.: The psychology of ageing. Copyright 1962 by Scientific American, Inc.

ers who are satisfied on their jobs. There is a sharp drop in formal participation in the early twenties, especially among hard-pressed married couples; there is a climb to a peak in the middle years, a slight drop off, and then a sag in the sixties.

The family-centered woman will now find that her social life can be "other directed" and can take on a more creative aspect rather than simply being an extension of her mother role. Cultivation of new friends and enjoyment of friends of long standing are often a pleasant aspect of life now. Visiting friends without an eye to the clock and the tyranny of what to have for dinner or what time to pick the children up can be a rewarding social aspect for the woman whose family is now fairly independent. Church-related social life with its often-attendant social service aspect may become more significant. Pressure of time and finances that did not allow for this activity previously are possibly the reason for this increased involvement. The way in which a person adjusts to changes in his social life depends on the way in which he has adjusted to the physical and emotional changes that are occurring.

The middle-aged individual finds himself with more freedom from responsibility and the job; this in turn leaves him often with more money to spend and more leisure time. Some people use this leisure time as an extension of interests, broadening their scope with enrichment and fulfillment in new activities. But many people engage in activities that do not offer a worthwhile return, and others drift into boredom and dissatisfaction. The manner in which a person conducts himself in middle age depends on the way he has conducted his whole life.

A major period of adjustment in this time of life is the loss of status—an area that affects the middle class more than others. Educated people of the middle class reach this time of life later than others because in getting their education they put off having children until later; therefore they are older when the children leave the home.

However, these same people started at the beginning of their marriage to build status. They view status as wealth, a professional or business career, a home, a boat, two cars, lovely children, tennis and golf trophies—the list can be endless. These are status symbols that one can and often does lose in middle life. Forced retirement or younger men in the office can replace the middle-aged man or lessen his authority. The children marry and move out, and often the home is then too big for the couple to keep up so that it is sold for a smaller house or even an apartment. Generally, the older person's physical being eliminates the role of an athlete, therefore no more trophies or awards.

This shows the importance of building up good interpersonal relationships throughout life. Making friends by being thoughtful, kind, and generous is the kind of status that cannot be taken away during middle life. The college athlete who helped and respected his teammates will be remembered long after he made the winning touchdown. The people from the big house with the swimming pool who were kind and helpful to their neighbors will be remembered even after the big house and pool are gone. The best insurance for an emotionally rich and satisfying old age is to build a vast store of interests that are varied and not dependent on the conditions that old age automatically removes and to work with people in such a way that the individual keeps their respect and his own self-respect.[10]

Stability of personality traits

Personality traits are relatively fixed by the time a person reaches middle adulthood. The adult personality is a product of the interaction of biological forces, life space, and the individual's own ego organization. These forces reach a culmination by middle age, and changes do not come readily. Since the adult has had much practice over the years in learning role behavior, this role behavior becomes an attitudinal and perceptive set that is not easily modified. Most people perseverate in habits, opinions, and attitudes; that is, they become deeply ingrained in their personality. They will resist, as a rule, any change that tends to threaten their practices and percepts.[11]

For some reason many people still like to believe that they can change their personal orientation at will. Some harbor a desire, fostered by sentimentalists, that a new life awaits the person who will only change his way of thinking, believing, or feeling. This can be accomplished, but *only* by the intervention of experiences that happen to be appropriate to the needs and physical capacities of the person involved. People do not change by themselves. Interaction with an outside agency or event or series of events is necessary to accomplish change and, unless such interaction is dramatic or traumatic, little discernible change may result. A major change in personality of the middle-aged adult is unlikely.

Most people in the middle adult years have settled down and become ethnocentric in their personal adaptations. Some people (a minority) are more flexible and open to change. Education, diversified experiences, and an open society are desirable and necessary exposures that make possible the great expectations for personality growth and accomplishment in the middle adult years.

A series of large-scale investigations of the social and psychological aspects of middle age and aging were carried out over a ten-year period under the sponsorship of The Committee on Human Development of the University of Chicago.[12] Cross-sectional data gathered on more than 700 men and women, ages 40 to 70 years, revealed seven psychological attributes or characteristics that were related to overall adjustment and mental health of the middle-aged person.

These characteristics include the following:

1. Cathectic or emotional flexibility, the capacity to shift emotional investments from one person to another and from one activity to another.
2. Mental flexibility, the capacity to use experience and prior mental sets as provisional guides rather than as fixed, inflexible rules in the solution of new problems.
3. Ego differentiation, the capacity to pursue and to enjoy a varied set of major activities in life and not to rely entirely on one or two life roles.
4. Body transcendence, the capacity to feel whole and happy because of one's social and mental powers and to avoid preoccupation with health, physique, and bodily comfort.
5. Ego transcendence, the capacity to engage in a direct, gratifying manner with the people and events of daily life with a strong concern for the well-being of others and not with self-centered desires.
6. Body satisfaction, the degree of satisfaction one subjectively feels with one's body.
7. Sexual integration, the capacity to mesh one's sexual desires with other aspects of life, among them affection for the sex partner and an integration of sexual and other motivations in social relationships.

Personality adjustment in the middle years appears to be related to the individual's capacity to properly utilize these seven characteristics. Emotional flexibility is needed because middle age is a period when parents die, children leave home, and the individual's circle of friends begins to be broken by death. He needs to be able to reinvest his emotions in others and to redefine existing relationships. Mental flexibility is needed in middle age to be able to work out a set of answers to life. The impact of retirement can be lessened by a good capacity for ego differentiation, permitting the individual to take up new roles. Body transcendence, ego transcendence, and body satisfaction are needed to be able to move beyond the self so that one's interests can lie in others rather than self. Sexual integration becomes necessary because of the "change of life" that occurs in middle age. There is no question that the transition from young adulthood to middle adulthood is equal in difficulty to any other period of transition in the growth and development of people.

Emotional crises of middle age

There are three significant crises that come to many during middle adulthood—children leaving the home, middle-age affairs, and identity crises.

Children leaving the home. One of the major events in a person's life, which brings the realization that an individual is in middle age, is the time when the children leave the home. Most children become fully independent on graduation from college or on their marriage. This can be a time of happiness and reward, or it can be a time of heartbreak and disillusionment.

Too often during parenthood the adult, especially the mother, will focus all of her attention on the children, sometimes at the expense of ignoring her spouse. Most adults do not even realize that they are doing this, and thus it is a traumatic occasion when the last child leaves the home. The husband and wife will really see each other for the first time in twenty or twenty-five years. All too often they are shocked by what they see. They have changed gradually, but the change is not noticed until this time. The only bond between them, the children, is no longer there. Many people at this stage believe that their life is over; there is nothing more to be done so they will wait for old age and eventually death. Some parents take a different approach by encouraging continued dependency of their children by making mother's house too readily available and father's pocketbook too easily opened.

The couples who manage this period gracefully are those who have kept their interest and love for each other alive and also have common interests and hobbies. Therefore, when they find themselves alone again, they can enjoy each other and often view it as a second honeymoon. Many find that at this time they can afford to travel and take up activities which they missed when they were young and struggling. These are the people who believe that the spouse's needs take precedence over those of the children. This not only leads to a happier middle age for the parents but can help to prevent the development of self-centered children.

Middle-aged affairs. In recent years there has been a sharp rise in divorces between middle-aged couples. Many people are shocked to find friends who have been married for twenty-five or thirty years and who seemed to have had a good marriage, suddenly get divorced. Much of this drifting apart is because the partners have lost touch with each other during parenthood and no longer have a common bond.

Some middle-aged adults suddenly find themselves trapped by their lives and their marriage. They try to recapture some of their youth and experience the "good life" before they are too far over the hill. This feeling of entrapment usually hits women in their middle forties and men in their late forties. Some people in middle age suffer through an identity crisis, and sometimes they lose sight of their values temporarily by engaging in extramarital affairs. These affairs often do not depend on what the husband or wife is like—in fact, many of these people still love their spouse deeply. Yet they jeopardize their marriage, their business prestige, and their relations with friends by seeking "the romance of a bygone era."

Sometimes the spouse never learns of the

extramarital affair. Some, when they do learn, forgive and forget—but too often it leads to divorce after many years of marriage.[13]

Identity crisis. With rapid technology and social changes and with today's emphasis on youth, many of today's middle-aged adults are faced with the question of their position in society. They are in a period of extreme internal and external pressures. They become uncertain of values; some feel bored, restless, dissatisfied, self-involved, and hemmed in by society.

The middle-aged person is suddenly faced with the shortness of life. He can choose to handle it in two ways, either to start new resolutions and activities or to begin the long, slow decline. Either way, the person's self-concept is challenged, especially his physical image. He asks himself, "Am I really young at heart, or do I have one foot in the grave?" Many psychologists see similar traits between adolescence and middle age, such as the sexual change, identity crisis, and uncertainty of the role expected of them.

The ways of handling this crisis are as varied as the individuals themselves. Some indulge in hypochondria; others try to act like their college children; many find new interests and hobbies; and still others find a change in jobs, careers, or houses. A poll of this age group reveals that the middle-aged adult does not really want to be young again and have to suffer through the struggling of the young. He believes that he has done his work and now deserves the freedom to enjoy it.[14]

When a person reaches this age, he enjoys the freedom of expressing himself unselfconsciously. He does not depend on peer acceptance. Most adults realize that they will not impress their peers or their juniors by being false so that they usually are honest. They can indulge in their whims and be a little eccentric without offending anyone. Possibly the greatest pleasure of middle age is the acceptance of one's limitations without surrender, the right to relax without giving in. Life *can* begin at 40 years for the one who has learned to give up inhibitions brought on by false social and personal values.

Mental characteristics

Contrary to popular belief, mental functions, if used, are at a peak in middle age. Cerebral capacities deteriorate slowly and only begin to weaken at the age of 70 years. Many cultures, in fact, look to their middle-aged population for wisdom and judgment. Studies now reveal that a person's general intellectual capacity is as great in middle age as it was when the person was younger. (See Fig. 13-1, lower chart.)

The adult who has used his mind actively and productively throughout his years will have a highly refined ability to use these powers through the middle years and later perhaps. The adult who has "completed" his education with the last formal class attended will be subject to a more rapid rate of deterioration of these powers. Since the growth of the mind is a product of many outside factors, it is possible for the adult to grow intellectually through involvement in subjects and activities other than those of an academic nature.

However, most middle-aged people do not make full use of their intellectual power; they cling to the old idea that "You can't teach an old dog new tricks." To most it is a convenient excuse to not make use of their capabilities. Many older people find that they have trouble learning new ideas and techniques, but these people have not lost their recall or their ability to learn. They have merely become "rusty," or they refuse to change their life patterns to allow for study time and work.

When an adult enrolls in a class, it often takes him a few weeks to adjust to the demands of learning; he has trouble remembering what he has heard or read. Unfortunately, many people get discouraged or quit at this time, but those who stay with it soon reach a high level of proficiency. A person at the age of 45 years learns at nearly the same rate and in the same manner as he did at 25 years. The only difference is that he emphasizes accuracy rather than speed as he gets older.[15]

Lehman[16] provided information regarding the sciences, medicine, philosophy, arts, practical invention, and other areas. He found that within fields of endeavor the maximum production rate for quality work occurred during the age decade of 30 to 39 years. The rate of creative production did not decline rapidly after the peak years, however. It was gradual at most ages—more gradual for lesser quality products than for higher quality products. Lehman's study showed that creativity varied within different fields of endeavor. For instance, in the study of philosophy the peak age of quality production was from age 60 to 64 years; the highest quality productions in science occurred from 35 to 40 years; for athletes it was 29 years; for soldiers and explorers it was 47 years; for historians, judges, and naturalists it was 54 years; and the overall peak was at 38 years of age. The use of fine motor coordination improves gradually to the early fifties, and mental and spiritual insights increase to about the age of 65 years. However, top speed is at about the age of 30 years, and top energy usage is at about the age of 35 to 38 years.

Tyler[17] makes the following observations concerning the maintenance of decline of various mental abilities (1) a gradual decline in all types of measurable ability sets in after the age of 30 years but does not become significant until well after 50 years, (2) sensory and perceptual abilities decline most and earliest, (3) motor abilities hold up well until late middle age, but there is a change in the methods by which the tasks are done, (4) decline in learning ability varies with the type of material to be learned, and (5) there are wide individual differences so that in any age group some persons are superior to the average for groups much younger.

Vocational status

The peak of vocational success for men comes during middle age, in the forties and early fifties. After the age of 35 years men are more stable in their jobs and are skilled to avoid acts that cause accidents. Between the ages of 30 and 34 years men show stable employment of 40%, upward mobility of 33%, and downward mobility of 3%.[18]

Most people reach their peak of income in the 40- to 45-year age bracket. There are fewer accidents by the older worker than by the younger worker, and the older worker has less absenteeism from work. It is at this time that men attain their greatest power and prestige in the business world. For both men and women it can be a time of great accomplishments in their lives.

It would seem that man's vocational adjustment problems are over, but for some people middle age brings new complications. Dissatisfaction with the present job, instability, restlessness, and loss of child-rearing responsibilities prompt many men to make a vocational change at this time of life. However, most of these "vocational change" seekers are individuals who have never really fulfilled their vocational desires and goals. He soon finds out that such a change is almost impossible and impracticable, unless the job change is closely related to his present position. Soon the desire to change jobs diminishes and is replaced by a desire to remain in the same occupation until retirement.

The vocational adjustment problem of middle age is as serious for women today as for men, if not more so. At present almost one half the women between the ages of 35 and 55 years are in the labor force.[19]

Many reasons can be cited for the overflow of middle-aged women desiring work outside the home. The various labor-saving devices permit them to care for their home in much less time than in the past. Earlier marriages, earlier childbearing, and smaller families ready the middle-aged woman for employment outside the home. The increase in cost of living and the desire for a better standard of living demand more money than the husband can bring home; thus the wife is willing to take a job to have some of the finer things in life.

Without question the opportunity for women to earn money outside the home is security in itself. If the time were to arise that she would need to be self-supporting (through divorce or death of the husband), she could carry on with much less frustration.

As the latter years of middle age bring retirement into focus, it is conceivable that retirement benefits from both husband's and wife's company retirement plan, in addition to Social Security benefits, will make the "golden years" most enjoyable.

THE CHANGE OF LIFE

In the middle years a change occurs for men and women. Climacteric (andropause), the change of life in men, and menopause, the change of life in women, are the cause of much anxiety in the minds of both sexes. The concerns and fears of the change of life are without scientific reason. Every period of life, from childhood to old age, has its joys and trials. This change of life is no different; it has its compensations and can become an era of great fulfillment leading to years of happiness and serenity.

What is it?

At a certain time in middle adulthood the body will undergo certain physical changes that are associated with the gradual inability of certain glands to secrete the hormones that they provided earlier. The word *menopause,* used to designate the change-of-life period in women, comes from the Greek words "month" and "cessation." It refers to that time in a woman's life when there is a pause in the menses, a cessation of the monthly reproductive function. The word *climacteric* comes from two Greek words meaning "rung of a ladder" and "a critical time." In popular usage it is applied to a change in men, although the word *andropause* would be more appropriate to indicate the change in men. The term *change of life* for both men and women denotes the leaving of one phase of life and the beginning of a new one.

Symptoms of menopause begin with major hormonal shifts that take place in the woman between the ages of 40 and 55 years. Out of 903 cases investigated in 1967 the average age at which there was a complete cessation of menses was 47.3 years.[20] Only 3.5% of the cases occurred before the age of 40 years; 20% occurred between 40 and 44 years; 44% occurred between 45 and 49 years; 30% occurred between 50 and 54 years; and only 1.5% occurred at the ages of 55, 56, or 57 years. It usually takes two to four years for menopause to be completed. There is some indication of a hereditary pattern for the onset of menopause. All things being equal, daughters generally begin and end menopause in the same manner and at the same age as their mothers.

Symptoms of menopause

During menopause, there is a reduction of action of the ovaries, affecting other glands and producing symptoms that can be disturbing to a woman. In about 75% of women menopausal disturbances are either absent or minor. Only about 25% of women need medical therapy.[21]

Menopause starts with a change in a women's menstrual pattern. One of the following four things will happen: (1) there will be a general slowing down of flow of blood without irregularity; (2) there will be an irregularity of timing with skipped periods; (3) there will be an irregularity of timing and an irregularity in the amount of flow; or (4) there will be an abrupt cessation of menstruation. The usual pattern is skipped periods, with the periods coming farther apart until there may be only one period in six months.

Inside the woman's body certain changes take place. The ovaries become smaller; no longer do they secrete ova regularly as before. The Fallopian tubes, having no more eggs to transport, also become smaller and shorter. The uterus hardens and shrinks. The vagina shortens and loses some of its elasticity. The urine is even different in its hormonal content. The internal changes all concern the reproductive system because there is no longer a need for this function.[22]

There are other internal physical symptoms that have nothing to do with the reproductive system. The spleen and lymphatic glands decrease in size. There is an increased tendency to constipation due to the changes in the wall of the intestine. There may be urinary incontinence.

The symptoms noticed most by women are the external physical ones. There are many symptoms, however, and not all will occur in every woman. Some women will experience one or two symptoms; some women will experience the symptoms for several years, some for several months, and some not at all.

One of the most common and most talked-about symptom is the hot flushes, sometimes called hot flashes. Most symptoms, including the hot flush, involve the nervous system and the blood. During a hot flush, the body becomes warm and there is excessive perspiration followed by chilliness. These hot flushes may involve only the face and neck, or they may extend over the whole body. They occur frequently during the months when periods are missed. They usually stop after the menses stop completely. They are never fatal, but they are probably the most annoying of all the symptoms. They usually last only a minute or so and can be controlled by medication.

There are many other symptoms. The breasts eventually become smaller and flabby. The body contour changes, and there is often a tendency to become obese. This may be checked by a careful diet. However, some women get progressively thinner. The hair on scalp and external genitalia becomes thinner. The labia may lose their firmness and become flabby. Muscles, especially of the upper arms and legs, may lose their elasticity and strength. Itchiness, particularly after bathing, may occur. Insomnia occurs frequently, and headaches are common. Certain male characteristics may appear, such as hair growth at the mouth's corners or upper lip. This can be helped by prescribed hormones. These symptoms are the ones that occur most frequently.

Hormonal deficiency, causing many of the physical and psychological symptoms of menopause, has been greatly reduced in the past several years by the use of estrogen replacement therapy. However, hormonal therapy helps only those complaints that are related directly or indirectly to hormonal deficiency. A woman who has reached menopause may have other reasons to feel the depression and general psychological upset that can be part of her life at this time.

In addition to the various physical symptoms there are also psychological ones, but, again, not every woman experiences psychological symptoms. Usually if a woman is well adjusted mentally and emotionally before menopause, she will have no problems. However, if a woman has been poorly adjusted or unhappy, she may have mental problems during menopause (Table 13-2).

Psychologically, the cessation of menstruation for some women is a state of anxiety that is related to the woman's concept of herself as a human being. Some women, since they no longer can bear children, believe that they are losing their usefulness. This symbolizes aging to some, and they become emotionally upset about it. This loss of reproductive power may even be equated with castration and connected to the castration complex.[23] Many women be-

Table 13-2. Women's attitudes and views toward menopause*

	PERCENT
The worst thing about middle age	
Losing your husband	52
Getting older	18
Cancer	16
Children leaving home	9
Menopause	4
Change in sexual feelings and behavior	1
What I dislike most about being middle-aged	
Getting older	35
Lack of energy	21
Poor health or illness	15
Feeling useless	2
None of these	27
The best thing about the menopause	
Not having to worry about getting pregnant	30
Not having to bother with menstruation	44
Better relationship with husband	11
Greater enjoyment of sex life	3
None of these	12
The worst thing about menopause	
Not knowing what to expect	26
The discomfort and pain	19
Sign of getting older	17
Loss of enjoyment in sexual relations	4
Not being able to have more children	4
None of these	30
How menopause affects a woman's appearance	
Negative changes	50
No effect	43
Positive changes	1
No response	6
How menopause affects a woman's physical and emotional health	
Negative changes	32
No effect	58
Positive change or improvement	10
How menopause affects a woman's sexual relations	
Sexual relations become more important	18
No effect	65
Sexual relations become less important	17

*Modified from Neugarten, B.: Vita Humana 6: 140-151, 1963.

come saddened because they see themselves aging in a youth-oriented society.

What happens to the woman who will not let herself get old? She will become especially interested in youth and their ideas. She will try to think like them and dress like them. She will want to be admired and loved by many young men. She will begin to wonder if her old husband is really worth hanging onto. She may be laying the groundwork for marital unhappiness.

Some women believe that with the menopause comes the end of their attractiveness, thus the end of their sex life. Their children are grown and married. They no longer feel needed. They no longer use their leisure time advantageously. They just worry. What happens to these women who cannot adjust? Some women drink to solve their problems. Some seek out "loving" men. Some avoid a social life of any kind—they isolate themselves. Some women cry all the time and are usually depressed.

The larger majority of women do not have these psychological problems because their lives have been filled with usefulness, happiness, charm, self-appreciation, and accomplishment. They have been emphasizing values and interests in life that can be pursued with vigor at any age.

When is menopause over? This is an interesting question. No one knows exactly when ovulation will end for any woman. She may not have a period for five or six months and then another may occur. Most authorities agree that menopause has been completed if there has been no menstrual period for one year. With the end of ovulation also usually comes the end of the physical symptoms. If they do not end, they are caused by something other than menopause.

Middle-aged pregnancy is uncommon as women approach menopause. The "change-of-life" baby is a possibility but not the usual occurrence for the woman who begins noticing changes in the menstrual cycle. One study indicated that, in general, pregnancy after 47 years of age is highly unlikely; another study stated that pregnancy in women over 50 years of age is "extremely rare."[24] During the time of irregular periods, it is difficult to know when ovulation takes place. Conception would be possible, but the whole combination of events would be unexpected and unlikely. When middle-aged pregnancy becomes a reality, particularly if the child is the first conceived, there is a greater tendency for longer labor due to the loss of elasticity of the cervix and vagina. There is a higher risk of the over 40-year-old mother producing a child with some defect. The rate of mongolism in the offspring of younger mothers is one in 600, whereas the rate of mongolism in the offspring of older mothers rises to one in every fifty births. Spontaneous abortions are frequent in women who become pregnant after the age of 40 years. Some doctors who believe that menopause is over when there has been no menstrual period for twelve months still suggest that some type of birth control be continued for another twelve months.

What about men?

There is really no such thing as a "male change" in the literal sense of the word. There is no physical change in the male comparable to the change in the female. Some emotional changes occur in men around middle age, but these can be attributed to progressive aging and to diminishing sexual desire.[25] The main change is in the man's thinking patterns and self-image. This is not the result of hormonal deficiency—androgen levels decline very slowly. The reproductive function does not end, and sperm manufacture continues with no sudden change until old age. Fertility is not interfered with even when sperm production slows. Fatherhood is possible until extremely late in life. Possible loss of sex drive and potency is more a matter of the mind than a set of physical facts.

Psychologically, there are two facts that may suggest a kind of male climacteric. First, some men have almost neurotic reactions to middle age. They do not want to be old, and like some women they try to look and act very young. Some even shed their wives and marry women ten or twenty years younger. Second, some men have depressive reactions, but they occur about ten or fifteen years later in men than in women, around the ages of 55 to 65 years. These are probably due to fatigue, retirement, boredom, financial problems, or fear of sex impotency.

However, in about one of every 100 men there is a period of changing years in which their reproductive powers suddenly end. When this happens, it is due to primary testicular failure. The discomforts of this disease are similar to the symptoms of menopause in women. The cure is slow and expensive because it is an illness and does not occur naturally like menopause.[26]

Sex in middle age

The years between the ages of 20 and 30 are ones in which sexual capacity and drives are greatest. However, with the aging process and physiological changes the male experiences a gradual decline in sexual behavior at about his fifty-fifth year. It is at this stage in some men that sexual pleasures leave the desirous state, and sex serves only as an outlet. This can best be illustrated by the male who seeks youthful sex partners to regain his self-esteem and shelter his declining virility. Kinsey[27] reports that at 60 years of age only 5% of males in his study were inactive sexually. By the age of 70 years nearly 30% were inactive, but 70% were active. There is usually little decrease in sexual interest, but there may be a decrease in sexual activities due to pressures or psychological attitudes (Fig. 13-2).

Decline in female sexual interest and activity usually begins earlier than in the male. It is a time of extreme sensitivity to her environment, irritability, and physical changes. She is aware of these changes.

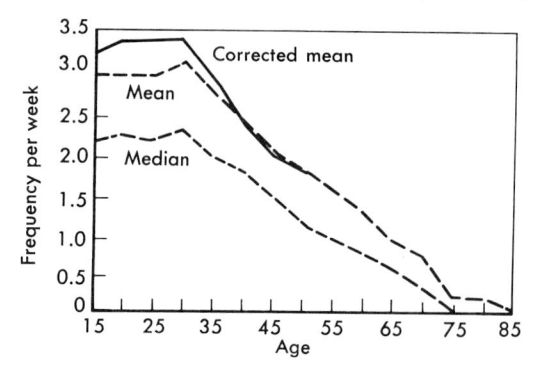

Fig. 13-2. Frequency of sexual outlet declines with age. (Modified from Kinsey, A. C., Pomeroy, W. B., and Martin, C. E.: Sexual behavior in the human male, Philadelphia, 1948, W. B. Saunders Co.)

Her ovaries cease to produce ova, and her appearance begins to show the signs of age. The woman who is unable to cope with the problems this phase brings can resort to sexual preoccupation and seeking young men or can become emotionally upset over her new role in life.

During the change, it is a good time for a woman to take stock of her sexual self and to ascertain if she has really reached the pinnacle of marital bliss with her husband. It must be emphasized that women who have always enjoyed marital relations to the fullest may expect to continue to do so; those who have never achieved sexual fulfillment now have an opportunity to "try again."

There is one condition that will prevent a woman from having sexual pleasure during or after menopause; it may even cause severe pain. This is dyspareunia, or painful intercourse. During and after menopause (and in some women approaching this time of life), an insufficient quantity of female sex hormone (estrogen) causes the lining of the vagina to thin out and become raw and painful to the touch. The administration of estrogen by injection, by mouth, and/or by suppositories in the vagina will thicken the epithelium lining of the vagina and repair the damage.[28]

The extent and degree of waning sex energy in middle-aged men and women vary with the individual's state of mind and physical fitness. The so-called change of life tends to intensify existing body disorders and permit others to occur. More often than not a woman's mental and emotional disturbance over menopause does more harm than the process itself. Anxiety has been proved to be the prime danger to the well-being of a man or woman during this period.

STUDY GUIDE

1. What is it like to be an adult 31 to 45 years of age? What are the sociological, psychological, and physiological factors involved?
2. What is meant by "the years of stability" or "the maintenance years"?
3. Review the developmental tasks of middle adulthood. They will need to be derived from the section with that title. Do the tasks appear to you to be more philosophical in nature?
4. What's so bad about becoming 40 years old? What's so great about it?
5. What physical changes occur during middle adulthood?
6. There are seven psychological characteristics in the middle years of adulthood that are related to overall adjustment. What are these attributes, and how do they contribute to good mental health?
7. Are adults of middle age capable of doing good reasoning and thinking? Are they beginning to lose or deteriorate in mental abilities?
8. What happens to cause menopause? Why does it happen? How does it show itself? What understanding is needed by the woman involved and by those associated with her?
9. Should sex activities decline after the ages of 45 or 50 years because a couple may no longer be capable of reproducing? What seems to be the key to continued sex?

10. What is it like to be an adult 46 to 59 years of age? What are the sociological, psychological, and physiological factors involved?

REFERENCES

1. Havighurst, R. J.: Human development and education, New York, 1953, Longmans, Green & Co., Inc., p. 15.
2. Duvall, E. H.: Family development, Philadelphia, 1957, J. B. Lippincott Co., p. 399.
3. Middle age: the command generation, Time, pp. 50-54, July 29, 1966.
4. Bracken, P.: Middle age: for adults only, Read. Digest 95:86, Dec., 1969.
5. Tibbetts, C., and Donahue, W.: Aging in today's society, Englewood Cliffs, N. J., 1960, Prentice-Hall, Inc., p. 17.
6. Don't just sit there: walk, jog, run, Time 91:45, Feb. 23, 1968.
7. Tibbetts, op. cit., p. 105.
8. Wingate, M. J.: The years after fifty, New York, 1947, McGraw-Hill Book Co., p. 1.
9. Wilensky, H. L.: Orderly careers and social participation. In Peters, H. J., and Hansen, J. C.: Vocational guidance and career development, New York, 1968, The Macmillan Co., pp. 399-425.
10. Ruch, F. L.: Psychology and life, Glenview, Ill., 1953, Scott, Foresman & Co., p. 150.
11. Miles, W. R., and Miles, C. C.: Mental changes in normal aging. In Stieglitz, E. J., editor: Geriatric medicine, Philadelphia, 1949, W. B. Saunders Co., p. 100.
12. Neugarten, B. L.: Personality in middle and late life: empirical studies, New York, 1964, Atherton Press, pp. 16-42.
13. Middle age crises, McCall's 94:88, March, 1967.
14. Lynes, R.: A cool cheer for middle-aged, Look 31:46, Oct. 17, 1967.
15. Thorndike, E. L.: The general form of the curve of learning ability with age. In Thorndike, E. L., Bregman, E. O., Tilton, J., and Woodyard, E.: Adult learning, New York, 1928, The Macmillan Co.
16. Lehman, H. C.: Age and achievement, Princeton, N. J., 1953, Princeton University Press.
17. Tyler, L. E.: The psychology of human differences, New York, 1956, Appleton-Century-Crofts, pp. 338-365.
18. Birren, J. E.: The psychology of aging, Englewood Cliffs, N. J., 1964, Prentice-Hall, Inc., pp. 141, 203, 214.
19. How woman's role in the United States is changing, U. S. News World Rep., pp. 58-60, May 30, 1966.
20. Wharton, L.: The ovarian hormones, Springfield, Ill., 1967, Charles C Thomas, Publisher, p. 22.
21. Ibid., p. 30.
22. Smith, A.: The body, New York, 1968, Walker & Co., p. 77.
23. Chapman, D. J.: The feminine mind and body, New York, 1968, Citadel Press, Inc., p. 268.
24. Cooley, D. G.: Family medical guide, Des Moines, Iowa, 1966, Better Homes and Gardens, Meredith Press, p. 331.
25. Deutsch, H.: The psychology of women, New York, 1967, Grune & Stratton, Inc., p. 139.
26. Gray, M.: The changing years, Garden City, N. Y., 1967, Doubleday & Co., Inc., p. 188.
27. Kinsey, A. C., and others: Sexual behavior in the human male, Philadelphia, 1948, W. B. Saunders Co.
28. Ellis, A., and Abarband, A.: The encyclopedia of sexual behavior, vol. I, New York, 1964, Hawthorn Books, Inc., p. 726.

14 Later adulthood
Age of recompense

LATER ADULTHOOD: TO RETIRE GRACEFULLY

The person about whom I have chosen to write has always been dear to me. He is my father. At present he is 69 years old and is residing in a small town in upstate New York.

My dad had been employed by a communications company as an electronical engineer, a well-paying position that he held for his entire working career until his retirement. He found his work a constant challenge and was very happy at it.

He was always a great perfectionist and would not settle for anything unless it was correctly done. This also carried over into his home life, as could be expected. He was creative and spent much of his leisure time working out problems, making things for his work, and seeing if he could improve anything and everything in any way possible. Actually, it might be said that he did not permit himself to have any leisure time to relax.

To quote him, "Television was the biggest piece of trash ever invented." He thought that it kept people from expanding their knowledge to a useful degree. He also had little use for anyone who wasted his time and money "boozing it up" in the local tavern or puffing away on a cigarette. As he once said, "There is not enough time in life to throw it around carelessly." He was definitely a man geared to work—almost like a machine that never wanted to quit.

Dad furnished his wife and two children with a fairly new, middle-sized eight-room home that was located in a pleasant residential neighborhood. His wife, a former school teacher, was easy to get along with and generally agreeable. There never seemed to be any quarreling in the home. However, as in every household there were some disagreements, usually settled by mutual consent. They worked well together and seemed to complement each other's personalities. My brother and I were always consulted about anything of importance. It seemed as if our decisions weighed as heavily as those of our parents, but of course we knew this was not true. The family spent much time together and were quite happy.

As the retirement year grew nearer, Dad grew uneasy. He started to wonder what he would do with himself. He wrote down a list of his many hobbies and interests that might occupy his time after retirement. He also started making lists of engineering companies that would hire an "old man" to work for them. He discussed moving to Michigan and buying a farm for the sole purpose of raising hogs and experimenting with breeding. There were other ideas that passed through his mind, but they all seemed to be in hopes of finding a way out of being forced into retirement.

An outsider looking at Dad would most likely think that he was a calm man—a man who would have no difficulty adjusting to his retirement. It appeared that his financial standing would enable him to maintain his family and home and his interests would enable him to occupy his mind successfully. All of these things were true; however, it did not seem quite so easy to Dad at this time.

After much thought and worry, many lists, and a few applications to different engineering concerns the expected day of retirement arrived. To quote him, "One minute I am a useful working citizen, contributing to the welfare of my country, and the next minute I am no longer of any use to anyone." It was a discouraging thought for a man of his nature; however, that was his thought.

During the first couple of weeks, he found himself sitting around watching television, the "trash box" that he despised so much, and taking the dogs for their morning walk. He would trail around after mother, watching every move she made, seeing if he could be of help. However, he found that he was only getting in the way of her daily household chores. He started taking naps in the afternoon just as if he had become an old man at the precise time that his retirement went into effect. Actually, it was sad to see all of his talent and enthusiasm for life being wasted.

He had grown accustomed to feeling sorry for himself until four months after his retirement, when he received a phone call from an engineering associate of his. His associate wanted to employ him on a part-time basis for his own engineering concern. Of course, Dad accepted the position immediately. He had received his chance to become useful again. This new job required him to work for a period of ninety days, with the option of continuing in another area at the end of that period, providing the first job was acceptable.

The first job that he completed for his new company was acceptable. However, during the ninety days he found that there were many young men who were working successfully in engineering and would soon be doing the identical job that he had been doing for so long. He also found that he was not used to keeping up with the fast pace that was common in such a company. He started to realize that he was not as young as he wished. He also found that he enjoyed having leisure time when he desired it, and consequently he decided that it was not so bad to be retired after all. After realizing all of this he turned the second job offer down. He had finally made his own choice to accept retirement gracefully and, I might add, graciously.

At this point in life he was a changed man, but actually he had not changed at all. He again became the curious hard-working individual that he had been all of his life. The only thing that had changed was the location of his work. He had decided that with all of the equipment he had at home he could definitely keep himself busy. He wanted to tinker with those things that had always been a puzzle to him. He started making his own gadgets that worked electronically and made himself a beautiful stereo, which he housed in his own handmade cabinet. He took time to travel to different parts of the country that he had always wanted to see but never had time to go previously.

It seems likely that he would have made his adjustment to retirement sooner or later without the assistance of his acquaintance and the part-time job; however, I do believe that this opportunity helped to speed him on his way to successful adjustment. He was fortunate to have had a sufficient amount of money saved in preparation for retirement and also to have had many hobbies and interests in which to keep active. He had a feeling of self-worth that was temporarily discarded but was fortunately restored. I believe that he made his adjustment to retirement successfully and easily. Unfortunately, it is a difficult task for many people.

The process of aging and old age itself have become major topics of discussion, research, and speculation in recent years. One of the reasons for such activity is that more and more people are reaching old age. Approximately 4,000 Americans have their sixty-fifth birthday every day, and 10% of the population is over the age of 65 years. Western society has never experienced such a large percentage of its population living in retirement. The social, economic, and medical implications of this increased aged population are tremendous. Problems never before encountered are now facing a society that must not only learn how to live with a sizable number of its members in retirement but also how to incorporate this older segment of the population into the mainstream of life. For the most part the aged are people who still have vigor and vitality for life. To isolate and segregate them will only serve to force them into becoming "old" before their time.

Early adulthood was the period of the developing years, a time when expansion was taking place in all phases of life. At some point enough growth, development, and accumulation had taken place so that the individual became content to maintain his position and status in life, not pushing for any further major gain. The years of stability and status quo were ushered in. As designed by nature, there comes a time when enough change has taken place chronologically, as well as physically, so that the individual finds himself in a different role or status of life compared with that of the younger population. This time usually occurs at retirement.

From the time of retirement on the individual is in the age of recompense. This is a period when the major tasks of adulthood have either been completed or set aside, and a new role, that of an older member of society, is assumed. How gracefully, how happily, how effectively the new role is lived will depend on the capability of the individual to be graceful, happy, and effective. His past life will determine how smoothly or awkwardly he moves into this new stage and how well he can adapt to it. Recompense means a return for something done, suffered, or given. It is a compensation, in kind, for past efforts and services rendered. The age of recompense is the time when a person reaps the rewards of the kind of life he lived in earlier years.

The time span

Old age is the last major segment of the life-span, within which there exists a variety of patterns of well-being and aging (Table 14-1). Individual differences are probably greater at this time than at any other age. Not all older people are "old," and certainly they are not all senile. Most are highly capable in many ways for many years. Yet a characteristic of the age level is that as age increases, there comes a regression, a decrease in effective functioning of the various bodily systems. Physical and mental decline occur with considerable individual differences, but 60 to 65 years is usually set as the dividing line between middle and old age. Gerontologists have attempted to deal with this unreliable concept of "oldness" after 65 years by dividing old age into two groups: early old age, 65 to 74 years, and advanced old age, 75 years and above.[1] Physical age is a poor measure in determining the beginning of old age because there are many differences among individuals as to when aging actually begins. In most cases men and women of today, because of better living conditions and better medical care, do not show physical and mental characteristics of decline until the mid-sixties or even early seventies.

As the person grows older, he may have less strength, vigor, and speed of reaction, but he compensates for this by increase in skill. For example, an older person's reactions may slow down and cause him to be accident prone when driving, but he compensates for this by driving more slowly and not driving when road conditions are dangerous. This period of old age when the decline is slow and gradual and when compensations can be made for the declines is known as *senescence*. Senescence means to grow old and to show the characteristics of old age. Depending on the mental and physical decline, the person may become senescent in the late fifties or not until the late sixties. When the person has a more or less complete physical breakdown, mental disorganization, or loss of mental faculties, this is known as *senility*. In senility the person becomes careless, absentminded, eccentric, socially withdrawn, and poorly adjusted. This may occur early, or it may

Table 14-1. Physiological age and life-span differences*

REVERSIBLE		PERMANENT	
COMPARISON	YEARS	COMPARISON	YEARS
Country vs. city dwelling	+ 5	Females vs. males	+ 3
Married status vs. single, widowed, divorced	+ 5	Familial constitutions‡	
		2 grandparents lived to age 80 years	+ 2
Overweight		4 grandparents lived to age 80 years	+ 4
25% overweight group	− 3.6	Mother lived to age 90 years	+ 3
35% overweight group	− 4.3	Father lived to age 90 years	+ 4.4
45% overweight group	− 6.6	Both mother and father lived to age 90 years	+ 7.4
55% overweight group	−11.4		
67% overweight group	−15.1	Mother lived to age 80 years	+ 1.5
Or: an average effect of 1% overweight	− 0.17	Father lived to age 80 years	+ 2.2
		Both mother and father lived to age 80 years	+ 3.7
Smoking			
1 package cigarettes per day	− 7	Mother died at 60 years	− 0.7
2 packages cigarettes per day	−12	Father died at 60 years	− 1.1
Atherosclerosis		Both mother and father died at age 60 years	− 1.8
Fat metabolism			
In 25th percentile of population having "ideal" lipoprotein concentrations	+10	Recession of childhood and infectious disease over past century in Western countries	+15
Having average lipoprotein concentrations	0	Life Insurance *Impairment Study*	
		Rheumatic heart disease evidenced by:	
In 25th percentile of population having elevated lipoproteins	− 7	Heart murmur	−11
		Heart murmur + tonsillitis	−18
In 5th percentile of population having highest elevation of lipoproteins	−15†	Heart murmur + streptococcal infection	−13
		Rapid pulse	− 3.5
		Phlebitis	− 3.5
Diabetes		Varicose veins	− 0.2
Uncontrolled, before insulin, 1900	−35	Epilepsy	−20.0
		Skull fracture	− 2.9
Controlled with insulin		Tuberculosis	− 1.8
1920 Joslin Clinic record	−20	Nephrectomy	− 2.0
1940 Joslin Clinic record	−15	Trace of albumin in urine	− 5.0
1950 Joslin Clinic record	−10	Moderate albumin in urine	−13.5

*From Jones, H. B.: The relation of human health to age, place, and timing. In Birren, J. E., Imus, H. A., and Windle, W. F.: The process of aging in the nervous system, Springfield, Ill., 1959, Charles C Thomas, Publisher, p. 354.
†This 70% difference in distribution of lipoproteins, between 25% vs. 5% highest, is equivalent to a total of 25 years in relative displacement of physiological age.
‡As measured in 1900. These effects may be measurably less now, as environment is changing to produce greater differences between parents and progeny.

never occur. Most people become senescent rather than senile.[2]

Gerontology and geriatrics

The word *gerontology* refers to the biological science that studies the aging process of life from a physiological, pathological, psychological, sociological, and economic point of view. Geriatrics is the medical specialty of gerontology in which changes of the aging human system are studied and treated. Much study and attention are also paid to "the aging process," that is, how aging takes place. The problems of the aged are one thing, the process of aging is another.

Barron[3] discusses several factors that he believes account for most of the interest and development of gerontology and geriatrics in recent years. A major factor is the decline of the death rate in Western societies. In 1860 only 2.7% (860,000 people) of the American people were over 65 years of age. By 1950 the percentage had risen to 7.6% and by 1980, according to census estimates, there will be 12.1% (22 million people) in that age group. In 1970, 10 million people were over 73 years of age, and more than 13,000 were over 100 years of age. For every 100 persons over 65 years, fifty-seven are women and forty-three are men. The ratio of women to men changes from 120 women per 100 men for ages 65 to 69 years to more than 160 women for every 100 men at the age of 85 years and over. Since the life expectancy of people 65 years of age and over is nearly thirteen additional years, the problems of older people can be of major consequence for both sexes, but for women especially. Women should be taught how to be widows.

A second underlying factor for recent interest in gerontology is the vast array of problems that confront the aged. Many problems are brought on by a new adult role, problems of living, and changes that affect the well-being and life style of the individual.

A third factor for increased interest is that many individuals are not prepared or educated for old age. Oftentimes retirement is unplanned. People who have worked hard all their lives suddenly reach compulsory retirement age and find nothing but a void in their lives. They are unable to cope with their leisure time.

A fourth factor in the growth of gerontology and geriatrics has been the enactment of legislation on behalf of older people, including the Social Security Act, old age assistance, Medicare, and laws passed to prohibit discrimination against older workers.

A fifth factor is the long-festering dissatisfaction with almshouses, "poor farms," and homes for the aged as institutional forms of rehabilitation and terminal care. Newer forms, such as outpatient geriatric clinics, have been created. Seeing the state mental hospitals overcrowded with geriatric patients who no longer needed institutional care but who did require some form of rehabilitation before being placed in the community, the legislature of Pennsylvania established the South Mountain Geriatric Center to provide this service. They seek to rehabilitate the elderly to independent self-help care and then place them in foster homes.

The impressive increase in the number and variety of clubs and fraternal organizations by and for the aged is a sixth factor for new interest in geriatrics. Golden Age Clubs and similar "senior citizens" organizations are principally social and seek to overcome the detrimental by-products of isolation in old age. The Townsend Clubs and other political pressure groups seek to influence all kinds of legislative action. All of these groups provide a measure of group therapy that helps to meet some of the needs of the aged.

The seventh factor is the evolving awareness of the traditional professions who have an interest in the problems of the elderly. More and more professional organizations of medicine, psychology, social science, nursing, and housing have formed committees and divisions to deal with the problems and needs of the aged.

Finally, gerontology and geriatrics have increased their activities in research. Systematic exploration into the aging processes and its problems is now being conducted in every conceivable discipline. Two of the major areas of current research are aging and the diseases of old age. There are still a great many unanswered questions in this area, however. For example, some of the pressing questions include: What are the factors that influence the rate of aging? What potentials and capacities do older people possess? What methods are most appropriate in the care of the senile aged person?

LIFE IN LATER ADULTHOOD

G. Stanley Hall,[4] a pioneer researcher and writer of developmental psychology, observes that the young should prudently plan for maturity. He raises the question, "Should not forty plan for eighty, or at least sixty, just as intently as twenty does for forty?" His point is well taken. Life after the age of 60 years is so completely different from that at any other age level. It would be advisable to prepare for such things as retirement, retirement living, and eventualities brought on by changes, decline, and losses.

Developmental tasks

Old age is no different from other age levels when it comes to having special adaptations that need to be made and special tasks to be achieved if the individual wishes to live effectively, happily, and confidently on that age level. The only difference is that the developmental tasks of old age are the final or ultimate ones in life and revolve about the conditions of life in that time period. The person must accept the concept and the fact of retirement. Furthermore, he must adjust to living on Social Security and/or small retirement income. Both of these tasks will require a change in personal attitudes and concepts. Learning how to live in retirement, that is how to occupy leisure time so that life is pleasant, will require some thought. Some people manage this problem by establishing contact with organizations for retirees and sharing with others of the same age group whatever benefits the organizations can offer. The elderly couple will also have to become closer companions to each other and learn how to intermesh their lives without getting on each other's nerves.

It will be necessary for the individual to reevaluate his self-concept and personal identity in light of the new role he plays in life. A workable, personal philosophy of life, including a view about death and eternity, will probably be evolved. A major task will be to accept physical changes and their limitations by learning to conserve strength and resources when necessary. Other specific developmental tasks include finding satisfactory housing on retirement income, maintaining interest in people outside the family, maintaining some degree of family ties with children and grandchildren, taking care of elderly relatives, being able to cope with bereavement and widowhood, and continuing to meet social and civic responsibilities by being involved in society and its affairs.

Advent of retirement

Retirement is generally thought of as the time when old age begins. The age of 65 years has been established in American society as the common retirement age. Apparently, this age was rather arbitrarily established by Congress when it first provided for old age benefits under the Social Security Act, and everyone else went along with the idea.

Perhaps the most important immediate result of retirement is what some have chosen to call "retirement shock." This condition may further be identified as a period of great personal crisis and turmoil, not unlike that which an individual faces during late adolescence or early adulthood when he is faced with the responsibility of finding a meaningful field of endeavor. More frequently, it is the prospect of retirement rather than retirement itself that leads to a morbid state of mind. This "shock" or feeling of estrangement manifests itself in many ways. Doubts about one's future usefulness, financial worries because of reduced income, and the emptiness felt because of the lack of social intercourse are only a few ramifications of the retirement shock phenomenon.

Everyone must have some feeling of apprehension concerning his future usefulness to society. Satisfactions once derived from a job well done are now removed from the immediate experience and can now only be used as the material for reflection. This would seem to be especially true for a person engaged in a helping or service occupation, where much or all of the person's time was spent helping other people. Occupations such as teaching, the ministry, medicine, and social work would seem to fall into this category. On the other hand, an industrial-type occupation, where the worker is a small part of an assembly-line process, would give him little opportunity to see the results of his labor, and therefore little personal satisfaction would result. In this respect perhaps the shock of retirement is not as great for the person who is engaged in an industrial type of occupation.

Financial matters preoccupy many people of postretirement age. It is possible that this is the most realistic concern of old age. After being financially independent for forty-five or fifty years most elderly people dread the possibility of not being able to support themselves. As a result, they have a tendency to become rather parsimonious with their financial resources. We know of several persons who went into great depth trying to figure out how they were going to live on their retirement income. Every penny was counted. Fixed expenditures were figured out. Often the person would say things like, "I have to stop subscribing to the newspaper," or "I'll have to give up smoking." It should be emphasized, however, that for many old people retirement incomes are inadequate for current prices, and becoming miserly is an economic necessity. On the other hand, it is also true that less income is needed in retirement. Income needs decrease by 40% to 60% because of the decrease in employment-related activities, social activities, and even in clothing and eating needs.

The theory of disengagement states that one of the elements of aging is a decreased amount of social interaction between the elderly and their former social life space. In this regard, retirement represents perhaps the most important occurrence in the process of disengagement. Often the worker's associates constitute the bulk of his social acquaintances. The severance of the associations with the people with whom he works may also mean a corresponding loss in more general social activity. Here, then, is another source of shock to which the retiree needs to adjust.

As more and more is being learned about the specific problems of retirement, increased attention is being focused on the problem of forced retirement. Researchers are finding that many of the problems associated with retirement are the results of individual differences and the state of "readiness" for the transition. Some of the country's largest employers are split "down the middle" on whether or not retirement should be compulsory at the age of 65 years.[5]

Those who support compulsory retirement argue their position with the following point of view: It is the fairest way and avoids giving a worker the stigma of being "washed up" while someone else the same age is kept on; it is a painless way of getting rid of those who have outlived their usefulness; finally, compulsory retirement opens promotion opportunities for younger men.

Those who are opposed to compulsory retirement but in favor of discretionary retirement insist the following: It is necessary to keep people of great value for longer than the age of 65 years; the valuable people will fall into the hands of the competition if released; some people will be forced into unhappy idleness. W. Ferguson Anderson,[6] University of Glasgow Department of Medicine, maintains that in the age group of 60 to 80 years is an "immense potential of knowledge, skill and experience." It would be the ultimate in wastefulness to retire all people because they are 65 years old.

Frederic Lewis, Inc., New York City.

Each of the preceding arguments has some merit, but perhaps the ideal situation would be to treat each worker as the individual he is, instead of adhering to all-inclusive policies that will benefit some and adversely affect others. Employers need to reexamine their present policies and come up with plans that will most benefit the employees in their own situations.

When a person retires voluntarily, presumably he does so because he believes that he will be happier in retirement than continuing as a member of the labor force. Granted he may be dissatisfied with his job or have some motive other than the primary motive of entering into a better way of life with retirement. In any case, if the decision to retire is his, the chances are that he enters retirement without the feeling of having outlived his usefulness to society that so often accompanies compulsory retirement.

A most obvious and prevalent form of segregation of old persons is the fixing of a chronological age at which it is compulsory to abandon their jobs, or above which employers will not hire them. This practice clearly applies a classification that is irrelevant to the efficiency of any given individual, to the need for his services, or to his own needs. A worker who is told that his employment is being terminated involuntarily on age alone may suffer an affront to his personal dignity and status. He enters retirement with a resentment toward the society that forced him into it. He would rather be at his job and will find it difficult to generate any interest in new activities. Time is likely to hang heavily on his hands, and instead of enjoying retirement, he will tend to brood over the injustice done to him.

Whether or not a person wishes to retire, the time does eventually come. Ideally, retirement should come gradually, with a tapering off of job activity. Some company executives, if they happen to be owners or part owners of the company, are able to do this. Professional people are often able to slow down and move out gradually. But most people cannot do this; therefore, it would seem advisable to begin making retirement plans long before the time actually arrives—to anticipate and overcome as many of the problems of retirement as possible.

An individual should prepare himself for retirement in the same way that he would prepare himself for any other undertaking. Planning should start in a practical and positive way while the worker is still on the job. He should cultivate a wholesome attitude toward retirement. It is vitally important that he look at retirement from the forward-looking position of "retiring to" rather than "retiring from." In this way the retiree will possess the optimism and adaptability necessary to cope with the various problems he will almost certainly have to face.

In preparing himself, it should be remembered that security in retirement is a balance of three things: physical security—reasonably good health to be able to do the things he really wants to do; activity security—a program and the opportunity for satisfying and rewarding accomplishments; financial security—having sufficient money to make it possible to achieve these goals. Of the three, activity security usually receives the least consideration during the planning, yet it is extremely important.

Bernard Isaacs,[7] consultant geriatrician at the Glasgow Royal Infirmary, says that much of the physical and mental ill health of old men can be traced to their retirement. There is no easy solution to the problem of enforced leisure in retirement, but many forward-looking attempts are being made to meet the difficulties. These include courses in preparation for retirement, in which workers approaching retirement are given an understanding of the financial, social, and psychological changes that they can anticipate and are advised about how to make constructive use of their leisure. Some firms encourage retired workers to return to the factory and offer them part-time employment in a special workshop. In some areas local authorities and voluntary groups provide workshops and craft centers where the skills of the retired worker can still be used.

Ewald W. Busse,[8] Director of The Center for the Study of Aging and Human Development at Duke University Medical Center, Durham, North Carolina, urges a "social career" for the retired person. The young person has a student career, the adult has an economic career, and if the older person has a social career, it will provide him with an orderly work pattern as well as the concomitant personal recognition and respect in his community. This corresponds with the activity theory, which states that health in old age is improved through mental and physical activity and is a countermeasure to the disengagement theory, which believes that there is significant withdrawal from activities and a reduction in social interaction at that time. The elderly can and should make valuable contributions to society.

Social aspects

One of the most important things an older person must do is to keep active. An old proverb says: "It is difficult to remain at peace in idleness." A life of doing nothing will only lead to increased emptiness. Work, to some degree, should continue. Most women can continue to cook, look after their husbands, and take care of the house. Men and women should start some of the projects that they have put off for so long. Reading, travel, visits to art museums, and developing new talents are all important in old age. Although it is important for a person to keep active and alert, he must also know when to stop, even if he is just taking a walk.

Friends and family. As a person develops, he becomes part of a social unit. He is a member of a family, and he has friends who add satisfaction and joy to his life. The social life of old people is narrowed increasingly by the loss of work associates, the death of relatives, friends, and spouse, and poor health, which restricts their participation in social activities. There are three types of social relationships that are affected by aging: close personal friendships, such as husband and wife, siblings, and friends from childhood days; friendship cliques made up of couples banded together in a social crowd when they were younger; and formal groups or clubs. Once broken, these social relationships are rarely replaced in old age. Also, as the elderly person's interest in self increases, interest in other people decreases. Married people are socially more active in old age than are those who are single or widowed, and those from upper socioeconomic groups are more socially active than those from lower socioeconomic groups.

To the elderly person his family makes up the nucleus of his social life. The older he becomes, the more he must rely on his family for companionship. His friends have either died or are physically unable to do things with him. He cannot keep pace with younger friends and, as a result, is no longer a welcome member of a younger group. Thus the old person must limit his social contacts to family members or to individuals of his own age. This means generally a group of intimate friends, many of whom have been friends since childhood or young adulthood days. One advantage of living in a social institution is that it provides the great advantage of opportunities for social contacts with contemporaries. The elderly person's contemporaries have interests, problems, and physical traits in common with his. However, many elderly people resist making this adjustment and, as a result, cut themselves off from social contacts.

Many communities are trying to meet the social needs of the aged by starting social clubs for them with activities planned to fit into their interests and capacities. Those who take advantage of any opportunities they have for social participation and who make an effort to retain old friendships or establish new ones, not only make a better adjustment to old age than do those who are socially inactive but find old age a far happier period of life than they had anticipated when they were younger. As is true at every age, the social needs of the individual at that period of his life must be met to his satisfaction if he wants to be happy.

Housing. A place in which to live poses yet another problem. Most older people prefer to live in their own dwellings. The next acceptable arrangement would be to live with someone of the same sex. Most widows think that it would not be wise to live with married sons or daughters. Living with relatives often causes overcrowding, annoying situations caused by small children, and tense situations with the children. In today's society, however, family belongingness, in many cases, is being replaced by community belongingness, which is making the individual less dependent on his family.

There are a few main prerequisites of good housing for older people. Housing should provide as much independence and privacy as possible, while still being near other older people and proper medical facilities.[9] Older people need greater warmth and freedom from drafts and often other types of controls such as air pollution and humidity controls. Proper illumination is also important because the eyes of older people are slower to adjust to changes in light; therefore each room that they use should have the same intensity of light. Noise level is a problem that many people do not realize. Older people, especially those with a vision problem, become most annoyed and tense when there is too much silence because they depend on their hearing for sensory input. As older people gradually lose their hearing, they must adjust sound volume to a higher level.

At present a popular notion is that the best way to spend one's retirement years is to move into the "sunshine belt." The results are by no means conclusive, but many "transplanted" people find little or no real satisfaction in moving away. What many of them need most is the friendship and concern of family and close friends. Moving away generally results in serious feelings of loneliness for these people. Coping with an unfamiliar environment just adds one more complication to an already complicated problem for some people.

On the other hand, a new environment for some people is definitely beneficial. A "retirement community" or a temporary "Florida-for-the-winter" type of venture may be just the potion some people need to regain vitality and interest in life; but it is not for everybody.

The aged and their children. The aged often have definite opinions concerning their relationships with their children. In a study at Cornell University by Streib[10] 84% of the parents of adult children believed that the children should visit often; 82% wanted the children to write often. Many of the feelings that older individuals experience are vicarious ones. Because of this, they feel a deep need to keep in close touch with their children and to continue to share their experiences. At the same time the grandparents do not want to interfere in their children's lives.

The aged think that their children should be expected to "help some" in financial assistance but "not a great deal." Many of the children, however, want the parents to apply for old age assistance, even though the children themselves could help.

Most aging parents consider their relationship with their children to be satisfactory. They have reached some kind of mutual agreement and know how each stands. They have a list of acceptable responses from their children that are usually met. Many elderly individuals, when surveyed, present a picture entirely different from that usually thought of in connection with the elderly. Instead of a lonely person sitting around in a rocking chair, Streib found a group of people who were useful both to themselves and society with a wide range of interests that many younger people do not have.

Probably the time of greatest conflict between aged parents and their children is at retirement. One should remember that retirement at the age of 65 years means that the "children" are probably about 45, 40, or 35 years old—at the peak of adulthood. The retiring couple are having their problems adjusting their thoughts and attitudes to the idea of retirement. They are uncertain and indecisive. They worry out loud about their concerns and try to reason out their problems from all angles. They may come up with "logical" answers, but they never seem to do anything about them. They are on a merry-go-round with their concerns and do not know how to get off. The children always seem to see things more clearly, "It's so obvious," and they are quick to give them opinions, "You should move out of this big house into a smaller place, maybe an apartment, where you won't have as much housekeeping to do." "You should move here (or there) ..." for any number of reasons that make sense to the children. Yet the old couple are reluctant to act. It becomes most exasperating to their children.

This would be the moment for the children to step back and examine what is happening. Their parents are at a point in life where they are contemplating major changes and moves. On the one hand the move seems so sensible, yet on the other hand the "feel" is not quite right, thus the hesitancy. It should be recognized that not all good decisions can be based on cold, hard facts alone. People are not machines. They are warm-blooded human beings with feelings, sentimental attachments, and maybe even fears. Children must keep in mind that just because their parents of retirement age find it hard to make decisions about where to live and what to do, this is no indication that their parents have become enfeebled and have lost their powers of intellectual reasoning and judgment. The parents should be allowed to move at their own pace. It is surprising how, in spite of all the concerns, they work things out. Children should not interfere unless asked specifically to do so. Even then, they should not be upset if their advice is not taken. The final decision should rest with the parents.

William T. Swaim, Jr.,[11] a former administrator of Presbyterian Homes of Central Pennsylvania, has written much on the aged and their lives. He gives some tips in *What Shall We Do With Granny?*

1. Let Granny do what she wants to do, even if it kills her. She is not as vulnerable as you think.
2. Do not expect perfection.
3. Make due allowance for any words or actions that may be caused by cerebral changes.
4. Treat Granny as a person. Let her make her own decisions. Respect her interests and needs.
5. Be demonstrative. Shake hands, hug her, kiss her.
6. Learn to listen long and smile even if you've heard it all before.
7. Do everything possible to build up her ego.
8. Impart information, tell her why, if you must change her mind or wishes.
9. Do not ruin your own health and happiness to minister to her nursing needs if they are beyond your capabilities.
10. Encourage Granny to remain employed as long as possible.
11. If Granny desires to remarry, remember "It is not good that man should be alone."
12. Move heaven and earth to keep Granny living with her own furniture and amid familiar scenes and faces as long as possible.
13. Do not force three-generation living which may deny Granny privacy, quiet and independence.
14. Make it easy and delightful for Granny to share chores.
15. Let her go to a home for the aging if that is her desire.
16. Welcome old age. Let your study of Granny's personality remind you to grow older graciously.
17. Have respect for Granny's age. Nurses should not call elderly patients by their first names.

Health maintenance

Any advice to the elderly concerning the maintenance of good health consistently includes suggestions for an adequate diet. Increasingly, evidence points to the necessity for the aged to be vitally concerned about their eating habits. The report of the White House Conference on Aging[12] indicates that individuals in 53% of the households containing people over 60 years of age had generally inadequate diets. Of concern, especially in recent years, has been the diet and its relationship to cardiac problems. As a result, physicians have almost always put their older patients on low-fat, high-protein diets.

Older people have the tendency to neglect their diets for a variety of reasons. Sadly, this neglect can frequently be traced to inadequate incomes. As a consequence, these people eat inexpensive foods that invariably are of the high-calorie, low-protein variety. Another common reason why people often do not receive adequate food is the preparation necessary for a nourishing, well-balanced meal. Often the person sees no real reason to go to a lot of "fuss" for just himself or perhaps one other person. As a result, shortcuts are taken and an inadequate diet results.

Another danger concerning the diet is that often elderly people have a tendency to overeat. They do not seem to realize that their caloric requirements are probably decreasing as the years pass, and the excess calories they consume simply turn into fat. This, then, becomes one more factor in the eventual deterioration of health. Physicians will frequently prescribe light exercise for their elderly patients. The exercise or activity is beneficial physically and also mentally because it helps the older person to avoid the "illness of idleness."

Accidents and safety

Older people have a disproportionate share of accidents that cause bodily injury or death. This is especially true for accidents that occur in the home. They also have an extremely high accident rate on the highway when the total number of miles driven is taken into consideration. A 1957 study showed that persons 65 years of age and older made up 9% of the total population but accounted for 28% of all accidental deaths and 20% of all accidents causing bodily injury.[13]

Complicating the matter is the fact that the recuperative processes take much longer for the older person. The study done in 1957 showed that the average hospital stay for those 65 years old and older was 24.1 days compared with 17 days for the total population and 4.8 days for children under 15 years of age.

It has been found that safety devices, especially those which help the older person maintain balance, have contributed significantly to their physical and mental well-being. In addition, care should be taken to remove all accident "traps" that may cause the elderly to fall, such as loose carpets. A small amount of concern on the part of the family and neighbors of the elderly person may save him from dangers he does not realize exist and to which he is therefore extremely susceptible.

AGE LEVEL CHANGES

As with all age levels, later adulthood has characteristics that are peculiar to it. Many changes take place in old age and if the types and numbers of these changes are carefully considered, they will be found to be no greater or more drastic than those of other age levels.

Physical characteristics and changes

It is true that physical changes do occur with aging and that they are in the direction of deterioration. Individual differences are so great, however, that no two individuals of the same age are necessarily at the same state of deterioration. Within the same person there are also variations in the rates of aging of different structures. Different parts of the body resist aging more than others, and the various abilities fade at different rates.

The physical condition of the aging person depends on his psychological temperament, his manner of living, his hereditary constitution, and also factors in the environment. Hereditary constitution plays a major role as a cause of physical change. Aging changes appear at different ages for different individuals, but within a family the rate of aging shows a high correlation for the different family members. Individuals with a small build have been found to live longer than those with larger builds.[14] Secondary causes that have significant influences on the rate of physical decline include faulty diet, malnutrition, gluttony, emotional stresses, overwork, passivity, infections, drug or alcohol intoxications, traumas and endocrine disorders. Environmental conditions such as heat and cold also influence the rate of aging.

Some age changes such as wrinkles, graying hair, stooping shoulders, reduced agility and speed of motion, decrease in strength, decrease in the steadiness of the hands and legs, and more difficulty in moving about are obvious in the aging individual. Some changes such as thinning hair and varicose veins can be upsetting to those who find it difficult to adjust to changes in physical appearance. The acceptance or rejection of aging is responsible for psychological aging, and the rate of psychological aging is directly related to how well an individual will accept change.

Wrinkling of the skin is caused by the loss of elastic tissue and the fatty layer. The skin does not snap back as readily when stretched. If you pinch the skin on the back of an older person's hand, you will see how it has lost much of its elasticity. The skin also has increased sensitivity to changes in temperature. Since automatic regulation of bodily functions no longer takes place as promptly as previously, older persons often "feel the cold more." The sense of touch also declines with age because there is a general drying, wrinkling, and toughening of the skin.

During the period of senescence, the sensory functions seem to be one of the first areas of the body to deteriorate. Hearing begins to decline about the age of 65 years. First affected in hearing is the ability to hear very high tones, and as time goes on, the level of auditory acuity becomes progressively lower. There is also a decline in the individual's vision as he grows older—few people over 60 years of age see well without glasses. This decline is usually caused by deterioration of the cornea, lens, iris, retina, and optic nerve. Color perception and the power of the eye to adjust to different levels of light and dark are reduced. There is a gradual loss of orbital fat so that eventually the eyes appear sunken, the blink reflex is slower, and the eyelids hang loosely because of poorer muscle tone.

The sense of smell and taste are also reduced in function during these advancing years. One reason for poor taste ability is the decrease in the number of taste buds in the mouth to 36% of those in the younger person, and even these buds are not as keen as they were during childhood and adolescence.[15] Due to the faltering of the senses of smell and taste, the older person will become easily upset about certain things associated with these senses. For example, he will complain that the food has no taste, even though much preparation has gone into the meal.

Vocal changes are partly caused by the hardening and decreased elasticity of the laryngeal cartilages. The voice becomes more highly pitched, and in advanced old age it becomes less powerful and is restricted in range. Singing and public speaking show deterioration earlier than do normal speaking voices in younger individuals. Speech becomes slower, and pauses become longer and more frequent; slurring often occurs due to pathological changes in the brain.

The skeleton gives shape and firmness to the body, provides attachments for the muscles, protects important organs such as the brain, heart, and lungs, and together with the striated muscles provides man with a leverage system for pushing and lifting. Full stature is reached by the late teens or early twenties. Afterward there is little or no change in the length of the individual bones, although there may be a slight loss in overall height in old age, brought about by atrophy of the discs between the spinal vertebrae. As age progresses, the chemical composition of the bone changes; the bones become less dense and more brittle. This increases the risk of breakage late in life. Movement of the joints becomes stiffer and more restricted, the incidence of diseases affecting these parts of the body increases with age, and the skeleton may suffer from cumulative effects of damage and disease.

In our contacts with the aged we have noticed an increase in this stiffness as the individuals begin to withdraw from activity It therefore seems reasonable to follow the advice so often given—that you do as little as possible for them so that they will be forced to exercise their joints and keep them functioning for a longer time. As soon as someone begins to assist some elderly persons, they stop doing things for themselves and become dependent on others.

In adult life teeth may cause pain and discomfort; the gums recede, and the teeth become yellowish. Loss of teeth or changes in their appearance may bring home the fact that the individual is aging physically. Having to resort to dentures often means that, at least temporarily, the person cannot eat or sleep as well, which may cause dismay and embarrassment. A person's disposition can be affected greatly. Changes in the jaws and face associated with old age are primarily consequences of reduction in size, and many of the facial evidences of old age may be prevented by proper care or replacement of teeth.

The functional capacities of a 30-year-old man and a 75-year-old man are compared in Table 14-2. After the age of 30 years there is a gradual and small reduction in the speed and power of muscular contractions and a decreased capacity for sustained muscular effort due to biochemical changes in the protein molecules of the fibers. Muscles begin to lose their strength in the middle years. After about the age of 50 years the number of active muscle fibers steadily decreases, and eventually the typical diminished appearance of the older person occurs. The involuntary smooth muscles that operate under the autonomic nervous system are affected only slightly, as compared to the other structures. They appear to function without difficulty even until late senescence. The ligaments, however, do tend to contract and harden, causing the familiar hunched-over body position.

The digestive system also seems to alter with age; in fact, complaints about the digestive system are among the most common of all the complaints of the aged. There is a reduction in the amount of saliva, gastric juices, and enzyme action, thus upsetting the digestion process. Because the digestive system is highly sensitive to emotional disturbances, anxieties and worries that ac-

Table 14-2. Functional capacity of an average 75-year-old man compared to 100% functional capacity of a 30-year-old man*

PHYSICAL CHARACTERISTIC	COMPARATIVE PERCENTAGE
Nerve conduction velocity	90
Body weight for males	88
Basal metabolic rate	84
Body water content	82
Blood flow to brain	80
Maximum work rate	70
Cardiac output (at rest)	70
Glomerular filtration rate	69
Number of nerve trunk fibers	63
Brain weight	56
Number of glomeruli in kidney	56
Vital capacity	56
Hand grip	55
Maximum ventilation volume (during exercise)	53
Kidney plasma flow	50
Maximum breathing capacity (voluntary)	43
Maximum oxygen uptake (during exercise)	40
Number of taste buds	36
Speed of return to equilibrium of blood acidity	17
Also: Less adrenal and gonadal activity Slower speed of response Some memory loss	

*From Shock, N. W.: The physiology of ageing. Copyright 1962 by Scientific American, Inc. All rights reserved.

company old age will play an important part in bringing about stomach deterioration.

Of all the organs in man's body, the heart and the blood vessels are the ones in which aging produces the most detrimental changes. Most of the other organs, such as the lungs, kidneys, and brain, would probably last for 150 years if they were assured an adequate blood supply. The heart and arteries are the weakest link in the chain of life.[16]

Aging affects the heart in several ways. The muscles in the heart tend to become stringy and dried out with the passage of time. Deposits of a brown pigment within the cells of the heart tend to restrict the passage of blood and impede the absorption of oxygen through its walls. The heart shrinks in size during the normal course of aging, and the fat in the heart increases. The valves of the heart lose their elasticity, and deposits of calcium and cholesterol may further decrease their efficiency. The heart of an older person pumps 70% as much blood as that of a young man. These changes in themselves are not necessarily dangerous, provided the heart is treated with the respect it deserves and not subjected to the stress of physical effort more appropriate to the young.

In later life many heart diseases involve the coronary artery, which has a tendency to harden and narrow and may become partially blocked. It is the site of many heart attacks brought on by increased physical effort or emotional stress. Hardening of the coronary artery may also be responsible for increased blood pressure, reducing the flow of blood to most parts of the body. Poor circulation of blood, whatever the cause, may result in trouble or breakdown of the kidneys and other organs. Poor circulation to the brain causes many personality deviations in older persons.

There are some structural changes in the nervous system and brain that occur as the person ages. Although there is little functional change in the nerves, the nerve tissue will be gradually replaced by fibrous cells. There will be a slower reaction and reflex time. The folds of the brain become less prominent, possibly resulting in decreased circulation of blood within the brain. There might be a decrease in the total number of cells, but the brain functions normally unless its blood supply is blocked, even briefly. The cortical area of the brain responsible for organizing the total perceptual processes often experiences degenerative changes. A person afflicted with cerebral arteriosclerosis will show some atrophy of brain tissue.

There is some evidence that homeostasis is less efficient in older people. If stabilizing mechanisms become sluggish, the physiological adaptability of the individual is reduced. Wounds heal more slowly. It takes longer for the breathing and heart rate to return to normal. Heat losses are less quickly restored. Sleep habits may undergo a change. The thyroid gland is smaller, resulting in a lower rate of basal metabolism. The pancreas loses some of its ability to produce the enzymes that are used in sugar and protein metabolism. Most glands function at close to normal rates all through life.

Another effect of aging is the reduction of respiratory efficiency. There is a decrease of oxygen utilization due to a decrease in the size of the lungs in senescence. Some functioning air sac membrane is replaced by fibrous tissue, interfering with the exchange of gases within the lungs. Maximum lung capacity in old age is 56%, and breathing capacity is 43%. Moderate exercise is ideal for keeping oxygen intake and blood flow at their level of highest potential, thus slowing down the aging and deterioration process.

In summary, according to Wolff,[17] the ten most common physical characteristics of biological aging are (1) an increase in connective tissue, (2) the disappearance of cellular elements in the central nervous system, (3) the loss of elastic properties in the connective tissue, (4) a reduction in the number of normally functioning cells, (5) an increase in fatty tissue, (6) a decrease in the utilization of oxygen, (7) a decrease in the volume of air expired by the lungs, (8) an overall decrease in muscular strength, and (9) a decrease in the excretion of hormones, especially by the sex and adrenal glands.

These changes in the body do not necessarily mean that the healthy aged person cannot function within normal limits. It does mean that there is less resistance to physical stress and less ability to recuperate. There is no single change that is of supreme major importance. It is the accumulation of changes that will be meaningful.

Sexuality. Generally, society tends to think that sexual activity is limited to young through middle-aged individuals. Some people have the misconception that age automatically puts a stop to sexual thoughts and relations. This, however, is not the case. Some people believe that it is wrong for older persons to think about or engage in sexual activity. These attitudes may hinder an older person's sex life if he believes them. Although a person is physically able to participate in sex activity, mentally he may not think this way and thus inhibit all sexual activity. Kinsey[18] has described sexuality in older people realistically. He believes that interest and desire of sex do not decline with age and that the aged have sexual needs and seek erotic outlets just as do younger people.

Kinsey's research found that more than three fourths of 50- and 60-year-old couples maintain sexual relations, although they do not engage in sexual activity as frequently. Sexual activity can continue throughout life, but it does become less frequent throughout married life. Thus at the ages of 50 and 60 years the pattern of infrequency is a continuation of a pattern generated over the years.

Research has disclosed the potency, that

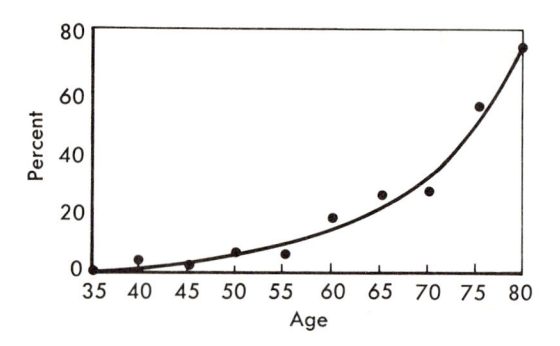

Fig. 14-1. Age of onset of impotence. (Modified from Kinsey, A. C., Pomeroy, W. B., and Martin, C. E.: Sexual behavior in the human male, Philadelphia, 1948, W. B. Saunders Co.)

is, capability of erection, of males during old age (Fig. 14-1). The findings are that about four out of five men are still potent at the age of 60 years, about 70% at 70 years, and at least 25% at 80 years.[19] Sexuality is not a set factor depending solely on age for its deterioration or discontinuance. This information would seem to indicate that if a man has good health, adequate opportunities, and is not conditioned by society, he may remain potent as long as he lives.

Factors in aging

Although the aging process is gradual, it is sometimes speeded up, starting during adolescence and increasing with the advent of disease. A person with a severe handicap will often age much faster and earlier than a person who is not handicapped. Even with the so-called "normal" person there is always a difference in the rate of aging due to the combined forces of biological, psychological, and sociological factors.

Many people do not realize that environmental factors play a large part in aging. Environmental factors include the people and attitudes that surround the individual. Activity tends to slow down the aging process, but insecurity, lack of someone to talk to, and a strange environment may speed up the aging process.[20]

Throughout life the body is exposed to a procession of accidents, illnesses, and stress, such as a bout of pneumonia, a broken leg, a severe burn, or a period of great psychological stress. The cumulative effect of such "biological insults" may well hasten aging.[21] Ionizing radiation is cumulative and even in the smallest doses decreases the lifespan. Radiation may be accumulated from medical and dental x-ray treatment, cosmic rays, and even the luminous dial of a wristwatch.

Malnutrition is a major contributor to physical deterioration. An older person oftentimes "loses his appetite" and will not eat much. His diet may not be adequate, since he may not be eating the proper foods or not be eating enough of them. Poor eating habits may accelerate aging. In some people the connective tissue becomes increasingly hard and impervious, and this may interfere with the distribution of nutrients and the disposal of wastes. Genetic inheritance definitely plays a role. People with long-lived parents have a somewhat greater life expectancy than people with short-lived parents. One theory supports the view that there is a certain length of time, genetically determined, in which the body has to function. A timing device within the organism causes tissues and organ systems to break down at specific times.

Functional activity of the cells seems to be all-important to the aging process. Cells sometimes make errors when they reproduce. This leads to an accumulation of mutant cells that are unable to survive or cells that may become malignant. Occasionally, aberrations in cells activate the immune mechanism, which in turn reacts against these cells and seeks to destroy them. Ordinarily, the immune mechanism only reacts against bacteria and viruses. One theory states that poisonous by-products arise from the activity of the body, depositing metabolic "clinkers," which eventually block the transporting of nutrients within the cells.[22]

Nature apparently has a built-in mechanism or factors that promote aging. Growing old is part of the natural developmental process. Biological aging is marked by a lowering metabolic rate, which slows down energy exchange. This in turn makes general health more precarious. Almost all bodily systems deteriorate in both their functional and structural efficiency. Structural decline occurs in the blood vessels, heart, and circulatory system in general. The capacity of the lungs at the age of 60 years is only half of that at 30 years. Therefore less oxygen gets into the system and fewer nutrients and fluids are circulated throughout the body, permitting degenerative diseases and illnesses to occur and exist with a diminished capacity of bodily resources to overcome them.

Much has been written in recent years about the value of exercise in maintaining good health and in slowing down aging. An interesting study is being conducted by Herbert de Vries[23] of the University of Southern California's Gerontology Center on this topic. He and his team took a mobile laboratory designed for research in the physiology of exercise and aging to a retirement community in Laguna Hills, California. Over 125 older men volunteered to work out in his program. Statistics indicated dramatic improvement in physical conditioning of the subjects, who followed a program of modified Royal Canadian Air Force calisthenics, jogging, walking, a static stretching routine, and swimming. For the group, maximum oxygen increased 9.2% and oxygen pulse (a measure of cardiovascular function) improved 8.4%. Oxygen intake appears to be the key to endurance fitness. De Vries is developing a pharmacopoeia of exercise that will be used by physicians to determine the kind and amount of exercise that an individual should have.

There appears to be an upper age limit for human beings. The life-span of anyone who reaches the age of 65 years has not been increased more than a half year since

1900. People are not living to be 200 years old, in spite of medical advances. Scientists have pretty much given up the idea of increasing man's life-span in older age and are now concentrating on making the latter years of life a time that has less debilitating disease.[24]

Mental changes

Lack of mental alertness is common in many older people. "I just can't remember anything. I am becoming so forgetful," said one elderly person. There are two major reasons for this forgetfulness. First, it may be organically caused by a deterioration of the arteries, commonly called hardening of the arteries. When blood flow is impaired, the brain ceases to receive the nourishment necessary for effective functioning of cognitive processes. The other reason is an apparent loss of interest in current events. Often older people take refuge in their memories of previous undertakings in which they were successful. In spite of the fact that an older person may score lower on intelligence tests than before, the ability to learn declines slowly in senescence. Age changes in the ability to learn are small under most circumstances. When differences do appear, they do not seem to be readily attributed to a change in the capacity to learn but rather to a change in the processes of perception, set, attention, motivation, and physiological state of the organism, including that of disease states.[25]

Studies indicate that the ability to learn is approximately the same at the age of 80 years as it is at 12 years. If the aged want to learn, they can. Learning may be slower, but it can be accomplished. It is false therefore to say, "An old dog cannot learn new tricks." The Duke University Center for Study of Aging and Human Development[26] has exhaustively tested the learning ability of the aged. The researchers conclude that the aged can learn, but more slowly than the young. They state that the older person's goal is more to avoid failure than to gain success. However, certain changes in the brain can make a difference in thinking along the "flexibility-rigidity" continuum. This person becomes more rigid and less capable of doing the problem-solving reasoning that requires a broad dimension of thought.

An elderly person attacks a problem differently than a younger person, tending to refer back to his own previous experience in his attempt to solve problems. If this approach is appropriate, he can cope effectively with the situation; but if it is inappropriate, the older person often misunderstands the problem and makes frequent mistakes because of his misconceptions and misinterpretations. He adopts a literal instead of a hypothetical approach to solving problems with logical implications.

In training situations the old person seems to be more involved and shows more care and greater concentration than a younger person. In working to minimize the risk of error, he usually sacrifices speed to stress accuracy. There is a slowing down of mental action and sensorimotor speed due to delay within the central nervous system. The slower performance of the elderly on many tasks is not necessarily due to a loss of capacity for the task but, rather, is caused by insufficient time for the slowed cerebral processes to be completed.[27]

The most noticeable symptoms of mental decline in old age are the deterioration of memory for recent events and the gradual loss of the power of attention. Perceptual accuracy shows a decline in the older person and is due to the decline of the peripheral sense organs. The motor skills deteriorate next, followed by intellectual functions. The elderly person is not as efficient intellectually as he was in earlier years.

During senescence, however, not all aspects of intellectual functioning decline at the same rate. In most cases the person's intelligent use of vocabulary and the recall of general information are not affected until the later years of senile decline. Verbal skills seem to deteriorate more slowly than mathematical skills. Judgment and imagination generally do not decline as rapidly as memory and attention.[28] Little is known about the difference between men and women in the way that intelligence is affected by aging. Existing evidence suggests that the age changes are the same for both sexes.

In a twelve-year study conducted by the National Institutes of Health and the Philadelphia Geriatric Center[29] with regard to the correlation between intelligence and longevity, it was found that the subjects who lived longest functioned at a higher intellectual level than those who died before the study was completed. Of the original forty-seven volunteers, twenty-three survived until the end of the study (1968), with an average age of 81 years at that time. Intelligence tests used were the Wechsler Adult Intelligence Scale (WAIS) and the Raven Progressive Matrices Test. The researchers found "no significant decline" on the test performances and actually saw "significant increases in ability" for the vocabulary and picture arrangement subtests of the WAIS. Therefore for these forty-seven men survival seemed to be associated with retention of intellectual vigor and capabilities.

Keeping active apparently is of vital importance not only for one's physiological well-being but also for helping to retain intellectual capabilities. The word *active* applies both to mental activity and to physical activity through a regular fitness routine.

Psychological changes

Older people need tangible relationships and experiences that will bolster their waning ego and provide them with evidence that will help them to sustain their identity.[30] Psychological changes in senescence are a result of a developmental process in which the psychological phenomena may be morbid at one moment and adaptive at another. The older person faces a variety of stresses, comparable to a combat soldier in a struggle to protect himself. The soldier's personal inclinations for preservation often run counter to what the cultural milieu demands of him. However, the soldier still receives some support from his culture. The older person, however, receives little or no support from society in his struggle for ego survival. This is because society, as a whole, is poorly informed as to what is appropriate behavior for the older individual and what to do to help him.

The essential task of the ego is to enable the individual to adapt to the outside world and to cope with the progressive losses of aging, such as loss of physical capacities, loss of modes for release of basic drives, losses in a culture oriented to the future and to youth, and some loss of the sex drive. Changes in ego, as the result of aging, lead old people to seek new sources of gratification to shore up their declining self-esteem. They are essentially seeking the love, respect, and gratification that they have difficulty in acquiring from other people. These needs are intensified at a time when their availability is diminished.

As the person changes intellectually and physically, so will personality change as well. The elderly person who is in contact with reality can easily see that younger people are taking a place in the world that his generation formerly occupied. He also realizes that he is now dependent on the younger person, whereas the younger person was once dependent on him. As his sensory acuity deteriorates, his effective contacts with the outside world are reduced. Many of his friends are suffering with old age diseases or are dead, and thus the older person finds himself lonely, isolated, and preoccupied with himself and with small matters that may not even involve him.

The older person is usually a lonely person. Most people 65 years or older are divorced, single, or widowed. The individual who has been single throughout life will not experience as much loneliness because he has been accustomed to it throughout his life, but the person who was married early in life and enjoyed love, devotion, and constant companionship throughout his earlier life will have a different reaction. If a loved one is lost, this results in a sense of loneliness that seems unbearable, and the years ahead seem full of nothing but emptiness, unless of course the person can grasp reality and adjust to it. In later years, even in cases when both spouses are alive, an elderly person will show a certain amount of depression and moodiness.

The psychological aspect of depression is sadly a part of the life of many elderly people. Concerned with himself, a depressed person lacks suitable judgment of his own self-worth. Depression in old age may be evident by feelings of uselessness, of loneliness, of being a burden, of hopelessness, and too often, of being unneeded. Depression is often accompanied by regressive behavior; it also shows somatic symptoms of fatigue, loss of appetite and weight, constipation, insomnia, and dryness of the mouth. This is an extremely important point to remember because many so-called losses of health could be due to the individual's state of depression.

Gitelson[31] lists six patterns of psychological responses or adjustment to stress situations that have resulting emotionality. His list includes (1) a decreased memory for recent events, (2) a sharpened memory for the past when life was beautiful, (3) a self-assertive attitude that is compensation for insecurity, (4) mild depression caused by isolation and loneliness, (5) introversion and increased sensitivity, and (6) anxiety caused by the loss of friends of the same age group. A person's emotions are influenced by psychological tensions such as feelings of uselessness, insecurity, fear of economic dependency, inferiority, possible permanent physical disability, and the thought that the future holds nothing but death. All of these help to bring on the aging process more quickly.

The preceding characteristics are some of the major emotional changes that influence personality during senescence. It is important to note, however, that the process of aging is a secondary rather than the prime cause of these changes, which is the pressures experienced by the individual in the environment. Some of these pressures are changed attitudes of younger persons and former associates, loss through illness and death of former friends, forced retirement from occupational status, and the apathetic attitude of society toward elderly people. These are responsible for the appearance of most of the undesirable emotional and personality characteristics in the aged.

DYING AND DEATH

In considering dying and death the matter of individual differences once again is important. Some people truly seem to be unconcerned. They "trust in the Lord" and have faith that, no matter how they die, after death (in Heaven) they will not only be reunited with loved ones who have "gone before" but will see God "face to face." Others regard this view as scientifically and intellectually unrealistic, and they matter-of-factly (and without fear) insist that the only life human beings have is here on earth. Certain individuals, probably those who have seen loved ones suffer in their last days, state that they are not afraid of death itself but are afraid of the event of dying. Still others, who may not fear the act of dying, have a fear of the cessation of life. They dread the thought of nothingness, of ceasing to exist, of being in everlasting, dreamless sleep.

Concerns of death

Death is a difficult concept for the young adult to comprehend. He thinks of death occasionally but does not linger on the thought. He can appreciate traumatic deaths, brought on by accidents, but deaths due to illness or organic failures seem to be something that happens only to "older people." In middle adulthood the notion of death comes closer to home. Few adults in their forties or fifties will not have experienced the death of at least one of their parents. The 40-year-old person also begins to read in the papers about someone not many years older than himself who died; at 50 years he is surprised at how many people of his age and younger have died. In late adulthood he is greatly concerned to realize how many friends and associates are dying, and this notion may become phobic. The first thing many older adults read in the newspaper is the obituary column. We recall an elderly person telling us, "You know, of all the charter members of the church, there are only five of us left." Later, "Now there are only two of us left." Finally, "I am the only surviving member that helped found this church." This kind of a realization must have some emotional impact on the individual. The interesting thing is that in spite of these thoughts, most older people continue to make the most of their days as best they can.

Lieberman[32] found that death as a salient theme only occurs frequently when the aged individual is within close proximity to death, not throughout all of old age. Elderly people living in a stable environment approach death as if they had made peace with many issues, including death. These people do not have a denial or avoidance attitude toward death. On the other hand, persons living in unstable settings regard death as a disruption. They view the approach of death more anxiously and have not formulated any personal philosophy to deal with it. His data suggests that death is not a prime issue of the very aged. Several authorities have found that the dying elderly are not afraid of dying and death. Cicely Saunders[33] of St. Joseph's Hospice in London (a lodging for the terminally ill), although acknowledging the fact that every case is different, insists that most deaths come quietly and peacefully. When other terminally ill patients see this occurring to those about them, they become relieved of their own anxieties and are able to discuss death openly and without fear. Saunders believes that (1) the patient should not be in pain—it should always be controlled, (2) the physician and others should be ready to discuss dying and death when the patient wishes it, (3) the patient must always be aware of "personal, caring contact," and (4) when death comes, it should be with dignity, and the patient should not be alone.

Kastenbaum and Weisman,[34] reporting on the psychological autopsies of 100 cases, indicated that the commonly held assumption that old people lose contact with reality when they are dying is a fallacy. The behavior and conversation of most of these persons seemed to be influenced by the recognition of impending death and by an attitude of acceptance or readiness. Kastenbaum defines the psychological autopsy as an interdisciplinary effort to reconstruct the preterminal and terminal phases of a recently deceased patient.

Coming to terms with death

Undoubtedly, as more and more people live longer lives, researchers will continue to try to learn more about dying and death and what can be done to make the final phase of life less fearsome and more natural. Elisabeth Kuebler-Ross,[35] whose seminars on death at the University of Chicago have attracted much attention, expresses the view that the terminally ill can teach people much about the anxieties, fears, and hopes in the last stages of life. In her seminars dying patients are interviewed, and their responses and needs are noted and evaluated. She states unequivocally that patients who are terminally ill should be told the truth, but no judgment should be given as to the length of time until death. Furthermore, the physician should let the patient know that he will not give up but will use all of the new drugs, treatments, and techniques available, with patient, family, and physician all joining in the battle, "no matter the end result." She has found that dying patients go through five stages: denial, resentment ("Why me?"), bargaining, depression, and finally, acceptance. She believes that the seminars (including students in medicine, theology, sociology, and psychology) have helped to change the atmosphere and bring death out of the "conspiracy of silence" and into the open, to the benefit of all involved.

Not everyone can come to terms with death as did Abraham Maslow. He had just finished an important piece of work when he suffered a near-fatal heart attack, and in discussing it afterward he stated that since he had really "spent" himself and had done the best he could do, it would have been a good time to die—a "good ending." He believed that his life after that was a bonus, and everything—flowers, babies, friendships, the very act of living—became more beautiful; he had a "much-intensified sense of miracles." Maslow,[36] who had been Chairman of the Department of Psychology at Brandeis University and was President of the American Psychological Association in 1968, stated in the last tape recording that he made just before his death: "If you're reconciled with death or even if you are pretty well assured that you will have a good death, a dignified one, then every single moment of every single day is transformed because the pervasive undercurrent—the fear of death—is removed."

Religion ties in the individual to past, present, and future. Through understanding, growth, and participation the healthy aging person can attain a stature, intellectually and spiritually, that can bring fulfillment in the evening of life. Research shows that the elderly person increases favorable attitudes toward religion as he grows older. Belief that there is an afterlife is held by two thirds of those who are 65 years old and by 100% of those at the age of 90 years. As a person's age increases past 65 years, listening to church services over the radio also increases. Attending church and reading the Bible weekly increases up to the age of 80 years, declining somewhat thereafter.[37] This decline is not due to lack of interest but to the decline of physical powers, which limit mobility and amount of reading. As a person grows older, there is an increase in the feelings of security afforded by religion, especially among women.

STUDY GUIDE

1. What is it like to be an adult of 60 to 75 years of age? What are the sociological, psychological, and physiological factors involved?
2. What is meant by the "age of recompense"?
3. Why have gerontology and geriatrics become such a significant area for research in recent years?
4. Review the developmental tasks of later adulthood. Can you see these tasks being pursued by your parents, your grandparents, or other older adults whom you know?
5. The advent of retirement has been a traumatic experience for many people. How much should be done for the person approaching retirement to help him (her or them) to make a satisfactory transition? How much should they do for themselves? Is the age of 20 years too early to do some planning for retirement? At what age would you begin—25, 30, 35, 40, 45, 50 years?
6. Housing is a problem for many elderly people. What alternatives are available for the varying tastes, needs, or economic capabilities?
7. What appears to be a central cause of physical changes that begin to take place in later adulthood? Note that old age spans a number of years, and the beginning years are not like the later years.
8. Which intellectual traits seem to hold and not deteriorate in old age, and which ones do not hold?
9. Is there an identity problem in old age?
10. A discussion concerning death is distasteful to some people, yet death

touches everyone in one way or another. What does the research state concerning the aged and their views of death?
11. What is it like to be over 75 years of age? What are the sociological, psychological, and physiological factors involved?

REFERENCES

1. Butler, R. N., and Lewis, M. I.: Aging and mental health: positive psychosocial approaches, St. Louis, 1973, The C. V. Mosby Co., p. 3.
2. Hurlock, E. B.: Developmental psychology, New York, 1968, McGraw-Hill Book Co., p. 785.
3. Barron, M. L.: The aging American, New York, 1962, Thomas Y. Crowell Co., p. 441.
4. Hall, G. S.: Senescence, New York, 1922, D. Appleton & Co., p. xiii.
5. Lang, G., editor: Old age in America, New York, 1961, H. W. Wilson Co., p. 53.
6. Anderson, W. F.: Potentials of the elderly, In Alpert, H.: World scientists analyze aging, Harvest Years 9:33, 1969.
7. Isaacs, B.: An introduction to geriatrics, London, 1965, Bailliere, Tindall & Cassell, Ltd., pp. 172-173.
8. Busse, E. W.: Viewpoint, Geriatrics 24:42-44, Sept., 1969.
9. Vivrett, W. K.: Housing and community settings for older people. In Tibbitts, C., editor: Handbook of social gerontology, Chicago, 1960, University of Chicago Press, pp. 549-587.
10. Streib, G. F.: The older person in a family context. In Handbook of social gerontology, 1960, pp. 478-485.
11. Swaim, W. T., Jr.: What shall we do with Granny? Dillsburg, Pa., 1963, Presbyterian Homes of Central Pennsylvania.
12. Federal Council on Aging: White House Conference on Aging chart book, Washington, D. C., 1961, Government Printing Office, p. 60.
13. Lang, op. cit., p. 102.
14. Pressey, S. L.: Potentials of age: an exploratory field study, Genet. Psychol. Monogr. no. 56, pp. 159-205, 1957.
15. Arey, L. B., and others: The numerical and topographical relation of taste buds to circumvallate papillae through the life span, Anat. Rec. 64:9-25, 1935.
16. Deropp, R. S.: Man against aging, New York, 1960, St. Martin's Press, Inc., p. 186.
17. Wolff, K.: The biological, sociological and psychological aspects of aging, Springfield, Ill., 1959, Charles C Thomas, Publisher, p. 7.
18. Kinsey, A. C., and others: Sexual behavior in the human male, Philadelphia, 1948, W. B. Saunders Co., p. 68.
19. Ibid., p. 68.
20. Cottrell, F.: A young science looks at aging, Business Week, p. 118, Aug. 26, 1967.
21. Boehm, G. A. W.: The search for ways to keep youthful, Fortune 71:139, March, 1965.
22. Snyder, A. J.: Why do we grow old? Today's Health 41:51, July, 1963.
23. Boehm, op. cit., p. 139.
24. Hamilton, A.: How to grow young, Parade, pp. 10-25, April 27, 1969.
25. Birren, J. E.: The psychology of aging, Englewood Cliffs, N. J., 1964, Prentice-Hall, Inc., p. 169.
26. The old in the country of the young, Time 96:51, Aug. 3, 1970.
27. Isaacs, op. cit., p. 154.
28. Bromley, D. C.: The psychology of human aging, Baltimore, 1966, Penguin Books, Inc., p. 226.
29. Birren, J. E., Butler, R. N., Greenhouse, S. W., Sokoloff, L., and Yarrow, M. R., editor: Human aging, Public Health Pub. no. 986, Washington, D. C., 1968, Government Printing Office.
30. Weiss, R.: Changes in the ego as the result of aging, Geriat. Focus 3:1, Aug. 15, 1964.
31. Gitelson, M.: Emotional problems of elderly people, Geriatrics 3:54-55, 1948.
32. Lieberman, I.: Social setting determines attitudes of aged to death, Geriat. Focus 6:1-6, No. 1, 1967.
33. Saunders, C.: The amount of truth. In Pearson, L., editor: Death and dying, Cleveland, 1969, The Press of Case Western Reserve University, pp. 49-78.
34. Kastenbaum, R., and Weisman, A. D.: The psychological autopsy: a reconstruction of deathbed attitudes and behavior in old age, Geriat. Focus 6:2, Feb. 15, 1971.
35. Kuebler-Ross, E.: Viewpoint: dying can teach the living, Geriatrics 24:26-34, Dec., 1969.
36. Maslow, A.: Editorial, Psychol. Today 4:16, Aug., 1970.
37. Cavan, R. S., Burgess, E. W., Havighurst, R. J., and Goldhamer, H.: Personality adjustment in old age, Chicago, 1949, Science Research Associates, Inc., p. 58.

Glossary

A

aberration A general term for any deviation from the normal or typical.

accommodation The tendency to change one's schema or operations or to make new ones to include new objects or experiences enabling a higher level of thinking. Term is used by Piaget in his theory on cognitive development. See also **assimilation**.

actualization-fulfillment theory The version of the fulfillment theory of personality, holding that the personality force is in the form of an inherited blueprint determining the person's special abilities. Term *self-actualization* was used by Maslow.

actualizing tendency The potential for the fullest development that, under appropriate circumstances, will occur.

adjustment Process and behavior that a person uses to satisfy his internal needs and cope effectively with environmental, social, and cultural demands.

adolescence The developmental period beginning with the onset of major pubertal changes and continuing until adult maturity.

adrenals A pair of ductless or internal secretion glands attached to the kidneys and secreting epinephrine and cortin, important in emergency and stress situations.

adulthood The stage of the human life cycle that begins when the individual achieves biological and psychological maturity and ends with the gradual onset of old age.

affect An overall term comprising feeling, mood, and emotion.

afterbirth The placenta, its attached membranes, and the rest of the umbilical cord, delivered in the final stages of labor.

age, mental (MA) The level of development in intelligence, particularly, is the age level at which the child has the attained capacity to function intellectually. The term should be obtained from the results of a mental test.

age norm The average for a given age as revealed by sample group performances at this age.

aggression Feeling and behavior of anger or hostility.

alienation A feeling of estrangement from and hostility toward society or familiar persons, based in part on a discrepancy between expectations and promises and in part on the actual experience of the role one is playing.

alleles Pairs of genes on corresponding chromosomes that affect the same traits. When the two alleles are identical, a person is said to be homozygous for that trait. When the alleles carry differing instructions, he is said to be heterozygous for that trait.

altruism Deep unselfish concern for others often expressed in charitable activities.

ambivalence Simultaneously holding conflicting reactions toward a person or object.

amnion The translucent sac in which the developing prenatal organism lies.

amniotic fluid The fluid in the amnion in which the developing prenatal organism is suspended; it protects the organism from external pressure.

anal stage In psychoanalytic theory the second stage of psychosexual development, during which the child's interest centers on anal activities such as those related to toilet training. See also **genital stage; oral stage; phallic stage**.

androgens Male sex hormones, produced primarily by the testes.

anencephaly The lack of a brain at birth.

anoxia A severe deficiency in the supply of oxygen to the tissues, especially the brain, causing damage to their structural integrity.

anterior pituitary gland The front part of the pituitary gland, an endocrine gland situated at the base of the brain. The anterior pituitary produces hormones that regulate growth and other hormones that regulate the functions of the other endocrine glands.

anxiety A feeling of uneasiness or distress that arises when a person is torn by inner conflict because of incompatible motives, or when he feels apprehension over a possible threat to himself.

aphasia The loss or impairment of the ability to use speech resulting from lesions in the brain.

apperception A mental process for interpreting and assimilating a new experience or behavior in the experimental background (apperceptive schema).

aptitude The potential ability to perform certain tasks or functions effectively in certain situations if given proper training or opportunity to develop skill or learning.

aspiration, level of The intensity of striving for achievement, or the standard by which a person judges his own activity in reference to expected end results.

assimilation The incorporation of new objects and experiences into a structure or schemata in the mind to be used later in problem-solving situations. See also **accommodation.**

asymmetrical One side of the physique, object, or figure lacks similarity or correspondence with the other side.

atrophy Progressive decline of a part, its decrease in size, or possible degeneration.

attention The focusing of perception on a certain stimulus while ignoring others. Needed for learning to take place.

attitude An acquired persistent tendency to feel, think, or act in a certain way.

autism A schizophrenic syndrome characterized by absorption in fantasy to the exclusion of interest in reality and in others.

axillary hair Underarm hair.

B

babbling Speech patterns found in infants, comprising repetitious sequences of alternating consonants and vowels.

behavior Any kind of reaction, including complex patterns of feeling, perceiving, thinking, and willing, in response to internal or external, tangible or intangible stimuli.

behaviorism The school of psychology holding that the proper object of study in psychology is behavior alone, without reference to consciousness. Behavior theorists are particularly interested in learning mechanisms.

behavioral sciences Those disciplines that study the various aspects of human living. Psychology, sociology, and social anthropology are considered to be the major behavioral sciences. However, the evolution of the interdisciplinary approach to the study of behavior has introduced certain aspects of history, economics, political science, physiology, zoology, and physics into the field of the behavioral sciences.

binocular disparity The incongruent views the two eyes receive because of their different positions in space.

binocular fusion The integration of the two different views of the eyes.

birth injury Temporary or possibly permanent injury to the infant that occurs during the birth process. Many disabilities are attributed to brain damage occurring as a result of birth injury.

blastocyst The cluster of cells that begins to differentiate itself into distinct parts during the germinal period of prenatal development.

blastula The cluster of cells that make up the prenatal organism in the first few days after conception.

body stalk During the germinal period of prenatal development, the structure that differentiates to become the embryonic disc and the umbilical cord.

breech delivery A birth in which the baby's buttocks appear first, then his legs, and finally his head.

C

catharsis The relief of feelings, particularly negative ones, through talking, playing, drawing, or painting; it is a technique used in psychology and psychiatry.

central nervous system (CNS) The brain and spinal cord.

cephalocaudal development The progressive growth of the body parts in the direction from the head to the feet.

cervix The canal connecting the vagina and the uterus.

cesarean section A surgical operation through the walls of the abdomen and uterus for the purpose of delivering a child.

character The acquired ability to act and conduct oneself in accordance with a personal code of principles based on a scale of values, and facility in doing so.

chorion The protective and nutrient cover of the amnion, which contains the developing organism in the womb.

chorionic villi Capillaries that link the developing umbilical veins and arteries of an embryo with the uterine wall; they eventually become part of the placenta along with the surrounding maternal tissues.

chromosome The minute threadlike body within the nucleus of the cell that carries many DNAs, RNAs, proteins, and genes and transmits hereditary traits.

chronological age (CA) Age in calendar years.

classical conditioning An experimental method in which a conditioned stimulus is paired with an unconditioned stimulus to condition a particular response.

climacteric The period marking the end of the time at which women can conceive, and for men the time at which there is a significant decline in sexual virility. The term *menopause* is generally used for women instead of *climacteric*.

cognition Knowing the world through the use of one's perceptual and conceptual abilities.

cognitive development The development of a logical method of looking at the world, utilizing one's perceptual and conceptual powers.

cognitive processes The operations or routines that the mind performs including the encoding of information, the storage and retrieval of information in memory, the generation of hypotheses, their evaluation according to criteria, and inductive and deductive reasoning.

coitus Sexual intercouse.

compensation A defense mechanism in which the individual works especially hard to avoid defeat or failure (direct compensation) or turns to another area of endeavor to allay anxiety (indirect compensation).

concept A type of symbol that represents a set of common attributes among a group of other symbols or images.

conception The merging of the spermatozoon and ovum in human fertilization.

conceptualization The process of concept formation in which various items are grouped into units on the basis of commensurable characteristics.

concrete operational stage The stage of cognitive development that occurs from about 7 to 12 years of age and during which the child develops the operations of conservation, class inclusion, and serialization.

conditioning A mode of training whereby reinforcement (reward or punishment) is used to elicit desired (rewarded) responses.

conduct That part of a person's behavior, including insufficiencies and reverses, which is guided by ethical, moral, or ideological standards.

confabulation An attempt to fill in the gaps of memory without awareness of the falsification involved.

conflict An intrapsychic state of tension or indecision due to contrary desires, ungratified needs, or incompatible plans of action; also between conscious and unconscious choices.

congenital Referring to characteristics and defects acquired during the period of gestation and persisting after birth as distinguished from heredity.

connective tissue Fibers that lie between cells of the body.

consciousness Cognizance of the immediate environment plus the ability to utilize encoding, memory, and logic at will.

conservation The realization that one aspect of something (e.g., quantity) remains the same, while another aspect is changed (e.g., shape, position). Used by Piaget.

constitution The organization of organic, functional, and psychosocial elements within the developing person that largely determines his condition.

contraception The prevention of pregnancy by artificial means.

control group A group used for comparison with an experimental group with the exception that the independent variable is not applied to the control group.

conventional stage A stage of moral development in which the individual strives to maintain the expectations of his family, group, or nation, regardless of the consequences. See also **postconventional stage; preconventional stage.**

correlation The relationship between two variables as measured by the correlation coefficient.

correlation coefficient A statistical index for measuring correspondence in changes occurring in two variables. Perfect correspondence is $+1.000$; no correspondence is 0.000; perfect correspondence in opposite directions is -1.000.

critical periods Specific times in development during which a child is best able to learn a specific lesson; also, in fetal development, crucial times at which various specific physical features and organs develop; detrimental environmental influences during those periods can adversely affect organic development.

culture The man-made aspects of human environment—customs, beliefs, institutions, modes of living—including the attitudes and beliefs held, and acted on, by a specific group of people about aspects of living that they consider important.

D

defense mechanism Any habitual response pattern that is spontaneously used to protect oneself from threats, conflicts, anxiety, frustration, and other conditions that a person cannot tolerate or cope with directly.

deoxyribonucleic acid (DNA) The complex molecules of which genes are composed; thought to be responsible for genetic inheritance.

dependence The desire or need for supporting relationships with other persons. See also **independence.**

development A process involving all the orderly

changes that occur during progress toward maturity.

developmental task A specific learning problem that arises at a particular stage of life and that an individual must accomplish to meet the demands of his culture. Developmental tasks vary with one's age and persist as objectives throughout life. The nature of the developmental task is such that one learning is related to, merges into, and forms the basis for the next learning.

differentiation The process by means of which structure, function, or forms of behavior become more complex or specialized; the change from homogeneity to heterogeneity.

disequilibrium According to Piaget, disequilibrium exists whenever the mind is confronted with inconsistencies or gaps in knowledge and a change is needed from one level of understanding to another to attain a more clearly delineated structure of knowledge; e.g., movement is toward a state of relative equilibrium of cognitive structures.

dizygotic (DZ) twins Twins who develop from two separate eggs; fraternal twins. See also **monozygotic (MZ) twins**.

dominant gene A gene whose hereditary characteristics always prevail.

Down's syndrome A congenital physical condition associated with mental retardation, characterized by thick, fissured tongue, flat face, and slanted eyes.

drive The tension and arousal produced by an ungratified need and directed toward a chosen object or end.

dynamic Refers to forces and potent influences that are capable of producing changes within the organism or personality.

dysfunction Disturbance or impairment of the functional capacity of an organ or system, including mental abilities.

E

ectoderm The outermost cell layer in the embryo from which structures of the nervous system and skin are developed.

EEG Electroencephalogram or electroencephalograph. A graphic record of the electric activity of the brain obtained by placing electrodes on the skull.

egg cell See ovum.

ego The conscious core of personality that exercises control demanded by the superego and directs drives and impulses of the id in accordance with the demands of reality.

ego identity According to Erik Erikson, a clear and continuing sense of who one is and what one's goals are.

embryo The form of prenatal life from the second to the eighth week. The period of the embryo follows the germinal period and is succeeded by that of the fetus.

embryology The study of the development of the individual from conception to birth.

embryonic disc During the germinal period, the part of the prenatal organism that will eventually become the embryo.

emotion A conscious state of experience, characterized by feeling or excitement that is accompanied and frequently preceded by specific physiological changes and frequently resulting in excitation of the organism to action. Emotions are the physiological forms that result from one's estimate of the harmful or beneficial effects of stimuli.

empathy The emotional linkage that characterizes relationships between individuals; the ability to sense the feelings of others.

encoding To transfer from one system of communication into another. In the perceptual process it is the point wherein the message or meaning is translated into behavior that is deemed an appropriate response to the stimuli.

endocrine glands The ductless glands of internal secretion, such as the pituitary, thyroid, and adrenals, that secrete hormones into the bloodstream or lymph system.

endoderm The innermost of the three cell layers of the embryo from which most of the visceral organs and the digestive tract are developed.

epistemology The branch of philosophy that is concerned with discovering the nature of knowledge and knowing.

equilibration According to Piaget, the coordination of cognitive level with environmental output so as to reduce disequilibrium.

estrogens Female sex hormones, produced primarily in the ovaries.

estrous cycle The periodic waxing and waning of sexual desire and receptivity, with accompanying physiological changes, in the female animal.

ethical relativity The doctrine stating that different cultures or groups hold different fundamental moral values and that these values cannot themselves be judged as more or less adequate or more or less moral.

ethics Moral values and ideals. See also **morality**.

etiology The investigation of origins, causes, and factors contributing to a trait, attitude, or disease.

euphoria An intense, subjective sensation of vigor, well-being, and happiness that may exist despite some problem or disability.

existentialism The philosophy that man forms his own nature in the course of his life, with man's *situation in the universe seen as purposeless or irrational.*

experiential freedom According to Carl Rogers, the subjective sense that one is free to choose among alternative courses of action in defining one's life.

extended family The family that consists of three generations—children, parents, grandparents, and even aunts and uncles—under the same roof. See also **nuclear family**.

extrovert A type of personality whose thoughts, feelings, and interests are directed chiefly toward persons, social affairs, and other external phenomena.

eye-hand coordination The ability to coordinate vision with motor activities so that one can accurately reach for and grasp objects.

F

Fallopian tube Either of the tubes that carries the ovum from the ovaries to the uterus.

fantasy A function of imagination marked by engagement in vicarious experiences and hallucinatory actions; reveries, daydreaming.

fertilization The union of an egg cell with a spermatozoon.

fetus The prenatal human organism from approximately eight weeks after conception to birth. See also **embryo**.

fixation The persistence of infantile, childish, pubertal, or adolescent response patterns, habits, and modes of adjustment throughout successive phases of development.

formal operational stage According to Jean Piaget, the fourth stage of thought, which begins at about 12 years of age. It is the period during which logical thinking begins and is the final step toward abstract thinking and conceptualization. See also **concrete operational stage; preoperational stage; sensorimotor stage**.

formal rules Statements of relations between units or classes that are always true and specifiable, such as the rules of mathematics.

fraternal twins See **dizygotic (DZ) twins**.

frustration The experience of distress induced by failures and by thwarting of attempts to gratify one's needs or ambitions.

fully functioning person Carl Rogers' term for an individual characterized by openness to experience, existential living, organismic trusting, experiential freedom, and creativity.

G

G-factor The common root of intellectual behavior that runs through the functioning of those specific subabilities identified by various authorities. G-factor is not general intelligence but the pervasive element in all types of intelligence.

galvanic skin response (GSR) A change in the electrical resistance of the skin.

gamete A sex cell; an egg or a sperm.

genes The basic units of heredity, carried in the chromosomes.

genetics The branch of biology concerned with the transmission of hereditary characteristics.

genital organs The male and female sex organs.

genital stage In psychoanalytic theory the final stage of psychosexual development, during which heterosexual interests are dominant. This stage begins in adolescence and lasts throughout adulthood. See also **anal stage; oral stage; phallic stage**.

genotype The characteristics of an organism that are inherited and that can be transmitted to offspring; also, the traits or characteristics common to a biological group. See also **phenotype**.

geriatrics The medical study and care of aging persons.

germinal period The first stage of prenatal development. It is roughly the first two weeks after conception, during which time the developing individual is primarily engaged in cell division. See also **embryo; fetus**.

gerontology The study of the improvement of the life habits of aging persons; the psychology and sociology of aging.

gestation period The amount of time the prenatal organism spends in the uterus; the period from conception to birth.

gonadotrophic hormones Secretions of the anterior pituitary that stimulate activity in the gonads.

gonads The sex glands; the ovaries in females and the testes in males.

group, reference The group a person belongs to or is interested in belonging to, e.g., peer groups, usually with a molding influence on the individual.

growth Strictly speaking, the addition of height and weight through simple physical accretion; sometimes used interchangeably with development, which includes the foregoing but also embraces the improvement of function.

H

habit An acquired or learned pattern of behavior, relatively simple and regularly used with facility, which leads to a tendency to use such acts rather than other behavior.

habituation The process of becoming accustomed to a particular set of circumstances or to a particular stimulus.

handedness The tendency to use either the right or the left hand predominantly.

hedonism A psychological or philosophical system of motivation explaining all behavior and con-

duct in terms of seeking pleasure and avoiding pain.
heredity The totality of characteristics biologically transmitted from parents and ancestors to the offspring at conception.
heterogeneous A term used to describe any group of individuals or items that show great differences in reference to some significant criterion or standard.
heterosexuality Attraction or interest toward members of the opposite sex.
homeostasis The tendency to preserve a stable or constant internal state, despite fluctuations of bodily conditions and external stimulations.
homogeneous A term used to describe any group of individuals or items that show great similarity or low variability in the qualities or traits considered.
homosexual Centered on the same sex; marked by a tendency to find sexual and erotic gratification with a person of the same sex.
hormone A specific chemical substance produced by an endocrine gland, which brings about certain somatic and functional changes within the organism.
hypothesis A tentative interpretation of a complex set of phenomena or data on the basis of supportive facts or findings.

I

id According to Freud, that part of the personality consisting of primitive instincts toward sexuality and aggression. The id seeks immediate gratification regardless of the consequences but is held in check by the superego. See also **ego; superego.**
ideal A standard approaching some level of perfection, usually unattainable in practice.
identical twins See **monozygotic (MZ) twins.**
identification The process by which a person takes over the features of another person whom he admires and incorporates them into his own personality.
identity A sense of one's self.
imprinting The alteration of an apparently instinctive behavior that occurs at a certain, extremely early critical period of development; e.g., ducklings from an incubator will follow a man or dog as though they were following a mother duck.
impulsivity Uncontrolled action; acting without first thinking.
independence Self-reliance.
independent variable The variable that is controlled by the experimenter to determine its effect on the dependent variable.
infancy The stage of human development lasting from birth until the organism is able to exist independently of its mother, capable of feeding itself, of walking, and of talking, usually until the age of 2 years.
informal rules Statements of imperfect relations between two or more units or classes. See also **formal rules.**
innate Existing before birth and accounting for a particular trait or characteristic.
instinct Unlearned, biologically based behavior.
intelligence The ability to conceptualize effectively and to grasp relationships; also, according to Jean Piaget, the coordination of operations.
intelligence quotient The index or rate of mental development. The ratio of mental to chronological age as expressed in the formula: Mental age divided by chronological age, times 100, equals IQ. IQ must be regarded as an indication rather than a measure, since different tests yield different results and performance fluctuates.
internalization The incorporation of beliefs, attitudes, and ideas into the personality so that they become part of one's makeup.
introvert Orientation inward toward the self rather than toward association with others.

J

juvenile Pertaining to an older child or adolescent.

K

kibbutz An Israeli collective farm or settlement.
Klinefelter's syndrome A congenital physical condition in men that occurs when the individual has two X chromosomes and one Y chromosome. The symptoms include sterility, small testes, small femalelike breasts, and usually mental retardation.
knee-jerk reflex See **patellar reflex.**

L

lability In psychology the tendency to shift erradically from one emotional state to another. See also **stability.**
language An abstract system of word meanings and syntactic structures that facilitate communication.
lanugo hair A fine, woolly fuzz that appears briefly on the fetus in the later months of development.
latency period In psychoanalytic theory a stage in psychosexual development that appears between the phallic and genital stages and during which sexual drives become temporarily dormant; usually begins about the age of 4 or 5 years and lasts until adolescence.
learning A relatively permanent modification of behavior resulting from experience.
level of significance In the T test expression of the confidence with which a null hypothesis can be

rejected, usually expressed as a decimal fraction. If the desired result could occur by chance one in twenty times, the level of significance is .05.

libido According to Freud, a basic psychological energy inherent in every individual; this energy supplies the sexual drive, whose goal is to obtain pleasure.

life expectancy The number of years, based on a statistical average, that a person is expected to live in a given culture.

life style The particular and unique pattern of living that characterizes the individual. It is a product of one's capacities, abilities, social milieu, family experiences, and the values one holds.

longitudinal study A study technique in which the same individual is examined over a long period or over a complete developmental stage.

love In the general sense an intense emotional response involving a feeling of affection toward a person or persons. According to John B. Watson, it, along with fear and rage, is one of the inherent or primary emotions.

M

maternal deprivation Disturbance of the mother-infant relationship in which the infant is rejected or abandoned, thus disrupting the usual physical and emotional mother-infant bonds.

matrix A framework or enclosure that gives form, meaning, or perspective to what lies within it.

maturation Developmental changes manifested in physiological functioning primarily due to heredity and constitution; organismic developments leading to further behavioral differentiation.

median The measure of central tendency that has half of the cases above it and half below it; the fiftieth percentile.

meiosis The process of cell division in which the daughter cells receive half the normal number of chromosomes, thus becoming gametes.

memory The mental activity of reliving past events. It can be considered as having two functions: the storage of experience for a period of time and the revival of that information at a later time.

menarche The first occurrence of menstruation.

menopause The period in a woman's life when menstruation ceases.

menstrual age The age of a prenatal organism calculated from the first day of its mother's last menstrual period.

menstruation The cyclic discharge of blood and discarded uterine material that occurs in sexually mature females.

mental age The knowledge of concepts or the ability to perform tasks appropriate to a certain chronological age as determined by specific tests. Mental age is thus a unit of mental measurement that, like IQ, is a relative measure. A child of any age whose tested performance equals that of an average 8-year-old is said to have a mental age of 96 months (8 × 12 months).

mental retardation A condition of mental deficiency, usually defined as being below 75 in IQ.

mesoderm The middle of the three fundamental layers of the embryo that forms a basis for the development of bone, muscle structure, alimentary canal, and various digestive glands.

metabolism The physicochemical changes within the body for supplying, repairing, and building up (anabolism) and for breaking down and removing (catabolism).

mongolism See **Down's syndrome**

monozygotic (MZ) twins Twins who develop from the same fertilized ovum; identical twins. See also **dizygotic (DZ) twins.**

moral judgments Judgments as to the rightness or wrongness of actions.

morality A sense of what is right and wrong.

mores Social norms of behavior invested with great moral importance. They involve matters of health, sex, religion, property, and other activities that are deemed important.

Moro response The newborn infant's involuntary response to having his head fall backward—he stretches his arms outward and brings them together over his chest in a grasp gesture.

motivation A general term referring to factors within an organism that arouse and maintain behaviors directed toward satisfying some need or drive or toward accomplishing a goal.

motive Any factor that stimulates or contributes to a conscious effort toward a goal.

motor skill Any skill, such as walking or riding a bicycle, that requires muscular coordination.

myelin sheath A white fatty covering on many neural fibers that serves to channel impulses along fibers and to reduce the random spread of impulses across neurons.

myelinization The process by which neural fibers acquire a sheath of myelin.

N

need Any physicochemical imbalance within the organism due to a lack of particular nutrients that arouses tension and drives. By analogy, psychological and personality needs are recognized. Primary or genetically determined needs and derived needs (generated by the operation of primary needs) are usually distinguished.

negative reinforcement In operant conditioning the termination of an aversive stimulus as the result of a response. See also **positive reinforcement**.

negativism A primary mode of expressing one's own will by persistent refusal to respond to suggestions from parental and authority figures.

neonate A newborn infant.

neuromuscular Pertaining to both nerve and muscle, their structure and functions.

neurosis A mental disorder that prevents the victim from dealing effectively with reality; it is characterized by anxiety and partial impairment of functioning.

normative Based on averages, standards, values, or norms.

nuclear family The family, rather typical in the United States, that consists of only parents and children. See also **extended family**.

nurture The impact of environmental factors on child growth and development. Nurture is usually contrasted with nature in describing development.

O

oedipal conflict According to Freud, a conflict that appears during the phallic stage. It consists of sexual attraction to the parent of the opposite sex and hostility toward the parent of the same sex.

ontogenesis Origin and development of an individual organism and its functions from conception to death. See also **phylogenesis**.

openness to experience According to Carl Rogers, the state in which every stimulus from the organism or the external environment is freely relayed through the individual without distortion by defenses.

operant conditioning A type of conditioning in which an organism's responses change as a result of the application of reinforcement or reward. It is based on the principle that organisms tend to engage in behavior that succeeds in producing desirable outcomes.

operation According to Jean Piaget, the mental action one performs in adapting to the environment.

oral stage In psychoanalytic theory the first stage of psychosexual development. In this stage gratification centers around the mouth and oral activities. See also **anal stage; genital stage; phallic stage**.

organismic age The average of all basic measures of a person's development at a particular time, such as carpal development, dental development, height, and weight. Often it includes achievement and educational, mental, and social age.

orgasm A period of intense physical and emotional sensation usually resulting from stimulation of the sexual organs, as in sexual intercourse, and generally followed in the male by the ejaculation of semen.

ovaries The female reproductive organs in which egg cells or ova are produced.

ovum The female reproductive cell, sometimes called the egg; the plural of ovum is ova.

P

parallel play The side-by-side play of two or more children with some independence of action yet heightened interest because of each other's presence.

parasocial speech In a young child, talking to one's self. This behavior, thought to be social in origin, occurs most frequently when others are listening or when the child encounters difficulties.

parturition The act of bringing forth the young; delivery of the baby.

patellar reflex The involuntary response that occurs when the patellar tendon is tapped, commonly known as the knee-jerk reflex.

patterns of behavior Organized ways of behaving in certain situations.

peer Any individual of about one's same level of development and therefore equal for play or any other mode of association.

peer group The group of persons who constitute one's associates, usually of the same age and social status.

penis The male copulatory organ.

percentile The rank of a given measure in a theoretical group of 100. High rank is indicated by 99, meaning that the individual exceeds 99 out of 100 subjects in the measure concerned; middle average would be 50.

percept The unit of immediate knowledge of what one perceives.

perception The awareness of one's environment obtained through interpreting sense data.

perfection-fulfillment theory The version of the fulfillment theory of personality maintaining that the personality force which takes the form of internalized but culturally universal ideals of what is good and meaningful in life. See also **personality, fulfillment theory of**.

personality An individual's characteristic pattern of behavior and thought, including an accordant self-concept and a set of traits consistent over time.

personality, fulfillment theory of The theory maintaining that maturity lies in the full expression of one psychological force, lying within the individual. See also **actualization-fulfillment theory; perfection-fulfillment theory**.

phallic stage In psychoanalytic theory the third stage of psychosexual development, during which gratification centers on the sex organs. The Oedipal conflict also manifests itself during this stage. See also **anal stage; genital stage; oral stage.**

phenotype The observable characteristics of an organism. See also **genotype.**

phenylketonuria (PKU) An error of metabolism caused by a recessive gene that gives rise to a deficiency in a certain enzyme. It can cause mental retardation if it is not caught in time.

phylogenesis Evolution of traits and features common to a species or race; rehearsal of the prehistory of man. See also **ontogenesis.**

placebo An inert preparation often used as a control in experiments.

placenta The organ that forms in the uterine lining and through which the developing prenatal organism receives nourishment and discharges waste.

positive reinforcement In operant conditioning the presentation of a rewarding consequence contingent on the desired response. See also **negative reinforcement.**

postconventional stage A stage of moral development in which the individual defines moral values and principles in relation to their validity and application rather than in relation to the dictates of society or of any particular group. It is characterized by self-chosen ethical principles that are comprehensive, universal, and consistent. See also **conventional stage; preconventional stage.**

postpartum Immediately after birth; the first week of life.

preconventional stage A stage of moral development in which the child responds to cultural rules and labels of good and bad only in terms of the physical or hedonistic consequences of obeying or disobeying the rules. See also **conventional stage; postconventional stage.**

prenatal Before birth; the stage of human development lasting from conception to birth.

preoperational stage According to Jean Piaget, the stage in a child's development occurring from 18 months to 7 years of age, during which he begins to encounter reality on the representational level. See also **concrete operational stage; formal operational stage; sensorimotor stage.**

problem solving Thinking directed toward the goal of solving a problem.

projection A type of defense mechanism characterized by the tendency to blame others or external circumstances for one's own shortcomings or failures. May attribute to others his own qualities and traits.

proximodistal development The progressive growth of the body parts in a center-to-periphery direction. See also **cephalocaudal development.**

psychoanalysis A method of psychotherapy developed by Sigmund Freud. Psychoanalysis has been subsequently extended to include the theoretical foundations of Jung, Adler, Rank, Sullivan, Horney, and their followers. It emphasizes the techniques of free association and transference and seeks to give the patient insight into his unconscious conflicts and motives.

psychoanalytic theory The basis of the school of psychology that emphasizes the development of emotions and their influence on behavior. It postulates a theory of the development and the structure of personality.

psychological growth Personality change; the increasing of inner differentiation and integration, the acquisition of autonomy and flexibility, and the development of new capacities for self-determination.

psychosexual development In Freudian theory, the sequence of stages through which the child passes, each characterized by the different erogenous zones from which the primary pleasure of the stage is derived. See also **anal stage; genital stage; oral stage; phallic stage.**

psychosis Severe mental disorder.

psychosomatic Pertaining to the effects of psychological and emotional stress on health and pathology; indicating that a phenomenon is both psychic and bodily.

psychotherapy The various techniques for the systematic application of psychological principles in the treatment of mental or emotional disturbance or disorder.

pubertal Pertaining to anything related to the developmental period of puberty.

puberty The period of life during which an individual's reproductive organs become functional and secondary sexual characteristics appear.

pubescent Pertaining to an individual in the early part of puberty or to anyone who exhibits significant characteristics of that period of maturation.

pubic hair Hair that appears in the genital area during adolescence.

Q

quickening The first fetal movements that a mother can readily perceive.

R

race An aggregate of persons who share a set of genetically transmitted and physically identifiable characteristics.

rage An emotional response involving intense anger and feelings of hostility. According to John B.

Watson, it, along with fear and love, is one of the inherent or primary emotions.

rationalization To rationalize; a dynamism of self-defense whereby a person justifies his activities or conduct by giving rational and acceptable, but usually untrue, reasons; the opposite of rational thought.

reaction formation A defense mechanism involving the replacement in consciousness of an anxiety-inducing impulse or feeling by its opposite.

readiness The combination of growth development and experience that prepares an individual to acquire a skill or understanding with facility.

recall The form of remembering in which previously learned material is reproduced with a minimum of cues. See also **recognition.**

recessive gene A gene whose hereditary characteristics will not prevail when paired with a dominant gene.

recognition The form of remembering in which the previously learned material is merely recognized as such without actually being recalled. See also **recall.**

reference groups The groups that affect in substantial measure the individual's personal goals and behavior. The groups to which he belongs and wants to belong.

regression Returning, because of frustrating experiences, to an earlier and less mature level of behavior and personality functioning than that previously achieved.

reinforcement In operant conditioning the experimental procedure of immediately following a response with a reinforcer.

representational level The level of cognitive development at which the child begins to use symbols as well as images.

repression In psychoanalytic theory the defense mechanism of forcefully rejecting unpleasant memories or impulses from conscious awareness.

retrolental fibroplasia Condition in which an opaque fibrous membrane develops on the posterior surface of the lens; occurs chiefly in premature infants subjected to high oxygen concentration.

reversibility The transformation by which a person is able to return to the starting point of a problem or situation after an operation had changed it. (Piaget)

Rh factor An agglutinizing factor present in the blood of most humans; when introduced into blood lacking the factor, antibodies form. Such a situation occurs when an organism with Rh-positive blood inherited from its father resides within a mother whose blood is Rh negative. A first-born child is rarely affected, but subsequent children may require transfusions.

ribonucleic acid (RNA) RNA molecules playing the role of a messenger or transfer agent for vital DNA functions by lining up amino acids in ribosomes to form proteins according to a particular sequence.

role See **sex roles; social role.**

role conflict The situation in which a person is expected to play two or more roles that he cannot integrate into his self-system.

rooting reflex The newborn infant's involuntary movement of his mouth toward any source of stimulation in the mouth area.

rote learning Memorization in which the task is to commit the various components of the material to memory with little or no understanding, requiring only the ability to later reproduce what has been learned in the exact form in which it was presented.

rubella German measles. Rubella in a pregnant woman can cause damage to the developing child if she contracts it during the first three months of pregnancy.

S

schizophrenia A form of psychosis in which the patient becomes withdrawn and apathetic. Hallucinations and delusions are common.

sebaceous Fatty, oily; sebaceous glands secrete oily matter for lubricating hair and skin.

secondary sex characteristics Physical characteristics that appear in humans around the age of puberty and that are sex differentiated but not necessary for sexual reproduction. Such characteristics include breast development and the appearance of pubic hair in girls and the appearance of facial and pubic hair, enlargement of the penis, and deepening of the voice in boys.

self-actualization According to Abraham Maslow, the need to develop one's true nature and fulfill one's potentialities.

self-concept The individual's awareness of and identification with his organism, cognitive powers, and modes of conduct and performance, accompanied by specific attitudes toward them.

self-direction Independent selection of goals and of the proper means and actions to attain them.

self-esteem The amount and quality of the regard that a person has toward himself.

self-realization The lifelong process of unhampered development marked by self-direction and responses in terms of one's capabilities or potentialities.

semen The fluid produced by the male testes that contains the spermatozoa.

senescence The period of old age.

senility Significant loss of physical and cognitive functions in old age or preceding it.

sensorimotor reflexes The basic reflex repertoire

*with which the infant is born—the Moro response, rooting reflex, patellar reflex, and so on.

sensorimotor stage According to Jean Piaget, the stage in a child's cognitive development during which he is essentially involved in perfecting his contact with the objects that surround him. It generally occurs from birth to 2 years of age. See also **concrete operational stage; formal operational stage; preoperational stage.**

sex roles Patterns of behavior deemed appropriate to each sex by society.

sibling A brother or sister.

sickle cell anemia A form of anemia (a blood condition) in which abnormal red blood corpuscles of crescent shape are present.

skeletal age A measure of the maturity of the skeleton, determined by the degree of ossification of bone structures.

skelic index The index that measures the ratio of lower limb length to sitting height.

social age Age measured in terms of an individual's social habits relative to society's expectations.

social class A social stratum or category differentiated from other such strata on the basis of such economic considerations as wealth, occupation, and property ownership. See also **socioeconomic class.**

social deprivation The lack of economic, educational, and cultural opportunities.

social role A set of expectations or evaluative standards associated with an individual or a position.

socialization The process by which individuals pass through age-graded social roles whose requirements they must learn.

socioeconomic class A grouping of people on a predetermined scale of prestige according to their social and economic status. Such status is based on many factors, including nature of occupation, kind of income, moral values, family genealogy, social relationships, area of residence, and education. See also **social class.**

sociogram A graphic representation of social preferences within a group; a mapping of preferences and rejections in social behavior.

sociometry The graphical or columnar representation of interpersonal attractions or avoidances in group situations. The study of reactions and avoidances between individual members of a social group. The study of interpersonal relationships—person to person, person to group, and group to group—pursued through tabulations or the plotting of lines of attraction, indifference, or dislike.

somatic Pertaining to the body or organism.

sperm The male germ cell, or spermatozoon, containing chromosomes, DNA, RNA, protein, and other substances.

standard deviation A statistical technique for expressing the extent of variation of a group of scores from the mean. It is a distance on a curve of probability, of which the first unit in both directions from the mean includes 68.3% of the total group of scores. About 99.7% of the scores are within three standard deviations in each direction from the mean.

startle response A reaction to stimuli in infants outwardly characterized by eye widening, jaw dropping, cooing, squealing, or crying and inwardly characterized by changes in heart rate, respiration, and galvanic skin potential.

stimulus Any form of environmental energy capable of affecting the organism.

sublimation A dynamism of self-defense whereby the energies of a basic, socially unacceptable drive are redirected into a higher and socially more acceptable plane of expression.

superego A psychoanalytic term which refers to the part of the personality structure that is built up by early parent-child relationships and helps the ego to enforce the control of primitive instinctual urges of the id; later functions as a moral force; analogous to an early form of conscience.

surrogate mother Someone or something that takes the place of a mother in an organism's life.

T

temperament The general nature, behavioral style, or characteristic mood of the individual; usually thought to have a physical or constitutional basis.

tension A state of acute need, deprivation, fear, apprehension, etc., that keeps an organism or certain organs in a state of intensified activity, e.g., adrenal glands.

terminal illness A disease that results in death.

testes The male reproductive organs in which spermatozoa are manufactured; testicles.

thalidomide A drug once used by women during pregnancy to assuage morning sickness; it caused birth defects in the limbs of children.

thinking The active process of conceptualization, involving integrating percepts, grasping relationships, and asking further questions.

thumb opposition The ability to oppose the thumb to the fingers and to bring the fingertips in contact with the ball of the thumb.

thyroxin A hormone produced by the thyroid gland; it regulates metabolism.

toxemia Blood poisoning. The presence of poisonous or infective matters in the bloodstream.

tracking The act of following an object with one's eye.

trait A distinctive and enduring characteristic of a person or his behavior.

trauma Any somatic or psychological damage to the individual, including stressful and terrifying experiences.

Turner's syndrome A congenital physical condition resulting from the individual's having only one X chromosome and no Y chromosomes. The afflicted individual looks like an immature female and is characterized by a lack of reproductive organs, abnormal shortness, and mental retardation.

U

umbilical cord The cord that connects the prenatal organism with the placenta. The embryo receives nourishment from the blood that is supplied by the arteries within the cord that connects the placenta and the fetus.

unconscious The area of motivational structure and thought process of which the person is not directly aware.

universal principles Moral propositions that are the end point of an unchanging ethical developmental sequence. They are of an absolute nature as opposed to beliefs or standards developed or determined by a reasoning approach to morality.

uterus The female organ in which the prenatal organism develops and is nourished prior to birth.

V

vagina The female genital canal (passage) extending from the uterus to the vulva. It is a copulatory organ.

value The worth or excellence found in a qualitative appraisal of an object by reliance on emotional and rational standards of the individual or of selected reference groups.

viability Capability for maintaining life. A fetus is viable after twenty-eight weeks, since it can then usually be kept alive if born prematurely.

vernix caseosa A sebaceous deposit covering the fetus due to secretions of skin glands.

W

Wechsler Adult Intelligence Scale A widely used individual intelligence test.

Wetzel grid A graphical representation of the longitudinal development of an individual in height and weight, devised by N. C. Wetzel. Rather than making interpersonal comparisons, as on height-weight charts, the grid takes into account variations in basic body build.

womb See uterus.

X

X chromosome A chromosome that, when paired with another X chromosome, programs a gamete to develop as a female.

Y

Y chromosome A chromosome that determines an individual will be male.

yolk sac A nonfunctional sac that forms during the germinal period of human prenatal development.

youth A stage of the human life cycle experienced by persons who are psychologically and physically mature but who are not sociologically mature, in that they have not made any commitments to career or family. This stage intervenes between adolescence and adulthood.

Z

zygote As used in the present work, a new individual formed by the union of male and female gametes; the resultant globule of cells during the first phase of prenatal development after conception and lasting approximately two weeks.

REFERENCES

Developmental psychology today, Del Mar, Calif., 1971, CRM Books.

English, H. B., and English, A. C.: A comprehensive dictionary of psychological and psychoanalytical terms, New York, 1958, David McKay, Inc.

Hinsie, L. E., and Campbell, R. J.: Psychiatric dictionary, ed. 3, New York, 1960, Oxford University Press, Inc.

Pikunas, J.: Human development: a science of growth, New York, 1969, McGraw-Hill Book Co.

Taber, C. W.: Taber's cyclopedic medical dictionary, ed. 11, Philadelphia, 1970, F. A. Davis Co.

Index

A

Aberration, chromosomal, 11-13
Ability, motor, in late childhood, 152-153
Acceptance, peer, in middle adolescence, 202-203
Accidents in later adulthood, 296
Accommodation, Piaget's theory of, 75
Activities
    of late childhood, 152-153
    play, developmental sequences of, 116
Adaptation, Piaget's theory of, 75
Adaptation syndrome, general, 15
Adaptive behavior, 10
Adjustive behavior, 6, 10
Adjustment
    mental health, in late childhood, 150
    personal, in marriage, 251-252
Adolescence, 169
    in disadvantaged environments, 215-217
    early, 167-194; *see also* Puberty
        daydreaming in, 192
        developing heterosexuality in, 182-184
            observations on, 184-185
        developmental tasks of, 170
        emotional characteristics of, 177-179
        fads and fashions in, 188-189
        gangs (groups) in, 187
        height in, 173-175
        intellectual abilities in, 192-193
        interests in, 187-188
        masturbation in, 186
        moral awakening in, 193
        motor awkwardness in, 176
        music in, 187, 188
        peer group influence in, 179-180
        personal problems and concerns in, 189-192
        petting in, 186-187
        physical development in, 170-177
        sexual awareness in, 185-187
        social development in, 179-187
        weight in, 174-175
    late; *see* Adulthood, young
    maturation sequence in
        for boys, 173
        for girls, 172
    middle and later, 195-218
        affection in, 210

Adolescence—cont'd
    middle and later—cont'd
        anger in, 210
        conflicts with family in, 200-201
        conformity in, 202-203
        crushes in, 206
        delinquency in, 213
        emotional characteristics in, 210-211
        emotional maturity in, 211
        emotionality in, 209-211
        envy in, 210
        establishing heterosexual relationships in, 202-206
        fear in, 210
        gangs in, 216
        happiness in, 210
        intellect in, 208-209
        jealousy in, 210
        love relationships in, 206-208
        mental characteristics in, 208-209
        moral and spiritual growth in, 211-212
        parent-child conflicts in, 200
        peer acceptance in, 202-203
        physical growth and development in, 198-199
        "popularity syndrome" in, 201
        problems in, 212-215
            personal, 213-215
        self-identity in, 211
        sequential pattern of dating in, 203-206
        worry in, 210
Adrenal glands, 16
Adult, unmarried, 258-259
Adulthood
    early, 238-263
        developmental tasks in, 240
        maturity in, 259-261
        personal independence in, 240-242
    emerging, 220-237
    later, 284-307
        accidents and safety in, 296
        age changes in, 296-304
        depression in, 304
        developmental tasks of, 289
        families in, 294-295
        friends and family in, 293
        health in, 295-296

Index

Adulthood—cont'd
  later—cont'd
    housing in, 293-294
    life in, 289-296
    mental changes in, 302-303
    physical characteristics of, 296-300
    psychological changes in, 303-304
    religion in, 306
    sexuality in, 300
    social characteristics of, 293-295
  middle, 264-283
    change of life in, 278-282
    developmental tasks of, 266-268
    emotional crises in, 275-276
    identity crisis in, 276
    infidelity in, 275-276
    life in, 270-278
    mental characteristics of, 276-277
    physical characteristics of, 270-272
    pregnancy in, 280-281
    sex in, 281-282
    social characteristics in, 272-273
    stability of personality traits in, 273-275
    versus youth cult, 268-270
    vocational status in, 277-278
  young, 220-237
    achievement of emotional independence in, 225-226
    culture of, 234-235
    development in, 224-226
    developmental tasks in, 224-225
    government in, 235-236
    identity in, 226-228
      in minority groups, 227-228
    intellectual growth in, 225
    moral development in, stages in, 230-231
    music in, 234-235
    physical growth in, 225
    self-image in, 226-227
    and society, 231-236
    uncertainty in
      moral, 228-229, 230-231
      religious, 229-230
Affection in middle adolescence, 210
Affective development in late childhood, 162-164
Age changes in later adulthood, 296-304
Aged and their children, 294-295
Aging
  characteristics of, 299-300
  factors in, 300-302
Amniotic sac, 33
Andropause, 278
Androsperms, 30
Anger
  in early childhood, 119
  in middle adolescence, 210
Anoxia, 58
Anxiety in late childhood, 163
Apgar score for newborn, 49
Arm movements of neonate, 67
Aschheim-Zondek test of pregnancy, 29
Assimilation, Piaget's theory of, 75
Associative play, 117

Attention, seeking, by infant, 96
Attitudes, student and parent, on recent issues, 223
Auditory-verbal development in early childhood, 108
Automobile, conflict over use of, 201
Autonomy as opposed to control in parent-child relationships, 201-202
Autosomes, 30
Awareness
  psychosexual, in late childhood, 155-156
  sexual
    in early adolescence, 185-187
    in late childhood, 154-157
Awkwardness, motor, in early adolescence, 176

B

Babbling and lalling, 84-86
Babinski reflex, 67
Baby, birth of, 42-59
Behavior
  adaptive, 10
  adjustive, 6, 10
  coping, 10
  in early childhood, 118-120
  genetic foundations of, 10-13
  imitation of, in early childhood, 120
  moral, of infant, 91-92
  prenatal, 32-40
  social, in late childhood, 157-160
Behavioral characteristics of neonate, 64-65
Bereavement, 256
Birth
  of baby, 42-59
  conditions present at, affecting development, 53-59
  kinds of, 48-49
  process of, 43-49
Birth defects, 54-57, 58
Birth weight, low, prematurity and, 58-59
Birthmarks, 54
Black families, 215-216
Blastocyte, 32
Body growth
  in early childhood, 102-103
  in middle childhood, 128
Body movements
  control of, in infant, 95
  of neonate, 66-69
Breech presentation, 48

C

Career development, 242-243
Cells
  germ, 10
  sex, 24-25
  somatic, 10
Centering, 111
Central nervous system, 14
Cephalocaudal sequence of growth, 2-3
Cervix, 26
Cesarean section, 48
Change of life in middle adulthood, 278-282
Changes, physical, at puberty, 173-177

Character development in middle childhood, 143-145
Chemicals and gene mutation, 12
Childhood
　early, 100-123
　　anger in, 119
　　auditory-verbal development in, 108
　　behavior in, 118-120
　　body growth in, 102-103
　　cognitive development in, 110-114
　　concepts in, 112-113
　　developmental tasks of, 102
　　emotions in, 118-120
　　imitation of behavior in, 120
　　jealousy in, 119
　　morality in, 122-123
　　motor characteristics of, 103-105
　　organization of personality in, 120-122
　　perceptual pattern for receiving, interpreting, learning, and responding, 105
　　personality identification in, 121
　　physical characteristics of, 103
　　play in, 115-118
　　psychosocial development in, 115-120
　　social development in, 115-118
　　value judgment system in, beginnings of, 121-122
　late, 147-166
　　activities of, 152-153
　　affective development in, 162-164
　　anxiety in, 163
　　dating in, 159
　　developmental tasks of, 149
　　emotional characteristics of, 163-164
　　family relationships in, 159-160
　　friendships in, 158-159
　　groups in, 157-158
　　health in, 152
　　height in, 150, 151
　　mental characteristics of, 160-161
　　mental health adjustment in, 150
　　moral development in, 162-164
　　motor ability in, 152-153
　　physical characteristics of, 149-152
　　physical growth and motor development in, 149-154
　　psychosexual development and awareness in, 155-156
　　school learning in, 160-162
　　sexual awareness and sex information in, 154-157
　　sexual learning in, 156-157
　　social behavior in, 157-160
　　social independence in, 159-160
　　social structure in, 157-158
　　spiritual development in, 164-165
　　teeth in, 151-152
　　understanding of God in, 164-165
　　weight in, 150, 151
　middle, 125-145
　　body growth in, 128
　　character development in, 143-145
　　developmental tasks of, 127

Childhood—cont'd
　middle—cont'd
　　emotional characteristics of, 141-143
　　fear in, 142
　　intelligence in, 134-138
　　language in, 134-138
　　logical thought in, 137-138
　　mental characteristics of, 135-137
　　moral characteristics of, 143-145
　　motor skills in, 128-129
　　peer culture in, 131, 132-134
　　personality development in, 138-139
　　physical development in, 127-129
　　play in, 132-134
　　play interests in, 133
　　self-concept in, 139-140
　　sex roles in, 133-134, 140-141
　　sex typing in, 140-141
　　social characteristics of, 130-132
　　social growth in, 129-134
　　thought in, 134-138
　moral development in, Piaget's studies on, 144
Child-parent relationships
　conflicts in, in middle adolescence, 200
　control as opposed to autonomy in, 201-202
　and development, 20
Children
　aged and, 294-295
　development of language in, 85
Chromosomal aberration, 11-13
Chromosomes, 25, 27
　helix of, 11
Cleft lip, 54
Cleft palate, 54
Climacteric, 278, 281
Clubfoot, 54
Clubhouses, 157
Code, genetic, 11, 13
Cognition, 75
Cognitive development
　in early childhood, 110-114
　of infant, 61-80
　in late childhood, 160-162
　Piaget's sensorimotor stage of, 76-78
　Piaget's system of, 75-76
　preconceptual stage of, 111
College and marriage, 245
Compatibility theory of marriage, 248
Complementary needs theory of marriage, 248
Concepts
　in early childhood, 113-114
　formation of, 112
　of morality in early childhood, 122-123
Concrete operations, Piaget's stage of, 134-135
Conditions at birth affecting development, 53-59
Conflicts in middle adolescence
　with family, 200-201
　parent-child, 200
Conformity in middle adolescence, 202-203
Congenital heart disease, 54
Congenital urinary tract defects, 55
Control
　of body movements in infant, 95

Control—cont'd
    as opposed to autonomy in parent-child relationships, 201-202
Coping behavior, 10
Cord, umbilical, 34-35
Crawling, 72
Creeping, 72
Crises
    emotional, in middle adulthood, 275-276
    identity, in middle adulthood, 276
    in marriage, 255-257
Crowning of baby's head, 44-47
Crushes in middle adolescence, 206
Culture
    teen, 187-189
    youth, 234-235
Curiosity of infant, 96-97

D

Darwinian reflex, 67
Dating
    in late childhood, 159
    sequential pattern of, in middle adolescence, 203-206
Daydreaming in early adolescence, 192
Death and dying, 304-306
Defects
    birth, 54-57, 58
    urinary tract, congenital, 55
Defense mechanism, 7
Delinquency in middle adolescence, 213
Delivery(ies)
    forceps, 48
    kinds of, 48-49
Deoxyribonucleic acid, 10-13
Depression in later adulthood, 304
Determination of sex, 30-31
Development, 2
    affective, in late childhood, 102-105
    auditory-verbal, in early childhood, 108-109
    career, 242-243
    character, in middle childhood, 143-145
    cognitive; see Cognitive development
    conditions at birth affecting, 53-59
    ego, and sex role development, 140
    emotional, in infancy, 87-88
    five areas of, 1, 2
    foundations of, 1-23
    of head, 3
    of heterosexuality in early adolescence, 182-184
        observations on, 184-185
    intellectual, Piaget's stages of, 134
    of intelligence, 74-78
    of language, 114-115
        in children, 85
    moral; see Moral development
    motor; see Motor development
    parent-child relationship and, 20
    of perceptual processes, 78-80
    personality, in middle childhood, 138-139
    physical; see Physical characteristics
    physiological basis of, 10-18

Development—cont'd
    prenatal, 24-40
        embryonic period in, 34-36
        influences on, 49-53
        period of fetus in, 36-40
        period of zygote in, 32-34
    primitive impulses and, 22
    principles of, 2-5
        specific, 3-4
    psychosexual, in late childhood, 155-156
    psychosocial
        in early childhood, 115-120
        in infancy, 82-98
        stages of, 89
    psychosocial influences of, 18-22
    pubertal, 170-177
    sensorimotor process in, 106-108
    sex role, and ego development, 140
    social; see Social characteristics
    spiritual, in late childhood, 164-165
    in young adulthood, 224-226
Developmental sequences of play activities, 116
Developmental tasks, 4-5
    of early adolescence, 170
    in early adulthood, 240
    of early childhood, 102
    of late childhood, 149
    of later adulthood, 289
    of middle adulthood, 266-268
    of middle childhood, 127
    of newlyweds, 250-251
    in young adulthood, 224-225
Diabetes, 55
Diagnosis of pregnancy, 29
Differentiation, 3
Directionality, 108
Disadvantaged environments, adolescence in, 215-217
Disease
    fibrocystic, 56, 58
    heart, congenital, 54
Divorce, 256-257
Dizygotic twins, 31
DNA (deoxyribonucleic acid), 10-13
Down's syndrome, 12-13
Dropout, social, 231-233
Drugs
    effect of, on fetus, 51-52
    and gene mutation, 12
    use of, 233-234
Dying and death, 304-306
Dyspareunia, 282

E

Echolalia and true speech, 86
Eclampsia, 52
Economic independence, 242
Ego, 94
    development of, and sex role development, 140
Egocentric speech, 86-87
Egocentrism, 111
Embryonic period in prenatal development, 34-36

Emotional characteristics
  of early adolescence, 177-179
  in infancy, 87-88
  of late childhood, 163-164
  in middle adolescence, 210-211
  of middle childhood, 141-143
Emotional crises in middle adulthood, 275-276
Emotional independence, achievement of, in young adulthood, 225-226
Emotional maturity in middle adolescence, 211
Emotional stress, effect of, on fetus, 52-53
Emotionality in middle adolescence, 209-211
Emotions in early childhood, 118-120
Endocrine glands, 16-17
Environments, disadvantaged, adolescence in, 215-217
Envy in middle adolescence, 210
Epididymis, 27
Episiotomy, 44
Erythroblastosis fetalis, 51, 55
Exploration by infant, 96-97
Exploratory play, 132
Exteroceptors, 13

F

Fads in early adolescence, 188-189
False labor, 44
Family(ies)
  black, 215-216
  conflicts with, in middle adolescence, 200-201
  in later adulthood, 293
  relationships with, in late childhood, 159-160
  as socializing agent, 19-20
Fashions in early adolescence, 188-189
Fear
  in middle adolescence, 210
  in middle childhood, 142
Female gametes and organs, 25-26
Fertility rate, 257
Fertilization, 28-29
Fetus
  effects on
    of drugs, 51-52
    of emotional stress, 52-53
    of smoking, 52, 53
  growth of, 37
  narcotics and, 51-52
  period of, in prenatal development, 36-40
Fibrocystic disease, 56, 58
Fitness, physical, in middle adulthood, 271
Flushes, hot, 279
Follicle, Graafian, 26
Forceps delivery, 48
Formal operations, period of, Piaget's, 209
Friends
  in late childhood, 158-159
  in later adulthood, 293

G

Galactosemia, 56
Gametes
  female, 25-26
  male, 26-28

Gangs; *see also* Groups
  in early adolescence, 187
  in late childhood, 157-158
  in middle adolescence, 216
  in young adulthood, 227-228
Gene mutation, 11-12
General adaptation syndrome, 15
Genetic code, 11, 13
Genetic foundations of behavior, 10-13
Geriatrics, 287-289
Germ cells, 10
German measles, 50
Gerontology, 287-289
Glands
  endocrine, 16-17
  prostate, 27
God, understanding of, in late childhood, 164-165
Gonadotrophin, human chorionic, 29
Government and youth, 235-236
Graafian follicle, 26
Gradients, growth, 2-3
Grasping reflex, 72-73
Groups; *see also* Gangs
  minority, identity in, 227-228
  peer, in middle childhood, 131, 132-134
Growth, 2
  cephalocaudal sequence of, 2-3
  of fetus, 37
  gradients of, 2-3
  intellectual, in young adulthood, 225
  moral and spiritual, in middle adolescence, 211-212
  physical
    in early childhood, 102-103
    in middle adolescence, 198-199
    in middle childhood, 128
    and motor development in late childhood, 149-154
    in young adulthood, 225
  proximodistal sequence of, 3
  social, in middle childhood, 129-134
Gynosperms, 30

H

Handedness, 104
Happiness
  marital, predictors of, 248-250
  in middle adolescence, 210
Head
  development of, 3
  movements of, of neonate, 67
Health
  in late childhood, 152
  in later adulthood, 295-296
Heart disease, congenital, 54
Height
  in early adolescence, 173-175
  in late childhood, 150, 151
  of neonate, 63
Helix, chromosomal, 11
Heredity, 10-13
Heterosexual relationships, establishing, in middle adolescence, 202-206

Heterosexuality, developing, in early adolescence, 182-184
  observations on, 184-185
Hierarchy of basic values, 260-261
Hippies, 232
Homeostasis, 5-7
Homogamy theory of marriage, 248
Hoodlums, 232
Hormones, 17
Hot flushes, 279
Housing in later adulthood, 293-294
Human chorionic gonadotrophin, 29
Human development; *see* Development
Hydrocephaly, 56, 58

I

"Ideal mate" theory of marriage, 248
Identical twins, 31
Identification, personality, in early childhood, 121
Identity in young adulthood, 226-228
  in minority groups, 227-228
Identity crisis in middle adulthood, 276
Imaginative play, 118
Imitation
  of behavior in early childhood, 120
  verbal, by infant, 97
Imitative play, 132
Impulses, primitive, and development, 22
Income, loss of, and marriage, 255
Incompatibility in marriage, 254
Independence
  economic, 242
  emotional, achievement of, in young adulthood, 225-226
  from home, achievement of, 199-202
  personal, in early adulthood, 240-242
  problems in seeking, 200
  social, 241
    in late childhood, 159-160
Individuality, 1-2
Inducing labor, 49
Infancy; *see also* Infant
  emotional development in, 87-88
  locomotion in, 69-72
  motor development of, 69-74
  postural control in, 69-72
  psychosocial development of, 82-98
Infant; *see also* Infancy
  attention seeking by, 96
  control of body movements by, 95
  curiosity of, 96-97
  exploration by, 96-97
  moral behavior of, 91-92
  motor and cognitive development of, 61-80
  physical satisfaction of, 95-96
  physiological stability of, 95
  self-assertiveness by, 97-98
  social development of, 88-91
  speech and language of, 84-87
  toilet training of, 92-93
  verbal imitation by, 97
Infections, maternal, 50

Infidelity
  in marriage, 255-256
  in middle adulthood, 275-276
Information, sex, in late childhood, 154-157
Intellectual abilities in early adolescence, 192-193
Intellectual development, Piaget's stages of, 134
Intellectual growth in young adulthood, 225
Intellectual operations, mastering, 208-209
Intelligence
  development of, 74-78
  in middle childhood, 134-138
  socioeconomic influence on, 192-193
Interests of early adolescents, 187-188
Interoceptors, 13
Intuitive thought, 111

J

Jealousy
  in early childhood, 119
  in middle adolescence, 210

K

Klinefelter's syndrome, 13
Knee jerk, 67

L

Labor
  false, 44
  inducing, 49
  mechanisms of, 45-47
  stages of, 44-48
  true, 43-44
Lalling and babbling, 84-86
Language
  development of, 114-115
    in children, 85
  of infant, 84-87
  in middle childhood, 134-138
Lanugo, 39
Laterality, 108
Learning, 7-10
  perceptual-motor processes for, 105-110
  school, in late childhood, 160-162
  sexual, in late childhood, 156-157
  to walk, 73-74
Leg and trunk movements of neonate, 67-69
Life
  beginning of, 24-29
  change of, in middle adulthood, 278-282
  in later adulthood, 289-296
  in middle years, 270-278
Lightening, 43
Limbs, missing, 56
Lip, cleft, 54
Living, efficient, basic processes related to, 5-10
Locomotion in infancy, 69-72
Logical thought in middle childhood, 137-138
Loss of income and marriage, 255
Love, meaning of, 245-246
Love relationships in middle adolescence, 206-208

M

Male gametes and organs, 26-28

Marriage, 243-258
  and college, 245
  crisis in, 255-257
  early, 206
  happiness in, predictors of, 248-250
  incompatibility in, 254
  infidelity in, 255-256
  loss of income and, 255
  personal adjustment in, 251-252
  problems in, 252-255
  reasons for, 244-245
  sex in, 252
  theories of, 248
Marriage partner, accepting, 248
Masturbation, 186
Mating, 243
Maturation, 4, 17-18
  sequence of
    in boys, 173
    in girls, 172
Maturing intellectual operations, 208-209
Maturity
  in early adulthood, 259-261
  emotional, in middle adolescence, 211
  traits of, 259-260
Measles, German, 50
Mechanism
  defense, 7
  of labor, 45-47
Menarche, 171-172
Menopause, 278
  symptoms of, 278-281
Menstruation, 26
  cessation of, 279-280
Mental changes in later adulthood, 302-303
Mental characteristics
  of late childhood, 160-161
  in middle adolescence, 208-209
  of middle adulthood, 276-277
  of middle childhood, 135-137
Mental health adjustment in late childhood, 150
Minority groups, identity in young adulthood in, 277-278
Mongolism, 57
Monozygotic twins, 31
Moral awakening in early adolescence, 193
Moral development
  in childhood, Piaget's studies on, 144-145
  of infant, 91-92
  in late childhood, 162-164
  in middle adolescence, 211-212
  of middle childhood, 143-145
  in young adulthood, 230-231
Moral uncertainty in young adulthood, 228-229
Morality, concepts of, in early childhood, 122-123
Moro reflex, 67-68
Mother
  infections in, 50
  nutrition of, 49-50
Motivation, 7, 8
Motor awkwardness in early adolescence, 176
Motor development
  in early childhood, 103-105

Motor development—cont'd
  in infancy, 69-74
  of infant, 61-80
  in late childhood, 149-154
  in middle childhood, 128-129
Mouth and throat response of neonate, 67
Movements, body, of neonate, 66-69
  arm and head, 67
  control of, 95
  leg and trunk, 67-69
Music
  in early adolescence, 187, 188
  in young adulthood, 234-235
Mutation, gene, 11-12

N

Narcotics and fetus, 51-52
Nature and origins of personality, 93-98
Negativism, 116
Neonate, 63-69
  Apgar score for, 49
  arm and head movements of, 67
  behavioral characteristics of, 64-65
  body movements of, 66-69
  height of, 63
  leg and trunk movements of, 67-69
  mouth and throat response of, 67
  physical characteristics of, 63-64
  reflexes of, 66-69
  sensory abilities of, 65-66
  vision of, 65-66
  weight of, 64
Nervous system, 13-16
  central, 14
  major structures of, 14
  peripheral, 14-15
Newborn; *see* Neonate
Newlyweds, developmental tasks in, 250-251
Nutrition of mother, 49-50

O

Oogenesis, 25
Organization
  of personality in early childhood, 120-122
  visual-motor, in early childhood, 109-110
Organs
  female, 25-26
  male, 26-28
Origins and nature of personality, 93-98
Ovaries, 16
Ovulation, 26
Ovum, 24-25
Oxytocin, 49

P

Palate, cleft, 54
Pancreas, 16
Parallel play, 116
Parathyroid gland, 16
Parental attitudes on recent issues, 223
Parent-child relationships
  conflicts in, in middle adolescence, 200
  control as opposed to autonomy in, 201-202

Index

Parent-child relationships—cont'd
  and development, 20
  in late childhood, 159-160
Parenthood, 257-258
Parents
  achievement of independence from, in middle adolescence, 199-202
  types of, 202
Parent–teen-ager relationship, 180-182
Partner, marriage, accepting, 248
Pathways, sensory-motor, relationship to perceptual process, 15
Peer acceptance in middle adolescence, 202-203
Peer culture in middle childhood, 131, 132-134
Peer group
  influences of, in early adolescence, 179-180
  in socialization, 20-21
Perception, 79
  visual-motor, in early childhood, 109-110
Perceptual pattern for receiving, interpreting, learning, and responding, 105
Perceptual process, 15-16
  development of, 78-80
  relationship to sensory-motor pathways, 15
Perceptual-motor processes for learning, 105-110
Period
  of formal operations, Piaget's, 209
  of prenatal development
    embryonic, 34-36
    fetal, 36-40
    zygote, 32-34
Peripheral nervous system, 14-15
Personal adjustment in marriage, 251-252
Personal independence in early adulthood, 240-242
Personal problems of middle adolescence, 213-215
Personality
  development of, in middle childhood, 138-139
  emergence of, 94-98
  nature and origins of, 93-98
  organization of, in early childhood, 120-122
  stability of, in middle adulthood, 273-275
Personality identification in early childhood, 121
Petting in early adolescence, 186-187
Phenylketonuria, 53, 57
Physical changes at puberty, 173-177
Physical characteristics
  in early adolescence, 170-177
  of early childhood, 103
  of late childhood, 149-152
  of later adulthood, 296-300
  of middle adulthood, 270-272
  of middle childhood, 127-129
  of neonate, 63-64
Physical fitness in middle adulthood, 271
Physical growth
  in late childhood, 149-154
  in middle adolescence, 198-199
  in young adulthood, 225
Physical satisfaction of infant, 95-96
Physiological basis of development, 10-18
Physiological demands of body, 7
Physiological stability of infant, 95

Piaget, Jean
  period of formal operations, 209
  sensorimotor stage of cognitive development, 76-78
  stage of concrete operations, 134-135
  stages of intellectual development, 134
  studies on moral development in childhood, 144-145
  system of cognitive development, 75-76
  theory of accommodation, 75
  theory of adaptation, 76
  theory of assimilation, 75
Pituitary gland, 16
Placenta, 34
Play
  associative, 117
  development of, and concept of possession, 117
  in early childhood, 115-118
  exploratory, 132
  imaginative, 118
  imitative, 132
  in middle childhood, 132-134
  parallel, 117
  testing, 132-133
Play activities, developmental sequences of, 116
Polydactyly, 55
"Popularity syndrome" in middle adolescence, 201
Possession, concept of, and development of play, 117
Postadolescence; see Adulthood, young
Postural control in infancy, 69-72
Preadolescence, 170; see also Childhood, late
Preconceptual stage of cognitive development, 111
Predictors of marital happiness, 248-250
Preeclampsia, 52
Pregnancy, 29-32
  Aschheim-Zondek test of, 29
  diagnosis of, 29
  middle-aged, 280-281
  signs of, 29
  toxemia of, 52
Prehension, 72-73
Prematurity and low birth weight, 58-59
Prenatal development, 24-40
  and behavior
    embryonic period in, 34-36
    period of fetus in, 36-40
    period of zygote in, 32-34
  influences on, 49-53
Preoperational thought, 111-112
Prepuberty, 170
Primary sex characteristics, 171
Primitive impulses and development, 22
Principles of development, 2-5
  specific, 3-4
Problems
  in early adolescence, 189-192
  marital, 252-255
  in middle and later adolescence, 212-215
    personal, 213-215
  in seeking independence, 200
Process(es)
  basic to efficient living, 5-10

Process(es)—cont'd
  birth, 43-49
  perceptual, 15-16
    development of, 78-80
    relationship to sensory-motor pathways, 15
  perceptual-motor, for learning, 105-110
  sensorimotor, in development, 106-108
  of socialization, 19
Propinquity theory for marriage, 248
Proprioceptors, 13
Prostate gland, 27
Proximodistal sequence of growth, 3
Psychological changes in later adulthood, 303-304
Psychological needs, 7
Psychosexual development and awareness in late childhood, 155-156
Psychosocial development
  in early childhood, 115-120
  in infancy, 82-98
  stages of, 89
Psychosocial influences of development, 18-22
Puberty, 153-154, 167-194; *see also* Adolescence, early
  development in, 170-177
  onset of, 170-173
  physical changes at, 173-177
Puberty rites, 197
Pubescence, 170
Purchases, teenage, 217-218

Q
Quickening, 38
Quinine, 51

R
Radiation and gene mutation, 12
Receptors, 13
Reflex
  Babinski, 67
  Darwinian, 67
  grasping, 72-73
  Moro, 67-68
  of neonate, 66-69
Reflexive vocalization, 84
Relationships
  heterosexual, establishing, in middle adolescence, 202-206
  love, in middle adolescence, 206-208
  parent-child; *see* Parent-child relationship
  parent–teen-ager, 180-182
Relativism, 123
Religion in later adulthood, 306
Religious uncertainty in young adulthood, 229-230
Retirement, advent of, 289-292
"Retirement shock," 289
Rh factor, 50-51
RhoGAM, 51
Ribonucleic acid, 11, 13
Rites, puberty, 197
RNA (ribonucleic acid), 11, 13
Rubella, 50

S
Safety in later adulthood, 296

Satisfaction, physical, of infant, 95-96
School as socializing agent, 21
School learning in late childhood, 160-162
Score, Apgar, for newborn, 49
Secondary sex characteristics, 171
Self-assertiveness by infant, 97-98
Self-concept in middle childhood, 139-140
Self-direction, 241-242
Self-ideal, 122
Self-identity in middle adolescence, 211
Self-image in young adulthood, 226-227
Self-reliance, 241
Self-structure, 21-22
Self-sufficiency, 241
Senescence, 286
Senility, 286-287
Sensorimotor processes in development, 106-108
Sensorimotor stage of cognitive development, Piaget's, 76-78
Sensory abilities of neonate, 65-66
Sensory-motor arc, 13
Sensory-motor pathways, relationship to perceptual process, 15
Sequence of growth
  cephalocaudal, 2-3
  proximodistal, 3
Sequential pattern of dating in middle adolescence, 203-206
Sex
  determination of, 30-31
  in marriage, 252
  in middle age, 281-282
Sex cells, 24-25
Sex characteristics, 171
Sex role
  development of, and ego development, 140
  in middle childhood, 133-134, 140-141
Sex typing, 141
Sexual awareness
  in early adolescence, 185-187
  and sex information in late childhood, 154-157
Sexuality
  in later adulthood, 300
  and sexual learning in late childhood, 156-157
Shock, "retirement," 289
Show, 44
Sickle-cell trait, 57
Signs of pregnancy, 29
Single adults, 258-259
Skills, motor, in middle childhood, 128-129
Smoking, effect of, on fetus, 52, 53
Social characteristics
  of early adolescence, 179-187
  of early childhood, 115-118
  of infant, 88-91
  of late childhood, 157-160
  in later adulthood, 293-295
  of middle adulthood, 272-273
  of middle childhood, 130-132
Social dropout, 231-233
Social growth in middle childhood, 129-134
Social independence, 241
  in late childhood, 159-160

Index

Social structure in late childhood, 157-158
Social trust, 241
Socialization, 18-21
    family in, 19-20
    peer group in, 20-21
    process of, 19
    school in, 21
    society in, 21
Socialized speech, 86-87
Society
    as socializing agent, 21
    and youth, 231-236
Socioeconomic influence on intelligence, 192-193
Somatic cells, 10
Speech
    egocentric and socialized, 86-87
    of infant, 84-87
    in middle childhood, 137-138
    true, echolalia and, 86
Spermatogenesis, 27
Spermatozoa, 27-28
Spermatozoon, 24
Spina bifida, 57, 58
Spiritual development
    in late childhood, 164-165
    in middle adolescence, 211-212
Stability
    of personality traits in middle adulthood, 273-275
    physiological, of infant, 95
Stages
    of concrete operations, Piaget's, 134-135
    of intellectual development, Piaget's, 134
    of labor, 44-48
Stress, emotional, effect of, on fetus, 52-53
Student attitudes on recent issues, 223
Sucking, 67
Suggestibility of feelings, 120
Superego, 122
Supertwins, 31-32
Syndactyly, 55
Syndrome
    Down's, 12-13
    Klinefelter's, 13
    Turner's, 13
Syphilis, 50

T

Tantrums, temper, 97-98
Tasks, developmental; see Developmental tasks
Teen culture, 187-189
Teenage purchases, 217-218
Teen-ager–parent relationships, 180-182
Teeth in late childhood, 151-152
Telephone, conflict over use of, 188, 201
Temper tantrums, 97-98
Test of pregnancy, Aschheim-Zondek, 29
Testes, 16
Testing play, 132-133
Thalidomide, 12, 51
Theories
    of marriage, 248
    Piaget's; see Piaget, Jean

Thought
    intuitive, 111
    logical, in middle childhood, 137-138
    in middle childhood, 134-138
    preoperational, 111-112
Threat, youth cult, 268-270
Throat and mouth response of neonate, 67
Thyroid gland, 16
Toilet training, 92-93
Toxemia of pregnancy, 52
Training, toilet, 92-93
Trophoblast, 33
True labor, 43-44
Trunk and leg movements of neonate, 67-69
Trust, social, 241
Turner's syndrome, 13
Twins, 31-32

U

Umbilical cord, 34-35
Uncertainty in young adulthood
    moral, 228-229
        stages of, 230-231
    religious, 229-230
Universality, 1-2
Unmarried young adult, 258-259
Urinary tract defects, congenital, 55
Uterus, 25-26

V

Value judgment system
    beginnings of, in early childhood, 121-122
    need for, 211-212
Values, basic, hierarchy of, 260-261
Vas deferens, 27
Verbal imitation by infant, 97
Vertex presentation, 48
Villi, 34
Vision of neonate, 65-66
Visual-motor organization and perception in early childhood, 109-110
Vocalization, reflexive, 84
Vocational status in middle adulthood, 277-278

W

Walk, learning to, 73-74
Walking, development of, 72
Water bag, rupture of, 44
Weight
    birth, low, prematurity and, 58-59
    in early adolescence, 174-175
    in late childhood, 150, 151
    of neonate, 63
Womb, 25-26
Worry in middle adolescence, 210

Y

Youth; see Adulthood, young
Youth cult threat, 268-270
Youth culture, 234-235
Youth market, 217-218

Z

Zygote, 32-34

mature relations with age mates
achievem of ♂/♀ role
accept physique
em. indep. from parents
economic indep.
occupation
intel skills   civil competence
responsible behavior
values

essay
4-10
10-14
Piaget & Erikson